CONTENT, COGNITION
COMMUNICATION

Content, Cognition, and Communication

Philosophical Papers II

NATHAN SALMON

CLARENDON PRESS · OXFORD

OXFORD
UNIVERSITY PRESS

Great Clarendon Street, Oxford OX2 6DP

Oxford University Press is a department of the University of Oxford.
It furthers the University's objective of excellence in research, scholarship,
and education by publishing worldwide in

Oxford New York

Auckland Cape Town Dar es Salaam Hong Kong Karachi
Kuala Lumpur Madrid Melbourne Mexico City Nairobi
New Delhi Shanghai Taipei Toronto

With offices in

Argentina Austria Brazil Chile Czech Republic France Greece
Guatemala Hungary Italy Japan Poland Portugal Singapore
South Korea Switzerland Thailand Turkey Ukraine Vietnam

Oxford is a registered trade mark of Oxford University Press
in the UK and in certain other countries

Published in the United States
by Oxford University Press Inc., New York

© in this volume Nathan Salmon 2007

The moral rights of the author have been asserted
Database right Oxford University Press (maker)

First published 2007

All rights reserved. No part of this publication may be reproduced,
stored in a retrieval system, or transmitted, in any form or by any means,
without the prior permission in writing of Oxford University Press,
or as expressly permitted by law, or under terms agreed with the appropriate
reprographics rights organization. Enquiries concerning reproduction
outside the scope of the above should be sent to the Rights Department,
Oxford University Press, at the address above

You must not circulate this book in any other binding or cover
and you must impose this same condition on any acquirer

British Library Cataloguing in Publication Data

Data available

Library of Congress Cataloging in Publication Data

Data available

Typeset by Laserwords Private Limited, Chennai, India
Printed in Great Britain
on acid-free paper by
Biddles Ltd., King's Lynn, Norfolk

ISBN 978–0–19–928272–2
ISBN 978–0–19–928472–6 (Pbk.)

1 3 5 7 9 10 8 6 4 2

These volumes are lovingly dedicated to my daughter,
Simone Becca Salmon,
the loveliest person it has been my honor to know.

Volume II Contents

Acknowledgments viii
Introduction to Volume II xi

PART I. DIRECT REFERENCE

1. A Millian Heir Rejects the Wages of *Sinn* (1990)   3
2. Reflexivity (1986)   32
3. Reflections on Reflexivity (1992)   58
4. Demonstrating and Necessity (2002)   67
5. Are General Terms Rigid? (2003)   100
6. A Theory of Bondage (2006)   113

PART II. APRIORITY

7. How to Measure the Standard Meter (1987)   141
8. How *Not* to Become a Millian Heir (1991)   159
9. Relative and Absolute Apriority (1993)   169
10. Analyticity and Apriority (1993)   183

PART III. BELIEF

11. Illogical Belief (1989)   193
12. The Resilience of Illogical Belief (2006)   224
13. Being of Two Minds: Belief with Doubt (1995)   230
14. Relational Belief (1995)   249
15. Is *De Re* Belief Reducible to *De Dicto*? (1998)   270

PART IV. SEMANTICS AND PRAGMATICS

16. Assertion and Incomplete Definite Descriptions (1982)   291
17. The Pragmatic Fallacy (1991)   298
18. The Good, the Bad, and the Ugly (2004)   309
19. Two Conceptions of Semantics (2004)   340

Bibliography of Nathan Salmon, 1979–2006   351
Index   355

Acknowledgments

Each of the following is reprinted by permission of the original publisher.

1. 'A Millian Heir Rejects the Wages of *Sinn*', in C. Anthony Anderson and Joseph Owens, eds, *Propositional Attitudes: the Role of Content in Logic, Language, and Mind* (Stanford, Calif.: Center for the Study of Language and Information, Stanford University, 1990), pp. 215–247.
2. 'Reflexivity', *Notre Dame Journal of Formal Logic*, vol. 27, no. 3 (July 1986), pp. 401–429, published by Notre Dame University.
3. 'Reflections on Reflexivity', *Linguistics and Philosophy*, vol. 15, no. 1 (February 1992), pp. 53–63, published by Springer.
4. 'Demonstrating and Necessity', *The Philosophical Review*, vol. 111, no. 4 (October 2002), pp. 497–537, published by Cornell University.
5. 'Are General Terms Rigid?', *Linguistics and Philosophy*, 28 (2005), pp. 117–134, published by Springer.
6. 'A Theory of Bondage', *The Philosophical Review*, vol. 115, no. 4 (October 2006), published by Cornell University.
7. 'How to Measure the Standard Meter', *Proceedings of the Aristotelian Society*, n.s., vol. 88 (1987/1988), pp. 193–217, published by Blackwell Publishing.
8. 'How *Not* to Become a Millian Heir', *Philosophical Studies*, vol. 62, no. 2 (May 1991), pp. 165–177, published by Springer.
9. 'Relative and Absolute Apriority', *Philosophical Studies*, vol. 69 (1993), pp. 83–100, published by Springer.
10. 'Analyticity and Apriority', in J. E. Tomberlin, ed., *Philosophical Perspectives, 7: Language and Logic* (Atascadero, Calif.: Ridgeview, 1993), pp. 125–133.
11. 'Illogical Belief', in J. E. Tomberlin, ed., *Philosophical Perspectives, 3: Philosophy of Mind and Action Theory* (Atascadero, Calif.: Ridgeview, 1989), pp. 243–285.
12. 'The Resilience of Illogical Belief', *Noûs*, forthcoming 2006, published by Blackwell Publishing.
13. 'Being of Two Minds: Belief with Doubt', *Noûs*, vol. 29, no. 1 (January 1995), pp. 1–20, published by Blackwell Publishing.
14. 'Relational Belief', in Paolo Leonardi and Marco Santambrogio, eds, *On Quine: New Essays* (Cambridge University Press, 1995), pp. 206–228.
15. 'Is *De Re* Belief Reducible to *De Dicto*?' in A. A. Kazmi, ed., *Meaning and Reference* (*Canadian Journal of Philosophy* Supplementary Volume 23, 1997, University of Calgary Press, 1998), pp. 85–110.

16 'Assertion and Incomplete Definite Descriptions', *Philosophical Studies*, vol. 42, no. 1 (July 1982), pp. 37–45, published by Springer.
17 'The Pragmatic Fallacy', *Philosophical Studies*, vol. 63, no. 1 (July 1991), pp. 83–97, published by Springer.
18 'The Good, the Bad, and the Ugly', in A. Bezuidenhout and M. Reimer, eds, *Descriptions and Beyond* (Oxford University Press, 2004), pp. 230–260.
19 'Two Conceptions of Semantics', in Zoltan Szabo, ed., *Semantics and Pragmatics* (Ithaca, N.Y.: Cornell University Press, 2004).

Introduction to Volume II

The present volume and its companion encompass most of the papers I wrote during the two decades since I left ivy to return to sunnier shores. Together with my previous books, *Reference and Essence* (second edition, Prometheus Books, 1981, 2004) and *Frege's Puzzle* (second edition, Atascadero, Calif.: Ridgeview, 1986, 1991), these volumes represent my thought to date on a variety of topics philosophical. I am grateful to Ernest Sosa, who first suggested that I compile the collection. With his suggestion came the realization: 'If not now, when?'

I have been deeply influenced by the writings of two dead, white, European males: Gottlob Frege and Bertrand Russell. I have also been deeply influenced by intellectual interactions with a number of remarkable American philosophers I have been privileged to know personally. Deserving of special mention are my former teachers, Tyler Burge, Keith Donnellan, Donald Kalish, and most especially, Alonzo Church, David Kaplan, and Saul Kripke. Standing on the shoulders of giants, the view has been breathtaking. For more than a quarter century I have strived—not always successfully—to strike a happy balance between independent thought and recognition of the fascinating and deeply significant insights of extraordinarily gifted minds. The pages that follow are a result of that endeavor.

In his second lecture on *The Philosophy of Logical Atomism*, Russell said, 'the point of philosophy is to start with something so simple as not to seem worth stating, and to end with something so paradoxical that no one will believe it'. Presumably, each of the transitions among the steps that lead from simple triviality to the paradoxically incredible must be like the starting point itself: so simple as not to seem worth stating. (Far too often in contemporary philosophy, this feature of the enterprise is undervalued, even ignored.) There is more to philosophy than the paradox of the heap, of course, and no one has demonstrated that better than Russell. Still, Russell's work often did conform to his succinct characterization of philosophy as the attempt to derive the incredible from the trivial. My own objective has often been similar to Russell's—more modest undoubtedly, but only somewhat. It has been to proceed by a sequence of obviously valid inferences (though not always uncontroversial) from clearly correct premises (though not generally indubitable) to a significant but unpopular thesis (though not typically incredible), or at least a rather surprising one.

In short, I have sought to establish (and insofar as possible, to prove) the surprising. If I should be accused of valuing this philosophical style because it is what I do, rather than the other way around, I shall take it as a compliment. I have argued for theses that fly in the face of conventional wisdom not because those theses are unfashionable, but because they are in each case, to the best of my ability to make a determination, the unrecognized, unappreciated truth of the matter. How far I have succeeded is for the reader to decide.

PART I

The first part of the present volume is concerned with the theory of direct reference. Frege and Russell held that an ordinary proper name functions fundamentally like a definite description (in English, a singular noun phrase beginning with the definite article 'the', or instead with a possessive adjective, as with 'Ryan's daughter'). For Frege this meant that a name expresses as its semantic content a *Sinn* (traditionally translated as *sense*)—a conceptual 'mode of presentation', or manner of specification, which determines the name's designatum to be whatever uniquely fits that manner of specification. Russell also held, though Frege did not, that besides ordinary proper names there are, or at least there could be, *logically proper names*, i.e. terms about which it is true that the semantic content is instead simply the object designated, nothing more and nothing less. The semantic content of a sentence employing a Russellian logically proper name is a *singular proposition*—a proposition that is about the name's designatum by virtue of including that very designatum, rather than a Fregean sense, as a constituent. The paradigm of a logically proper name is an individual variable, whose only semantic content, under an assignment of a value, is its assigned value. A variable must be a logically proper name; otherwise quantification into a context of propositional attitude would not express a *de re* attitude. Suppose, for example, that Jones believes of the planet Venus, *de re*, that it is a star, by virtue of believing that the Evening Star is a star. Then the sentence,

$(\exists x)[x$ is the second closest planet to the sun & Jones believes that x is a star$]$,

should express something true. By standard quantificational semantics, this sentence is true if and only if its component open sentence,

Jones believes that x is a star

is true under the assignment of the second closest planet to the sun as value for the variable 'x', i.e., if and only if Venus satisfies the open sentence. And this is so, in turn, if and only if Jones believes the proposition expressed by the simpler open sentence 'x is a star' under the same assignment of Venus as the value of 'x'. Although Venus is specified as *the second closest planet to the sun* in being assigned to 'x', the variable is not *ipso facto* assigned that manner of specification as its content. If it were, then the proposition expressed by 'x is a star' under the assignment would be that the second closest planet to the sun is a star—which Jones does not believe. Instead, the variable functions as a logically proper name of its value. Accordingly, the semantic content of an open sentence, like 'x is ingenious but ingenuous', under an assignment of a value to the free variable 'x', is the singular proposition about that assigned value that he or she (or it) is ingenious but ingenuous.

Saul Kripke and Keith Donnellan demonstrated, to my mind beyond a reasonable doubt, that ordinary proper names function very differently from definite descriptions—whether definite descriptions are taken to be singular terms, as with Frege, or taken to be quantifiers, as with Russell. Kaplan demonstrated, again I think conclusively, that ordinary demonstratives are essentially Russellian logically proper names. A few philosophers, myself included, have argued for the doctrine of *Millianism*—that ordinary proper names too are Russellian logically proper names. One argument for this, provided in 'A Millian Heir Rejects the Wages of *Sinn*', comes directly from the analysis of *de re* attitudes. Analogously with quantification into an attribution of belief, in order for 'Jones believes of the second closest planet to the sun that it is a star' to be true, the sub-sentence 'Jones believes that it is a star' must be true under the anaphoric assignment of the second closest planet to the sun, i.e., Venus, to the pronoun 'it' as its designatum. The proposition expressed by 'It is a star' under this assignment must be the singular proposition about Venus that it is a star; otherwise the original sentence would be *de dicto* rather than *de re*. Hence the 'it' is a logically proper name. As goes the variable, so goes the pronoun, and so too the constant. For the only difference between a variable and a constant is that the latter is constant while the former is variable (and whatever differences follow from this). The constant is married, while the variable is playing the field. A variable is basically a constant wannabe. (Or is it the other way around?) If either is a logically proper name, so is the other. Just as the variable '*x*' is a logically proper name of its assigned designatum—and similarly the anaphoric pronoun 'it'—so too is the name 'Venus'.

Several chapters of the present volume are concerned with Millianism. In 'Reflexivity' and 'Reflections on Reflexivity', I argue that Millianism should maintain a genuine distinction between the proposition that Cicero admires Tully and the proposition that Cicero is a self-admirer. 'Are General Terms Rigid?' answers the title question: As with singular terms, some general terms are rigid designators, some not.

'Demonstrating and Necessity' concerns the nature of both bare demonstratives, like 'that' used deictically, and complex demonstratives, i.e. demonstrative phrases of the form '*that F*'. Following Frege, Kaplan has argued that the demonstrative itself is essentially incomplete and that the demonstration that typically accompanies the use of a demonstrative is an essential component of the complete expression uttered, which is a demonstrative-*cum*-demonstration. I argue contrary to Frege and Kaplan that the demonstrative itself (whether bare or complex) is the complete expression, whereas the accompanying demonstration is an additional feature of the context of utterance. Some interesting consequences of this alternative to Kaplan's account are explored, focusing on a unified solution to Frege's Puzzle (*How can the informative* $\ulcorner \alpha = \beta \urcorner$, *if true, differ at all in content from the uninformative* $\ulcorner \alpha = \alpha \urcorner$?), as it arises with demonstratives as well as proper names.

'A Theory of Bondage' presents a non-classical account of the semantics of expression-occurrences in accordance with Frege's admonition that the designation and semantic content of an expression must be relativized to that expression's position within a sentence. The theory is brought to bear on the binding of variables and on recent fallacious arguments concerning anaphoric pronouns and quantification into compound designators.

PART II

'How to Measure the Standard Metre', 'How *Not* to Become a Millian Heir', 'Relative and Absolute Apriority', and 'Analyticity and Apriority' concern particular consequences of Millianism with respect to the semantic-epistemological status of certain special kinds of sentences. Kripke has forcefully argued that certain true identity sentences of the sort invoked in Frege's Puzzle—including 'Hesperus is Phosphorus' and 'Cicero is Tully'—express necessary truths even though they are synthetic and *a posteriori*. His arguments appear to have persuaded the philosophical community. He has also forcefully argued that certain sentences made true through a special kind of terminological stipulation, including Wittgenstein's example, 'The Metre Stick (assuming it exists) is exactly one metre long at time t_0' (which Wittgenstein evidently thought neither true nor false), express contingent truths that are knowable *a priori*. Kaplan has made a similar claim about certain indexical sentences whose truth is guaranteed by the indexical logic, e.g., 'I am here now'.

I agree that these sentences (most of them, anyway) are of a rather special and peculiar sort. I argue that the identity sentences arising in Frege's Puzzle, while they do indeed express necessary truths, are in fact *analytic*, in the sense that they are true solely as a consequence of pure semantics, without invoking any non-semantic facts, and the necessary truths they express are in fact knowable *a priori*. (I believe this notion of sentential truth solely by virtue of pure semantics underlies the traditional conception of analyticity.) Turning Kaplan and Kripke on their heads, I also argue that while Wittgenstein's metre sentence and indexical-logically true sentences do indeed typically express contingent truths, those truths are not in general *a priori*. Instead many of them are *a posteriori* even though the sentences in question are analytic, contrary to Kripke's characterization. (Kaplan's example of 'I am here now' is not even analytic; it is synthetic *a posteriori*.) In 'Demonstrating and Necessity' I offer what I believe is a purer example of the same general phenomenon of the analytic-contingent-*a posteriori*: 'That student (if existent) is a student.'

PART III

'Illogical Belief', 'The Resilience of Illogical Belief', 'Being of Two Minds', 'Relational Belief', and 'Is *De Re* Belief Reducible to *De Dicto*?' develop and continue a substantial project undertaken in *Frege's Puzzle*: the reconciliation of Millianism with a host of problems posed by locutions of propositional attitude, especially by attributions of belief. Chief among these problems is the apparent failure of substitution of co-referential names (or relevantly similar devices). Apparent substitution failures include substitutions within iterations (a problem originally introduced by Benson Mates), as in 'Tyler disbelieves that Pierre believes that London is pretty.' Also addressed at length is Quine's question in 'Quantifiers and Propositional Attitudes' concerning belief *de re*, and Kripke's question 'A Puzzle about Belief' concerning belief *de dicto*. Quine asks whether Ralph believes of Ortcutt, *de re* ('relationally'), that he is a spy, when Ralph believes *de dicto* ('notionally') that the man in the brown hat is a spy but also that the man seen at the beach is not a spy, and when, unbeknownst to Ralph, both men are Ortcutt. Kripke asks whether Pierre believes *de dicto* that London is pretty when he evidently believes (also *de dicto*) that the city known to Frenchmen as '*Londres*' is pretty whereas the city known to its own denizens as 'London' is not, and when, unbeknownst to Pierre, these cities are one.

The first step toward solving all of these problems is to recognize that insofar as one believes a singular proposition about a person, place, or thing that one fails to recognize, one likewise fails to recognize the very singular proposition one believes. As a result, one's failure to recognize some person, place, or thing nearly inevitably results in one harboring cognitively dissonant attitudes without realizing it toward one and the same proposition about that person, place, or thing—for example, believing the proposition while also disbelieving, doubting, or suspending judgment in taking it to be a distinct and independent proposition. It may be supposed that if someone has cognitive access to each of a pair of things, x and y (which may or may not be the same), and he or she takes them to be distinct, then there are distinct ways of taking something, or *guises*, g_1 and g_2, such that he or she has cognitive access to x under g_1 and has cognitive access to y under g_2. Belief of a proposition is a cognitive attitude toward that proposition, but whether one bears this attitude is relative to the guise under which one apprehends the proposition. Just as Ralph believes that Ortcutt is a spy under one of that proposition's guises while failing to believe it under another, so Pierre believes that London is pretty under one of that proposition's guises while failing to believe under another. An exactly similar situation can obtain with regard to the propositions that Cicero is Cicero, that Venus is Venus, that Superman is Superman.

To believe of something x, *de re*, that it is such-and-such is to believe the singular proposition about x that it is such-and-such. It is in this sense, but only in this sense, that *de re* belief is reducible to *de dicto*. To believe a proposition p is to believe it under some guise or other. To disbelieve p is to believe its denial under some guise or other. One suspends judgment about p if there is a proposition guise under which one fails either to believe or to disbelieve p. One doubts whether p if one either disbelieves p or suspends judgment about p under some guise. Though it is logically impossible to believe and fail to believe one and the same proposition, one can easily believe while also disbelieving or suspending judgment with regard to the same proposition, by believing it under one guise and doubting under another.

Specifically, Ralph believes of Ortcutt that he is a spy even while also doubting whether Ortcutt is a spy, and Pierre believes that London is pretty even while doubting whether London is pretty. Worse than that, contrary to Quine and contrary to Kripke, Ralph and Pierre believe straightforwardly contradictory propositions: that Ortcutt is a spy and Ortcutt is not a spy; and that London is pretty and London is not pretty. Ralph would not express his belief with the words 'Ortcutt is a spy and Ortcutt is not a spy', nor would Pierre express this belief with the words 'London is pretty and London is not pretty.' Indeed, both would dissent from such a formulation, precisely because both rightly disbelieve the relevant proposition taking it thus presented, as an explicit contradiction. Instead, Ralph expresses his belief by uttering 'He is a spy, but he isn't', pointing with the first 'he' to the man in the brown hat, with the second to Ortcutt at the beach. Similarly, Pierre expresses his belief with the words '*Londres* is pretty but London is not', not realizing that this sentence expresses a contradictory proposition. He is in no position to infer, for example, (and he does not, indeed could not, believe) the trivial consequence that London is both pretty and not pretty. In order to draw even the simplest inferences—in order to recognize the validity of the inference of *that London is both F and G* from *that London is F and London is G*, or the inference of *that London is pretty* from *that it is not the case that London isn't pretty*, or even the inference of *that London is pretty* from itself—one must recognize the relevant proposition as it occurs within and among premises and conclusion. Absence such recognition, one is unable to reason in a way that would be second nature in the presence of such recognition. We justifiably criticize or censure someone for being illogical only when his or her failure to reason correctly is not a direct result of recognition failure.

From the present point of view, Kripke's puzzle is reducible to Quine's. Or is it the other way around? Either way, they are essentially the same. So are their solutions.

PART IV

The papers in this section are all about the distinction between meaning and use, or more generally, the distinction between semantics and pragmatics. The delineation of the exact relationship between meaning and use is extremely difficult, and (partly as a result) highly controversial. Blurring of the distinction is commonplace, even fashionable. Worse, respect for the distinction has been suppressed through professional authoritative abuse. It is my considered judgment that the most common source of error in the philosophy of language—and consequently the most important impediment to progress—has long been, and remains, the mistaking of pragmatic phenomena as properly semantic. Confusion between semantics and pragmatics is rampant. In these papers I defend the legitimacy of the distinction with special reference to a widely discussed distinction between two kinds of uses of descriptive phrases.

It is ironic that the theory of direct reference—most directly applicable to simple proper names, individual variables, pronouns, and indexical (context-sensitive) words—embarked from its least promising turf: the definite description. If there are any singular terms to which the direct-reference theory does *not* apply, and instead an essentially Fregean account directly applies, they are definite descriptions. (A version of the Fregean theory applies also to predicates and to whole sentences.) Nevertheless, the contemporary incarnation of direct-reference theory began in 1966 with the publication of Keith Donnellan's seminal 'Reference and Definite Descriptions'. Donnellan pointed to a distinction between significantly distinct ways of using a definite description. On the *referential use*, the speaker has a particular individual object in mind, which is presumed to answer to the description, and the speaker's use is directed toward that object, as that to which the speaker is referring. An *attributive use*, by contrast, is not directed toward any object in particular. Instead, in using 'the such-and-such', the speaker intends primarily to make a general remark to the effect that (or to ask a general question whether, etc.) whoever or whatever is (uniquely) such-and-such is thus-and-so. An attributive use of a description yields the familiar Russellian truth conditions for the sentence uttered. Donnellan argued that a referential use, by contrast, results in the sentence expressing a singular proposition about the object the user has in mind, regardless of whether that object actually answers to the description used. Others, notably Kripke, objected that the referential-attributive distinction is entirely pragmatic, and has no bearing on such semantic issues as content or truth conditions for the sentence uttered.

In 'Assertion and Incomplete Definite Descriptions' and 'The Pragmatic Fallacy', I argue that whenever asserting that the such-and-such is thus-and-so, by uttering a sentence with exactly this content, the speaker typically also asserts a singular proposition about the such-and-such, to the effect that he, she, or it is thus-and-so. In 'The Good, the Bad, and the Ugly', some interesting consequences are investigated, while still other types of uses of definite descriptions are examined. One alleged consequence that it is fallacious to draw, however, is that the sentence uttered expresses the singular proposition with respect to the context of the speaker's utterance. The sentence does one thing, the speaker another. The distinction between what the sentence says (or designates) and what its user says highlights two competing conceptions of the enterprise known as semantics, explored in 'Two Conceptions of Semantics'. On the speech-act centered conception (perhaps the dominant conception at the turn of the millennium), the designation of a term, the truth-value of a sentence, the semantic content of an expression—all of these fundamentally derive from what the speaker accomplishes in using the expression. On the expression-centered conception, inherited from Frege and Russell—and to which I remain fiercely loyal—an expression's semantics enjoys a kind of autonomy from the speaker, allowing for the possibility of divergence, even widespread and systematic deviation, between what the expression and its user mean.

PART I
DIRECT REFERENCE

1

A Millian Heir Rejects the Wages of *Sinn* (1990)

It is argued, in sharp contrast to established opinion, that the linguistic evidence arising out of propositional-attitude attributions strongly supports Millianism (the doctrine that the entire contribution to the proposition content of a sentence made by a proper name is simply the name's referent) without providing the slightest counter-evidence. This claim is supported through a semantic analysis of such *de re* attributions as 'Jones believes of Venus that it is a star.' The apparent failure of substitutivity of co-referential names in propositional-attitude attributions is shown to be evidentially irrelevant through consideration of analogous phenomena involving straightforward synonyms.

I

In *Frege's Puzzle* [27] I defended a Millian theory of the information contents of sentences involving proper names or other simple (noncompound) singular terms. The central thesis is that ordinary proper names, demonstratives, other single-word indexicals or pronouns (such as 'he'), and other simple singular terms are, in a given possible context of use, Russellian 'genuine names in the strict logical sense'.[1] Put more fully, I maintain the following anti-Fregean doctrine: that the contribution made by an ordinary proper name or other simple singular term to securing the information content of, or the proposition expressed by, declarative sentences (with respect to a given possible context of use) in which the term occurs (outside of the scope of nonextensional operators, such as quotation marks) is just the referent of the term, or the bearer of the name (with respect to that context of use). In the terminology of *Frege's Puzzle*, I maintain that the *information value* of an ordinary proper name is just its referent.[2]

The present chapter has benefited from discussions with Mark Richard and Stephen Schiffer, from comments by Graeme Forbes and Timothy Williamson, and from discussions at Birkbeck College, London and Oxford University (where portions of the essay were presented as talks in May 1988), and at the University of Minnesota conference on *Propositional Attitudes: the Role of Content in Logic, Language, and Mind*, October 1988.

[1] See Russell's 'Knowledge by Acquaintance and Knowledge by Description' [22] and 'The Philosophy of Logical Atomism' [23].

[2] Throughout this chapter, I use the term 'Millian' broadly to cover any theory that includes this doctrine. (The term derives from Kripke, 'A Puzzle About Belief' [13].) I0 do not use the term in the

Another thesis that I maintain in *Frege's Puzzle*—and which both Frege and Russell more or less accepted—is that the proposition that is the information content of a declarative sentence (with respect to a given context) is structured in a certain way, and that its structure and constituents mirror, and are in some way readable from, the structure and constituents of the sentence containing that proposition.[3] By and large, a simple (noncompound) expression contributes a single entity, taken as a simple (noncomplex) unit, to the information content of a sentence in which the expression occurs, whereas the contribution of a compound expression (such as a phrase or sentential component) is a complex entity composed of the contributions of the simple components.[4] Hence, the contents of beliefs formulatable using ordinary proper names, demonstratives, or other simple singular terms, are on my view so-called *singular propositions* (David Kaplan), i.e., structured propositions directly about some individual, which occur directly as a constituent of the proposition. This thesis (together with certain relatively uncontroversial assumptions) yields the consequence that *de re* belief (or *belief of*) is simply a special case of *de dicto* belief (*belief that*). To believe *of* an individual x, *de re*, that it (he, she) is F is to believe *de dicto* the singular proposition about (containing) x that it (he, she) is F, a proposition that can be expressed using an ordinary proper name for x. Similarly for the other propositional attitudes.

---

more restricted sense of a theory that includes the (apparently stronger) thesis that the reference of a simple singular term completely exhausts the 'linguistic function' of the term (whatever that means). John Stuart Mill himself was almost certainly not a Millian, strictly speaking, but his philosophical view of proper names is very much in the spirit of Millianism—enough so for genuine Millians, such as myself, to be counted his heirs.

[3] This separates the theory of *Frege's Puzzle*, together with the theories of Frege, Russell, and their followers, from contemporary theories that assimilate the information contents of declarative sentences with such things as sets of possible worlds, or sets of situations, or functions from possible worlds to truth values, etc.

Both Frege and Russell would regard declarative sentences as typically reflecting only *part of* the structure of their content, since they would insist that many (perhaps even most) grammatically simple (noncompound) expressions occurring in a sentence may (especially if introduced into the language by abbreviation or by some other type of explicit 'definition') contribute complex proposition-constituents that would have been more perspicuously contributed by compound expressions. In short, Frege and Russell regarded the prospect of expressions that are grammatically simple yet semantically compound (at the level of content) as not only possible but ubiquitous. Furthermore, according to Russell's Theory of Descriptions, definite and indefinite descriptions ('the author of *Waverley*', 'an author', etc.), behave grammatically but not semantically (at the level of content) as a self-contained unit, so that a sentence containing such an expression is at best only a rough guide to the structure of its content. Russell extends this idea further to ordinary proper names and most uses of pronouns and demonstratives. This makes the structure of nearly any sentence only a very rough guide to the structure of the sentence's content. The theory advanced in *Frege's Puzzle* sticks much more closely to the grammatical structure of the sentence.

[4] There are well-known exceptions to the general rule—hence the phrase 'by and large'. Certain nonextensional operators, such as quotation marks, create contexts in which compound expressions contribute themselves as units to the information content of sentences in which the expression occurs. Less widely recognized is the fact that even ordinary temporal operators (e.g., 'on April 1, 1986' + past tense) create contexts in which some compound expressions (most notably, open and closed sentences) contribute complexes other than their customary contribution to information content. See 'Tense and Singular Propositions' [29]. In addition, compound predicates are treated in *Frege's Puzzle* as contributing attributes, as single units, to the information contents of sentences.

Here I will elaborate and expand on certain aspects of my earlier defense of Millian theory, and present some new arguments favoring Millianism. It is commonly held that Millianism runs afoul of common-sense belief attributions, and other propositional-attitude attributions, in declaring intuitively false attributions true. Ironically, the main argument I shall propose here essentially relies on common-sense belief attributions and the semantics of the English phrase 'believes that'. I shall argue, in sharp contrast to established opinion, that the seemingly decisive evidence against Millianism from the realm of propositional-attitude attributions is no evidence at all, and is in fact evidentially irrelevant and immaterial. If I am correct, common-sense propositional-attitude attributions, insofar as they provide any evidence at all, strongly support Millianism without providing even the slightest counter-evidence (in the way that is commonly supposed).

Historically, the most influential objection to the sort of theory I advocate derives from Frege's notorious 'Hesperus'–'Phosphorus' puzzle. The sentence 'Hesperus is Phosphorus' is informative; its information content apparently extends knowledge. The sentence 'Hesperus is Hesperus' is uninformative; its information content is a 'given'. According to my theory, the information content of 'Hesperus is Hesperus' consists of the planet Venus, taken twice, and the relation of identity (more accurately, the relation of identity-at-t, where t is the time of utterance). Yet the information content of 'Hesperus is Phosphorus', according to this theory, is made of precisely the same components, and apparently in precisely the same way.[5] Assuming a plausible principle of compositionality for propositions, or pieces of information—according to which if p and q are propositions that involve the very same constituents arranged in the very same way, then p and q are the very same proposition—the theory ascribes precisely the same information content to both sentences. This seems to fly in the face of the fact that the two sentences differ dramatically in their informativeness.

This puzzle is easily transformed into an argument against Millian theory, by turning its implicit assumptions into explicit premisses. The major premiss, which I call *Frege's Law*, connects the concept of informativeness (or that, in Frege's words, of 'containing a very valuable extension of our knowledge') with that of cognitive information content (what Frege called '*Erkenntniswerte*', or 'cognitive value'):

If a declarative sentence S has the very same cognitive information content as a declarative sentence S', then S is informative if and only if S' is.

A second premiss is the compositionality principle for propositions. A third critical premiss consists in the simple observation that whereas 'Hesperus is Phosphorus' is informative, 'Hesperus is Hesperus' is not. Assuming that the information contents of 'Hesperus is Phosphorus' and 'Hesperus is Hesperus' do not differ at all in structure

---

[5] It has been argued, however, that the information content of a sentence is a function not only of the information-values and the sequential order of the information-valued parts but also of the very logical structure of the sentence as a whole, and that therefore, since the two identity sentences differ in logical structure, the modes of composition of the information values of their parts are different from one another. See Putnam [17], especially note 8 (also in [29], pp. 157n10). For response, see Church [2]; Scheffler [31] (pp. 42n7); Soames [33]; and Salmon [27] (pp. 164–165n4).

or mode of composition, it follows that they differ in their constituents.[6] This points to a difference in information value between the names 'Hesperus' and 'Phosphorus'. Since these names are co-referential, it cannot be that the information value of each is simply its referent.

As I pointed out in *Frege's Puzzle* (pp. 73–76), there is a very general difficulty with this Fregean argument: an exactly similar argument can be mounted against any of a wide variety of theories of information value, including Frege's own theory that the information value of a term consists in an associated purely conceptual representation. It happens that I, like Hilary Putnam, do not have the slightest idea what characteristics differentiate beech trees from elm trees, other than the fact that the English term for beeches is 'beech' and the English term for elms is 'elm'.[7] The purely conceptual content that I attach to the term 'beech' is the same that I attach to the term 'elm', and it is a pretty meager one at that. My concept of elm wood is no different from my concept of beech wood. Nevertheless, an utterance of the sentence 'Elm wood is beech wood' would (under the right circumstances) be highly informative for me. In fact, I know that elm wood is not beech wood. At the same time, of course, I know that elm wood is elm wood. By an argument exactly analogous to the one constructed from Frege's puzzle about the informativeness of 'Hesperus is Phosphorus' we should conclude that the information value of 'elm' or 'beech' is not the conceptual content.[8]

---

[6] See the previous note. There is considerable conflict, however, between Putnam's stance described therein and his more recent concession in his 'Comments' on Kripke's 'A Puzzle about Belief' [19] (p. 285), that 'certainly Frege's argument shows meaning cannot just *be* reference'.

[7] This particular example is due to Putnam, whose botanical ignorance cannot possibly exceed my own. See 'Meaning and Reference' [18] (p. 704).

[8] I had made this same general point earlier in a review of Leonard Linsky's *Names and Descriptions* [154] (p. 451). There, however, I labored under the illusion that the original Fregean argument is sound.

It may be objected that my concept of elm trees includes the concept of being called 'elms' in English, and perhaps even the concept of being a different genus from the things called 'beeches' in English, making the purely conceptual contents different after all. Even setting aside the question of whether such differences can show up in a purely conceptual representation, this objection is mistaken. In the relevant sense of 'conceptual content', such concepts as that of being called 'elm' in English are not part of the conceptual content I attach to the term 'elm'. Not everything one believes about elms can be part of the information value of the term 'elm', or of the conceptual representation attached to the term 'elm', as the notion of conceptual representation is intended in Fregean theory. Otherwise, every sentence S that is sincerely uttered by someone and that involves the word 'elm' (not in the scope of quotation marks or other such devices) would be such that the conditional ⌜If there are any elms, then S⌝ is analytically true for the speaker. One could not acquire new beliefs expressed by means of the term 'elm', and hence one could not change one's mind about anything expressed in terms of 'elm' (e.g., that Jones is standing by an elm tree), without literally changing the subject. In particular, there are compelling reasons for denying that any concept like that of being called such-and-such in English can be part of the information value of terms like 'elm' and 'beech'. It is not analytic, for example, that elms are called 'elm' in English. (That 'elm' applies to elms in English is a nontrivial piece of information about English. Things might have been otherwise, and it is not 'given' or known *a priori* what the expression 'elm' applies to in English.) Whatever the information value of 'elm' is, there are terms in other languages that have the same information value—e.g., the German words '*Ulme*' and '*Rüster*'. The information value of these German terms does not include any concept of what things of that kind

This argument employs the same general strategy, and mostly the very same premisses (including Frege's Law and the compositionality principle for propositions), as the original Fregean argument in connection with 'Hesperus' and 'Phosphorus'. This generalized Fregean strategy may be applied against virtually any minimally plausible and substantive theory of information value. In this particular application of the generalized strategy, the relevant informative identity statement is not even true, but that does not matter to the general strategy. The truth of an informative identity statement is required only in the application of the general argument against theories that locate information value, at least in part, in reference. In the general case, only informativeness is required. False identity statements are always informative—so informative, in fact, as to be misinformative. Thus, virtually any substantive theory of information value imaginable reintroduces a variant of Frege's puzzle (or else it is untenable on independent grounds, such as Kripke's modal arguments against orthodox Fregean theory).

The sheer scope of the generalized Fregean strategy—the fact that, if sound, it is applicable to virtually any substantive theory of information value—would seem to indicate that the strategy involves some error. That the generalized strategy does indeed involve some error can be demonstrated through an application of the generalized strategy to a situation involving straightforward (strict) synonyms for which it is uncontroversial that information value is exactly preserved. Suppose that foreign-born Sasha learns the words 'ketchup' and 'catsup' not by being taught that they are perfect synonyms, but by actually consuming the condiment and reading the labels on the bottles. Suppose further that, in Sasha's idiosyncratic experience, people typically have the condiment called 'catsup' with their eggs and hash browns at breakfast, whereas they routinely have the condiment called 'ketchup' with their hamburgers at lunch. This naturally leads Sasha to conclude, erroneously, that ketchup and catsup are different condiments that happen to share a similar taste, color, consistency, and name. He thinks to himself, 'Ketchup is a sandwich condiment, but no one in his right mind would eat a sandwich condiment with eggs at breakfast; so catsup is not a sandwich condiment.' Whereas the sentence 'Ketchup is ketchup' is uninformative for Sasha, the sentence 'Catsup is ketchup' is every bit as informative as 'Hesperus is Phosphorus'. Applying the generalized Fregean strategy, we would conclude that the terms 'catsup' and 'ketchup' differ in information value for Sasha. But this is clearly wrong. The terms 'ketchup' and 'catsup' are perfect synonyms in English. Some would argue that they are merely two different spellings of the very same

---

are called in English. A German speaker may know what an elm is—may have a concept of an elm tree—without having the foggiest idea what elms are called in English. Also, for most terms, such as 'tree', 'table', 'anthropologist', 'green', etc., it is distinctly implausible to suppose that the information value of the term includes the concept of being so-called in English. Each is perfectly translatable into any number of languages. The typical German speaker knows what a tree is—has the concept of a tree—even if he or she does not have any opinion as to the English term for a tree. There is no reason why 'elm' should be different from 'tree' in this respect. See Kripke, *Naming and Necessity* [12] (pp. 68–70) and 'A Puzzle about Belief' [13] (note 12), and my *Frege's Puzzle* (pp. 163–164n2).

English word.[9] Most of us who have learned these words (or these spellings of the single word) probably learned one of them in an ostensive definition of some sort, and the other as a strict synonym (or as an alternative spelling) of the first. Some of us learned 'ketchup' first and 'catsup' second; for others the order was the reverse. Obviously, it does not matter which is learned first and which second. Either word (spelling) may be learned by ostensive definition. If either may be learned by ostensive definition, then both may be. Indeed, Sasha has learned both words (spellings) in much the same way that nearly everyone else has learned at least one of them: by means of a sort of ostensive definition. This manner of acquiring the two words (spellings) is unusual, but not impossible. Sasha's acquisition of these words (spellings) prevented him from learning at the outset that they are perfect synonyms, but the claim that he therefore has not learned both is highly implausible. Each word (spelling) was learned by Sasha in much the same way that some of us learned it. Even in Sasha's idiolect, then, the two words (spellings) are perfectly synonymous, and therefore share the same information value. Since this contradicts the finding generated by the generalized Fregean strategy, the generalized Fregean strategy must involve some error. This discredits the original Fregean argument.[10]

What is the error? It is tempting to place the blame on Frege's Law. In Sasha's case, the sentences 'Catsup is ketchup' and 'Ketchup is ketchup' have the very same information content, yet it seems that the first is informative and the second is not. This would be a mistake. A sentence is *informative* in the sense invoked in Frege's Law only insofar as its information content is a 'valuable extension of our knowledge', or is knowable only *a posteriori*, or is not already 'given', or is nontrivial, etc. There is some such property P of propositions such that a declarative sentence S is informative in the only sense relevant to Frege's Law if and only if its information content has P. Once the informativeness or uninformativeness of a sentence is properly seen as a derivative semantic property of the sentence, one that the sentence has only in virtue of encoding the information that it does, Frege's Law may be seen as a special instance of Leibniz's Law, the doctrine that things that are the same have the same properties:

---

[9] Indeed, a similar example could be constructed using the American and British spellings of 'color', or even differing *pronunciations* of 'tomato'.

[10] The argument given here involving the terms 'ketchup' and 'catsup' is related to Kripke's 'proof' of substitutivity using two Hebrew words for Germany, and to his argument involving 'furze' and 'gorse', in the conclusion section of 'A Puzzle about Belief' [13]. All of these arguments are closely related to Church's famous arguments from translation. (See especially 'Intensional Isomorphism and Identity of Belief' [2].) For further discussion of the relation between the position taken in Kripke's article on belief and the position defended here see *Frege's Puzzle* (pp. 129–132), and 'Illogical Belief' [28].

The example of Sasha, like the 'beech'–'elm' example, demonstrates that the difficulty involved in Frege's puzzle is more general than it appears, arising not only on my own theory of information value but equally on a very wide range of theories, including various Fregean theories. This is not peculiar to Frege's puzzle. Although I will not argue the case here, a great many criticisms that have been leveled against the sort of account I advocate—perhaps most—are based on some difficulty or other that is more general in nature than it first appears, and that equally arises on virtually any substantive theory of information value in connection with the example of Sasha's understanding of the synonyms 'ketchup' and 'catsup'. (*Cf.* 'Illogical Belief'.) Perhaps I will elaborate on this matter in later work.

if the information content of S is the information content of S', then the information content of S has the informative-making property P if and only if the information content of S' does. Since Frege's Law is a logical truth, it is unassailable.

By the same token, the sentence 'Catsup is ketchup' is definitely not informative *in this sense*. The proposition it semantically contains is just the information that ketchup is ketchup, a proposition that clearly lacks the relevant informative-making property P. The sentence 'Catsup is ketchup', unlike the sentences 'Ketchup is ketchup' and 'Catsup is catsup', is 'informative' in various other senses. If uttered under the right circumstances, the former can convey to someone like Sasha that the sentence itself is true, and hence that the words (or spellings) 'ketchup' and 'catsup' are English synonyms, or at least co-referential. To someone who already understands 'ketchup' but not 'catsup', an utterance of the sentence can convey what 'catsup' means. These pieces of linguistic information about English do have the informative-making property P, but in order for a sentence to be informative in the relevant sense its very information content itself must have the informative-making property P. It is not sufficient that utterances of the sentence typically impart information that has P, if that imparted information is not included in the semantic information content of the sentence. The question of information value concerns semantically contained information, not pragmatically imparted information.

Exactly analogously, once the word 'informative' is taken in the relevant sense, thereby rendering Frege's Law a truth of logic, one of the other crucial premises of the original Fregean argument against Millian theory is rendered moot. Specifically, with the word 'informative' so understood, and with a sharp distinction between semantically contained information and pragmatically imparted information kept in mind, the assumption that the sentence 'Hesperus is Phosphorus' is informative *in the relevant sense* requires special justification. To be sure, an utterance of the sentence typically imparts information that is more valuable than that typically imparted by an utterance of 'Hesperus is Hesperus'. For example, it may impart the nontrivial linguistic information about the sentence 'Hesperus is Phosphorus' itself that it is true, and hence that the names 'Hesperus' and 'Phosphorus' are co-referential. But presumably this is not semantically contained information. The observation that 'Hesperus is Phosphorus' can be used to convey information that has the informative-making property P does nothing to show that the sentence's semantic content itself has the property P. It is by no means obvious that this sentence, stripped naked of its pragmatic impartations and with only its properly semantic information content left, is any more informative in the relevant sense than 'Hesperus is Hesperus'. I claim that the information content of 'Hesperus is Phosphorus' is the trivial proposition about the planet Venus that it is it—a piece of information that clearly lacks the informative-making property P. It is by no means certain, as the original Fregean argument maintains, that the difference in 'cognitive value' we seem to hear between 'Hesperus is Hesperus' and 'Hesperus is Phosphorus' is not due entirely to a difference in pragmatically imparted information. Yet, until we can be certain of this, Frege's Law cannot be applied and the argument does not get off the ground. In effect, then, the original Fregean argument begs the question, by assuming that the typical impartations of 'Hesperus is Phosphorus' that have the informative-making property P are included in the very information content. Of course, if one fails to draw the distinction between semantically contained and pragmatically imparted information (as so many philosophers have), it is small wonder that information pragmatically imparted by 'Hesperus is Phosphorus' may be mistaken for semantically contained information. If the strategy of the original Fregean argument is ultimately to succeed, however, a further argument must be given to show that the information imparted by 'Hesperus is Phosphorus' that makes it seem informative is, in fact, semantically contained. In the meantime, Frege's 'Hesperus'–'Phosphorus' puzzle is certainly not the conclusive refutation of Millian theory that it has been taken to be. For all that the Fregean strategy achieves, some version of Millianism may be the best and most plausible theory available concerning the information value of proper names.

II

What evidence is there in favor of the Millian theory? One extremely important consideration comes by way of the paradigms of nondescriptional singular terms: individual variables. A related consideration involves pronouns. Consider the following so-called *de re* (as opposed to *de dicto*), or *relational* (as opposed to *notional*), propositional-attitude attribution, expressed in the formal mode by way of quantification into the nonextensional context created by the nonextensional operator 'that':

(1) $(\exists x)[x = $ the planet Venus & Jones believes that x is a star].

Such a *de re* locution might be expressed less formally in colloquial English as:

(1') Jones believes of the planet Venus that it is a star.

What is characteristic of these *de re* locutions is that they do not specify how Jones conceives of the planet Venus in believing it to be a star. It is left open whether he is thinking of Venus as the first heavenly body visible at dusk, or as the last heavenly body visible at dawn, or instead as the heavenly body he sees at time t, or none of the above. The Fregean (or 'neo-Fregean') theorist contends that this lack of specificity is precisely a result of the fact that the (allegedly sense-bearing) name 'Venus' is positioned outside of the scope of the oblique context created by the nonextensional operator 'believes that', where it is open to substitution of co-referential singular terms and to existential generalization. What is more significant, however, is that another, non-sense-bearing singular term is positioned within the scope of the nonextensional context: the last bound occurrence of the variable 'x' in (1), the pronoun 'it' in (1'). Consider first the quasi-formal sentence (1). It follows by the principles of conventional formal semantics that (1) is true if and only if its component open sentence

(2) Jones believes that x is a star

is true under the assignment of the planet Venus as value for the variable 'x'—or in the terminology of Tarski, if and only if Venus *satisfies* (2). The open sentence (2) is true under the assignment of Venus as value of '*x*' if and only if Jones believes the proposition that is the information content of the complement open sentence

(3) *x* is a star

under the same assignment of Venus as the value of '*x*'.

A parallel derivation proceeds from the colloquial *de re* attribution (1'). Sentence (1') is true if and only if its component sentence

(2') Jones believes that it is a star

is true under the anaphoric assignment of Venus as referent for the pronoun 'it'. As with the open sentence (2), sentence (2') is true under the assignment of Venus as the referent of 'it' if and only if Jones believes the information content of

(3') It is a star

under this same assignment.

Now, the fundamental semantic characteristic of a variable with an assigned value, or of a pronoun with a particular referent, is precisely that its information value is just its referent. The referent-assignment provides nothing else for the term to contribute to the information content of sentences like (3) or (3') in which it figures. In fact, this is precisely the point of using a variable or a pronoun rather than a definite description (like 'the first heavenly body visible at dusk') within the scope of an attitude verb in a *de re* attribution. A variable with an assigned value, or a pronoun with a particular referent, does not have in addition to its referent a Fregean sense—a conceptual representation that it contributes to semantic content. If it had, (3) and (3') would semantically contain specific general propositions, under the relevant referent-assignments, and (2) and (2') would thus be notional rather than relational. If (2) and (2'), used with reference to Venus, are to be relational—if they are to fail to specify how Jones conceives of Venus—the contents of (3) and (3') under the assignments of Venus to '*x*' and 'it' can only be the singular proposition about Venus that it is a star, the sort of proposition postulated by the Millian theory. This means that the information value of the variable or the pronoun must be its referent.

What is good for the variable or the pronoun, under an assigned referent, is good for the individual constant. Indeed, the only difference between a variable and a constant is that the variable varies where the constant stands fast. The semantics for a given language fixes the reference of its individual constants. It happens that some particularly useful operators, included in the usual mathematical languages, operate simultaneously on a certain kind of simple singular term and a formula, by surveying the various truth values that the operand formula takes on when the operand singular term is assigned different referents (and the rest of the sentence remains fixed), and then assigning an appropriate extensional value to the whole formed from the operator and its two operands. (Technically, the extension of such an operator is a function from the extension of its operand formula with respect to its operand term to an appropriate extension for the compound formed by attaching the operator to an appropriate term and a formula—where the extension of a formula S_v *with respect to* a term v is a function that assigns to any assignment of a referent to v the corresponding truth value of S_v under that referent-assignment.) If a given language includes operators of this sort, it is natural for it to include also special singular terms that are not coupled with a particular referent to which they remain faithful, and that are instead allowed to take on any value from a particular domain of discourse as temporary referent. These special singular terms are the individual variables, and the operators that induce their presence are the variable-binding operators. Individual variables are singular terms that would be individual constants but for their promiscuity. Conversely, then, individual constants are singular terms that would be variables but for their monogamy. The variability of a variable has nothing whatsoever to do with the separate feature that the variable's information value, under an assignment of a referent, is just the assigned referent. It is the simplicity of the variable that gives it the latter feature; the variability only guarantees that the information value also varies. Once the variable is assigned a particular value, the variable becomes, for all intents and purposes pertaining to that assignment, a constant. Hence, if the open sentence (3), under the assignment of Venus as the value of 'x', semantically contains the singular proposition about Venus that it is a star, then the closed sentence

   a is a star,

where 'a' is an individual constant that refers to Venus, semantically contains this same proposition. Assuming that the individual constants of natural language are the proper names, single-word indexical singular terms, and other (closed) simple singular terms, the considerations raised here support the Millian theory.[11]

There is an alternative way of looking at the same result. All of us are accustomed to using special variables or pronouns that have a restricted domain over which they range. In ordinary English, the pronoun 'he' often ranges only over males, the pronoun 'she' only over females. Among special-purpose technical languages, some variables range only over numbers, some only over sets, some only over times. The domain over which a variable ranges (at least typically) must be non-empty, but it can be quite small in size. In standard extensional second-order logic, for example, the range of the second-order variables 'p', 'q', and 'r' is the pair set consisting of (representatives of) the two truth values. Could there be variables whose range is a unit set? Of course there could. Why not? Except that it would be odd to call such

---

[11] The foregoing argument is closely related to a somewhat different argument advanced in *Frege's Puzzle* (pp. 3–7) for the conclusion that so-called *de re* propositional-attitude attributions, such as (1) and (1'), attribute attitudes toward singular propositions. (This is not a premiss of the argument; it is a conclusion.) The latter argument was derived from a similar argument of David Kaplan's involving modality in place of propositional attitudes. The new argument is an argument by analogy: Individual constants are relevantly analogous to individual variables and pronouns, differing only in their constancy; hence, so-called *de dicto* propositional-attitude attributions involving proper names also attribute attitudes toward singular propositions. This argument by analogy to variables and pronouns occurred to me sometime in late 1980, and although it is not proffered in *Frege's Puzzle*, it was this argument more than any other that actually convinced me of the highly contentious thesis that the information value of a proper name, or any other closed simple singular term, is simply its referent and nothing more. The argument of the following section occurred to me immediately thereafter. (*Cf. Frege's Puzzle*, p. ix.) A version of the latter of these is proffered in *Frege's Puzzle* (pp. 84–85, 114–118, and *passim*).

terms 'variables'. Their range is too restrictive to allow for genuine *variation*, in an ordinary sense; they are maximally restricted. Let us not call them 'variables', then. What should we call them? We could call them 'invariable variables'. (This has the advantage that it emphasizes the exact analogy with the less restrictive variables.) Alternatively, we could call them 'constants'. In fact, we do. The proper names and demonstratives of ordinary language might be seen as nothing other than the hypothesized 'invariable variables'. Proper names and unrestricted variables are but the opposite limiting cases of a single phenomenon.[12]

III

This sort of consideration favoring the sort of account I advocate is complemented by a new application of a general form of argument that has been suggested, and usefully exploited, by Saul Kripke.[13]

What compelling evidence is there that the proper names of ordinary language are not simply the hypothesized invariable variables? We have seen that the original Fregean argument from the alleged informativeness of 'Hesperus is Phosphorus' is illegitimate, or at least seriously incomplete. What other evidence is there? An alternative argument against Millian theory derives from the apparent failures of substitutivity in propositional-attitude attributions. Consider the familiar story of Jones and his ignorance concerning the planet Venus. Jones sees a bright star in the dusk sky, before any other heavenly body is visible, and is told that its name is 'Hesperus'. Subsequently he sees another bright star in the dawn sky, later than any other heavenly body is visible, and is told that its name is 'Phosphorus'. What Jones is not told is that these are one and the very same heavenly body, the planet Venus. Although Jones believes the

---

[12] I know of no convincing evidence that proper names (and natural-language simple singular terms generally, other than pronouns) are not invariable pronominals. The fact that proper names do not seem to be grammatically bindable by quantifier (or other) antecedents cannot be taken as conclusive refutation of the thesis that names are maximally restricted variables. Since quantification employing such variables would not differ in truth value from the unquantified open sentence, binding such variables would serve no useful purpose; the natural evolution of language would have little reason to introduce a device for binding these special invariable pronominals. In any event, the general argument in the text does not require the premise that proper names are variables of a special sort (maximally restricted); it requires only the premise that names are sufficiently *analogous* to (unrestricted) variables—together with the usual semantics governing existential quantification, conjunction, and identity (or the natural semantics governing anaphora in English locutions of the form ⌜Of *a*, ... it ... ⌝), and the further premise that a (closed or open) sentence of the form ⌜*a* believes that *S*⌝ is true (under an assignment of values to variables) if and only if the referent of *a* believes the information content of *S*. See the previous note.

[13] *Cf.* Kripke, *Naming and Necessity* [12] (pp. 108). Kripke's general methodological observation is given in more detail in 'Speaker's Reference and Semantic Reference' [14] (especially p. 16). Kripke does not explicitly consider applying the general strategy specifically to substitutivity-failure objections to Millianism. Whereas he clearly regards such objections as inconclusive at best (see his 'A Puzzle about Belief' [13]), I am not certain that he would endorse this particular application of the 'schmidentity' strategy to showing the substitutivity phenomena evidentially irrelevant. (I hope that he would.)

proposition that Hesperus is Hesperus, he seems not to believe (and indeed to disbelieve) the proposition that Hesperus is Phosphorus. That is, upon substitution of 'Phosphorus' for the second occurrence of 'Hesperus' in the true sentence

(4) Jones believes that Hesperus is Hesperus

we obtain the evidently false sentence

(5) Jones believes that Hesperus is Phosphorus.

The apparent failure of substitutivity in propositional-attitude attributions is generally taken by philosophers to constitute a decisive refutation of the sort of account I advocate. But the very phenomena that appear to show that substitutivity fails would arise even if the Millian theory were absolutely correct (for standard English) and substitutivity of co-referential proper names in propositional-attitude attributions were uniformly valid. In particular, the same feeling of invalidity in connection with substitution in such attributions as (4) would arise even in a language for which it was stipulated—say, by an authoritative linguistic committee that legislates the grammar and semantics of the language, and to which all speakers of the language give their cooperation and consent—that the theory of *Frege's Puzzle* is correct. Suppose, for example, that such a committee decreed that there are to be two new individual constants, 'Schmesperus' and 'Schmosphorus'. (I am deliberately following the genius as closely as possible.) It is decreed that these two words are to function exactly like the mathematician's variables 'x', 'y', and 'z' as regards information value, except that they are to remain constant (with whatever other differences this key difference requires)—the constant value of the first being the first heavenly body visible at dusk and the constant value of the second being the last heavenly body visible at dawn. Suppose further that some English speakers—for example, the astronomers—are aware that these two new constants are co-referential, and hence synonymous. Nevertheless, even if our character Jones were fully aware of the legislative decree in connection with 'Schmesperus' and 'Schmosphorus', he would remain ignorant of their co-reference. Jones would dissent from such queries as 'Is Schmesperus the same heavenly body as Schmosphorus?' Would those who are in the know—the astronomers—automatically regard the new constants as completely interchangeable, even in propositional-attitude attributions? Almost certainly not. English speakers who use 'ketchup' and 'catsup' as exact synonyms but who do not reflect philosophically on the matter—and even some who do reflect philosophically—may be inclined to assent to the sentence 'Sasha believes that ketchup is a sandwich condiment, but he does not believe that catsup is.'[14] On reflection, however, it emerges that this sentence expresses a logical impossibility, since the proposition that catsup is a sandwich condiment just is the proposition that ketchup is a sandwich condiment. Similarly, speakers who agree to abide by the legislative committee's decree about 'Schmesperus' and 'Schmosphorus' and who recognize that these two terms are co-referential—especially if these speakers

---

[14] For similar claims, see for example Burge's 'Belief and Synonymy' [10]. Burge explicitly disagrees with my contention that such claims express logical impossibilities.

do not reflect philosophically on the implications of the decree in connection with such *de re* constructions as (1)—might for independent pragmatic reasons be led to utter or to assent to such sentences as 'Jones believes that Schmesperus appears in the evening, but he does not believe that Schmosphorus does' and 'Jones believes that Schmesperus is Schmesperus, but he does not believe that Schmesperus is Schmosphorus.' The astronomers may be led to utter the latter sentence, for example, in order to convey (without knowing it) the complex fact about Jones that he agrees to the proposition about Venus that it is it, taking it in the way he would were it presented to him by the sentence 'Schmesperus is Schmesperus' but not taking it in the way he would were it presented to him by the sentence 'Schmesperus is Schmosphorus'. The astronomers would thus unknowingly speak in a way that conflicts with the usage to which they have agreed. This, in turn, would lead to their judging such belief attributions as 'Jones believes that Schmesperus is Schmosphorus' not only inappropriate but literally false, and to the unmistakable feeling that substitution of 'Schmosphorus' for (some occurrences of) 'Schmesperus' in such attributions as 'Jones believes that Schmesperus is Schmesperus' is logically invalid. Insofar as the same phenomena that give rise to Frege's puzzle about identity sentences and to the appearance of substitutivity failure would arise even in a language for which the theory advanced in *Frege's Puzzle* was true by fiat and unanimous consent (and do in fact arise with respect to such straightforward strict synonyms as 'ketchup' and 'catsup'), these phenomena cannot be taken to refute the theory.

IV

The anti-Millian argument deriving from the apparent failure of substitutivity is closely related to the original Fregean argument about the informativeness of 'Hesperus is Phosphorus'. The analogue of the questionable premiss that 'Hesperus is Phosphorus' is informative is the assertion that (5) is false (or that 'Hesperus is Phosphorus' does not correctly give the content of one of Jones's beliefs, etc.). This premiss too, I claim, is incorrect.[15] However, this premiss, unlike its analogue in

---

[15] I do not deny the initial intuitive force of the premisses that 'Hesperus is Phosphorus' is informative and that (5) is false; I argue that they are nevertheless erroneous, and I propose an explanation for their initial pull. My rejection of these premisses is by no means a standard position among Millians. A more common Millian reaction is to concede these premisses, and to challenge instead the relevant analogue of Frege's Law—for example, the common and extremely plausible assumption that if 'Hesperus' has the same information value as 'Phosphorus' (as Millianism requires), then (4) is true if and only if (5) is. (The assumption has been challenged merely on the grounds that Millianism is not committed to it. Such a reaction misjudges the force of the Fregean argument: the assumption is independently compelling, and taken in conjunction with the other premisses, it precludes Millianism. The Millian is under the gun to reject either this premiss or one of the others as untrue, and to motivate his or her rejection of the offending premiss.) It has been argued, for example, that whereas (5) attributes belief of a proposition, it does not attribute belief of the very content of 'Hesperus is Phosphorus' (i.e., the singular proposition about Venus that it is it). This merely evades the general problem. Consider instead the parallel assumption that if 'Hesperus is Phosphorus' has the same information (proposition) content as 'Hesperus is Hesperus', then the former correctly gives the content of one of Jones's beliefs if and only if the latter does.

the original Fregean argument, does not simply beg the question. The intuition that (5) is false (according to the story) is strong and universal. We have seen that this intuition cannot be regarded as decisive—or even evidentially relevant—regarding the question of the actual truth value of (5), since (for some reason) the intuition of falsity would arise in any case. But there are forceful reasons for deeming (5) false, and the intuition of falsity must be addressed and explained. A full reply to the objection from the apparent failure of substitutivity involves greater complexities.[16]

In *Frege's Puzzle*, I propose the sketch of an analysis of the binary relation of belief between believers and propositions (sometimes Russellian singular propositions). I take the belief relation to be, in effect, the existential generalization of a ternary relation, *BEL*, among believers, propositions, and some third type of entity. To believe a proposition p is to adopt an appropriate favorable attitude toward p when taking p in some relevant *way*. It is to agree to p, or to assent mentally to p, or to approve of p, or some such thing, when taking p a certain way. This is the *BEL* relation. The third relata for the *BEL* relation are perhaps something like *modes* of acquaintance or familiarity with propositions, or *ways* in which a believer may take a given proposition. The important thing is that, by definition, they are such that if a fully rational believer adopts conflicting attitudes (such as belief and disbelief, or belief and suspension of judgment) toward propositions p and q, then the believer must take p and q in different ways, by means of different modes of acquaintance, in harboring the conflicting attitudes towards them—even if p and q are in fact the same proposition. More generally, if a fully rational agent construes objects x and y as distinct (or even merely withholds construing them as one and the very same—as might be evidenced, for example, by the agent's adopting conflicting beliefs or attitudes concerning x and y), then for some appropriate notion of a *way* of taking an object, the agent takes x and y in different ways, even if in fact $x = y$.[17] Of course, to use a distinction of Kripke's, this formulation is far too vague to constitute a fully developed *theory* of ways-of-taking-objects and their role in belief formation, but it does provide a *picture* of belief that differs significantly from the sort of picture of propositional attitudes

---

This assumption is virtually as certain as Frege's Law. Yet common sense dictates that 'Hesperus is Hesperus' does, and 'Hesperus is Phosphorus' does not, correctly give the content of one of Jones's beliefs (since Jones sincerely and reflectively assents to the first while dissenting from the second, etc.). Cf. *Frege's Puzzle* (pp. 5–6, 87–92, and *passim*).

[16] I provide only an outline of my reply here. See *Frege's Puzzle* (especially pp. 80–118) for the details.

[17] An appropriate notion of a way of taking an object is such that if an agent encounters a single object several times and each time construes it as a different object from the objects in the previous encounters, or even as a different object *for all he or she knows*, then each time he or she takes the object in a new and different way. This is required in order to accommodate the fact that an agent in such circumstances may (perhaps *inevitably will*) adopt several conflicting attitudes toward what is in fact a single object. One cannot require, however, that these ways-of-taking-objects are rich enough by themselves to determine the object so taken, without the assistance of extra-mental, contextual factors. Presumably, twin agents who are molecule-for-molecule duplicates, and whose brains are in exactly the same configuration down to the finest detail, may encounter different (though duplicate) objects, taking them in the very same way. Likewise, a single agent might be artificially induced through brain manipulations into taking different objects the same way. Cf. *Frege's Puzzle* (p. 173n1).

advanced by Frege or Russell, and enough can be said concerning the *BEL* relation to allow for at least the sketch of a solution to certain philosophical problems, puzzles, and paradoxes involving belief.[18]

In particular, the *BEL* relation satisfies the following three conditions:

(a) *A* believes *p* if and only if there is some *x* such that *A* is familiar with *p* by means of *x* and *BEL*(*A*, *p*, *x*);[19]
(b) *A* may believe *p* by standing in *BEL* to *p* and some *x* by means of which *A* is familiar with *p* without standing in *BEL* to *p* and all *x* by means of which *A* is familiar with *p*;
(c) In one sense of 'withhold belief', *A* withholds belief concerning *p* (either by disbelieving or by suspending judgment) if and only if there is some *x* by means of which *A* is familiar with *p* and not-*BEL*(*A*, *p*, *x*).

These conditions generate a philosophically important distinction between withholding belief and failure to believe (i.e., not believing). In particular, one may both withhold belief from and believe the very same proposition simultaneously. (Neither withholding belief nor failure to believe is to be identified with the related notions of disbelief and suspension of judgment—which are two different ways of withholding belief, in this sense, and which may occur simultaneously with belief of the very same proposition in a single believer.)

It happens in most cases (though not all) that when a believer believes some particular proposition *p*, the relevant third relatum for the *BEL* relation is a function of the believer and some particular *sentence* of the believer's language. There is, for example, the binary function *f* that assigns to any believer *A* and sentence *S* of *A*'s language, the *way A* takes the proposition contained in *S* (in *A*'s language with respect to *A*'s context at some particular time *t*) were it presented to *A* (at *t*) through the very sentence *S*, if there is exactly one such way of taking the proposition in question. (In some cases, there are too many such ways of taking the proposition in question.)

According to this account, (5) is true in the story of Jones and the planet Venus, since Jones agrees to the proposition that Hesperus is Phosphorus when taking it in a certain way—for example, if one points to Venus at dusk and says (peculiarly enough) 'That is that', or when the proposition is presented to him by such sentences as 'Hesperus is Hesperus' or 'Phosphorus is Phosphorus'. That is,

BEL[Jones, that Hesperus is Phosphorus, *f*(Jones, 'Hesperus is Hesperus')].

Jones also withholds belief concerning whether Hesperus is Hesperus. In fact, according to my account, he believes that Hesperus is not Hesperus! For he agrees

---

[18] The *BEL* relation is applied to additional puzzles in 'Reflexivity'[26].
[19] I do not claim that a sentence of the form ⌜*A* believes *p*⌝ is exactly synonymous with the existential formula on the right-hand side of the 'if and only if' in condition (a). I do claim that condition (a) is a (metaphysically) necessary, conceptually *a priori* truth. (See note 5 above concerning the contents of predicates. It may be helpful to think of the English verb 'believe' as a *name* for the binary relation described by the right-hand side of (a), i.e., for the existential generalization on the third argument-place of the *BEL* relation.) My claim in *Frege's Puzzle* (p. 111) that belief may be so 'analyzed' is meant to entail that condition (a) is a necessary *a priori* truth, not that the two sides of the biconditional are synonymous. (My own view is that something along these lines is all that can be plausibly claimed for such purported philosophical 'analyses' as have been offered for ⌜*A* knows *p*⌝, ⌜*A* perceives *B*⌝, ⌜*A* (nonnaturally) means *p* in uttering *S*⌝, etc.)

to the proposition that Hesperus is not Hesperus, taking it in the way he would were it presented to him by the sentence 'Hesperus is not Phosphorus'. That is,

BEL[Jones, that Hesperus is not Hesperus, f(Jones, 'Hesperus is not Phosphorus')],

and hence, assuming Jones is fully rational, it is not the case that

BEL[Jones, that Hesperus is Hesperus, f(Jones, 'Hesperus is Phosphorus')].

As noted above, these consequences of my account do not conform with the way we actually speak. Instead it is customary when discussing Jones's predicament to say such things as 'Jones does not realize that Hesperus is Phosphorus; in fact, he believes that Hesperus is *not* Phosphorus.' It is partly for this reason that the anti-Millian's premiss that (5) is false does not simply beg the question. Yet, according to my account, what we say when we deny such things as (5) is literally false. In fact, (5)'s literal truth conditions are, according to the view I advocate, conditions that are plainly fulfilled (in the context of the Jones story). Why, then, do we not say such things, and instead say just the opposite? Why is it that substitution of 'Phosphorus' for 'Hesperus'—or even of 'Schmosphorus' for 'Schmesperus'—*feels* invalid in propositional-attitude attributions? Some explanation of our speech patterns and intuitions of invalidity in these sorts of cases is called for. The explanation I offer in *Frege's Puzzle* is somewhat complex, consisting of three main parts. The first part of the explanation for the common disposition to deny or to dissent from (5) is that speakers may have a tendency to confuse the content of (5) with that of

(5′) Jones believes that 'Hesperus is Phosphorus' is true (in English).

Since sentence (5′) is obviously false, this confusion naturally leads to a similarly unfavorable disposition toward (5). This part of the explanation cannot be the whole story, however, since even speakers who know enough about semantics to know that the fact that Hesperus is Phosphorus is logically independent of the fact that the sentence 'Hesperus is Phosphorus' is true, and who are careful to distinguish the content of (5) from that of (5′), are nevertheless unfavorably disposed toward (5) itself—because of the fact that Jones demurs whenever the query 'Is Hesperus the same heavenly body as Phosphorus?' is put to him.

The second part of my explanation for (5)'s appearance of falsity is that its denial is the product of a plausible but mistaken inference from the fact that Jones sincerely dissents (or at least does not sincerely assent) when queried 'Is Hesperus Phosphorus?', while fully understanding the question and grasping its content, or (as Keith Donnellan has pointed out) even from his expressions of preference for the Evening Star over the Morning Star. More accurately, ordinary speakers (and even most nonordinary speakers) are disposed to regard the fact that Jones does not agree to the proposition that Hesperus is Phosphorus, when taking it in a certain way (the way it might be presented to him by the very sentence 'Hesperus is Phosphorus'), as sufficient to warrant the denial of sentence (5). In the special sense explained in the preceding section, Jones withholds belief from the proposition that Hesperus is Phosphorus, actively failing to agree with it whenever it is put to him in so many words, and this fact misleads ordinary speakers, including Jones himself, into concluding that Jones harbors no favorable attitude of agreement whatsoever toward the proposition in question, and hence does not believe it.

The third part of the explanation is that, where someone under discussion has conflicting attitudes toward a single proposition that he or she takes to be two independent propositions (i.e., in the troublesome 'Hesperus'–'Phosphorus', 'Superman'–'Clark Kent' type cases), there is an established practice of using belief attributions to convey not only the proposition agreed to (which is specified by the belief attribution) but also the way the subject of the attribution takes the proposition in agreeing to it (which is no part of the semantic content of the belief attribution). Specifically, there is an established practice of using such a sentence as (5), which contains the uninteresting proposition that Jones believes the singular proposition about Venus that it is it, to convey furthermore that Jones agrees to this proposition *taking it in the way he would were it presented to him by the very sentence 'Hesperus is Phosphorus' (assuming he understands this sentence)*. That is, there is an established practice of using (5) to convey the false proposition that

BEL[Jones, that Hesperus is Phosphorus, f (Jones, 'Hesperus is Phosphorus')].

V

An unconventional objection has been raised by some self-proclaimed neo-Fregeans against versions of Millianism of the sort advanced in *Frege's Puzzle*. It is charged that such theories are, at bottom, versions of a neo-Fregean theory.[20] Ironically, this unorthodox criticism is invariably coupled with the further, standard criticism that such versions of Millianism are problematic in some way or other that neo-Fregean theory is not (for example, in counting sentence (5) true). The fact that this more familiar criticism is directly contrary to the newer criticism is all but completely ignored. More importantly, this more recent criticism betrays a serious misunderstanding of the gulf that separates Frege's theory from that of Mill or Russell.

It should be said that the theory of *Frege's Puzzle* does indeed follow Frege's theoretical views in a number of significant respects. First and foremost, the theory sees the information value (contribution to proposition-content) of such compound expressions as definite descriptions as complexes whose constituents are contributed by the component expressions and whose structure parallels the syntactic structure of the compound itself. Although my theory has been called 'neo-Russellian', it departs radically from the theory of Russell in treating definite descriptions as genuine singular terms, and not as contextually defined 'incomplete symbols' or quantificational locutions. In addition to this, a semantic distinction is observed, following Frege's distinction of *Bedeutung* and *Sinn*, between a definite description's referent and the

---

[20] The charge has been made both in oral discussion and in print. See Forbes [5] (pp. 456–457), Smith [32], and Wagner [34] (p. 446). A very similar charge was apparently first made by Gareth Evans, in Section VI of his 'Understanding Demonstratives' [3] (pp. 298–300). Although Evans's criticism was aimed at John Perry's views on demonstratives, a great deal of my reply to my own critics extends to Evans's criticism of Perry.

description's information value. A similar distinction is maintained for predicates, sentential connectives, quantifiers, other operators, and even for whole sentences. The referent of a predicate is taken to be its semantic characteristic function from (sequences of) objects to truth values; the information value is taken to be something intensional, like an attribute or concept. Sentences are viewed entirely on the model of a definite description that refers (typically nonrigidly) to a truth value. The content ('information value') of a sentence is taken to be a proposition—the sort of thing that is asserted or denied, believed or disbelieved (or about which judgment is suspended), etc., something that is never-changing in truth value. The account of predicates, sentences and the rest as referring to their extensions is defended by means of the principle of extensionality (the principle that the referent of a compound expression is typically a function solely of the referents of the component expressions and their manner of composition). In all of these respects, the theory advanced in *Frege's Puzzle* self-consciously follows Frege.

There remains one crucial difference, however: the information value of a simple singular term is identified with its referent. This major plank makes the theory Millian (or 'neo-Russellian'), and hence severely and deeply anti-Fregean.

Although a great deal of attention has been paid to the differences between Russell and Frege over the question of whether it is false that the present king of France is bald, their disagreement on this question is dwarfed in significance by their disagreement over the information values of simple proper names. This primary bone of contention emerged in correspondence in 1904, even before Russell came to herald his Theory of Descriptions, which later supplemented his Millianism.[21] Russell answered Frege's protest that Mont Blanc with its snowfields cannot be a constituent of the 'thought', or information, that Mont Blanc is more than 4000 meters high, arguing that unless we admit that Mont Blanc is indeed a constituent of the content of the sentence 'Mont Blanc is over 4000 meters high' we obtain the absurd conclusion that we know nothing at all concerning Mont Blanc. Although Frege apparently made no attempt at a response (Russell did not seem to be fully apprehending Frege's remarks), one can be certain that he did not regard Russell's vision of the proposition that Mont Blanc is over 4000 meters high as merely a minor departure from his own sense-reference theory. There can be no real doubt that Frege would have vigorously denounced all versions of Millianism as completely inimical to his theoretical point of view.[22]

---

[21] In Frege's *Philosophical and Mathematical Correspondence* [8] (pp. 163, 169–170; also in Salmon and Soames, *Propositions and Attitudes* [30], pp. 56–57).

[22] The (allegedly) neo-Fregean charge that my account is ultimately Fregean is sometimes coupled with (and perhaps predicated on) an extraordinary interpretation of Frege, advanced by Evans (in 'Understanding Demonstratives' [3], and in *The Varieties of Reference* [4] (pp. 22–30 and *passim*), on which Frege is supposed to have held that typical nonreferring proper names have no Fregean sense and that declarative sentences involving such names (in ordinary extensional contexts, or in 'purely referential position'), while they appear to express thoughts, do not really do so. This highly unorthodox interpretation is based heavily on what seems a tendentious reading of an ambiguous passage in Frege's *Posthumous Writings* [7] (p. 30). Evans and his followers may have been misled by Frege's unfortunate term 'mock thought' (the translators' rendering of Frege's '*Scheingedanke*', which might also be translated as 'sham thought' or 'pseudo-thought'), and by his

What, then, is the rationale for the charge that my version of Millianism is, at bottom, a neo-Fregean theory? My critics have not been absolutely clear on this point. The charge appears to stem from my acknowledgment of something like *ways of taking objects*, and my reliance on them to explain away the appearance of falsity in connection with such propositional-attitude attributions as (5). To this somewhat vague and general criticism, a specific and detailed response was offered in *Frege's Puzzle*.[23] To begin with, my ways-of-taking-objects do not have all of the features that characterize Fregean senses. (See below.) Even if they had, however, they play a significantly different role in my theory. My analogy to the philosophy of perception (pp. 122–125) illustrates the anti-Fregean nature of my view (despite its acknowledgment of sense-like entities): Whereas my theory is analogous to the naive theory that we perceive external objects—apples, tables, chairs—Fregean theory is analogous to the sophisticated theory that the only objects of genuine perception are percepts, visual images, auditory images, and so on. The naive theorist of perception sees the 'sees' in 'Jones sees the apple' as expressing a relation between perceivers and external objects, and its

habitual use of the term 'fiction' in an artificially broad sense—roughly, as a term for any piece of discourse or line of thought (whether of fiction, in the ordinary sense, or otherwise) in which senses occur without *Bedeutungen* and/or in which sentences or their thought contents occur that are either without truth value or not put forward as true. (This use of 'fiction' is not especially remarkable for a mathematician/logician/philosopher keenly interested in truth and its properties.) Evans evidently thought that Frege regarded any such discourse on the model of genuine fiction, and as only seeming to have cognitive content.

In the same work by Frege appear numerous passages that unambiguously preclude Evans's unconventional interpretation. *Cf.*, for example, pp. 118, 122, 194, and especially 191–192, 225. Similar remarks occur in '*Über Sinn und Bedeutung*', in English in [9], pp. 162–163. Curiously, Evans dismisses these passages as 'dubiously consistent with the fundamentals' of Frege's post-1890 philosophy of semantics, although Evans fails to cite any passage which is uncontroversially post-1890 and in which Frege unambiguously asserts something straightforwardly inconsistent with these passages (something that uncontroversially entails that the sense of an ordinary proper name depends for its existence on the object it determines). This interpretive stance makes it difficult to imagine what Evans and his followers would accept as convincing evidence that Frege did not hold the theory they attribute to him. (In fact, Frege's use of the phrase 'mock proper name' or 'pseudo proper name'—for nonreferring but nevertheless real singular terms—in the central passage cited by Evans would, even by itself, tend to indicate that Evans's reading of this very passage is not faithful to Frege's intent. *Cf.* also Frege's 'Thoughts' [6] (p. 38), where Frege speaks of 'mock assertions' made either by actors on the stage—'it is only acting, only fiction'—or in poetry, where 'we have the case of thoughts being expressed without being actually put forward as true', not for lack of the thoughts themselves but for lack of 'the requisite seriousness' on the speaker's part.) In any event, Frege unambiguously denied (*Posthumous Writings* [7], pp. 187, 225) that the referent of a proper name like 'Mont Blanc' or 'Etna' is involved in any way in the name's information value; Frege's *explicit* theory (whether internally consistent or not, and whether compatible with any secret doctrines or not) is therefore diametrically opposed to Millianism. (*Cf.* Salmon, *Reference and Essence* [25] (pp. 9–23), and *Frege's Puzzle* (pp. 46–50, 63–65, 78). John McDowell, who appears to follow Evans's misreading of Frege, nevertheless disagrees with Evans's notational-variant charge on these, or related, grounds. See McDowell's 'Engaging with the Essential' [15] (p. 61), and '*De Re Senses*' [16] (especially p. 104*n*15).) The important point as far as the present discussion is concerned is that (whatever Frege's real views were) my own view is a form of genuine Millianism.

[23] A number of passages in *Frege's Puzzle* are devoted to pointing out significant advantages of my version of Millianism over Fregean theory (and hence significant differences between them). *Cf.* pp. 2–7, 66–71 (and *passim*), and chapter 9, especially pp. 119–126. See also note 18 above.

grammatical direct object 'the apple' as occurring in purely referential position and referring there to the apple. By contrast, the sophisticated theorist sees the 'sees' as expressing a relation between perceivers and mental objects, and 'the apple' as referring *in that context* to Jones's visual apple image. The two theories disagree fundamentally over *what is perceived*. The naive theorist need not deny that internal sensory images play a role in perception. He or she may even propose an analysis of perceptual relations (like seeing) that involves existential generalization over mental objects. Why not? Perception obviously does involve experience; there need be no quarrel over such trivial and extremely general matters. The fundamental disagreement over the objects of perception remains. This disagreement will manifest itself not only in differing interpretations of such sentences as 'Jones sees the apple', but often even in differing judgments concerning its truth value (for instance when Jones is hallucinating).

Likewise, I do not quarrel with Fregeans over the trivial question of whether belief and disbelief involve such things as conceptualizing. Our fundamental disagreement concerns the more substantial matter of *what is believed*—in particular, the question whether what is believed is actually made up entirely of such things as 'ways of conceptualizing'. The *ways of taking objects* that I countenance are, according to my view, not even so much as mentioned in ordinary propositional-attitude attributions. In particular, on my view, a 'that'-clause makes no reference whatsoever to any way of taking the proposition that is its referent, and a 'that'-clause whose only singular terms are simple (such as the one occurring in (5)) makes no reference whatsoever to any way of taking (or conceiving of, etc.) the individuals referred to by those terms. Consequently, ways-of-taking-objects are not mentioned in (an appropriate specification of) the truth conditions of such an attribution. The only way they come into the picture at all is that in some cases, a certain sort of analysis of the propositional attribute designated by the relevant predicate (e.g., belief) involves existential generalization over them—and even this is not true in all cases. There are many propositional locutions that are not attitudinal as such, and that consequently do not involve ways-of-taking-objects in the way that belief does—for example, 'The laboratory test indicates that Mary has contracted the disease' or better still 'It is necessary that Mary is human' (perhaps even 'Jones asserted that Venus is a star'). In short, my ways-of-taking-objects have nothing whatsoever to do with the semantic content of ordinary sentences, and consequently they have nothing whatsoever to do with the semantics of propositional attributions, even attributions of propositional attitude. Ways-of-taking-objects hail from philosophical psychology, not from philosophical semantics.

By contrast, for the Fregean, ways of conceptualizing objects are explicitly referred to in, and pivotal to the truth conditions of, all propositional attributions. I sharply disagree with the Fregean who claims that alethic modality—or even that laboratory tests—involve such things as conceptualizing in just the same way that belief does. (Consider the Fregean account of such valid inferences as 'The physician believes whatever the laboratory test indicates, and the test indicates that Mary has contracted the disease; hence the physician believes that Mary has contracted the disease', or 'It is necessary that Mary is human, and Jones believes that Mary is human; hence Jones believes at least one necessary truth.')[24] My fundamental disagreement with Fregeans over the objects of propositional attitude is manifested not only in our differing interpretations of propositional-attitude attributions, but often even in different judgments concerning their truth value. (Recall the conflict between the charge that my version of Millianism is neo-Fregean, and the more orthodox Fregean criticisms of Millianism.)

Fortunately, Graeme Forbes has provided a somewhat more detailed account of how my view is supposed to 'dissolve' into a neo-Fregean theory.[25] It is especially instructive to examine his rationale for this criticism.

Forbes exploits the fact that the neo-Fregean is not shackled by the letter of Frege's specific views, and may preserve the general spirit of Frege's theoretical point of view while departing in various details. Forbes proposes two ways in which a neo-Fregean theory can converge, in certain respects, with my version of Millianism.[26] One thing the neo-Fregean may do is to regard a belief attribution ⌜Jones believes that S⌝, as uttered by a given speaker, as asserting not that Jones stands in the belief relation specifically to P, where P is the 'thought' (proposition) that is the sense of S in the speaker's idiolect, but instead that Jones stands in the belief relation to some thought or other that is relevantly *similar* to P. In this way, the neo-Fregean might find his or her way to delivering the same (somewhat liberal) verdicts as I do with respect to various controversial propositional-attitude attributions (presumably, such as (5)).

Forbes's second proposal suggests a particular way of fleshing out the similarity relation involved in the first proposal, one that is designed to ensure that the neo-Fregean's verdicts will always coincide exactly with mine. It is well-known that Fregean theory runs into difficulty with such *de re* constructions as (1) or (1'). Although Frege himself was largely tacit concerning constructions involving *belief of*, a number of neo-Fregeans have proposed various ways of accommodating them within the spirit of Fregean theory. The most famous (and I believe the most compelling) of these neo-Fregean proposals is still David Kaplan's from 'Quantifying In' [10].[27] For present purposes, we shall modify Kaplan's proposal slightly. As can be gleaned

---

[24] Notice also the relative lack of hesitation in substituting for 'Mary' in 'The test indicates that Mary has contracted the disease' any other proper name Mary may have, or even the pronoun 'she' accompanied by ostension to Mary. Where ways-of-taking-objects obviously play no role, they do not matter to what we say in ascribing attitudes. Notice also our reluctance to substitute 'the woman who spent 17 years studying primate behavior in the wild'. Where ways-of-taking-objects obviously do play a role, they do matter to what we say.

[25] Forbes [5] (p. 457).

[26] Although Forbes does not treat these two proposals as two parts of a single proposal, I shall treat them in unison in this reconstruction of his criticism. Forbes's overall criticism is considerably more effective when his two proposals are united into a single proposal, and I believe that doing so does not necessarily conflict with Forbes's intentions. Either proposal taken alone leaves obvious and significant (not merely notational) differences between the resulting (so-called) neo-Fregean account and my version of Millianism.

[27] Kaplan himself has long since given up on neo-Fregean attempts to accommodate the effects of direct reference.

from the previous section, the Fregean's difficulty with such constructions as (1) arises from a lack of genuine Fregean sense in connection with the open sentence (3), taken under an assignment of a value to x. Kaplan's analysis (as here modified) reconstrues (1) in such a way that (3) is no longer regarded as a proper (i.e., semantic) constituent. Specifically, the open sentence (2) is analyzed into the following:

(6) $(\exists \alpha)[\alpha$ *represents* x to Jones & Jones believes ⌜α is a star⌝],

where the special representation relation designated in the first conjunct is such as to entail that α is an individual concept (a sense appropriate to a singular term) that determines x as its referent, and where the quasi-quotation marks occurring in the second conjunct are sense-quoting marks that function in a manner analogous to standard quasi-quotation marks with respect to (i.e., without attempting to quote the sense of) the sense variable 'α'.[28] (Think of this analysis as resulting from a contextual definition for open 'that'-clauses, analogous to Russell's contextual definition for definite descriptions—complete with scope distinctions, the definiendum's lack of 'meaning in isolation', and all the rest.) It is a (fairly) straightforward matter to extend this analysis of such quasi-formal *de re* constructions as (1) to such informal constructions as (1'): The neo-Fregean analysis of (2') is obtained from (6) by substituting the pronoun 'it' for the free variable 'x'.[29] Replacing the bound occurrence of (2) in (1) by its analysis (6) (or the scattered occurrence of (2') in (1') by a nonscattered occurrence of its analysis), we obtain something equivalent to

(7) $(\exists \alpha)[\alpha$ *represents* Venus to Jones & Jones believes ⌜α is a star⌝],

The neo-Fregean is struck by the fact that this analysis of (1) and (1') is significantly similar to my proposed analysis of

(8) Jones believes that Venus is a star.

It is a small step to obtain (7) from (8). One need only extend Kaplan's analysis further, to cover all cases in which a simple singular term—whether a variable or pronoun, or even a proper name or demonstrative—occurs free in a propositional-attitude attribution. We thus obtain a special neo-Fregean theory, one according to which (8) asserts that Jones stands in the belief relation to some thought or other to the effect ⌜α is a star⌝, where α is a sense that represents Venus to Jones. Thus (8) is counted true both by this theory and by my version of Millianism. Similarly, (5) is seen on this theory as asserting that Jones stands in the belief relation to some

---

[28] Strictly speaking, different analyses result from different choices for the representation relation.
[29] Notice that the proposed analyses of such constructions as (2) and (2'), if sound, would effectively block the argument given in Section II above in connection with (1) and (1')—by falsifying the premise that an open sentence of the form ⌜a believes that S⌝ is true under an assignment of values to variables if and only if the referent of a, under the assignment, believes the content of S, under the assignment. (See note 13 above.) The argument takes (2) and (2') at face value, rather than as contextually defined in terms of quantification and quasi-sense-quotation. Kaplan's analysis allows the neo-Fregean to eschew singular propositions altogether, even in the semantics of *de re* constructions. But how plausible is it—independently of the Fregean motivation for the analysis—that (3) is not a (semantic) constituent of (2)?

thought or other to the effect ⌜α is β⌝, where each of α and β is a sense that represents Venus to Jones. Thus (5) is also counted true, as with my Millianism. Therefore, Forbes argues, my version of Millianism dissolves, for all intents and purposes, into this special neo-Fregean theory—with my talk of 'singular propositions' and 'ways of taking objects' merely a notational variant of the neo-Fregean's talk of 'representation' and 'individual concepts'.[30]

One significant difficulty with this neo-Fregean proposal is that it does not validate such apparently valid inferences as 'Smith believes that Bush will win the presidency, and so does Jones; hence there is something (some proposition) that both Smith and

---

[30] A full development of this (allegedly) neo-Fregean theory would involve David Kaplan's procedure of *articulation*, described in 'Opacity' [11] (p. 270).

I have not followed Forbes's proposal in detail. Forbes (on my reconstruction—see note 27) suggests instead that my Millianism be taken to be a notational variant of a neo-Fregean theory according to which (8) asserts that Jones stands in the belief relation to some thought or other to the effect ⌜α obtains⌝, where α represents the entire singular proposition about Venus that it is a star to Jones. This proposal is thwarted, however, in case Jones believes Venus to be a star (so that (8) is, on my view, true), but—perhaps because of Jones's philosophical skepticism concerning singular propositions in general—he does not also believe this singular proposition to obtain (so that Forbes's suggested construal of (8) is false). An analogous difficulty arises if the belief that the singular proposition obtains is replaced with the belief that Venus has the property of being a star. (Suppose Jones is skeptical of properties.)

Forbes's proposed (alleged) version of neo-Fregeanism follows his own in substituting the singular proposition about Venus that it is a star for its truth value as the referent of the sentence 'Venus is a star', and likewise in substituting the property of being a star for (the characteristic function of) its extension as the referent of the predicate 'is a star'. These planks disqualify Forbes's theory as genuinely neo-Fregean. Furthermore (as Alonzo Church and Kurt Gödel independently showed), assuming extensionality, each plank precludes the conjunction of the following two plausible principles: (a) that a definite description refers to the individual that uniquely answers to it, if there is one; (b) that trivially equivalent expressions are, if not strictly synonymous, at least close enough in meaning as to ensure their having the same referent. Forbes apparently rejects both of these principles. In fact, he adopts a Russellian account both of definite descriptions and of modal contexts. These various anti-Fregean elements strongly invite the countercharge that Forbes's so-called neo-Fregean theory collapses into a neo-Russellian theory. (But see below.)

A more literal reading of Forbes's proposal is that my assertion that '(8) is true if and only if there is a way of taking the singular proposition about Venus that it is a star such that Jones agrees to this proposition when taking it that way' is merely a notational variant of the neo-Fregean's thesis that the *de re* attribution 'Jones believes of the state of affairs of Venus's being a star that it obtains' is true if and only if there is some state-of-affairs concept α that represents Venus's being a star to Jones and Jones believes ⌜α obtains⌝. This interpretation construes my assertions ostensibly assigning truth conditions to (8) as really making disguised reference to a different sentence altogether, and as assigning the truth conditions to this other sentence instead of to (8). I find this interpretation incredible, and assume it is not what Forbes intends. More likely, he means that my analysis of belief, together with the neo-Fregean analysis of *de re* locutions, make my use of (8) into a notational variant of the neo-Fregean's use of 'Jones believes of the state of affairs of Venus's being a star that it obtains'. (Analogously, Evans (*Varieties of Reference* [4]) seems to propose that Perry's use of such an attribution as (8) is a notational variant 'at best' of the neo-Fregean's use of something like (1').) But this would hardly make my (or Perry's) theory of (8) into a notational variant of the neo-Fregean's theory of *the very same sentence* (8)—we would still disagree concerning its truth conditions—unless the envisaged neo-Fregean goes further and construes (8) as a paraphrase of something like the relevant *de re* attribution. The proposal in the text represents my attempt to construct the strongest possible case for the spirit of Forbes's (and Evans's) criticism while staying as much as possible within the spirit of Fregean theory (and the bounds of plausibility).

Jones believe.'[31] This constitutes one fairly dramatic difference between the proposed theory and my version of Millianism. But there are more fundamental differences.

Does the proposed neo-Fregean theory even agree with my version of Millianism on every question of propositional-attitude attribution, without exception, as it is designed to do? On my theory, any propositional attribution involving a proper name within the scope of the 'that'-operator is deemed equivalent to the corresponding *de re* construction in which the name is moved outside the scope of the 'that'-operator. (For instance, (8) is true if and only if (1') is.) Thus Forbes's proposed neo-Fregean theory succeeds in echoing the verdicts of my version of Millianism only insofar as neo-Fregean analyses along the lines of Kaplan's succeed in capturing the truth conditions of *de re* constructions. Several direct-reference theorists (including Kaplan) have mounted an impressive case that Kaplan-style neo-Fregean analyses fail in this attempt. Hilary Putnam's Twin-Earth argument suffices to demonstrate the point.[32] Oscar believes his friend Wilbur to be stingy, while Oscar's exact doppelganger on Twin Earth, Oscar$_{TE}$, likewise believes his friend Wilbur$_{TE}$ to be stingy. Duplicates in every detail, Oscar and Oscar$_{TE}$ believe the very same Fregean (nonsingular) thoughts. Neither Oscar nor Oscar$_{TE}$ is in possession of any Fregean individual concept (in which only senses occur as constituents) that differentiates between Wilbur and Wilbur$_{TE}$, and consequently neither possesses a Fregean sense that determines the relevant friend as referent independently of context. Assuming that the objects of belief (whether Fregean thoughts or Russellian singular propositions) and their constituents determine their objects (truth values, individuals, etc.) independently of context,[33] each believes something *de re* that

---

[31] Strictly speaking, this depends on the details of Forbes's neo-Fregean proposal. (The proposed theory certainly does not validate the inference 'Smith believes that Bush will win the presidency, and so does Jones; hence there is some proposition to which both Smith and Jones stand in the belief relation.') Forbes has confirmed in personal correspondence that the intended theory does not validate the inference in the text—on the most straightforward reading of its conclusion—and instead allows only the much weaker conclusion that Smith and Jones believe propositions of the same type. (He proposes taking this weaker conclusion as an alternative reading of the conclusion in the text.)

[32] 'Meaning and Reference' [18] (pp. 700–704 and *passim*). *Cf. Frege's Puzzle* (pp. 66–67, 70, 176n7).

[33] This assumption is shared by both Frege and myself. As Frege noted, propositions, or 'complete thoughts,' (unlike indexical sentences or their conventional meanings—or their senses-in-abstraction-from-context) do not change in truth value, or in the objects they concern, when placed in different settings within a single possible world. The alternative would be an account that allows that one subject A may believe one and the very same proposition (complete thought) p as another subject B, yet A's belief of p is correct, or concerns C, while B's belief of p is incorrect, or does not concern C—because of their differing contexts. Any such indexical account of propositions (as opposed to sentences or their meanings) evidently gets things wrong. For suppose p is the alleged 'indexical thought' believed by both Oscar and Oscar$_{TE}$ to the effect ⌜α is stingy⌝, where α is the relevant (complete) 'indexical individual concept'. Notice first that p cannot be the thought that Wilbur is stingy, since Oscar$_{TE}$ does not believe that thought (in his context, whatever that means), or any other thought concerning Wilbur. (The thought that Wilbur is stingy has nothing whatever to do with Wilbur$_{TE}$—on Twin Earth or anywhere else. It is definitely *not* indexical.) Nor is p the thought that *this* person here [pointing to Wilbur] is stingy, for precisely the same reason. Evidently, we do not express p (in our dialect) with the words 'Wilbur is stingy' or 'He [pointing to Wilbur]

the other does not. Oscar's belief concerning Wilbur is therefore irreducible to his beliefs of Fregean (nonsingular) thoughts. The sentence 'Oscar believes that Wilbur is stingy', which is true on my theory, is deemed false by the proposed neo-Fregean theory. The theories are thus diametrically opposed on a key issue.

The Twin-Earth thought experiment illustrates a further, and more central, divergence between my theory and Fregean theory. The way in which Oscar takes Wilbur is presumably exactly the same as the way in which Oscar$_{TE}$ takes Wilbur$_{TE}$—despite the fact that Oscar's thought of Wilbur that he is stingy and Oscar$_{TE}$'s thought of Wilbur$_{TE}$ that he is stingy concern different individuals. By contrast, for the Fregean, each individual concept determines a unique object, or nothing at all. Oscar's thought that Wilbur is stingy and Oscar$_{TE}$'s thought that Wilbur$_{TE}$ is stingy, if they were to have such thoughts concerning different individuals, would have to contain different individual concepts; the sense that Oscar attaches to the name 'Wilbur' would have to be different from the sense that Oscar$_{TE}$ attaches to the same name. This is made impossible by the fact that Oscar and Oscar$_{TE}$ are exact duplicates.[34] This sort

---

is stingy'. Nevertheless, barring singular propositions, p is supposed to be the thought that Oscar expresses (in his idiolect) with these words (or with these words-accompanied-by-pointing). Similarly for Oscar$_{TE}$—otherwise, they would not have the same nonsingular thoughts, and consequently would not be exact duplicates. Thus, on most theories (including orthodox Fregean theory and most of its contemporary variations), Oscar should be able to utter the words 'My Twin-Earth counterpart believes with me that Wilbur is stingy' truthfully (thereby attributing to Oscar$_{TE}$ a belief of p). But he cannot. The alleged indexical thought p, therefore, does not exist. (The fact that Oscar cannot truthfully say 'Oscar$_{TE}$ believes that Wilbur is stingy' might be urged as evidence in favor of the theory described in the text! On that theory, coupled with indexical thoughts, Oscar could truthfully say 'Oscar$_{TE}$ does not believe that Wilbur is stingy, but the sentence "Wilbur is stingy" does correctly give the content, in my idiolect, of one of Oscar$_{TE}$'s beliefs.' But taking the argument in this way would be perverse. The point of the argument is precisely that the thought that Oscar expresses with the words 'Wilbur is stingy' in his idiolect is no more indexical than the thought that we express in our dialect.)

[34] I can find no plausible way out of this problem for the Fregean. A favored response to this difficulty by self-proclaimed neo-Fregeans has been the postulation of special senses the grasping of which leaves no distinctive trace in one's inner (wholly internal, 'purely psychological') state of consciousness—so that exact duplicates like Oscar and Oscar$_{TE}$, whose inner states are exactly the same, nevertheless grasp different 'individual concepts'. This move faces a serious dilemma: Either the postulated 'senses' involve nonconceptual objects (presumably the objects they determine, or their surrogates) as constituents—and are thus individuated by their means—or they do not. If the former, the postulation amounts to the adoption of precisely the sort of theory against which Frege (post-1890) rebelled, while misleadingly couching this anti-Fregean theory in Fregean terminology and labeling the theory with the misnomer 'neo-Fregean'. An 'object-involving sense'—a Fregean *Sinn* with nonconceptual components—is a *contradiction in adjecto*; the hypothesized theory is the proverbial wolf in sheep's clothing. (See note 22 above. The arguments of the preceding sections apply equally against this anti-Fregean theory. See also *Frege's Puzzle* (p. 67–70).) If the latter, the response seems little more than a desperate attempt to stipulate or hypothesize what is intuitively impossible, or even conceptually incoherent. The very notion of a concept (*qua* graspable content) seems to include as a necessary condition that those concepts actively grasped or apprehended by someone at any given time, if free of constituents not themselves grasped by the mind, are determined by the grasper's inner state of consciousness—in the sense that such a concept is grasped by someone if and only if it is also grasped by anyone in exactly the same inner state. Actively grasping a purely conceptual concept just *is* a matter of (or, at least, supervenes on) being in a particular inner mental state. *Cf.* the last paragraph of 'Thoughts' [6] (p. 54), where Frege says that grasping or believing a thought is 'a process in the inner world of a thinker', and that 'when

of consideration points up a crucial difference—in many respects *the* crucial difference—between my ways-of-taking-objects (which are not precluded from determining their objects only contextually) and Fregean senses (which, since they are information values, cannot do so). (See note 18 above.)

The neo-Fregean might attempt to remedy this serious difficulty with his or her attempt to accommodate *de re* constructions, by tinkering with the Kaplan-style analysis (for example, by relaxing the determination requirement on representation). I remain doubtful that this can be successfully accomplished in a plausible manner without resorting to singular propositions, or the like. But suppose I am wrong and the neo-Fregean can find Fregeanistically acceptable necessary-and-sufficient conditions for *de re* belief and other *de re* propositional attributes, including alethic necessity. (Committed neo-Fregeans might suppose that this *must* be possible.) Would this show that my version of Millianism is simply a notational variant of a suitably designed neo-Fregean theory? Certainly not. Even if (1′) is true with respect to a possible circumstance if and only if Jones believes some Fregean thought or other of such-and-such a sort in that possible circumstance—so that, on my view, (8) is also true exactly on the same Fregean condition—still (8), according to my account, does not *say* that this Fregean condition is fulfilled. On my view, (8) asserts a certain relationship—the belief relationship—between Jones and the singular proposition about Venus that it is a star. It does not merely *characterize* Jones's belief as being of some Fregean thought *or other* of such-and-such a special sort; it *specifies* a particular belief and attributes it to Jones. In short, even if the neo-Fregean's promise can be kept by adjusting the Kaplan-style analysis (a very big 'if'), the suitably designed neo-Fregean theory ascribes to (8) a very different semantic content from that ascribed by my version of Millianism. The neo-Fregean's semantic truth conditions for (8) are, at best, *a priori* and metaphysically necessarily equivalent to my own. They are not identical.

Finally, we must consider whether the suitably designed theory would be neo-Fregean. It is true, of course, that a neo-Fregean need not follow the master in every detail. (I do not know of any follower of Frege, for instance, who has not shied away from Frege's views concerning the concept *horse*.) But there must be some limit as to how much departure still qualifies as neo-*Fregean*. Certainly the theory of Russell, for example, differs too extensively from that of Frege on central issues to qualify as neo-Fregean. (It is worth noting in this connection that Russell

---

a thought is grasped, it . . . brings about changes in the inner world of the one who grasps it'. See also *Reference and Essence* [25] (pp. 56–58, 65–69). If Oscar's believing ⌜α is stingy⌝ is a 'process in Oscar's inner world', where α is a purely conceptual individual concept representing Wilbur, and Oscar$_{TE}$ is in exactly the same inner state, how can he fail to believe exactly the same thing? On the other hand, if grasping the postulated individual concepts is not just a matter of being in a particular inner mental state, the entire account becomes quite mysterious. What exactly are these postulated entities—and what is the justification for calling them 'senses' or 'purely conceptual concepts' that the mind 'grasps', when the (alleged) act of grasping them leaves no distinguishing trace in one's inner state? (Contrast our concepts of *blue, down, left*.) Is there any plausible reason to suppose that there are such concepts that are pure yet traceless? What would *grasping* such an entity amount to, over and above one's inner state? Is there any plausible reason to believe that the mind engages in such activity?

too recognized certain nonsemantic elements from philosophical psychology in his correspondence with Frege over the proposition that Mont Blanc is over 4000 meters high. It is highly doubtful that Frege saw this as simply another way of saying what he himself was saying.) The sort of theory that Forbes envisions (on this reconstruction of his criticism) is a theory that denies that the 'that'-operator occurring in (8) is functioning there merely as a device for sense-quotation, in the same way that it functions in 'Jones believes that the first heavenly body visible at dusk is a star'; specifically, it denies that (8) asserts a relationship between Jones and the sense of the sentence 'Venus is a star'. Furthermore, the theory denies that (8) specifies a particular belief and attributes it to Jones, claiming instead that (8) merely characterizes Jones's belief as being one or another of a particular sort. Most significantly, the theory construes any occurrence of a simple singular term (even of a proper name) within the scope of the 'that'-operator in a propositional attribution (even in an attribution of propositional attitude) as completely open to substitution by any co-referential simple singular term. The theory is specifically designed to have the consequence that Jones believes that Hesperus is Hesperus if and only if he also believes that Hesperus is Phosphorus. It draws no significant distinction at all, in fact, between the ostensibly *de dicto* (8) and the patently *de re* (1'). Otherwise it would be very different from my version of Millianism—obviously so—and hence unsuited to support Forbes's charge of mere notational variance. I submit that there is not enough of Frege's overall theoretical point of view left here for this (would-be) theory to warrant the epithet 'neo-Fregean'.[35] The same would be true of any of its notational variants.

Nor is the envisioned theory a version of Millianism exactly. It is more a curious admixture, a strange brew made up of elements of both Fregeanism and Millianism. I do not claim that one (perhaps even an erstwhile Fregean) could not find reason to adopt this strange theory; I claim only that doing so would involve abandoning too much of the spirit of orthodox Fregean theory for the proponent to qualify as a neo-Fregean. Indeed, if (much to my surprise) genuinely Fregean necessary-and-sufficient conditions are eventually found for the *de re*, I would urge any committed anti-Millian to give the envisioned blend of Fregeanism and Millianism serious consideration as a superior alternative to neo-Fregeanism. Given greater flexibility, however, I would strongly advise against its adoption. Some version of genuine Millianism is much to be preferred. (This was the moral of Sections II and III above.)

---

[35] Essentially this same point is made, on similar grounds, by Mark Richard, 'Taking the Fregean Seriously' [21] (pp. 221–222). There, and also in 'Attitude Ascriptions, Semantic Theory, and Pragmatic Evidence' [20] (pp. 247–248), Richard makes the related criticism of (something like) the envisaged 'neo-Fregean' theory that, since it validates substitution of co-referential names, it lacks one of the primary motivations for the original Fregean theory of senses. (Here Richard also recognizes that the envisaged theory and Millianism assign different, even if equivalent, truth conditions to such propositional-attitude attributions as (8).)

REFERENCES

[1] Burge, T. (1978). 'Belief and Synonymy', *Journal of Philosophy*, 75: 119–138.
[2] Church, A. (1954). 'Intensional Isomorphism and Identity of Belief', *Philosophical Studies*, 5(5): 65–73. Also in N. Salmon and S. Soames (eds), *Propositions and Attitudes* (Oxford: Oxford University Press, 1988).
[3] Evans, G. (1981). 'Understanding Demonstratives', in H. Parret and J. Bouveresse (eds), *Meaning and Understanding* (Berlin and New York: De Gruyter).
[4] Evans, G. (1982). *The Varieties of Reference* (Oxford: Oxford University Press).
[5] Forbes, G. (1987). 'Review of Nathan Salmon's *Frege's Puzzle*', *The Philosophical Review*, 96(3): 455–458.
[6] Frege, G. (1918). 'Thoughts', in N. Salmon and S. Soames (eds), *Propositions and Attitudes* (Oxford: Oxford University Press, 1988). Originally appeared in English in *Mind* 65 (1956): 289–311.
[7] Frege, G. (1979). *Posthumous Writings*. H. Hermes, F. Kambartel, and F. Kaulbach (eds), P. Long and R. White (trans.) (Chicago: University of Chicago).
[8] Frege, G. (1980). *Philosophical and Mathematical Correspondence*. G. Gabriel, H. Hermes, F. Kambartel, C. Thiel, and A. Veraart (eds) (Chicago: University of Chicago Press).
[9] Frege, G. (1984). *Collected Papers on Mathematics, Logic, and Philosophy*. Brian McGuinness (ed.) (Oxford: Basil Blackwell).
[10] Kaplan, D. (1969). 'Quantifying In', in D. Davidson and G. Harman (eds), *Words and Objections: Essays on the Work of W. V. Quine* (Dordrecht: Reidel). Also in L. Linsky (ed.), *Reference and Modality* (Oxford: Oxford University Press, 1971).
[11] Kaplan, D. (1986). 'Opacity', in L. E. Hahn and P. A. Schilpp (eds), *The Philosophy of W. V. Quine* (La Salle: Open Court).
[12] Kripke, S. (1972). *Naming and Necessity* (Cambridge, Mass.: Harvard University Press).
[13] Kripke, S. (1979). 'A Puzzle about Belief', in A. Margalit (ed.), *Meaning and Use* (Dordrecht: Reidel). Also in N. Salmon and S. Soames (eds), *Propositions and Attitudes* (Oxford: Oxford University Press, 1988).
[14] Kripke, S. (1979). 'Speaker's Reference and Semantic Reference', in P. French, T. Vehling, and H. Wettstein (eds), *Contemporary Perspectives in the Philosophy of Language* (Minneapolis: University of Minnesota Press.
[15] McDowell, J. (1981). 'Engaging with the Essential', *Times Literary Supplement*, (January 16, 1981): 61–62.
[16] McDowell, J. (1984). '*De Re* Senses', in C. Wright (ed.), *Frege: Tradition and Influence* (Oxford: Basil Blackwell).
[17] Putnam, H. (1954). 'Synonymity and the Analysis of Belief Sentences', *Analysis*, 14: 114–122. Also in N. Salmon and S. Soames (eds), *Propositions and Attitudes* (Oxford: Oxford University Press, 1988).
[18] Putnam, H. (1973). 'Meaning and Reference', *Journal of Philosophy*, 70: 699–711.
[19] Putnam, H. (1979). 'Comments', in A. Margalit (ed.), *Meaning and Use* (Dordrecht: Reidel).
[20] Richard, M. (1986). 'Attitude Ascriptions, Semantic Theory, and Pragmatic Evidence', *Proceedings of the Aristotelian Society*, 87: 243–262.
[21] Richard, M. (1988). 'Taking the Fregean Seriously', in D. Austin (ed.), *Philosophical Analysis: A Defense by Example* (Dordrecht: Reidel).
[22] Russell, B. (1911). 'Knowledge by Acquaintance and Knowledge by Description', Chapter X of *Mysticism and Logic and Other Essays* (London: Longmans, Green and Company). Also

in N. Salmon and S. Soames (eds), *Propositions and Attitudes* (Oxford: Oxford University Press, 1988).

[23] Russell, B. (1918). 'The Philosophy of Logical Atomism', in R. C. Marsh (ed.), *Logic and Knowledge* (London: George Allen and Unwin, 1956). Also in D. Pears (ed.), *The Philosophy of Logical Atomism* (La Salle: Open Court, 1985).

[24] Salmon, N. (1979). 'Review of Leonard Linsky's *Names and Descriptions*', *Journal of Philosophy*, 76(8): 436–452.

[25] Salmon, N. (1981). *Reference and Essence* (Princeton: Princeton University Press, and Oxford: Basil Blackwell).

[26] Salmon, N. (1986). 'Reflexivity', *Notre Dame Journal of Formal Logic*, 27(3): 401–429. Also in N. Salmon and S. Soames (Oxford: Oxford University Press, 1988).

[27] Salmon, N. (1986). *Frege's Puzzle* (Cambridge, Mass.: MIT Press).

[28] Salmon, N. (1989). 'Illogical Belief', in J. Tomberlin (ed.), *Philosophical Perspectives 3: Philosophy of Mind and Action Theory* (Atascadero, Calif.: Ridgeview).

[29] Salmon, N. (1989). 'Tense and Singular Propositions', in J. Almog, J. Perry, and H. Wettstein (eds), *Themes from Kaplan* (Oxford: Oxford University Press).

[30] Salmon, N. and Soames, S. (eds) (1988). *Propositions and Attitudes* (Oxford: Oxford University Press).

[31] Scheffler, I. (1955). 'On Synonymy and Indirect Discourse', *Philosophy of Science*, 22(1): 39–44.

[32] Smith, A. D. (1988). 'Review of Nathan Salmon's *Frege's Puzzle*', *Mind*, 97(385): 136–137.

[33] Soames, S. (1987). 'Substitutivity', in J. J. Thomson (ed.), *On Being and Saying: Essays for Richard Cartwright* (Cambridge, Mass.: MIT Press).

[34] Wagner, S. (1986). 'California Semantics Meets the Great Fact', *Notre Dame Journal of Formal Logic*, 27(3): 430–455.

2

Reflexivity (1986)

In 1983 Mark Richard formulated a new and interesting problem for theories of direct reference with regard to propositional-attitude attributions.[1] The problem was later discovered independently by Scott Soames, who recently advanced it[2] as a powerful objection to the theory put forward by Jon Barwise and John Perry in *Situations and Attitudes*.[3] Interestingly, although both Richard and Soames advocate the fundamental assumption on which their philosophical problem arises, they disagree concerning the correct solution to the problem. In this paper I discuss the Richard–Soames problem, as I shall call it, as well as certain related problems and puzzles involving reflexive constructions in propositional-attitude attributions. I will treat these problems by applying ideas I invoked in *Frege's Puzzle*[4] defending a semantic theory that shares certain features with, but differs significantly from, that of Barwise and Perry. Unlike the theory of *Situations and Attitudes*, the theory of *Frege's Puzzle* has the resources without modification to solve the Richard–Soames problem and related problems.

I

In setting out the Richard–Soames problem, we make some important assumptions. First, we make the relatively uncontroversial assumption that a monadic predicate ⌜believes that S⌝, where S is a declarative sentence, is simply the result of filling the second argument place of the dyadic, fully extensional predicate 'believes' with the term ⌜that S⌝. Furthermore, it is assumed that the contribution made by the dyadic predicate 'believes' to securing the information content (with respect to a time t) of, or the proposition expressed (with respect to t) by, a declarative sentence in which the

---

Many of the ideas in this chapter were first urged by me in correspondence with David Kaplan, Mark Richard, and Scott Soames in February 1984. There was also a discussion of some of these issues with Joseph Almog, Kaplan, and Soames, and some later correspondence with Alonzo Church. Although there was not the time before original submission to receive reactions or comments on the present chapter, it has benefited from these earlier exchanges.

[1] M. Richard, 'Direct Reference and Ascriptions of Belief', *Journal of Philosophical Logic* 12 (1983), 425–452.

[2] 'Lost innocence', *Linguistics and Philosophy* 8 (1985), 59–71.

[3] MIT Press, 1983.

[4] Ridgeview, 1986.

predicate occurs (outside of the scope of any nonextensional devices, such as quotation marks) is a certain binary relation between believers and propositions, the relation of believing-at-t,[5] and that a term of the form ⌜that S⌝ refers (with respect to a possible context of use c) to the information content (with respect to c) of the sentence S itself. More accurately, the following is assumed:

(B) A monadic predicate of the form ⌜believes that S⌝, where S is an (open or closed) sentence, correctly applies (with respect to a possible context of use and an assignment of values to individual variables) to all and only those individuals who stand in the binary belief relation (at the time of the context in the possible world of the context) to the information content of, or the proposition expressed by, S (with respect to that context and assignment).

On this assumption, a sentence of the form ⌜a believes that S⌝, where a is any singular term, is true if and only if the referent of a stands in the belief relation to the information content of S. Thesis (B) is generally agreed upon by Fregeans and Russellians alike, and is more or less a commonplace in the literature of the theory of meaning, and of the philosophy of semantics generally.

In addition to thesis (B), we assume that ordinary proper names, demonstratives, other single-word indexicals (such as 'he'), and other simple (noncompound) singular terms are, in a given possible context of use, Russellian 'genuine names in the strict logical sense'.[6] Put more fully, we assume the following anti-Fregean thesis as a hypothesis:

(R) The contribution made by an ordinary proper name, demonstrative, or other simple singular term to securing the information content of, or the proposition expressed by, declarative sentences (with respect to a given possible context of use) in which the term occurs (outside of the scope of nonextensional operators, such as quotation marks) is just the referent of the term, or the bearer of the name (with respect to that context of use).

In various alternative terminologies, it is assumed that the *interpretation* (Barwise and Perry), or the *Erkenntniswerte* (Frege), or the *content* (David Kaplan), or the *meaning* (Russell), or the *semantic value* (Soames), or the *information value* (myself) of a proper name, demonstrative, or other simple singular term, with respect to a given context, is just its referent.

It is well-known that the thesis that ordinary proper names are Russellian, in this sense, in conjunction with thesis (B), gives rise to problems in propositional-attitude attributions, and is consequently relatively unpopular. (Even Russell rejected it.) Thus, thesis (R) is hardly the sort of thesis that can legitimately be taken for granted as accepted by the reader. However, I defend thesis (R) at some length and in some detail

---

[5] The idea of indexing, or relativizing, the notion of information content to times (independently of contexts) is due to M. Richard, 'Tense, Propositions, and Meanings', *Philosophical Studies* 41 (1982), 337–351. The idea that the contribution made by a predicate to information content is something like a temporally indexed attribute is defended in *Frege's Puzzle* and stems from Richard's idea of indexing information content to times.

[6] B. Russell, 'The Philosophy of Logical Atomism', in R. C. Marsh (ed.), *Logic and Knowledge* (George Allen and Unwin: London, 1956), 177–281; also pp. 35–155 in Russell's *The Philosophy of Logical Atomism*, ed. D. Pears (Open Court: La Salle, 1985).

in *Frege's Puzzle*. Moreover, the thesis has gained some long overdue respectability recently, and it cannot be summarily dismissed as obviously misguided. It is (more or less) accepted by Barwise–Perry, Kaplan, Richard, Soames, and others. One standard argument against the thesis—the argument from apparent failure of substitutivity in propositional-attitude contexts—has been shown by Kripke[7] to be inconclusive at best, and the major rival approaches to the semantics of proper names and other simple singular terms have been essentially refuted by Keith Donnellan, Kripke, Perry, and others.[8] The Richard–Soames problem is a problem that arises only on the assumption of thesis (*R*), and it is a problem for this thesis. It is not a problem for alternative approaches, such as those of Frege or Russell, which have much more serious problems of their own. Thesis (*R*) is to be taken as a hypothesis of the present paper, its defence given elsewhere. The conclusions and results reached in the present paper on the assumption of thesis (*R*) may be regarded as having the form 'If thesis (*R*) is true, then thus-and-so.' The present paper, in combination with *Frege's Puzzle*, allows for the all-important *modus ponens* step.

One version of the Richard–Soames problem can be demonstrated by the following sort of example, derived from Richard's. Suppose that Lois Lane, who is on holiday somewhere in the wilderness, happens to overhear an elaborate plot by some villainous misanthrope to expose Superman to Kryptonite (the only known substance that can harm Superman) at the Metropolis Centennial Parade tomorrow. She quickly rushes for the nearest telephone to warn Superman, but suddenly remembers that the nearest telephone is one day's journey away. As luck would have it, she happens to be standing in front of an overnight mail delivery service outlet. She quickly scribbles a note warning of the plot to harm Superman—a note that absolutely, positively has to get there overnight. She has no address for Superman (or so she believes), but she does have Clark Kent's address, and she (thinks she) knows that Clark planned to spend all day tomorrow at his apartment. Now the following sentence is true:

(1*a*) Lois believes that she will directly inform Clark Kent of Superman's danger with her note.

By the assumption of theses (*B*) and (*R*), it would seem that the following sentence contains the very same information as (1*a*), and hence must be true as well:

(1*b*) Lois believes that she will directly inform Superman of Superman's danger with her note.

---

[7] S. Kripke, 'A Puzzle about Belief', in A. Margalit (ed.), *Meaning and Use* (D. Reidel: Dordrecht, 1979), 239–275.

[8] See K. Donnellan, 'Proper Names and Identifying Descriptions', in D. Davidson and G. Harman (eds), *Semantics of Natural Language* (D. Reidel: Dordrecht, 1972), 356–379; S. Kripke, *Naming and Necessity* (Harvard University Press and Basil Blackwell, 1972, 1980); also in D. Davidson and G. Harman (eds), *Semantics of Natural Language* (D. Reidel: Dordrecht, 1972), 253–355, 763–769; and J. Perry, 'The Problem of the Essential Indexical', *Nous* 13 (1979), 3–21. For a summary of the major difficulties with the views of Frege and Russell, see N. Salmon, *Reference and Essence* (Prometheus Books, 1981, 2004), chapter 1. Further problems with the Frege–Russell view in connection with propositional attitudes are discussed in *Frege's Puzzle*, ch. 9 and *passim*.

Richard argues, however, that although (1*a*) is true in this example, (1*b*) cannot be true. For if (1*b*) were true, then the following sentence would also be true:

(1*c*) Lois believes that there is someone *x* such that she will directly inform *x* of *x*'s danger with her note.

That is, if (1*b*) were true, then Lois would also believe that someone or other is such that she will inform him of *his own* danger with her note, since this follows trivially by existential generalization from what she believes according to (1*b*). Yet Lois believes no such thing. (Recall that Lois believes that she has no address for Superman.) Of course, Lois hopes that Clark will relay the warning to Superman before it is too late, but she has not formed the opinion that she herself will directly inform someone of his own danger with her note. To put it another way, it is simply false that Lois believes that there is someone with the special property that he will be directly informed by her of his own danger with her note. On the contrary, what she believes is that she will inform someone of *someone else's* danger with her note. Thus (1*a*) is true, though (1*b*) would seem to be false. This poses a serious problem for any theory—such as the theory formed from thesis (*R*) coupled with thesis (*B*) and some other natural assumptions—that claims that (1*a*) and (1*b*) have exactly the same information content, or even merely that they have the same truth value.

Using a similar example, Soames provides a powerful argument against semantic theories of a type that identify the information contents of declarative sentences with sets of *circumstances* (of some sort or other) with respect to which those sentences are either true or untrue (or equivalently, with characteristic functions from circumstances to truth values)—such as the possible-world theories of information content (David Lewis, Robert Stalnaker, and many others) or the 'situation' theory of *Situations and Attitudes*. The argument is this: the following sentence concerning a particular ancient astronomer is assumed to be true (where reference to a language, such as 'English', is suppressed):

(2*a*) The astronomer believes: that 'Hesperus' refers to Hesperus and 'Phosphorus' refers to Phosphorus.

Hence according to thesis (*R*) in conjunction with thesis (*B*) and some natural assumptions, the following sentence, which allegedly contains the very same information as (2*a*), must also be true:

(2*b*) The astronomer believes: that 'Hesperus' refers to Hesperus and 'Phosphorus' refers to Hesperus.

But if (2*b*) is true, and thesis (*B*) is also true, then on certain assumptions that are either trivial or fundamental to a set-of-circumstances theory of information content, the following is also true:

(2*c*) The astronomer believes: that something or other is such that 'Hesperus' refers to it and 'Phosphorus' refers to it.

Assuming thesis (*B*), the additional assumptions needed to validate the move from (2*b*) to (2*c*) on any set-of-circumstances theory of information content are: (i) that a believer's beliefs are closed under *simplification* inferences from a conjunction to either of its conjuncts, i.e. if x believes p *and* q, then x believes q; and (ii) that the conjunction of an ordinary sentence S (excluding nonreferring singular terms and nonextensional devices such as the predicate 'does not exist') and any existential generalization of S is true with respect to exactly the same circumstances as S itself.

Now (2c) is tantamount to the claim that the astronomer believes that 'Hesperus' and 'Phosphorus' are co-referential. Yet certainly (2c) is no consequence of (2a). Indeed, we may take it as an additional hypothesis that (2c) is false of the ancient astronomer in question. Since (2a) is true and (2c) is false, it is either false that if (2a) then (2b)—contrary to the conjunction of theses (B) and (R)—or else it is false that if (2b) then (2c)—contrary to the conjunction of (B) and any set-of-circumstances theory of information content. Now (B) and (R) are true. Therefore, Soames argues, any set-of-circumstances theory of information content is incorrect. As Soames points out, the problem points to a fundamental error in the theory of *Situations and Attitudes*, which accepts both (B) and (R) as fundamental, thereby ensuring the validity of the move from (2a) to (2b), as well as the assumptions that validate the move from (2b) to (2c).

In the general case, we may have the first of the following three sentences true and the third false, where a and b are co-referential proper names, demonstratives, other simple singular terms, or any combination thereof, and R is a dyadic predicate:

(3a) c believes that aRb

(3b) c believes that aRa

(3c) c believes that $(\exists x)xRx$.

The Richard–Soames problem is that (3b) appears to follow from (3a), and (3c) appears to follow from (3b). Since (3a) is true and (3c) false, something has got to give.

II

Now (3b) is either true or false. Hence it is either false that if (3a) then (3b), or else it is false that if (3b) then (3c). Both Richard and Soames accept thesis (R). Insisting that if (3b) then (3c), Richard maintains that it is false that if (3a) then (3b), thereby impugning thesis (B).[9] Accepting thesis (B) as well as (R), Soames argues instead that 'there is a principled means of blocking' the move from (3b) to (3c) while preserving (B).

There is a certain intuitive picture of belief advanced by Barwise and Perry (*Situations and Attitudes*, chapter 10) and which is independently plausible in its own right. This is a picture of belief as a cognitive state arising from internal mental states that derive information content in part from causal relations to external objects. Soames points out that on this picture of belief, the following is indeed true if (3b) is:

(3d) $(\exists x)$ c believes that xRx.

---

[9] 'Direct Reference and Ascriptions of Belief', pp. 440–442 and *passim*. He constructs (pp. 444–445) a semantics for belief attributions that conflicts with thesis (B).

Soames adds:[10]

However, [on this picture of belief] there is no reason to think that [the referent of *c*] believes the proposition that something bears *R* to itself. Since none of the agent's mental states has this as its information content, he does not believe it.

Quine distinguishes two readings of any sentence of the form ⌜*c* believes something is ϕ⌝—what he calls the *notional* and the *relational* readings. The notional reading may be spelled out as ⌜*c* believes: that something or other is ϕ⌝. It is the Russellian secondary occurrence or small-scope reading. The relational reading may be spelled out as ⌜*c* believes something in particular to be ϕ⌝, or more perspicuously as ⌜Something is such that *c* believes: that it is ϕ⌝. It is the Russellian primary occurrence or large-scope reading. In Quine's terminology, Soames claims that the notional reading of ⌜*c* believes something bears *R* to it⌝ does not follow from the relational. Quine demonstrated some time ago that the relational reading of ⌜*c* believes something is ϕ⌝ does not in general follow from the notional reading, with his clever example of 'Ralph believes someone is a spy'. Soames may be seen as arguing that, on a certain plausible picture of belief, there are cases in which the reverse inference also fails. Since the appearance of Quine's influential writings on the subject, it is no longer surprising that the notional reading does not imply the relational. It is at least somewhat surprising, however, that there could be converse cases in which the relational reading is true yet the notional reading false. This is what Soames is arguing.

My own view of the Richard–Soames problem favors Soames's account over Richard's. Thesis (*B*) is supported by strong linguistic evidence. It provides the simplest and most plausible explanation, for example, of the validity of such inferences as:

John believes the proposition to which our nation is dedicated.
Our nation is dedicated to the proposition that all men are created equal.
Therefore, John believes that all men are created equal.

Furthermore, although a number of philosophers have proposed a variety of truth-condition assignments for belief attributions contrary to thesis (*B*), these alternative truth-condition assignments often falter with respect to belief attributions that involve open sentences as their complement 'that'-clause, and that are true under some particular assignment of values to individual variables or to pronouns—for example, 'the astronomer believes that *x* is a planet' in 'There is something *x* such that *x* = Venus and the astronomer believes that *x* is a planet' or 'the astronomer believes that it is a planet' in 'As regards Venus, the astronomer believes that it is a planet'.[11] Thesis (*B*) should be maintained to the extent that the facts allow, and should not be abandoned if Soames is correct that there is a principled means of solving the Richard–Soames problem while maintaining (*B*).

By contrast, Soames's proposals for solving the problem invoke essentially some of the same ideas advanced and defended in *Frege's Puzzle*. There I develop and defend

---

[10] 'Lost Innocence', p. 62.
[11] Richard 'Direct Reference and Ascriptions of Belief' is one exception.

thesis (R) (and, to a lesser extent, thesis (B)), as well as the view (which Russell himself came to reject) that the contents of beliefs formulatable using ordinary proper names, demonstratives, or other simple singular terms, are so-called singular propositions (Kaplan), i.e. structured propositions directly about some individual which occurs directly as a constituent of the proposition. I take propositions to be structured in such a way that the structure and constituents of a proposition are directly readable from the structure and constituents of a declarative sentence containing the proposition as its information content. By and large, a simple (noncompound) expression contributes a single entity, taken as a simple (noncomplex) unit, to the information content of a sentence in which the expression occurs, whereas the contribution of a compound expression (such as a phrase or sentential component) is a complex entity composed of the contributions of the simple components.[12] One consequence of this sort of theory is that, contrary to set-of-circumstances theories of information content, there is a difference, and therefore a distinction, between the information content of the conjunction of an ordinary sentence S and any of its existential generalizations and that of S itself. This disables the argument that applied in the case of a set-of-circumstances theory to establish the (alleged) validity of the move from (3b) to (3c).

Unfortunately, this difference between the two sorts of theories of information content does not make the problem disappear altogether. There is an interesting philosophical puzzle concerning the logic and semantics of propositional-attitude attributions that is generated by the Richard–Soames problem, a puzzle that arises even on the structured-singular-proposition sort of view sketched above.

Soames slightly misstates the case when he says that (on the intuitive picture of belief as deriving from certain mental states having information content), 'there is no reason to think that (3c) is true'. For in fact, even though (1c) and (2c) are false in the above examples, there are very good reasons to think that they are true. One excellent reason to think that (1c) is true is the fact that (1b) is true, and one excellent reason to think that (2c) is true is the fact that (2b) is true. In general, it is to be expected that if a sentence of the form $\ulcorner c$ believes that $\phi_a\urcorner$ is true, then so is $\ulcorner c$ believes that $(\exists x)\phi_x\urcorner$, where a is a singular term that refers to something, ϕ is an ordinary extensional context (excluding such predicates as 'does not exist'), and ϕ_a is the result of substituting (free) occurrences of a for free occurrences of 'x' uniformly throughout ϕ_x. There is a general psychological law to the effect that subjects typically tend to believe the existential generalizations of their beliefs. Herein the puzzle arises. Even if the conjunctive proposition *'Hesperus' and 'Phosphorus' refer to Hesperus and*

---

[12] The reason for the phrase 'by and large' is that there are important classes of exceptions to the general rule. Certain nonextensional operators, such as quotation marks, create contexts in which compound expressions contribute themselves as units to the information content of sentences in which the quotation occurs, and other nonextensional operators, such as temporal operators, create contexts in which some compound expressions contribute complexes other than their customary contribution to information content (see n. 5, above). In addition, we shall see below that a compound predicate formed by abstraction from an open sentence is regarded as contributing something like an attribute, taken as unit, rather than a complex made up of the typical contributions of the compound's components.

there is something that 'Hesperus' and 'Phosphorus' refer to is not the same proposition as the simpler proposition *'Hesperus' and 'Phosphorus' refer to Hesperus*, if the astronomer believes that 'Hesperus' and 'Phosphorus' refer to Hesperus, then it seems he ought to believe that there is something that 'Hesperus' and 'Phosphorus' refer to. And if Lois believes that she will inform Superman of his danger with her note, then it seems she ought to believe that there is someone whom she will inform of his danger with her note. It is precisely for this reason that Richard rejects (1*b*), even though he does not endorse a set-of-circumstances theory of information content and favors the structured-singular-proposition account.

Perhaps if a subject is insane or otherwise severely mentally defective, he or she may fail to believe the (validly derivable) existential generalizations of his or her beliefs, but we may suppose that neither Lois Lane nor the astronomer suffer from any mental defects. We may even suppose that they are master logicians, or worse yet, that they have a perverse penchant for drawing existential generalization (EG) inferences as often as possible. They go around saying things like 'I'm tired now; hence, sometimes someone or other is tired' and 'Fred shaves Fred; hence someone shaves Fred, Fred shaves someone, and someone shaves himself.' In this way, it can be built into the example that the truth of (1*b*) is an excellent reason to believe in the truth of (1*c*), and the truth of (2*b*) is an excellent reason to believe in the truth of (2*c*). For such EG-maniacs, one might expect that it is something of a general law that every instance of the following schema is true:

(L$_1$) If c believes that ϕ_a, then c believes that something is such that ϕ_{it},

where c refers to the subject, a is any referring singular term of English, ϕ_{it} is any English sentence in which the pronoun 'it' occurs (free and not in the scope of quotation marks, an existence predicate, or other such operators) and which may also contain occurrences of a, and ϕ_a is the result of substituting (free) occurrences of a for (free) occurrences of 'it' throughout ϕ_{it}. In fact, one might expect that it is something of a general law that every instance of (L_1) is true where c refers to any normal speaker of English, even if he or she is not an EG-maniac.

I maintain with Soames that the sentences ⌜If (1*b*) then (1*c*)⌝ and ⌜If (2*b*) then (2*c*)⌝ constitute genuine counterexamples to this alleged general law. But even if the principle that every instance of (L_1), as formulated, is true is thereby refuted, surely something very much like it, some weakened version of it, *must be* true—even where the referent of c does not have a perverse penchant for existential generalization. For the most part, in the typical kind of case, it would be highly irrational for someone to fail to believe the existential generalizations of one of his or her beliefs. Neither Lois Lane nor the astronomer is irrational in this way. The conditionals ⌜If (1*b*) then (1*c*)⌝ and ⌜If (2*b*) then (2*c*)⌝ are not typical instances of schema (L_1), but it is not enough simply to point out how they are atypical and to leave the matter at that. It is incumbent on the philosopher who claims that these instances of (L_1) fail, to offer some alternative principle that is *not* falsified in these cases and thereby accounts for the defeasible reliability, and the *prima facie* plausibility, of the alleged general law.

This is not a problem special to set-of-circumstances theories of information content. It is equally a puzzle for the structured-singular-proposition sort of theory that

I advocate and that Soames proposes in his discussion of the Richard–Soames problem. It is a puzzle for the conjunction of theses (*B*) and (*R*), irrespective of how these theses are supplemented with a theory of information content.

III

There is a second, and surprisingly strong, reason to suppose that (1*c*) and (2*c*) are true. The general puzzle posed by the Richard–Soames problem can be significantly strengthened if we exploit a simple reflexive device already present to a certain degree in standard English.

Given any simple dyadic predicate Π, we may form a monadic predicate ⌜*self*-Π⌝ defined by

$$(\lambda x)x\Pi x,$$

in such a way that ⌜*self*-Π⌝ is to be regarded as a simple (noncompound) expression, a single word. In English, this might be accomplished by converting a present tensed transitive verb *V* into a corresponding adjective and prefixing 'self-' to obtain a reflexive adjective; e.g. from 'cleans' we obtain 'self-cleaning', from 'indulges', 'self-indulgent', from 'explains', 'self-explanatory', and so on. The contribution made by a term of the form ⌜*self*-Π⌝ to the information content, with respect to a time *t*, of a typical sentence in which it occurs is simply the reflexive property of bearing *R* to oneself at *t*, where *R* is the binary relation semantically associated with Π.[13] Assuming thesis (*R*), if *a* is a proper name or other simple singular term and *R* is the binary relation semantically associated with Π, then the information content, with respect to *t*, of the sentence ⌜*self*-Π(*a*)⌝ is the singular proposition made up of the referent of *a* together with the property of bearing *R* to oneself at *t*.

Consider again the move from (3*a*) to (3*b*), where *a* and *b* are co-referential proper names, *R* is a simple dyadic predicate, and (3*a*) is true:

(3*a*) *c* believes that *aRb*.

(3*b*) *c* believes that *aRa*.

As Soames points out, (on a plausible picture of belief) the following relational, or *de re*, attribution follows from (3*b*):

(3*d*) (∃*x*) *c* believes that *xRx*.

---

[13] The '*self*'-prefix defined here may not correspond exactly to that of ordinary English. In English, the term 'self-cleaning' may apply, with respect to a time *t*, to an object even if that object is not cleaning itself *at t* (say, because it is unplugged or switched off for the moment), as long as the object is the *sort* of thing at *t* that cleans itself at appropriate times. Similarly, someone is self-indulgent at *t* if and only if he or she is the sort of person at *t* that has at some appropriate times the feature of indulging oneself, even if he or she is not doing so at *t*. The '*self*'-prefix defined here is such that ⌜*self*-*R*⌝ applies to an object with respect to *t* if and only if the object bears *R* to itself at *t*.

In fact, a somewhat stronger *de re* attribution also follows from (3*b*), by exportation:[14]

$(\exists x)[x = a \,\&\, c$ believes that $xRx]$,

or less formally:

(3*b′*) *c* believes of *a* that it *R* it.

Now from this it would seem to follow that:

(3*e′*) *c* believes of *a* that it *R* itself.

From this (perhaps together with some general psychological law) it would seem to follow further that:

(3*f′*) *c* believes of *a* that *self-R*(it),

with the predicate ⌜*self-R*⌝ understood as explained above. Finally by importation, we may infer:

(3*f*) *c* believes that *self-R*(*a*).

For example, suppose that, owing to certain miscalculations, the astronomer comes to believe that Hesperus weighs at least one thousand tons more than Phosphorus. Now every step in the following derivation follows by an inference pattern that is either at least apparently intuitively valid or else sanctioned by the conjunction of theses (*B*) and (*R*), or both:

(4*a*) The astronomer believes that Hesperus outweighs Phosphorus.

(4*b*) The astronomer believes that Hesperus outweighs Hesperus.

(4*b′*) The astronomer believes of Hesperus that it outweighs it.

(4*e′*) The astronomer believes of Hesperus that it outweighs itself.

(4*f′*) The astronomer believes of Hesperus that it is self-outweighing.

(4*f*) The astronomer believes that Hesperus is self-outweighing.

One could continue the sequence of inferences from (4*f*) all the way to:

(4*c*) The astronomer believes that there is something such that it outweighs it,

---

[14] The unrestricted rule of exportation has been shown invalid, or at least highly suspect, by the fallacious inference 'The shortest spy exists and Ralph believes: that the shortest spy is a spy; therefore Ralph believes of the shortest spy: that he or she is a spy.' From the conclusion of this inference one may validly infer 'There is someone whom Ralph believes to be a spy', which intuitively does not follow from the initial premiss. This instance of exportation fails because the exported term, 'the shortest spy', is a definite description. The theory formed from the conjunction of theses (*B*) and (*R*) requires the validity of exportation with respect to belief attributions, provided the rule is restricted to proper names, demonstratives, or other simple singular terms. Hence, the theory must accept the inference from (3*b*) to (3*b′*) (assuming the tacit premiss ⌜$(\exists x)[x = a]$⌝). Similarly, the theory is committed to the validity of importation, inferring ⌜*c* believes: that ϕ_a⌝ from ⌜*c* believes of *a*: that ϕ_{it}⌝, under the same restriction on *a*.

by invoking some corrected, weakened version of the law mentioned above (the alleged law that every appropriate instance of (L_1) is true), to pass from (4*f*) to:

(4*g*) The astronomer believes that there is something such that it is self-outweighing,

from which (4*c*) appears to follow directly. But there is no need to extend the derivation this far. A problem arises at least as soon as (4*f*). For unless the astronomer is insane, or otherwise severely mentally defective, (4*f*) is obviously false. The astronomer would not ascribe to Venus the reflexive property, which nothing could possibly have, of weighing more than oneself. Hence, in moving from a sentence to its immediate successor, somewhere in the derivation of (4*f*) we move from a truth to a falsehood. Where? The moves from (4*a*) to (4*b*′) and from (4*f*′) to (4*f*) are validated by the conjunction of theses (*B*) and (*R*), and both of the remaining transitions commencing with (4*b*′) are based on inference patterns that (assuming ordinary folk psychology and that the astronomer is normal) seem intuitively valid.

One may harbour some residual doubts about the exportation move from (4*b*) to (4*b*′) and/or the importation move from (4*f*′) to (4*f*). The theory formed from the conjunction of theses (*B*) and (*R*) requires the validity of both of these inferences, so that if either is invalid the theory is false. In fact, however, these inferences are not essential to the present puzzle. The exportation inference takes us on a detour that some may find helpful, though one may bypass the *de re* 'believes of' construction altogether. Instead, we may construct the following alternative derivation from (4*b*):

(4*b*) The astronomer believes that Hesperus outweighs Hesperus.
(4*e*) The astronomer believes that Hesperus outweighs itself.
(4*f*) The astronomer believes that Hesperus is self-outweighing.

If the inference from (4*b*′) to (4*e*′) is valid, then by parity of reasoning so is the inference from (4*b*) to (4*e*). And if the inference from (4*e*′) to (4*f*′) is valid, then by parity of reasoning so is the inference from (4*e*) to (4*f*). Hence, if the derivation of (4*f*′) from (4*b*′) via (4*e*′) is legitimate, then so is the derivation of (4*f*) from (4*b*) via (4*e*). But (4*f*) is false. Therefore, it would seem, so is (4*b*). Sentence (4*a*), on the other hand, is true. This raises anew doubts about the independently suspicious move from (4*a*) to (4*b*), or more generally, the move from (3*a*) to (3*b*), thereby impugning once again the conjunction of theses (*R*) and (*B*).

The new puzzle, then, is this: according to the conjunction of theses (*B*) and (*R*), (4*b*) follows from (4*a*) together with the fact that 'Hesperus' and 'Phosphorus' are co-referential proper names. Now in the sequence ⟨(4*b*), (4*e*), (4*f*)⟩, each sentence appears to follow logically from its immediate predecessor. Alternatively in the sequence ⟨(4*b*′), (4*e*′), (4*f*′)⟩, each sentence appears to follow logically from its immediate predecessor, and furthermore, according to the conjunction of (*B*) and (*R*), (4*b*) entails (4*b*′), and (4*f*′) entails (4*f*). One way or another, we seem to be able to derive (4*f*) from (4*a*), together with the fact that 'Hesperus' and 'Phosphorus' are co-referential proper names. Yet in the example, (4*a*) is plainly true and (4*f*) plainly false. Where does the derivation go wrong?

I call this *the puzzle of reflexives in propositional attitudes*. Here again, the problem posed by the puzzle is especially pressing for any set-of-circumstances theory of information content. In fact, the problem is even more pressing than the Richard–Soames problem for such theories, if that is possible. One difference between the Richard–Soames problem and the puzzle of reflexives in propositional attitudes is that what is said to be believed at the final step of the derivation, in this case step (3f), is not merely a consequence of, but is *equivalent to*, what is said to be believed in (3b). In fact, any circumstance in which an individual x bears R to x is a circumstance in which x has the reflexive property of bearing R to oneself, and vice versa. There is no need here to make the additional assumption that belief is closed under simplification inferences. Any set-of-circumstances theory of information content, in conjunction with thesis (B), automatically validates the derivation of (3f) from (3b). The problem thus also points to a fundamental error in the theory of *Situations and Attitudes* which includes both theses (B) and (R) as fundamental, thereby validating the full derivation of (3f) from (3a) without any further assumptions concerning belief. The puzzle of reflexives in propositional attitudes, however, is not peculiar to set-of-circumstances theories, and arises on any theory of information content that incorporates the conjunction of theses (B) and (R), including the structured-singular-proposition theory that I advocate. The difference is that the structured-singular-proposition view (in conjunction with (B) and (R)), unlike the theory of *Situations and Attitudes*, is not committed by its very nature to the validity of the derivation of (4f) from (4b). It is just that each step in the derivation of (4f) from (4b) is independently plausible.

IV

The puzzle of reflexives in propositional attitudes is related to a paradox that concerns quantification into belief contexts and that was discovered some time ago by Alonzo Church.[15] Unlike the former puzzle, however, Church's paradox presents a serious problem in particular for the theory of structured singular propositions.

As a matter of historical fact, as of some appropriate date, King George IV was acquainted with Sir Walter Scott, but was doubtful whether Scott was the author of *Waverley*. We may even suppose that George IV believed at that time that Scott did not write *Waverley*. Yet, Church notes, if quantification into belief contexts is taken as meaningful in combination with the usual laws of the logic of quantification and identity, then the following is provable as a logical theorem using classical Indiscernibility of Identicals (Leibniz's Law):

(5) For every x and every y, if George IV does not believe that $x \neq x$, if George IV believes that $x \neq y$, then $x \neq y$.

---

[15] 'A Remark concerning Quine's Paradox about Modality', Spanish translation in *Analisis Filosofico* 2. 1–2 (May–November 1982), 25–34; in English in N. Salmon and S. Soames, (eds), *Propositions and Attitudes* (Oxford University Press, 1988).

Mimicking the standard proof in quantified modal logic of the necessity of identity, Church remarks that although it is not certain, it was very likely true as of the same date that:

(6) For every x, George IV does not believe that $x \neq x$,

since it is very likely that George IV did not believe anything to be distinct from itself. Taking (6) as premiss, we may derive:

(7) For every x and every y, if George IV believes that $x \neq y$, then $x \neq y$.

We are thus apparently led to ascribe to King George's beliefs the strange 'power to control the actual facts about x and y'. Since Scott is in fact the author of *Waverley*, this derivation of (7) from (6) seems to preclude King George's believing, as of the same date, that Scott did not write *Waverley*. The derivation thus constitutes an unacceptable paradox, not unlike Russell's paradox of naïve set theory (set theory with unrestricted comprehension). Church concludes that this provides a compelling reason to reject the meaningfulness of quantification into belief contexts.[16]

As quantification into belief contexts goes, so goes the theory of structured singular propositions as potential objects of belief. Church's paradox thus poses a serious difficulty for the theory that I advocate. But it also poses a serious difficulty for any theory, including any set-of-circumstances theory, that purports to make sense of *de re* constructions or quantification into belief contexts. Furthermore, the paradox is quite independent of the conjunction of theses (*B*) and (*R*). Whether these are true or false, the paradox arises as long as quantification into belief contexts is regarded as meaningful.

V

It is precisely to treat philosophical puzzles and problems of the sort presented here that I proposed the sketch of an analysis of the binary belief relation between believers and propositions (sometimes Russellian singular propositions) in *Frege's Puzzle*. I take the belief relation to be, in effect, the existential generalization of a ternary relation,

---

[16] He compares his result to the derivation in standard quantified modal logic of the contrapositive of the necessity of identity: If any x and y can be distinct, they are. He likewise cites the derivability of this principle (which he calls 'a variant of Murphy's Law') as providing a reason for rejecting the meaningfulness of quantification into modal contexts.

Church seems to allow that on the theory of structured singular propositions as potential objects of belief (which he calls 'the principle of transparency of belief' and which he regards as a doubtful theory), a power to control the actual facts about x and y with one's beliefs would not be surprising and could be explained. Unfortunately, he does not provide the alleged explanation. I am unsure what he has in mind with his remarks in this connection. Speaking as one who is deeply committed to the theory in question, I would find such a power surprising in the extreme and utterly inexplicable. I see the problem as one of how to reconcile the derivation of (7) with the obvious fact that no such power exists (and the fact that (7) may even be false in the case of Sir Walter Scott and the author of *Waverley*).

BEL, among believers, propositions, and some third type of entity. To believe a proposition p is to adopt an appropriate favorable attitude toward p when taking p in some relevant *way*. It is to agree to p, or to assent mentally to p, or to approve of p, or some such thing, when taking p a certain way. This is the *BEL* relation. The third relata for the *BEL* relation are something like *proposition guises*, or *modes* of acquaintance with propositions, or *ways* in which a believer may be familiar with a given proposition. Of course, to use a distinction of Kripke's, this formulation is far too vague to constitute a fully developed *theory* of belief, but it does provide a *picture* of belief that differs significantly from the sort of picture of propositional attitudes advanced by Frege or Russell, and enough can be said concerning the *BEL* relation to allow for at least the sketch of a solution to certain philosophical puzzles, including the original puzzle generated by the Richard–Soames problem.

In particular, the *BEL* relation satisfies the following three conditions:

(i) A believes p if and only if there is some x such that A is familiar with p by means of x and $BEL(A, p, x)$.

(ii) A may believe p by standing in *BEL* to p and some x by means of which A is familiar with p without standing in *BEL* to p and all x by means of which A is familiar with p.

(iii) In one sense of 'withhold belief', A withholds belief concerning p (either by disbelieving or by suspending judgment) if and only if there is some x by means of which A is familiar with p and not-$BEL(A, p, x)$.

These conditions generate a philosophically important distinction between withholding belief and failure to believe (i.e. not believing). In particular, one may both withhold belief from and believe the very same proposition simultaneously. (Neither withholding belief nor failure to believe is to be identified with the related notions of disbelief and suspension of judgment—which are two different ways of withholding belief, in this sense, and which may occur simultaneously with belief of the very same proposition in a single believer.)

It happens in most cases (but not all) that when a believer believes some particular proposition p, the relevant third relatum for the *BEL* relation is a function of the believer and some particular *sentence* of the believer's language. Consider for example the binary function f that assigns to any believer A and sentence S of A's language, the *way* A takes the proposition contained in S (in A's language with respect to A's context at some particular time t) were it presented to A (at t) through the very sentence S. Then (assuming t is the time in question) Lois believes the proposition that she will inform Clark Kent of Superman's danger with her note by virtue of standing in the *BEL* relation to this proposition together with the result of applying the function f to Lois and the particular sentence 'I will inform Clark Kent of Superman's danger with my note.' That is, in the example the following is true:

BEL(Lois, that she will inform Clark Kent of Superman's danger with her note, f[Lois, 'I will inform Clark Kent of Superman's danger with my note']).

On the other hand, the following is false:

BEL(Lois, that she will inform Superman of his danger with her note, *f* [Lois, 'I will inform Superman of his danger with my note']).

Similarly, assuming the astronomer in Soames's example spoke English:

BEL(the astronomer, that 'Hesperus' refers to Hesperus and 'Phosphorus' refers to Phosphorus, *f* [the astronomer, ' "Hesperus" refers to Hesperus whereas "Phosphorus" refers to Phosphorus']),

but not:

BEL(the astronomer, that 'Hesperus' refers to Hesperus and 'Phosphorus' refers to Hesperus, f [the astronomer, ' "Hesperus" and "Phosphorus" both refer to Hesperus']).

In *Frege's Puzzle* the *BEL* relation and the function *f* are invoked in various ways to explain and to solve some of the standard (and some nonstandard) problems that arise on the sort of theory I advocate. This device is also useful with regard to the original puzzle that arises from the Richard–Soames problem and the puzzle of reflexives in propositional attitudes.

In the first example, (1*c*) is false, since Lois does not adopt an appropriate favorable attitude toward the proposition that there is someone whom she will inform of his own danger with her note, no matter how this proposition might be presented to her. That is, there is no *x* such that Lois stands in *BEL* to the proposition that she will inform someone or other of his own danger with her note and *x*. Similarly, in Soames's example. (2*c*) if false, since the astronomer does not adopt the appropriate favorable attitude toward the proposition that 'Hesperus' and 'Phosphorus' are coreferential, no matter how this proposition might be presented to him. He does not stand in *BEL* to this proposition and any *x*.

What about (1*b*) and (2*b*)? These are indeed true in the examples. Consider the first example. Sentence (1*a*) is true by hypothesis. Now notice that if Superman were somehow made aware of the truth of (1*a*), then he could truthfully utter the following sentence:

(1*b*I) Lois believes that she will directly inform me of my danger with her note.

In fact, (1*b*I) yields the only natural way for Superman to express (to himself) the very information that is contained in (1*a*). But if (1*b*I) is true with respect to Superman's context, then (1*b*) is true with respect to ours. Both (1*b*I), taken with respect to Superman's context, and (1*b*), taken with respect to ours, are true precisely because Lois adopts the appropriate favorable attitude toward the proposition about Superman, i.e. Clark Kent, that she will inform him of his danger with her note. Lois assents to this information when she takes it the way she would if it were presented to her through the sentence 'I will inform Clark Kent of Superman's danger with my note.' Hence, she believes it. Similarly, the astronomer inwardly assents to the proposition about Hesperus, i.e. Venus, that 'Hesperus' refers to it and 'Phosphorus' refers to it, when it is presented to him through the sentence ' "Hesperus" refers to Hesperus whereas "Phosphorus" refers to Phosphorus'. Hence (2*b*) is true.

In fact, in the examples Lois also believes that she will *not* inform Superman of his danger with her note, and the astronomer that 'Hesperus' and 'Phosphorus' do *not* both refer to Hesperus, since:

BEL(Lois, that she will not inform Superman of his danger with her note, f [Lois, 'I will not inform Superman of his danger with my note'])

and:

BEL(the astronomer, that 'Hesperus' and 'Phosphorus' do not both refer to Hesperus, f [the astronomer, ' "Hesperus" and "Phosphorus" do not both refer to Hesperus']).

Both Lois and the astronomer thus (unknowingly) believe some proposition together with its denial.[17]

One reason so many instances of schema (L_1) are true, although it fails in these special cases, is that the schema approximates the following weaker schema, all (or at least very nearly all) of whose instances are true, and which is not falsified in these special cases:

(L_2) If $(\exists p)BEL(c, p, f[c, `\phi_a`])$, then $(\exists q)BEL(c, q, f[c,$ 'Something is such that ϕ_{it}']),

where c refers to a normal speaker of English, a is any referring singular term of English, ϕ_{it} is any English sentence in which the pronoun 'it' occurs (free and not in the scope of quotation marks, an existence predicate, or other such operators) and which may also contain occurrences of a, and ϕ_a is the result of substituting (free) occurrences of a for (free) occurrences of 'it' throughout ϕ_{it}. I submit that the similarity of the former schema (L_1) to something like schema (L_2) is a major source of the plausibility of the alleged general law concerning the former. Schema (L_2) is not falsified in these special cases, even if Lois and the astronomer are normal speakers of English, since Lois does not agree to the proposition that she will inform Superman of his danger with her note when she takes it in the way she would if it were presented to her through the sentence 'I will inform Superman of his danger with my note', and the astronomer does not agree to the proposition that 'Hesperus' and 'Phosphorus' refer to Venus when it is presented to him through the sentence ' "Hesperus" and "Phosphorus" refer to Hesperus.'[18]

---

[17] That is, neither Lois nor the astronomer knows (in the example) that she or he believes some proposition together with its denial. On the other hand, Lois does know that she believes that she will inform Superman of his danger with her note and will not inform Superman of his danger with her note, and the astronomer does know that he believes that 'Hesperus' refers to Venus and 'Phosphorus' refers to Venus and 'Hesperus' and 'Phosphorus' do not both refer to Venus. Furthermore, each presumably knows that these propositions are contradictory—though neither knows that she or he believes a contradictory proposition. Sorting these matters out is a delicate task made extremely difficult by relying on the term 'believes' without the use of some expression for the full ternary BEL relation. Cf. *Frege's Puzzle*, ch. 8.

[18] Soames has offered an account not unlike this one in response to my urging on him that, as Richard originally presented the problem, it poses a serious difficulty for the theory of structured singular propositions as well as for the set-of-circumstances theories. See 'Lost Innocence', p. 69 n. 12. The notion of a 'belief state' invoked there (which seems to have been derived from 'The Problem of the Essential Indexical' and *Situations and Attitudes*) plays a role analogous to the third relata of the BEL relation in my account, the *ways* in which one may be familiar with, or take, a

VI

Even if this resolves the original puzzle generated by the Richard–Soames problem for the structured-singular-proposition account of information content, it does not yet lay to rest the puzzle of reflexives in propositional attitudes, not to mention Church's ingenious paradox concerning quantification into belief contexts.

Richard's proposal to solve the original puzzle by blocking the initial inference from (3*a*) (together with the fact that *a* and *b* are co-referential proper names or other simple singular terms) to (3*b*) would equally block the puzzle of reflexives in propositional attitudes. This proposal involves relinquishing thesis (*B*), and is motivated by the threat of the alleged derivability of falsehoods such as (1*c*) from (1*b*). But I argued above that thesis (*B*) is supported by strong linguistic evidence, and should be maintained insofar as the facts allow. We have seen that the account of belief in terms of the *BEL* relation effectively blocks the move from (1*b*) to (1*c*), while retaining thesis (*B*) and while also affording an explanation (or at least the sketch of an explanation) for the *prima facie* plausiblity of the move. If there is a solution to the problem of reflexives in propositional attitudes, it does not lie in the rejection of thesis (*B*).

Ruth Barcan Marcus has argued that, in at least one ordinary sense of 'believe', it is impossible to believe what is impossible.[19] Marcus would thus claim that (4*a*) is false to begin with, since the astronomer cannot 'enter into the belief relation' to the information, which is necessarily misinformation, that Hesperus outweighs

proposition. See *Frege's Puzzle*, ch. 9 n. 1, for some brief remarks comparing the third relata of the *BEL* relation (proposition guises, or modes of acquaintance with propositions) with Perry's notion of a belief state.

In response to the Richard–Soames problem, Barwise and Perry seem to have abandoned the idea that the information content ('interpretation') of a declarative sentence, with respect to a context, is the set of situations (or type of situation) with respect to which the sentence is true (with 'situation' understood in such a way that any situation with respct to which it is true that 'Hesperus' and 'Phosphorus' both refer to Venus is one with respect to which it is also true that there is something referred to by both 'Hesperus' and 'Phosphorus'). In fact, Barwise and Perry seem to have moved significantly in the direction of structured singular propositions and an account of the Richard–Soames problem similar (in certain respects) to the one advanced here and to the one advanced by Soames (see 'Shifting Situations and Shaken Attitudes', *Linguistics and Philosophy* 8 (1985), 105–161 (also available as the Stanford University Center for the Study of Language and Information Report No. CSLI-84-13), pp. 153–158, esp. pp. 156–157). If so, this move constitutes an important concession to Soames. However, Barwise and Perry (if I understand them correctly) couple this move with the surprising claim (p. 158) that there is a significant sense in which the information content of 'Something or other is referred to by both "Hesperus" and "Phosphorus"' is not a consequence of that of 'Venus exists and "Hesperus" refers to it and "Phosphorus" refers to it'. If this is to be understood as a claim about the logic of the information contents of these sentences, surely the claim must be rejected, and the doctrine of structured singular propositions as the information contents ('interpretations') of sentences and the objects of belief, coupled with classical logic, is much to be preferred over the newer theory of Barwise and Perry.

[19] 'A Proposed Solution to a Puzzle about Belief', in P. French, T. Uehling, and H. Wettstein (eds), *Midwest Studies in Philosophy, vi. The Foundations of Analytic Philosophy* (University of Minnesota Press, 1981), 501–510, esp. 503–506, and 'Rationality and Believing the Impossible', *Journal of Philosophy* 80, 6 (June 1983), 321–338.

Phosphorus. However, one of Marcus's arguments for this, perhaps her main argument, appears to be that where a and b are co-referential names, if (3a) is true so is (3c), and in a great many cases where one is inclined to hold an instance of (3a) true even though ⌜aRb⌝ encodes necessarily false information ((4a) for example), (3c) is patently false, because ⌜$(\exists x)xRx$⌝ (e.g. 'Something outweighs itself') encodes information that is not only impossible but patently unbelievable.[20]

Marcus's view that one cannot believe what cannot be true is highly implausible, and I believe, idiosyncratic. It often happens in mathematics and logic that owing to some fallacious argument, one comes to embrace a fully grasped proposition that is in fact provably false. Sometimes this happens even in philosophy, more often than we care to admit. In our example, we may suppose that, for some particular number n, the astronomer comes to believe the proposition that Hesperus weighs at least n tons, and also the proposition that Phosphorus weighs no more than $(n - 1,000)$ tons. He embraces these two propositions. It is very implausible to suppose that the fact that their conjunction is such that it could not be true somehow prevents the astronomer from embracing that conjunction, along with its component conjuncts, or that the astronomer is somehow prevented from forming beliefs on the basis of inference from his two beliefs, as in (4a).

More important for our present purpose is that Marcus's argument for the falsehood of (4a), at least as the argument is interpreted here, has to be mistaken. Otherwise, one could also show that (1a) and (2a) are false in the original examples. For although the proposition that Lois will inform someone of his own danger with her note is not unbelievable, it is plain in the example that it is not believed by Lois, i.e. (1c) is plainly false. If Marcus's argument for the impossibility of believing the impossible were sound, then by parity of reasoning it would follow that (1a) is false. Similarly, although the proposition that 'Hesperus' and 'Phosphorus' are co-referential is believable, in fact true, it is a hypothesis of the example that the astronomer does not believe it, i.e. (2c) is stipulated to be false. If Marcus's claim that (3c) is true if (3a) is true were itself true, it would follow that (2a) is false. But (1a) and (2a) are plainly true in these examples. There must be something wrong, therefore, with Marcus's argument, at least as I have interpreted it here.

What is wrong is precisely the claim that (3c) is true if (3a) is. Since it is incorrect, this claim cannot give us a way out of the present problem. In fact by shifting from (4a)–(4f) to another example, we can remove the feature that what is said to be believed at step (a) is such that it could not be true. Thus from 'Lois believes that

---

[20] See 'A Proposed Solution to a Puzzle about Belief', p. 505, and 'Rationality and Believing the Impossible', p. 330. Marcus's argument focuses on the special case where R is a predicate for numerical distinctness. She writes: 'If I had believed that Tully is not identical with Cicero, I would have been believing that something is not the same as itself and I surely did not believe that, a blatant impossibility, so I was mistaken in claiming to *have* the belief [that Tully is not Cicero]', and, '[believing that London is different from Londres] would be tantamount to believing that something was not the same as itself, and surely I could never believe *that*. So my belief claim [my claim that I believed that London is not Londres] was mistaken....'. These arguments evidently rely on the premiss that if (3a) then (3c) (or perhaps on the premiss that if (3a) then [the existential generalization on a of (3e′)], i.e. if c believes that a and b are distinct, then c believes *of* something that it is distinct from itself).

Clark Kent disparages Superman while Superman indulges Clark Kent' we may construct a parallel and equally fallacious derivation of 'Lois believes that Superman is self-disparaging and self-indulgent.' Marcus's unusual contention that it is impossible to believe the impossible, whether correct or incorrect, is simply irrelevant to this example.

What, then, is the solution to the puzzle of reflexives in propositional attitudes for the theory of structured singular propositions?

In the example, (4*b*) and (4*b'*) are true, whereas (4*f*) and (4*f'*) are false. Any temptation to infer (4*f*) from (4*b*), or (4*f'*)(4*b'*), can be explained using the *BEL* relation and the function *f* in a manner similar to the explanation given above in connection with the *prima facie* plausibility of inferring (3*c*) from (3*b*). In any case, either the inference from (4*b*) to (4*e*) (and therewith the inference from (4*b'*) to (4*e'*)) is fallacious, or the inference from (4*e*) to (4*f*) (and therewith the inference from (4*e'*) to (4*f'*)) is. Which is it?

Answering this question involves taking sides in a current controversy concerning the identity or distinctness of propositions of the form *x bears R to x* and *x bears R to itself*. If the propositions that Hesperus outweighs Hesperus and that Hesperus outweighs itself are the very same, then the inference from (4*b*) to (4*e*) is valid by classical Indiscernibility of Identicals (or Leibniz's Law) together with thesis (*B*), and the inference from (4*e*) to (4*f*) must then be rejected. If, on the other hand, these propositions are not the same and instead the proposition that Hesperus outweighs itself is the same (or very nearly the same) as the proposition that Hesperus is self-outweighing, then the inference from (4*e*) to (4*f*) is unobjectionable and the inference from (4*b*) to (4*e*) must be rejected.

As noted in Section III above, the advocate of a set-of-circumstances theory of information content is committed to the claim that propositions of the form *x bears R to x* and *x bears R to itself* are exactly the same, since any circumstance in which *x* bears *R* to *x* is one in which *x* bears *R* to itself, and vice versa. Thus, M. J. Cresswell, a set-of-possible-worlds theorist, has recently claimed that:[21]

> on any reasonable account of propositions, the proposition that Ortcutt loves himself ought to be the same as the proposition that Ortcutt loves Ortcutt.

This, however, is far from the truth. In fact, there are compelling reasons to distinguish a proposition of the form *x bears R to x* from the proposition *x bears R to itself*. One sort of consideration is the following: we must distinguish between the reflexive property of exceeding oneself in weight and the simple relational property of exceeding the planet Venus in weight. The former is an impossible property; it is quite impossible for anything to possess it. The latter property, on the other hand, is fairly widespread; a great many massive objects (e.g. the stars) possess it—although, of course, it is quite impossible for Venus to possess it. Now the sentence 'Hesperus outweighs itself' seems to ascribe to Hesperus, i.e. Venus, the impossible property of weighing more than oneself, rather than the simple relational property of weighing more than Venus. It seems to say about Venus what 'Mars outweighs itself' says about

---

[21] *Structured Meanings: The Semantics of Propositional Attitudes* (MIT Press, 1985), p. 23.

Mars—that it has the reflexive property of exceeding oneself in weight—and not what 'Mars outweighs Venus' says about Mars. If one wants to ascribe to Venus the simple relational property of weighing more than Venus, rather than the impossible property of weighing more than oneself, one may use the sentence 'Hesperus outweighs Hesperus' (among others). It says about Venus what 'Mars outweighs Venus' says about Mars—that it weighs more than Venus—instead of what 'Mars outweighs itself' seems to say about Mars. If one prefers, it ascribes the relation of exceeding-in-weight to the ordered pair of Venus and itself. In either case, the proposition contained in 'Hesperus outweighs Hesperus' is not the same as what seems to be the proposition contained in 'Hesperus outweighs itself'.[22] Contrary to any set-of-circumstances account of propositions, the proposition about Venus, that it weighs more than it, is a different proposition from the proposition about Venus that it is self-outweighing, although they are, in some sense, logically equivalent to one another.[23]

---

[22] The argument presented thus far has been emphasized by D. Wiggins in a number of writings. See e.g. 'Identity, Necessity and Physicalism', in S. Körner (ed.), *Philosophy of Logic* (University of California Press, 1976), 96–132, 159–182, esp. 164–166; and 'Frege's Problem of the Morning Star and the Evening Star', in M. Schirn (ed.), *Studies on Frege*, ii. *Logic and the Philosophy of Language* (Bad Canstatt: Stuttgart, 1976), 221–255, esp. 230–231.

Wiggins credits the argument to Peter Geach, and claims to have extracted the argument from Geach *Reference and Generality* (Cornell University Press, 1962), p. 132. This, however, is a serious misinterpretation of Geach, whose view is precisely the denial of Wiggins's view that sentences of the form ⌜a bears R to a⌝ and ⌜a bears R to itself⌝ contain different information, or express different propositions. See e.g. Geach, 'Logical Procedures and the Identity of Expressions', in id. *Logic Matters* (University of California Press, 1972), 108–115, esp. 112–113. If I read Geach correctly, his view is that a sentence such as 'Hesperus outweighs Hesperus' ascribes to Venus the reflexive property of weighing more than oneself, as does the sentence 'Hesperus outweighs itself', rather than the simple relational property of weighing more than Venus. (*Cf.* the treatment of the contents of sentences with recurring expressions in H. Putnam, 'Synonymy, and the Analysis of Belief Sentences', *Analysis* 14, 5 (April 1954), 114–122; also in Salmon and Soames, *op. cit.* See also *Frege's Puzzle*, pp. 164–165 n. 4.) The argument in *Reference and Generality* is intended to show not that 'Marx contradicts himself' differs in information content from 'Marx contradicts Marx' (which Geach rejects), but that the 'himself' in 'Marx contradicts himself' is not a singular term referring to Marx. The argument for this conclusion (which Wiggins presumably also believes) is part of a defence of Geach's general view that pronouns occurring with antecedents are typically not referring singular terms. (I disagree with Geach both concerning the semantic analysis of sentences such as 'Hesperus outweighs Hesperus' and 'Marx contradicts Marx', as does Wiggins, and concerning typical (nonreflexive) pronouns with antecedents, though the latter issue is not germane to the topic of the present discussion.)

The same (or very nearly the same) misinterpretation of Geach's argument in *Reference and Generality* occurs in G. Evans, 'Pronouns, Quantifiers and Relative Clauses (I)', in M. Platts (ed.), *Reference, Truth and Reality*, (Routledge and Kegan Paul: London, 1980), 255–317, esp. 267–268, although Evans admits that the view he attributes to Geach has been unambiguously denied by Geach in a number of places. (Oddly, Evans cites references to, and even quotes, writings in which Geach clearly denies the view that Evans attributes to him.) It might be said that in accusing Geach of misinterpreting Geach, Evans takes on the very property he attributes to Geach—although Evans does not misinterpret himself.

[23] The response to the Richard–Soames problem in 'Shifting Situations and Shaken Attitudes' suggests that Barwise and Perry might similarly respond to the puzzle of reflexives in propositional attitudes by claiming that 'Hesperus outweighs Hesperus' and 'Hesperus is self-outweighing' differ in information content (have different 'interpretations'). See n. 18 above. Such a move would constitute a repudiation of the idea, fundamental to *Situations and Attitudes*, that the information content ('interpretation') of a sentence is the set of situations (or type of situation) with respect to

The astronomer in the example believes the former and not the latter. Neither the sentence 'Hesperus outweighs Hesperus' nor the sentence 'Hesperus outweighs itself' can be regarded as somehow containing *both* of these propositions simultaneously (as might be said, for example, of the conjunction 'Venus has the simple relational property of weighing more than Venus and also the reflexive property of weighing more than oneself'). Each sentence contains precisely one piece of information, not two. Neither is ambiguous; neither is a conjunction of two sentences with different (albeit equivalent) information contents.[24] Similar remarks may be made in connection with Cresswell's example of 'Ortcutt loves Ortcutt' and 'Ortcutt loves himself'.

This conception of reflexive propositions of the form *x bears R to itself* involves rejecting the otherwise plausible view that the reflexive pronoun 'itself' in 'Hesperus outweighs itself' refers anaphorically to the planet Venus. Instead, the pronoun might be regarded as a predicate-operator, one that attaches to a dyadic predicate to form a compound monadic predicate. Formally, this operator may be defined by the following expression:[25]

$(\lambda R)(\lambda x) x R x.$

The alternative conception of propositions of the form *x bears R to itself* involves treating reflexive pronouns instead as anaphorically referring singular terms. On this view, in order to ascribe to Venus the reflexive impossible property of weighing more than oneself, it is not sufficient to use the sentence 'Hesperus outweighs itself'. Instead, one must resort to some device such as the predicate 'is self-outweighing'.

There can be no serious question about the possibility of an operator such as the one defined above. The displayed expression definitely captures a *possible* operator on dyadic predicates. There is no reason why English (and other natural languages) could not contain such an operator, and there is no *a priori* argument that standard English does not have this operator. The question is whether the reflexive pronouns

---

which the sentence is true—with the term 'situation' understood in such a way that any situation with respect to which it is true that Venus outweighs Venus is one with respect to which it is also true that Venus is self-outweighing, and vice versa. Any attempt to modify their view to accommodate the fact that 'Hesperus outweighs Hesperus' and 'Hesperus is self-outweighing' differ in information content would clearly constitute a concession to the structured-singular-proposition sort of theory advocated in *Frege's Puzzle*.

However, this move might be coupled with the claim that there is a significant sense in which the second information content ('interpretation') is no consequence of the first. They might even claim that there is a significant sense in which these information contents are independent and neither implies the other. Here again, if either of these claims is to be understood as concerning the logic of the information contents of 'Hesperus outweighs Hesperus' and 'Hesperus is self-outweighing', they must surely be rejected. Insofar as the newer theory of Barwise and Perry includes one or both of these claims, the doctrine of structured singular propositions coupled with the denial of each of these claims (and with classical logic) is much the preferable theory.

[24] This part of the argument is intended as a rejoinder to Evans's response in 'Pronouns, Quantifiers and Relative Clauses', p. 268.

[25] *Cf. Reference and Generality*, pp. 136–137. In the theoretical apparatus of *Frege's Puzzle*, the contribution to information content made by (i.e. the 'information value' of) the displayed expression is the *operation* of assigning to any class K of ordered pairs of individuals the class of individuals i such that the reflexive pair $\langle i, i \rangle \in K$.

of standard English ('itself', 'himself', 'myself', 'oneself', etc.) are expressions for this operator, rather than anaphorically referring singular terms.

This is not a metaphysical question about the essential natures of propositions, but an empirical question about the accidents of standard English semantics. It is a question, moreover, for which decisive linguistic evidence is difficult to produce, since on either hypothesis the information content of 'Hesperus outweighs itself' is logically equivalent to the content yielded by the rival hypothesis (although writers on both sides of this dispute have advanced what they take to be compelling evidence for their view).

Assuming that the semantic analysis presented above of sentences such as 'Hesperus outweighs Hesperus' is at least roughly correct, the claim that propositions of the form *x bears R to x* and *x bears R to itself* are the same is tantamount to the empirical claim that the reflexive pronouns of standard English are singular terms and not expressions for the predicate-operator defined above, whereas the claim that the proposition *x bears R to itself* is not the same as *x bears R to x* but instead goes with *x is self-R* is tantamount to the empirical claim that the reflexive pronouns are expressions for the predicate-operator and not singular terms. This issue cannot be settled by *a priori* philosophical theorizing about the nature of propositions. A complete solution to the puzzle of reflexives in propositional attitudes thus turns on answering a difficult empirical question concerning the meanings of reflexive pronouns in standard English.

VII

The time has come to face the music. How can the theory of structured singular propositions solve Church's paradox concerning quantification into belief contexts?

Fortunately, some of the ideas discussed in the preceding sections bear directly on Church's paradox. Notice first that (7), taken literally, does not ascribe any power to King George or his beliefs *per se*. Nor does it ascribe to George an infallibility concerning the distinctness of distinct individuals x and y. It merely states a generalization concerning every pair of individuals x and y believed distinct by King George. In Humean terminology, it merely states a *constant conjunction* between any pair of individuals being believed distinct by King George and their actually being distinct. As Hume noted, there is no idea of power contained in that of constant conjunction. Analogously, the sentence 'All crows are black' merely states a generalization, or constant conjunction, concerning all crows. The idea that something's being a crow somehow *makes it* black arises only when this sentence is regarded as having the status of biological law, rather than that of a purely accidental generalization.

Likewise, the conclusion (7) can be regarded as ascribing a power or nomological regularity to King George's beliefs only if (7) is regarded as having the status of a law ascribing some special law-governed feature to George IV and his beliefs, rather than as an accidental constant conjunction. Now in deriving (7), we took (6) as our only premiss. Thus (7) may be regarded as stating some sort of law only if (6) may be.

Church remarks that, even though (6) is not certain, it is very likely. This observation may support a plausible view of (6) as some sort of psychological law concerning George IV and his beliefs. In this way, (7) would emerge as a law ascribing a nomological feature to King George's beliefs. Since no such law in fact obtains, and may even be falsified by the very case of Sir Walter Scott and the author of *Waverley*, the meaningfulness of quantification into belief contexts, and therewith the theory of structured singular propositions, would be thereby discredited.

On the theory that I advocate, however, (6) is not only not very likely, as of some particular date during King George's acquaintance with Scott, it is very likely false.

It may seem as if denying (6) is tantamount to saying that George IV believed of some x that it is distinct from itself, and this seems a serious charge indeed. If an interest in the law of identity can hardly be attributed to the first gentleman of Europe, it is nothing short of blasphemy to attribute to him an interest in denying that law. In claiming that (6) is very likely false, as of some appropriate date, I mean no disrespect. Sentence (6) can easily be false even though King George is, of course, entirely rational—in fact, even if he were (what is beneath his dignity) a master of classical logic. If there was some time when George IV was acquainted with Scott and nevertheless believed after reading a *Waverley* novel that Scott was not the author, then (6) is false with respect to that time. If this be disputed, imagine instead that George IV confronted Scott at a book-signing ceremony, at which Scott truthfully proclaimed his authorship of *Waverley* but disguised himself in order to conceal his identity as Sir Walter Scott. Suppose the disguise succeeded in fooling even King George.[26] Let George IV say with conviction, pointing to the disguised author, 'He is not Sir Walter Scott'. In this case, (6) is decisively false. George IV is in the same unfortunate position as that of the ancient astronomer who believed of Venus that it is distinct from it.

Why, then, does Church claim that (6) is very likely? My conjecture is that Church confuses (6) with:

(6′) For every x, George IV does not believe that $(\lambda x')[x' \neq x'](x)$

or with:

(6″) For every x, George IV does not believe that x is self-distinct,

where the term 'self-distinct' is understood in accordance with the definition of the '*self*'-prefix given in Section III above. Both of these are indeed extremely likely—nay (I hasten to add), virtually certain. On the theory that I advocate, the pair of open sentences

$$x \neq x$$

and

$$(\lambda x')[x' \neq x'](x)$$

---

[26] As a matter of historical fact, Scott did conceal his authorship of *Waverley*, and George IV did wish to know whether Scott indeed wrote *Waverley*. Hence Russell's clever example.

(or 'x is distinct from x' and 'x is self-distinct'), although logically equivalent, must be sharply distinguished as regards the propositions expressed under any particular assignment of a value to the variable 'x'. Under the assignment of Scott to 'x', the singular proposition contained in the first open sentence is believed by George IV in the book-signing example, the second is not. The extreme likelihood of (6′) and (6″) does not extend to (6).

Whereas sentences (6′) and (6″) are similar to, and easily confused with sentence (6), the former sentences do not concern King George's doxastic attitudes toward the propositions involved in sentence (6). They concern propositions of the form *x is self-distinct* (which ascribe the plainly impossible property of self-distinctness to particular individuals x) rather than propositions of the form *x is distinct from x* (which ascribe the relation of distinctness to reflexive pairs of individuals $\langle x, x \rangle$). Sentences (6′) and (6″) provide adequate explanation why George IV is disinclined to answer affirmatively when queried 'Is Sir Walter self-distinct?', but the substitution of these sentences for Church's (6) does not show sufficient appreciation for the fact that King George is similarly disinclined when queried 'Is Sir Walter distinct from Sir Walter?', or when any other similarly worded question is posed. These considerations give rise to a second potential confusion that could also lead one to conclude erroneously that (6) is true or at least very likely. By invoking the ternary *BEL* relation, something even closer to (6) may be assumed as at least very likely:

(6‴) For every x, if there is a y such that George IV is familiar with the proposition that $x \neq x$ by means of y, then there is a y' such that George IV is familiar with the proposition that $x \neq x$ by means of y' and not-*BEL*(George IV, that $x \neq x, y'$).

That is, either George IV is not familiar at all with the proposition that $x \neq x$ (in which case he does not believe it) or he withholds belief concerning whether $x \neq x$, either by disbelieving or by suspending judgment. (See the third condition on the *BEL* relation in Section V above.) Although (6‴) is not certain, it is very likely true as of the date in question, and this yields an explanation for King George's failure to assent to 'Sir Walter is distinct from Sir Walter'. But (by the first and second conditions on *BEL*) it does not follow that (6) itself is true or even likely.

It is entirely an empirical question whether (6) itself is true. There is no reason in advance of an actual investigation to suppose that (6) is even probably true.[27] By the same token, however, even if (6) is in fact very unlikely, it might well have been true throughout King George's lifetime. In some perfectly plausible alternative history of the world, it is true. If (6) were true, (7) would be as well. What then? Are we only contingently rescued from paradox in the actual world by the contingent falsity of (6)?

Even if (7) were true, it would not state a law ascribing some strange property to King George's beliefs. It would state a purely contingent constant conjunction concerning every pair of individuals x and y, an accidental generalization that happens to

---

[27] This contrasts sharply with the analogous principle involved in the standard proof in quantified modal logic of the necessity of identity: For every x, it is not possible that $x \neq x$. This is a logical truth, and therefore an *a priori* certainty. Unlike (7), the necessity of identity (or equivalently, Murphy's Law of Modality) is a genuine law (in this case, a law of logic).

be true not by virtue of some nomological feature of King George IV and his beliefs, but because—fortunately for King George—(6) happens to be true. No power to control the actual facts about x and y would be ascribed to King George's beliefs. If (6) were true (and Scott still had written *Waverley*), it would have to be true as well that King George does not believe that Scott is not the author of *Waverley*, and that George IV is not otherwise mistaken about the distinctness of any other pairs of identical objects of his acquaintance. The derivation of (7) from (6) would be sound, but it would no more constitute an unacceptable paradox than the so-called 'paradoxes of material implication' constitute unacceptable paradoxes concerning 'if . . ., then'. In fact, since (7) employs the material 'if . . ., then', Church's paradox concerning quantification into belief contexts is a version of one of the 'paradoxes of material implication'.

VIII

What is the nature of the connection among the Richard–Soames problem, the puzzle of reflexives in propositional attitudes, and Church's 'paradox' concerning quantification into belief attributions?

It is important to notice that, unlike the original puzzle generated by the Richard–Soames problem, neither the puzzle of reflexives in propositional attitudes nor Church's paradox makes essential use of existentially general beliefs, such as those ascribed in (1*c*), (2*c*), or (4*c*), or that denied in:

George IV does not believe that for some x, $x \neq x$.

Instead, the puzzle of reflexives in propositional attitudes and Church's paradox essentially employ beliefs whose formulation involves reflexive devices, such as the reflexive pronoun 'itself' and the '*self*'-prefix defined above. Conversely, the original puzzle, as constructed by means of sentences such as (1*b*), (2*b*), and (4*b*), makes no explicit use of beliefs whose formulations involve reflexive pronouns or other such devices. In lieu of such beliefs, the original puzzle employs beliefs whose formulations involve repeated occurrences of the same, or otherwise anaphorically related, bound variables or pronouns: the occurrences of '*x*' in (3*c*), the occurrences of 'it' in (2*c*) and (4*c*), the 'whom' and 'his' in (1*c*). In each case, these recurrences, or similarly related occurrences, are bound together from *within* the belief context. If I am correct, Church's 'paradox' results, in part, from a confusion of a belief involving recurrences of the same variable bound together from *outside* the belief context with a belief involving a reflexive device. Nothing with the force of any of these puzzles is generated if we confine ourselves to beliefs involving recurrences of the same proper name, as in (1*b*), (2*b*), and (4*b*), or beliefs involving recurrences of the same variable or pronoun bound together from without, as ascribed in (3*d*) and (4*b*′) and denied in (6), and keep them sharply separated from beliefs involving reflexive devices or variables or pronouns bound together from within. On the theory formed from the conjunction of theses (*B*) and (*R*), sentences (1*b*), (2*b*), (4*b*), and (4*b*′) are all straightforwardly true. It appears likely, therefore, that the general phenomenon that gives rise to all three of these puzzles centers on some important element that is common to beliefs whose formulations involve reflexive devices and beliefs whose formulations involve recurrences of variables or pronouns bound together (from within any belief attribution), but absent from beliefs whose formulations involve recurrences of proper names or of free variables or pronouns (bound together from without the belief attribution).

Wherein is this common element of reflexivity? The question is significantly vague, and therefore difficult to answer. Some of the apparatus of *Frege's Puzzle*, however, points the way to a possible response.

In *Frege's Puzzle* the binding of a variable is regarded as involving the abstraction of a compound monadic predicate from an open sentence. Thus '($\exists x$)("Hesperus" refers to x and "Phosphorus" refers to x)' is seen on the model of 'Something is such that "Hesperus" refers to it and "Phosphorus" refers to it', and '($\exists x$)(x outweighs x)' is seen on the model of 'Something is such that it outweighs it', where in each case the initial word 'something' is a second order predicate and the remainder of the sentence is the abstracted compound monadic predicate to which 'something' is attached. In fact, the abstracting of a predicate from an open sentence of formal logic using Church's 'λ'-operator might be understood on the model of transforming an 'open' sentence such as 'I love *it* and *it* loves me' (with both occurrences of '*it*' functioning as 'freely' as a free variable of formal logic) into the corresponding closed monadic predicate 'is such that I love it and it loves me'.

Compound monadic predicates formed by variable-binding (or pronoun-binding) abstraction from open sentences are treated in *Frege's Puzzle* as yielding an exception to the general rule that the contribution to information content made by (i.e. the 'information value' of) a compound expression is a complex entity made up of the contributions of the components. Instead such compound predicates are taken as contributing a semantically associated temporally indexed property, taken as a unit. (See note 5.) Thus, the (closed) abstracted predicate 'is an object x such that "Hesperus" refers to x and "Phosphorus" refers to x' is regarded as contributing, with respect to a time t, simply the property of being referred to at t by both 'Hesperus' and 'Phosphorus', and the (closed) abstracted predicate 'is an object x such that x outweighs x' is regarded as contributing, with respect to t, the property of outweighing oneself at t. The proposition contained, with respect to t, by 'Something is such that it outweighs it' (or 'Something is an object x such that x outweighs x') is taken as being composed of this latter property together with the contribution made by 'something' (to wit, the property of being a nonempty class at t).

The properties of being referred to at t by 'Hesperus' and also by 'Phosphorus' and of outweighing oneself at t contain the element of reflexivity that also arises when using the '*self-*'prefix, defined in Section III above by means of the binding of a recurring variable. The dyadic-predicate-operator defined in Section VI above in connection with the question of the meanings of reflexive pronouns also involves the binding of a recurring variable, and thereby also involves this element of reflexivity. Some such aspect of the binding of recurring variables and pronouns seems to provide the link among the Richard–Soames problem, the puzzle of reflexives in propositional attitudes, and Church's paradox concerning quantification into belief contexts.

3
Reflections on Reflexivity (1992)

Although two or more are often lumped together as if they were the same, or virtually the same, at least five different theories should be sharply distinguished concerning the contributions to propositional content made by the pronouns occurring in sentences like the following:

(1) John loves himself
(2) John loves his wife.

Linguists will note that in both sentences the pronoun—either 'himself' or 'his'—is c-commanded by 'John'.[1]

In 'Reflexivity' I cited M. J. Cresswell as one theorist (among many) who claims that (1) expresses the same proposition as 'John loves John'. On the Simple Anaphor Theory the pronoun occurrence in (1) or (2) is simply another singular term, one that takes on the same semantic content as its antecedent, referring anaphorically to John. The Simple Anaphor Theory treats (1) as expressing the proposition that John loves John, and (2) as expressing the proposition that John loves John's wife. We may represent these propositions as:

⟨*C*('John'), *C*('John'), *C*('loves')⟩
⟨*C*('John'), *C*('the wife of'), *C*('John'), *C*('loves')⟩,

where *C* is the semantic content function for English.[2] Fancier representations are possible, but this will suffice for the present purpose. By adopting this form of representation I follow the Frege–Russell tradition in assuming that the semantic content of a sentence is not, for example, the set of possible worlds with respect to which the sentence is true, but rather a structured, composite entity whose constituents are

---

The present chapter was written largely in response to a draft of a version of McKay (1991), and to Soames (1989/90). I appreciate the comments provided by Thomas McKay and by a second, anonymous referee.

[1] The notion of c-command from theoretical linguistics corresponds, roughly, to the logician's notion of *scope*. An expression occurrence in a sentence c-commands a nonoverlapping expression occurrence in that sentence iff the first branching node that dominates the first constituent also dominates the second.

[2] Alternatively, the pronoun may be regarded as inheriting a modified (e.g., intensionally rigidified) content from its antecedent, which serves to 'fix the reference' of the pronoun, in something like Kripke's sense.

(roughly) the semantic contents of the sentential components. As a facilitating expedient we may further assume that 'John' is a Millian term that directly refers to John. We may then represent the two propositions as:

⟨John, John, the loving relation⟩

⟨John, the concept *wife-of*, John, loving⟩.[3]

Nothing that I shall argue here depends on the Millian assumption that the name 'John' contributes its referent to the propositions contained by sentences in which the name occurs; my central points are compatible with the Fregean thesis that 'John' instead contributes a *Sinn* that is thoroughly descriptional, or purely conceptual, in nature.

Contrary to the interpretation of several readers, 'Reflexivity' does not reject the Simple Anaphor Theory. The misunderstanding may have arisen because I gave reasons there for rejecting this analysis and presented a rival analysis. I cannot overemphasize that I do not know of any decisive refutation of the Simple Anaphor Theory. My own view is that sentences like (1) and (2) may be ambiguous, that the Simple Anaphor Theory may well capture one anaphoric reading (even if not the only, or even the most natural, reading), and that it is even possible, contrary to popular belief, that the Simple Anaphor Theory correctly gives the only legitimate reading of these sentences (aside from the indexical or deictic reading of (2)).

Whereas it remains a genuine possibility that the Simple Anaphor Theory correctly captures one reading for sentences like (1) and (2), I am inclined to believe that it does not give the whole story. My general dissatisfaction with the Simple Anaphor Theory stems from the fact that it leaves out the element I call *reflexivity* that seems present in (1) and (2), at least on one reading. The other four theories that I shall distinguish attempt to accommodate the reflexivity evidently intrinsic to these sentences.

On the Linked Anaphor Theory, as on the Simple Anaphor Theory, the pronouns occurring in (the alleged reflexive readings of) (1) and (2) are anaphoric singular terms that derive their content and reference from their antecedents, but their anaphoric character is also alleged to be something that itself shows up in the propositions expressed by (the relevant readings of) (1) and (2). The propositions are held to contain some further element indicating the 'linkage'—or identification—between John's occurrences therein (or, if one prefers, between the occurrences of the Fregean sense of 'John' therein). This further propositional element might be represented through something like lines-of-connection, as follows:[4]

⟨John, John, the loving relation⟩
    |_____|

⟨John, the concept *wife-of*, John, loving⟩.
    |_____|

---

[3] This method of representing propositions is developed further in my *Frege's Puzzle*, Appendix C, pp. 143–151.

[4] Cf. *Frege's Puzzle*, pp. 156, 164 and *passim*.

The second proposition, for example, might be thought of as having something like the following import, where 'α' and 'β' are two distinct names having the same semantic content as 'John': α loves β's wife, *and furthermore, that wife-lover is the same as that one whose wife is loved*. Something like this theory was proffered in the mid-1950s by Hilary Putnam, and more recently by David Kaplan and William Taschek—for sentences like 'John loves John' and 'John loves John's wife' in which a singular term recurs (perhaps in addition to sentences like (1) and (2)).[5]

I know of no decisive evidence against the Linked Anaphor Theory, though there is one sort of consideration that inclines me against it. The relational proposition that is represented as ⟨John, Mary, the loving relation⟩ may be said to attribute the property of loving Mary to John (or to ascribe the property to John, or to predicate the property of John, etc.). It might also be said to attribute the property of being loved by John to Mary. It does not do either of these things, however, in the same direct way that the proposition ⟨John, the property of loving Mary⟩ does the first, since the attributed property and the individual to whom the property is attributed occur as the sole elements of the latter proposition. Let us say that the second proposition *directly attributes* the property of loving Mary to John.[6] Whereas the proposition ⟨John, Mary, loving⟩ may be regarded as directly attributing the binary loving relation to the ordered pair ⟨John, Mary⟩, and as thereby indirectly attributing the property (singularly attribute) of loving Mary to John, it does not directly attribute any property to any individual. Then the Linked Anaphor theory apparently does not capture the intuition that (1) directly attributes to John the same property that 'James loves himself' directly attributes to James, to wit, the Narcissistic property of loving oneself. Similarly, (2) seems directly to attribute to John the property of loving one's own wife. On the Linked Anaphor Theory, these reflexive properties make no appearance in the semantically contained propositions; they evidently must be *inferred*, as logical consequences, from the information actually present in those propositions.[7]

A closely related problem, or potential problem, with the Linked Anaphor Theory is that, on the view that the Simple Anaphor Theory is incorrect because (1) and

---

[5] Putnam (1954); Kaplan (1990, p. 95n6); Taschek (1991). Kaplan has suggested calling these lines-of-connection *Putnam wires*. Putnam's idea that the very logical structure of a sentence makes a contribution to the sentence's semantic content in the manner proposed is criticized in Soames (1987) and in Salmon (1986a, pp. 164–165n4).

The theory proffered in McKay (1991) seems similar in many respects to the Linked Anaphor Theory. McKay evidently regards the syntactic relation of c-command between 'John' and the pronoun (rather than any piece of notation like a word or phrase) as providing the linkage component of the proposition.

[6] The latter proposition may be expressed in English by 'John is someone who loves Mary'. The former might be expressed by 'John and Mary are such that the first loves the second'. This leaves open the question: Which proposition is expressed in English by 'John loves Mary'? (There is a brief discussion in Salmon (1981, p. 20); see especially footnote 19.)

[7] This sort of consideration focuses on the subtle, but very real, differences that separate the complex proposition that α *loves the wife of* β, *and furthermore that wife-lover is the same as that one whose wife is loved* from the seemingly simpler proposition that α *is an own-wife-lover*. The first, for example, is essentially relational while the second is essentially single-subject/monadic-predicate. It is even possible for someone to entertain and believe the first without believing or entertaining the second.

(2) have reflexive readings, the predicates 'loves himself' and 'loves his wife' (on the alleged reflexive readings) would seem to be closed predicates, complete and fully determinate in themselves as regards both content and extension, without an attached grammatical subject to serve as antecedent. Both the Simple Anaphor Theory and the Linked Anaphor Theory fail to achieve this result. On those theories, the pronouns in (1) and (2) derive their content and reference from their antecedents (the relevant occurrence of 'John').[8]

On the Polyadic-Predicate Operator Theory, the pronouns occurring in (1) and (2) are not singular terms at all—anaphoric or otherwise. They designate a higher-order entity. In the simplest kind of case, they designate the function that maps any binary relation R between individuals to (the characteristic function of) the class of individuals that reflexively bear R to themselves, $(\lambda R)(\lambda x)[xRx]$. On this theory, the 'himself' in (1) and the 'him' implicit in (2), on the alleged reflexive readings of these sentences, are expressions for this higher-order function, and they designate it non-anaphorically.

A special case of the Polyadic-Predicate Operator Theory, the Dyadic-Predicate Operator Theory for certain reflexive pronoun occurrences, is the rival theory (rival to the Simple Anaphor Theory) presented in Salmon (1986b). Some readers have erroneously thought that I endorse the theory there. Salmon (1986b) takes no sides on the question of whether the Polyadic-Predicate Operator Theory is correct, for reflexive pronouns or for other pronouns. In fact, however, the Polyadic-Predicate Operator Theory has difficulties which make it almost certainly false.

---

[8] Since the anonymous referee was confused concerning my claim that the predicates 'loves himself' and 'loves his wife' are incomplete on the Anaphor theories, the editor has suggested that I include a word of caution to the reader. The referee evidently misunderstood me to be claiming that on the Anaphor theories, the predicates 'loves himself' and 'loves his wife' are open expressions (like 'loves x' and 'loves the wife of x' with the variable 'x' occurring free) and their occurrences (or their pronoun occurrences) in (1) and (2) remain free (unbound), so that (1) and (2) are deemed open formulas ('open sentences') on the Anaphor theories. I am not making any of these claims. The Anaphor theories need not regard anaphors on the model of a bound, or bindable, occurrence of an open expression (like a variable), and indeed it is probably a mistake to do so. Even if anaphors are so regarded, they should probably also be seen as bound in some way by their antecedents. (In that case, singular-term antecedents would emerge as a sort of quantifier, in the manner of Richard Montague.)

Accepting that the Anaphor theories treat the predicates of (1) and (2) as open expressions, the referee defended the Anaphor theories by arguing that, on any theory that sees the phenomenon of anaphora as incorporating a syntactic linkage between an anaphor and its antecedent, it is indeterminate whether the predicates are free or bound in (1) and (2). This is also incorrect. Indeed, if it were correct, it would point to a serious defect, rather than a virtue, in the Anaphor theories, since it is determinate that (1) and (the relevant reading of) (2) are (closed) sentences.

The incompleteness of an anaphoric expression removed from its anaphoric setting is not the same phenomenon as the openness of an expression containing a free variable. In many respects it is more like the incompleteness of a demonstrative expression ('loves *him*') considered in abstraction from any accompanying demonstration that might fix its content and extension in a particular context of utterance. My criticism of the Anaphor theories does not challenge their ability to accommodate the completeness of the *sentences* (1) and (2). Instead I challenge their ability to accommodate the completeness of certain *predicates*, considered in isolation from any larger expression in which those predicates occur.

First, it makes pronouns generally—including reflexive pronouns—radically ambiguous, between pronominal singular terms on the one hand (at least for their indexical use and for occurrences not c-commanded by antecedents), and polyadic-predicate-operator expressions on the other. In fact, the Polyadic-Predicate Operator Theory regards the several (explicit or implicit) occurrences of 'he' and 'him' in a complex sentence like the following as somehow forming a single, albeit scattered, polyadic-predicate operator:

S: John, with his wife's help, fooled his sister into thinking that he was ill.

In this case, the scattered predicate operator would operate on the extension of a complex four-place predicate—even though the needed predicate does not seem to occur as a separate, unified component of the original surface sentence S. All of this is implausible purely as a matter of English syntax.[9]

Moreover, the Polyadic-Predicate Operator Theory fails to achieve the desired results as regards content. The motivation for the Polyadic-Predicate Operator Theory is the intuition—more or less shared by Peter Geach,[10] David Wiggins,[11] Tanya Reinhart,[12] and many others—that (1) and (2) express the same propositions as those expressed by:

(1′) $(\lambda x)[x \text{ loves } x](\text{John})$

(2′) $(\lambda x)[x \text{ loves } x\text{'s wife}](\text{John})$.

These propositions are represented here as:

P1: ⟨John, the reflexive property of loving oneself⟩

P2: ⟨John, the reflexive property of loving one's own wife⟩.

Instead of these desired propositions, the Polyadic-Predicate Operator Theory delivers the (respectively logically equivalent) propositions expressed by:

$(\lambda R)(\lambda x)[xRx](\text{loves})(\text{John})$

$(\lambda R)(\lambda x)[xRx]((\lambda yz)[y \text{ loves } z\text{'s wife}])(\text{John})$.

These propositions (which might be expressed in English by 'John has the reflexivization of loving' and 'John has the reflexivization of loving the wife of') would be represented here as:

⟨John, O, the binary loving relation⟩

⟨John, O, the binary relation of loving the wife of⟩,

---

[9] The needed predicate might be formulated in a quasi-formal version of English as '$(\lambda xyzu)[x,$ with y's wife's help, fooled z's sister into thinking that u was ill]'. It is not easy (and perhaps not even possible) to formulate the needed predicate in standard English. Perhaps the following will do: 'are four individuals such that the first, with the help of the second's wife, fooled the third's sister into thinking that the fourth was ill'. (See the discussion of the Abstraction Operator Theory below.)

[10] Geach (1962, ch. 5, pp. 108–143, especially p. 132 and *passim*); Geach (1965, pp. 112–113).

[11] Wiggins (1976a, pp. 230–231); Wiggins (1976b, pp. 164–166).

[12] Reinhart (1983, pp. 150–160).

where O is the content of the predicate-operator expression '$(\lambda R)(\lambda x)[xRx]$' (perhaps something like the operation of assigning to any binary relation R between individuals the characteristic function of the class of individuals that reflexively bear R to themselves). Here again, the propositions delivered by the theory do not directly attribute reflexive properties; the desired properties make no appearance in the relevant propositions, and must be inferred on the basis of the information actually present in those propositions.

It would appear that the Polyadic-Predicate Operator Theory, extended to cover pronouns c-commanded by singular-term antecedents generally, is advocated by Scott Soames. He proposes extending the Dyadic-Predicate Theory presented in Salmon (1986b) into a theory according to which

anaphoric pronouns with c-commanding singular term antecedents are not themselves singular terms, but rather are abstraction operators which combine with predicates of the sort illustrated by ['__ loves __'s mother'] to produce predicates ... represented by ['$(\lambda x)[x$ loves x's mother]']. In the simplest cases the effect of the anaphoric pronoun is to map a two-place relation R onto the corresponding one-place property of being an object o to which R applies reflexively—i.e. of being an object o such that R applies to the pair $\langle o, o \rangle$.[13]

Evidently the term 'antecedent' must be given a nonstandard sense here, since the pronouns are alleged on this theory not to be anaphoric terms.

Soames's characterization of the proposed theory as an extension of the Dyadic-Predicate Operator Theory of Salmon (1986b) and his characterization of the pronoun in (2) as having the effect of mapping a binary relation onto the corresponding reflexive property, strongly support an interpretation on which he is defending a version of the Polyadic-Predicate Operator Theory. On the other hand, Soames's use of the phrase 'abstraction operator' instead of 'predicate operator', and his subsequent discussion, suggest that he may have in mind a variant of the Polyadic-Predicate Operator Theory. According to the fourth theory considered here, the pronoun 'him' in (2) is a genuine predicate-abstraction operator, which forms a monadic predicate for loving one's own wife when attached to the gappy expression '__ loves __'s wife'. Although Soames calls this gappy expression a 'predicate', it would in fact play the role of an *open formula*, like 'x loves x's wife', with gaps serving as separate occurrences of a single free variable.

This Abstraction Operator Theory duplicates the syntactic implausibility of the Polyadic-Predicate Operator Theory by treating gappy expression's like '__ with __'s wife's help, fooled __'s sister into thinking that __ was ill' as unified, semantically

---

[13] Soames (1989/90, p. 204). Soames seems to suggest (p. 204n11) that Salmon (1986b) explicitly rejected the extension of the theory from the special case of reflexive pronouns to pronouns c-commanded by singular-term antecedents generally. In the passage that Soames cites, however, I made only the weaker claim that the Polyadic-Predicate Operator Theory is incorrect for some nonreflexive pronoun occurrences (besides pronouns of laziness). I had in mind pronouns occurring indexically and so-called E-type or *donkey* pronoun occurrences, which are not c-commanded by their antecedents. (I do not presuppose that the latter sort of pronoun occurrences are not simply special cases of indexical pronoun occurrences.)

significant constituents of sentences like S above.[14] The Abstraction Operator Theory compounds the syntactic implausibility by treating this gappy expression not as a closed predicate but as an open formula with its gaps serving as bindable free-variable occurrences. The Abstraction Operator Theory also apparently shares with the Linked Anaphor Theory the undesirable feature that English predicates like 'loves himself' and 'loves his wife', on their alleged reflexive readings, are not complete and determinate in themselves as regards content and extension without an attached antecedent. Unlike the situation on the Linked Anaphor Theory, in which the incompleteness of these predicates arises from lack of a content and referent provided by an antecedent, here the incompleteness arises from lack of the antecedent's syntactic position—an additional gap, which needs to be bound by the alleged pronominal abstraction operator. On the Abstraction Operator Theory, the 'himself' in (1) functions like the abstraction phrase '(λx)' in '$(\lambda x)[x$ loves $x]$', forming a monadic predicate from an open formula. It cannot abstract the monadic predicate from the dyadic predicate 'loves', nor from the 'open' expression 'loves __';[15] it requires an open *formula* '__ loves __' with two gaps (the analogue of 'x loves x').

The final theory discussed here, the Bound Variable Theory, succeeds where the previous theories fail. On the Bound Variable Theory, (1) has precisely the same content as (1'), (2) precisely the same as (2'), and the pronouns in (1) and (2) function as variables bound by a 'λ'-abstraction operator—like the final occurrences of 'x' in (1') and (2'). The Bound Variable Theory simultaneously achieves the following results: (i) a complex sentence like S above is not regarded as somehow containing a scattered polyadic-predicate operator or predicate-abstraction operator and a complex, polyadic predicate or gappy open formula to serve as the operator's operand; (ii) predicates like 'loves himself' and 'loves his wife' are closed expressions, determinate in content and extension without an attached antecedent; (iii) the pronouns in (1) and (2) are singular terms; (iv) the pronouns in (1) and (2) may be regarded as anaphors; and (v) (1) expresses P1 and (2) expresses P2, thereby directly attributing reflexive properties. Although the pronouns in (1) and (2) may be seen as anaphors on the Bound Variable Theory, the theory has an additional feature stressed by Geach: (vi) it is a mistake to ask for the referent or designation of the pronoun occurrences in (1) and (2) —just as it is a mistake to ask for the referent of 'x' in (1') or (2') (even under an assignment of values to variables).[16]

---

[14] Soames says that he is 'assuming that gap-containing formulas of arbitrary complexity may be counted as predicates that receive semantic interpretations which are operated on by abstraction operators' (p. 204n11).

[15] There are indeed open predicates that correspond to the gappy expression 'loves __', e.g. '$(\lambda y)[y$ loves $x]$' or 'is someone who loves x'. But abstraction on the free variable does not yield a monadic predicate for loving oneself (a predicate corresponding to 'loves himself'). Instead it yields an operator that attaches to a singular term to form a monadic predicate. (Attached to 'John' it yields a predicate for the property of loving John.)

[16] *Pace* Geach, result (vi) does not preclude the possibility of assigning a referent to other sorts of occurrences of pronouns (e.g., indexical or 'donkey' occurrences).

Something similar to the Bound Variable Theory has been advocated by Geach, Reinhart, and others. If (1) and (2) indeed have reflexive readings that the Simple Anaphor Theory fails to capture (as I am inclined to believe), then the Bound Variable Theory would appear to be the most likely of the theories discussed here to yield the correct analysis of those readings. The only problem with the theory that I can see (aside from the fact that it posits a potentially controversial reading—the alleged reflexive reading—for (1) and (2)) derives from the fact that it carries the burden of positing an invisible abstraction operator in the predicates of (1) and (2), on their alleged reflexive (closed) readings.[17] One might explain the invisible abstraction operator in the predicates of (1) and (2) by positing a reflexive–nonreflexive ambiguity in (1) and (2), incorporating the Simple Anaphor Theory for the nonreflexive reading, and declaring that the reflexive reading is shorthand for something involving an abstractor phrase like 'is someone who' or 'is something that'. If (1) and (2) have reflexive readings (and I am inclined to think they do), it is not immediately objectionable to regard the sentences, on those readings, as shortened versions of

John is someone who loves himself

John is someone who loves his wife.

Here the pronouns 'himself' and 'his' are to be construed in conformity with the Simple Anaphor Theory. They are anaphoric here not on 'John', but on the bound variable 'who' (or on its trace, in Chomsky's sense).

The Bound Variable Theory does not require Geach's view that all pronoun occurrences other than pronouns of laziness (even so-called E-type or *donkey* occurrences) are bound variables. There are always the indexical or deictic occurrences. Still, a similar hypothesis might even accommodate a reflexive reading for sentences in which an anaphoric pronoun occurrence is not c-commanded by its antecedent, as in:

If John married Joan, then John loves her.

Anyone who marries Joan loves her.

Soames claims (pp. 204–205n11) that the Bound Variable Theory provides a 'different but empirically equivalent way of conceptualising' his own proposal. However, the failure of either the Polyadic-Predicate Theory or the Abstraction Operator Theory to achieve results (i), (iii), (iv) and (vi) would seem to demonstrate that they are not alternative conceptualizations of the Bound Variable Theory. (On the Abstraction Operator Theory, the pronouns in (1) and (2) can be seen as designating a certain 'abstraction' function, which assigns a class of individuals, or the characteristic function thereof to a function from variable-value assignments to truth values. Recall also that the Polyadic-Predicate Operator Theory fails to achieve result (v), and the Abstraction Operator Theory apparently fails to achieve result (ii).)

[17] McKay (1991) offers a similar criticism of the Polyadic-Predicate Operator Theory. Soames (pp. 204–205n11) characterizes the Bound Variable Theory as treating the pronouns in (1) and (2) 'as variables bound by lambda operators introduced at the stage in the evaluation of the sentence at which the antecedent of the pronoun is specified'. I do not know what this means exactly, but whatever it means, it is probably incorrect. The syntax of (1) and (2) should not depend on notation introduced (presumably as constituents of *other* expressions) only at various stages in their 'evaluation'.

The former sentence, for example, on its alleged reflexive reading, is supposed to express something like that Joan is loved-by-John-if-married-by-John. The alleged reflexive reading of these sentences, however, seems strained. It is questionable whether the Bound Variable Theory should be extended this far.[18]

REFERENCES

Geach, P. T.. 1962, *Reference and Generality*, Cornell University Press, Ithaca.

—— 1965, 'Logical Procedures and the Identity of Expressions', *Ratio* 7; reprinted in Geach's *Logic Matters*, University of California Press, pp. 108–115.

Kaplan, David. 1990, 'Words', *Proceedings of the Aristotelian Society*, pp. 93–119.

McKay, Thomas. 1991, 'Representing *De Re* Beliefs', *Linguistics and Philosophy* 14, 711–739.

Putnam, Hilary. 1954, 'Synonymity, and the Analysis of Belief Sentences', *Analysis* 14, pp. 114–122, reprinted in Salmon and Soames (1988), pp. 149–158.

Reinhart, Tanya. 1983, *Anaphora and Semantic Interpretation*, University of Chicago Press, Chicago.

Salmon, Nathan. 1981, *Reference and Essence*, Princeton University Press, Princeton, New Jersey and Basil Blackwell, Oxford.

—— 1986a, *Frege's Puzzle*, Ridgeview, Atascadero, California.

—— 1986b, 'Reflexivity', *Notre Dame Journal of Formal Logic*, 27, 401–429; reprinted in Salmon and Soames (1988), pp. 240–274.

Salmon, Nathan and Soames, Scott (eds). 1988, *Propositions and Attitudes*, Oxford Readings in Philosophy, Oxford.

Soames, Scott. 1989/90, 'Pronouns and Propositional Attitudes', *Proceedings of the Aristotelian Society*, 90, Part 3, pp. 191–212.

—— 1987, 'Substitutivity', in J. J. Thomson (ed.), *On Being and Saying: Essays for Richard Cartwright*, MIT Press, pp. 99–132.

Taschek, William. 1991, 'Belief, Substitution, and Logical Structure', unpublished.

Wiggins, David. 1976a, 'Frege's Problem of the Morning Star and the Evening Star', in M. Schirn (ed.), *Studies on Frege II: Logic and the Philosophy of Language*, Bad Canstatt, Stuttgart, pp. 221–255.

—— 1976b, 'Identity, Necessity and Physicalism', in S. Korner (ed.), *Philosophy of Logic*, University of California Press, Berkeley, California, pp. 96–132, 159–182.

---

[18] *Cf.* Soames (1989/90, pp. 211–212). McKay objects that the proposed account does not seem to extend to more complex cases, like 'Mary wants the money that John left to his wife'. The anonymous referee made a similar criticism using the sentence 'Seeing himself promoted would be good for John's self-image'. These constructions, however, do not present insurmountable obstacles to the proposed account. They may be regarded as shortened versions of the following:

Mary wants the money which is such that John is someone who left it to his wife
Being someone who sees himself promoted would be good for John's self-image.

If the Bound Variable Theory is applied to the allegedly problematic sentences, its point is precisely that these sentences have readings something like those given by the displayed sentences, so that the pronouns 'him' and 'himself' are not referring singular-term occurrences anaphoric on 'John' but variable occurrences bound by an abstraction operator.

4

Demonstrating and Necessity (2002)

I

My title is meant to suggest a continuation of the sort of philosophical investigation into the nature of language and modality undertaken in Rudolf Carnap's *Meaning and Necessity* (University of Chicago, 1947, 1956) and Saul Kripke's *Naming and Necessity* (Harvard University Press, 1972, 1980). My topic belongs in a class with meaning and naming. It is *demonstratives*, i.e., expressions like '*that* darn cat' or the pronoun 'he' used deictically (in contrast to its use either as a bound variable or as a 'pronoun of laziness'). A few philosophers deserve particular credit for advancing our understanding of demonstratives and other indexical (i.e., context-dependent) words. Though *Naming and Necessity* is concerned with proper names, not demonstratives, it opened wide a window that had remained mostly shut in *Meaning and Necessity* but which, thanks largely to Kripke, shall forevermore remain unbarred. Understanding of demonstrative semantics grew by a quantum leap in David Kaplan's remarkable work, especially in his masterpiece 'Demonstratives' together with its companion 'Afterthoughts'.[1] In contrast to the direct-reference propensities of these two contemporary figures, Gottlob Frege, with his uncompromisingly thoroughgoing intensionalism, shed important light on the workings of demonstratives in '*Der Gedanke*'—more specifically, in a few brief but insightful remarks from a single paragraph concerning tense and temporal indexicality.

Frege and Kaplan are especially concerned with Frege's Puzzle. As it applies to demonstratives, the Puzzle may be posed thus: How can 'This is that', if true, differ at all in content from an utterance of 'That is that' while pointing with two hands straight ahead to the same thing? Kaplan lifts much of his theory of demonstratives from Frege's remarks, yet disagrees with Frege concerning the Puzzle's solution. This results in a fundamental tension in Kaplan's observations concerning demonstratives.

The present chapter was written to be delivered in part at the University of San Marino 2001 Conference on David Kaplan's Contribution to Philosophy. I am grateful to the discussants there, especially Kaplan, for their challenging comments (all of which I believe are answered here), and to the participants in my seminar at UCSB during Fall 2000 for their role as initial sounding board for most of the ideas presented here. I am also grateful to the referees for *The Philosophical Review*, to my audience at an American Philosophical Association, Pacific Division meeting (2002), and especially to my commentator, Ben Caplan, for their insightful reactions and comments.

[1] In J. Almog, J. Perry, and H. Wettstein, eds, *Themes from Kaplan* (Oxford University Press, 1989), pp. 481–614.

68   *Direct Reference*

   Kaplan distinguishes among three semantic values for a single expression: *extension*, *content*, and *character*. Extension is essentially Frege's notion of *Bedeutung*. The extension of a singular term is its *designatum*, i.e., the designated object for which the term stands; the extension of a sentence is either truth or falsity. Content corresponds closely to Frege's notion of *Sinn* or sense, and coincides with Russell's notion of what he called 'meaning'. It also corresponds to Strawson's notion of the statement made in using a sentence. The content of a declarative sentence is the proposition expressed, the content of a singular term is its contribution to the content of sentences in which it occurs. The content of an expression determines its extension with respect to discourse about various scenarios, and in particular, with respect to any possible 'circumstance of evaluation', i.e., any possible world at a particular time. Indexicals reveal a need for a third layer of semantic value. An indexical sentence like 'I'm busy now' expresses different propositions on different uses. Some of these propositions may be true and others false. Likewise, when the sentence 'It is rainy today' is uttered one day and again the following day, the propositions asserted are different. Even if the extensions (in this case, the truth-values) happen to be the same, the propositions asserted still *might have* differed in truth-value—there are possible scenarios in which the same propositions determine different truth-values—and even a merely possible divergence in truth-value is sufficient to establish distinctness of the propositions expressed. Yet the sentence uttered is not ambiguous in regard to linguistic meaning; it is univocal. The meaning, which remains constant among different utterances, generates a distinct proposition for each distinct day on which the sentence is uttered, *to wit*, the proposition about that day to the effect that *it* is rainy. The character of an expression determines what content is expressed with respect to any particular context.[2]

   A competent speaker need not know the extension of an expression (e.g., the truth-value of a sentence) in order to understand the expression properly. But neither must a competent speaker always know the content. The detective who stumbles upon an unsigned note containing the words 'The loot will be deposited in a Swiss account the

---

[2] Kaplan's three-tiered theory of character, content, and extension is inadequate. The eternal nature of contents—e.g., the fact that a given proposition is unwavering in its truth value—argues in favor of separating the possible world of a circumstance from the time, and drawing a four-way distinction among semantic values by inserting a semantic value—what I call the *content base*—between the levels of character and (proper) content. Content bases are proposition-like entities except for being non-eternal. Such things are sometimes called *states of affairs*. I call them *proposition matrices*. Kaplan's notion of character is replaced by a semantic value, which I call *program*, that assigns content bases to contexts:

Level 4:	*program*
Level 3:	*content base* with respect to c
Level 2:	*content* with respect to c and t
Bottom:	*extension* with respect to c, t, and w

The content of 'I am hungry', when uttered by me at t, is the eternal proposition that I am hungry at t, whereas the content base is a proposition matrix—a recurring state of affairs that, although frequent, is not quite eternal. See my 'Tense and Singular Propositions', in *Themes from Kaplan*, pp. 331–392. I will ignore the need for this significant modification of Kaplan's scheme in what follows when there is no danger of any resulting serious confusion of the relevant issues.

day after tomorrow' understands the sentence but cannot know which proposition it was used to express without knowing the extension of 'tomorrow'. What a competent speaker must know to understand the sentence (as opposed to understanding the speaker's speech act) is the character, and it is the character which is best identified with the *meaning*. An expression is *indexical* if its character determines different contents depending on the context.[3]

Among indexicals, Kaplan distinguishes between demonstratives, which require an accompanying demonstration (e.g., a fingerpointing or hand gesture), and 'pure indexicals', which do not (like 'I' or 'tomorrow').[4] Moreover, according to Kaplan, demonstrations function rather like context-dependent definite descriptions: when performed ('mounted') in a particular context, a demonstration takes on a representational content that determines an object with respect to a possible circumstance. Which content is taken on depends on the context; which object is determined depends on the circumstance. Kaplan calls the demonstrated object the *demonstratum* of the demonstration (in the relevant circumstance), e.g., the person, place, or thing pointed to in an act of ostension.

II

As mentioned, Frege made insightful observations concerning tense and indexicality. He wrote:

[in some cases] the mere wording, which can be made permanent by writing or the gramophone, does not suffice for the expression of the thought. ... If a time indication is made in present tense, one must know when the sentence was uttered to grasp the thought correctly. Thus the time of utterance is part of the expression of the thought. If someone wants to say today what he expressed yesterday using the word 'today', he will replace this word with 'yesterday'. Although the thought is the same, the verbal expression must be different to compensate for the change of sense which would otherwise be brought about by the different time of utterance. The case is the same with words like 'here' and 'there'. In all such cases, the mere wording, as it can be written down, is not the complete expression of the thought; one further needs for its correct apprehension the knowledge of certain conditions accompanying the utterance, which are used as means of expressing the thought. Pointing the finger, gestures, and glances may belong here too. The same utterance containing the word 'I' will express different thoughts in the mouths of different people, of which some may be true and others false.[5]

Tyler Burge argues that this passage strongly supports an interpretation on which there is a very nearly explicit distinction in Frege's thought about language very much

---

[3] More accurately, an indexical determines different *content bases* depending on context. See the preceding note 2.

[4] In 'Afterthoughts' Kaplan proposes replacing demonstrations with 'directing intentions' (pp. 582–590 and *passim*). Though the distinction remains somewhat unclear, I believe that nothing said here is affected if the proposed replacement is made throughout.

[5] *'Der Gedanke,' Beiträge zur Philosophie des deutschen Idealismus* (1918), translated by P. Geach and R. H. Stoothoff as 'Thoughts', in Frege's *Logical Investigations* (New Haven: Yale University Press, 1977). An alternative translation of the quoted passage occurs there, at p. 10.

like Kaplan's—not merely the celebrated dichotomy of sense and designatum, but a distinction among those two and, thirdly, conventional linguistic meaning.[6] Here again, the distinction among these three is said to be revealed by indexicals. Indexical words like 'yesterday', 'there', and the demonstratives express different senses with respect to different contexts of use. The linguistic meaning of an indexical remains constant among different uses, and determines what sense the expression takes on with respect to a possible use, whereas the sense determines what the expression designates. Since the sense shifts with context while the linguistic meaning remains the same, the sense is different from the meaning.

Burge's interpretation is evidently based on a misreading of the quoted passage. Frege explicitly denies that an indexical by itself expresses a sense that determines the relevantly designated object, let alone a different such sense in different contexts. Rather, it is supposed to be the indexical *supplemented by the associated contextual element* that expresses the relevant sense. In an utterance of a sentence involving an indexical, Frege observes, what expresses a proposition (a 'thought') is not the sentence itself—the 'mere wording' which might be written down or recorded onto an audiocassette—but the wording taken together with certain accompanying elements, like the time of utterance or an ostension, things that cannot be 'made permanent' by writing them down or by recording the spoken word. In such cases, the mere wording itself is, in an important sense, essentially incomplete. What expresses the proposition is neither the uttered words nor the conditions accompanying the utterance, but the words and the conditions working in tandem. Indeed, Frege says that the conditions form part of the expression of the proposition, as if what *really* plays the role of a sentence—what actually expresses the proposition—is a hybrid entity made up of syntactic material (words) together with such supplementary contextual material as a time of utterance or a gesture of the hand. According to Frege, the union of sentence and context accomplishes what neither can do without the other. Frege makes his position even clearer in 'Logic in Mathematics' (1914):

I can use the words 'this man' to designate now this man, not that man. . . . The sentences of our everyday language leave a good deal to guesswork. It is the surrounding circumstances that enable us to make the right guess. The sentence I utter does not always contain everything that is necessary; a great deal has to be supplied by the context, by the gestures I make and the direction of my eyes. A concept-word combined with the demonstrative pronoun or definite article often has in this way the logical status of a proper name in that it serves to designate a single determinate object. But then it is not the concept-word alone, but the whole consisting of

---

[6] Tyler Burge, 'Sinning Against Frege', *The Philosophical Review*, 88, 3 (July 1979), at pp. 398–432. Burge argues that Frege's three-way distinction is partially non-semantic, because Frege's notion of *sense* is epistemic or cognitive rather than semantic. I am unpersuaded, partly for reasons to be set out shortly. Though Fregean propositions ('thoughts') are mentally apprehended objects of propositional attitude, Frege's notion of sense is no less semantic than Kaplan's notion of content or Alonzo Church's notion of sense. Indeed, the former is a good deal more semantic than, for example, Strawson's notion of the statement made in an utterance. (*Cf.* my 'Two Conceptions of Semantics', in Z. Szabo, ed., *Semantic versus Pragmatics* (Oxford University Press, 2005).) The Fregean sense of an expression is precisely what, on Frege's theory, the expression (as supplemented by various contextual elements) expresses and what, in turn, determines the same expression's *Bedeutung*. The last is a properly semantic notion if anything is.

the concept-word together with the demonstrative pronoun and accompanying circumstances which has to be understood as a proper name.[7]

Let us call these hybrid expressions-*cum*-contextual-elements *supplemented expressions*—e.g., *supplemented words, supplemented sentences*, etc. And let us call the expression that requires supplementation by a contextual element a *mere expression* (a mere word, etc.). Where there is no danger of confusion, we may call the latter entity simply an *expression*—although doing so evidently conflicts to some extent with the spirit of Frege's account, on which it is not the mere indexical sentence but the non-syntactically supplemented sentence that serves as 'the expression' of a proposition. Let us call Frege's claim that it is not the mere words themselves but the union of the mere indexical sentence with non-syntactic material that expresses the proposition, *the syntactic incompleteness thesis*.

The syntactic incompleteness thesis precludes Burge's interpretation. If a mere indexical does not express a sense that determines the relevantly designated object, and instead only the supplemented indexical does, then neither does the mere indexical have a linguistic meaning that assigns it such senses with respect to contexts of use. It is very much in keeping with the spirit of Fregean semantic theory to ascribe linguistic meaning to supplemented expressions. But the same indexical differently supplemented yields *different* supplemented expressions, evidently with different linguistic meanings. The supplemented indexical 'tomorrow'⌢today (the word supplemented by this very day), insofar as it functions as a meaningful expression itself, evidently means something very different from 'tomorrow'⌢tomorrow. As 'tomorrow' is uttered on different days, and the sense that determines the designated day shifts, so the time that supplements the word also shifts; hence so does the supplemented word and its meaning. Conversely, the meaning of 'tomorrow'⌢t is held fixed only by holding the supplementing time t fixed, hence also the sense that determines the designated day (the one after that of t). This blurs the line between the linguistic meaning and the sense of a supplemented expression, effectively eliminating any pressure to distinguish between them. If there remains any such distinction here, it threatens to be a distinction without a difference.

If the mere indexical or the mere present-tensed verb does not express a sense that determines the relevantly designated object, it does not follow that the mere expression does not express any sense at all. Does the mere indexical have a sense on Frege's view? If it does not, then its role is completely *syncategorematic*, i.e., it is then a contextually defined 'incomplete symbol' having no content itself yet affecting the content of the larger expressions of which it is a part (the supplemented word and the supplement sentence in which it occurs)—like a right parenthesis or a crucially placed comma. But as a matter of general philosophical policy, Frege eschews syncategorematicity wherever it is not excessively implausible to do so. Instead Frege very likely viewed mere indexicals as designating *functions*—those 'unsaturated' entities in Frege's ontology that stand in need of supplementation—and he regarded the

---

[7] Frege's *Posthumous Writings*, H. Hermes, F. Kambartel, and F. Kaulbach, eds, P. Long and R. White, trans (University of Chicago Press, 1979), p. 213.

supplementing contextual element, the time of utterance or a hand gesture, as a name of the argument to the designated function.[8] A demonstration functions as a name of its demonstratum, whereas the time of an utterance might serve in the utterance as a name of itself. The mere word 'yesterday' could be taken to designate a function from a time t (which supplements the mere word, designating itself) to the day before t. Correspondingly, the word 'now' would designate the identity function restricted to times, just as a mere demonstrative like 'that' or 'he' would designate the identity function on demonstrata. Accordingly, the sense of the mere demonstrative would be the identity function on the senses of demonstrations.[9] A mere demonstrative would thus express a sense (albeit not a concept, in Alonzo Church's sense, of the object designated by the supplemented demonstrative), and its sense would remain constant among various utterances, determining the designata for those utterances, precisely as the linguistic meaning intuitively does. This interpretation—which is both a plausible reading of the passage and true to the general spirit of a Fregean philosophy of semantics—does not merely fail to support Burge's attribution to Frege of a three-way distinction like Kaplan's. It strongly suggests that Frege *rejected* the postulation a level of semantic value distinct from sense which yields a sense for various contexts. By regarding the mere indexical as an expression for an identity function, and any contextual elements as separate designating parts of the completed expression, one eliminates the need to postulate an additional semantic value beyond sense and designatum. The task that Kaplan's character was designed to perform is held to be accomplished instead by the context-independent sense of the mere indexical.[10]

---

[8] I am indebted to observations made by Kripke, who suggested this interpretation and cited some of these points against Burge's reading of Frege in a seminar at Princeton around 1980.

[9] The time of utterance would have to present itself in a particular way in order to designate itself (perhaps as the current time, the time being, or the *specious present*, etc.), since on Fregean theory all designation is secured by means of a sense. Times of utterance, *qua* self-referential 'expressions', would thus provide rare exceptions to the Fregean dictum: *There is no backward road from designatum to sense.*

A complication arises from Frege's explicit assertion that 'today'⌢yesterday has the same sense as 'yesterday'⌢today. The designated day is the same, but sameness of sense of the supplemented words would require that the sense of 'today' applied to yesterday should yield the very same value as the sense of 'yesterday' applied to today—i.e., $^\wedge$today$^\wedge$(yesterday) = $^\wedge$yesterday$^\wedge$(today) (where '∧' is a sense-quotation mark). It is difficult (at best) to reconcile this with Frege's tendency to treat the senses of compound expressions as (metaphorically) being *composed* of the senses of the component expressions. (How can the sense of 'yesterday' be a component of the proposition expressed by a sentence using the word 'today'?) On the other hand, as several commentators have noted (including Burge and Kaplan), Frege's assertion seems directly contrary to his original motivation for postulating sense as distinct from designatum. But see note 14 below.

[10] Burge says (p. 399*n*) that his interpretation of Frege as contrasting his notion of sense with the properly semantic notion of linguistic meaning is further supported by the following passage from Frege's '*Logik*' (probably 1897). But the passage supports, and even strongly suggests, the very different interpretation offered here:

Words like 'here' and 'now' achieve their full sense always only through the circumstances in which they are used. If someone says 'It is raining' the time and place of utterance have to be supplied. If a sentence of this kind is written down it often no longer has a complete sense because there is nothing to indicate who uttered it, and where and when ... the same sentence does not always express

III

Although Kaplan's account of indexicals owes much to Frege, it differs from Frege's in important respects. First and foremost, the content of an indexical word is taken to be the designatum itself, rather than a concept of the designatum (in Church's sense). Furthermore, a mere indexical word like 'yesterday' is said by Kaplan to designate the relevant object—in this case, the day before the time of utterance—not a function from times to days. The word takes on, relative to a context of use, a content that determines the designated object with respect to the context. The time of the context serves to determine the content. Though Frege assigns a different designatum to the mere word, he also allows that the supplemented word designates the relevant day. One may wonder whether there is any non-arbitrary way to choose between saying with Frege that the word 'yesterday' *supplemented by* the time of utterance designates the day before the supplementing time, and saying instead with Kaplan that 'yesterday' designates *with respect to* a context the day before the context. Can it make any difference whether we say that a word plus a context designates a given object, or instead that the word designates the object 'relative to' or 'with respect to' the context?

From a purely formal perspective the different ways of speaking amount to the same thing. Either way we assert a ternary relation between a word, a context, and an object. But from a broader philosophical perspective, Kaplan's manner of speaking better captures the underlying facts. There are linguistic intuitions governing the situation, and on that basis it must be said that the word 'yesterday' (the *mere* word) designates a particular day—which day depending on the context of utterance—not a function from times to days. The intuition is unshaken even among sophisticates who, through proper training, have acquired the intuition that, for example, the

---

the same thought, because the words require supplementation to obtain the complete sense, and this supplementation can vary according to the circumstances. (Frege's *Nachgelassene Schriften*, H. Hermes, F. Kambartel, and F. Kaulbach, eds, Felix Meiner: Hamburg, 1969, at p. 146. An alternative English translation occurs in Frege's *Posthumous Writings*, p. 135.)

Burge also says (p. 400) that his interpretation is neutral concerning whether it is the indexical expression itself (e.g., the word 'that') or the accompanying circumstance (a demonstration) that actually expresses the sense that determines the relevant designatum. One way or the other, the sense associated with the indexical relative to the context varies with the context, whereas the meaning of the indexical itself remains constant among all its relevant uses. The reasoning is mistaken. There is more than one sense 'associated' with the indexical relative to a context of use: there is the sense of the indexical itself, and there is that of the supplemented indexical. Insofar as it might be a third sense, there is also that of the contextual supplement—which, like the supplemented indexical, functions as a distinct expression from the mere indexical. It is irrelevant that different demonstrations will express different senses (as Frege undoubtedly held). Crucial to Burge's interpretation is the claim that the indexical itself ('that') does not, by Frege's lights, express a sense that remains unchanged with variations in context. But Frege is best seen as holding precisely that the mere indexical's sense remains unchanged despite changes in the accompanying contextual elements (and the senses thereby expressed).

exponentiation in the numerical term '7^2' (and likewise the word 'squared' in 'seven squared') designates a particular mathematical function.[11]

It is preferable, both theoretically and conceptually, to see the ternary relation between word, context, and object as the relativization to context of the binary relation of designation between word and object, rather than as assigning a semantic value to a cross-bred mereological union of word and context. One unwelcome consequence of Frege's syntactic incompleteness thesis is the damage it inflicts on the syntax of an indexical language. The material that supplements the mere word to form the supplemented expression does not itself have a genuine syntax as such. It is not that such entities as times and gestures *could* not have their own syntax. In *Über Sinn und Bedeutung* Frege observes that 'it is not forbidden to take any arbitrarily produced event or object as a sign for anything'. A highly systematic mode of composition of such signs, and with it a generative grammar, could be cleverly devised, or might even evolve through usage. Although the expressions that make up a sign language, for example, cannot be 'made permanent' by writing them down or by audio recording, still sign language itself has its own definite syntax. But as a matter of sociological linguistics, such aids to communication as times of utterance and fingerpointings do not have an obvious and recognizable syntax. On Frege's account, a language with indexicals recruits elements from beyond conventional syntax in order to express propositions. What manages to express a proposition in such a language is not something that can be recorded by writing or the gramophone, at least not in its entirety. It is partly syntactic and partly contextual. Natural-language syntax becomes a fine theoretical mess.

In sharp contrast, one welcome consequence of relativizing the semantic relations of designation, and of expressing a content, to context is the recognition of a third kind of semantic value—Kaplan's character—that at least approximates the intuitive notion of *meaning*. Frege's account avoids the claim that utterances on different days of the word 'yesterday' are of a single univocal expression with different designata, but only at a serious cost: the cost of misinterpretation. Frege imputes univocality by interpreting the word in such a manner that it allegedly designates the same thing on each occasion of use—that designated thing being a function and not an 'object', in Frege's sense. Though the word's meaning intuitively remains constant from one use to the next, that same word (not some *other* expression) also *does in fact* have different designata, and therefore also different contents, on different occasions of use.

There is a closely related reason why Kaplan contends that an indexical is monogamous in meaning while promiscuous in designation, a reason pertaining to Frege's Puzzle in connection with indexicals. Frege recognizes that 'Today is Smith's birthday', uttered one day, expresses the same proposition as 'Yesterday was Smith's

---

[11] Frege maintained that it is not the exponent itself (and not the word 'squared') that designates the relevant function, but the incomplete expression '__^{2}' (likewise, '____ squared'). On the interpretation suggested here, Frege saw the mere word 'yesterday' as also being incomplete, its argument place to be filled not with a syntactic entity but with the time of utterance (*qua* self-designating 'expression').

birthday' uttered the next. Yet, as Kaplan notes, Frege apparently overlooks that the two sentences can differ in informativeness or 'cognitive value' (*Erkenntniswerte*). Contrary to Frege's assertion, the information conveyed in an utterance at 11:59:59 pm of the former sentence is different from that conveyed in an utterance of the latter only seconds later. An auditor who does not keep a close eye on an accurate clock is apt to find the two assertions incompatible. But how can the two utterances differ in cognitive value when the very same proposition is asserted in each?

Kaplan's explanation proceeds in terms of the characters of the two sentences. There is an important yet generally overlooked aspect of character, one that I believe Kaplan invokes in his solution to Frege's Puzzle in connection with indexicals, even if only implicitly. (He does not articulate it in precisely the way I shall here.) It is that the character has a contextual perspective on content. More elaborately, *the character specifies the content with respect to a given context of use in a particular manner, describing it in terms of its special relation to the context.* To illustrate, the particular English sentence 'I had a fever yesterday' is governed by the following content rule:

(*CR1*) With respect to any context *c* the (English) content of 'I had a fever yesterday' is the proposition composed of the (English) contents of 'I', 'had a fever', and 'yesterday' with respect to *c*.

This rule fixes content for any context. Taking this together with such further English semantic facts as that the content of 'yesterday' with respect to a context is the day before the context, then 'multiplying through', one derives a content rule of a rather special form, one that *fixes the character*:

(*CR2*) With respect to any context *c* the (English) content of 'I had a fever yesterday' is the singular proposition about the agent of *c*, and about the day before *c*, that the former had a fever on the latter.

I call this rule 'character-building'. Unlike the content rule (*CR1*), (*CR2*) *specifies* the content of the sentence with respect to any context as a particular appropriately non-linguistic function of the context, instead of merely fixing the content by reference to the semantics of component expressions. It thereby gives the character.[12] Every utterance has a speaker and typically at least one auditor or reader, whom I shall call a 'speakee'. When a speaker utters 'I had a fever yesterday' in a context *c*, the speakee who understands the sentence (and thus knows its character-building content

---

[12] Other specifications of the content, even as a function of context, do not fix the character. There is an exactly analogous distinction between a meta-linguistic biconditional in a theory or definition of truth, like ' "Snow is white" is true-in-English iff "is white" applies in English to the English designatum of "snow" ', and those special theorems called *'T'-sentences* that appropriately fix the non-semantic truth conditions. Kaplan represents an expression's character in his formal apparatus by the function-in-extension from contexts to contents fixed by a content rule, but further remarks (e.g., 'Demonstratives', p. 505) suggest that the character is something more like the function-in-intension expressed by the character-building content rule. For present purposes an expression's character may be identified with the meta-proposition expressed by its character-building content rule, as distinguished from the other content rules. One who does not know this meta-proposition does not understand the expression. (David Braun makes a similar observation, but a significantly different positive proposal, in 'What is Character?' *Journal of Philosophical Logic*, 24 (1995), pp. 227–240.)

rule (*CR2*)) is thereby presented a particular proposition. The proposition in this case is singular, directly concerning a particular agent (the speaker) and a particular day (the preceding). But the sentence itself, *via* its character, presents the proposition to the speakee 'by description' (in Russell's sense), in terms of its relation to the very context *c*—specifically (and roughly), as *the singular proposition about the agent of this very context, and about the day before this very context, that he/she had a fever that day*. The speakee who has been paying even minimal attention, by knowing which day and agent are in question, easily determines which singular proposition was expressed. The speakee therewith apprehends that proposition. The speakee is acquainted with the proposition, yet that acquaintance is obtained through identification of the objects given in a context-specific description. The meaning of the sentence *describes* a singular proposition in terms of the context, and two separate things occur as a result: the utterance issues in the speaker's assertion of that very proposition; and the attentive speakee thereby makes the acquaintance of the presented proposition.[13]

Return now to the utterances of 'Today is Smith's birthday' one day and 'Yesterday was Smith's birthday' the next. The same content is presented differently by the different characters. It is presented in the first context *c* as *the singular proposition about the day of the time of this very context c that it is Smith's birthday*, whereas it—the very same proposition—is presented in the second context *c′* as *the singular proposition about the day before this very context c′ that it is Smith's birthday*. The two different descriptions of the same proposition in terms of its relations to two different contexts reflect the different characters' separate contextual perspectives. Kaplan proposes identifying the 'cognitive value' ('*Erkenntniswerte*') of an expression with its

---

[13] *Cf.* 'Demonstratives', pp. 529–532, 597. Kaplan does not articulate the issues concerning knowledge by description and acquaintance as I have. He sees the matter in terms of a supplemented demonstrative's potential for having a different content while retaining its character, in that the same demonstration has different demonstrata in different contexts. I think of the matter instead in terms of the descriptive manner in which the character-building content rule presents the content as a function of context. The difference between the two perspectives is subtle but significant. (See also note 21 below.) To illustrate, Kaplan has introduced the name 'Newman-1' (not an indexical) for whoever will be the first child born in the twenty-second century (in 'Quantifying In', in D. Davidson and J. Hintikka, eds, *Words and Objections: Essays on the Work of W. V. Quine* (Dordrecht: D. Reidel, 1969), pp. 206–242, at 228–229). Kaplan agrees that 'Newman-1' has no semantic potential for having a different content (unlike the corresponding '*dthat*'-term), since the content is the same no matter the context. Still, its character-building content rule presents that content in a special manner (albeit not as a non-constant function of context):

With respect to any context *c* the (English) content of 'Newman-1' is whoever will be the first child born in the 22nd century, if there will be a unique such person, and nothing otherwise.

The character's perspective on content underlies the phenomenon that has been called 'the essential indexical' in explaining behavior by invoking indexical reports of certain beliefs or other attitudes (e.g., the belief that one's pants are on fire). *Cf.*, John Perry, 'The Problem of the Essential Indexical', *Noûs*, 13 (1979), pp. 3–21; reprinted in N. Salmon and S. Soames, eds., *Propositions and Attitudes* (Oxford University Press, 1988), pp. 83–101. If I am correct, however, a contextual perspective on content is quite inessential to what is semantically expressed by 'I do believe that my pants are on fire'.

character—the way the content is presented as a function of context—rather than with the content.[14]

IV

As mentioned, Kaplan's attention to Frege's Puzzle also motivates his distinction between demonstratives and the so-called pure indexicals. Since different syntactic occurrences of the same demonstrative can converge on the same designatum (hence the same content) yet differ in cognitive value, Kaplan reasons, the characters of those different occurrences must be different. But how can the characters differ when the two occurrences are of the very same univocal vocable?

Kaplan's solution: It is the same vocable, but different expressions. Kaplan's account of demonstratives, as contrasted with 'pure' indexicals, can be summed up in a pair of succinct theses:

KT1: Although incorrect about pure indexicals, Frege's syntactic incompleteness thesis is correct with respect to demonstratives; but

KT2: As with all indexical words, the propositions expressed by sentences invoking supplemented demonstratives are singular rather than general.[15]

---

[14] The idea of accounting for cognitive value in terms of meaning rather than content (or the 'statement' made) is found in P. F. Strawson, 'On Referring', sec. V(*b*), where he says:

[O]ne becomes puzzled about what is being said in these sentences [sentences like 'Today is Smith's birthday' and 'Yesterday was Smith's birthday']. We seem ... to be referring to the same [thing] twice over and either saying nothing about [it] and thus making no statement, or identifying [it] with [itself] and thus producing a trivial identity.

The bogy of triviality can be dismissed. This only arises for those who think of the object referred to by the use of an expression as its meaning, and thus think of the subject and complement of these sentences as meaning the same because they could be used to refer to the same [thing].

Is Frege stymied here? Perhaps not. If the problem for him cited in note 9 above can be solved, he might accommodate the alleged difference in informativeness between 'Today is Smith's birthday' and 'Yesterday was Smith's birthday' through his doctrine of *indirect sense* (*ungerade Sinn*). In fact, Kaplan's identification of the cognitive value of a sentence with its character, *qua* a kind of description of the relevant proposition, is highly reminiscent of Frege's notion of indirect sense. *Cf.* my 'A Problem in the Frege–Church Theory of Sense and Denotation', *Noûs*, 27, 2 (June 1993), pp. 158–166; and 'The Very Possibility of Language: A Sermon on the Consequences of Missing Church', in C. A. Anderson and M. Zeleny, eds, *Essays in Memory of Alonzo Church* (Boston: D. Reidel, forthcoming).

[15] Kaplan sometimes uses the term 'utterance' for the supplemented expression, reserving the term 'sentence' for the mere sentence. This terminological difference should not eclipse the fact that on Kaplan's view, as on Frege's, it is the supplemented sentence, not the mere sentence, that expresses a proposition when occurring in a context. (See note 24 below.)

Kaplan overstates *KT2* by saying that 'indexicals, pure and demonstrative alike, are directly referential' (*ibid.*, p. 492). This statement gives the misleading impression that the fact that indexical words are directly referential (in Russell's terminology, *logically proper names*; in Kripke's, *Millian*) obtains somehow in virtue of their context-sensitivity. Both the statement and the misleading suggestion are refuted by the context-dependence of such non-rigid phrases as 'his wife' and 'my hometown'. Also, indexical sentences typically express contingent truths and falsehoods ('He lives in Princeton, New Jersey'), hence do not rigidly designate their truth-value. By contrast, indexical *words* are directly referential not by virtue of their context-sensitivity, but presumably because their extensions are not secured through a semantic computation (as with definite descriptions and

The attribution of *KT1* is based on numerous passages in 'Demonstratives' and in its forerunner, 'Dthat'.¹⁶ In both of these works, sentences invoking demonstratives are uniformly given with a bracketed specification immediately following the demonstrative of a demonstration. The demonstration that completes the mere demonstrative is typically (not always) performed by the agent of the context, and this demonstration is supposed to serve as a component of the sentence that it accompanies. As Kaplan observes ('Demonstratives', pp. 490–491), demonstratives are unlike other indexicals in this respect. A demonstration of oneself is completely superfluous in an utterance of 'I' or 'me', and a demonstration of anything else is completely infelicitous. By contrast, a typical demonstrative is essentially incomplete without an accompanying demonstration. Not vacuous; incomplete. A demonstrative *can* be used vacuously, by performing a demonstration with no unique demonstratum. What designates, or fails to designate, is not the demonstrative itself but a supplemented demonstrative, a demonstrative-*cum*-demonstration. An unsupplemented demonstrative—the mere word—is not even a candidate for designating. In effect, it is grammatically incomplete. As Kaplan puts it:

> Demonstratives are incomplete expressions which must be completed by a demonstration (type). A complete sentence (type) will include an associated demonstration (type) for each of its demonstratives. (*ibid.*, p. 527)

Kaplan tentatively accepts a 'Fregean theory of demonstrations', on which demonstrations have a character, and express an individual concept as content with respect to a context, and on which the demonstration's content determines a demonstratum with respect to a circumstance (i.e., with respect to a world at a time). Demonstrations are, in these respects, exactly like indexical definite descriptions. The demonstration fixes the designatum of the supplemented demonstrative, hence also its content. With this in mind, Kaplan proposes a sanitized demonstration-free model of how the natural-language demonstrative works: a mere indexical, '*dthat*', which is supplemented not by a demonstration but by a singular term to form a complete singular term. Kaplan's '*dthat*' is intended to represent our natural-language demonstrative 'that', except that it accepts accompanying supplemental specifications of anything whatsoever as demonstratum—even of something that cannot be strictly demonstrated (because, for example, it is nowhere to be found in the context)—as long as the supplemental specification is strictly verbalized:

> *Dthat* [the suspicious-looking guy I saw yesterday wearing a brown hat] is a spy.

---

sentences) but given by a default semantic rule for all simple (e.g., single-word) singular terms, indexical or otherwise: the Russellian rule that *designatum = content*.

¹⁶ In P. Cole, ed., *Syntax and Semantics 9: Pragmatics* (Academic Press, 1978), pp. 221–243; reprinted in P. French, T. Uehling, Jr., and H. Wettstein, eds, *Contemporary Perspectives in the Philosophy of Language* (Minneapolis: University of Minnesota Press, 1979), pp. 383–400.

The content of this sentence is to be the singular proposition about the suspicious-looking guy the agent saw the day before wearing the relevant brown hat—Bernard J. Ortcutt, to give him a name—that he is a spy.[17] Kaplan writes:

'*Dthat*' is simply the demonstrative 'that' with the following singular term functioning as its demonstration. (*ibid.*, pp. 521–522)

I regard my '*dthat*' operator as representing the general case of a demonstrative. . . . I regard the treatment of the '*dthat*' operator in the formal logic . . . as accounting for the general case. (*ibid.*, p. 527)

Though the content of the complete singular term is the designatum (Ortcutt himself), the actual meaning should be given by a character-building content rule. Kaplan suggests the needed content rule by saying that '*dthat*' is 'a special demonstrative which requires completion by a description and which is treated as a directly referential term whose referent is the denotation of the associated description' (*ibid.*, p. 521). He then liberalizes by allowing the supplemental expression to be any singular term, definite description or otherwise. Earlier in 'Dthat', he wrote: 'I would like to count my *verbal* demonstration . . . as part of the sentence type' (p. 237). The content rule suggested by these remarks can be stated thus:

(D) With respect to any context c the content of the singular term $\ulcorner dthat[\alpha]\urcorner$ is the designatum with respect to c, if there is one, of the component operand singular term α (i.e., the designatum, if any, of α with respect to c and the particular circumstance c_W-at-c_T of c). Otherwise $\ulcorner dthat[\alpha]\urcorner$ has no content.[18]

In effect, (D) constitutes a contextual definition of '*dthat*'. Taking (D) together with such further semantic facts as that 'yesterday' designates the day before the context and 'multiplying through', the character-building content rule for the particular term '*dthat* [the suspicious-looking guy I saw yesterday wearing a brown hat]' is obtained:

(CR3) With respect to any context c the Kaplish content of '*dthat* [the suspicious-looking guy I saw yesterday wearing a brown hat]' is, if anything, the suspicious-looking guy whom the agent of c saw in the possible world of c wearing a brown hat on the day before c.[19]

The semantic rule (D) also yields the following corollaries (*Cf.* 'Demonstratives', pp. 520–522):

---

[17] A complex demonstrative like 'that man' may be seen as the combination of a mere demonstrative with a sortal term, standing in need of further supplementation by a demonstration which is facilitated by the sortal. Thus an utterance of 'He is a spy' is a natural-language analogue of: '*Dthat* [the male x: x is suspicious-looking & x is wearing a brown hat] is a spy.'

[18] *Cf.* the designation rule 11 of the inductive definition of extension ('truth and denotation') in 'Demonstratives', pp. 545–546.

[19] See note 12 above. The result of instantiating the meta-linguistic variable 'α' in (D) to the quotation-name of 'the suspicious-looking guy I saw yesterday wearing a brown hat' is a content rule that fixes the function-in-extension from contexts to contents, but does not express the actual character. By contrast, the 'multiplied through' character-building content rule displayed in the text fixes the intended function-in-intension, thereby expressing the relevant character.

(*D1*) The singular term ⌜*dthat*[α]⌝ is indexical—i.e., its content depends on and varies with the context.

(*D2*) With respect to any context ⌜*dthat*[α]⌝ is directly referential—i.e., its content with respect to a context, if any, is simply its designatum with respect to that context.

(*D3*) With respect to any context ⌜*dthat*[α]⌝ rigidly designates the designatum, if any, of α with respect to that context, and is otherwise a rigid non-designator.

Corollary (*D3*) demonstrates that '*dthat*' is, *inter alia*, an intensional operator. The content and designatum of ⌜*dthat*[the φ]⌝ with respect to a given context *c* and a given circumstance *w*-at-*t* is the designatum of ⌜theφ⌝ with respect to the circumstance of *c*, never mind the given circumstance *w*-at-*t*. The '*dthat*'-operator is thus a *rigidifier*. With respect to any context, '*dthat* [the suspicious-looking guy I saw yesterday wearing a brown hat]' rigidly designates whoever *in that context* is the suspicious-looking guy the agent saw wearing a brown hat on the day before the context. The operator is in this respect analogous to the modal operator 'actually': 'Actually, the suspicious-looking guy I saw yesterday wearing a brown hat is a spy' is true with respect to a context *c* and a possible world *w* if and only if the suspicious-looking guy that the agent of *c* saw wearing the relevant brown hat on the day before *c* is (at the time of *c*) a spy *in the possible world of c*, even if he is not a spy in *w*.[20]

As mentioned, Kaplan intends his '*dthat*'-operator as a kind of idealized, thoroughly syntactic model of natural-language demonstratives, which require supplementation by actual demonstrations rather than by singular terms. Kaplan sees in a single deictic utterance of 'that' a pair of component 'expressions': the mere word and the supplemental demonstration. Although the demonstration has a content, that content forms no part of the content of the supplemented sentences in which it figures. The content rule governing supplemented demonstratives is modeled after (*D*):

(T_K) With respect to any context *c* the (English) content of the supplemented English demonstrative 'that'⌢δ (where δ is a demonstration) is the demonstratum with respect to *c*, if there is one, of δ, and nothing otherwise.[21]

Demonstratives on Kaplan's theory are thus content operators, in that the designation of a supplemented demonstrative with respect to a circumstance *w*-at-*t* depends not merely on the demonstratum of the supplementing demonstration with respect to

---

[20] But see note 24 below.

[21] This rule is stated (slightly differently) in 'Demonstratives', p. 527, where Kaplan says that it 'gives the character' of a supplemented ('complete') demonstrative. The latter assertion contradicts my exposition, on which the instantiation of the variable 'δ' in (T_K) to a particular demonstration yields a content rule that is not character-building. (A character-building rule would specify the content with respect to *c* as *the such-and-such in c*, where the demonstration's content is: *the such-and-such*. See notes 12 and 19 above.) As I see it, the rule (T_K) itself is instead Kaplan's contextual definition of the mere word 'that'. Have I misinterpreted Kaplan? Or is his claim that (T_K) gives the character of a supplemented demonstrative an oversimplification of his view? (It does *fix* the character, specifying the character by description.)

w-at-t but on the content. (It is the demonstratum determined by that content with respect to a different circumstance, *viz.*, the circumstance c_W-at-c_T of the context of utterance.) But demonstratives are counter-examples to a strong compositionality principle, on which the content of a compound expression is formed from the contents of the component expressions. This feature of Kaplan's account is brought into focus by (D). The content of '*dthat* [the suspicious-looking guy I saw yesterday wearing a brown hat]' is not formed from the content of its component operand—contrary to what one might have expected on the basis of the general behavior of English compound expressions. The content is the guy himself.

V

By distinguishing supplemented demonstratives in virtue of their demonstrations, Kaplan provides a solution to Frege's Puzzle (as it applies to demonstratives) that builds on the idea that the cognitive value of an indexical is its character rather than its content. A supplemented demonstrative 'that'$^\frown\delta$ presents its content/designatum in a context c, roughly, as *the such-and-such in this very context*, where the content of the accompanying demonstration δ is: *the such-and-such*. Supplemented demonstratives whose supplementary demonstrations differ in content differ themselves in character, in the way their content/designatum is presented as a function of context. The different completions of the sentence 'That is that', even though they share the same content, differ in informativeness because of a difference in meaning. The same proposition is presented two different ways, by means of different supplemented sentences with different characters: one time as *the singular proposition about the such-and-such in this very context and about the so-and-so in this very context, that they are one and the very same*; and a second time (pointing to the same object simultaneously with two hands) as *the singular proposition about the such-and-such in this very context that it is itself*. The same proposition is given by distinct descriptions of it in terms of different relations that it bears to the same context, descriptions invoking the contents of the distinct accompanying demonstrations.

Kaplan briefly considers an alternative account that does away with Frege's syntactic incompleteness thesis even for demonstratives, treating all indexical words on a par (pp. 528–529). Kaplan calls this alternative *the Indexical theory of demonstratives*. I shall call it *the Bare Bones Theory*. On this theory, a context of use is regarded as including alongside an agent (to provide content for 'I'), a time ('now'), a place ('here'), and any other such features, a demonstratum—or better yet, a sequence consisting of first demonstratum, second demonstratum, and so on, in case a single demonstrative is repeated in a single context with different designata, as in 'That$_1$ [pointing to a carton] is heavier than that$_2$ [a different carton]'. Demonstratives on the Bare Bones Theory function according to a very simple character-building content rule:

(T_n) With respect to any context c the content of the nth occurrence in a sentence of 'that' is the nth demonstratum (if any) of c.

This semantic rule imputes different characters to the demonstrative occurrences in 'That is that', since there are contexts in which the first demonstratum is one thing, the second demonstratum another. According to the Bare Bones Theory, the meaning (character) of a sentence like 'That is heavier than that' presents its content with respect to a context as *the singular proposition about the first and second demonstrata, respectively, of this very context, that the former is heavier than the latter*. This contrasts sharply with Kaplan's theory, on which the content is presented instead by means of the contents of the supplemental demonstration, as *the singular proposition about the such-and-such in this context and about the so-and-so in this context, that the former is heavier than the latter*. The Bare Bones Theory makes no place in semantics for the demonstration that accompanies the use of a demonstrative, and consequently misses the epistemologically significant content-demonstratum distinction. Kaplan favors this distinction as providing a more satisfying solution to Frege's Puzzle with regard to demonstratives, *How can an utterance of 'That$_1$ is that$_2$', if true, differ at all in content from an utterance of 'That$_1$ is that$_1$'?* He says:

> The Fregean theory of demonstrations may be extravagant, but compared with its riches, [the Bare Bones Theory] is a mean thing ... the Fregean idea that the very demonstration might have picked out a different demonstratum seems to me to capture more of the epistemological situation than the [Bare Bones] Indexicalist's idea that in some contexts the first and second demonstrata differ.   (*ibid.*, pp. 528–529)

VI

We looked at some grounds for favoring an account of indexicals on which contextual features are regarded as indices to which the semantic relations of designation and content are relativized over Frege's idea that such features instead form part of the expression. All of these grounds extend straightforwardly to demonstratives. There is first the damage inflicted upon English syntax. This is the main reason, or at least one very important reason, for the retreat from 'that' to '*dthat*', with the resulting well-behaved syntax of a sort that we students of language have come to treasure. But foremost, there is this: linguistic intuition demands that a demonstrative has a single context-sensitive meaning that assigns different designata, and hence also different contents, on different occasions of use. On Kaplan's theory, in sharp contrast, each utterance of 'that' with a different designatum is an utterance of a different term with a different character or meaning. In fact, as with Frege, each utterance of 'that' accompanied by a different demonstration with a different content is an utterance of *a different term with a different meaning*—even if the demonstrata in that context are exactly the same. (The character is represented by the function that assigns to any context the demonstratum in that context of the particular accompanying demonstration; *cf.* (*D*) above.) One might say that the demonstrative 'that' is highly ambiguous on Kaplan's account, its precise meaning depending on the content of the accompanying demonstration. This is not merely somewhat counter-intuitive; it is obviously incorrect. As with all indexicals, the designatum of 'that', and therefore also the content, depends on the context, but the English meaning is the same on each occasion of use.[22]

It is not quite correct, however, to say that a demonstrative is ambiguous on Kaplan's account. More accurately, precisely the opposite is true: the mere demonstrative—the word itself—is utterly meaningless in isolation. One feature of Kaplan's operator '*dthat*' that is easy to overlook but that makes it a highly implausible model for natural-language demonstratives like 'that' is that the former is, by stipulation, a syncategorematic 'incomplete symbol'. The content and designatum of the compound term ⌜*dthat*[α]⌝ is a function of the content of its operand α (*viz.*, the designatum thereby determined), but the '*dthat*'-operator itself has no character or content (no 'meaning in isolation'). Natural-language demonstratives, in sharp contrast, have a meaning that remains fixed for each use and determines its content in that use.

This is one respect in which Kaplan's account is inferior to Frege's. As we have seen, Frege easily accommodates the fact that a demonstrative has a fixed yet context-sensitive meaning by taking the mere demonstrative to designate a function from features of context to appropriate designata. By contrast, semantically '*dthat*' is not (as its syntax would have us expect) a *functor*. It might appear that Kaplan could improve his account significantly by following Frege's lead and taking '*dthat*' to be a functor for the identity function, and by analogy, taking 'that' to designate the identity function on demonstrata. For numerous reasons such a modification is not open to Kaplan. One immediate problem—in fact, an immediate *reductio* of Frege's account—is that in the typical case a supplemented demonstrative is, according to that account, a non-rigid designator. Its designatum is simply the demonstratum of the supplementing demonstration, and thus varies from one possible world to the next. This conflicts with Kaplan's thesis *KT2* and his semantic corollary (*D3*).

It might be thought that although Kaplan cannot follow Frege in taking a demonstrative to designate the identity function on demonstrata, this only goes to show that he must seek a different sort of function. As noted above, '*dthat*' is, *inter alia*, an intensional operator. An appropriate designatum for '*dthat*', therefore, cannot operate on the mere designatum of its operand. Analogously, an appropriate designatum for a natural-language demonstrative cannot be a function on the mere demonstratum of the supplementing demonstration. Instead, for any context c there is the aptly suited function $@^i_c$ that assigns to any individual concept (any content suitable for either a definite description or a demonstration) the object determined by that concept in the particular circumstance c_W-at-c_T of c (and to any non-concept itself). An account of '*dthat*' as designating $@^i_c$ with respect to c could be made to yield exactly the right intension (function from circumstances to designata) for

---

[22] Other writers have made this observation about Kaplan's account—for example, Howard Wettstein, 'Has Semantics Rested on a Mistake?' *Journal of Philosophy*, 83, 4 (April 1986), pp. 185–209, at 196*n*. David Braun presses a related point in 'Demonstratives and Their Linguistic Meanings', *Noûs*, 30, 2 (June 1996), pp. 145–173, at 149–150. Braun assumes that Kaplan holds that a mere demonstrative is devoid of character while nevertheless having a univocal meaning, and objects that this is inconsistent with Kaplan's proposed identification of linguistic meaning with character. An alternative interpretation is provided in the next paragraph of the text.

supplemented '*dthat*'-terms. In fact, doing so would make '*dthat*' an indexical modal functor exactly analogous to the sentential operator 'actually' (whose extension with respect to a context c is the function $@^p_c$ that assigns to any proposition its truth-value in the particular possible world c_W of c). Kaplan's thesis *KT1* virtually cries out for $@^i_c$ to serve as the mere demonstrative's designatum.[23]

Yet Kaplan is barred from taking '*dthat*' and natural-language demonstratives to be functors. The problem is that the propositions expressed by sentences invoking '*dthat*' could not then be singular propositions—any more than the contents of sentences beginning with 'actually' are truth-values rather than propositions (although again, this could be made to yield exactly the right intension). Instead of Ortcutt himself, the proposition expressed by '*Dthat* [the suspicious-looking guy I saw yesterday wearing a brown hat] is a spy' would include among its constituents, if '*dthat*' were semantically a functor, the content of the operand description 'the suspicious-looking guy I saw yesterday wearing a brown hat' as well as the content of the functor itself (perhaps something like the *operation* of assigning to any such individual concept the individual it determines in the particular circumstance c_W-at-c_T). This violates (*D2*) and would thus destroy *KT2*, and therewith tarnish the spirit of Kaplan's general account. The cost of mediation between *KT1* and *KT2* is not cheap: a demonstrative is regarded as a syncategorematic incomplete symbol, as mere punctuation.[24]

---

[23] The character of a demonstrative might be represented on this proposal by the function that assigns to each context c the corresponding function $@^i_c$. Alternatively, the character might be identified with the appropriate function from singular-term characters to directly-referential-singular-term characters (e.g., from the character of 'the suspicious-looking guy I saw yesterday wearing a brown hat' to that of the corresponding '*dthat*'-term).

David Braun in 'Demonstratives and Their Linguistic Meanings' (see note 22 above) makes a proposal similar to the second identification of characters mentioned above. The similarity is superficial. Braun's specific proposal has at least two significant defects. First, Braun takes the arguments of the functions he identifies with the meanings of demonstratives to be demonstrations themselves rather than their characters. This would be analogous to taking the meaning of 'the mother of' to be a function from its singular-term arguments (instead of their meanings) or the character of 'not' to be a function from sentences. This defect might be forgivable, if demonstrations are arguably part of a universal language (unlike singular terms). More important, Braun's central idea is to assign an additional kind of 'meaning' to mere demonstratives: a fourth semantic value beyond character, content, and extension (of the supplemented demonstrative). By contrast, the proposal in the text (to be rejected presently) assigns a character, content, and extension to a mere demonstrative itself. The character of the mere demonstrative determines that of the supplemented demonstrative from that of a given supplemental demonstration, whereas the content or extension of the mere demonstrative determines that of the supplemented demonstrative from the content (in both cases) of the demonstration.

[24] Kaplan explicitly acknowledges some of these points in 'Afterthoughts', pp. 579–582. Discomfort over the cost of mediation seems to have prompted a disorderly retreat from *KT1*. Kaplan says that, precisely because the singular term is meant to be directly referential, he had intended the designating term to be simply the word '*dthat*', rather than the compound expression ⌜*dthat*[the ϕ]⌝, and that the supplemental description ⌜the ϕ⌝ was to be merely a 'whispered aside' which was 'off the record' (p. 581; Kaplan adopted these latter phrases from suggestions by Kripke and me, respectively). Since the supplemental term is no part of the term '*dthat*', he says, as originally intended '*dthat*' is not a rigidifier of something else but a term unto itself. He writes:

> The word '*dthat*' was intended to be a surrogate for a true demonstrative, and the description which completes it was intended to be a surrogate for the completing demonstration. On this

Another problem with Frege's account, inherited by the envisaged account of demonstratives as designating $@^i{}_c$, is that the mere demonstrative is 'context-sensitive'

> interpretation '*dthat*' is a syntactically complete singular term that requires no *syntactic* completion by an operand. (A 'pointing', being extra-linguistic, could hardly be a part of syntax.) The description completes the *character* of the associated occurrence of '*dthat*', but makes no contribution to content. Like a whispered aside or a gesture, the description is thought of as off-the-record (i.e., off the *content* record). It determines and directs attention to what is being said, but the manner in which it does so is not strictly part of what is asserted. . . . '*Dthat*' is no more an operator than is 'I' . . . The referent of '*dthat*' is the individual described . . . It is directly referential.
> Although Frege claimed that the context of use was part of 'the means of expression' of a thought, he never, to my knowledge, attempted to incorporate 'the pointing of fingers, hand movements, glances' into logical syntax. Can an expression such as the description in a '*dthat*'-term appear in logical syntax but make no contribution to semantical form? It would be strange if it did. But there is, I suppose, no strict contradiction in such a language form. (pp. 581–582)

These remarks are at once curious and maddening. Kaplan's labeling the prospect of a non-compositional compound expression 'strange' creates the misimpression that his account of designating demonstratives treats them otherwise. I shall make several points in response and clarification, though I suspect that a much expanded discussion is required. First, Kaplan introduced his expression '*dthat*' in 'Dthat' and again in 'Demonstratives' explicitly *stipulating* that it requires completion by a supplemental term, typically a description. He also explicitly said that natural-language demonstratives analogously require completion, by a demonstration instead of a description. (See the quotes supporting the attribution of thesis *KT1* and the content rules (*D*) and (*T*$_K$) above.) And indeed, it cannot be merely the expression '*dthat*', but *must* be its union with a supplemental term—thus, a compound expression—that has a character of the appropriate sort. Contrary to Kaplan's remark, the supplemental description makes an essential contribution to content: It *fixes* the content. Without the supplemental term, '*dthat*' is semantically impotent. (Ironically, Kaplan repeatedly acknowledges this point in 'Demonstratives', both with regard to '*dthat*'-terms and with regard to natural language, e.g., at pp. 490–491, and even in 'Afterthoughts', e.g., at p. 588.) To see the point clearly, let the reader attempt to formulate an appropriate content rule like (*D*) above, except assigning content to the expression '*dthat*' rather than to ⌜*dthat*[α]⌝, while treating the supplemental term α as neither a component expression nor as a component of the context, but instead merely as a 'whispered aside' (whatever that would be) that makes no contribution to content. Similarly for (*T*$_K$) and the supplemental demonstration. In whatever sense it is true, as Kaplan says above, that the supplemental term α 'completes' the character, it is equally true (if not even more so) that '*dthat*' alone is incomplete without a supplemental term and that the complete term has the form ⌜*dthat*[α]⌝.

All of this is perfectly compatible with the further fact that the content of the supplemental term forms no part of the content of the completed term. Otherwise (*D*) itself should be formally inconsistent—as should be Kaplan's own informal formulation of this same content rule (p. 521). So too should be (*T*$_K$), which Kaplan explicitly endorses (p. 527). In fact, Kaplan's acknowledgment above of the consistency of the envisioned prospect is tantamount to an acknowledgment that there is no valid argument from the non-compositionality of content of a complete '*dthat*'-term to the supplemental term's not being an essential component expression. On the contrary, the envisioned consistent prospect is the very reality Kaplan has produced with his operator. There does seem to be a kind of inconsistency—not in the operator as stipulated, but between the very two paragraphs quoted above. In fact, the very notion of a demonstrative that is on the one hand non-compound and univocal, but on the other variable in character depending on the designata of 'whispered asides', is straightforwardly inconsistent.

The remarks in 'Afterthoughts', pp. 579–582, fail to provide a coherent interpretation of 'Demonstratives'. I conclude that Kaplan, on reflection, has misjudged his own original intent for '*dthat*' above (and his own theory of demonstratives!) and that the theory is the one explicitly proffered in 'Demonstratives' (at pp. 521–527 and *passim*): that the complete term is the supplemented term comprised by the union of the mere demonstrative with a supplemental demonstration.

on Frege's account only in the sense that its sense and designatum are functions from contextually variant elements. The central insight of Kaplan's account of indexicality is that indexicality is not a matter of expressing functions from contextually variant elements, but a matter of taking on *different contents altogether* in different contexts. This observation goes significantly beyond Hans Kamp's original insight that indexicality requires *double indexing* of extension both to contexts and to circumstances which may vary independently of context. Not only does the extension, but also the *content*, of an indexical depend upon, and vary with, a context of use.[25] On Frege's account, the content of 'that' is the same in every context: the identity function on demonstration contents. Although 'context-sensitive' in one obvious sense—the function in question is a function on a contextually variant element—a mere demonstrative on Frege's account is not indexical in Kaplan's sense. Likewise, although on Frege's account a supplemented demonstrative, 'that'⌢δ, is 'context-dependent' in one obvious sense—the argument to the function designated by 'that' is given by the demonstration δ—it is not indexical in Kaplan's sense. It is crucial to Kaplan's account that the supplemented demonstrative be indexical. The content of 'that'⌢δ in any context is the demonstratum of δ *in that context*, and consequently varies with the context. For these various reasons (and more), Kaplan is barred from taking the mere demonstrative—the word itself—to have a meaning in isolation.

But the demonstrative 'that' is surely not meaningless in isolation. It has a definite meaning, one that remains unchanged from one utterance to the next, a meaning that is shared by demonstratives in other languages. And as with any indexical, the meaning of a demonstrative looks to the context to secure a content, and thence, a designatum. Far from being an 'incomplete symbol', a demonstrative—the word itself—is a designating singular term if anything is. When Ralph points to Ortcutt and declares, 'He is a spy!' the word 'he' surely designates Ortcutt. Furthermore, even if the pointing itself is regarded as somehow designating Ortcutt, intuitively it is the word 'he' *rather than some hybrid consisting of the word and the pointing* that semantically designates Ortcutt. Again, Kaplan's account of demonstratives as syncategorematic punctuation, rather than as fully designating singular terms, is not merely somewhat counter-intuitive. It is clearly incorrect.

Does Frege's Puzzle provide adequate grounds to segregate demonstratives from indexical words like 'I' and 'yesterday' in requiring Frege's syntactic incompleteness thesis? Kaplan's complaint concerning the alternative Bare Bones Theory has considerable force. The mere fact that separate occurrences of a demonstrative within a single context frequently differ in their demonstrata is not an adequate explanation of the apparent informativeness of 'That = that', any more than the apparent informativeness of 'Hesperus is Phosphorus' is adequately explained by noting that a single object typically has one name rather than two. Even sophisticated speakers aware of the co-designation of two occurrences of 'that' in a particular context deem it possible to believe that $that_1$ is the same as itself without believing that it is $that_2$. Frege's Puzzle is concerned with the contents of such sentences as 'Hesperus is Phosphorus' and 'This is that' and not merely with their syntax. The Puzzle is: How can

---

[25] So does the content base. (See note 2 above.)

the expressed propositions differ in the ways that they do from those expressed by 'Hesperus is Hesperus' and by an utterance of 'That = that' while pointing to the same object twice in the same way—as, perhaps, by pointing simultaneously with both hands?[26] Kaplan's explanation in the case of demonstratives is that the complete sentence is supplemented by distinct demonstrations with distinct contents, and though the two supplemented demonstratives have the same content in the relevant context, they differ in the manner in which they semantically present their common content as a function of context. The Bare Bones Theory also distinguishes the two occurrences of 'that' in regard to meaning, but that difference is described in terms of the different sequential order in which their demonstrations are performed, ignoring the epistemologically crucial contrast between the actual contents of those demonstrations. And, it should be added, the Bare Bones Theory *cannot* provide any explanation in terms of character or content of the *uninformativeness* of an utterance of 'That is that' while pointing with both hands, nor of the *difference* in informativeness between the two utterances of 'That is that', since the sentence is assigned the same character and the same content.

The Bare Bones Theory attempts to solve Frege's Puzzle by postulating distinct words with distinct meanings where there is only one word with one meaning. At bottom, this is the same general strategy employed in both Frege's and Kaplan's solutions. It is a strategy forced on anyone attempting to solve the Puzzle in terms of meaning. But it violates a linguistic variation on Occam's Razor: *Thou shalt not multiply meanings beyond necessity.* Worse, it flagrantly violates a further, particularly imposing variation of Occam's Razor: *Thou shalt not multiply expressions beyond plausibility.* Kaplan laments the fact that his preferred solution to the puzzle about 'That$_1$ = that$_2$' does not extend to 'Hesperus is Phosphorus', since the two names, unlike the supplemented demonstratives, share the same character (*ibid.*, pp. 562–563). Rather than contort our linguistic intuitions in order to accommodate an explanation that does not in any event work in the general case, it would be wiser to extract from the case of proper names an important lesson concerning Frege's Puzzle and devices of direct reference generally: *The epistemologically significant ways in which the same proposition is differently presented, or differently taken, are not always a matter of semantics* (*linguistic meaning*).

The sins of the Bare Bones Theory are not limited to its violation of the linguistic variations on Occam's Razor. That theory ignores demonstrations altogether, and consequently ignores their properly semantic role in the proper use of a demonstrative. One potential problem with the Bare Bones Theory is that *a demonstration's demonstratum need not be active or even present in the context.* This point is illustrated by one of Kaplan's examples (used for a slightly different purpose). I may demonstrate Alonzo Church by pointing to a photograph while uttering 'He

---

[26] *Cf.* my *Frege's Puzzle* (Atascadero, Calif.: Ridgeview, 1986, 199), especially pp. 57–60, 87–92. Performing the very same demonstration of the same object twice over in a single utterance of 'That is that' is in fact very difficult to accomplish. For convenience, I assume throughout that pointing simultaneously with both hands is a way of accomplishing this feat (though this assumption is strictly false).

was one of the greatest thinkers of the 20th century.' Regrettably, Church himself is not present or active in the context; only the photograph is. But the demonstratum is no mere photograph. It is the photograph's subject: Church himself. At most, Church is *present by proxy*, his photograph representing him not merely in the standard way that a picture represents but also standing in for him. The demonstratum of a particular demonstration may be neither present in the context nor an active participant, nor even present by proxy.[27] Consider the following discourse fragment:

> (*i*) Do you recall the suspicious-looking guy we saw yesterday wearing a brown hat? (*ii*) Well, I think: he's a spy.

Although the 'he' in (*ii*) is anaphoric, it is not a variable bound by its grammatical antecedent in (*i*), but a syntactically free term designating Ortcutt. Of course, the pronoun 'he' does not designate Ortcutt no matter what the context. The anaphora here is of a peculiar variety. In effect, the 'he' in (*ii*) is a demonstrative and the definite description in (*i*) plays the role of accompanying demonstration.[28] The demonstratum is entirely absent from, and inactive in, the context; the demonstrative 'he' succeeds all the same. In general, the demonstratum of a particular demonstration need not be present by proxy nor *connected* to the context in any significant ('real') manner, e.g., causally. The demonstratum may be *merely* that which is demonstrated—witness Kaplan's '*dthat*'-operator, which may be supplemented by material that designates an object from long, long ago and far, far away, merely 'by description' (as in 'Consider whoever was the last child born in the nineteenth

---

[27] I am thinking here of a context as the setting or environment in which an utterance occurs, rather than as the proposition, or set of propositions, assumed by all conversational participants. The case of the answering machine demonstrates that a contextual parameter need not be at the location of the context at the time of the context, since the agent of the utterance of 'I am not here now' is typically asserting a truth. Though the agent of the context of such an utterance is, in some sense, absent from the context, he or she is nevertheless playing an active, or 'real', role in the context—there is an assertion *in absentia* by the agent—and I conjecture that it is this fact that warrants including the absent agent as a contextual parameter. By contrast, the demonstratum of a particular demonstration may be entirely passive, utterly inert, a *mere* demonstratum. (Thanks to Ben Caplan for forcing me to be more explicit about this matter.)

The pronouns 'he', 'she', and 'that' may differ in this respect from the special demonstrative 'this', for which the designatum is arguably always present in the context of use (or present by proxy?). If something closely resembling the Bare Bones Theory is applicable to 'this', it is so because of some such special restriction governing its appropriateness. (In effect, the Bare Bones Theory may mistake 'that' for 'this'. Or is it the other way around?)

[28] Contrary to Kaplan's claim (echoing Peter Geach) that anaphoric pronouns may be seen invariably as bound variables (*ibid.*, p. 572). Perhaps the issue of whether the 'he' in (*ii*) is a bound variable is to some extent terminological. But the terminology of 'bound' and 'free' is not without constraints. If it is insisted that the 'he' is a bound variable, then what is the variable-binding operator that binds it to its grammatical antecedent? The 'his' in 'No author inscribed his book' is not a designating *occurrence*; it is genuinely a bound variable. By contrast, the 'he' in (*ii*) designates Ortcutt. Nor is the 'he' a 'pronoun of laziness' or an abbreviation for the description in (*i*). The speaker's suspicion is not merely a *de dicto* thought to the effect that whoever is a uniquely suspicious-looking guy seen the day before wearing the relevant brown hat is a spy. It is *de re* concerning Ortcutt: that *he* is a spy. All indications are that the 'he' in (*ii*), although anaphoric, is syntactically free, with its grammatical antecedent functioning as a kind of verbalized demonstration.

Century. It would have been possible that *he* or *she* be born instead in the twentieth Century').

As mentioned, Church's photograph may be employed as a stand in for Church himself. Another feature of the context which is no less relevant to understanding my use of 'he' is my demonstration of Church *via* the photograph. Frege and Kaplan put the demonstration directly into the expression to form a peculiar hybrid: 'he'⌒pointing-at-the-photograph. But the demonstration does not belong in the expression. I say we take it back. My alternative proposal is that we put the demonstration exactly where it has belonged all along: in the context. Intuitively, the speaker's hand gestures, fingerpointings, and glances of the eye are features of the context of use, every bit as much as the identity of the speaker and the time and place of the utterance. Consider again Frege's insightful observations: 'Thus the time of utterance is part of the expression of the thought ... The case is the same with words like "here" and "there". In all such cases, the mere wording, as it can be written down, is not the complete expression of the thought; one further needs for its correct apprehension the knowledge of certain conditions accompanying the utterance, which are used as means of expressing the thought. Pointing the finger, gestures, and glances may belong here too.' I agree with Frege, as against Kaplan, that gestures and fingerpointings belong together with the time and place of an utterance; I disagree with Frege, and Kaplan, that they go into the expression uttered. Rather, they are equally features of the conditions of an utterance that fix the contents of uttered indexicals. My proposal is that a context of use be regarded as sometimes including a demonstration among its features, along with an agent, a time, a place, and a possible world. Not the bare demonstratum, but the demonstration with all its representational content.[29]

Better yet, since the same demonstrative may recur within a single sentence or stretch of discourse, each time accompanied by a different demonstration ('That one goes between that one and that one'), the context should include an *assignment* of a demonstration for each syntactic occurrence of a demonstrative in a sentence—the first occurrence, the second, and so on.[30] This fuller notion of a context provides a different explanation from that of Frege–Kaplan of the sense in which demonstratives without accompanying demonstrations are *incomplete*. The demonstrative itself is

---

[29] Kaplan objected (in San Marino) that the demonstration should not go into the context instead of the expression, for otherwise a possible context can include a demonstration completely different from the one performed by the context's agent in the context location at the context time in the context world. This prospect is avoided by restricting the admissible ('proper') contexts to those n-tuples $< c_A, c_T, c_W, \ldots, c_D >$ such that the demonstration c_D is mounted at time c_T in possible world c_W (etc.). It is far from obvious, however, that such a restriction is desirable. Is the sentence 'That object (assuming it exists) is now being demonstrated', for example, to be regarded as true solely by the logic of 'to demonstrate'?

[30] One might wish to let the context assign demonstrations to each demonstrative occurrence in an entire argument. The particular argument 'He is taller than him; hence, he is shorter than him' can be uttered with accompanying demonstrations that ensure the truth of the conclusion given the truth of the premise. ('He$_1$ is taller than him$_2$; hence, he$_2$ is shorter than him$_1$'.) Still, the form of words evidently yields an invalid argument. Compare: 'He is taller than him; hence, he is neither shorter than nor the same height as him.'

a complete expression, fully assembled and ready to go. Strictly speaking, it is the *context* that is incomplete. Or if you prefer, it is the *occurrence* of the demonstrative in the defective context that is incomplete, because of a contextual deficiency. It is like the use of 'now' in a timeless universe ('before' the Big Bang?), or the use of 'there' in Oakland, California—fully complete expressions occurring in defective contexts.[31]

The demonstration included in a context need not be an actual fingerpointing, or any action or event in the usual sense. The demonstration can be entirely verbalized—witness the discourse fragment displayed above. Kaplan should formalize this by putting the description from (*i*) directly into (*ii*) thus:

(*ii'*) I think that *dthat* [the male *x*: *x* is a suspicious-looking guy & we saw *x* yesterday wearing a brown hat] is a spy.

If the description in (*i*) is replaced by 'the present Secretary of State', Kaplan would need to make a corresponding adjustment to (*ii'*). But there is no intuitive justification for this dramatic departure from surface syntax. The description in (*i*) does not occur in (*ii*), which is a complete sentence by itself. Instead, (*i*) is part of the context in which (*ii*) occurs ((*i*) is the *verbal* context for the occurrence of (*ii*)), and the description in (*i*) is associated with the 'he' in (*ii*), playing the role of accompanying demonstration. As already mentioned, the description in (*i*) is a verbalized demonstration. If the description is replaced by another, the context for (*ii*) is changed, and hence so too its content. But (*ii*) itself remains the same complete sentence with the same English meaning.[32]

---

[31] Gertrude Stein on seeing her childhood town after it had been torn down: 'There is no *there* there.'

Braun ('Demonstratives and Their Linguistic Meaning') objects to taking demonstrations as aspects of context on the question-begging grounds that doing so obliterates Kaplan's contrast between demonstratives and the so-called pure indexicals. On the contrary, this is precisely one important reason for putting demonstrations into the context, exactly where they belong. Braun also notes that, unlike other aspects of context (e.g., time and place), demonstrations are typically produced under the voluntary control of the agent and are not themselves the contents of the demonstratives they accompany. Here again, these are insufficient grounds to banish demonstrations from their proper place. Demonstrations have important features in common with such contextual aspects as time and place: they are all recognizable as features of the circumstances surrounding an utterance that fix the contents of uttered indexicals.

[32] It is for similar reasons that substitution of 'Barbarelli' for 'Giorgione' fails in 'Giorgione was so-called because of his size'. Substitution alters the context for the demonstrative 'so'.

The construction in the text raises particularly perplexing issues. Consider the following variant:

(*i''*)Consider whoever is the shortest spy in the world; (*ii''*)he or she is certainly a communist.

It seems undeniable that the speaker has asserted *of* the shortest spy, *de re*, that he or she is a communist, since the semantic content of (*ii''*) is precisely that very singular proposition. Kaplan concludes (contradicting his earlier arguments in 'Quantifying In'—see note 13 above) that a mastery of the semantics of such directly designating devices as demonstratives enables speakers to form beliefs of singular propositions, and even to gain singular-propositional knowledge *a priori* (e.g., about the shortest spy that he or she is a spy, or about the first child to be born in the twenty-second century that he or she will be born in the twenty-second century), in the absence of any 'real' connection to the object in question ('Dthat', p. 241; 'Demonstratives', p. 560*n*; 'Afterthoughts', p. 605). This conclusion leads almost directly to a form of the controversial thesis of *latitudinarianism* with regard to *de re* belief. But even if *de re* assertion (assertion of the singular

Importantly, the distinction between so-called pure indexicals and demonstratives is a matter of incompleteness not in the expressions, but in their contexts. Demonstratives and 'pure' indexicals alike are full-fledged indexicals, complete expressions unto themselves. The demonstratives 'this' and 'that' are every bit as complete and purely indexical as 'you' and 'I', as pure as freshly fallen snow. The negative side effects of the syntactic incompleteness thesis are avoided. The strictures of the linguistic variations of Occam's Razor are respected. Forget the Bare Bones Theory. Here is an *Indexical Theory of Demonstratives* worthy of the epithet.

VII

As mentioned, this Indexical Theory conforms with the linguistic variations of Occam's Razor which Kaplan's theory flaunts.[33] But how does Frege's Puzzle with regard to demonstratives fare?

The sentence 'That is that' has a single meaning. The sentence is univocal but indexical, expressing different identity propositions in different contexts—some necessarily true, others necessarily false. The invariant meaning presents the content expressed in a given context with its contextual perspective, (roughly) as *the singular proposition about the demonstrata of the separate demonstrations assigned by this very context to the first and second syntactic occurrences of 'that', that they are one and the very same*. One might regard this as a lean and mean way of presenting content as compared with the riches of Kaplan's theory with its multiplicity of demonstration contents. But to see matters thus is to draw a hasty conclusion on the basis of a serious oversight concerning the communicative situation.

One may still appeal to the contents of accompanying demonstrations on the Indexical Theory in an account of *Erkenntniswerte*. The speakee understands the sentence merely by knowing the relevant character-building content rule. But in witnessing the utterance, the attentive speakee observes not only the sentence uttered but also the demonstrations that are assigned to distinct utterances of demonstratives. Indeed, the speakee must observe the demonstrations to grasp the

---

proposition) is in fact accomplished through such means, it by no means follows that *de re* belief, let alone *de re* knowledge, follows suit. On the contrary, firm intuitions derived from ordinary language show otherwise. *Cf.* my 'The Good, the Bad, and the Ugly', in A. Bezuidenhout and M. Reimer, eds, *Descriptions and Beyond* (Oxford University Press, 2004).

[33] Kaplan observes that there is 'a kind of standard form for demonstrations' accompanying a typical utterance of a demonstrative: such demonstrations have a character like that of a definite description of the form, *the individual that has appearance A from here now*, where the mentioned appearance is 'something like a picture with a little arrow pointing to the relevant subject' (pp. 525–526). This is plausible. However, by building excess material into the linguistic meaning of the demonstrative Kaplan inevitably misclassifies some utterances of synthetic sentences as being utterances of analytic sentences, e.g., 'He (if there is such a thing) has appearance *A* from here now'. Though this sentence is true, a full mastery of its meaning does not by itself give one the knowledge that it is inevitably true, as Kaplan's account implies. Its truth crucially depends on non-linguistic, empirical information: that the demonstrated male appears a particular way from the speaker's perspective at the time of the utterance. This information is supplied with the demonstration; it is built into the context of the utterance, not into the expression uttered. (*Cf.* note 31 above.)

speech act adequately, since knowing which proposition was asserted—knowing what is said—requires knowing which object was demonstrated. Awareness of the context provides the speakee with a special handle on the demonstrations assigned to each utterance. This ancillary empirical knowledge about which demonstrations are performed in the particular context allows the speakee to make substitutions into the character-building content rule's mode of presentation of the content, plugging in particular demonstrations, with their particular contents, for the meta-level concept *the demonstration assigned by this very context*. Instead of taking the proposition in terms of its relation to the context, the speakee now takes the proposition in terms of its relation to the particular demonstrations observably included in the context. In effect, the speakee converts knowledge by description of the proposition in terms of the context into knowledge by description in terms of the demonstration, exchanging knowledge by context-specific description for knowledge by demonstration-specific description. The latter, in turn, provides acquaintance with the proposition itself. The epistemic situation is not unlike learning the color of Alonzo Church's hair by being told that Church's hair was the color of snow while simultaneously being shown what snow looks like.

When the speaker utters 'That is that' pointing to the same object with both hands simultaneously, the context assigns the very same demonstration to both syntactic occurrences of 'that'. In such contexts, the proposition expressed is taken by the attentive speakee as a trivial self-identity—in effect, as *the singular proposition about the demonstratum of δ that it is itself*. This special way of taking the proposition is given not by the character itself, which presents the proposition in terms of its relation to the context, but by the character in tandem with the context *that includes the observable demonstration δ*. There are other contexts that assign distinct demonstrations that happen to converge on the same demonstratum. In such contexts, the proposition is taken by the attentive speakee as an identification between objects differently demonstrated—as *the singular proposition about both the demonstratum of δ_1 and the demonstratum of δ_2, that they are one and the very same*. Pairs of contexts, one of each sort, may yield exactly the same singular proposition—resulting in Frege's Puzzle. With regard to such context pairs, the uttered sentence 'That is that' not only expresses the same content but retains the same meaning. The relevant character-building content rule presents the proposition in terms of the same relations to the respective contexts—as a singular proposition about the demonstrata of whatever demonstrations are assigned to utterances of 'that' by the relevant context. In observing those demonstrations, the attentive speakee is enabled to take the proposition in the distinct contexts in terms of its relation to those very demonstrations. The different ways in which the same proposition is taken—what I have elsewhere called *proposition guises*[34]—are provided not by the character-building content rule itself, but in the contents of the demonstrations assigned by the particular context of use. In short, the difference lies not in the semantics but in the contexts, which assign distinct demonstrations to the syntactic occurrences of 'that' and thereby provide the attentive speakee with contrasting

---

[34] *Cf.* my *Frege's Puzzle*, especially chapters 8–9.

perceptual perspectives on what is in fact the same proposition presented *via* the same meaning in the distinct contexts.

This contrasts with Kaplan's account, on which the same mere words are uttered, yet different sentences with different meanings (the different characters resulting from different demonstrations with different contents). While proposition guises can be a matter of linguistic meaning, they are not always so. Where demonstratives are used, they are a matter of ancillary knowledge, of non-linguistic perceptual perspective. The semantics of demonstratives on the proposed Indexical Theory makes essential reference to demonstrations, which are assigned to syntactic occurrences of demonstratives by the context. But that reference is exclusively by description. The semantics makes no essential reference to the *contents* of those demonstrations, even if they are crucial to the communicative and epistemic situation. The Indexical Theory provides no semantic distinction on which to hang the different ways in which the same proposition might be taken differently in different utterances of 'That is that'. The various proposition guises are not given in the semantics. They are given in the context—or more accurately, in the union of meaning and context.

In 'Afterthoughts', Kaplan says that he accepted the Fregean theory of demonstrations in 'Demonstratives' in part because 'the Fregean idea that *that very demonstration* might have picked out a different demonstratum, an idea that depended on the separability of a demonstration from a particular context, seemed to track very closely the cognitive uncertainties of "that$_1$ is that$_2$". This cognitive value appears in character, and thus as an aspect of meaning' (p. 588). The Indexical Theory I propose demonstrates that the Fregean idea does not require the detachment of the demonstration from context. Nor must the relevant 'cognitive uncertainties' be an aspect of meaning. Meaning has a role to play, and an important role it is. But the epistemologically crucial *ways of taking things* are given in the context rather than the character-building content rule. Direct-reference theorists who share my skepticism regarding Frege's Solution to Frege's Puzzle with regard to 'Hesperus' and 'Phosphorus'—including Kaplan (*ibid.*, pp. 562–563, 598)—should not be troubled by this aspect of my proposed account. On the contrary, in respecting the strictures of the linguistic variations of Occam's Razor while locating the proposition guises provided through the use of demonstratives in non-semantic, contextual aspects of their use, the account points the way to a similarly non-semantic account of the cognitive role played by proper names, natural-kind terms, and other devices of direct reference.[35]

VIII

I have not argued that Kaplan's operator '*dthat*' could not be added to a natural language like English, or even that it would be undesirable to do so. Quite the contrary, it has already proved itself a very useful addition to philosophical English. What I am

---

[35] See note 13 above. A name whose designation is fixed by description has a character of a rather special form. In the case of a typical name, the character-building content rule specifies the content for (every context) by name rather than by description.

asserting is that the operator provides an inaccurate and seriously misleading model of standard uses of the English demonstrative 'that'. Unlike '*dthat*', which is syncategorematic, the English demonstrative 'that' is standardly used as a complete singular term that semantically designates the relevant demonstratum with respect to a context. In other standard uses, the English word 'that' is not itself a singular term but part of a so-called complex demonstrative, 'that *F*', which is a complete, fully designating singular term. It might be better to view the bare demonstrative 'that' as a diminution or abbreviation of the demonstrative phrase 'that object' or 'that thing', making space for the complex phrase 'that *F*' as the underlying general case. There are other uses of phrases of the same surface form as complex demonstratives on which those phrases seem to be instead stylistically altered definite descriptions. ('David is still hoping to encounter that pupil who will surpass him.') There may also be uses of words like 'that' and 'she' on which they function nearly enough like '*dthat*'—as perhaps, 'A teacher gave Rudolf a low grade and David doubts whether she (the same teacher) graded fairly.' Such uses deviate from the standard case.[36]

---

[36] A frequently heard objection to the hypothesis that compound expressions of a given category (e.g., definite descriptions) are singular terms is that expressions of the given category can be coherently quantified into (i.e., they can contain a variable bound by an external quantifier) while genuine singular terms cannot. The objection evidently originated with Benson Mates, 'Descriptions and Reference', *Foundations of Language*, 10, 3 (September 1973), pp. 409–418, at p. 415, but has been endorsed or echoed by others (*e.g.*, Stephen Neale, *Descriptions*, Cambridge, Mass.: MIT Press, 1990, at p. 56n28). The objection typically relies on a λ-abstraction theorem, to the effect that any sentence ϕ_β containing a genuine singular term β in extensional position, and which is the result of uniformly substituting β for the free occurrences of a variable α in the open formula ϕ_α, is true only if the designatum of β satisfies ϕ_α. (The assumed abstraction theorem is not generally stated this precisely, if it is stated at all. Mates may rely on an alternative semantic principle: that any sentence ϕ_β of a restricted class C, and containing a genuine singular term β in extensional position, is true only if β designates. The class C might exclude such problematic formulas as ⌜β does not exist⌝.) The objection has been applied to complex demonstratives—for example, by Ernest Lepore and Kirk Ludwig in 'The Semantics and Pragmatics of Complex Demonstratives', *Mind*, 109, 433 (April 2000), pp. 200–241, at pp. 205–206, 210–222, and *passim* (where something like the assumed abstraction theorem is explicitly applied): 'It is difficult to see how to make sense of quantification into complex demonstratives on the assumption that they are referring terms. . . . [The abstraction theorem] renders mysterious how the material in the nominal could interact semantically with the rest of the [quantified] sentence' (pp. 205–206). . . . 'Examples of apparently coherent quantification into the nominals of complex demonstratives supply some of the most important evidence for denying that they are referring terms' (p. 219). *Cf.* Jeffrey King, *Complex Demonstratives* (Cambridge, Mass.: MIT Press, forthcoming), at pp. 10–11, 20–22.

It should be noted in response that complex demonstratives seem especially immune to this objection, since quantification into them is, at best, odd. If the open phrase 'that man she sees at the podium' is used genuinely demonstratively in 'At least one woman here admires that man she sees at the podium' (not as a stylistically altered definite description), the sentence is indeed true if and only if the relevant demonstratum satisfies the matrix 'At least one woman here admires x', and the objection collapses. (The example is from Lepore and Ludwig.) *Cf.* Barry Taylor, 'Truth-theory for Indexical Languages', in M. Platts, ed., *Reference, Truth, and Reality* (London: Routledge & Kegan Paul, 1980), pp. 182–198, at pp. 195–196; and Neale, 'Term Limits', in J. Tomberlin, ed., *Philosophical Perspectives, 7: Language and Logic* (Atascadero, Calif.: Ridgeview, 1993), pp. 89–123, at p. 107. More importantly, if it were sound, the assumed abstraction principle would establish more generally that the very notion of an *open designator* (a designating expression containing a free variable) is semantically incoherent. Despite the objection's popularity, ordinary mathematical notation is rife with counter-examples to the abstraction 'theorem': '$x + 3$', 'x^2', etc.

Following Kaplan's lead, I here introduce an artificial operator, '*zat*'. Unlike its predecessor '*dthat*', the '*zat*'-operator does not have the logical form of a functor. But like '*dthat*', neither is it a singular term. Like the logician's inverted iota, it is a variable-binding operator that forms singular terms from open formulas: '(*zat x*)(*x* is a man & *x* looks suspicious)'. It is not required, however, that the open-formula matrix, '*x* is a man & *x* looks suspicious', be uniquely satisfied for the '*zat*'-term to be a 'proper' demonstrative, i.e., to designate. The meaning of a '*zat*'-term is determined by the following replacement for (*D*) (as well as for (T_n)):

(Z) With respect to any assignment of values to variables *s* and any context *c*, the content of an occurrence of the demonstrative term $\ulcorner(zat\,\alpha)\phi_\alpha\urcorner$ is the demonstratum of the demonstration assigned to that occurrence in *c*, provided there is such a demonstratum and it satisfies ϕ_α with respect to *c* (i.e., provided ϕ_α is true under the modified version of *s* that assigns the demonstratum to α and is otherwise the same as *s*, with respect to both *c* and the particular circumstance c_W-at-c_T of *c*). Otherwise $\ulcorner(zat\,\alpha)\phi_\alpha\urcorner$ has no content.[37]

As with '*dthat*', the '*zat*' operator is a content operator, in that the designatum of $\ulcorner(zat\,\alpha)\phi_\alpha\urcorner$ with respect to a circumstance *w*-at-*t* must satisfy the matrix formula ϕ_α with respect to a different circumstance, *viz.*, that of the context. Also like '*dthat*'-terms, '*zat*'-terms are not compositional with regard to content. Though $\ulcorner(zat\,\alpha)\phi_\alpha\urcorner$ is a compound term, the content of its matrix formula ϕ_α (under the assignment of values to its free variables) generally forms no part of the content of the '*zat*'-term itself (under that same value assignment), which, provided it satisfies the operand, is simply the demonstratum assigned to the term by the context. The semantic rule (Z) yields the following corollaries, analogous to (D1)–(D3) above:

(Z1) The complex demonstrative $\ulcorner(zat\,\alpha)\phi_\alpha\urcorner$ is indexical.

(Z2) With respect to any context $\ulcorner(zat\,\alpha)\phi_\alpha\urcorner$ is directly referential.

The most glaring counter-example is the paradigm of an open designator: the individual variable. The objection is in fact based on an elementary confusion. Designation for an open term (whether compound or a variable) is relative to an assignment of values to its free variables. The variable '*y*' is a genuine singular term if anything is. Its designatum (under the assignment of, say, David Kaplan as value) may fail to satisfy the particular open formula '∼(*y*)(*y* is a person ⊃ *x* is ingenious)' (let this be ϕ_α, with $\alpha =$ '*x*') even though the sentence that results by substituting '*y*' for '*x*' is true—precisely because the newly introduced occurrence of '*y*' is captured by the quantifier, making its value irrelevant. The mistaken abstraction 'theorem' can be corrected, and even generalized: An assignment *s* of values to variables satisfies a formula ϕ_β [of the restricted class C] containing a *free occurrence* of a singular term β in extensional position, and which is the result of uniformly substituting *free occurrences* of β for the free occurrences of a variable α in ϕ_α, if and only if the modified value-assignment *s'* that assigns to α the designatum of β under *s*, and is otherwise the same as *s*, satisfies ϕ_α. This corrected version effectively blocks the objection. (There is likewise a corrected, generalized version of Mates's apparent assumption: *An assignment s of values to variables satisfies a formula* ϕ_β *[of the restricted class C] containing a **free occurrence** of singular term* β *in extensional position only if* β *designates under s*.) Cf. my 'Being of Two Minds: Belief with Doubt', *Noûs*, 29, 1 (1995), pp. 1–20, at 18*n*26.

[37] By stipulation, '*zat*'-terms are genuine singular terms. Their stipulated content rule (Z) allows for the possibility of quantification in. (See the previous note.)

(Z3) With respect to any context an occurrence of $\ulcorner(zat\,\alpha)\phi_\alpha\urcorner$ rigidly designates the demonstratum of the demonstration assigned to it in that context, provided such a demonstratum satisfies ϕ_α with respect to c. Otherwise it is a rigid non-designator.

Accordingly, I propose that Kaplan's content rule (T_K) be replaced with the following as governing standard uses of demonstratives:

(T) With respect to any context c, the (English) content of an occurrence of the complex demonstrative 'that'⌒NP is the demonstratum of the demonstration assigned to that occurrence in c, provided: (i) there is such a demonstratum; and (ii) NP applies to it with respect to c. Otherwise 'that'⌒NP has no content. (NP may be deleted to form a bare demonstrative, in which case condition (ii) is regarded as vacuously fulfilled, or simply deleted.)

This rule yields the same corollaries for natural-language complex demonstratives: 'that' is a content operator; complex demonstratives are not compositional with regard to content; they are indexical, directly referential, rigid.[38] It is presumably Kaplan's intent that his alternative content rule (T_K) is to be extended to cover supplemented complex demonstratives, 'that'⌒NP⌒δ, by including (T)'s condition (ii).[39] This natural extension of (T_K) makes the mere (unsupplemented) complex

---

[38] Stefano Predelli, in 'Complex Demonstratives and Anaphora', *Analysis*, 61, 1 (January 2001), pp. 53–59, challenges those who deny that complex demonstratives are compositional with regard to content to explain how the anaphoric pronoun 'her' in 'That man talking to Mary admires her' (uttered while pointing to one of several men talking to Mary) obtains its content. It is tempting to suppose that any anaphoric pronoun occurrence whose antecedent is a singular term simply inherits as its content the very content contributed by its antecedent to the content of the sentence in which the antecedent occurs. But according to (T), the antecedent term in this case contributes no component to the content of the complex demonstrative in which it occurs.

In response I note that the naive rule of content inheritance is falsified in cases in which the antecedent is a singular term that is not directly referential, as perhaps in 'The number of planets is such that, necessarily, *it* is odd' and 'Ralph believes of the man seen at the beach that *he* is a spy.' If the naive rule were correct (and if, contrary to Russell, the definite-description antecedents are singular terms), these sentences would be *de dicto* rather than *de re*. A more promising rule of anaphora—applicable even to anaphoric pronouns whose antecedents are singular terms that are not directly referential—is that *a simple (non-reflexive) anaphoric pronoun occurrence whose antecedent is a singular term, if it is not itself a bound variable, typically takes as its content the object customarily designated by its antecedent*. There is no requirement that the antecedent contribute its customary content to the content of the sentence in which the antecedent occurs. Although this rule is also subject to counter-examples, it is applicable to a significantly wider range of cases than the naive rule of content inheritance and it seems likely that some restricted variant is correct. Consider: 'That man talking to the actress honored here tonight admires her.' Although I hold the description 'the actress honored here tonight' does not contribute its customary content to that of the sentence in question, and instead merely contributes toward a restriction on admissible contents for the complex demonstrative, the description itself has a customary designatum (assuming it is a singular term), and it is that customary designatum, though she makes no appearance in the content of the demonstrative itself, that the anaphoric pronoun takes as its content.

[39] He says of (T_K) that 'obvious adjustments are to be made to take into account any common noun phrase which accompanies or is built-in to the demonstrative' (*ibid.*, p. 527). Kaplan is interpreted as incorporating condition (ii) by Emma Borg, 'Complex Demonstratives', *Philosophical Studies*, 97 (2000), pp. 229–249, at 242, where a designation rule entailed by my content rule (T) is

demonstrative 'that'⌢NP syncategorematic, i.e., a contextually defined incomplete symbol.[40] Utterances of the same mere complex demonstrative accompanied by demonstrations of differing content are utterances of strictly different expressions with different meanings. On my alternative proposal, by contrast, a complex demonstrative is a complete singular term each use of which is an utterance of *a single expression with a single meaning*—though its content varies with context and its use is felicitous only in those contexts in which it is accompanied by a demonstration.

We have already seen numerous philosophically significant consequences of regarding natural-language complex demonstratives in accordance with (*T*), i.e., on the model of '*zat*'-terms: Frege's syntactic incompleteness thesis is rejected; the purity of natural-language syntax is not threatened; complex demonstratives are not syncategorematic; they are both meaningful and univocal; they designate the right object, etc. A treatment of complex demonstratives on the model of '*zat*'-terms yields further philosophically significant consequences. The semantic corollary (*Z3*) in particular imposes three conditions worthy of special note. Not surprisingly, complex demonstratives are rigid designators.[41] More interesting, a complex demonstrative

---

defended at some length. A similar designation rule, though couched within the Bare Bones Theory, is proffered by David Braun, 'Structured Characters and Complex Demonstratives', *Philosophical Studies*, 74 (1994), pp. 193–219, at p. 209.

[40] Whereas the mere complex demonstrative 'that'⌢NP is devoid of character, content, and designatum, the content of the completed expression 'that'⌢NP⌢δ is defined to be the demonstratum of δ (in the context), if there is a unique such demonstratum and NP applies to it (with respect to the context), and to be nothing otherwise.

[41] In the sentence 'If there had been an atheist elected to the US Senate, then that Senator's atheism would have been concealed during the political campaign' (on its most natural reading) the phrase 'that Senator' is evidently not correctly formalized using '*zat*'. Yet it is a rigid designator. The sentence seems to have a form something like that of 'For every possible individual *i*, if *i* had been an atheist who was elected to the US Senate, then *i*'s atheism would have concealed during the political campaign.' Though not a demonstrative phrase, the variable '*i*' is a rigid designator of its value under any value-assignment. Simple individual variables are rigid designators *par excellence*. (By contrast, see note 28 above.)

The same remark applies to analogous bound-variable uses of pronouns ('. . ., then *he* would have concealed his atheism . . .'; *cf.* note 38 above). Michael McKinsey, in 'Mental Anaphora', *Synthese*, 66 (1986), pp. 159–175, uses an example like the following to argue that such pronouns are not rigid (p. 161): 'An atheist was once elected to the US Senate, but his atheism had been concealed during the political campaign.'

According to McKinsey, the pronoun designates different possible individuals with respect to different possible worlds—*to wit*, whoever in that world is an atheist elected to the US Senate. The argument is echoed by Scott Soames, in his review of Gareth Evans' *Collected Papers*, in *Journal of Philosophy*, 86, 3 (March 1989), pp. 141–156, at p. 145, and endorsed by Stephen Neale, in 'Descriptive Pronouns and Donkey Anaphora', *Journal of Philosophy*, 87, 3 (March 1990), pp. 113–150, at p. 130, and again in *Descriptions*, at p. 186. It assumes, following Evans, that such pronoun occurrences (so-called 'donkey' pronouns) are unbound singular terms or descriptions. *Pace* Evans, McKinsey, et al., there is every indication that the pronoun here is (as Peter Geach maintains), or at least is naturally taken to be, a bound variable—like the last occurrence of '*i*' in 'It was once the case that for some atheist *i*, *i* was elected to the US Senate but *i*'s atheism had been concealed during the political campaign'. (In this case the pronoun 'his' might be regarded as bound by the restricted quantifier 'an atheist'. But compare this with the plural pronoun in 'Few current atheists have been elected to the US Senate, and their atheism was concealed during the political campaign.' Though also a bound variable, the 'their' is bound not by the restricted quantifier

'that F' cannot literally (semantically) designate anything that is not an F. The phrase might be used by a speaker to designate something that is not an F, but this is a matter of 'speaker reference' as opposed to 'semantic reference'. Such a 'referential' use is, from the point of view of English semantics, a misuse.[42] More interesting yet, a complex demonstrative 'that F' may designate something with respect to a possible world w even though the designated object is not an F in w, as long as it is *actually* an F—for example, 'If we had not lowered admission standards, then *that graduate student* would not be in graduate school today.'[43] No component of the content of an atomic sentence of the form 'That F is G' expresses about the demonstratum that it is F. Yet this is logically entailed. In fact, the sentence presupposes of the demonstratum that it is F, in that unless this is a fact the sentential subject is vacuous and the sentence is without truth value.[44]

There is another noteworthy consequence. The following English sentence is *analytic*, in the sense that it is true by virtue of semantics alone:

S: That graduate student (if there is any such thing) is a graduate student.[45]

The analyticity of S lies behind the logical validity of the argument, 'Every graduate student is full of angst; therefore that graduate student (assuming he/she exists) is full of angst.'[46] Although analytic, the content of S in any context is hardly a necessary truth.[47] Indeed, its contingency is a likely source of considerable anxiety for the

'few current atheists' but, as it were, by a related unarticulated restricted universal quantifier. The sentence is true iff: (*i*) few individuals who satisfy the open sentence 'X are current atheists' also satisfy the open sentence 'X have been elected to the US Senate'; and (*ii*) those individuals that satisfy both 'X are current atheists' and 'X have been elected to the US Senate' also satisfy the further open sentence 'Their atheism was concealed during the political campaign'.) For any simple pronoun occurrence, if it is a bound variable it is also an occurrence of a rigid designator. Consider: 'A girl sprang from the particular gametes s and e, and it is a necessary truth that whoever sprang from s and e did not spring instead from the entirely different particular gametes s' and e'' vs. 'A girl sprang from the particular gametes s and e, and it is a necessary truth that *she* did not spring instead from s' and e'''. Consider also substituting 'that girl' for 'she'. (The foregoing remarks have benefitted from discussion with Alan Berger, who realized independently that McKinsey's argument is incorrect.)

[42] *Cf.* 'The Good, the Bad, and the Ugly'.

[43] Contrary to Lepore and Ludwig (pp. 222–226), this is not a matter of demonstrative phrases always, or typically, taking wide scope: 'Consider: *That graduate student* is not in graduate school today. The proposition is, of course, false. But its falsity is quite accidental. Indeed, it would have obtained if we had not lowered our admission standards.'

[44] If the demonstratum is not F, the sentence 'That F does not exist' is a true negative existential. Such things are rare. *Cf.* my 'Nonexistence', *Noûs* 32 (1988): 277–319.

[45] I assume here that the parenthetical antecedent is false if the demonstrative 'that graduate student' lacks a designatum.

[46] *Cf.* Borg, *op. cit.*, pp. 239–241. Any theory that assigns logical attributes to propositions rather than to sentences or their meanings (such as is defended by Kripke) is unable to accommodate the validity of this inference, assuming (T), without S as an additional premise. Such theories miss the important distinctions illustrated by S.

[47] Again, contrary to Lepore and Ludwig (*ibid.*, pp. 213, 222–226). In any context in which the demonstratum is a graduate student, the fact or state of affairs described by S could have been otherwise. (Philosophers indoctrinated in the Quinean tradition may have a tendency to misconstrue 'necessary' as a term for analyticity—a semantic notion—rather than for the peculiarly metaphysical notion of a fact or state of affairs that *could not have been otherwise*.)

demonstrated student. More surprisingly, *S*, although analytic, expresses an *a posteriori* truth. For consider a typical context in which the demonstratum is a particular graduate student, David. How does one come to know the following *de re* fact about David: that he—that very individual (if he exists at all)—is in graduate school? In any number of ways. One might observe his lifestyle, follow him around the university, confiscate his computer disks, subpoena his transcripts, record his nocturnal mutterings. Not, however, by *a priori* reflection on the issue.[48]

---

[48] Kaplan mentions similarly analytic though typically contingent sentences of the form ⌜*dthat*[α] = α⌝—he specifically mentions 'He is the male at whom I am now pointing' (see note 29 above)—claiming that all such sentences are *a priori* (*ibid.*, pp. 518, 538–539). (Braun, 'Structured Characters', pp. 211–212, 215–216, considers an example exactly like *S*, correctly deeming it logically valid. Braun does not discuss its epistemological status.) Kaplan offers as an explanation of the existence of such contingent yet (allegedly) *a priori* truths that alethic modal attributes (metaphysical necessity, possibility, contingency, etc.) are attributes of propositions whereas apriority and aposteriority are attributes of proposition-characters (i.e., of characters that, given a context of use, yield a proposition) or of sentences, not propositions. This confuses epistemological matters (apriority) with properly logico-semantic matters (analyticity), and thus misses one of the important philosophical lessons of demonstratives. Though the sentence '*Dthat* [the only member of the UCSB Philosophy Department born in Los Angeles] is the only member of the UCSB Philosophy Department born in Los Angeles' is analytic-in-Kaplish—and hence, known to be true solely on the basis of pure Kaplish semantics—there is no learning the contingent fact described thereby (*to wit*, that I am the only UCSB philosopher born in Los Angeles) except through epistemic appeal to experience.

The same considerations apply against Kripke's contention in *Naming and Necessity* (pp. 54–56, 63) that 'The Standard Meter is exactly one meter long at t_0' is contingent *a priori*. See notes 13 and 32 above. Such sentences should be deemed *analytic* even though the facts described are neither necessary nor (*pace* Kaplan and Kripke) *a priori*. Although the existence of analytic truths that are both contingent and *a posteriori* is a straightforward consequence of direct-reference theory—*S* is as good an example as any—the aforementioned confusion between epistemological and properly logico-semantic matters has obscured the fact. *Cf.* my 'How to Measure the Standard Meter', *Proceedings of the Aristotelian Society*, 88 (1987/1988), pp. 193–217; and especially 'Analyticity and Apriority', in J. Tomberlin, ed., *Philosophical Perspectives, 7: Language and Logic* (Atascadero, Calif.: Ridgeview, 1993), pp. 125–133.

5

Are General Terms Rigid? (2003)

I

On Kripke's intended definition, a term designates an object x *rigidly* if the term designates x with respect to every possible world in which x exists and does not designate anything else with respect to worlds in which x does not exist. Kripke evidently holds in *Naming and Necessity*, hereafter *N&N* (pp. 117–144, *passim*, and especially at 134, 139–140), that certain general terms—including natural-kind terms like 'water' and 'tiger', phenomenon terms like 'heat' and 'hot', and color terms like 'blue'—are rigid designators solely as a matter of philosophical semantics (independently of empirical, extra-linguistic facts). As a consequence, Kripke argues, identity statements involving these general terms are like identity statements involving proper names (e.g., 'Clark Kent = Superman') in that, solely as a matter of philosophical semantics, they express necessary truths if they are true at all. But whereas it is reasonably clear what it is for a (first-order) singular term to designate, Kripke does not explicitly say what it is for a *general* term to designate.[1] General terms are standardly treated in modern logic as predicates, usually monadic predicates. There are very forceful reasons—due independently to Church and

---

The present chapter was presented to the interdisciplinary Princeton Workshop on Semantics in May 2003, where Robert May was commentator. I am grateful to May and the other discussants for their reactions, especially Scott Soames. I am also grateful to May for subsequent correspondence. I respond below to what I take to be his central criticisms. The reader is hereby cautioned, however, that I do not know the extent to which those criticisms represent his current thinking. Thanks go also to Alan Berger, Delia Graff, and Teresa Robertson for discussion.

[1] The phrase 'singular term' is used throughout as a meta-linguistic term for any object-language expression of a certain logical *type*—specifically, any first-order expression whose primary logico-semantic function is to designate (with respect to a given context, time, place, and possible world, and under a given assignment of values to variables) a single individual, and which attaches to (or fills an argument place of) a first-order predicate to form a (open or closed) formula. A general term, by contrast, is of a logical type that is potentially applicable (with respect to semantic parameters) to any number of individuals.

In the English sentence 'Tony is a tiger', 'Tony' functions as a singular term, 'tiger' as a general term. (See note 13 concerning the copula.) Proper names, personal pronouns, and individual variables are taken to be paradigm cases of singular terms, whereas common nouns, most adjectives (other than determiners), and intransitive verbs are taken to be paradigm cases of general terms. In the spirit of the literature on possible-world semantics and rigid-designator theory (dating back at least as far as John Stuart Mill), I assume for the most part that an English first-order definite description, ⌜the *NP*⌝, is a singular term—ignoring the prospect that it is instead (in the rival spirit of Bertrand Russell and Richard Montague) a first-order uniqueness-restricted quantifier equivalent to ⌜a unique *NP*⌝.

Gödel, and ultimately to Frege—for taking predicates to designate their semantic extensions.[2] But insofar as the extension of the general term 'tiger' is the class of actual tigers (or its characteristic function), it is clear that the term does not rigidly designate its extension, since the class of tigers in one possible world may differ from the class of tigers in another. What, then, is it for 'tiger' to be rigid?

In his recent book, *Beyond Rigidity* (Oxford University Press, 2002), Scott Soames considers the two interpretive hypotheses that he deems the most promising, strongly favoring one of the two (pp. 249–263, 287–288, and *passim*). On the preferred interpretation, a general term is *rigid*, by definition, if it expresses a property (e.g., being a tiger) that is essential to anything that has it at all, i.e., a property of an object that the object could not fail to have (except perhaps by not existing). Soames characterizes this hypothesis as a 'natural extension' to predicates of *N&N*'s definition of singular-term rigidity.[3] I deem it a non-starter. One obvious problem with the proposal is that color terms then emerge as non-rigid, contrary to Kripke's apparent labeling of them as rigid. Also the definition does not provide any obvious candidate to be the rigid designatum of a predicate like 'is a tiger'. The proposal might be based on a notion of *poly-designation*, whereby a predicate 'designates' one by one each of the things individually to which the predicate correctly *applies* semantically, i.e., each of the elements of the semantic extension.[4] A predicate for an essential property applies to anything *x* that has the property in question with respect to every world in which *x* exists, while a predicate for an accidental property does not do this. But an essential-property predicate equally applies to the other things *y* in its extension besides *x*, *and does so with respect to worlds in which x does not exist*. This interpretation, therefore, does not fit the intended definition of rigid designation.

If the predicate 'is a tiger' is to be regarded as designating the property of being a tiger (rather than as multiply designating each individual tiger, and rather than as designating the class of actual tigers), then it would appear that any predicate should be seen as designating the property that it expresses. But in that case, every predicate, even 'is a bachelor', emerges as a rigid designator, since the attribute (property or

---

[2] *Cf.* my *Reference and Essence* (Princeton University Press and Basil Blackwell, 1981), at pp. 48–52. The *metaphysical extension* of a property *P* (in a possible world *w* at a time *t*) = $_{def}$ the class of possible objects that have *P* (in *w* at *t*). The *semantic extension* of a predicate Π (with respect to semantic parameters) = $_{def}$ the metaphysical extension of the property semantically expressed by Π (with respect to those same parameters). The *metaphysical intension* of a property *P* = $_{def}$ the function that assigns to any possible world *w* (and time *t*) the metaphysical extension of *P* in *w* (at *t*). The *semantic intension* of a predicate Π = $_{def}$ the metaphysical intension of the property semantically expressed by Π.

[3] *Cf.* pp. 251–252. Soames defended this interpretive hypothesis at an international conference on Kripke's work at the *Instituto de Investigaciones Filosóficas, Universidad Nacional Autónoma de México*, Mexico City, October 1996, which Kripke and I both attended. The other interpretive hypothesis that Soames considers is mentioned below in note 11.

[4] Soames does not explicitly suggest this. On the contrary, he says repeatedly that a natural-kind predicate designates a natural kind. It is difficult to reconcile this idea with Kripke's labeling of natural-kind terms as rigid designators, on Soames's proposed interpretation of the latter. (My best guess is that Soames attempts to provide a reconstruction of the notion of rigidity for general terms that is divorced from the notion of designation.) *Cf.* Monte Cooke, 'If "Cat" is a Rigid Designator, What Does it Designate?', *Philosophical Studies*, 37 (1980), pp. 61–64.

relation) expressed by a predicate with respect to a possible world does not vary from world to world. Nothing special about natural-kind predicates, color predicates, etc. has been identified to demarcate them from the rest. So it is that *N&N* leaves us with the question: What is for a general term to be a rigid designator?[5]

One way to proceed that is more promising than the failed strategies Soames considers would be to define a notion of designation (*simpliciter*) for both singular and general terms in such a way that, applying the intended definition of rigid designation *as is*, without modification, a natural-kind general term (and a color general term, a natural-phenomenon general term, etc.) designates its designatum rigidly whereas some other sorts of general terms designate only non-rigidly.[6] What object, then, should a general term like 'tiger' be said to *designate*? And which contrasting sorts of general terms designate only non-rigidly?

The first question has an obvious and natural response: The term 'tiger' designates the species, *Tiger (Felis tigris)*. In general, a biological taxonomic general term should be seen as designating a biological taxonomic kind (a species, a genus, an order, or etc.), a chemical-element general term ('gold') should be seen as designating an element (gold), a chemical-compound general term as designating a compound (water), a color general term as designating a color (red), a natural-phenomenon general term as designating a natural phenomenon (heat), and so on. The semantic content of a single-word general term might then be identified with the designated kind (or the designated substance, phenomenon, etc.). So far, so good. But now the threat is faced anew that every general term will emerge as a rigid designator of some appropriately related universal or other. If 'bachelor' designates the gendered marital-status category, *Unmarried Man*, it does so rigidly. Even a common-noun *phrase*, like 'adult male human who is not married', emerges as a rigid designator.

II

Such is the notion of designation for general terms that I proposed in *Reference and Essence* (pp. 52–54, 69–75), and which I continue to believe is fundamentally correct.[7] Soames objects on the grounds that 'there is no point in defining a notion of rigidity for predicates according to which all predicates turn out, trivially, to be rigid' (p. 251).[8] Ultimately he decides that there is no notion of rigidity that is simultaneously analogous to singular-term rigidity, a natural extension of singular-term

---

[5] *Cf. Reference and Essence*, pp. 44–54.

[6] Soames complains (p. 248) that Kripke's original definition of rigidity is restricted to singular terms. I see no conclusive evidence of this in Kripke's writings. I assume instead that the notion of designation *simpliciter* that Kripke invokes extends to general terms (as does, for example, the notion of designation invoked in the work of Carnap). I believe Kripke intended his definition of rigidity to apply to general as well as singular terms. (It is possible that *N&N* uses the word 'reference' for the special case of singular-term designation.)

[7] See also Joseph Laporte, 'Rigidity and Kind', *Philosophical Studies*, 97, 3 (2000), pp. 293–316.

[8] On Soames's 'Extended Millianism' (pp. 278–279), the content of a natural-kind phrase like 'matter sample composed exclusively of molecules consisting of two hydrogen atoms and one oxygen atom' is a property, whereas the content of a single-word natural-kind term like 'water' is a natural kind (which Soames identifies with the metaphysical intension of a property). This account

Are General Terms Rigid? 103

rigidity to general terms, and a notion on which certain general terms (especially, natural-kind terms) are rigid but many other general terms are non-rigid (p. 263). And this, he argues, paves the way for a 'demotion of the status of rigidity in Kripke's overall semantic picture' of terms singular and general (p. 264).

I sharply disagree. It is true that Kripke's thesis that proper names and certain general names alike, including natural-kind terms, are rigid designators is secondary to a more fundamental thesis: that these names are *non-descriptional*.[9] However, the corollary that they are therefore rigid is correct, and its philosophical significance should not be missed or undervalued. Soames's discussion suffers from a failure to distinguish sharply between a general term like 'tiger' and its corresponding predicate, 'is a tiger'. Even if every common count noun (whether a single word or a phrase) emerges as a rigid designator on my counter-proposal, it does not follow that every general term is rigid. As Bernard Linsky noted in an unduly neglected paper, some general terms, in fact, are manifestly non-rigid.[10] This is most evident with certain English definite descriptions. Definite descriptions are typically singular terms—or alternatively (following the great philosopher-lord), quantificational expressions that go around impersonating singular terms—but some English definite descriptions, unlike ordinary singular terms, function rather as if they were adjectives or, more likely, mass-noun phrases. One example is the description 'the color of the sky', as it occurs in the sentence

(*P*1) My true love's eyes are the color of the sky.

Soames sees the definite description in the predicate of (*P*1) as a singular term rather than a general term (p. 261).[11] Yet the copula 'are' here cannot be the

---

makes room for a distinction between descriptionality (connotativeness) and non-descriptionality for some general terms analogous to John Stuart Mill's insights concerning definite descriptions and proper names, though only among natural-kind general terms and the like. (Mill, by contrast, classified all general terms as 'connotative'.) Although Soames opposes extending this account to all general terms—presumably on the ground that doing so would render even an institutional-kind term like 'bachelor' a rigid designator—there is no obvious principled reason why single-word non-natural-kind terms should differ from single-word natural-kind terms (and single-word color terms, single-word natural-phenomenon terms, etc.) in this respect. I suspect there is no such deviation. See notes 14 and 23 below.

[9] Or not descriptional in a certain way; cf. *Reference and Essence*, chapters 1–2, especially pp. 14–23, 32–36, 42–44, 54–56.

[10] Bernard Linsky, 'General Terms as Designators', *Pacific Philosophical Quarterly*, 65 (1984), pp. 259–276. See also John Heintz, *Subjects and Predicables* (The Hague: Mouton, 1973), at p. 88. Although my account differs significantly in certain details from Linsky's (cf. note 22 below), I have benefited from his observations. In particular, as Linsky notes, it is highly likely that the notion of a general-term definite description (a 'definite ascription') underlies Kripke's labeling of certain contrasting general terms as *rigid designators*. (See note 25 below concerning Kripke's reaction to this alternative to Soames's preferred account.)

[11] More accurately, he sees the description as a quantifier phrase, which he 'assimilates to the broader class of singular terms' (p. 316*n*17). Soames neither sees the description in (*P*1) as a general term nor assimilates it to one.

I presented my objections to Soames's proposed interpretation of *N&N*, as well as this counter-proposal regarding designation, in the discussion following Soames's paper at the 1996 *Universidad Nacional Autónoma de México* conference on Kripke. (See note 3 above.) There is some discussion

pluralization of the 'is' of identity, since the color blue is a single universal whereas the speaker's lover's eyes are two particulars, and hence not both identical to a single thing. Nor can the copula be the so-called 'is' of constitution. One might argue that the copula in (*P*1) is a fourth kind of 'is', over and above the 'is' of predication, the 'is' of identity, and the 'is' of constitution: the dyadic *'is' of possession*. Soames is evidently committed to positing such an alternative sense. This rather strained account raises the question of why 'to have' should come to masquerade as 'to be'. It is considerably more plausible that the 'are' in (*P*1) is the very same copula that occurs in

(*C*) My true love's eyes are blue

to wit, our old and dear friend, the 'is' of predication (in its pluralized conjugation). This common form of 'be' cannot coherently combine with an English expression functioning as a (first-order) singular term to form a meaningful English predicate. Any English term (or English expression that functions as a term when occurring in a predicate) that combines with the 'is' of predication to form a monadic predicate, must function as a general term in the predicate so formed.[12] (I take these principles to be partly 'criterial' of the distinction between singular and general terms.) Just as the adjective 'blue' is a general term in (*C*), so the definite description 'the color of the sky' is a general term in (*P*1). The former rigidly designates the color blue; the latter designates the color non-rigidly.

How can a definite description combine with the 'is' of predication while designating something? In the same way as the adjective 'blue' or the mass noun 'water'. Let us formally represent the copula in 'is blue' as a predicate-forming operator on adjectives (whether single words or adjective phrases) and mass nouns, '*is*{ }', and let us represent the 'is a' in 'is a tiger' as a similar predicate-forming operator on count nouns, '*is-a*{ }', so that the predicate 'is blue' is formalized as '*is*{blue}' and the predicate 'is an albino tiger' as '*is-a*{albino tiger}'.[13] The term 'the color of the sky' may then be formally rendered as a second-order definite description:

in Soames that was evidently prompted by my objections and counter-proposal, but in which he considers instead a significantly different proposal (one which I reject), according to which a general term ('predicate') is to be labeled *rigid*, or *non-rigid*, according as some relevantly associated *singular* term is rigid or not (pp. 364n9, 260–262, 289–292, 307–311). Soames objects that on the counter-proposal he considers, every general term ('predicate') is rigid. This contradicts the very point of (*P*1), as it is intended. (Soames does not consider the prospect that the description 'the color of the sky' functions as a general term rather than a singular term.)

[12] See note 1. Numerous linguists and philosophers have argued that a first-order definite description following the verb 'be' is at least often a general term (or 'predicate'), and the copula the 'is' of predication rather than the 'is' of identity. See, for example, George Wilson, 'On Definite and Indefinite Descriptions', *The Philosophical Review*, 87 (1978), pp. 48–76; and Delia Graff, 'Descriptions as Predicates', *Philosophical Studies*, 102, 1 (January 2001), pp. 1–42. If a first-order definite description can combine with the 'is' of predication to form a monadic predicate, then the description must function predicatively in the predicate so formed rather than as a singular term.

[13] In light of the previous note, it might be advisable to introduce also a third predicate-forming operator, '*is-the*{ }', whereby '*is-the*{author of *Waverley*}' is equivalent to '*is-a*{unique author of *Waverley*}'.

I remain neutral here concerning whether the copula in 'Tony is a tiger' is the 'is' of predication or the 'is' of identity ('is identical with some tiger'). If it is the latter, the predicate-forming operator '*is-a*' may have a complex definition invoking existential quantification and identity. Some device

$(\iota F)[\textit{is-a}^2\{\text{color}\}(F) \ \& \ \textit{is}\{F\}(\text{the sky})]$,

where 'F' is a variable ranging over appropriate universals. (The superscript '2' indicates that the resulting predicate is second order.) As a second-order term, the description designates even while combining felicitously with the 'is' of predication.[14] Indeed, so understood, (C) is a straightforward logical consequence of (P1) taken together with the empirical premiss,

(P2) Blue is the color of the sky.

This inference is best seen as a special instance of Leibniz's Law, or Substitution of Equality. In the words of a great English poet, it's easy if you try. According to (P2), the color blue is identical with the color of the sky. Since the speaker's true love's eyes are the color of the sky, it follows by Substitution that those same eyes are blue. All you need (besides love) is to see the copula in (P2) for what it surely is: an 'is' of identity, attached to general terms instead of singular terms, and forming a sentence that is true if and only if the terms flanking the 'is' are co-designative.

Formalization of the inference might help to make the point:

(P1') $(x)[\textit{is-a}\{\text{eye of my true love}\}(x) \to \textit{is}\{(\iota F)[\textit{is-a}^2$
$\{\text{colour}\}(F) \ \& \ \textit{is}\{F\}(\text{the sky})]\}(x)]$

(P2') blue $=^2 (\iota F)[\textit{is-a}^2\{\text{colour}\}(F) \ \& \ \textit{is}\{F\}(\text{the sky})]$

∴ (C') $(x)[\textit{is-a}\{\text{eye of my true love}\}(x) \to \textit{is}\{\text{blue}\}(x)]$

(Then again, it might not.) The copula in (P2) is evidently the same 'is' of identity that occurs in the conclusion of 'There are exactly three volumes of Russell and Whitehead's *Principia Mathematica*; therefore, three is the number of volumes of *Principia Mathematica*.' Soames contends instead (pp. 364n9, 289–290) that the syllable/vocable 'blue' represents a pair of English homonyms: one an adjective (blue$_1$), the other a noun (blue$_2$) that is parasitic on the adjective. This perspective yields a markedly different rendering of the inference:

(P1'') $(x)[x \text{ is an eye of my true love} \to \textit{Is}(x, (\iota y)[y \text{ is a color} \ \& \ \textit{Is}(\text{the sky}, y)])]$

may still be needed, however, to convert the count noun into a predicate, as for example in:

$$(\lambda F)(\lambda x)[(\exists y)(\{F\}\text{-}\textit{izes}(y) \ \& \ x = y)]$$

where the '-*izes*' operator applies to a count noun to yield a predicate. (See note 22.) Since an analysis of indefinite descriptions combined with 'be' to form a monadic predicate does not eliminate the need for converting a count noun into a predicate, it may be more plausible to see the indefinite article in such constructions as syncategorematic—a purely cosmetic grammatical convenience (or inconvenience!)—rather than as signaling its alternative function as an existential-quantificational operator.

[14] Using this formal device one may even form non-rigid count-noun general terms, e.g.

$(\iota F)[\textit{is-a}^2\{\text{gendered marital-status category}\}(F) \ \& \ \textit{is-a}\{F\}(\text{Hugh Hefner})]$.'

This application of the device to count nouns does not obviously correspond to any legitimate construction of English, but neither is there any obvious reason why such a construction could not be appended to English. (Sentences like (P1) might be taken as evidence that English already has some characteristics of a second-order formal language.)

($P2''$) $\text{blue}_2 = (\iota y)[y \text{ is a color } \& \text{ } Is(\text{the sky}, y)]$

∴ (C'') $(x)[x \text{ is an eye of my true love} \to x \text{ is blue}_1]$,

where the dyadic predicate '*Is*' occurring in the premises represents the alleged '*is*' *of possession*. This argument, however, is invalid as it stands. The argument (and also the parallel invalid argument obtained by interchanging the major premiss and conclusion) may be validated by supplementing the premises with a striking Carnapian 'meaning postulate' (perhaps as a tacit premiss): 'Something is blue iff it is blue', taken in the alleged sense of

($P3$) Something is$_{predication}$ blue$_1$ iff it is$_{possession}$ blue$_2$,

and formalized as

($P3''$) $(x)[x \text{ is blue}_1 \leftrightarrow Is(x, \text{ blue}_2)]$.

But how plausible is it that both of the words 'is' and 'blue' making up the English predicate are ambiguous (quite independently of a third meaning, the 'is' of identity), and in such a way that, solely as a matter of English semantics, the predicate applies under one meaning exactly when it applies under the other as well? Indeed, solely as a matter of English semantics, the two alleged readings would have to be *logically equivalent*—sharing not only the same semantic extension, and not only the same modal intension, but even the very same logical content, i.e., the same function from models to intensions.[15] This degree of duplication—duplication of spelling, phonetics, structure, etc., and in addition, duplication of logical content—strongly suggests that something has gone wrong in the analysis. Rather than exposing an unnoticed convergence, our distinction without a difference more likely indicates an erroneous proliferation ('is$_{predication}$ blue$_1$' *vs.* 'is$_{possession}$ blue$_2$'). The fact that the word 'blue' can occur alternatively as a noun or as an adjective does not imply that the word is ambiguous with regard to semantic extension or intension, let alone that there are two words 'blue' rather than one—let alone that there is in addition to the standard 'is' of predication another predicative 'is', the alleged 'is' of possession. To quote Kripke (slightly out of context): 'It is very much the lazy man's approach to philosophy to posit ambiguities when in trouble.... [The] ease of the move should counsel a policy of caution: Do not posit an ambiguity ... unless there are really compelling theoretical or intuitive grounds to suppose that an ambiguity really is present' ('Speaker's Reference and Semantic Reference', p. 19).

---

[15] See my 'On Content', *Mind*, 101, 404 (October 1992), pp. 733–751, concerning the relevant notion of logical content. As I use the term, the *logical content* of an expression e is the function that assigns to any model Z for the language, the principal semantic value (classically the extension, in modal logic the intension) of e in Z. Meaningful expressions are logically equivalent when, and only when, they have the same logical content. For example, '$(p \vee q) \wedge \sim (p \wedge q)$' and '$\sim (p \equiv q)$' have the same logical content—since they have the same truth table—even if they do not have the same semantic content *simpliciter* (i.e., even if they express different propositions).

III

Robert May has argued in response to these considerations that insofar as 'the color of the sky' is to be classified either as a singular term or as a general term, it is a singular term even in (P1).[16] He endorses this conclusion on the ground that definite descriptions are nominal phrases that can occur in positions occupied by singular terms—as, for example, in 'Max and the color of the sky are two of my favorite things.' In addition, May cites the particular sentences, 'Max is the man for the job' (due to James Higgenbotham) and the sarcastically understated 'Max isn't the best cook in town', as further examples—allegedly like (P1)—of the 'is' of predication combined with an English singular term rather than a general term to form an English monadic predicate.

As a rejoinder to May's objections, and in order to clarify the position I am defending, I offer the following observations:

(*i*) The possibility of grammatically occupying singular-term position is a necessary condition on singular terms, not a sufficient condition. Mass terms in English, for example, can occur in singular-term position ('Water is H_2O', 'Max and gin are two of my favorite things'), but they also occur in general-term position, combining with the 'is' of predication to form English monadic predicates ('The liquid in this cup is water'). Likewise, canonical color terms and number terms ('three') can occur in singular-term position (as in (P2) and 'Nine is the number of planets'), but they also combine with predicational 'be' to form a predicate (as in (C) and 'The planets are nine'[17]). Contrary to May, the latter is something singular terms cannot do, at least not while functioning as singular terms, or even as first-order restricted quantifiers in the manner of Russell and Montague. (See note 1 above. The fact that mass terms and the like can occur grammatically in singular-term position in addition to general-term position might be taken as independent grounds for recognizing at least some general terms as *second-order singular terms*.)

(*ii*) English also includes sentences like 'What I am is nauseous', in which the subject is a general term—or, at least, would appear to be one. Indeed, this sentence appears to be an identity statement, and its subject a second-order definite description (or, alternatively, a second-order restricted quantifier). Insofar as English includes second-order definite descriptions, phrases like 'the color of the sky', 'Henry's favorite beverage', and 'the chemical compound composed of two parts hydrogen, one part oxygen' are as good candidates as any.[18] Although these descriptions can occur

---

[16] 'Comments on Nathan Salmon, "Are General Terms Rigid?"', presented to the 2003 Princeton Workshop on Semantics.

[17] The predicate formed by combining 'be' with a canonical number term might be regarded as *multi-adic* (rather than as monadic, or dyadic, etc.). More accurately, such numerical predicates should be seen as applying collectively rather than individually (or equivalently, as applying to pluralities or multiplicities, i.e., to groups having a number which may be other than one). See my 'Wholes, Parts, and Numbers', in J. Tomberlin, ed., *Philosophical Perspectives 11: Mind, Causation, and World* (Atascadero, Calif.: Ridgeview, 1997), pp. 1–15.

[18] The threat of Russell's Paradox applies pressure to see some definite descriptions as differing from others in logical form, despite sharing the same syntactic form. The kinds that come readily

in singular-term position, they also combine with the 'is' of predication to form monadic predicates, wherein they cannot function as singular terms. In fact, at least some of these same definite descriptions appear to function as mass-noun phrases and/or as color-term noun phrases. (Consider (*P2'*) and 'Water is the chemical compound composed of two parts hydrogen, one part oxygen'.) As such, these descriptions would be general terms rather than singular.

(*iii*) The copula in May's examples—'Max is the man for the job' and 'Max isn't the best cook in town'—is normally and plausibly construed as the 'is' of identity rather than the 'is' of predication. For example, 'Max is the man for the job' is logically equivalent to its converse, 'The man for the job is Max', and also to Russellian paraphrases of its identity construal—'Someone is both a unique man for the job and Max', 'Max, and no one else, is a man for the job', etc. Likewise, 'Max is the man for the job' supports Leibniz's-Law substitution, e.g., 'Therefore, Max speaks Japanese iff the man for the job speaks Japanese.' By contrast, (*P*1), on its relevant reading, is not equivalent to *'Something is both a unique color of the sky and each of my true love's eyes.'[19] Neither does (*P*1) support logical substitution (e.g., #'Therefore, my true love's eyes have cataracts iff the color of the sky has cataracts'). Since the copula in (*P*1), on its relevant reading, cannot be read as the 'is' of identity, and should be read instead as the 'is' of predication, the definite description does not function in (*P*1) as a singular term.

(*iv*) May's claim that some first-order definite descriptions, like 'the man for the job', can combine with the 'is' of predication to form an English monadic predicate, rather than with the 'is' of identity, is controversial. (See notes 12 and 13 above.) If the thesis is correct, the description in the predicate so formed is equivalent to a predicative indefinite description—as perhaps the indefinite description in 'is a unique man for the job'. A predicative indefinite description (e.g., the phrase 'a tiger' in the predicate 'is a tiger') is not a singular term, and does not function as one in its containing predicate. May's examples therefore cannot be instances of a monadic predicate formed by combining the 'is' of predication (functioning as such in the predicate) with a singular term (functioning as such in the predicate).[20]

---

to mind are always of the following sort (*R*): *a kind K that is not itself something of kind K*. The species, *Tiger*, for example, is not itself a tiger. (Indeed, precious few kinds are not of this kind (*R*).) Consider now the very kind just specified: the kind (*R*) such that, necessarily, something is of (*R*) iff it is a kind *K* that is not itself something of kind *K*. The preceding definite description, despite its syntax, cannot be first-order on pain of contradiction (assuming that it designates a kind, and assuming obvious logical properties of definite descriptions).

[19] The converse of (*P*1), *'The color of the sky are my true love's eyes', is acceptable only in stylized discourse, wherein it is a stylistic variant of the original (and the copula functions as the converse of the 'is' of predication).

[20] May contends that the definite description in 'Henry is the best man for the job' may be seen as functioning simultaneously as a first-order singular term and predicatively. He argues that this dual function is illustrated by the definite description in 'Oscar considers Henry the best man for the job.' This sentence provides no clear support for the claimed schizophrenia. On the contrary, the description cannot function in the latter sentence as a customary-mode singular term. If it did, it would support Leibniz's-Law substitution, but it does not. (If Oscar judges Henry the best man for the job, while the best man for the job is in fact the man who is having an illicit affair with Oscar's wife, it does not follow that Oscar considers Henry the man who is having an illicit affair

(v) That 'blue' and 'the color of the sky' are general terms is a fact about logical form. It is not a fact about syntactic form—or about *grammar* in a syntactic sense of the term (which does not conform to current usage in theoretical linguistics). The following sentences, on their standard readings, have the same syntactic form.

(1) Henry's favorite shirt is the color of the sky

(2) Henry's favorite color is the color of the sky

Each is a copular sentence constructed from a definite description of the form ⌜Henry's favorite N⌝ as subject, the appropriate conjugation of the verb 'be' as copula, and the definite description 'the color of the sky' as predicate nominal. Nevertheless, they differ sharply in logical form. Sentence (1) is a monadic predication, whereas sentence (2) is (equivalent to) an identity/equation, on a par with ($P2$) and with May's examples (e.g., 'Max is the man for the job'). Correspondingly, (2) is logically equivalent to its converse and supports Leibniz's-Law substitution; (1) is not and does not.

It would be a mistake to infer that, since they differ in logical form, (1) and (2) also differ in syntactic/grammatical form. Compare the following two sentences, on their standard readings.

(3) Henry's favorite shirt is blue

(4) Henry's favorite color is blue

These sentences are semantically related exactly as (1) and (2). All four sentences, (1)–(4), share a common syntactic structure. Like the pair (1) and (2), (3) and (4) differ in the replacement in their subjects of 'shirt' by 'color' (count nouns both), and are otherwise structurally identical. Here the lexical switch in the subject issues a categorial (non-structural) switch in the predicate. The word 'blue' occurs as an adjective in (3), as a noun in (4), reflecting the change in logical form. This grammatical switch in the predicate does not occur with (1) and (2). As already noted, abstracting from their meanings and their logic—which are indeed very different—(1) and (2) share the same syntactic analysis in terms of both constituent structure and lexical and phrasal categories. Yet the same change in logical form that occurs in (3) and (4) also occurs in (1) and (2), where it is concealed behind a veil of superficial syntactic similarity. Though 'the color of the sky' is a nominal phrase, it

---

with Oscar's wife.) Neither does the description in 'Oscar considers Henry the best man for the job' function straightforwardly predicatively—e.g., in the manner of the indefinite description in the predicate 'is a unique best man for the job'. For, again, if the description functioned in the manner of a customary-mode, predicative, uniqueness-restricted, indefinite description, it would support logical substitution. Rather the description occurs in a non-extensional context of cognitive attitude; its function in 'Oscar considers Henry the best man for the job' is the same as in 'Oscar thinks that Henry is the best man for the job.' As Frege has taught us, the description here is not a singular term designating its customary designatum. Rather it is in *ungerade* (oblique, indirect) mode, designating its *ungerade* designatum, which is its customary content. Moreover, as Frege also noted, the customary content is (in some sense) objectual rather than function-like, so that the description also does not function predicatively. In sharp contrast, the description in ($P1$) is in customary mode, wherein it designates its customary designatum, the color blue.

plays exactly the same logico-semantic role in (1) and (P1) that the adjectival 'blue' plays in (3) and (C)—a role reflected in the grammar of the word but not in that of the description.[21]

Here again, contrary to May, recognition that the copula in (P1), on its standard reading, is the same 'is' of predication that occurs in (3) and (C) reveals that the predicate nominal in (P1)—regardless of its syntax—is a general term, since a term that combines with the 'is' of predication (without an intervening article) to form a monadic predicate cannot function as a singular term in the predicate so formed.

(*vi*) Having misclassified 'the color of the sky' as a (first-order) singular term, May is prepared to classify the copula in (1) and (P1) as an expression that sometimes operates on a singular term to form a monadic predicate. The predicate-forming operator '*is*{ }' in (P1′) and (C′) is not an operator of this sort. On the other hand, the envisioned 'is' of possession in (P1″) is exactly that. And indeed, May defends the second analysis of the argument about my true love's eyes. May's stance thus fails to appreciate the implausibility of its commitments, e.g., that each of the words making up the English predicate 'is blue' has two separate readings (independently of a third meaning—the 'is' of identity), but only in such a way that, solely as a matter of English semantics, the two resulting readings of the predicate are logically equivalent.

Given that the noun/adjective 'blue' designates the color blue, that the definite description 'the color of the sky' designates the color of the sky, and the empirical fact that the sky is blue, the general terms 'blue' and 'the color of the sky' are co-designative.[22] (No surprises here.) But whereas the former is surely rigid, the latter

---

[21] The original version of the present paper, to which May replied, used the word 'adjectival', inadvisably, in a logico-semantic (and consequently artificially broad) sense, to include any term whose logical form allows it to combine with the 'is' of predication, without an intervening article, to form a monadic predicate (one that is not logically equivalent to the result of combining instead with the 'is' of identity). If I am correct, this class includes at least mass terms and some second-order definite descriptions, which are nominals rather than adjectival. Some of May's original criticisms were directed at showing that the central example, 'the color of the sky', is grammatically not an adjective phrase but uniformly a noun phrase. This observation, though correct, is irrelevant to my argument.

It is at least likely that each of (1)–(4) has a non-standard, surrealistic reading on which it has the same logical form that its pair-mate has on its standard reading. Thus (1) might be read as expressing that a certain particular (a shirt) and a certain universal (a color) are one and the very same thing; (2) might be read as expressing the alternative category mistake that a certain universal is colored. (Some deny that (1)–(4) have these alternative readings. But the very fact that one can routinely dismiss such readings as category mistakes seems to indicate that we have *some* understanding of the sentence on the purported alternative reading. Mere gibberish does not express a category mistake or anything else.) Insofar as each of the sentences has an alternative, surrealistic reading in addition to its standard reading, the ambiguity of (3) is grammatically signaled by a toggle between adjectival and nominal 'blue'. Similarly for (4). There is no such toggle accompanying the ambiguity in (1), nor that in (2). The point of the contrast between (1) and (2) is not that they cannot be read as having the same logical form. It is, rather, that whatever logical form, or forms, (1) may have is a matter of its semantics, not its syntax, and similarly for (2). The syntactic form of (1) and (2) is the same, and constant, throughout.

[22] Though the general-term description 'the color of the sky' designates blue, the corresponding predicate 'is the color of the sky' semantically expresses the property of having the same color as the sky, as opposed to the more specific property of being blue (in color). The two properties share the same metaphysical extension—*to wit*, the class of all blue things—but they differ in metaphysical

designates red with respect to some worlds, making (*P2*) contingent. (Again, no surprise.) If the copula in (*P2*) is indeed an 'is' of identity to be placed between general terms, then Kripke's claim is vindicated that identity statements in which rigid general terms occur are, unlike (*P2*) but like identity statements involving proper names, necessary if true at all. Examples are close at hand: 'Furze is gorse'; 'Gold is *Au*'; 'Water is H_2O'. As already noted, even some descriptional general terms, like 'adult male human who is not married', are rigid designators. Still, non-rigid general terms are everywhere. These include such definite descriptions as 'the species that serves as mascot for Princeton University', 'the liquid compound that covers most of the Earth', 'the most valuable of elemental metals', 'the color of the sky' and so on.[23]

It was once maintained by many that a general term like 'blue' is synonymous with a description like 'the color of the sky', that 'water' is synonymous with a description, such as perhaps 'the colorless, odorless, potable, thirst-quenching liquid

---

extension in some counter-factual worlds, and so differ in metaphysical intension. It is important to notice also that whereas 'the color of the sky' is a non-rigid general term, the gerund phrase 'being the color of the sky' evidently rigidly designates a particular property—that of having the same color as the sky.

In 'Bob and Carol and Ted and Alice', David Kaplan says, 'almost all single words other than particles seem to me to be rigid designators' (p. 518*n*31). He once suggested to me (in conversation) that whereas the common noun 'tiger' rigidly designates the species, the corresponding predicate 'is a tiger' rigidly designates the property of being a tiger. *Cf.* his 'Afterthoughts' to 'Demonstratives', in *Themes from Kaplan*, at pp. 580–581*n*30. On this view, whereas 'the color of the sky' may be a non-rigid general term, its corresponding predicate 'is the color of the sky' is rigid—all the more reason to distinguish sharply between a general term and its corresponding predicate. Linsky holds, by contrast, that 'is the color of the sky' (non-rigidly) designates the property of being blue, rather than (rigidly) designating the property of having the same color as the sky (*op. cit.*, p. 270). I prefer to regard the predicate 'is the color of the sky' as designating its extension (non-rigidly, of course) while expressing the property of having the same color as the sky, as the predicate's semantic content. On this view the copula/operators formalized above may be taken as designating (with respect to a possible world and time) the function that assigns to any universal its metaphysical extension (in that world at that time)—making each copula/operator roughly analogous to the functor 'the metaphysical extension of'.

[23] Some definite descriptions are rigid, e.g., 'the even prime integer'. In *N&N*, Kripke calls such descriptions *rigid de facto*, in contrast to proper names, which are termed *rigid de jure* (p. 21*n*). There is a question whether the rigidity of 'bachelor' is *de jure* or *de facto*. (*Cf.* note 8 above.) The word 'tiger' is presumably rigid *de jure*, something like a logically proper name of the species. By contrast, the general-term description 'the gendered marital-status category *K* such that necessarily, someone is of *K* iff: he is an adult & he is male & he is human & he is unmarried' is rigid *de facto*. Perhaps an English common noun phrase (*sans* article/determiner) is typically synonymous with a general-term description of the particular form: *the Φ-kind/category K such that necessarily, something is of K iff it is such-and-such & it is thus-and-so & . . .*. This would explain exactly how common noun phrases—and hence also single words that are definably synonymous with such phrases (if such there be)—are descriptional, while simultaneously explaining why they are nevertheless uniformly rigid. A modification of this form would be required for noun phrases employing adjectives like 'suspected', 'alleged', etc. (*Cf.* note 14 above.)

The word 'bachelor' seems to me, on the other hand, rather like a logically proper name, rather than a description, of the gendered marital-status category, *Unmarried Man*. If that is how it does function, then its rigidity is *de jure* and, contrary to the common view, it is not strictly synonymous with the corresponding description, even though it is closely tied to the description—as the name 'Hesperus' is closely tied to some description of the form 'the first heavenly body visible at dusk from location *l* at time *t*'.

that fills oceans, lakes, and streams', and that 'pain' is synonymous with a description of the form 'the physiological state that occupies such-and-such causal/functional role'. Some consequences of these views are that 'The sky is blue' and 'The oceans are filled with water' express necessary, *a priori* truths, whereas 'Water is the chemical compound of two parts hydrogen, one part oxygen' and 'Pain is the stimulation of C-fibers' expresses contingent identities. Today we know better—many of us anyway—thanks in large measure to *N&N*'s lasting insight that 'blue' and 'water' and 'pain' are, and the allegedly synonymous general-term descriptions are not, rigid designators in the original sense of that term.[24] The relevant notion of general-term rigidity results directly from recognizing expressions like 'blue', 'water', 'the color of the sky', and 'the liquid that sustains terrestrial life' as general terms designating appropriate universals (colors, substances, etc.), and then applying Kripke's definition of rigidity without modification—with the result that some general terms are rigid, some not. This notion is analogous to singular-term rigidity in every way that matters.[25]

---

[24] *Cf.* David Lewis, 'Mad Pain and Martian Pain', in his *Philosophical Papers I* (Oxford University Press, 1983), pp. 122–132; and Soames, pp. 364–365n12.

[25] Responding to my comments during the discussion of Soames's presentation at the 1996 *Universidad Nacional Autónoma de México* conference (see notes 3, 11 above), Kripke said that this proposed interpretation of *N&N* on general-term rigidity is basically correct. Soames reports that in November 1997, when he presented what is essentially the same interpretation proposed in the book with Kripke in attendance, Kripke this time expressed sympathy with Soames's assessment that there is no notion of rigidity for general terms relevantly analogous to singular-term rigidity (p. 366n22). I am puzzled by the apparent inconsistency between Kripke's response in Mexico City and his reported response only one year later. My confidence is unshaken, however, that the counter-proposal correctly indicates an extremely close analogy between singular and general terms, and with it a general notion of rigidity applicable to some (but not all) terms of either sort.

6

A Theory of Bondage (2006)

I

Let A be an assignment of values to variables on which Marlon Brando is the value of 'x', and Shirley MacLaine is the value of 'y'. In classical semantics, the open formula ('open sentence')

(1) $(\exists x)(y$ is a sister of $x)$

is true under our value-assignment A iff there is some element or other i of the universe over which the variables range such that

(2) y is a sister of x

is true under the value-assignment $A^{'x'}{}_i$, a variant of A that assigns i instead of Brando as value for 'x' and is otherwise the same as A (and so assigns Shirley MacLaine as value for 'y'). In Tarski's terminology, A *satisfies* (1) if and only if some modified value-assignment $A^{'x'}{}_i$ of the sort specified satisfies (2). Assigning Warren Beatty as value for 'x' does the trick.

This simple example demonstrates a fact not often recognized: The quantifier phrase '$(\exists x)$' is non-extensional. This follows from the fact that it is not truth-functional. Under the original value-assignment A, '$(\exists x)(x \neq x)$' is every bit as false as its matrix, '$x \neq x$', yet (1) is true even though its matrix is false. The non-extensionality of a quantifier phrase is a surprising but trivial consequence of the way the quantifier works with a variable. The truth-value of (2) under A, and for that matter also the designatum of 'x' under A, are irrelevant to the truth-value of (1) under A. What matters are the designata of 'x' and 'y', and therewith the truth-value of (2), under modified value-assignments $A^{'x'}{}_i$. The original value-assignment A does not satisfy (2), but the value-assignment $A^{'x'}{}_{Beatty}$ does, and that is sufficient for A to qualify as satisfying (1). We achieve satisfaction by offering Brando's role to Beatty.

The present chapter owes a great deal to David Kaplan, Saul Kripke, the late Alonzo Church, and the late Donald Kalish, who taught me of many things discussed herein. I thank Alan Berger, Teresa Robertson, Zoltán Gendler Szabó, and the anonymous referee for *The Philosophical Review* for their comments. I am also grateful to my audiences at the UCLA Workshop in Philosophy of Language during Spring 2004, at the 2005 European Conference in Analytic Philosophy 5 in Lisbon, Portugal, and at the Universities of Groningen and of Amsterdam, the Netherlands, for their reactions to some of the material.

Under A, 'x' designates Brando and 'y' designates MacLaine. The variables 'x' and 'y' both occur in (1). The original value-assignment A satisfies (1), although the particular value of 'x' under A and the particular truth-value of (2) under A, do not matter in the slightest. When evaluating (1) under A, MacLaine is present while Brando is nowhere on the set. Under A, (1) makes no mention of Brando. He has nothing to do with the success of (2) under $A^{'x'}{}_{\text{Beatty}}$. Why does he still receive billing? More to the point, how is it that under A (1) makes no mention of Brando even though 'x', which occurs twice therein, designates Brando?

Frege admonished that *one should never ask for the designatum or content of an expression in isolation, but only in the context of a sentence.* This is his celebrated Context Principle.[1] Extrapolating from Frege's prohibition, we should not inquire after the designatum of 'x' under A. Instead we should inquire after the designatum of *the second 'x' in (1)*—as distinct, for example, from the 'x' in (2). If ever there was a case in which Frege's Context Principle has straightforward application, this is it: the bound variable. So let us follow Frege's considered advice and ask: If 'x' *as it occurs in (1)* does not designate Brando under A, what exactly is the 'x' in (1) doing? Likewise, what is the extension of (2), under A, *as (2) occurs in (1)*?

Classical Tarski semantics does not specify what the second 'x' in (1) designates under the original assignment. This is because the second 'x' in (1) is not the *variable* 'x', which designates Brando under A. It is a bound *occurrence* of 'x', which does not. Classical semantics imputes semantic extensions to expressions (under assignments of values to variables), not to their occurrences in formulae. Classical semantics does not abide by the Context Principle. But Frege's admonition has a point. One reason for departing from classical semantics—and one possible motivation for the Context Principle—is the desire for universal principles of *extensionality* for designation and of *compositionality* for semantic content. (According to extensionality, the extension of a compound expression is a function of the extensions of its meaningful components, including the designata of the component designators. According to compositionality, the semantic content of a compound expression is a function of the contents of the meaningful components.) Even more important is our intuition concerning what is actually being mentioned in a particular context. Consider, for example, the following fallacious inference:

> In 1999, the President of the United States was a Democrat.
> The President of the United States = George W. Bush.
> Therefore, in 1999, George W. Bush was a Democrat.

The invalidity is partially explained by noting that whereas the definite description in the second premiss designates Bush, there is no mention of Bush in the first premiss. The argument's two occurrences of the phrase 'the President of the United States' thus do not designate the same thing. Though perhaps incomplete, the explanation is intuitive, even satisfying.

---

[1] *The Foundations of Arithmetic*, J. L. Austin, trans. (Evanston, Ill.: Northwestern University Press, 1968), pp. x, 71, 73.

The Context Principle is not a blanket injunction against assigning semantic values to expressions *simpliciter*. Frege regarded the attributing of semantic values to expressions as legitimate only to the extent that such attribution is derivative from semantic attribution to those expression's occurrences in sentences. One need not adopt Frege's attitude in order to make perfectly good sense of attributing a semantic content and a designatum to an expression-occurrence. From the perspective of classical semantics, semantic attribution to occurrences may be regarded as derivative from the metalinguistic T-sentences (and similar meta-theorems) derived from basic semantic principles. According to Frege, whereas 'Ortcutt is a spy' *customarily* designates a truth-value, the *occurrence* in 'Ralph believes that Ortcutt is a spy' instead designates a proposition (*Gedanke*). Similarly we may choose to say that whereas 'the President of the United States' customarily designates Bush, its occurrence in the major premiss above instead designates the function that assigns to any time t, the person who is President of the United States at t. The semantic value of the description that bears on the truth-value of the sentence is not Bush, but this function.[2]

My primary objective in what follows is to sketch a proper and natural way of doing quantificational semantics on expression-occurrences. I do this, in part, in the hope of warding off confusion that has resulted from doing occurrence-based quantificational semantics in improper or unnatural ways. In the closing sections below, I apply the occurrence-based semantic apparatus to two separate, seemingly unrelated, contemporary controversies. I do this not because one must adopt occurrence-based semantics in order to obtain the right results in connection with those controversies. On the contrary, in both cases classical expression-based semantics suffices both to obtain and to justify those results, while occurrence-based semantics supplements the case. I do this, rather, because the two controversies are in fact closely related to one another: each is fueled almost entirely by the same pernicious misconception in occurrence-based semantics. In both cases, one needs to get a handle on occurrence-based semantics to see clearly what went wrong on the wrong side of the controversy, and hence in order to provide a full and definitive response.

At least as important—quite apart from and independently of these particular controversies—occurrence-based semantics illuminates. It upholds intuitions about what is actually mentioned, or at least what is not actually mentioned, in sentences like 'The temperature is rising' (Barbara Partee[3]) and 'In 1999, the President of the United States was a Democrat.' It reveals thereby what is right about the analysis of the fallacy mentioned two paragraphs up. As Frege knew, occurrence-based semantics

---

[2] Hence I reject Donald Davidson's appeal to 'pre-Fregean semantic innocence', which I believe is based largely (though not entirely) on a confusion between expression-based and occurrence-based semantics. See the closing paragraph of his 'On Saying That', *Synthese*, 19, 1968–69, pp. 130–146. (See note 20 below.)

[3] *Cf.* Richard Montague's treatment of this sentence in his 'The Proper Treatment of Quantification in Ordinary English', in J. Hintikka, J. Moravcsik, and P. Suppes, eds, *Approaches to Natural Language: Proceedings of the 1970 Stanford Workshop on Grammar and Semantics* (Dordrecht: D. Reidel, 1973), pp. 221–242, at p. 240.

reveals that there is a sense in which principles of extensionality and compositionality are upheld, at least in spirit (perhaps even in letter), despite the presence of nonextensional devices (e.g., modal operators, temporal operators, 'believes that', or quotation). More important for my present purpose, occurrence-based semantics illuminates just what is going on when a quantifier binds a variable. Properly executed, occurrence-based quantificational semantics directly contradicts prevailing views about bound variables and pronouns. Occurrence-based quantificational semantics also reveals that principles of extensionality and compositionality are upheld with regard to the binding of variables despite the non-extensionality (strictly speaking) of quantifier phrases. It reveals how Frege could have accommodated variable-binding, and more important how he should have done so. It also reveals how Fregean functions from objects to truth-values (*'Begriffe'*), and even Russellian functions from objects to singular propositions ('propositional functions'), emerge from constructions involving bound variables. Even if the Context Principle is wrong and classical expression-based semantics is the 'right' or preferred way to do semantics—as I believe—it remains that expression-based semantics is, as Frege insisted, a less discriminating by-product, or sub-theory, of occurrence-based semantics. This alone justifies the present investigation.

Important Cautionary Note: Throughout this chapter I distinguish very sharply between an expression (e.g., the variable '*x*') occurring in a sentence or formula and the occurrence itself (e.g., the second occurrence of '*x*' in (1)). Equivalently, I draw a sharp distinction between ascribing certain semantic attributes to an expression (of a particular language or semantic system) *per se* and ascribing those attributes to the expression 'as it occurs in', or relative to a particular *position* in a larger expression (e.g., a sentence) or stretch of discourse.[4] *It is essential in what follows that the reader be ever vigilant, paying extremely close attention to the distinction between expressions themselves and their occurrences*. Many philosophers of language who think, habitually and almost instinctively, in terms of expression-occurrences and their semantic values— especially Fregean and linguistics-oriented philosophers—habitually and almost instinctively reinterpret remarks explicitly about expressions occurring in a sentence as concerning not the expressions but their occurrences. Nearly everyone who thinks about expressions at all typically has at least some inclinations of this sort. How many letters are there in the name 'Nathan'? The reader with even the slightest inclination to give the incorrect answer 'six' is implored to remain on the alert and to make every

---

[4] An expression-occurrence standing within a formula must not be confused with a token of the expression, such as an inscription or an utterance. A token is a physical embodiment, physical event, or other physical manifestation of the expression (type). An occurrence of an expression is, like the expression itself, an abstract entity. For most purposes, an expression-occurrence may be regarded as the expression *together with* a position that the expression occupies within a larger sequence of expressions.

In contemporary philosophy of language it has become a common practice to attribute semantic values neither to expressions themselves nor to their occurrences but to expression-utterances. I regard this *speech-act centered conception of semantics* a giant leap backward, lamentable in the extreme. See my 'Two Conceptions of Semantics', in Z. G. Szabó, ed., *Semantics versus Pragmatics* (Oxford University Press, 2005), pp. 317–328.

A Theory of Bondage 117

effort in what follows to let intellect overcome inclination, instinct, and habit; else much of what is said will inevitably be seriously misunderstood.[5]

II

I assume the classically defined notion of semantic extension in what follows. Context Principle enthusiasts may take this to be Frege's notion of *default* or *customary Bedeutung*. In developing an occurrence-based semantics of variable-binding, I take my cue from Frege's theory of indirect (oblique, *ungerade*) contexts.

The variables occurring in (2) occur exclusively free there. Assignments of values to variables are assignments of designata to free occurrences. Under the original assignment A, the 'x' in (2)—that is, the occurrence of 'x' in (2)—designates Brando, the 'y' in (2) MacLaine. These are the default or customary designata of the variables 'x' and 'y' under A, i.e., the designata of occurrences in extensional position and not within the scope of a variable-binding operator.[6] The variables have their customary extensions in (2), and (2) is thereby false under A. Not all occurrences of variables have their customary extensions. Some occurrences deviate from the default value. On a natural extrapolation from Frege's explicit remarks, the occurrence of 'x' in 'Ralph believes that x is a spy' has its indirect designatum (*ungerade Bedeutung*), under a value-assignment, designating its customary or default sense. This is because the 'x' is within the scope of an occurrence of 'believes that', which induces a *semantic shift*, whereby expressions take on their indirect designata in lieu of their customary designata. Alonzo Church has developed this idea by considering assignments of customary-sense values ('individual concepts') to variables instead of customary-designatum values.[7]

---

[5] The letters in 'Nathan' are four: 'A', 'H', 'N', and 'T'. Two of these occur twice, making six letter-occurrences in all.

With some trepidation, I follow the common vernacular in speaking of 'bound variables' in a sentence where what are mentioned are actually bound *occurrences*, or of 'the initial quantifier of', or 'the "he" in' a sentence, etc., where what is mentioned is actually an *occurrence* of a quantifier or the pronoun. I have taken care to see that my usage unambiguously decides each case. For example, there is only one lower-case, italic letter 'x', and only one English word 'he', but there are infinitely many occurrences of either, so that any talk of 'the bound variables' (plural) of a formula containing no variable other than 'x', or of '*the* "he" ' (with definite article) in a sentence, can not sensibly concern expressions.

[6] Positions within quotation marks and similar devices, including 'believes that', are not extensional. An occurrence of a wfe ζ is said to be *within the scope of* an occurrence of a variable-binding-operator phrase $\ulcorner(B\alpha)\urcorner$, where **B** is a variable-binding operator and α is a variable, if the latter occurrence is the initial part of an occurrence of a wfe of the form $\ulcorner(B\alpha)\phi\urcorner$, where ϕ is a formula, and the former occurrence stands within that occurrence of $\ulcorner(B\alpha)\phi\urcorner$. (It may be assumed that the universal quantifier is '$\forall$', and as a notational convenience is routinely deleted, so that a universal-quantifier phrase written $\ulcorner(\alpha)\urcorner$ is of the form $\ulcorner(B\alpha)\urcorner$.)

[7] 'The Need for Abstract Entities in Semantic Analysis', *American Academy of Arts and Sciences Proceedings*, 80 (1951), pp. 100–112. Church does not follow Frege's Context Principle. Church's semantics is on expressions, not on their occurrences. He therefore does not distinguish between designatum and customary designatum, or between sense and customary sense, and has no notion of indirect designatum or indirect sense.

Fortunately, the matter of indirect designation does not concern us here. Our concern is with the semantics of ordinary bound variables. The outline is the same. The '*x*' in (2) is a free occurrence, and consequently it has its customary extension in (2). But neither occurrence of '*x*' in (1) has its customary extension in (1). This is because both occurrences ('the two bound variables in (1)') are within the scope of an occurrence of a shift-inducing operator.

Quantifiers are variable-binding operators. Like 'believes that', variable-binding operators induce the variables they bind to undergo semantic shift, but a shift of a different sort from intensional or 'indirect' (oblique) operators. The occurrences of '*x*' in (1) are no longer in default mode, designating their customary extension. They are in bondage. Classical semantics—the semantics of expressions, as opposed to their occurrences—is the customary semantics of default semantic values: the semantics of free occurrences. Classical semantics is thus the semantics of freedom. Bound variables have their *bondage semantics*, in many respects analogous to the semantics of indirect occurrences. One could say that the special kind of semantic shift that occurs when a quantifier binds a variable is precisely what variable-binding *is*.

If a free variable has its default or customary extension, which is simply its value under a value-assignment, then what is the extension of a bound variable (of the *occurrence*, not the variable of which it is an occurrence)? A bound variable ranges over a universe of discourse. It is not that Brando is nowhere on the set. It is that he is part of a cast of thousands. Ranging is not the same thing as designating. The definite description 'the average man', as it occurs in 'The average man sires 2.3 children in his lifetime', does not designate a peculiar biological being that has *very* peculiar offspring. It ranges over a universe of relatively normal biological beings, each with a definite whole (non-fractional) number of relatively normal offspring. The description does not *designate* this universe; it *ranges* over it. Similarly, the bound variable does not designate the universe over which it ranges.

Bound occurrences of different variables of the same sort range over the same universe. Does the variable also designate? A standard view is that free variables (and occurrences of compound designators containing free variables) designate, whereas bound variables do not. An analogous view is generally assumed with regard to natural-language pronouns like 'he': deictic occurrences and some 'pronouns of laziness' designate, whereas bound-variable anaphoric occurrences do not. Peter Geach, for example, criticizes 'the lazy assumption that pronouns, or phrases containing them, can be disposed of by calling them "referring expressions" and asking what they refer to'.[8] He says of anaphoric pronoun-occurrences. 'It is simply a prejudice or a blunder to regard such pronouns as needing a reference at all.'[9] Geach's thesis that anaphoric pronoun-occurrences other than pronouns of laziness do not designate is supported by his contention that such pronoun occurrences are bound variables and his insistence that bound variables do not designate. This attitude (which I once shared) betrays a lack of analytical vision. With regard to the issue

---

[8] Geach, 'Ryle on Namely-Riders', *Analysis*, 21, 3 (1960–1961); reprinted in *Logic Matters* (Oxford: Basil Blackwell, 1972), pp. 88–92, at 92.

[9] Geach, *Reference and Generality* (Ithaca, N.Y.: Cornell University Press, 1962), at pp. 125–126, and *passim*.

of whether anaphoric pronoun-occurrences designate, the prejudice or blunder, I contend, is on Geach's side. He is not alone.

A bound variable has its *bondage extension*, which is different from the variable's customary extension. In general, an occurrence of a meaningful expression in extensional position and not within the scope of a variable-binding operator has its customary extension under a value-assignment, whereas a bound occurrence has its bondage extension.[10] The central idea is given by the following principle of identification, analogous to Frege's identification of *ungerade Bedeutung* with customary sense: *The extension of a bound occurrence of an open expression in otherwise extensional position is the function from any potential value of the bound variable to the expression's customary extension under the assignment of that value.* It is this function, rather than the extension of the open expression, that bears on the truth-value of sentences in which the open expression occurs bound.

More accurately, the extension of an occurrence depends on the number of variable-binding operators governing it. Let us call the extension, under a value-assignment s, of an *occurrence* of a well-formed expression ζ within the scope of an occurrence of a variable-binding-operator phrase $\ulcorner(B\alpha)\urcorner$—where **B** is a variable-binding operator and α is a variable—and not within the scope of any other occurrence of a variable-binding-operator phrase or other nonextensional operator, *the bondage extension of ζ with respect to α under s*. Our theory of bondage starts with, and builds upon, the following principle.

A_1: The bondage extension of a well-formed (open or closed) expression ζ with respect to a variable α, under a value-assignment s, is (λi)[the customary extension of ζ under $s^\alpha{}_i$]—i.e., the function that maps any element i of the universe over which α ranges to the customary extension of ζ under the modified value-assignment that assigns i to α and is otherwise the same as s.[11]

The bondage extension of the variable 'x' with respect to itself is the identity function on the universe over which 'x' ranges.[12] Each distinct variable with the same range

---

[10] When a quantifier or other variable-binding operator 'quantifies into' an open expression—i.e., when an occurrence of the open expression includes a variable occurrence bound by an external quantifier-occurrence, or other variable-binding operator-occurrence—I say that the external quantifier-occurrence, or other variable-binder occurrence, in addition to binding the variable occurrence, also binds the containing open-expression occurrence itself. The effect is that a quantifier (or other variable-binder) is said to *bind* not only variables, but also the open expressions that the quantifier (binder) 'quantifies into'. Thus the quantifier-occurrence in '$(\exists x)(x^2 = 9)$' is said to bind not only the two occurrences of 'x' but also the occurrence of 'x^2' and even the occurrence of '$x^2 = 9$'. *Cf.*, D. Kalish, R. Montague, and G. Mar, *Logic: Techniques of Formal Reasoning* (Oxford University Press, 1964, 1980), at pp. 206, 311–312.

[11] This function is the customary extension of $\ulcorner(\lambda\alpha)[\zeta]\urcorner$ under s. Compare: The indirect extension of 'Snow is white' is the customary sense—the proposition that snow is white—which is the customary extension of 'that snow is white'. (Frege: 'In indirect discourse the words have their indirect designata (*ungerade Bedeutungen*), which coincide with what are customarily their senses. In this case then the clause has as its designatum a thought (*Gedanke*), not a truth-value; its sense is not a thought but is the [customary] sense of the words "the thought that ..." ' *Über Sinn und Bedeutung*.)

[12] By contrast, though the occurrence of 'y' in '$(\exists x)Fy$' is free, its extension under a value-assignment s is, strictly speaking, not the customary designatum. It is the bondage extension of

thus has the same bondage extension, under any given value-assignment, with respect to itself.

Variables are not the only expressions that have bondage extension. Any well-formed expression that has extension does. (See note 10 above.) Occurrences of open formulae bound through an internal variable-occurrence range over a universe of truth-values. (OK, so it is a baby universe.) The bondage extension of a formula is what Frege misleadingly called a *concept* ('*Begriff*'), i.e., a function from objects to truth-values. Thus the extension of the occurrence of 'x is bald' in '$(\exists x)(y$ is a sister of x & x is bald)', under any particular value-assignment, is the function that maps any bald individual to truth ('the True') and any non-bald individual to falsehood ('the False'). More generally, the bondage extension of a formula ϕ with respect to a variable α, under a value-assignment s, is the characteristic function of the class of objects i from the range of α such that ϕ is true under $s^{\alpha}{}_i$. For most purposes, the bondage extension may be identified with this class, in lieu of its characteristic function.

The extension of a doubly bound occurrence of a doubly open expression, like 'x is a sister of y' or 'x loves y', must be sensitive to the particular manner in which its internal variables are bound in a particular occurrence. Otherwise '$(x)(\exists y)(x$ loves $y)$' collapses together with '$(y)(\exists x)(x$ loves $y)$'. How shall this be accomplished?

Let α and β be variables, and let $\phi_{(\alpha, \beta)}$ be any formula in which both α and β occur free. Suppose an occurrence of $\phi_{(\alpha, \beta)}$ is within the scope of a quantifier-occurrence on β that is itself within the scope of quantifier-occurrence on α. That is, suppose we are considering a doubly embedding formula of the form

$$(\mathbf{B}\alpha)(\ldots (\mathbf{C}\beta)[\ldots \phi_{(\alpha, \beta)} \ldots] \ldots)$$

Whereas the occurrence of $\phi_{(\alpha, \beta)}$ still ranges over a universe of truth-values, it occurs here doubly bound: by **B** with respect to α and by **C** with respect to β. We call the extension, under a value-assignment s, of an *occurrence* of a well-formed expression ζ in extensional position within the scope of an occurrence of a variable-binding-operator phrase ⌜($\mathbf{C}\beta$)⌝, itself within the scope of an occurrence of a variable-binding-operator phrase ⌜($\mathbf{B}\alpha$)⌝—where **B** and **C** are variable-binding operators and α and β are variables—but not within the scope of any other occurrence of a nonextensional operator, *the double bondage extension of ζ with respect to $<\alpha, \beta>$ under s*. Doubly bound occurrences are governed by the following principle.

A$_2$: The double bondage extension of a well-formed (open or closed) expression ζ with respect to an ordered pair of variables $<\alpha, \beta>$, under a value-assignment s, is $(\lambda i)(\lambda j)$[the customary extension of ζ under $s^{\alpha\beta}{}_{ij}$]—i.e., the function that maps any element i from the range of α to the function that maps any element j from the range of β to the customary

---

'y' with respect to 'x', which is the function that maps any element i of the universe over which 'x' ranges to the customary designatum of 'y' under the modified value-assignment $s^{\alpha}{}_i$. This is the constant function to the customary designatum, s('y'), defined over the range of 'x'. For most purposes, this may be replaced with s('y') itself.

extension of ζ under the doubly modified value-assignment that assigns i to α, j to β, and is otherwise the same as s.[13]

This singular function to singular functions may be replaced with its corresponding binary function. In the special case where ζ is a formula $\phi_{(\alpha,\,\beta)}$, the latter function maps any pair of objects, i and j (from their respective ranges), to the truth-value of $\phi_{(\alpha,\,\beta)}$ under $s^{\alpha\,\beta}_{\,i\,\,j}$. For most purposes, we may go further and replace this binary function with the class of ordered pairs that it characterizes.

The double bondage extension of the variable 'x' with respect to the pair $<$'x', 'y'$>$ is not the same as its double bondage extension with respect to the converse pair $<$'y', 'x'$>$. This is just to say that the extension of a bound occurrence of a variable within the scope of a pair of variable-binding operator-occurrences depends on the order of the variable-binding operator-occurrences. Replacing singular functions to singular functions with binary functions, the extension of the second 'x' in '$(x)(\exists y)(x$ loves $y)$' is the binary function, *the former of i and j*, the extension of the second 'y' (indeed of both occurrences of 'y') is the binary function, *the latter of i and j*. By contrast, the extension of the second 'x' in '$(y)(\exists x)(x$ loves $y)$' is the function, *the latter of i and j*, the extension of the second 'y' the function, *the former of i and j*.[14]

The process iterates. The occurrence of the open formula 'x is positioned between y and z' in '$(z)(\exists x)(\exists y)(x$ is positioned between y and $z)$' ranges over a universe of truth-values. Its extension is the *triple bondage extension* with respect to the ordered triple $<$'z', 'x', 'y'$>$. The general notion of *n*-fold bondage extension is defined as follows.

Def : For $n \geq 0$, the *n-fold bondage extension* of a wfe ζ *with respect to* an *n*-tuple of variables $<\alpha_1, \alpha_2, \ldots, \alpha_n>$, *under* a value-assignment $s =_{def}$ the extension under s of an

---

[13] This function is the customary extension of $\ulcorner (\lambda\alpha)(\lambda\beta)[\zeta]\urcorner$ under s.
[14] The notion of double bondage extension, and the distinction between it and customary designation, is relevant to resolving Kit Fine's development of Russell's *antinomy of the variable*, in 'The Role of Variables', *The Journal of Philosophy*, 100 (December 2003), pp. 605–631. The problem, as Fine poses it, is this: 'How is it that any two variables ranging over a given universe have the same semantic role and yet have a different semantic role?' As he develops the problem, the question becomes 'How is it that there is no cross-contextual difference in semantic role between the variables 'x' and 'y', and yet there is a cross-contextual difference in semantic role between the pair $<$'x', 'y'$>$ and the pair $<$'x', 'x'$>$?' (p. 608). Our theory of bondage provides one possible response to Fine's question. The extension of each of the occurrences of 'x' in '$(\exists x)(x$ loves $x)$' is the bondage extension of 'x' with respect to itself: the identity function on the universe over which 'x' ranges. This is equally the extension of the occurrences of 'y' in '$(\exists y)(y$ loves $y)$'. Here is one sense in which there is no 'cross-contextual difference in semantic role' between 'x' and 'y'. By contrast, the occurrences of 'x' and 'y' in '$(\exists x)(\exists y)(x$ loves $y)$', though they range over the same universe, differ in extension. The double bondage extensions of 'x' and 'y' with respect to $<$'x', 'y'$>$ are neither of them the same as the single bondage extension of 'x' with respect to itself, or that of 'y' with respect to itself. Here is one sense in which there is a 'cross-contextual difference in semantic role' between the variables in '$(\exists x)(\exists y)(x$ loves $y)$' on the one hand, and those in '$(\exists x)(x$ loves $x)$' or in '$(\exists y)(y$ loves $y)$' on the other.
  The apparent dichotomy here is illusory. The single bondage extension of 'x' with respect to 'x' is *not* the same as that of 'y' with respect to 'x'. (See note 12 above.) And while the double bondage extension of 'x' with respect to $<$'x', 'y'$>$ is not the same as that of 'y' with respect to the same pair $<$'x', 'y'$>$, it *is* the same as that of 'y' with respect to the converse pair $<$'y', 'x'$>$. Furthermore, the double bondage extension of 'y' with respect to $<$'x', 'y'$>$ is the same as that of 'x' with respect to the reflexive pair $<$'x', 'x'$>$.

occurrence of ζ within the scope of exactly *n* occurrences of variable-binding-operator phrases, ⌜($\mathbf{B}_1\alpha_1$)⌝, ⌜($\mathbf{B}_2\alpha_2$)⌝, ..., ⌜($\mathbf{B}_n\alpha_n$)⌝, *in that order*, and not within the scope of any other occurrence of a nonextensional operator.

Identifying the 0-fold bondage extension with the customary extension, the basic tenet of our theory of bondage may be characterized by the following recursion:

A_0: The 0-fold bondage extension of a well-formed (open or closed) expression ζ with respect to the 0-tuple <—>, under a value-assignment *s*, is the *customary extension* of ζ under *s*.

$A_{(n+1)}$: For $n \geq 0$, the $(n+1)$-fold bondage extension of a well-formed (open or closed) expression ζ with respect to an $(n+1)$-tuple of variables $<\alpha_{(n+1)}, \ldots, \alpha_2\alpha_1>$, under a value-assignment *s*, is (λi)[the *n*-fold bondage extension of ζ with respect to the sub-tuple obtained by deleting $\alpha_{(n+1)}$ under the value-assignment *s′* that assigns *i* to $\alpha_{(n+1)}$ and is otherwise the same as *s*].[15]

This function may be replaced by its corresponding $(n+1)$-ary function. In the special case where ζ is a formula, the latter function maps an appropriate $(n+1)$-tuple to ζ's truth-value under the assignment of those objects as the values of the externally bound variables. For most purposes, we may go further and replace this function with the class of ordered $(n+1)$-tuples that it characterizes. The notions of bondage extension and of double bondage extension, characterized above, fall out as special cases of this recursion.[16]

There are the makings here of a hierarchy analogous to Frege's hierarchy of indirect senses. Our hierarchy is completely harmless. The $(n+1)$-fold bondage extension gives back the *n*-fold bondage extension once the free variables of ζ have been exhausted.[17]

---

[15] This function is the customary extension of ⌜$(\lambda\alpha_{(n+1)})\ldots(\lambda\alpha_2)(\lambda\alpha_1)[\zeta]$⌝ under *s*. The recursion principles, A_0 and $A_{(n+1)}$, might be taken as axioms. This construal may seem more appropriate for the latter principle than the former, which is plausibly construed instead as a definition of 'customary extension'. (See note 6.) What entity the customary extension of an expression is can be determined by invoking the classical characterization of extension *simpliciter*.

[16] Let a particular $(n+1)$-ary function f from objects to truth values be the $(n+1)$-fold bondage extension of a formula ϕ_α with respect to a sequence of variables $<\beta_1, \beta_2, \ldots, \beta_n, \alpha>$, under a value-assignment *s*. Then:

(*i*) The *n*-fold bondage extension of the universal generalization ⌜$(\alpha)\phi_\alpha$⌝ with respect to $<\beta_1, \beta_2, \ldots, \beta_n>$, under *s*, is an *n*-ary function f_Π that maps $j_1, j_2, \ldots, j_n$ to truth if every element *i* from the range of α is such that $f(j_1, j_2, \ldots, j_n, i)$ = truth, and that maps $j_1, j_2, \ldots, j_n$ to falsehood if at least one element *i* from the range of α is such that $f(j_1, j_2, \ldots, j_n, i)$ = falsehood; and

(*ii*) The *n*-fold bondage extension of the existential generalization ⌜$(\exists\alpha)\phi_\alpha$⌝ with respect to $<\beta_1, \beta_2, \ldots, \beta_n>$, under *s*, is an *n*-ary function f_Σ that maps $j_1, j_2, \ldots, j_n$ to truth if at least one element *i* from the range of α is such that $f(j_1, j_2, \ldots, j_n, i)$ = truth, and that maps $j_1, j_2, \ldots, j_n$ to falsehood if every element *i* from the range of α is such that $f(j_1, j_2, \ldots, j_n, i)$ = falsehood.

A universal generalization ⌜$(\alpha)\phi_\alpha$⌝ is true under a value-assignment *s* iff the class characterized by the extension of its occurrence of φ_α under *s* (i.e., the bondage extension of ϕ_α with respect to α under *s*) is universal. An existential generalization ⌜$(\exists\alpha)\phi_\alpha$⌝ is true under *s* iff the class characterized by the extension of its occurrence of ϕ_α under *s* is non-empty.

[17] See notes 11 and 12 above. By contrast, on Frege's hierarchies of multiply indirect extensions, the $(n+1)$-fold indirect extension is the *n*-fold indirect sense—which, as Russell noted in his

Consider a concrete example. Suppose the universe over which the variables 'x' and 'y' range is the set of people. The occurrence of 'x loves y' in '$(x)(\exists y)(x$ loves $y)$' ranges over a universe of truth-values. Its extension is the double bondage extension of 'x loves y' with respect to $<$'x', 'y'$>$. This is the binary function that maps pairs of people to truth if the first person loves the second, and to falsehood otherwise. The extension of the occurrence of '$(\exists y)(x$ loves $y)$' in '$(x)(\exists y)(x$ loves $y)$' is the bondage extension of '$(\exists y)(x$ loves $y)$' with respect to 'x': the characteristic function of the class of lovers. The sentence is true iff this class is universal over the set of people. By contrast, the extension of the occurrence of 'x loves y' in '$(y)(\exists x)(x$ loves $y)$' is the double bondage extension of 'x loves y' with respect to $<$'y', 'x'$>$. This is the binary function that maps pairs of people to truth if the second person loves the first, and to falsehood otherwise. The extension of the occurrence of '$(\exists x)(x$ loves $y)$' in '$(y)(\exists x)(x$ loves $y)$' is the bondage extension of '$(\exists x)(x$ loves $y)$' with respect to 'y': the characteristic function of the class of beloveds. The sentence is true iff this class is universal over the set of people.

One may choose to follow Frege in saying that any expression that has an extension *designates* the extension. For Frege, this entails that any expression-occurrence that has an extension—whether it is the customary extension or a non-customary extension—is a designator of that extension. Then a bound occurrence of an open expression (such as an individual variable) has its *bondage designatum* with respect to a variable (on an analogy to Frege's notion of *ungerade Bedeutung*, or indirect designatum), which is simply the bondage extension. A singly bound variable (the occurrence) would thus designate the identity function on the universe over which the variable (the expression) ranges. In the standard, and most natural, possible-worlds semantics of modality, the range of the individual variables varies from one possible world to the next. (A so-called possibilist, or fixed-universe, modal semantics is an alternative option.) Whereas a free occurrence of 'x' is a rigid designator under a value-assignment of its value, a singly bound occurrence of 'x' (on a variable-universe modal semantics) would be regarded as designating identity functions on different universes with respect to different possible worlds. The variable 'x', which occurs bound in (1), is itself rigid, but its occurrences in (1) (unlike the occurrence of 'y'), insofar as they are designators, are non-rigid.

If one holds with Frege that an expression designates its extension, one may say that the open formula (1) *customarily designates* truth under A. As already noted, our original value-assignment A does not satisfy (2); (2) customarily designates falsehood under A. But falsehood is not what (2) designates *as it occurs in (1)*. Like the occurrences of 'x' in (1), the occurrence of (2) in (1) is bound, through its occurrence of 'x', by the initial quantifier occurrence. It therefore ranges over a universe of truth-values. Under A, the occurrence of (2) in (1) designates (non-rigidly) the characteristic function of the class of MacLaine's siblings. And (1) designates truth under A as long as (and only as long as) this class is non-empty.

---

infamous 'Gray's *Elegy*' argument, is a new entity, entirely distinct from the n-fold indirect extension.

III

The foregoing is an outline of a Fregean extensional-semantic theory for both bound and free expression-occurrences. It can be extended into a Fregean theory of sense for bound and free expression-occurrences. To do so in a thoroughgoing Fregean manner, one should follow Church's idea of considering assignments of customary-sense values to variables in lieu of assignments of customary-designatum values.

Russell's intensional-semantic theory avoids this. On a Russellian theory, variables are *logically proper names*, or *directly referential*. That is, the semantic content ('meaning') of a variable, under an assignment of values to variables, is simply the variable's designatum (the assigned value) rather than a sense. The content of (2) under A is the false singular proposition about MacLaine and Brando, that she is a sister of his. Suppose that the universe over which 'x' ranges is the set of people. Then the content of (1) under A is a somewhat different, more general proposition, having just two components. The first component is the propositional function that maps anyone i to the singular proposition that MacLaine is a sister of i. Or it is the concept (or something similar) corresponding to this, that of *having MacLaine as sister*. The second component is the content of '$(\exists x)$'.[18] The proposition so constituted is the singular proposition about MacLaine that she is a sister of someone or other.

This is a theory of semantic content for expressions, not for expression-occurrences. Russellian intensional semantics violates *strong compositionality*, according to which the semantic content of a compound expression is not only a function of, but indeed a composite entity whose components *are*, the semantic contents of the compound expression's meaningful components. The Russellian content of 'x'—of the variable itself—is, in some natural sense, a component of the Russellian content of (2), but it is no part of the Russellian content of (1), even though 'x' itself is as much a component of (1) as it is of (2). Likewise, the Russellian content of (2) is not a component of the Russellian content of (1).

To satisfy extensionality and compositionality, the notion of a component of a compound expression must be understood to be not an *expression* but an *expression-occurrence*. So understood, it is not unreasonable to hope to satisfy compositionality, and even strong compositionality. What we seek is a kind of hybrid Frege–Russellian intensional occurrence-based semantics—a Russellian theory of content that conforms to Frege's Context Principle.

Here is an excessively brief sketch. In Frege–Russellian occurrence-based semantics, what we have been calling 'the content of 'x' ' under a value-assignment is the *customary content* of 'x', i.e., the content of its free occurrences (not within quotation marks or the like). Bound variables have their bondage semantics. Suppose again that the universe over which the variables 'x' and 'y' range is the set of people.

---

[18] This might be the concept of being a non-empty class, or the second-order propositional function Σ that maps any first-order propositional function F to the proposition that F is 'sometimes true', i.e., that F yields a true proposition for at least one argument, or the corresponding concept, or something similar.

The customary content of the open formula 'x loves y' under an assignment of values to variables is a singular proposition about the values of 'x' and 'y'. This proposition is the content of free occurrences of 'x loves y', not of bound occurrences. The occurrence of 'x loves y' in '$(y)(\exists x)(x$ loves $y)$' is in bondage, ranging over a universe of singular propositions. Its content, under an assignment s of values to variables, is the *double bondage content* of 'x loves y' with respect to <'y', 'x'> under s. This is the function that maps a pair of people, i and j, to the customary content of 'x loves y' under the doubly modified value-assignment $s^{'x'}{}_j{}^{'y'}{}_i$ that assigns j as value for 'x' and i as value for 'y', and is otherwise the same as s—i.e., the binary Russellian propositional function (λij)[the singular proposition that j loves i]. More accurately, the content of the occurrence of 'x loves y' in '$(y)(\exists x)(x$ loves $y)$' is the binary-relational concept, *being loved by*, that corresponds to the double bondage content.

The content of the occurrence of '$(\exists x)(x$ loves $y)$' in '$(y)(\exists x)(x$ loves $y)$' is the bondage content of '$(\exists x)(x$ loves $y)$' with respect to 'y'. This is the propositional function (λi)[the singular proposition that someone or other loves i]. Or rather, the content of the occurrence of '$(\exists x)(x$ loves $y)$' in '$(y)(\exists x)(x$ loves $y)$' is the concept corresponding to this propositional function: that of *being loved by someone or other*. This concept is composed of the content of the occurrence of 'x loves y' and the customary content of '$(\exists x)$', the latter being the second-order concept, *someone or other*. The customary content of '$(y)(\exists x)(x$ loves $y)$' is the proposition composed of the content of the occurrence of '$(\exists x)(x$ loves $y)$' and the customary content of '(y)': that everyone is loved.

Similarly, the singular proposition that we have been calling 'the content of (2)' under a value-assignment is the customary content of (2), i.e., the content of its free occurrences, not of its bound occurrences. The occurrence of (2) in (1) is in bondage, ranging over the universe of singular propositions of the form, *Maclaine is a sister of i*, (i.e., the class of propositions p such that for someone i, $p =$ the singular proposition about MacLaine and i, that she is a sister of i.) The content under A of the occurrence of (2) in (1) is (λi)[the customary content of (2) under the modified value-assignment $A^{'x'}{}_i$]. This is the Russellian propositional function that maps i to the singular proposition that MacLaine is a sister of i. Or rather, the content under A of the occurrence of (2) in (1) is the concept corresponding to this propositional function, that of *having MacLaine as sister*.

Russellian occurrence-based semantics obtains as customary content for (1) under A the same proposition that Russell's expression-based semantics obtains as (1)'s content (*simpliciter*) under A. Unlike the latter, occurrence-based semantics does this *by composition*, generating a proposition by combining the semantic contents of the sentence's meaningful components—not the component expressions but the component occurrences.

IV

Unlike classical Russell–Tarski expression-based semantics, the Frege–Russell occurrence-based semantics sketched above evidently conforms to Frege's Context

Principle and to (modestly restricted) principles of extensionality, compositionality, and even strong compositionality.[19] I should nevertheless strongly advise classical semantics to continue disregarding the Context Principle. This is not because I think it incorrect to attribute semantic values to expression-occurrences. The two approaches, though different, are not intrinsically in conflict. Contrary to the Context Principle, semantics may be done either way. Semantics may even be done both ways simultaneously, assigning semantic values both to expressions and to their occurrences within formulae or other expressions, and without prejudice concerning which is derivative from which. Frege's occurrence-based semantics in fact assigns semantic values both to expressions and their occurrences, even while honoring his Context Principle. His notions of customary designatum, indirect sense, doubly indirect designatum, and the like, are semantic values of the expression itself. The customary designatum is the designatum of the expression's occurrences in 'customary' settings, i.e., its occurrences that are in extensional position and not within the scope of a variable-binding operator. (See note 15.) And despite its pedigree, the Context Principle is not sacrosanct. Translating the term 'extension' of conventional expression-based semantics into 'customary extension', and so on for the other semantic terms ('designate', 'content', and so forth), occurrence-based semantics emerges as a conservative extension of conventional expression-based semantics. Occurrence-based semantics may be unorthodox and unconventional, but it is only somewhat unorthodox and only somewhat unconventional. As mentioned, expression-based semantics is its less discriminating by-product.

The principal reason I nevertheless advocate expression-based semantics over occurrence-based semantics is that the latter inevitably invites serious confusion. It led Frege to his view that each meaningful expression has not only a sense, but an indirect sense, and also a doubly indirect sense, and indeed an entire infinite hierarchy of indirect senses.[20] Occurrence-based semantics has also led to the miscataloging

---

[19] An actual proof that a modestly restricted principle of strong compositionality is satisfied (or falsified) awaits a suitable theory of concepts analogous to Zermelo–Frankel set theory.

[20] I argue this in 'On Indirect Sense and Designation' (unpublished). My attitude resonates somewhat with Rudolf Carnap's in *Meaning and Necessity* (University of Chicago Press, 1947, 1956), chapter III, especially §§29–32, pp. 124–144. (But see note 2 above.) Carnap calls expression-based semantics *the method of extension and intension*, and Frege's occurrence-based semantics *the method of the name-relation*. Carnap saw Frege's occurrence-based semantics as flowing naturally from his assimilation of semantic extension to 'the name-relation' between a singular term and its designatum. *Cf. ibid.*, §28, especially at p. 123. (Occurrence-based semantics *per se* does not require this assimilation. I believe the Context Principle also flows fairly naturally from a 'truth-conditional' semantics that does not assimilate extension to designation. I have set out occurrence-based semantics without assuming the assimilation.) A resolute advocate of the expression-based semantic method over Frege's occurrence-based semantics, Carnap points out that the expression-semantic notion of extension and Frege's notion of designation ('nominatum', *Bedeutung*), though they are very similar, are not to be identified; and likewise the expression-semantic notion of content ('intension') and Frege's notion of sense, though very similar, are not to be identified. 'A decisive difference between our method and Frege's consists in the fact that our concepts, in distinction to Frege's, are independent of the context' (p. 125). Still, Carnap noted, the expression-semantic notions of extension and content coincide, respectively, with Frege's notions of *customary* designatum and sense. (*Cf.* Carnap's principles **29-1** and **29-2**, pp. 125–126.) Carnap advises against doing semantics both ways simultaneously (pp. 128–129), and complains that Frege's method led him

of various terms. In particular, it has led to the misclassification of various non-compound singular terms as non-rigid, and of various compound terms (for example, complex demonstratives and 'that'-clauses in attributions of belief) as restricted quantifiers (often mislabeled *generalized quantifiers*). Though not Frege's, these errors have been committed by followers in Frege's footsteps, reinforcing a current *quantifiermania*. The misclassifications, and other confusions like them, come about when a philosopher of language fails to distinguish sharply between an expression and its occurrences.[21]

I shall first take up the misclassification of compound terms. This arises when a language philosopher erroneously imputes an open expression's customary semantics to the expression's occurrences in a sentence. I have in mind the recent rash of arguments to the effect that compound terms of a certain grammatical category (for example, 'that'-clauses), because they can be quantified into ('Every boy believes *that his dad is tougher than every other boys' dad*'), cannot be singular terms, or cannot be directly referential singular terms, and should be regarded instead as restricted quantifiers.

The general form of the argument originates with Benson Mates, who employed it as an objection to the Fregean (and Strawsonian/anti-Russellian) thesis that definite descriptions are compound singular terms, and that a definite description designates the individual that answers to the description if there is a unique such individual and

---

to postulate an insufficiently explained notion of indirect sense (p. 129) and leads ultimately to Frege's infinite hierarchies (pp. 131–132).

Russell had previously blamed the Fregean hierarchy not on occurrence-based semantics, but on the expression-semantic thesis that definite descriptions are singular terms. See note 17 above. My own view is that the hierarchy discredits neither the Context Principle nor the thesis that definite descriptions are singular terms, and is to be traced instead to the union of two fundamental principles of Fregean theory: that any expression-occurrence that has a designatum also has a sense, which is a concept of the designatum; and that the indirect designatum of an expression is the customary sense. See my 'On Designating', in *Mind*, 114, 456 (October 2005), pp. 1069–1133, reprinted in my *Metaphysics, Mathematics, and Meaning* (Oxford University Press, 2005), pp. 286–334; and also 'On Indirect Sense and Designation'.

There is an analog to the Fregean hierarchy in Church's elegant 'Logic of Sense and Denotation' ('LSD'), in Henle, Kallen, and Langer, eds, *Structure, Method and Meaning* (New York: Liberal Arts Press, 1951), pp. 3–24; *Noûs* (1973), pp. 24–33, 135–156. As Carnap recognizes (pp. 132, 137–138), however, the hierarchies in 'LSD' are not semantic values of single expressions. They are the senses of infinitely many *different* expressions.

[21] Since 1905 it has been illegitimate to presume without argument that definite descriptions are singular terms and not restricted quantifiers—even if it is at least as illegitimate, based largely on intuitions concerning what is mentioned, to presume without argument that definite descriptions are quantifiers and not singular terms. Some of the arguments of Russell and his followers have shaken confidence in the orthodox view that definite descriptions are singular terms. (See my 'On Designating'.) By contrast, the thesis that demonstratives and 'that'-clauses are singular terms remains quite plausible, also based largely on intuitions concerning what is mentioned, while the rival thesis that they are quantifiers remains enormously implausible. Many of the arguments of Kripke and others that names are not descriptions transfer easily to demonstratives and 'that'-clauses. In particular, that demonstratives are singular terms is common sense, and no persuasive evidence has been adduced that they are quantifiers. Specifically, as will be seen, the general argument presently to be considered provides no evidence whatever concerning demonstratives or 'that'-clauses. (I thank Zoltán Szabó for pressing me to address this. It should not be assumed that he agrees with my assessment.)

designates nothing otherwise, yielding a sentence with no truth-value.[22] Although initially plausible, the Fregean thesis apparently falters when a definite description is quantified into, as in:

(3) Every [some/at least one/more than one/exactly one/not one] male soldier overseas misses the only woman waiting for him back home.

If the definite description 'the only woman waiting for him back home' were a singular term, then (3) should not be true—indeed, on the Frege–Strawson theory, it should be neither true nor false—if the description has no designatum. But (3) could well be true, Mates argues, even though one cannot assign a designatum to the open definite description 'the only woman waiting for him back home' as occurring in (3), any more 'than one can assign a truth-value to "it is less than 9" as occurring in "If a number is less than 7, then it is less than 9".'[23]

Let us take a close look at the objection. As Mates notes, the definite description 'the only woman waiting for him back home' occurring in (3) is open. The pronoun 'him' occurring in the description corresponds to a variable bound by an external quantifier. The pronoun may be assigned any one of various soldiers as designatum. If the phrase 'the only woman waiting for him back home' is indeed a singular term, it designates different women under different such assignments. What about the *occurrence* of the description in (3)? Our theory of bondage demonstrates that Mates overstates the case when he says that one cannot assign anything to the occurrence as its designatum. The occurrence has its bondage extension with respect to 'him', and may be regarded as designating the function that assigns to any male the only woman waiting for him back home, if he left exactly one woman waiting for him back home, and assigns nothing otherwise. This much may be said, though: The occurrence of the description in (3) does not designate any particular woman who answers to the description.

---

[22] Mates, 'Descriptions and Reference', *Foundations of Language*, 10 (1973), pp. 409–418, at p. 415. The general form of argument has been employed or endorsed by several others during the past three decades. The following is a chronological partial bibliography: Gareth Evans, 'Reference and Contingency', *Monist*, 62 (1979), pp. 161–189, at pp. 169–170; Stephen Neale, *Descriptions* (Cambridge, Mass.: MIT Press, 1990), at p. 56n28; Neale, 'Term Limits', in J. Tomberlin, ed., *Philosophical Perspectives: Logic and Language*, 7 (Atascadero, Calif.: Ridgeview, 1993), pp. 89–123, at p. 107; Jeffrey King, 'Are Complex "That" Phrases Devices of Direct Reference?' *Noûs*, 33 (1999), pp. 155–182, at pp. 157–158, 161–162; Ernest Lepore and Kirk Ludwig, 'The Semantics and Pragmatics of Complex Demonstratives', *Mind*, 109 (2000), pp. 200–241, at pp. 205–206, 210–222, and *passim*; King, *Complex Demonstratives* (Cambridge, Mass.: MIT Press, 2001), at pp. xi–xii, 1, 10–11, 20–22; Kent Johnson and Ernest Lepore, 'Does Syntax Reveal Semantics? A Case Study of Complex Demonstratives', in J. Tomberlin, ed., *Philosophical Perspectives: Language and Mind*, 16 (Atascadero, Calif.: Ridgeview, 2002), pp. 17–41, at p. 31; and Jason Stanley, Review of Jeffrey King, *Complex Demonstratives*, *The Philosophical Review*, 111 (2002), pp. 605–609. *Cf.* my 'Being of Two Minds: Belief with Doubt', *Noûs*, 29 (1995), pp. 1–20, at p. 18n26, and 'Demonstrating and Necessity', *The Philosophical Review*, 111 (2002), pp. 497–537, at pp. 534–535n47; both reprinted in *Content, Cognition, Communication*.

[23] Before Mates, Geach had drawn a somewhat different conclusion from the same data: that the occurrence of the definite description in (3), since it does not designate, does not 'have the role of a definite description'. See his 'Ryle on Namely-Riders', at pp. 91–92 of *Logic Matters*; also 'Referring Expressions Again', *Analysis*, 24, 5 (1963–1964), reprinted in Geach's *Logic Matters*, pp. 97–102, at 99–100.

Now suppose (3) is true. How does it follow that the description occurring in (3) is not a singular term?

It does not—not without the aid of some additional semantic machinery. What does follow is that if definite descriptions are singular terms, the occurrence of the description in (3) does not designate the description's customary designatum under any particular designatum assignment. But no one ever said that it did. The Fregean thesis is that definite descriptions—the expressions themselves—are singular terms. If one is not careful to distinguish between an expression and its occurrences, one might misconstrue this as the thesis that every *occurrence* of a definite description designates the object that answers to the description. (Recall the Cautionary Note in Section I.) But it is well known that Frege, with his doctrine of indirect designation, rejected the latter thesis. For (3) to be true, every male soldier overseas must miss the woman who is value of the function designated by the occurrence of the definite description when that soldier is assigned as argument. As long as the function is defined for every male soldier overseas, this presents no particular problem.

To bridge the gap between the current sub-conclusion and the Fregean thesis in Mates's crosshairs, the objection tacitly invokes the following semantic theorem:

M: *Any sentence ϕ_β [of a restricted class C], containing an occurrence of a genuine singular term β not within the scope of an indirect, intensional, or quotational operator, is true [either true or false] only if that same occurrence of β designates the customary designatum of β.*[24]

Assuming Mates does not misconstrue the Fregean/Strawsonian thesis, his objection assumes (M) (or something very much like it) as its major premiss, or assumes that his Fregean opponent is committed to it. As we have noted, if the description 'the only woman waiting for him back home' is a genuine singular term, its occurrence in (3)—since an external quantifier-occurrence quantifies into it—does not designate the description's customary designatum under a particular designatum-assignment. Yet (3) may be true. Given (M), it directly follows that the description is not a genuine singular term.

The argument is fallacious. Other versions of Mates's objection are equally fallacious. Those other versions make, or require, semantic assumptions analogous, or otherwise very similar, to (M).[25] What the proponents of the style of argument generally fail to recognize is that, insofar as there are semantic theorems like (M) concerning singular terms, there are analogous semantic theorems concerning quantifiers,[26] as well as other sorts of expressions that have semantic extension.

---

[24] See note 6. The bracketed material represents variations or restrictions that Mates might have in mind. The restricted class C excludes such problematic sentences as ⌜β does not exist⌝ and things that entail it.

[25] The assumed semantic theorem is not generally stated precisely, if it is stated at all. In some applications a somewhat stronger semantic theorem is employed, for example:

(M+) *Any sentence ϕ_β, of the restricted class C, containing an occurrence of a genuine singular term β not within the scope of an indirect, intensional, or quotational operator, is true if and only if the designatum of that same occurrence of β satisfies the formula ϕ_α —where ϕ_β is the result of uniformly substituting occurrences of β for the free occurrences in extensional position of a variable α in ϕ_α.* (See the appendix.)

[26] Thus, for example: *Any sentence [of a restricted class C], containing an occurrence of universal generalization ⌜$(\alpha)\phi_\alpha$⌝ not within the scope of an indirect, intensional, or quotational operator, is true*

This makes for the possibility of an exactly analogous argument for the conclusion that quantifiers also cannot be quantified into, and therefore definite descriptions (or 'that'-clauses, and so forth.) are not quantifiers either, *or anything else for that matter.* Something has gone very wrong. Restricted quantifiers can be bound by other quantifiers—as, for example, in 'Every male soldier overseas misses *some woman waiting for him back home.*' For that matter, so can singular terms—witness the case of the individual variable. Somewhere a fatal error has been committed.

In every application of which I am aware, the assumed semantic 'theorem' is in fact false and the proponents of the target thesis (e.g., that definite descriptions or 'that'-clauses are singular terms) do not endorse it. If (M) were sound, it would establish more generally that the very notion of an occurrence of an open singular term bound ('quantified into') by an external quantifier is semantically incoherent. Despite the objection's popularity, ordinary mathematical notation is rife with counter-examples to its major premise—for example the 'x^2' in '$(\exists x)(x^2 = 9)$'. The most glaring counter-example is the paradigm of an open designator: the individual variable. To use Mates's own example, if the occurrences of 'y' in the true sentence '$(y)(y < 7 \supset y < 9)$' (let this be ϕ_β, with $\beta = $ 'y') designate anything, they designate not the customary designatum of 'y' under a particular value-assignment, but the bondage extension with respect to 'y' itself: the identity function on the range of 'y'. Yet the variable 'y' is a genuine singular term if anything is.[27] (See the appendix.)

The mistake directly results from imputing the semantic attributes of an expression to its occurrences, including even bound occurrences. The mistaken 'theorem' can be corrected, and even generalized:

M': *An assignment s of values to variables satisfies a formula ϕ_β, of the restricted class C, containing a free occurrence of a singular term β not within the scope of any nonextensional operator (other than classical variable-binding operators), only if that same occurrence of β designates the customary designatum of β under s.*

This corrected version effectively blocks the objection.[28] Fregean theory may also countenance a second variation of (M):

M'': *Any sentence ϕ_β [of a restricted class C], containing an occurrence of a genuine singular term β not within the scope of any nonextensional operator (other than classical variable-binding operators), is either true or false only if that same occurrence of β designates.*

---

only if the extension of that same occurrence of $\ulcorner(\alpha)\phi_\alpha\urcorner$ is truth if the extension of its occurrence of ϕ_α is the function that assigns truth to everything in the range of the variable α, and is falsehood otherwise.

[27] Let ϕ_α in $(M+)$ be the open formula '$(y)(y < 7 \supset x < 9)$', with $\alpha = $ 'x'. The customary designatum of 'y' under the assignment of 10 as value does not satisfy it.

[28] There are likewise corrected versions of the more elaborate assumptions mentioned in note 25 above. Thus:

$M+'$: *An assignment s of values to variables satisfies a formula ϕ_β, of the restricted class C, containing a free occurrence of a genuine singular term β not within the scope of any nonextensional operator (other than classical variable-binding operators), if and only if the modified value-assignment s' that assigns the designatum of that same occurrence of β under s as value for a variable α and is otherwise the same as s, satisfies the formula ϕ_α—where ϕ_β is the result of uniformly substituting free occurrences of β for the free occurrences of α in extensional position in ϕ_α.*

Each of these corrected versions effectively blocks the objection.

As mentioned earlier, according to the occurrence-based semantics sketched above, the occurrence of the open definite description in (3) designates a particular partial function.

It is a trivial matter to extend the theory of bondage from Section II above to include definite descriptions as singular terms, which, if open, can be quantified into. A definite description $\ulcorner(\iota\alpha)\phi_\alpha\urcorner$ customarily designates under a value-assignment s the unique object i that is an element of the class characterized by the extension of its occurrence of ϕ_α, if there is a unique such i, and customarily designates nothing under s otherwise. A free occurrence of a definite description in extensional position designates the description's customary designatum. The extension of a bound occurrence in otherwise extensional position is then the appropriate bondage extension.[29] One may consistently add the corrected Mates theorem (M') into the mix. On this theory of bondage, quantification into singular terms is not only permitted, it is encouraged.

Saul Kripke has sermonized, 'It is important, in discussion of logico-philosophical issues, not to lose sight of basic, elementary distinctions by covering them up with either genuine or apparent technical sophistication.'[30] The distinction between an expression and its occurrences is elementary and fundamental. The Fregean/Strawsonian thesis that Mates aims to refute is that definite descriptions are singular terms. It is no part of the Fregean thesis that every *occurrence*—even a bound occurrence—of a definite description in otherwise extensional position in a sentence designates the description's customary designatum. The latter thesis is neither Frege's nor Strawson's; it is Strawman's.

There remain significant differences between the Fregean theory sketched above and the Russellian theory that Mates and company prefer. If every male soldier overseas left exactly one woman waiting for him back home, and he does indeed miss her, then contrary to Mates, Frege's theory, no less than Russell's, deems (3) true. If every male soldier overseas left exactly one woman waiting for him back home, but at least one male soldier overseas does not miss the woman he left behind, then both Frege and Russell deem (3) false. But suppose at least one male soldier overseas left no woman, or two women, waiting for him back home. On Russell's theory, (3) is false in this third case as well as the second. On Frege's theory it is not, although it is not true either. This verdict is a straightforward result of (M') together with the theory's other semantic principles. The third case, not the first, is the deciding case. To this day, it remains unclear whether the falsity verdicts of Russell's theory, or those of Frege's, are the correct ones.

---

[29] Let a particular $(n+1)$-ary function f from objects to truth values be the $(n+1)$-fold bondage extension of a formula ϕ_α with respect to a sequence of variables $<\beta_1, \beta_2, \ldots, \beta_n, \alpha>$, under a value-assignment s. Then the n-fold bondage extension of the definite description $\ulcorner(\iota\alpha)\phi_\alpha\urcorner$ with respect to $<\beta_1, \beta_2, \ldots, \beta_n>$, under s, is the n-ary partial function f_i that maps $j_1, j_2, \ldots, j_n$ to the unique element i from the range of α such that $f(j_1, j_2, \ldots, j_n, i)$ = truth, if there is a unique such i, and is undefined otherwise.

[30] 'Is There a Problem about Substitutional Quantification?' in G. Evans and J. McDowell, eds, *Truth and Meaning* (Oxford University Press, 1976), pp. 325–419, at p. 408.

V

Besides the misclassification of various compound terms, there has also occurred a miscataloging of certain directly referential singular terms as non-rigid definite descriptions, again partly as a result of a failure to distinguish sharply between the term and its occurrence. Here the confusion is traceable to a larger confusion, between an entire sentence and its occurrence in a discourse. Consider the following discourse fragment:

(4) (*i*) A comedian composed the musical score for *City Lights*. (*ii*) He was multi-talented.

The particular sentence (4*ii*) is ordinarily regarded as an open formula with a free variable, 'he'. As Geach has noted, the pronoun evidently functions differently *as it occurs in (4)*. Geach takes the pronoun-occurrence to be a variable-occurrence bound by a prenex occurrence of the restricted existential quantifier 'a comedian', as in the following:

(4*G*) [a x: comedian(x)] (x composed the musical score for *City Lights* & x was multi-talented).[31]

Gareth Evans mounted solid evidence against Geach that the scope of 'a comedian' in (4) does not extend beyond (4*i*), and so the phrase does not bind the 'he' in (4*ii*)—this despite the fact that the 'he' is anaphoric upon the phrase 'a comedian'.[32] Following Evans, an anaphoric pronoun-occurrence whose grammatical antecedent is a quantifier-occurrence within whose scope that pronoun-occurrence does not stand is often called an *E-type pronoun* (alternatively a *donkey pronoun*, because of particular examples originally due to Walter Burley).[33] The 'he' in (4) appears to be a free occurrence of a closed singular term rather than a bound variable. *E*-type pronoun-occurrences, according to Evans, are 'assigned a reference and their immediate sentential contexts can be evaluated independently for truth and falsehood'. Evans takes the 'he' in (4) to be a rigid singular term whose reference is fixed by the

---

[31] *Reference and Generality*, at pp. 129*ff*.; and 'Quine's Syntactical Insights', at pp. 118–119 of *Logic Matters*.
[32] *Cf*. Gareth Evans, 'Pronouns, Quantifiers, and Relative Clauses (I)', *Canadian Journal of Philosophy*, 7 (1977), pp. 777–797; 'Pronouns', *Linguistic Inquiry*, 11 (1980), pp. 337–362. The analogous discourse fragment, 'Just two actors starred in *City Lights*. They were both multi-talented' is not equivalent to the quantified generalization 'Just two actors both: starred in *City Lights* and were multi-talented'. (The latter allows, while the former does not, that a third, non-multi-talented actor also starred in *City Lights*.) Many, including several critics, have followed Evans in concluding that the pronoun 'they' in the discourse fragment is an occurrence of a closed expression; hence too, by analogy, the pronoun in (4).
[33] In the vernacular of theoretical linguistics, the term '*E*-type pronoun' is used for an anaphoric pronoun-occurrence whose grammatical antecedent is a quantifier-occurrence that does not *c-command* that pronoun-occurrence. Linguists and linguistics-oriented philosophers almost invariably phrase this in terms of a 'pronoun' and its antecedent 'quantifier', where what are at issue are actually occurrences. (See note 5 above, and recall again the cautionary note to which it is appended.)

description 'the only comedian who composed the musical score for *City Lights*'. He thus represents (4) as having the following logical form:

(4*E*) (*i*) [a *x*: comedian(*x*)] (*x* composed the musical score for *City Lights*).

(*ii*) *dthat*[[the *y*: comedian(*y*)] (*y* composed the musical score for *City Lights*)] was multi-talented.

The bracketed expression in the first sentence is a restricted existential quantifier phrase, which may be read 'a comedian *x* is such that'. The innermost bracketed expression in the second sentence may be read 'the only comedian *y* such that'. The full '*dthat*'-term—which might be read '*that* comedian who composed the musical score for *City Lights*' (a closed expression)—is alleged to be the formal counterpart of the 'he' in (4*ii*).

Michael McKinsey, Scott Soames, Stephen Neale, and others argue that the 'he', as it occurs in (4), is not merely co-designative, but *synonymous* in content, with 'the only comedian who composed the musical score for *City Lights*'. For although the 'he' in (4) designates Charlie Chaplin with respect to the actual world, (4) may also be evaluated with respect to other possible worlds. Consider a possible world *W* in which, say, Buster Keaton composed the musical score for Chaplin's classic silent film. The discourse fragment (4) is true with respect to *W* iff Keaton is a multi-talented comedian in *W*, never mind Chaplin.[34] With respect to *W*, it is argued, the 'he' in (4) designates Keaton instead of Chaplin, just as the description does. The entire discourse fragment is thus depicted as having the following logical form, in contrast to (4*E*):

(4*M*) (*i*) [a *x*: comedian(*x*)] (*x* composed the musical score for *City Lights*).

(*ii*) [the *y*: comedian(*y*)] (*y* composed the musical score for *City Lights*) was multi-talented.

The full definite description in (4*Mii*) is alleged to be the formal counterpart of the 'he' in (4).[35]

The argument is mistaken. That the pronoun 'he' (the expression) is rigid is confirmed by positioning it in the scope of a modal operator-occurrence:

A comedian composed the musical score for *City Lights*. That he was multi-talented is a contingent truth.

---

[34] Insofar as the modal truth-conditions for (4) yield this result, the 'he' does not function in (4) as a demonstrative. By contrast with (4*ii*), the sentence '*Dthat*[the comedian who composed the musical score for *City Lights*] was multi-talented' is true with respect to a context *c* and a possible world *w* iff the comedian who *in the possible world of c* (rather than *w*) composed the musical score for *City Lights*, was multi-talented *in w*.

[35] This argument for the pronoun's non-rigidity is McKinsey's, in 'Mental Anaphora', *Synthese*, 66 (1986), pp. 159–175, at 161. It is echoed by Scott Soames, in his review of Gareth Evans's *Collected Papers*, in *The Journal of Philosophy*, 86 (1989), pp. 141–156, at 145. It is also endorsed by Stephen Neale, in 'Descriptive Pronouns and Donkey Anaphora', *The Journal of Philosophy*, 87 (1990), pp. 113–150, at p. 130, and again in *Descriptions* (Cambridge, Mass.: MIT Press, 1990), p. 186.

The second sentence here does not impute contingency to the fact that whichever comedian composed the music for *City Lights* was multi-talented. (something about chaplin himself: If it did, it would presumably be false.) Instead it expresses that, although in fact multi-talented, he might not have been.³⁶

This does not mean that Evans was right and Geach wrong. The pronoun-occurrence in (4) is more plausibly regarded as a variable-occurrence bound by a restricted quantifier implicit in (4*ii*), perhaps 'a comedian who composed the musical score for *City Lights*'. The entire discourse fragment is plausibly regarded as having an underlying logical form more like the following, where items in boldface correspond to explicit elements in the surface form (4):

(4′) (*i*) [a *x*: **comedian**(*x*)] (*x* **composed the musical score for** *City Lights*).
(*ii*) [a *y*: comedian(*y*); *y* composed the musical score for *City Lights*] (*y* **was multi-talented**).

The open formula '*y* was multi-talented' occurring in (4′*ii*) makes an explicit appearance in the surface form, as (4*ii*). The rest of (4′*ii*) does not. On this analysis, an *E*-type pronoun-occurrence is a species of bound-variable occurrence, as Geach has long maintained. In fact, the conjunction corresponding to (4′) is equivalent to (4*G*) (and to the second conjunct (4′*ii*) alone). Contrary to Geach, however, the anaphora between an *E*-type pronoun and its antecedent is not the same relation as that between a bound variable and its binding operator. Instead the *E*-type pronoun is bound by an absent operator recoverable from the antecedent.

One important advantage of this analysis over both (4*E*) and (4*M*) is that the mere grammar of (4) does not support an inference to a uniqueness claim of the sort presupposed or otherwise entailed by the use of '*the only* comedian that scored the music for *City Lights*'. Though this may not be obvious with (4) (since, typically, if someone scored the musical score for a particular film, then no one else did), it is with the following discourse:

A comedian panned the musical score for *City Lights*. He was jealous. Another comedian also panned the musical score for *City Lights*. He wasn't jealous; he was tone-deaf.

Another important difference is that there is no definite description in (4′) to be regarded as a formal counterpart of the 'he' in (4). There is no non-rigid designation of Chaplin in (4′). There is no designation at all of Chaplin in (4′), except by the variables '*x*' and '*y*' under appropriate value-assignments. The rigidity of 'he' suggests that its formal counterpart in (4′) is simply the last occurrence of '*y*'.³⁷

---

³⁶ *Cf.*, my 'Demonstrating and Necessity', *loc. cit.*, pp. 497–537, at pp. 536–537*n*52. My critique has benefited from discussion with Alan Berger, who realized independently that the arguments of Evans and McKinsey are incorrect. See his *Terms and Truth* (MIT Press, 2002), at pp. 171–178.

Though the pronoun 'he' is rigid, so-called laziness occurrences (in addition to bound occurrences) may be non-rigid. The occurrence in (4*ii*) is not a laziness occurrence.

³⁷ By contrast with (4), the two '*E*-type' pronoun-occurrences in 'If a man has a home, it is his castle' are more naturally taken as variable-occurrences bound by implicit universal-quantifier

A Theory of Bondage 135

Recall again the cautionary note of Section I. It is extremely important here to distinguish sharply between the English *sentence* (4*ii*) and its *occurrence* in the discourse-fragment (4). The former is the natural-language analog of an open formula. That is the sentence itself—an expression—whose logical form is given, nearly enough, by 'y was multi-talented'. The occurrence of (4*ii*) in (4) is a horse of a different color. Here the surface form of an occurrence is not a reliable guide to the logical form. The occurrence of (4*ii*) in (4) corresponds not merely to 'y was multi-talented' but to the *whole* of (4'*ii*), in which a restricted quantifier binds the open formula. Though superficially an occurrence of an open formula, the underlying logical form is that of a closed sentence, which 'can be evaluated independently for truth and falsehood'. In effect, the second sentence-occurrence in (4), though syntactically an occurrence of (4*ii*), is semantically an occurrence of (4'*ii*). One could say that the *sentence* (4*ii*) itself is bound in (4), though not by any element of (4*i*)—indeed, not by any element of the surface form of (4). One might even say that the occurrence of (4*ii*) in (4) is a *pro-clause of laziness*; although syntactically an occurrence of (4*ii*), it has the logical form of the whole consisting of (4*ii*) *together with a binding quantifier phrase*. The quantifier phrase itself, though invisible, is present behind the scenes.[38]

---

occurrences. Compare the account of Berger, *ibid.*, at pp. 159–189, 203–227. The analysis Berger provides for discourse-fragments like (4) looks to be a notational variant of (4'). (Berger has informed me that he is inclined to think it is.)

The anonymous referee for *The Philosophical Review* worries that although the two *E*-type pronouns in the following discourse are anaphorically linked to each other, on the analysis proposed here they are not co-bound by the same quantifier-occurrence:

(5) (*i*) I spoke to a philosopher yesterday. (*ii*) He sides with Geach against Evans. (*iii*) He lives in California.

Imagine the referee spoke with only two male philosophers yesterday, one of whom sides with Geach against Evans but does not live in California, the other lives in California but does not side with Geach against Evans. Then (5*ii*) and (5*iii*) are not both true.

The worry is misplaced. The underlying logical form of (5) is arguably given by:

(5') (*i*) [a x: **philosopher**(x)] (**I spoke to x yesterday**).
  (*ii*) [a y: philosopher(y); I spoke to y yesterday] (y **sides with Geach against Evans**).
  (*iii*) [a z: philosopher(z); I spoke to z yesterday; z sides with Geach against Evans] (z **lives in California**).

On this analysis each of the *E*-type pronouns is a bound variable. Whereas (5'*ii*) is true in the envisaged circumstance, (5'*iii*) is false—evidently in conformity with the English sentences they represent. The final occurrence of 'z' in (5'*iii*) is indeed co-bound with the second-to-last, as it should be, by the initial quantifier phrase '[a z]'. It is not co-bound with the occurrences of 'y' in (5'*ii*). Nor should it be. If the two *E*-type pronouns in (5) were co-bound variables, (5*ii*) would be an open sentence and, as such, would not have truth-value. (The conjunction corresponding to (5') is equivalent to the conjunct (5'*iii*) alone.)

[38] The discourse fragment mentioned *supra* in note 32 is plausibly regarded as having an underlying logical form given, nearly enough, by:

(*i*) [**just two** x: **actor**(x)] (x **starred in** *City Lights*).

(*ii*) [every y: actor(y); y starred in *City Lights*] (y **was multi-talented**).

The occurrence of 'they' corresponds to the final occurrence of 'y'. See the previous note. Consider, in contrast, the discourse fragment:

If the occurrence of 'y was multi-talented' in ($4'ii$) is to be regarded as having an extension, it has the open formula's bondage extension: the function that maps individuals in the range of 'y' who were multi-talented to truth and maps those who were not to falsehood. The whole of ($4'ii$)—and hence the occurrence of ($4ii$) in (4)—is true iff the class characterized by this function includes a comedian who composed the musical score for *City Lights*. As was noted, the occurrence of ($4ii$) in (4) is thus true with respect to the possible world W iff Keaton was multi-talented in W.

The very fact that the occurrence of ($4ii$) in (4) has these modal truth-conditions despite the rigidity of 'he' indicates that, contrary to Evans and several of his critics, the 'he' in (4) is not a closed-term occurrence but a bound variable. One can say with some justification that the 'he' in (4)—the occurrence—is a non-rigid designator. But this is not because the occurrence designates Chaplin with respect to one possible world and Keaton with respect to another. It does neither. Where it occurs free—as for example in a deictic use (and not as a pronoun of laziness)—'he' is a rigid designator of its customary extension under a designatum-assignment. If the pronoun-occurrence in (4) is to be regarded as designating at all, it designates the pronoun's bondage extension: the identity function on the range of 'he'. Insofar as the occurrence is non-rigid, it is so only because it has its bondage extension, ranging over different universes with respect to different possible worlds.

APPENDIX

Jeffrey King, as cited in note 22 above, applies a version of Mates's objection against the thesis that demonstratives are directly referential singular terms. Quantification into a complex demonstrative is odd at best. Although King assumes it is permissible, almost all his examples involve, or appear to involve, a stylistically altered definite description rather than a genuine demonstrative, e.g., 'Every professor cherishes that first publication of his.' (Compare with (3).) Where the phrase 'that first publication of his' occurs as a genuine demonstrative, it should be possible to delete the word 'first' by pointing to the publication in question. But this is problematic with King's example.

The issue is significant, but set it aside. King explicitly aims to establish the conclusion that at least some complex demonstratives (the expressions) are not singular

(i) A man and a woman starred in *City Lights*. (ii) The man was multi-talented.

If this does not entail that only one man starred in *City Lights* (... 'Another man who also starred in *City Lights* was not multi-talented'), its logical form is arguably given by,

(i) [a x: **man**(x)] (x starred in *City Lights*) **and** [a x: **woman**(x)] (x **starred in** *City Lights*).
(ii) [a y: man(y); y starred in *City Lights*] ([**the** z: **man**(z)]($z = y$) **was multi-talented**).

It is an interesting question under what circumstances a so-called E-type pronoun or similar occurrence is bound by an implicit (typically restricted) universal-quantifier occurrence and under what circumstances it is bound instead by an implicit existential-quantifier occurrence. In many cases, the issue might not be settled unambiguously—for example, 'Some senators are liars, but they have redeeming qualities.' It is possible that some E-type pronouns (occurrences) are pronouns of laziness rather than bound.

terms at all, let alone directly referential singular terms. His argument employs the following tacit premise: (*K*1) *Any sentence φ_β containing a directly referential occurrence of singular term β not within the scope of an indirect, intensional, or quotational operator expresses as its semantic content a singular proposition in which the designatum of that same occurrence of β occurs as a component.* The conclusion King derives using this premise is that bound occurrences of complex demonstratives are not *directly referential occurrences*, that is the occurrence's semantic content is not the expression's customary designatum. Although King evidently believes this refutes the target thesis, strictly speaking the target thesis is perfectly compatible with this conclusion—just as Mates's sub-conclusion before invoking (*M*) is compatible with the Fregean thesis that definite descriptions are singular terms. An additional premise is required to validate King's argument against the target thesis: (*K*2) *If a singular term β is directly referential, then every occurrence in a sentence of β not within the scope of an indirect, intensional, or quotational operator is a directly referential occurrence.*

King has confirmed in correspondence that he accepts (*K*2) as well as (*K*1). He adds that he believes both are partly stipulative, by virtue of the meaning of 'directly referential'. (He also adds that (*K*2), because it concerns expressions as well as expression-occurrences, is likely to confuse.) Taken together, (*K*1) and (*K*2) yield the direct-reference analogue of Mates's semantic theorem: (*K*) *Any sentence φ_β containing an occurrence of a directly referential singular term β not within the scope of an indirect, intensional, or quotational operator expresses as its semantic content a singular proposition in which the designatum of that same occurrence of β occurs as a component.* This theorem may be taken as premise in place of (*K*1) and (*K*2).

Jason Stanley has confirmed in correspondence that in his review he interprets King's objection as tacitly invoking (*K*) as a stipulative premise—or alternatively, (*K*1) and (*K*2). Stanley, *ibid.*, maintains that whereas Mates's original argument and others like it fail—essentially on the same grounds argued in the text above—King's variant of Mates's argument is nevertheless decisive against the thesis that demonstratives are directly referential singular terms. Stanley's position is based on his contention that an intensional semantics of content (as opposed to classical, extensional semantics in the style of Tarski) does not relativize content to assignments of values to variables. Contrary to Stanley, however, wherever there is variable binding, the natural method of systematically assigning contents involves doing so under value-assignments. Church's 'The Need for Abstract Entities in Semantic Analysis' and the Russellian intensional semantics sketched in Section III above both do so explicitly.[39] Mates's argument cannot be made to succeed simply by choosing to speak of the semantic *content* of a definite description occurrence and the individual of which that content is a concept, rather than speaking of the occurrence *designating* the individual.

Contrary to both King and Stanley, (*K*) is not an analytic or stipulative truth. In fact, it has extremely dubious consequences, for example that variables are not directly referential—assuming that a bound variable, since its semantic content is not

---

[39] *Cf.* also my *Frege's Puzzle* (Atascadero, Calif.: Ridgeview, 1986), at pp. 144–147.

the variable's customary designatum, is not a 'directly referential occurrence'. (This is how both King and Stanley understand the phrase.) More specifically, both (*K*2) and (*K*) are evidently falsified by the same paradigm-case as (*M*): bound variables. Furthermore, proponents of the direct-reference theory, though they may accept (*K*1), do not endorse either (*K*2) or (*K*)—again, witness the case of bound variables. Contrary to Stanley, King's argument and Mates's original argument thus evidently fail for the same general reason.[40]

Stanley responds that both (*K*2) and (*K*) are true despite bound variables because the lower-case letter '*x*' (*qua* variable) ambiguously represents two distinct expressions: '*x*'-bound and '*x*'-free. (He maintains that this alleged ambiguity is a corollary of (*K*).) The bondage extension of a variable is indeed distinct from its customary extension, and one might choose to express this (I believe misleadingly) by saying that the variable is *ambiguous*, having a *bondage reading* distinct from its *customary* or *default reading*. (It is incorrect to express this by saying that a bound occurrence and a free occurrence of '*x*' are occurrences of different *expressions*.) Expressing the point in terms of an 'ambiguity' between customary and bondage readings, however, is ineffective as a defense of King's objection. The bondage semantics of any open expression deviates from the customary semantics, for example, 'the only woman waiting for *him*', '*his* first publication', and so forth. Insofar as open expressions are deemed *ipso facto* ambiguous, the thesis that King's argument aims to refute is that demonstratives *on their customary readings* are directly referential singular terms. The alleged bondage reading is irrelevant.

---

[40] See note 28. There is a similarly corrected version of King's (*K*2): (*K*2′) *If a singular term β is directly referential, then every free occurrence in a sentence of β not within the scope of any nonextensional operator (other than classical variable-binding operators) is a directly referential occurrence.* As with the replacement of (*M*) by (*M″*), and (*M*⁺) by (*M*⁺′), correcting (*K*2) effectively blocks King's argument.

PART II

APRIORITY

7

How to Measure the Standard Meter (1987)

I

There is *one* thing of which one can say neither that it is one meter long, nor that it is not one meter long, and that is the Standard Meter in Paris.—But this is, of course, not to ascribe any extraordinary property to it, but only to mark its peculiar role in the language-game of measuring with a meter-rule.

So says Wittgenstein (*Philosophical Investigations* §50). Kripke sharply disagrees:

This seems a very 'extraordinary property', actually, for any stick to have. I think [Wittgenstein] must be wrong. If the stick is a stick, for example, 39.37 inches long (I assume we have some different standard for inches), why isn't it one meter long? (*Naming and Necessity*, Harvard University Press and Basil Blackwell, 1972, 1980, at p. 54).

Kripke goes on to argue that it not only would be correct to say of the Standard Meter that it is exactly one meter long, but the very fact about the Standard Meter that it is exactly one meter long, although it is only a contingent fact, is in some sense knowable *a priori*:[1]

We could make the definition more precise by stipulating that one meter is to be the length of S at a fixed time t_0.... [A] man who uses the stated definition [is] using this definition not to *give the meaning* of what he called 'the meter', but to *fix the reference*.... There is a certain length which he wants to mark out. He marks it out by an accidental property, namely that there is a stick of that length. Someone else might mark out the same reference by another accidental property.... Even if this is the *only* standard of length that he uses, there is an intuitive difference between the phrase 'one meter' and the phrase 'the length of S at t_0'. The first phrase is meant to designate rigidly a certain length in all possible worlds, which in the actual world happens to be the length of stick S at t_0. On the other hand, 'the length of stick S at t_0' does not designate anything rigidly.... [T]he 'definition', properly interpreted,

---

I am grateful to Graeme Forbes, Eli Hirsch, Saul Kripke, Mark Richard, and Timothy Williamson for their comments on an earlier draft.

[1] The present discussion is predicated on the common myth that the unit of length, one meter, was at one time fixed by the length of a particular bar used as a standard and kept in Paris. In reality, the Standard Meter is kept in Sevres, near Paris, and is considerably greater than one meter in length; the term 'meter' was defined as the length between two particular scratches that had been carefully cut into the bar. (How far apart? Wittgenstein: 'Don't ask'. Kripke: 'You want to know how far apart? One meter, what else?') The meter is no longer so defined. (Neither is the metre. Apparently it is now defined as the distance light travels in a certain fixed fraction of a second.)

does *not* say that the phrase 'one meter' is to be *synonymous* (even when talking about counterfactual situations) with the phrase 'the length of S at t_0' but rather that we have *determined the reference* of the phrase 'one meter' by stipulating that 'one meter' is to be a *rigid* designator of the length which is in fact the length of S at t_0. So this does *not* make it a necessary truth that S is one meter long at t_0....

What, then, is the *epistemological* status of the statement 'Stick S is one meter long at t_0' for someone who has fixed the metric system by reference to stick S? It would seem that he knows it *a priori*. For if he used stick S to fix the reference of the term 'one meter', then as a result of this kind of 'definition' (which is not an abbreviative or synonymous definition), he knows automatically, without further investigation, that S is one meter long. On the other hand, even if S is used as the standard of a meter, the *metaphysical* status of 'S is one meter long' will be that of a contingent statement, provided that 'one meter' is regarded as a rigid designator: under appropriate stresses and strains, heatings or coolings, S would have had a length other than one meter even at t_0.... So in this sense, there are contingent *a priori* truths. (*ibid.*, pp. 54–56.)

... The case of fixing the reference of 'one meter' is a very clear example in which someone, just because he fixes the reference in this way, can in some sense know *a priori* that the length of this stick is a meter without regarding it as a necessary truth. (*ibid.*, p. 63)[2]

Wittgenstein's claim that the sentence in question is unassertable because of the Standard Meter's 'peculiar role in the language-game' goes much further than the doctrine held by the empiricists that such definitions are devoid of proper cognitive, extra-linguistic factual content. By contrast with Wittgenstein, the empiricists argued that the sentence does indeed express *a priori* knowledge, but only because it does not express a *matter of fact* and instead expresses a *relation of ideas* (or a linguistic convention devoid of cognitive, factual content, etc.). Kripke's claim that the meter sentence is contingent *a priori* is significant, in part, because it contradicts this empiricist tradition. If Kripke is correct, the meter sentence expresses a matter of contingent fact. My chief concern in this paper, however, is not with the relation of either Wittgenstein's or Kripke's views to the doctrine of empiricism (vexing issues in themselves), but more directly with the apparent divergence between Kripke and Wittgenstein over the question of the assertability and epistemic justification of the meter sentence.

Either Wittgenstein is wrong or Kripke is wrong. For surely if one who defines 'meter' as the length of the standard S at t_0 can thereby know *a priori* that S is exactly one meter long at t_0, as Kripke claims, then *pace* Wittgenstein, one can correctly say of the standard that it is indeed one meter long at t_0. This follows from the trivial fact that knowledge entails truth and truth entails (is?) assertability. Who is right and who is wrong?

It must be admitted that Kripke has more plausibility on his side than Wittgenstein does. Still, my answer is that Kripke and Wittgenstein are probably both wrong to some extent. To the extent that Wittgenstein is wrong, some of what Kripke says

---

[2] In a footnote to this passage Kripke acknowledges that his claim that such sentences as 'Stick S is exactly one meter long at t_0' express *a priori* knowledge (for one who so fixes the reference of 'meter') may seem implausible, and that some version or variant of its denial may be true.

is right. More interestingly, the extent to which Kripke is right suggests that in *some* sense, a significant part of what Wittgenstein says may also be right. Frankly, I suspect Wittgenstein is ultimately completely wrong regarding the Standard Meter. Nevertheless, some of what I shall say here provides a measure of support (of some sort) for Wittgenstein's paradoxical observations concerning the Standard Meter. Specifically, I shall propose an epistemic paradox that might, to some extent, vindicate Wittgenstein's enigmatic remark. I make no claim, however, to be faithfully capturing Wittgenstein's intent. In the passage from which Wittgenstein's remark was extracted, he is discussing issues concerning our use of language as a means of representation, and is not explicitly concerned with the epistemological issues I will enter into here.

II

I argued in *Frege's Puzzle*[3] that the disputed meter sentence is (apparently contrary to Wittgenstein) true, but (apparently contrary to Kripke) contingent *a posteriori* rather than contingent *a priori*. In judging the sentence contingent, I followed Kripke in gainsaying the traditional empiricist claim that such definitional sentences do not express matters of extra-linguistic fact, but I went further than Kripke by rejecting even the less controversial (not to say *un*controversial) doctrine that such sentences express *a priori* knowledge.[4]

I shall not rehearse the full argument for aposteriority. Instead, I shall merely sketch the main premisses, and leave their defence as a homework exercise for the reader. (Warning: This exercise should not be attempted by the squeamish.) For this purpose let us call the length at t_0 of S (that is, the length one meter or 39.3701 inches), 'Leonard'. Leonard is an abstract quality, a species of the generic Lockean primary quality *length*. We assume that the measurement-term 'meter' is introduced in such a way that a phrase of the form ⌜α meters⌝, where α is a term referring to some number n, is itself a singular term referring to the length that is exactly n times as great as Leonard.[5] We assume further that the sentence 'The length at t_0 of S, if S exists, is

---

[3] Cambridge, Mass.: Bradford Books/MIT Press, 1986, pp. 140–142.

[4] For a similar rejection of a-priority for definitional sentences like Kripke's meter sentence, see Michael E. Levin, 'Kripke's Argument Against the Identity Thesis', *Journal of Philosophy*, 72, 6 (March 27, 1975), pp. 149–167, p. 152n; Alvin Plantinga, *The Nature of Necessity* (Oxford University Press, 1974), pp. 8–9n; and Keith Donnellan, 'The Contingent *A Priori* and Rigid Designators', in P. French, T. Uehling, and H. Wettstein, eds, *Contemporary Perspectives in the Philosophy of Language* (Minneapolis: University of Minnesota Press, 1979), pp. 45–60. My own argument, while not exactly the same as Donnellan's, owes a great deal to his and has much of the same flavor.

[5] The phrase ⌜α meters⌝ probably should not be regarded as a simple proper name. Whereas the '2' in the phrase '2 meters' seems to be replaceable by a variable for existential generalization on a sentence like 'The length of S is 2 meters', it is certainly not thus replaceable in a genuine name like 'R2-D2'. In *Frege's Puzzle*, I made the somewhat artificial assumption that the term 'meter' itself was a proper name referring to Leonard. A more plausible account parses the word 'meter' and its pluralization 'meters', as comprising a simple (non-compound) *functor* (like the 'squared' in the algebraic phrase 'three squared'), i.e., an operator that attaches to a singular term to form a new singular term. The functor would attach exclusively to number-terms ('three', '3',

one meter' has as its cognitive information content a Russellian *singular proposition* (David Kaplan) in which Leonard occurs directly as a constituent.[6] (This move in the argument presupposes a highly controversial theory of the nature of propositions, but Kripke is not prepared to reject it.) Let us call this singular proposition 'Peter'. For simplicity, we may assume that Peter has only two constituents: Leonard and the complex property of *being the length of S at t_0 if S exists*. (The fact that Peter actually has a somewhat more complex structure does not matter a great deal to the argument.) Peter is true in all and only those possible worlds in which the very stick S either does not exist at all, or does exist and has at t_0 the very length Leonard. To assert, believe, or know Peter is to assert, believe, or know of the length Leonard that if S exists, it is precisely *that* long at t_0. Therefore, the reference-fixer knows Peter, which is the cognitive content of the meter sentence, *a priori* only if he knows of Leonard without appeal to experience (beyond the experience needed merely to apprehend the proposition) that if S exists, it is precisely that long at t_0. That is, the reference-fixer knows the content of the meter sentence *a priori* only if he knows of Leonard that S, if it exists, is precisely that long at t_0, without his belief that this is so being justified by means of experience. Yet it would seem that no matter what stipulations one makes, one cannot know without resorting to experience such things as that S, if it exists, has precisely such-and-such particular length at t_0. It would seem that one must at least *look at* S's length, or be told that it is precisely that long, etc. Therefore, it would seem that the meter sentence is not *a priori* but *a posteriori*.[7]

---

etc., with grammar determining the propriety of the singular or plural form) to form a compound term referring to a specific length. The function referred to is a systematic assignment of lengths to numbers, and has the entire class of lengths as its range. Measuring the length of an object is a way of determining the (or at least a) number corresponding to the given length. Thus units of measurement (such as the meter or the gram) for a generic quality (such as length or mass) are seen as systematic assignments of particular species of the genus to numbers (something like Gödel-numbering, or its converse). Although I shall not pursue the matter in this chapter, the contrast between the two accounts of the logic of 'meter' is not altogether irrelevant to the issues discussed herein.

[6] I include the proviso 'if S exists' for the benefit of purists, who will point out that S's having Leonard as its length entails S's existence, and since one cannot know *a priori* that S exists, one therefore cannot know *a priori* that S has that length. The more cautious, conditional sentence does not entail S's existence, and indeed is a trivial consequence of 'S does not exist'. (This formulation presupposes a free logic.) In what follows, I will often ignore the complications that result from the inclusion of the proviso.

[7] Gareth Evans, in 'Reference and Contingency', *The Monist*, 62 (April 1979), pp. 161–189, defends Kripke's claim that such sentences as the meter sentence are *a priori*. Evans replaces Kripke's example with his own, in which a reference-fixer introduces the name 'Julius' for whoever uniquely invented the zip. Evans argues (pp. 172–173) that in putting forward such a sentence as 'If anyone uniquely invented the zip, Julius did' as not entailing the named entity's existence (see the preceding footnote), Kripke presupposes that the newly introduced name ('Julius') is a 'Fregean name', having descriptive content that may determine no referent. (The argument for this, which is largely implicit, appears to be that if the name contributed its referent, rather than a descriptive content, to the proposition expressed, then since a proposition cannot exist unless each of its constituents exist, the sentence could not be true with respect to a circumstance in which Julius does not exist.) Indeed, Evans defends the claim of a-priority by implicitly conflating the content of the sentence with something like that of the modally (nearly) equivalent, logically true

Notice that someone who has heard of the stick S but has not yet seen it could still introduce the term 'meter' by means of the description 'the length of S at t_0'.[8] If

---

sentence 'If anyone uniquely invented the zip, then the actual inventor of the zip did', in which the modal description 'the actual inventor of the zip', which has replaced the name 'Julius', has its indexical, modally rigid use. (See, for example, pp. 183–185, especially the last paragraph beginning on p. 184.) The alleged presupposition that the newly introduced name has descriptive content, in this sense, is something Kripke surely denies. Indeed, that proper names are not descriptive, in Evans's sense (even when their reference is fixed by description) might be regarded as the central thesis of *Naming and Necessity*. *Cf.* my *Reference and Essence* (Basil Blackwell and Princeton University Press, 1982), chapter 1, especially pp. 14–16, 21–23. Contra Evans, the use of free logic involves no presupposition to the contrary. (The implicit argument for the presupposition is inapplicable to the phrase 'one meter' in any case, since Leonard presumably exists in every possible circumstance. More important, the argument is unsound; Peter does not exist in any possible circumstance in which S does not exist, yet it is true with respect to any such circumstance. *Cf. Naming and Necessity*, pp. 21n, 78. For related discussion, see *Reference and Essence*, pp. 35–40, and my 'Existence', in J. Tomberlin, ed., *Philosophical Perspectives I: Metaphysics*, Atascadero: Ridgeview, 1987, pp. 49–108.) The central question before us is whether the meter sentence is *a priori* for the reference-fixer when the phrase 'one meter' is presumed to *lack* descriptive content, in the relevant sense, and is presumed instead to have been introduced in the way Kripke explicitly proposed. Evans's conflation of such a sentence with a logically true surrogate conflicts with one of the main premisses of the argument just presented: that (something like) Leonard itself occurs directly as a constituent of the content of the meter sentence, rather than being represented therein by the content of a description, so that knowledge of the fact described by the meter sentence is *de re* knowledge of Leonard that S, if it exists, is that long at t_0. (As I have said, Kripke is not prepared to reject this premiss.) I do not deny that the corresponding logically true sentence 'The length at t_0 of S, if it exists, is the actual length at t_0 of S' is contingent *a priori*. By the same token, however, knowledge of the fact it describes is not *de re* knowledge concerning Leonard. (See footnotes 10 and 11 below.)

[8] David Kaplan recommended that Russell's friend who had a trying exchange with a touchy yacht owner might have done something exactly like this in order to convey what the yacht owner refused to understand him as saying. See Kaplan's 'Bob and Carol and Ted and Alice', in J. Hintikka, J. Moravcsik, and P. Suppes, eds, *Approaches to Natural Language* (Dordrecht: D. Reidel, 1973), pp. 490–518, p. 501. If Kripke were correct that doing so makes the specification of the length of the object an *a priori* truth, the yacht owner's original reply would still be apt and Kaplan's recommended strategy would be unsuccessful. There is considerable tension between this passage from Kaplan and some of his other writings—e.g., in 'Dthat', in P. French, T. Uehling, and H. Wettstein, eds, *Contemporary Perspectives in the Philosophy of Language*, pp. 383–400, p. 397, and especially in 'Demonstratives', in J. Almog, J. Perry, and H. Wettstein, eds, *Themes from Kaplan* (Oxford University Press, 1987), sections XVII ('Epistemological Remarks') and XXII ('On Proper Names')—wherein something close to Kripke's position is explicitly endorsed.

My own view (which is similar in this respect to Donnellan's—see footnote 4 above) is that Kaplan's examples ('the shortest spy', 'the first child to be born in the twenty-second century', 'the length of your yacht') might be used to *demonstrate* that the reference-fixer in Kripke's story does not know of Leonard *a priori* that it is the length at t_0 of S (or that 'one meter' refers to it, in his present idiolect, etc.). In this I agree with Kaplan's former view, enunciated in 'Quantifying In', in L. Linsky, ed., *Reference and Modality* (Oxford University Press, 1971), pp. 112–144, at pp. 126–127, and especially 135. Unfortunately, the view has become controversial. In addition to Kaplan's more recent writings see Ernest Sosa, 'Propositional Attitudes De Dicto and De Re', *Journal of Philosophy*, 71 (December 1975), pp. 883–896. Quine's views have also taken a turn towards a kind of latitudinarianism much like Sosa's. See his 'Intensions Revisited', in P. French, T. Uehling, and H. Wettstein, eds, *Contemporary Perspectives in the Philosophy of Language*, pp. 268–274, at pp. 272–273. (But see footnote 17 below.) A more extreme latitudinarian view has also been endorsed, for example by Stephen Schiffer in 'The Basis of Reference', *Erkenntnis*, 13 (1978), pp. 171–206. (The paper, however, involves a curious

the reference-fixer in this case has a wildly mistaken impression as to S's actual length (and so uses the description *referentially*, in Donnellan's sense, to refer to a very different length), or has no opinion whatsoever regarding S's length (and so uses the description *attributively*), it would clearly be incorrect to describe him or her as knowing *a priori* of Leonard that S, if it exists, is exactly that long at t_0. It is only after the reference-fixer sees S's length for himself (or is told it, etc.) that the proposition Peter becomes a piece of knowledge. In his description of the reference-fixing situation, Kripke had in mind a case in which the reference-fixer sees S there in front of him and uses the description referentially to refer to that length.[9] In such a case, it is correct to say that the reference-fixer knows Peter, but, it would seem, only because he has had the experience needed to acquire this knowledge.

The reference-fixer can know without looking at (or being told, etc.) S's length that the length at t_0 of S, if it exists, is the length he means (in his present idiolect, as determined by his own overriding intentions) by 'one meter'. Perhaps this even qualifies as genuine *a priori* knowledge; it depends on whether one's knowledge of one's own intentions is ultimately justified by appeal to experience. For the sake of argument, let us agree that it is *a priori*. The reference-fixer could infer from this that the length at t_0 of S, if it exists, is one meter (and thereby know of Leonard that S, if it exists, is precisely that long at t_0) if only he knew of Leonard that the phrase 'one meter' refers to it (in his present idiolect, if S exists). But this is precisely what the reference-fixer apparently cannot know, without having an appropriate experience in which S plays a significant role. Pending this additional experience, all that the reference-fixer knows is the general proposition that the phrase 'one meter' refers (in his present idiolect) to whatever length S has at t_0, if S exists (and is non-referring otherwise).[10] In fact, the natural order of things is just the reverse: the reference-fixer

---

inconsistency on that point, among the definition in note 4, the proposal on p. 202, and the example on pp. 203–204.) Kripke has an example that, I believe, decisively refutes extreme latitudinarianism.

[9] This was confirmed by Kripke in conversation.

[10] If this is correct, the reference-fixer cannot know, without some experiential contact involving S, such basic semantic facts about his own word 'meter' as that the phrase 'one meter' refers (in his present idiolect) to one meter (if S exists, and is non-referring otherwise), or that the meter sentence is true (in his present idiolect) if and only if S (if it exists) is one meter long at t_0. In this sense, without additional experience involving S the reference-fixer does not even understand his word 'meter' or any sentence, such as the meter sentence, using (as opposed to mentioning) the word—though he may be in a position to use the word in *asserting* (without apprehending) propositions involving Leonard. (Perhaps, for this reason, use of the phrase 'his idiolect' may not be fully appropriate here; pending suitable experience involving S, the reference-fixer has introduced a version of English that he himself does not fully understand. There may be a weaker sense of 'understand' in which the reference-fixer 'understands' the word 'meter' simply by knowing that it was introduced in such a way that 'one meter' refers to whatever length S has at t_0, if S exists. But understanding 'meter' in this weak sense does not give one the basic semantic knowledge that 'one meter' refers, if S exists, specifically to one meter.) He can know, without experiencing S and simply by knowing a bit of semantics, that the metalinguistic *sentences* 'The phrase "one meter" refers in my present idiolect to one meter' and 'The sentence "S, if it exists, is one meter long at t_0" is true in my present idiolect if and only if S, if it exists, is one meter long at t_0' (in this perhaps extended sense of 'idiolect') are themselves true (in his present meta-idiolect). But his knowledge of these metalinguistic facts is in the same boat as his knowledge that the meter sentence itself is true. He

would ordinarily rely on additional experience to discover first that S has Leonard as its length at t_0, and then infer that 'one meter' refers to Leonard. Both pieces of knowledge are apparently *a posteriori*.

If the claim that the meter sentence is *a priori* is to be maintained in the face of these considerations, its defence must come from fastening onto an important epistemic distinction: the distinction between experience that plays a peculiar role in the *epistemic justification* of a belief (which is relevant to the question of whether the knowledge is *a priori* or *a posteriori*), and experience that merely serves to place the believer in a position to apprehend the proposition in the first place (by giving him or her the requisite concepts, for example), and does not play the relevant role in the epistemic justification of the belief. Thus, for example, the fact that one must have some experience in order to acquire the concept of a bicycle, and so to apprehend the proposition that all bicycles are bicycles, does not alter the fact that the proposition is known *a priori*. One might maintain that the reference-fixer's visual experience of S in the introduction of 'meter' likewise enables the reference-fixer to apprehend Peter but plays no further role in justifying that belief.

The case for apriority along these lines, however, is far from clear. The reference-fixer's visual experience of S *can* play an important role in enabling him to apprehend propositions directly concerning S, but it does play a crucial role in justifying his belief of Peter. Suppose the reference-fixer has got himself into a position of being

---

knows that these sentences are true, but pending the additional experience, he does not understand them—he does not know what they mean or what facts they describe (in the stronger sense)—and he does not know those facts themselves.

Donnellan's argument mentioned supra in footnote 4 is criticized by Evans, *op. cit.*, at pp. 171–176 and *passim*. Evans's criticism, however, seems to be based on a serious misunderstanding of the argument. Specifically, Evans charges (p. 173) that Donnellan's argument (which is, in this regard, essentially the same as the one involving Leonard and Peter) gratuitously assumes the doubtful thesis that the name 'Julius' in Evans's example (see footnote 7 above) cannot have been introduced through fixing its reference by means of the description 'the inventor of the zip' in such a way that 'Julius' is thereby given descriptive content, since one cannot understand this name unless it has a referent. Evans counters that a successful introduction of this sort is indeed possible, and has the consequence that the reference-fixer understands the name 'Julius' whether or not it has a referent. (Donnellan uses a different example.) By contrast, Donnellan explicitly allows, at pp. 47–49, that 'Julius' *could* be introduced as a 'descriptive name', in Evans's sense, stipulated to be shorthand for 'the actual inventor of the zip'. Who is to stop us from doing so? To repeat a point made above, the relevant question is whether the meter sentence is *a priori* when the phrase 'one meter' is presumed *not* to have been introduced as a shorthand description, and is presumed instead to have been introduced in the way Kripke explicitly proposed, without taking on descriptive content. (Perhaps Evans denies the legitimacy, or even the possibility, of stipulating the use of the word 'meter' in this way. But who is to stop us from doing so?) Moreover, Donnellan's general argument allows that a speaker can understand the phrase 'one meter' (in a strong sense of 'understand'), so introduced, even if it is non-referring—simply by learning that it is non-referring. What the argument denies is that the general sort of semantic knowledge acquired through introducing the word 'meter' in the way Kripke envisages (the knowledge that the phrase 'one meter' refers to whatever length S has at t_0, if S exists, and is non-referring otherwise) is sufficient, without additional sensory experience involving S, for the more specific semantic knowledge of Leonard that 'one meter' refers (if S exists) to it. Contrary to the impression created by Evans, the question of whether the former knowledge qualifies as *understanding* the word 'meter' is quite irrelevant to the argument. (Use of the word 'understand' in this connection is apt to cause confusion, in light of the potential ambiguity alluded to in the preceding paragraph.)

able to apprehend propositions directly concerning Leonard somehow *other than* by looking at *S* and conceiving of Leonard as the length of *S*. He comes into the situation of the introduction of 'meter' already grasping the generic concept of length. Suppose that he conceives of Leonard as '*this length here*', pointing to some object other than *S* yet having the very same length. Even if the reference-fixer came to believe of Leonard (so conceived) that *S*, if it exists, is also exactly that long at t_0, but did so somehow solely through contemplation and reflection on his concepts without experiential justification (i.e., not by estimating *S*'s length from its appearance etc.), he still could not properly be said to *know* this of Leonard. At best, it seems more like extremely lucky guesswork. It is only by seeing *S* and its length that the reference-fixer comes to know that *S* (if it exists) is just that long.

Whereas the reference-fixer's visual experience of *S* certainly plays a crucial role in the justification of his belief of Peter, it is arguable that the experience *need not* play the *sort* of role that would disqualify the belief from being *a priori* knowledge. The issue is quite delicate; a great deal depends on the exact meaning of '*a priori*'. It is even possible that the issue is, to some extent, merely verbal. Ordinarily, at least, it would be quite odd to say that one can know *a priori* concerning a certain length that a particular stick (if it exists) is exactly that long. I conjecture that Kripke, in his discussion, either failed to distinguish properly between the *a posteriori* content of the meter sentence, i.e. Peter, and the arguably *a priori* truth that the length at t_0 of *S* is referred to (in the reference-fixer's present idiolect) as 'one meter' (or something similar, such as the proposition that the meter sentence is true in the reference-fixer's idiolect), or else he failed to appreciate that the reference-fixer's visual experience of *S* in the very introduction of the term 'meter' is a crucial part of the justification for the reference-fixer's belief of Peter.[11]

---

[11] In *Frege's Puzzle* I allowed (p. 180) that Kripke had given at least the outline of a mechanism for generating certain contingent *a priori* truths through fixing the reference of a name by means of a definite description, in cases where the description is of a special sort that involves a *de re* (or *en rapport*) connection with the thing described. One example might be 'If I am visually perceiving anyone in the normal non-illusory way, then I am perceiving Irving', where 'Irving' is introduced by the speaker as a name for whoever he is visually perceiving. (This is derived from a similar example proposed by Kripke in a lecture at a conference on Themes from David Kaplan at Stanford University in March 1984, in which Kripke responded to Donnellan's argument and developed and modified his position on the contingent *a priori*.) Kripke has suggested (in the Stanford lecture, and more recently in conversation) that his meter example can be bolstered through the use of a suitable description, perhaps 'the length of the stick presented to me in the normal way by this visual perception', used with introspective ostension to a particular veridical visual perception of *S*.

Although it is quite unlikely, the speaker *could* come to believe the proposition that is the content of such a sentence without proper epistemic justification: Suppose, for example, that the speaker, who is offering a reward for the return of his lost pet cat named 'Sonya', is shown several cats that are indistinguishable from Sonya, and looking coincidentally at Sonya, thinks to himself (with more hope than justification) 'If I am visually perceiving a cat, then I am seeing none other than Sonya herself'—conceiving of Sonya not as '*this* cat I see here in front of me, whether or not it is Sonya' but in the more familiar, everyday manner in which he conceives of the beloved pet. Here the proposition in question is certainly not a piece of *a priori* knowledge, since it is not even a piece of knowledge. If the speaker were to come to believe this same singular proposition, this time conceiving of the cat in the former way rather than in the latter, the belief so formed would be epistemically justified in the appropriate manner. Since the speaker cannot be in a position to

I claimed in *Frege's Puzzle* that actual measurement of *S*'s length by someone is required in order for anyone to know that *S* has Leonard as its length. I did not mean that one must do the measuring oneself. One could be told *S*'s length by someone else who actually measured it, etc. But I thought that at some point an actual measurement by someone was required. Kripke allows in his discussion that the inch may already be in use as a unit of length, independently of the introduction of the meter by the reference-fixer. One function that is filled by the institution of using a unit of length, such as the inch, is that it provides *standard* or *canonical names* for infinitely many otherwise unnamed abstract entities (the particular lengths), exploiting names already in use for the numbers ('39.37 inches', etc.). It seems plausible that if one is a member of a community of speakers for whom there are one or more units of length in use at a particular time, then at least in the typical sort of case, one would count as knowing exactly how long a given object is only if one is in a position to specify the object's length correctly by means of one of its standard names, given in terms of a conventional unit and the (or at least a) correspondingly appropriate numerical expression. It would follow that one counts as knowing exactly how long *S* is at t_0 only if one is able to specify *S*'s length in some such manner as '39.37 inches' or '3.28 feet', etc. Having this ability would seem to depend on *S*'s length having been previously measured—either by oneself, or by an informant, or by someone else who is the ultimate source of the information.

By the time *Frege's Puzzle* made its appearance in print, I realized that this piece of reasoning was flawed by overstatement. When one looks at an ordinary, middle-sized object, one typically sees not only the object; one typically also sees *its length*. To put it more cautiously, one typically thereby enters into a cognitive relation to the length

---

conceive of the cat correctly in the former way unless he sees the cat, his occurrent visual experience of the cat would therefore play a crucial role in the epistemic justification of the belief so formed. In some sense, the speaker would know of the cat in this case that she ('*this* very cat') is the cat he is looking at (if such exists), in part, by *looking* at her. Nevertheless, it is arguable that if the speaker conceives of the cat in the former way (as 'this cat I see here, whoever she is' and not as 'my pet Sonya', etc.), then he believes the singular proposition in question by virtue of the fact that he believes the more general proposition, which is knowable *a priori*, that if he is visually perceiving a cat, then he is perceiving *whichever cat he is perceiving*—together with the external fact that he is perceiving Sonya. If the visual experience does not play the sort of role here that would make the example *a posteriori* rather than *a priori*, then it is arguable that Peter is knowable *a priori* after all—*provided that S* is conceived of not as 'the stick I learned of earlier' but in the appropriate *de re* manner as 'this stick here' (or 'the stick I see here in the normal way', etc.), and Leonard is conceived of not as 'the length of the stick I learned of earlier' nor even (as in Kripke's original example) as 'the length of this stick here' but as 'this *length* here', with ostension to *S*'s length *via S* itself. Otherwise, Peter is known by the reference-fixer only *a posteriori*. Against this, one may be inclined to maintain that, even if *S* and its length are so conceived, the reference-fixer knows only *a posteriori*, by seeing the stick's length, that the stick he sees in the normal way (if it exists) has the length he sees, so that Peter remains *a posteriori*. As I have said, though, the issue may be to some extent merely verbal. There is a great deal more to be said about this sort of case. (I am indebted to Eli Hirsch and to Kripke for fruitful discussion of these, and related matters. Kripke has informed me that he independently arrived at conclusions similar to many of those presented in this paper and discussed them in a lecture on these topics at Notre Dame University in 1986. I have not heard the Notre Dame lecture and am unsure as to the extent of agreement between us. There seems to be a good deal of convergence, though I have the impression that some significant differences between the account given in Kripke's Notre Dame lecture and the present treatment may remain.)

itself, a relation that is analogous in several respects to ordinary visual perception, but that (because perceiving subjects may stand in the relation to abstract qualities like lengths) may not correspond exactly with the relation, standardly called 'seeing', between perceivers and the concrete objects they see. One also typically thereby sees (perhaps in some other extended sense) *the fact* that the object has that very length. Of course, merely perceiving an object will not always result in such empirical knowledge. Perhaps in order to see an object's length one must be able to take in the object lengthwise, from end to end, in one fell swoop. Perhaps the visual presentation cannot be under circumstances that create optical illusions (such as might be created by surrounding the object with miniature artifacts, each reduced to the same scale, etc.). Perhaps not. In any case, if the reference-fixer does indeed see S under the required circumstances, he can thereby know of its present length, Leonard, that S is presently exactly that long.[12] No physical measurement is required beyond merely perceiving the object (taking it in lengthwise in one fell swoop, etc.). But some sensory experience in which S plays a crucial role seems to be required. The meter sentence is apparently *a posteriori*, even if physical measurement is not required for its verification.

The error in my argument for the necessity of measurement was the plausible assumption that to know of Leonard that S (if it exists) is exactly that long at t_0 is to know exactly how long S is at t_0 (provided it exists). I suppose that anyone who knows exactly how long a given object is ordinarily knows of its length that the object is exactly that long. But the converse is not universally true; one can know of an object's length, just by looking at the object (and its length, under appropriately favorable circumstances), that the object is exactly that long. Assuming there is a unit of length in use independently of the object in question, one does not thereby learn exactly *which* length the object's length is, as one would (for example) by physically measuring the object in terms of the conventional unit. Knowing exactly how long something is typically requires more than merely perceiving the object.

III

This brings us to Wittgenstein's paradoxical observation concerning the unassertability of the meter sentence. Wittgenstein claims that one can say of S neither that it is one meter long, nor that it is not one meter long. With part of this, there can be no quarrel. One assuredly cannot properly say of S that it is not one meter long, since that would be straightforwardly false. Why, then, can one not properly say of S that it is one meter long?

Let us modify Kripke's story slightly. Suppose there is no standard unit of length in use by the reference-fixer's community. Suppose the reference-fixer is a very clever caveman who is attempting to devise for the first time a precise method for specifying various lengths. He hits on the brilliant idea of establishing a convention of specifying every length whatsoever as a multiple (whole or fractional) of some one, specially

---

[12] Thus I cannot accept the argument proposed on my behalf by Ralph Kennedy in 'Salmon Versus Kripke on the *A Priori*', *Analysis*, 47, 3 (June 1987), pp. 158–161.

selected length, which will serve as the standard unit of length. He arbitrarily selects for this purpose the length at that moment t_0 of a particularly straight and sturdy stick S that he picks up from among a pile of sticks and holds in his hands. He calls its length 'one meter'. His fellow tribesmen agree to his scheme. The length at t_0 of stick S, i.e. Leonard, happens to be 39.3701 inches, though of course, no one is in a position prior to the reference-fixer's flash of brilliance to specify its length using inches or any other unit of measurement, since there was no such thing until the historic moment t_0. Using a compass and a straightedge, the reference-fixer carefully scratches calibrations onto the stick, marking them '$\frac{1}{2}$', '$\frac{1}{4}$', '$\frac{3}{4}$', etc., down to a very fine degree, say 128ths. The clever caveman knows that with this new tool, given any middle-sized object and sufficient time, anyone can now determine the object's length with a very high degree of precision. His people have a new prize possession, the only standard measuring rod on Earth. Soon the measuring rod is in such great demand that every household has its own, carefully crafted duplicate—each carefully measured against the original. A new institution has been born: measuring with a meter-rule.

Does the reference-fixer in this case know at t_0 that S is exactly one meter long? Yes, simply by looking at it. Surely he need not measure S against itself in order to determine its length as a multiple of the standard length. In fact, there is no clear sense to be made of the idea of measuring the standard itself by means of itself, or even against any of its facsimiles. Its length *is* the standard length, by stipulation. If the reference-fixer can know of S's length, Leonard, just by looking, that S is presently exactly that long, then in some sense he cannot fail to know that S's length is exactly one times that length—except by not seeing it under appropriately favorable circumstances. Physical measurement is not only unnecessary; the very notion is in some sense inapplicable to this case.[13]

But an interesting philosophical difficulty arises once we say that the reference-fixer does know that S is exactly one meter long. He has deliberately established a convention of measuring objects in order to determine their lengths, and of specifying those lengths as multiples of a standard unit of length. Within the framework of this institution or 'language-game', one counts as knowing *how* long something is (as opposed to merely knowing of its length that the object is that long), typically, if and only if one is in a position to specify its length correctly as a multiple of the standard length (for example, as '3 and 27/32 meters')—within the degree of precision epistemically accessible to the community in the current state of scientific knowledge. It would seem that anyone who can correctly specify that a given object is exactly n meters long (with sufficient epistemic justification, understanding what the specification means,

---

[13] Of course, one may later measure the standard against (say) one of its duplicates in order to check whether the standard has *changed* in length over time (or, as Kripke and James Tomberlin pointed out, in order to verify that it is indeed the original standard)—provided one has reason to believe that the duplicate itself has not changed in length. But we are here concerned with how the reference-fixer knows *at t_0* of Leonard that S is that long *at t_0*. The fact that the length of the standard does not remain fixed over time introduces a host of issues that are largely irrelevant to the purposes of this paper. The problem I shall discuss would arise even if S did not change in length over time and even if the reference-fixer knew this. For simplicity, I shall simply presuppose that the reference-fixer knows that S's length remains constant.

etc.) knows exactly how long that object is. Thus, if the reference-fixer knows that S is precisely one meter long, it would seem that he knows precisely how long S is. If Kripke's claim in this connection were correct, the reference-fixer would know exactly how long S is (provided it exists) *a priori*! This would be quite astonishing, but we have seen that Kripke's claim seems incorrect. In order to know that S is exactly one meter long, the reference-fixer must look at (or be told, etc.) S's length. However, we still get a rather curious result, not unlike Kripke's claim that the reference-fixer knows S's length *a priori*: if the reference-fixer knows without measuring and just by looking that S is precisely one meter long, then *he knows precisely how long S is without measuring and just by looking*.

Indeed, knowing that a given object's length is exactly n times that of another object (the standard) cannot give one knowledge of how long the first object is unless one already knows how long the second object is. If one knows only that the length of the first is n times that of the second without knowing how long the second object is, one knows only the proportion between the lengths of the two objects without knowing how long *either* object is. Thus, if measurement is ever to give one knowledge of how long an object is, one must already know how long the standard itself is. Yet we have just seen the reference-fixer could not have come to know exactly how long S is by actually measuring S. Physical measurement is out of the question. If he has this knowledge, he must have acquired it simply by *looking at S*'s length, under appropriately favorable circumstances.

Suppose the reference-fixer wishes to know exactly how long his spear is. Can he tell just by looking at its length, without taking the trouble to measure? It would seem not. Now that there is an institution of measuring with a meter-rule, he can do much better than estimating the spear's length solely on the basis of its visual appearance. He can physically measure it. In fact, it would seem that he *must* physically measure the spear if he wishes to know *exactly* how long it is. Why is measurement not equally required in order for him to know exactly how long S is? Because of its unique role in the language-game of determining length with a meter-rule. Measuring the stick itself is, in some sense, impossible. There is nothing to measure S against that is not itself measured ultimately against S.

The caveman could try to do the same thing for the spear that he did for S. He could scratch calibrations into the spear at its midpoint, and so on, proposing the spear as a second and rival standard of measurement. Would this little exercise make it possible for the caveman to know exactly how long the spear is just by looking at it, as he can in the case of S? If so, then it would seem that he does not need to measure *anything*—or at least any ordinary middle-sized object—in order to know precisely how long it is. He need only look at it and propose to use its length as a new unit of length. Clearly, this would defeat the purpose of the institution of measuring: it would violate the rules of the language-game. No, if the caveman wishes to know exactly how long his spear is, he must do much better than merely look at it and perform a little ritual. He must measure it against the standard S, or by proxy against one of the many facsimile measuring sticks that have since been constructed, etc.

This makes S epistemically quite unique *vis à vis* the reference-fixer. No other object is such that he can know precisely how long it is just by looking at it. Once an institution of measuring lengths is put into operation, knowing how long an object is—at least if the object is something other than the standard itself—requires a little elbow grease. This is true even of the duplicate measuring sticks. But how could S have become knowable in a way that no other object is knowable? The measuring rod S was chosen entirely arbitrarily by the reference-fixer to serve a special purpose: all lengths are to be specified as multiples of its length. Despite its 'peculiar role in the language-game', it is still a stick, a physical object subject to the same natural laws and knowable in the same way as any other. If the reference-fixer had selected some other stick in place of S as the standard—as well he might have—the other stick would play the special role in the language-game. Its length, rather than Leonard, would be the one in terms of which all others are to be specified. In order to know precisely how long S is, one would simply have to measure it (or be told by someone who measured it, etc.). The reference-fixer's accidental selection of S as the standard could not have made it knowable in some direct way, quite different from the way it would have been knowable if it had not been selected in the first place. The reference-fixer cannot simply *legislate* that he knows exactly how long S is, any more than he can legislate that he knows exactly how long his spear is. The accidents and whims of human history and culture do not alter the nature of our epistemic relations to external objects. The laws of epistemology (if there are any such things) are *universal*. They do not play favorites by singling out this or that arbitrarily selected, inanimate object as epistemically special. If the laws of epistemology say *in order that thou knowest how long a physical object is, thou shalt measure it*, they do not make an exception in the case of some favorite stick.[14]

Thus as soon as we say that the reference-fixer knows that S is one meter long, we are embroiled in a paradox. The language-game of measuring with a meter-rule involves a simple criterion for knowing how long something is. In order for the reference-fixer to know how long anything is, he must be able to specify its length in meters *and* he must know how long the Standard Meter is. Saying that he knows that S is exactly one meter long attributes to him knowledge of exactly how long the Standard Meter is. But he could not have acquired this knowledge through measurement. If he has such knowledge, he can only have acquired it by simply looking at S. This would require S to be what it cannot be: knowable in a unique way in which no other object is knowable and in which it itself would not be knowable if it had not been arbitrarily selected as the standard. These considerations invite the skeptical conclusion that the reference-fixer does not know after all that S is exactly one meter long. This, in turn, leads to an even stronger skeptical conclusion. For if the reference-fixer does not know how long S is, he cannot know, and cannot even

---

[14] Thus, apparently, the reasoning in *Frege's Puzzle* would not have been overstated if Kripke's example had included the feature that there are no rival units of length defined independently of the meter. As I said at the end of Section II above, if there is a rival system of measurement that supersedes the metric system, the reference-fixer's knowing of Leonard that S is exactly that long does not guarantee his knowing exactly how long S is. But where there is no rival system, to know that something is exactly n meters long is to know exactly how long it is, and knowing exactly how long something is apparently requires measurement. See footnote 19 below.

154   *Apriority*

discover, how long *anything* is. Measuring an object's length using S only tells him the ratio of that object's length to the length of S.

The problem leads to an even more disturbing result. Suppose we grab the bull by the horns and deny that the reference-fixer knows the length of S or of anything else. Even if we say merely that S is *in fact* exactly one meter long, while not suggesting that the reference-fixer knows this, we pragmatically implicate that *we* know that S is exactly one meter long, thereby opening the door to the same skeptical paradox. For if we know that S is exactly one meter long, then (assuming S's length were the ultimate unit of length-measurement, in terms of which all other such units are ultimately defined) we must have come to know precisely how long S is simply by looking at its length, without measurement. This would make S inexplicably unique, differing in epistemic accessibility from all other objects, and from what it would have been if it had not been selected as the standard, solely by virtue of the special role it has arbitrarily come to occupy as the result of an accident of human history and culture. Since this is impossible, we are drawn to the skeptical conclusion that we do not know, and cannot discover, how long anything is! If this argument is sound, we are epistemically unjustified in saying of S that it is exactly one meter long at t_0. This comes very close to Wittgenstein's enigmatic claim.

There is a more general form of skepticism, of which the problem of the Standard Meter is only a special case. Analogous skeptical doubts can be raised in connection with other standards, such as the period of the earth's rotation on its axis, midnight Greenwich time, and so on. We may call the general form of skepticism exemplified by these examples *Does-anybody-really-know-what-time-it-is skepticism*.

This general problem arises in a particularly sharpened form in connection with the transcendental number π. Let us assume that the Greek letter 'π' was introduced as a standard name for the ratio of the circumference of a circle to its diameter, analogously to the introduction of 'meter'. We may then raise questions analogous to those raised in connection with the Standard Meter. First, do mathematicians know that π is the ratio of the circumference of a circle to its diameter? Notice that this is separate from the question of whether mathematicians know that 'π' refers to the ratio of the circumference of a circle to its diameter—which clearly should be answered affirmatively. What we are asking here is whether there is any number that mathematicians know to *be* the ratio of the circumference of a circle to its diameter. Questions arise concerning the various modes of acquaintance by which mathematicians are familiar with π. If mathematicians conceive of π as the ratio of the circumference of a circle to its diameter, or even as the sum of a particular convergent series, is their (or *our*) knowledge of π not merely what Russell called 'knowledge by description'? Or are mathematicians also acquainted with π in some more direct fashion, something like the way in which we are acquainted with 3 or 4 (or even 3.1416)? Presumably, despite the doubts that this line of questions raises, many will insist that mathematicians do know of π that it is the ratio of the circumference of a circle to its diameter. Indeed, the conventional wisdom is that mathematicians know *a priori* that π is the ratio of the circumference of a circle to its diameter. Very well, then, do they know *exactly* what number this ratio is? What exactly is the value of 'π'? The very question seems to demand what it is impossible to produce: a specification of π by means of its full decimal expansion. Providing the decimal expansion of a particular constant is analogous to measuring a particular object to determine its length. It is not enough here (perhaps by contrast with the case of measuring) merely to be able to set upper and lower bounds within a desired (non-zero) margin of error. Whatever margin of error one chooses, there remain infinitely many numbers that have not yet been ruled out. Given that the ratio of the circumference of a circle to its diameter lies somewhere among infinitely many other numbers between these bounds, do mathematicians know which number it is? Since one cannot know the full decimal expansion of π, there seems to be a sense in which no one can know what number π is.[15] It would follow that no one knows, or can even discover, given the diameter of a circle as a rational number, what the circumference is, or what the internal area is, etc. The well-known formulas for computing these values yield only their proportion to the unknown quantity π.

The threat of Does-anybody-really-know-what-time-it-is skepticism gives a point (whether or not it is the intended point) to Wittgenstein's counsel that we not say of S that it is exactly one meter long. Our not saying this about S would indeed mark its peculiar role in the 'language-game' of determining how long objects are with a meter-rule. But how does this help to solve the paradox? It does not.[16]

IV

The paradox revolves around the epistemic notion of *knowing how long* a given object is. This concept is philosophically problematic in precisely the same way as the concept of *knowing who* someone is. In fact, both concepts should be seen as special cases of a more general epistemic notion: that of *knowing which F* a given *F* is, where '*F*' is some sortal. Knowing-who is the special case where '*F*' is 'person'; knowing-how-long is the special case where '*F*' is 'length'.[17] A number of philosophers have

---

[15] Even more analogous to the case of the Standard Meter is the transcendental number e, defined as the base of the logarithmic function whose derivative is the reciprocal function. Just as all lengths are specified in the metric system as multiples of Leonard, so all positive numbers are specified via the Napierian (or 'natural') logarithmic function as powers of e.

[16] 'This was our paradox: no course of action could be determined by a rule, because every course of action can be made out to accord with the rule.' The problem discussed in and around *Philosophical Investigations* §201 is not the same as the epistemological problem just presented. Wittgenstein's (alleged) paradox concerns the concept of following a rule, such as the rule (set of instructions) for determining the length of an object with a meter-rule; Does-anybody-really-know-what-time-it-is skepticism concerns the distinct concept of knowing which thing of a certain kind (e.g., which length) a specially designated thing of that kind is, and in particular, the question of whether the rule for determining length using a meter-rule applies in exactly the same way to the Standard Meter. Even if we have a solution to Wittgenstein's (alleged) paradox, the latter problem still arises.

[17] The relation of knowing which *F*, for a particular *F*, is a relation between a knower and (using the terminology of *Frege's Puzzle*) a singular-term information value, that is, either an individual ('knowing which *F a* is') or an intensional representation thereof ('knowing which *F* the φ is'). As in the special case of length, a distinction should be maintained between knowing of a given *F* that it is α and knowing which *F* is α. One may know of a given thief, without knowing who he or she is but simply by witnessing the crime, that he or she is the person stealing a certain book from the

held that the locution of 'knowing who' is highly interest-relative. Relative to some interests, simply knowing a person's name qualifies as knowing who he or she is: relative to other interests, it does not.[18] If this is correct, then the locution of 'knowing how long' is equally interest-relative. In some contexts, knowing a length's standard name in the metric system counts as knowing which length it is; in other contexts, it does not. One way of spelling out this idea (though not the only way) is to claim that the locution of 'knowing which F' is *indexical*, expressing different epistemic relations with respect to different contexts.[19]

Interest-relative notions can easily lead to paradox, if we shift our interests without noticing it. Epistemic notions, if they are interest-relative, lead to skeptical paradox. Someone whose epistemic situation remains unchanged may be correctly described, relative to one set of interests, as knowing something that, relative to another set, he or she cannot be correctly described as knowing. The appearance of contradiction is due to a sort of equivocation, similar to that typified by the sentence 'Now you see it; now you don't'. If the indexical (or interest-relative) theory of knowing which F is correct, the skeptic is not really denying what we claim when we claim to know something.

---

library. This distinction has often been blurred. See, for example, Donnellan, pp. 52, 57–58; Jaakko Hintikka, *Knowledge and Belief*, Ithaca: Cornell University Press, 1962, at pp. 131–132, and *passim*; and Quine, *loc. cit.* The distinction is upheld in Stephen Boër and William Lycan, *Knowing Who* (Cambridge, Mass.: Bradford Books/MIT Press, 1986), at pp. 132–133; David Kaplan, 'Opacity', in L. Hahn and P. A. Schilpp, eds, *The Philosophy of W. V. Quine* (La Salle: Open Court, 1986), pp. 229–289, at pp. 258–260; and Igal Kvart, 'Quine and Modalities De Re: A Way Out?', *Journal of Philosophy*, 79, 6 (June 1982), pp. 295–328, at pp. 300–301. *Cf.* also the closing paragraph of Section II above.

[18] *Cf.* W. V. Quine, p. 273.

[19] An alternative account would treat the locution 'knows which F' as non-indexical but implicitly ternary-relational, with an additional argument-place for a specification of a particular interest or purpose. *Cf.* the account given in Boër and Lycan, *op. cit.* (I am indebted to James Tomberlin for pointing out that the interest-relative theory need not take the form of an indexical theory.)

Kripke (in lecture) has proposed several examples that appear to demonstrate the dependency (in at least most contexts) of the concept of knowing which F on such contextual factors as one's training and whether a name has become standardized through cultural entrenchment. The thesis that knowing which F is (at least usually) dependent on such factors, however, is largely independent of the interest-relative theory (according to which someone whose cognitive relations to a given F remain unchanged might be correctly described relative to one set of interests as knowing which F the given F is, and relative to another set of interests as not knowing which F the given F is). I believe the former; I am inclined to believe the latter as well.

I am disinclined to believe the analogue of the interest-relative theory with respect to the separate phenomena of *de re* knowledge and *de re* belief. The view that *de re* belief is interest-relative is proffered by Ernest Sosa, *op. cit.*, and endorsed by Quine, *loc. cit. De re* belief, in my view, is simply belief of a singular proposition. In this (trivial) sense, my view makes *de re* belief into a species of *de dicto* belief, i.e. belief of a proposition. If the former notion were interest-relative, *ipso facto* so would be the latter. *Cf.* Kaplan, 'Opacity', *loc. cit.*, and Kvart, *loc. cit.* Some philosophers have held that knowledge generally (knowledge of a proposition or fact, and not merely the special case of knowing which F) is indexical. See, for example, Alvin Goldman, 'Discrimination and Perceptual Knowledge', *Journal of Philosophy*, 73, 20 (November 18, 1976), pp. 771–791; Stewart Cohen, 'Knowledge, Context, and Social Standards', *Synthese* (October, 1987), and 'How to be a Fallibilist', in J. Tomberlin, ed., *Philosophical Perspectives, 2: Epistemology* (Atascadero, Calif.: Ridgeview), pp.91–123.

The skeptic merely has different interests; he or she is changing the subject. There is no disagreement between us as to the facts of the matter.

It seems likely that the paradox outlined in the preceding section arises from some equivocation of this sort. In describing the caveman's situation, we invoke a notion of knowing-how-long for which a necessary and sufficient condition is, roughly, the ability to produce a standard name of the object's length, in terms of the standard unit, while understanding the meaning of that name. Within the confines of the caveman's language-game, knowing how long something is *just is* knowing the proportion of its length to Leonard. For every object but one, satisfying this condition requires actual physical measurement. but the reference-fixer *trivially* satisfies the necessary and sufficient condition for knowing how long S itself is, provided he sees its length. Knowing his own intention in introducing the term 'meter' gives the reference-fixer the ability to produce the standard name of S's length; seeing S's length gives him the understanding he needs of that standard name. (See footnote 10.) In the sense of 'measurement' in which knowing how long something is requires measurement against the standard, merely looking at the standard's length (under the appropriately favorable circumstances) counts as *measuring* the stick itself. In S's case, merely looking is a sort of limiting-case of measuring. The laws of epistemology are not violated; it is just that there are different ways of obeying them.

When we explicitly ask, on the other hand, whether the reference-fixer knows how long the standard itself is, we shift our focus from within the confines of his language-game to looking in on him from the outside. Without taking notice we have raised the ante. From our newer, broadened perspective, knowing how long S is seems to require physically measuring it against a higher standard—one that supersedes and overrides the reference-fixer's standard, one that (by hypothesis) is not available to the reference-fixer himself.

If we raise the same question with respect to our own, or our scientists', current standard, we may raise the ante beyond what anyone is currently in a position to pay. Perhaps there is a legitimate sense in which no one now knows *exactly* how long a meter is. Likewise, perhaps there is a sense in which no one *can* know exactly what number π is. But if there is a sense in which these instances of Does-anybody-really-know-what-time-it-is skepticism are true, what is true in this sense need not concern us. It is like shouting 'Fire!' in a crowded theatre merely because someone is lighting a cigarette. There is still the standard, everyday sense, in which everyone *of course* knows how long the Standard Meter is and everyone *of course* knows what number π is: the Standard Meter is exactly one meter long, and π is the ratio of the circumference of a circle to its diameter. We can expand on this by producing a meter-rule and thereby *showing* how long the Standard Meter is, or by producing a partial decimal expansion of π or instructions for computing its value to whatever number of places is desired. That is all one can have. To demand more than this is to change the rules of the game in such a way that nobody can win. At the other extreme, there are no doubt contexts in which it is true to say that the caveman knows how long his spear is just by looking at it. ('I'll get more respect when everyone sees how long my spear is.') The important fact is that we stand in such-and-such perceptual and cognitive relations to particular objects. In some (perhaps extended) sense of 'see', the caveman sees his spear's length by looking at the spear itself (lengthwise, in one fell swoop, etc.). Some of us are acquainted with π only by knowing an approximation to its decimal expansion. Perhaps there is even a (possibly metaphorical) sense of 'see' in which we may be said to see the ratio of the circumference of a circle to its diameter simply by looking at a diagram. In the end, what does it matter whether we dignify how we stand with the honorific 'knowing which F'?

If all of this is correct, there may be a better reason for not saying of the Standard Meter that it is exactly one meter long. In the circumstances of everyday, non-philosophical commerce, the proposition that the standard is just that long is something nearly everyone counts as knowing. But (in part for that very reason) merely uttering the sentence 'The Standard Meter is exactly one meter long' tends to raise the ante to a level at which its utterance becomes epistemically unjustified—and threatens to invoke the skeptic's favorite level, at which its utterance is in principle unjustifiable. If saying something that is trivially true leads us to say further things that sound much more alarming than they really are, it may be better to say nothing. In any event, this provides one sort of rationale for not saying of the Standard Meter that it is one meter long.

As I have said, however, I do not pretend that this rationale bears any significant resemblance to Wittgenstein's. It is unclear to me whether Does-anybody-really-know-what-time-it-is skepticism is connected with the issues discussed in and around *Philosophical Investigations* §50. If π occupies a unique role in the language-game of mathematics, analogous to the peculiar role of the Standard Meter in the language-game of measuring with a meter-rule, its peculiar role is (happily) not marked by any prohibition against saying that it is the ratio of the circumference of a circle to its diameter. Moreover, if the rationale I have suggested does bear some significant resemblance to Wittgenstein's, then his arresting remark itself is also something that sounds much more alarming than it really is, and in the absence of at least the minimal sort of explicit epistemological stagesetting I have provided here, is probably better left unsaid.

8

How *Not* to Become a Millian Heir (1991)

I

Millianism is a highly contentious doctrine in the theory of meaning. It is the thesis that the contribution made by an ordinary proper name to securing the information content of, or the proposition expressed by, a declarative sentence in which the name occurs (outside of the scope of such nonextensional operators as quotation marks), as the sentence is used in a possible context, is simply the name's referent (bearer) in the given use.[1] The unpopularity of the doctrine stems heavily—perhaps primarily—from the fact that it leads to a serious philosophical difficulty discovered by Gottlob Frege, and which I have dubbed 'Frege's Puzzle': Let a and b be distinct but co-referential proper names such that the identity sentence $\ulcorner a = b \urcorner$ contains information that is knowable only *a posteriori*, and can therefore be informative. Then how can this sentence $\ulcorner a = b \urcorner$ differ at all in cognitive information (propositional) content from $\ulcorner a = a \urcorner$, which is *a priori* and uninformative?

In *Frege's Puzzle*[2] I proposed an analysis according to which the puzzle relies on three components: (*i*) a compositionality principle that propositions formed in the very same way from the very same components are the very same proposition; (*ii*) the principle, which I call 'Frege's Law', that declarative sentences sharing the same cognitive information (propositional) content do not differ in informativeness or epistemological status; and (*iii*) the observation that there are co-referential proper names a and b (for example, 'Hesperus' and 'Phosphorus') such that $\ulcorner a = b \urcorner$ is

---

The present chapter is a sequel to my previous manual, 'How to Become a Millian Heir', *Nous*, 23, 2 (April 1989), pp. 211–220. I thank my daughter, Simone Salmon, who provided almost constant discouragement while I worked on the current manual. It was delivered as a talk to the University of Padua conference on Propositions in May 1990. Further manuals are contemplated.

[1] The term 'Millianism' is derived from Saul Kripke, 'A Puzzle about Belief', in N. Salmon and S. Soames, (eds), *Propositions and Attitudes* (Oxford Readings in Philosophy, 1988), pp. 102–148. I have formulated the doctrine in a neutral manner that accommodates various differing theories regarding the nature of propositions (whether they are structured Russellian propositions, sets of possible worlds, characteristic functions of such sets, etc.).

[2] Cambridge, Mass.: MIT Press/Bradford Books, 1986. For relevant background see also my 'Reflexivity', *Notre Dame Journal of Formal Logic*, 27, 3 (July 1986), pp. 401–429, also in *Propositions and Attitudes*, pp. 240–274; 'How to Measure the Standard Metre', *Proceedings of the Aristotelian Society*, New Series, 88 (1987/1988), pp. 193–217; 'Illogical Belief', in J. Tomberlin, (ed.), *Philosophical Perspectives, 3: Philosophy of Mind and Action Theory, 1989* (Atascadero, Calif.: Ridgeview, 1989), pp. 243–285; and 'A Millian Heir Rejects the Wages of *Sinn*', in C. A. Anderson and J. Owens, (eds), *Propositional Attitudes: The Role of Content in Logic, Language, and Mind* (Stanford: CSLI, 1990), pp. 215–247.

informative and *a posteriori* even though $\ulcorner a = a \urcorner$ is always uninformative and *a priori*. Together these assertions comprise the main premises of a powerful argument against Millianism. Most Millians, if forced to give direct response, would probably reject Frege's Law. And taken in one sense, I would agree. I argued, however, that properly understood, Frege's Law should be seen as analytic, and that the only objectionable assertion is the first half of (*iii*). There can be no co-referential names *a* and *b* such that $\ulcorner a = b \urcorner$ is either *a posteriori* or informative *in the only senses of 'a posteriori' and 'informative' that are relevant to Frege's Puzzle*.

Howard Wettstein and Kai-Yee Wong have recently argued independently that the Millian ought to embrace the first half of (*iii*) and reject the second half.[3] They claim that Millians (at any rate Millians of my ilk), if we are to be consistent, should maintain that for any proper name *a*—or at least any proper name that refers to an empirically observable entity like a person or a planet—the reflexive identity sentence $\ulcorner a = a \urcorner$ is typically neither *a priori* (in something like the traditional sense) nor trivial.

II

Wettstein makes this dramatic claim in the course of an argument that Millians should reject the view, which he calls 'the mental apprehension picture of reference', that using a proper name competently to refer to its referent requires special epistemic contact with the referent (either through the user's association of nontrivial individuating or other substantive properties with the name, or through a special causal connection with the referent). I quote at length:

Frege's data themselves—the idea that two names can, unbeknownst to the competent speaker, co-refer—don't seem all that dramatic. Is it, after all, so obvious, that we should know of any two co-referring names that they co-refer? But put Frege's data together with the mental apprehension picture and sparks fly ... [The] mental apprehension conception is what propels the puzzle. Were we to radically deny the former and adopt an epistemically innocent way of thinking about reference, as I have suggested we should, Frege's data would present no special problem ...

I argued above that Frege's puzzle, so called, is generated not by Frege's data alone, but only in conjunction with the mental apprehension conception of reference. Is it so obvious, I asked, that there is something deeply puzzling about the very idea that a speaker can be competent with two co-referring names, and not know that they co-refer? The radical

---

[3] Howard Wettstein, 'Turning the Tables on Frege: or How is it That "Hesperus is Hesperus" is Trivial?' in J. Tomberlin, (ed.), *Philosophical Perspectives*, 3: Philosophy of Mind and Action Theory, 1989, pp. 317–340; Kai-Yee Wong, '*A Priority* and Ways of Grasping a Proposition', *Philosophical Studies*, 62, 2 (May 1991). A caveat: Wettstein evidently accepts a weakened version of (*iii*). He allows that in some circumstances, which he regards as atypical, $\ulcorner a = a \urcorner$ can be trivial (and presumably *a priori*?) even when $\ulcorner a = b \urcorner$ is both true and informative. Though he does not acknowledge that this, together with (*i*) and (*ii*), is sufficient to generate the puzzle, he presumably joins other Millians in rejecting (*ii*). Wong is also concerned to defend a version of (*iii*) against my analysis. Wong's argument that I should reject the second half of (*iii*) is not put forward as a Millian solution to Frege's Puzzle.

change in perspective I've been encouraging makes even more dramatic the dissolution of the puzzle. ... If one can refer to something without anything like a substantive cognitive fix on the referent ..., then why should it be the slightest bit surprising that a speaker might be competent with two co-referring names, but have no inkling that they co-refer? ...

Rejecting [the mental apprehension picture], we can now see that there is no presumption whatever that co-reference should somehow be apparent to the competent user ...

Indeed, if there is any presumption to speak of here, it is ... that co-reference, except under unusual circumstances, will not be apparent ... What is ... surprising perhaps—and here we turn the tables on Frege—is that '$a = a$' identities are not, in general, trivial ... [The] mere presence of the same name, indeed the same name of the same party, surely does not make the identity trivial. (Wettstein 'Turning the Tables on Frege', pp. 331–332)

That Wettstein's diagnosis of Frege's Puzzle, and his related stance on the alleged informativeness of $\ulcorner a = a \urcorner$, are based on a misunderstanding of the import of the puzzle is proved by the fact that the puzzle arises with equal force even against versions of Millianism (such as Wettstein's) that explicitly reject the 'mental apprehension picture' of referential competence that Wettstein opposes (see note 3). Moreover the puzzle, in its usual formulations ('Hesperus'–'Phosphorus', 'Superman'–'Clark Kent', etc.), does not constitute an objection to orthodox Fregean theory, despite the latter's commitment to the offending picture of referring.[4] Wettstein is correct that competence in the use of a pair of co-referential names generally neither requires nor guarantees knowledge of their co-reference. Even without rejecting the offending picture of referring, however, this observation is not particularly puzzling. Indeed, in the younger days of his *Begriffsschrift*, Frege invoked the possibility of ignorance of co-reference, in tandem with something like the offending picture, as an essential part of a *solution* to Frege's Puzzle.[5] If anyone has ever argued that a competent user's failure to recognize the co-reference of two names in his or her repertoire, together with

---

[4] As I have argued elsewhere, a variant of the original puzzle can be mounted against orthodox Fregean theory, using a pair of (not necessarily co-referential) terms with respect to which a competent user associates the same purely qualitative concepts (in a particular way)—perhaps 'elm wood' and 'beech wood'. See my review of L. Linsky's *Reference and Descriptions*, *Journal of Philosophy*, 76, 8 (August 1979), pp. 436–452, at p. 451, and *Frege's Puzzle*, pp. 73–74; see also Takashi Yagisawa, 'The Reverse Frege Puzzle', in J. Tomberlin, (ed.), *Philosophical Perspectives, 3: Philosophy of Mind and Action Theory, 1989* (Atascadero, Calif.: Ridgeview, 1989), pp. 341–367. The point is echoed in Wettstein's article, though he evidently draws the wrong conclusion concerning the source of the original puzzle, by concentrating on such unusual variants of the original.

[5] In the usual ('Hesperus'–'Phosphorus', 'Superman'–'Clark Kent') cases, the offending picture yields a straightforward explanation of the speaker's failure to recognize the co-reference. It is only in the unusual sorts of cases mentioned in the previous note that a similar explanation may not be available, since these cases purport to refute stronger versions of the offending picture. Weaker versions of the offending picture (which do not require the user's association of fully individuating properties) remain perfectly compatible with the fact that, even in such cases, the user need not be aware of the co-reference, and such weaker versions of the picture do not turn this fact into a philosophical mystery. The offending picture need not purport to explain all cases of the general phenomenon.

principles like (*i*) and (*ii*), spell serious trouble for Millian theory, I am unaware of it. Certainly Frege did not.[6]

In missing the puzzle's point, Wettstein fails to appreciate the puzzle's force. The puzzle arises within Millian theory, and it is a puzzle for the Millian whether or not he or she rejects the picture of referential competence that Wettstein criticizes. Either way, Millian theory allows that the assertion that the names 'Hesperus' and 'Phosphorus' are coreferential is *a posteriori* and informative (to the competent user who is unaware of their co-reference). The puzzle arises from the fact that, evidently, a sentence like 'Hesperus is Phosphorus' (and its Leibniz's-Law consequences, e.g. 'Hesperus is a planet if Phosphorus is') is potentially informative, not merely because it may impart the *a posteriori* linguistic information about itself that it is true (and hence that 'Hesperus' and 'Phosphorus' are co-referential) but, in part, because the information (proposition) semantically *contained* in the sentence—the *nonlinguistic* information that Hesperus is Phosphorus—is *a posteriori*. In the very act of presenting the puzzle, the author of '*Uber Sinn und Bedeutung*' chastised the author of *Begriffsschrift* for mistaking the former information for the latter, and (as the Church–Langford translation argument demonstrates[7]) the later author was right to do so. The nontrivial character of the information that 'Hesperus' and 'Phosphorus' are co-referential is irrelevant to Frege's Puzzle.[8]

One might attempt to defend Wettstein's conflation of semantics with astronomy by pointing out that although the sentence 'Hesperus and Phosphorus are identical' differs in content from ' "Hesperus" and "Phosphorus" are co-referential', these two sentences cannot differ in informativeness for anyone competent in the use of the two names. For such a user knows that 'Hesperus' refers (in English) to Hesperus and that 'Phosphorus' refers to Phosphorus, and from these the bridge principle that *'Hesperus' and 'Phosphorus' are co-referential (in English) if and only if Hesperus is Phosphorus* trivially follows. This sort of consideration raises extremely delicate issues.[9] It is enough for present purposes to note that the observation that a competent user need not be aware of the co-reference of 'Hesperus' and 'Phosphorus' cannot be made to generate a problem for Millianism unless it is relied upon, assuming background knowledge of something like the bridge principle, to establish as a separate and further fact that

---

[6] One philosopher who may have held that competence in the use of a pair of co-referential names requires or guarantees knowledge of their co-reference is Ruth Barcan Marcus. See her contribution to the 'Discussion' of her 'Modalities and Intensional Languages' [*Synthese*, 13 (1961), pp. 303–322], in *Synthese*, 14 (1962), pp. 132–143, at p. 142. The seminal article under discussion contains perhaps the earliest incarnation of contemporary Millianism. See also Saul Kripke, *Naming and Necessity* (Harvard University Press, 1972, 1980), at p. 101. It is doubtful, however, that Marcus (who remains a Millian) retains the view about co-referential names that she expressed in the 1962 discussion. (It is unclear even whether she advocated it then.)

[7] Alonzo Church, 'On Carnap's Analysis of Statements of Assertion and Belief', *Analysis*, 10, 5 (1950), pp. 97–99; also in L. Linsky, (ed.), *Reference and Modality* (Oxford Readings in Philosophy, 1971), pp. 168–170.

[8] *Cf. Frege's Puzzle*, pp. 48–54, 58–60, 77–79.

[9] It is doubtless true that, in at least many such cases, the competent user of 'Hesperus' and 'Phosphorus' should know this bridge principle, but (as a thoroughgoing Millian) I deny that the competent user can always justifiably infer that the two names are co-referential from his knowledge that Hesperus is Phosphorus. See 'Illogical Belief', p. 278, note 19 for a brief discussion.

'Hesperus is Phosphorus' is informative, in the sense that its semantic content can be new information to one who already knows that Hesperus is Hesperus. It is the latter putative fact, and not the former observation, that generates the puzzle. It would be odd to attempt to establish the putative fact by means of the observation; indeed the putative fact seems obvious enough without supporting evidence, and is generally taken for granted.[10] Notice also that the same observation could not be used, in the same way, to establish the putative fact that 'Hesperus is Phosphorus' is *a posteriori*. For the bridge principle itself is also *a posteriori*.[11]

The contrasting sentence 'Hesperus is Hesperus', where both occurrences of the sequence of letters 'Hesperus' are used in the same way, with the same semantic reference, is *uninformative* in the only sense relevant to Frege's Puzzle: the proposition the sentence (so used) semantically contains is a trivial truism. The fact that it may not be

---

[10] *Cf. Frege's Puzzle*, pp. 77–78. Moreover, echoing a further point made in *Frege's Puzzle*, at pp. 12, 51, Wettstein says (p. 326) that his analysis of the puzzle focuses on variants that do not involve identity sentences, such as the puzzle that arises from consideration of 'Hesperus appears in the morning' (informative) and 'Phosphorus appears in the morning' (uninformative). I prefer the example: 'Hesperus is a planet if Phosphorus is' vs. 'Hesperus is a planet if Hesperus is.' (This example is due to Keith Donnellan, who used it for a somewhat different purpose. See my *Reference and Essence*, Princeton University Press and Basil Blackwell, 1981, p. 80. Donnellan's use of the example presupposed that the first sentence of the pair is *a posteriori*. See note 24 below.) It would be especially odd to use the fact that a competent user may be ignorant of the names' co-reference, together with the bridge principle, to establish that such pairs of sentences differ in informativeness (in the relevant sense).

[11] A number of writers (e.g., Quine and his followers) are confused that semantic theorems like the bridge principle mentioned here or so-called '*T*'-sentences ('"Snow is white" is true in English iff snow is white') are analytic, *a priori*, or otherwise trivial. That the bridge principle is *a posteriori* can be demonstrated by translating the (meta-English) formulation given here into another (meta-) language, preserving content. The demonstration can be made especially dramatic for the Millian who accepts that the proposition that Hesperus is Phosphorus is (identical with) the proposition that Hesperus is Hesperus, by translating into a language that has only one name for the planet Venus. *Cf.* Alonzo Church, 'Intensional Isomorphism and Identity of Belief', in N. Salmon and S. Soames, (eds), *Propositions and Attitudes*, pp. 159–168; and Saul Kripke, 'A Puzzle about Belief', *ibid.*, at pp. 133–134.

A related confusion, which is opposite in thrust, lies behind the idea (urged by Joseph Almog at the Padua conference) that a Millian of the sort mentioned in the previous paragraph can (perhaps even *should*) maintain that an English speaker who is competent in the use of the names 'Hesperus' and 'Phosphorus' does not automatically know that 'Hesperus is Phosphorus' means (expresses the proposition) that Venus is Venus. The competent user may be presumed to know the semantic fact that 'Hesperus is Phosphorus' means in English that Hesperus is Phosphorus. For a Millian (of the sort in question), this semantic fact just is the fact that 'Hesperus is Phosphorus' means in English that Venus is Venus. Again, a carefully selected translation into another language should prove to such a Millian that this fact is precisely what the competent user knows; it is not a *further* fact. (It does not follow that such a user can thereby know that 'Hesperus is Phosphorus' is true in English. See note 9 above.)

The confusion common to both cases is essentially that between the content of a sentence *S* and the independent metatheoretic information that *S* is true. (In both cases the *S* in question is itself a sentence of meta-English.) *Frege's Puzzle* emphasizes this distinction as a special case of the general distinction between the information semantically contained in a sentence *S* and information merely pragmatically imparted by utterances of *S*.

apparent on a given occasion that both occurrences of 'Hesperus' are being so used is irrelevant.[12]

III

Wong's challenge to my claim that 'Hesperus is Phosphorus' is *a priori* correctly focuses on the epistemological status of the semantically contained proposition. That proposition, according to Millianism, is the singular proposition about the planet Venus that it is it. On my account, this proposition consists of Venus taken twice and the binary relation of identity (more accurately, identity at *t*, where *t* is the present time). Furthermore, according to my account, when we grasp such a proposition, we take the proposition in some particular *way*, by means of something like a particular mode of familiarity with it. Though I was deliberately vague about what *ways of taking a proposition* are or amount to, it is critical to my attempt to rescue Millianism from puzzles like Frege's that whenever someone grasps a familiar proposition but fails to recognize it (as the one encountered on such-and-such earlier occasion, or as a trivial truism, etc.), he or she takes the proposition in a new and different way. I also said that a true proposition is *a priori* if it is in principle knowable solely on the basis of reflection on its components (conceptual or otherwise), without recourse to sensory experience, and that a true sentence is derivatively *a priori* if its semantically contained proposition is *a priori*.

Wong agrees, initially for the sake of argument, that my characterization of *a priority* more or less captures (or at least does not conflict with) the traditional notion.[13] His objection is that, given my account of our grasp of propositions in general, and given my account of the singular proposition about Venus that it is it in particular, that proposition does not satisfy my own characterization of *a priority*. For in order to know the proposition it is not sufficient on my account to reflect on its components, if one does not take the proposition in an appropriate way. In particular, taking this proposition in the way one would were it presented by the very sentence 'Hesperus is Phosphorus', an empirical investigation would be required to establish it as a piece of knowledge. Wong also questions the correctness of my characterization of *a priority*, arguing that, assuming my account of our grasp of propositions, '*a priority*, as an epistemic notion, should be sensitive to the ways in which a proposition is taken or grasped', so that 'it may be mistaken to characterize *a priority* as applying *primarily* to propositions, as Salmon does'.

---

[12] *Cf. Frege's Puzzle*, pp. 58–60. It is worth noting also that this same fact does not alter the triviality of the further fact that, however the sequence of letters is used, 'Hesperus' so used and 'Hesperus' so used are co-referential.

[13] Noel Fleming has pointed out to me that the characterization may be less restrictive than a traditional notion of *a priority* on which nonsensory introspective experience is also to be disallowed (thus declaring Descartes' *Cogito a posteriori* rather than *a priori*). This subtle distinction, significant though it is, is unimportant for the present discussion. A more careful characterization is suggested in 'How to Measure the Standard Meter', pp. 197–204. A useful catalogue of alternative notions of *a priority* may be found in the various readings collected in Paul K. Moser, (ed.), *A Priori Knowledge* (Oxford Readings in Philosophy, 1987).

My account of the structure of the singular proposition about Venus that it is it may be crucial to the objection. As Wong notes, others such as Ruth Barcan Marcus and Pavel Tichy had urged before me that the proposition semantically contained in 'Hesperus is Phosphorus' is *a priori*.[14] However, in so doing these writers drew no distinction between the singular proposition about Venus that it is it and the singular proposition about Venus that it is selfidentical.[15] The latter proposition, on my account, differs from the former in having only two components: Venus and the property of being selfidentical (at *t*).[16] One could not object, in the same way, that the singular proposition consisting of Venus and selfidentity is knowable only *a posteriori* if it is taken one way rather than another. Thus Marcus and Tichy may be immune from Wong's objection.

The objection depends on a misinterpretation of my characterization of *a priority*. Wong says that, given a natural understanding of the phrase 'in principle', 'to say that [a certain proposition] is in principle knowable solely on the basis of reflection is to say that, provided that one has the modicum of logicality needed and has reflected "hard enough" on [that proposition], one cannot fail to know [that proposition].' This does not accord with my intent. Indeed, any but the most trivial of mathematical theorems would almost certainly fail such a test. The notion of *a priority* does not demarcate a kind knowledge automatically attained once certain (nonexperiential) sufficient conditions are fulfilled. Instead it characterizes a kind of knowledge in terms of the *necessary* conditions for its attainment. The phrase 'on the basis of' does not mean merely the same as 'by means of'; it pertains to epistemic *justification*. A piece of knowledge is *a priori* if sensory experience need not play a certain key role in its justification. Exactly what this special role is may be extremely difficult to specify.[17]

---

[14] Ruth Barcan Marcus, 'A Proposed Solution to a Puzzle about Belief', in P. French, T. Uehling, and H. Wettstein, (eds), *Midwest Studies in Philosophy VI: The Foundations of Analytic Philosophy* (Minneapolis: University of Minnesota Press, 1981), pp. 501–510, at pp. 503–506, and 'Rationality and Believing the Impossible', *Journal of Philosophy*, 80, 6 (June 1983), pp. 321–338; Pavel Tichy, 'Kripke on Necessary A Posteriori', *Philosophical Studies*, 43 (1983), pp. 225–241.

[15] Marcus: 'If I had believed that Tully is not identical with Cicero, I would have been believing that something is not the same as itself and I surely did not believe that, a blatant impossibility, so I was mistaken in claiming to *have* the belief [that Tully is not Cicero]' (*op. cit.*, pp. 505–506); and '[believing that London is different from Londres] would be tantamount to believing that something was not the same as itself, and surely I could never believe *that*. So my belief claim [my claim that I believed that London is not Londres] was mistaken . . .' (p. 330). Tichy: 'All ['Hesperus is Phosphorus'] says is that Venus is selfidentical. . . . When [this sentence] is uttered, . . . [the] utterer merely refers to Venus, then refers to Venus over again and asserts that the former is identical with the latter. In other words, he imputes selfidentity to Venus. . . . Now it seems . . . obvious that this . . . truth is . . . knowable *a priori*. It is a case of the general *a priori* principle (embodied in an axiom of first-order logic) that every single thing is identical with itself. An empirical inquiry into Venus's selfidentity would clearly be a ludicrous exercise in futility' (p. 232).

[16] See 'Reflexivity'. For a penetrating critique of Tichy on independent grounds, see Curtis Brown, 'The Necessary A Posteriori: A Response to Tichy', *Philosophical Studies*, 45 (1984), pp. 379–397.

[17] Experience that may be needed merely to acquire one or more of the concepts involved in a given proposition (and hence to grasp it) does not preclude the proposition from being *a priori*. Even experience that is required in some more direct way in connection with the epistemic justification may be allowable. *Cf.* 'How to Measure the Standard Meter', pp. 201–203, and especially note 11, pp. 203–204.

If sensory experience can play no role at all, beyond merely enabling one to grasp the proposition in question (say, by giving one the requisite concepts), the proposition qualifies as *a priori*. This is what I claim for the singular proposition about Venus that it is it. It is a truth of logic. It may be that in order to know this logical truth without recourse to experience on must not take it a certain way (e.g. the way one might take it were it presented through the sentence 'Hesperus is Phosphorus'). One can know the proposition on the basis of reflection (including the faculty of reason) alone by taking it the way one would if one *stipulated* that one is considering a certain trivial truism—as in 'Consider the fact about Venus that it is it.' That fact is thus know*able* without recourse to sensory experience.[18]

Wong anticipates a reply along these lines. He responds that it is not clear that such a reply does not risk trivializing the notion of *a priority*, on the grounds that even a sentence like 'Peter is at location *l* at time *t*' might emerge as *a priori*, since its content can be expressible by the arguably logically true sentence 'I am here now'.[19] And indeed, *Frege's Puzzle* allowed (p. 180) that the latter sentence may be *a priori*. More recently, I have come to have doubts about this. In the first place, it would be decidedly mysterious if one could know of one's current location, without the slightest experiential contact with one's surroundings, that one is at that location.[20] There is no like mystery in the fact that one can know without such contact that one is wherever one is, and that the sentence 'I am here' is therefore true with respect to one's context (wherever that may be). In the second place, I have become convinced that the particular sentence 'I am here now', in its normal use, is not logically true, and that this is demonstrated by Gerald Vision's example of the standard telephone answering-machine message: 'I am not here now'. I believe this example is best thought of as a genuine case of *assertion in absentia*, in which the agent of the context is (just as he or she says) not present at the context of his or her speech act (and indeed, is generally not even aware at the time of performing it).[21] One can always invent an artificial sentence that succeeds where the natural-language sentence fails. Thus let

---

[18] Although my characterization of *a priority* does not explicitly mention that reflection may include deductive reasoning, *Frege's Puzzle* explicitly argued (p. 137, in a passage quoted by Wong) for the *a priority* of 'Hesperus is Phosphorus' on the grounds that the semantically contained proposition is fully knowable, with complete certainty, by reason alone. Wong evidently allows that, assuming my version of Millianism, the singular proposition about Venus that it is it is indeed knowable without recourse to experience when taking that proposition the way one would were it presented by the logically true sentence 'Hesperus is Hesperus'. See note 3.

[19] *Cf.* David Kaplan, 'On the Logic of Demonstratives', in *Propositions and Attitudes*, pp. 66–82, at pp. 67–68.

[20] This is not to say that one must know where one is or what time it is. *Cf.* 'How to Measure the Standard Meter'.

[21] A videotaped Last Will and Testament may provide a similar counterexample to the alleged logical truth of 'I exist now'. (Does one know *a priori* that one's speech act is not performed *in absentia*?)

An interesting exchange on this sort of alleged counterexample to the alleged logical validity of 'I am here now' appeared in the recent pages of *Analysis*. See Gerald Vision, ' "I am Here Now" ', *Analysis*, 45, 4 (October 1985), pp. 198–199; Julia Colterjohn and Duncan MacIntosh, 'Gerald Vision and Indexicals', *Analysis*, 47, 1 (January 1987), pp. 58–60; Paul Simpson, 'Here and Now', *Analysis*, 47, 1 (January 1987), pp. 61–62; and Gerald Vision, 'Antiphon', *Analysis*, 47, 2 (March 1987), pp. 124–128.

'C$_i$' indexically refer with respect to any context to the context itself. Then 'I am the agent of C$_i$' is perhaps a logical truth, since by semantics alone it is true with respect to every context, no matter what the range of possible contexts.[22] But by the same token, it is by no means clear that the semantically contained proposition is not *a priori*. Let 'Clarence' name a particular context in which Peter is agent. If 'I am the agent of C$_i$' is *a priori in the sense relevant to Frege's Puzzle*, then so is 'Peter is the agent of Clarence'. There is no problem here. Likewise, suppose I am wrong about 'I am here now'. If it is *a priori*, then so is 'Peter is at l at t' (provided the latter is true). But then if 'I am here now' is *a priori*, it is not at all obvious that the resulting *a priority* of 'Peter is at l at t' would trivialize the notion of *a priority*. Such sentences as 'Peter is 5'9" tall', 'Mary was born in Seattle', 'Water runs downhill', etc. would remain *a posteriori*. If it is supposed to be clear that 'I am here now' is logically true and yet 'Peter is at l at t' *not a priori* in the relevant sense, the result would be that some logically true sentences are not *a priori in the relevant sense* (and whose contents, with respect to particular contexts, are thus not themselves logical truths), and are only '*a priori*' in some alternative sense (e.g., in the sense that one can know by semantics alone that the sentence in question is true in every context). Such a result does not strike the present writer as untenable.[23]

Having said this much, I must add that I am not unsympathetic to Wong's suggestion that *a priority* and *a posteriority* might be taken as relative statuses, so that a single proposition may be said to be *a priori relative to* one way of taking it and *a posteriori relative to* another. Still, relativization of the notions of *a priority* and *a posteriority* does not replace the absolute notions. A true and knowable proposition is *a priori* in the absolute sense if and only if it is *a priori* relative to some ways of taking it, and *a posteriori* in the absolute sense if and only if it is not *a priori* relative to any way of taking it. It is this absolute notion of *a priority* that corresponds to the traditional notion—which is that of a property of propositions and not that of a binary relation between propositions and ways of taking them (or a property of pairs consisting of a proposition and a way of taking the proposition)—but the relativized notions, being more discriminating, doubtless deserve their own niche in general epistemology. As Wong suggests, the relativized notions may even form the basis of a justification, of sorts, for the traditional view held by Frege (and once endorsed by Kripke) that 'Hesperus is Phosphorus' is '*a posteriori*'.[24]

---

[22] For an example closer to 'I am here now', let 'here-now$_i$' indexically refer with respect to any context to the spacetime location of the context. Consider 'If C$_i$ has a spacetime location, it is here-now$_i$'.

[23] *Cf. Frege's Puzzle*, p. 177, note 1.

[24] Kripke has suggested such a defense. The idea may lie behind an intriguing footnote from Keith Donnellan, 'Kripke and Putnam on Natural Kind Terms', in C. Ginet and S. Shoemaker, (eds), *Knowledge and Mind* (Oxford University Press, 1983), pp. 84–104: 'If we distinguish a sentence from the proposition it expresses then the terms "truth" and "necessity" apply to the proposition expressed by a sentence, while the terms "*a priori*" and "*a posteriori*" are sentence relative. Given that it is true that Cicero is Tully (and whatever we need about what the relevant sentences express) "Cicero is Cicero" and "Cicero is Tully" express the same proposition. And the *proposition* is necessarily true. But looking at the proposition through the lens of the *sentence* "Cicero is Circero"

All the same, the proposition that Hesperus is Phosphorus is trivial, "given" information that is knowable *a priori* in the traditional (absolute) sense, and the sentence 'Hesperus is Phosphorus' is therefore uninformative and *a priori* in the only sense relevant to Frege's Puzzle.

the proposition can be seen *a priori* to be true, but through "Circero is Tully" one may need an *a posteriori* investigation' (p. 88*n*).

Kripke has suggested that Donnellan's position on the epistemological status of 'Hesperus is Phosphorus' may thus be closer to my own than I had recognized in *Frege's Puzzle* (p. 78). However, Donnellan has expressed misgivings about the account of propositional-attitude attributions in *Frege's Puzzle*. (*Cf.* the preface to *Frege's Puzzle*, at p. x, and Donnellan's 'Belief and the Identity of Reference', in P. French, T. Uehling, and H. Wettstein, (eds), *Midwest Studies in Philosophy XIV: Contemporary Perspectives in the Philosophy of Language II*, University of Notre Dame Press, 1989, pp. 275–288, at 277–278, 287*n*6.) Conversely, I have misgivings about taking *a priority* to be relative to sentences—instead of *ways of taking* propositions—in the light of examples like Kripke's 'Paderewski is Paderewski', with the first occurrence of the name used by Peter to refer to the musician and the second occurrence to the politician (from 'A Puzzle about Belief'). This is not the same as Wettstein's argument that such sentences, in such uses, are not trivial since a competent user like Peter may not know the linguistic fact that the sentence, so used, is true. The sentence, so used, is not only true but logically true, and expresses an *a priori* piece of trivia, even if Peter does not realize it—and even if that trivial proposition is '*a posteriori* relative to' the way Peter takes the proposition when the sentence is so used.

9

Relative and Absolute Apriority (1993)

I

The theory of direct reference is the theory that proper names and other simple singular terms are nondescriptional in content. Propounders and expounders have agreed that one of the theory's remarkable consequences, discovered by Kripke, is that such identity sentences as 'Hesperus is Phosphorus' and 'Cicero is Tully' semantically contain necessary truths even though they are *a posteriori* and informative.[1] Whereas the possibility of necessary *a posteriori* truth—of facts that could not have been otherwise yet cannot be known except by empirical means—is philosophically remarkable for its own sake, the claim that the direct-reference theory yields this consequence is especially dramatic. Gottlob Frege, in the opening paragraph of '*Über Sinn und Bedeutung*', noted the aposteriority and syntheticity of such sentences as 'Hesperus is Phosphorus' and 'Cicero is Tully' in generating what I call 'Frege's Puzzle', which forms the core of his principal argument against Millianism—a version of direct-reference theory according to which the sole contribution made by a proper name, as occurring in a typical context, to the proposition content of the sentence in which it occurs is its referent (bearer, denotation, designatum). Frege asks: *If Millianism is correct, how can 'Cicero is Tully' differ in epistemological status from the a priori 'Cicero is Cicero'?* Certainly there is considerable tension between direct-reference theory and the evident *a posteriori* informativeness of identity sentences like 'Cicero is Tully'. How is this apparent conflict to be resolved?

A word of caution: One can maintain that 'Cicero is Tully' is '*a posteriori*' or 'informative', and mean by this that the linguistic fact that the sentence 'Cicero is Tully' is true (in English) is a nontrivial fact that is knowable only on the basis of experience.[2] But it is hardly remarkable that there are necessary truths that are '*a*

I am grateful to Rod Bertolet and to my audience at UCLA in May 1991 for their comments on an earlier version of the present chapter.

[1] Saul Kripke, *Naming and Necessity* (Harvard University Press, 1972, 1980), pp. 20–21, 28–29, 104, 108–109, and *passim*. Kripke partially rescinds some of the relevant formulations from *Naming and Necessity*, in 'A Puzzle about Belief', in N. Salmon and S. Soames, eds, *Propositions and Attitudes* (Oxford University Press, 1988), pp. 102–148, at pp. 134–135, 147*n*44. The example of 'Cicero is Tully' is evidently due to John Stuart Mill, who argued that the sentence asserts that the names 'Cicero' and 'Tully' are co-referential (*A System of Logic*, Book I, Chapter V 'Of the Import of Propositions', Section 2).

[2] This, or some variation of it (e.g. the observation that it is *a posteriori* that 'Cicero' and 'Tully' are co-referential in English), is a common misinterpretation of the claim that a sentence like

posteriori' or 'informative' in this attenuated sense. Nor could the claim that 'Cicero is Tully' is '*a posteriori*' in that sense, once properly understood, be regarded as threatening the theory of direct reference. Which sentences of English are true, or necessary, is an empirical matter concerning the relationship between English and the world; all true sentences of English are '*a posteriori*' in the attenuated sense. By the same token, which sentences of English are true, or necessary, is, at least to a large extent, a contingent matter. The claim that 'Cicero is Tully' is necessary even though *a posteriori* and informative is philosophically significant, at least initially, because it concerns the means by which one might come to know the nonlinguistic, necessary truth that Cicero is Tully.

One pioneering direct-reference theorist provided (in a footnote) an intriguing account of how the claim that identity sentences like 'Cicero is Tully' are *a posteriori* might be reconciled with Millianism. Keith Donnellan says:

I introduce the expression 'exotic necessary truths' not just to dramatize the interest of Kripke's discovery [that certain sentences involving rigid designators turn out to express necessary truths although the fact that they express truths is to be learned by empirical means]. The more obvious term '*a posteriori* truths' obscures an important point. If we distinguish a sentence from the proposition it expresses then the terms 'truth' and 'necessity' apply to the proposition expressed by a sentence, while the terms '*a priori*' and '*a posteriori*' are sentence relative. Given that it is true that Cicero is Tully (and whatever we need about what the relevant sentences express) 'Cicero is Cicero' and 'Cicero is Tully' express the same proposition. And the *proposition* is necessarily true. But looking at the proposition through the lens of the *sentence* 'Cicero is Cicero' the proposition can be seen *a priori* to be true, but through 'Cicero is Tully' one may need an *a posteriori* investigation. ('Kripke and Putnam on Natural Kind Terms', in C. Ginet and S. Shoemaker, eds, *Knowledge and Mind*, Oxford University Press, 1983, pp. 84–104, p. 88 *n*)[3]

By contrast, in developing and defending a version of Millianism, I argued in *Frege's Puzzle* that such identity sentences as 'Cicero is Tully' are both *a priori* and uninformative—indeed analytic—since the proposition content of 'Cicero is Tully' is just the singular proposition about Cicero that he is him, a trivial truism that is in principle knowable with complete certainty solely on the basis of reflection (including

---

'Cicero is Tully' or 'Hesperus is Phosphorus' is *a posteriori* or informative. See, for example, Howard Wettstein, 'Turning the Tables on Frege or How is it that "Hesperus is Hesperus" is Trivial?' in J. Tomberlin, ed., *Philosophical Perspectives, 3: Philosophy of Mind and Action Theory* (Atascadero, Calif.: Ridgeview, 1989), pp. 317–339, especially pp. 331–334. I reply to Wettstein in 'How *Not* to Become a Millian Heir', *Philosophical Studies*, 62, 2 (May 1991), pp. 165–177, pp. 166–169.

[3] Donnellan is not confused regarding the point raised in the previous paragraph. The quoted passage speaks of what is involved in seeing the proposition that Cicero is Tully to be true. Donnellan drew the distinction between the claim that the semantic content of a sentence is knowable *a priori* and the claim that the fact that the sentence is true is knowable *a priori* in his earlier work 'The Contingent *A Priori* and Rigid Designators', in P. French, T. Uehling, and H. Wettstein, eds, *Contemporary Perspectives in the Philosophy of Language* (Minneapolis: University of Minnesota Press, 1977, 1979) pp. 45–60, p. 51. (Donnellan credits Alvin Plantinga and Michael Levin with having drawn the distinction in their earlier criticisms of Kripke. Ironically, Kripke had drawn a very closely related distinction, in *Naming and Necessity*, at pp. 102–103. *Cf.* my *Frege's Puzzle* (Atascadero, Calif.: Ridgeview, 1986, 1991), pp. 137–138.)

the faculty of reason), without recourse to any experience beyond what may be needed simply to be able to apprehend singular propositions involving Cicero.[4] Donnellan and I thus seem to have provided two competing Millian accounts of the epistemological status of such sentences as 'Cicero is Tully'. This raises the question of which account, if either, is correct.

II

It must be admitted that for such sentences as 'Cicero is Tully', understanding and reason alone are not sufficient without empirical investigation to reveal their truth. In order to know the proposition content independently of experience, one must also apprehend that proposition in a way that is sensitive to its special logical status. This fact, however, does not establish that such sentences are *a posteriori* rather than *a priori*. Even a straightforwardly analytic and *a priori* sentence can share the property that one must apprehend its content in a special way in order to know that proposition independently of experience. Kripke provides the basis for one such example:

A speaker ... may learn 'furze' and 'gorse' normally (separately), yet wonder whether these are the same, or resembling kinds. (What about 'rabbit' and 'hare'?) It would be easy for such a speaker to assent to an assertion formulated with 'furze' but withhold assent from the corresponding assertion involving 'gorse'. The situation is quite analogous to that of [a speaker who uses 'Cicero' and 'Tully' normally but sincerely and reflectively assents simultaneously to 'Cicero was bald' and 'Tully was not bald']. Yet 'furze' and 'gorse', and other pairs of terms for the same natural kind, are normally thought of as *synonyms*. ('A Puzzle about Belief', p. 134)

Kripke's speaker presumably learned the words 'furze' and 'gorse' on separate occasions by something like ostensive definitions, without thereby learning that the two words are co-extensional, let alone synonymous. Has the speaker therefore failed to learn one or both of the words? Not necessarily. Most of us learn one of the two words by ostensive definition, and the other as a word that is interchangeable with the first, in a sort of verbal (non-ostensive) definition. We might be told something like 'Furze is that stuff growing over there', and later ' "Gorse" is another word for furze.' Alternatively, we might be told 'Gorse is that stuff growing over there', and later ' "Furze"

---

[4] The argument is given in section B.1, pp. 133–138, of *Frege's Puzzle*. The phrases 'knowable by means of' and 'knowable on the basis of' pertain to the epistemic *justification* for the proposition in question. In saying that a proposition is knowable solely on the basis of reflection without recourse to (independently of) experience, one is denying that experience is required to play a certain key role in that justification. Specifying that key role in a philosophically significant way is by no means trivial. It is arguable, for example, that experience may be a necessary component of the epistemic justification for a given proposition in some way that does not disqualify the proposition from being *a priori*. It is possible that the terms '*a priori*' and '*a posteriori*', as used by philosophers, are ambiguous on this point. See my 'How to Measure the Standard Meter', *Proceedings of the Aristotelian Society*, New Series, 88 (1987/1988), pp. 193–217, at pp. 201–203 and especially pp. 203–204*n*. If experience is not required at all, beyond merely enabling one to apprehend the proposition in question (by giving one the requisite concepts, for example), then that proposition is unquestionably *a priori*. This is what I claim for the contents of 'Cicero is Tully' and similar identity sentences.

is another word for gorse.' If either of these words can be learned by ostensive definition, then both can be. Kripke's speaker has done so. If those words are indeed synonyms,[5] then the sentence 'Furze is gorse' is analytic and *a priori*. But Kripke's speaker, while assenting to 'Furze is furze', does not assent to 'Furze is gorse'. Why not? Not because the words are not synonyms in the speaker's idiolect. It is not as if he or she misunderstands 'gorse' to mean *heather*. The speaker has correctly learned both 'furze' and 'gorse'. If they are synonyms in English, they are therefore synonyms also in the speaker's idiolect. The problem is that the speaker does not realize that. He or she understands both 'Furze is furze' and 'Furze is gorse' without recognizing their synonymy. In particular, he or she understands 'Furze is gorse', but fails to recognize the proposition thus expressed as the logical truth that furze is furze.

The general phenomenon is not restricted to natural-kind terms. As I have argued elsewhere, someone may also fail to apprehend the content of the sentence 'Catsup is ketchup' in the right way if he or she learned 'ketchup' and 'catsup' independently—not by being told that they are synonyms but, for example, by consuming the condiment and reading the labels on the bottles, in a sort of ostensive definition.[6] The sentence 'Catsup is ketchup' is unquestionably analytic—despite the fact that the speaker, who correctly understood both words even before learning of the identity, might sincerely say, 'I'm fond of ketchup, but I find the taste of catsup repugnant.' In fact, it is arguable that 'ketchup' and 'catsup' are not two words, but alternative spellings of a single word. Indeed, a native Santa Barbaran who has learned in a physics lecture while studying in Oxford that 'colour' is the English word for the property of reflecting electromagnetic radiation in the visible spectrum may be surprised to learn the truth of 'Colour is color'. To push the point even further, the same Santa Barbaran, whose limited experience of tomatoes consists in seeing them sliced and put into salads, on later consuming a tomato-based sauce in Oxford could be similarly surprised to learn the truth of 'Tomatoes are tomatoes', if it is pronounced: To-**mae**-toes (American) are to-**mah**-toes (British, or American affectation). This despite the fact that, however it is pronounced, the sentence has the logical form of a valid sentence: All F's are F's.[7]

---

[5] J. L. Austin, who had a nose for detecting extremely subtle shades of meaning, had held that 'the natural economy of language' prevented there being two English words with exactly the same function, without even the slightest difference in meaning. John Searle reports that the example of 'furze' and 'gorse' was going around Oxford in the fifties as a counterexample to Austin's claim. Evidently Austin conceded that he could not find any difference in meaning between the two, declaring the pair a singular instance of authentic English synonyms.

[6] *Cf.* my 'How to Become a Millian Heir', *Nous*, 23, 2 (April 1989), pp. 211–220 p. 216f.

[7] *Cf.* my 'A Millian Heir Rejects the Wages of *Sinn*', in C. A. Anderson and J. Owens, eds, *Propositional Attitudes: The Role of Content in Language, Mind, and Logic* (Stanford, Calif.: CSLI, 1990), pp. 215–247, p. 221n10. The tomato example occurred to me serendipitously when giving the 'ketchup'/'catsup' example in Oxford. I was informed that the example did not work there, because 'catsup' is not used in British English. Not to despair, a resourceful member of the audience (who evidently consumed little ketchup herself) suggested, in her native pronunciation, that I replace 'catsup' with 'tomato sauce'.

See note 5 above. Some may see the presence of 'catsup' in American English as completely superfluous—'a dispensable linguistic luxury'—perhaps even as extravagant. But then America is often seen as the Land of Plenty of Excess, and luxuries of surplus do have their value. (Austin's

Sentences like 'Cicero is Tully', on my view, belong very much with these examples. If they are exotic philosophically, then they are not only exotically necessary but exotically analytic, *a priori*, and, in the relevant (semantic) sense, uninformative: They are analytic, *a priori*, uninformative sentences for which understanding and reflection does not suffice for recognition of their truth.[8] If 'Cicero is Tully' seems somehow more exotic than 'Ketchup is catsup', it is chiefly because the names 'Cicero' and 'Tully' are not mere etymological variations, so that one might more naturally come to learn both without thereby becoming aware of their co-reference. Even for etymologically unrelated co-referential names, however, one can—and indeed one very often does—learn one of the two names by means of its co-reference with the other. I suspect that this is precisely the way most of us learn the name 'Tully'.[9]

III

Quoting the passage from Donnellan, as well as passages from other pioneering direct-reference theorists and a passage from my former self, I claimed in *Frege's Puzzle* (pp. 78–79) that my account of the epistemological status of such sentences as 'Cicero is Tully' differed significantly from that of these other theorists.[10] Rod Bertolet and Saul Kripke have independently objected that Donnellan's account in terms of the sentence relativity of the concepts of apriority and aposteriority is in fact

---

intended thesis of 'the natural economy of language' may have been confined in scope to languages of more ascetic cultures.)

[8] Of course, 'Cicero is Tully', unlike 'Tomatoes are tomatoes', does not have the form of a logically valid sentence. All the more reason that a competent speaker can fail to recognize its semantic content as itself a truth of logic.

[9] This is even true for the peculiar case of 'Hesperus' and 'Phosphorus', in which individuating descriptions may be conventionally associated with the names ('the Evening Star' and 'the Morning Star'). Kripke says in *Naming and Necessity* (pp. 80–81) that it is a tribute to the education of philosophers that so many have held that the name 'Cicero', for the average person, means something like 'the man who denounced Catiline', since most speakers can only identify Cicero indefinitely as *a famous Roman orator*. Actually, most speakers who can use the name 'Cicero' probably cannot identify him even that well. More rare still is someone who has been introduced to the name 'Tully' without being told something like that it is simply 'another name of Cicero'. (*Cf.* Kripke's remarks concerning the case of 'Cicero'/'Tully' in 'A Puzzle about Belief', at pp. 110, 116. See also his remarks contrasting that case with 'Hesperus'/'Phosphorus', at pp. 146–147 n43.)

There may be a further reason that 'Cicero is Tully' may seem more exotic philosophically than 'Ketchup is catsup'. The former may also seem more exotic to some than 'Furze is gorse', even though 'furze' and 'gorse' are, like 'Cicero' and 'Tully', two words rather than alternative spellings of a single word. This may be related to the fact that 'furze' and 'gorse' are, like 'ketchup' and 'catsup', mass nouns rather than proper names. One may be thinking of them as general terms, rather than as simple singular terms. Seen in this light, 'Ketchup is catsup' probably does not have the form: $a = b$. Even on Mill's theory—as well as on my own—there is a systematic divergence between semantic content ('connotation') and extension ('denotation') for predicates and common nouns. This does not alter the fact, however, that on the Millian theory, 'Cicero' and 'Tully' are every bit as identical in meaning as any pair of synonymous common nouns. (What about 'rabbit' and 'hare'?)

[10] I would add to that set of quotations the following from David Kaplan: 'The Babylonians knew what Hesperus was, and knew what Phosphorus was, but didn't know that they were the same' ('Afterthoughts' to 'Demonstratives', in J. Almog, J. Perry, and H. Wettstein, eds, *Themes from Kaplan* (Oxford University Press, 1989): pp. 481–614, at p. 607).

entirely within, and in significant respects truer to, the spirit and fundamentals of my own theory.[11] For *a priori* knowledge involves knowledge, and knowledge involves belief. And *Frege's Puzzle* also argued that belief is the existential generalization (on the third argument place) of a ternary relation *BEL* among believers, propositions, and some third type of thing, perhaps something like *ways of taking propositions*. My account thus makes such epistemic concepts as apriority and aposteriority relative concepts. As I have just admitted, one must take the proposition content in a particular way in order to recognize that a given sentence is true without an empirical investigation, simply by understanding it (reflecting on its content, etc.).

I did not argue, however, that belief is sentence relative. In fact, I do not say that belief is a ternary relation. Belief, on my view (as on the views of Frege, Alonzo Church, *et al.*), is a binary relation between believers and propositions. If the concept of belief is considered to be a relative concept on my account, it is not *sentence* relative but *way-of-taking* relative: one believes a given proposition under one way of taking it but not under another (where we understand 'A believes p under x' to mean that $BEL[A, p, x]$). More generally, our 'epistemic access to propositions' (Bertolet) is not sentence relative but way-of-taking relative. For 'Paderewski'-type reasons, ways-of-taking propositions cannot be identified with sentences in a language (and indeed ways-of-taking things generally cannot be identified with expressions generally).[12] Sentences are too coarse-grained. Furthermore, even in the more typical case ('Cicero was talented' rather than 'Paderewski was talented'), a sentence in a language does not determine a unique way of taking its content except relative to a particular speaker.[13]

One can define, in a fairly natural and straightforward way, something like a sentence relative notion of sentential apriority—I shall call it *s*-apriority—in terms of the traditional (proposition-based rather than sentence-based) notion of apriority and my notion (proto-notion?) of a way of taking a proposition. We may say that a true sentence S is *s*-apriori with respect to a speaker A if something like the following obtains:

(D1) The proposition content of S (with respect to some [A's] context) is knowable [by A] by reflection (including deductive reasoning) while taking that proposition in the way A does when it is presented to A by means of (A's version of) S, without recourse to experience *and without taking the proposition in some alternative way*.[14]

---

[11] Rod Bertolet, 'Salmon on the A Priori', *Analysis*, 51, 1 (January 1991), pp. 43–48. Kripke first made the objection in a conversation concerning my claim that sentences like 'Cicero is Tully' are *a priori*. Kai-Yee Wong makes a similar criticism in '*A Priority* and Ways of Grasping a Proposition', *Philosophical Studies*, 62, 2 (May 1991), pp. 151–164. I reply to Wong in 'How *Not* to Become a Millian Heir', pp. 169–173.

[12] Saul Kripke, 'A Puzzle about Belief', pp. 130–131.

[13] *Cf. Frege's Puzzle*, pp. 75, 175–176 *n*5, and especially 120, 170*n*1, 173–174*n*1.

[14] Brackets indicate alternative formulations. We shall not be concerned here with the subtle differences that distinguish the corresponding alternatively defined notions. Some scholars would note that the notion of *s*-apriority must be relativized further to a particular language, since the same sentence S appears, or can appear, in multiple unrelated languages, each time with a completely different meaning. Any required relativization to a language will be suppressed throughout this discussion.

We would then say that a true sentence is *s-aposteriori with respect to A* if its content (with respect to some [*A*'s] context) is knowable [by *A*] but the sentence itself is not *s*-apriori with respect to *A*. One may similarly define, in a parallel manner, relative notions of *s*-informativeness and *s*-triviality. Then presumably, 'Cicero is Tully' would be *s*-aposteriori rather than *s*-apriori, and *s*-informative rather than *s*-trivial, with respect to someone who has learned the names 'Cicero' and 'Tully' but has not learned that they are two names of the same man. This comes mighty close to the claim that 'Cicero is Tully' is '*a posteriori*' and 'informative'.

We can also define absolute notions in terms of these relative notions. The most natural definition for absolute sentential *s*-apriority would be something like the following, where the metalinguistic variable '*S*' ranges over true sentences:

(*D*2) *S* is *s-apriori (simpliciter)* $=_{def.}$ *S* is [could be] *s*-apriori with respect to someone or other.

A true sentence would then be *s-aposteriori (simpliciter)* if its content (with respect to some context and time) is knowable but the sentence itself is not *s*-apriori (*simpliciter*), i.e. if it is not [could not be] *s*-apriori with respect to anyone. Alternatively, one might define an absolute notion of sentential *s*-apriority in terms of a sentence's being *s*-apriori with respect to *everyone* who understands the sentence. This yields a correspondingly wider notion of *s-aposteriority simpliciter*, defined in terms of a sentence's failing to be *s*-apriori with respect to someone or other. I choose the former definitions for the absolute notions, in part, because it seems more natural to say that a sentence is *s*-apriori, than it is to say that it is *s*-aposteriori, whenever it is *s*-apriori with respect to at least some speakers, even if it might turn out to be *s*-aposteriori with respect to other speakers. For in that case, the content is still know*able* independently of experience. Under the alternative definitions, situations like 'Ketchup is catsup' threaten to preclude any sentence from being deemed '*s*-apriori'.

IV

I willingly concede, and even insist, that all of these epistemic notions are perfectly legitimate, and indeed epistemologically significant. But I would also note several additional features. First and foremost, none of these notions is identical with the traditional, proposition-based notions of apriority and aposteriority. Second, strictly speaking the proposed relative notions are not sentence relative; they are speaker relative. (The '*s*' in '*s*-apriori' stands for 'speaker relative'.) Also, they are probably undefined for cases like that of 'Tomatoes are tomatoes' *vis à vis* my native Santa Barbaran, or of 'Paderewski is Paderewski' *vis à vis* Kripke's character Peter, who does not realize that the pianist and the statesman are one and the same. For there is no single way of taking the trivial proposition that Paderewski is Paderewski that counts as *the* way that Peter takes it when it is presented to him by means of the sentence 'Paderewski is Paderewski'. (There are at least three different ways that Peter might take the proposition when it is so presented to him, depending on how he thinks the sentence is intended: The pianist is the pianist; the statesman is the statesman;

the pianist is the statesman—if I may put the point this way.[15]) Furthermore, the proposed absolute notion of *s*-apriority does not support that claim that 'Cicero is Tully' is '*a posteriori*'. A scholar who understands the sentence 'Cicero is Tully' and knows that it is true (e.g. any philosopher of language who knows that 'Cicero' and 'Tully' are co-referential, and to whom the names both refer), at least if that scholar happens to be a Millian, may treat the names more or less interchangeably. Such a scholar is liable to take the proposition that Cicero is Tully, when thus expressed, in much the same way he or she would take it were it put instead by means of 'Cicero is Cicero'.[16] If such patently analytic sentences as 'Tomatoes are tomatoes' and 'Paderewski is Paderewski' are to be counted *s*-apriori, then so is 'Cicero is Tully'. Last but not least, the notions of *s*-apriority and *s*-aposteriority are no more (albeit no less) natural or fundamental to the spirit of my view of our cognitive access to propositions than is the corresponding name relative notion of love natural or fundamental to the spirit of Everyman's view of love. (According to the name relative notion of love, Mrs. Jones, who does not realize that the demented grave-robber she loves is none other than her husband, may be described as *loving someone qua* 'Jones the Ripper-Offer' but no longer *qua* 'Hubby Dear'.[17]) The proposed relative notions are derivative, contrived, nonbasic.

A less contrived notion would be a way-of-taking relative notion of sentential apriority. We may say that a true sentence *S* is *w-apriori with respect to* a way *x* of taking a proposition—or as I shall say instead, that *S* is simply *a priori with respect to x*—if something like the following condition obtains:

(*D3*) *x* is a way of taking the proposition content of *S* (with respect to some context and time) and that proposition is knowable [by the agent of the context] by reflection (including deductive reasoning) while taking the proposition in way *x*, without recourse to experience and without taking the proposition in some alternative way.

A true sentence would be *a posteriori with respect to* a way *x* of taking a proposition if the sentence's proposition content (with respect to some context and time) is knowable and *x* is a way of taking that proposition, but the sentence itself is not *a priori* with respect to *x*. We may thus say that whereas 'Paderewski is Paderewski' is *a priori* with respect to some ways of taking its proposition content, it is still *a posteriori* with respect to others (the pianist is the statesman).

These way-of-taking relative notions are arguably the basic ones on my view.[18] But even they are not identical with the traditional, proposition-based ones. (Compare the relationship between *BEL* and belief.) More importantly, they do not support

---

[15] *Cf.* the character Elmer *vis à vis* 'Bugsy Wabbit is Bugsy Wabbit', from *Frege's Puzzle*, pp. 93–94, and *passim*.

[16] See note 9 above. *Cf.* 'A Puzzle about Belief', at p. 116; and my 'Illogical Belief', in J. Tomberlin, ed., *Philosophical Perspectives, 3: Philosophy of Mind and Action Theory* (Atascadero, Calif.: Ridgeview, 1989), pp. 243–285, especially at 267–268.

[17] *Frege's Puzzle*, pp. 103–105.

[18] I say 'arguably'. Is the way-of-taking relative concept of love (on which Mrs. Jones loves her husband relative to one way of taking him but not relative to another) more basic in Everyman's conceptual scheme than the absolute concept of love? (Certainly there is a sense in which the relative concept *underlies* the absolute one.)

the claim that 'Cicero is Tully' is '*a posteriori*', any more than the proposed absolute notions of *s*-apriority and *s*-aposteriority do. As we saw above, although 'Cicero is Tully' is *a posteriori* with respect to some ways of taking its content, a Millian philosopher who both understands the sentence and knows that it is true is liable to take its content in a way with respect to which the sentence is *a priori* rather than *a posteriori*. The fact that the sentence is *a priori* with respect to at least one way of taking its content is sufficient for the sentence to be *a priori* (*simpliciter*)—otherwise even 'Tomatoes are tomatoes' and 'Paderewski is Paderewski' should be counted '*a posteriori*'. Accordingly, if the way-of-taking relative notions of sentential apriority and aposteriority are taken as basic, something like the following definition (where '*S*' ranges over true sentences) for absolute sentential apriority may be taken in place of more conventional definitions:

(*D*4) *S* is *a priori* (*simpliciter*) =$_{def.}$ *S* is [could be] *a priori* with respect to some way of taking a proposition.

As usual, a true sentence would be *a posteriori* (*simpliciter*) if its proposition content (with respect to some context and time) is knowable but the sentence itself is not *a priori* (*simpliciter*). Here this means that, although its content is knowable, the sentence is not [could not be] *a priori* with respect to any way of taking a proposition.

Recognition of the fact that 'Cicero is Tully' is *a priori simpliciter* is crucial to finding a philosophically satisfactory solution to Frege's Puzzle: In the relevant sense, 'Cicero is Tully' does not differ in epistemological status from 'Cicero is Cicero'. Combined with results obtained in earlier work, this yields the further result that the theory of direct reference does not have the consequence, which had been claimed, that there are (nontrivial) examples of necessary *a posteriori* sentences.[19] About the closest I am able to come to accommodating the claim that 'Cicero is Tully' is necessary even though '*a posteriori*' is to acknowledge that 'Cicero is Tully' is not only necessary but is also [could also be] *s*-aposteriori with respect to some speakers, in particular with respect to anyone who understands (his or her version of) the sentence without knowing that it is true.

I had criticized Donnellan's account on the grounds that it assumes that 'Cicero is Tully' and 'Cicero is Cicero' differ in epistemological status, judging 'Cicero is Tully' *a posteriori* even though 'Cicero is Cicero' is *a priori*.[20] I am persuaded, however, that

---

[19] *Cf.* G. W. Fitch, 'Are There Necessary *A Posteriori* Truths?', *Philosophical Studies*, 30 (1976), pp. 243–247. In *Reference and Essence* (Princeton University Press, 1981), I explored, and disputed, the claim (made by Hilary Putnam and others) that the direct-reference theory has the 'startling consequence' that sentences like 'Water consists of two parts hydrogen and one part oxygen' express necessary truths despite being *a posteriori*. This is not to say that the sentence is not necessary *a posteriori*. Various general principles of essentialism, when combined with direct reference and with uncontroversial, empirical observations, yield nontrivial examples of necessary *a posteriori* sentences. If we let '*S*' and '*E*' name the gametes from which I developed, the sentence 'Saul Kripke did not spring from *S* and *E*' may be another such example. (A trivial example of a necessary *a posteriori* sentence is 'Saul Kripke actually lives in Princeton, New Jersey'.)

[20] Contrary to Bertolet (p. 47), my criticism was not that Donnellan's account illicitly assumes that 'Cicero is Tully' and 'Cicero is Cicero' differ in content. Donnellan explicitly rejects that view, in the very passage quoted.

Donnellan should be interpreted instead as making a different claim, one which I may be able to accept. He may be saying, for example, merely that (as we now put it) 'Cicero is Tully' is [could be] *s*-aposteriori with respect to anyone who understands the sentence but does not know that it is true. If so, I was indeed wrong to group him with other direct-reference theorists (such as my former self) who have maintained that 'Cicero is Tully' is *a posteriori* (*simpliciter*). However, I would still urge the several points made in the opening paragraph of this section in response. The fact that 'Cicero is Tully' is *s*-aposteriori with respect to anyone who understands it without knowing that it is true does not distinguish that sentence from 'Ketchup is catsup'.

V

Though identity sentences like 'Cicero is Tully' are every bit as *a priori* as the theorems of mathematics, the original motivation for the claim that 'Cicero is Tully' is *a posteriori* probably did not focus on the epistemology of its content. One indication of this comes by way of the complementary claim that had been made by some direct-reference theorists—notably Kripke and David Kaplan—that sentences like 'The Standard Bar is exactly one meter long' and 'Newman-1 will be the first child born in the 22nd Century' are *a priori* despite their contingency, if the reference of the term 'meter' is fixed by the description 'the length of the Standard Bar' and if the name 'Newman-1' is similarly 'defined' as 'the first child to be born in the 22nd Century'.[21] Those who declare such sentences *a priori* may not have intended thereby to separate the propositional contents of those sentences on epistemological grounds from knowledge gained by measuring a bar's length or by looking at one's watch at the time of a birth. Direct-reference theorists who deem 'Cicero is Tully' *a posteriori*, or the 'meter' and 'Newman-1' sentences *a priori*, sometimes seem to mean something more *linguistic*. Their principal concern seems to be not with our knowledge of the contents of the sentences in question, but with the means by which we know that the sentences themselves are true. At the same time, they may mean something less *epistemological* than, for example, the observation that the truth in English of 'Cicero is Tully' is knowable only by means of experience. We have seen that the question of whether particular English sentences are true or false—even logically valid sentences—is an empirical matter. This is partly because the question of what any particular English sentence means is itself an empirical matter; even the Queen of England does not have innate knowledge of the language. What originally prompted the claim that the 'meter' and 'Newman-1' sentences are *a priori*, however, was the recognition that those sentences belong, in some sense, with those for which knowledge of the meaning—however empirical that knowledge may be—is sufficient to establish

---

[21] Kripke, *Naming and Necessity*, pp. 54–56, 63, 79*n*; David Kaplan, 'Dthat', in P. French, T. Uehling, and H. Wettstein, eds, *Contemporary Perspectives in the Philosophy of Language* (Minneapolis: University of Minnesota Press, 1977, 1979), pp. 383–400, at p. 397. Compare Kaplan, 'Demonstratives' and the 'Afterthoughts' thereto, at pp. 536–539, 550, 560, 597, 604–607. Kripke has modified his view of the epistemological status of sentences like the 'meter' and 'Newman-1' sentences since the appearance of *Naming and Necessity*.

their truth.[22] Likewise, the main point behind the claim that 'Cicero is Tully' is *a posteriori* may not be to mark that sentence off from the nonempirical sciences, but instead to mark it off from those sentences for which mere understanding is sufficient to establish their truth.

In what sense is our understanding of a sentence something that is sufficient in some cases and not in others to establish the sentence's truth? Understanding the mathematical equation '$5,278 + 3,639 = 8,927$' involves knowing that the equation is true in standard mathematical notation if and only if the sum of 5,278 and 3,639 is 8,927.[23] One can thereby establish the falsity of the equation by an *a priori* calculation. But this involves something beyond merely understanding the equation. It involves arithmetic. If the notion of *understanding being sufficient to establish truth* is to differ in extension from that of *semantic content being knowable independently of experience* by excluding both this case and 'Cicero is Tully', and by including the 'meter' and 'Newman-1' sentences, the former notion needs to be made more precise, or at least clearer.

Let us draw a distinction between *pure semantics* and *applied semantics*. It is a purely semantic fact about English that the definite description 'the inventor of bifocals' refers to (denotes, designates) the inventor of bifocals. It is also a semantic fact about English that 'the inventor of bifocals' refers to Benjamin Franklin. But the latter is a fact of applied semantics; it obtains partly in virtue of the nonlinguistic historical fact that it was Benjamin Franklin who invented bifocals. Similarly, whereas it is a purely semantic fact about English that 'Snow is white' is true if and only if snow is white, it is an applied semantic fact that 'Snow is white' is true. Certain sentences are special in that their truth value is settled entirely by pure semantics. It is a purely semantic fact about English for example that 'Cicero is Cicero' is true. For this fact is a logical

---

[22] Kripke says: 'What ... is the *epistemological* status of the statement ['The Standard bar is one meter long at time t_0'], for someone who has fixed the metric system by reference to [the Standard Bar]? It would seem that he knows it *a priori*. For if he used [the Standard Bar] to fix the reference of the term "one meter", then as a result of this kind of "definition" (which is not an abbreviative or synonymous definition), he knows automatically, without further investigation, that [the Standard Bar] is one meter long' (*Naming and Necessity*, p. 56). But what the reference-fixer knows automatically as a result of his reference-fixing definition is that the 'meter' sentence is true (in his own idiolect); he knows automatically without investigating the Standard Bar that however long it is, that length is designated by the phrase 'one meter'. He does not automatically know of that length that the bar is exactly (or even roughly) that long.

For extended discussion see the articles by Donnellan and me cited in notes 3 and 4 above. The burden of those articles was to criticize the claim that such sentences as the 'meter' and 'Newman-1' sentences semantically contain *a priori* truths. The interpretation that will be suggested in the present section of this paper therefore cannot capture the intended import of Donnellan's claim that the proposition about Cicero that he is him may be *a posteriori relative to* the sentence 'Cicero is Tully' even if it is *a priori* relative to 'Cicero is Cicero'.

[23] It is arguable that such metalinguistic '*T*'-sentences are not always true, since the object-language sentence involved may be neither true nor false—for example, ' "The present king of France is bald" is true in English if and only if the present king of France is bald.' Even for this case, however, understanding the sentence involves: (i) knowledge that the present king of France is bald if the sentence is true; and (ii) the ability to infer that the sentence is true from the fact that the present king of France is bald, if there were such a fact. (We ignore for present purposes cases in which the object-language sentence attempts to make a metalinguistic assertion.)

consequence of the purely semantic fact that 'Cicero is Cicero' is true if and only if Cicero is Cicero.

The notion of a sentence's truth being a fact of pure rather than applied semantics is, roughly, a notion of 'truth solely by virtue of meaning'.[24] The epistemologically charged term '*a priori*' is less appropriate for this notion than the more semantic epithet 'analytic'. Nevertheless, I have often felt that this form of analyticity as truth-by-virtue-of-pure-semantics may be what is meant by particular uses of '*a priori*'.[25] The notion does have an epistemological dimension: for any sentence whose truth value is a logical consequence of pure semantics, anyone competent in the language is *ipso facto* in possession of sufficient information to determine that truth value by logic—never mind that knowledge of pure semantics for a natural language, and hence competence in the language, is gained only by means of experience.

Correspondingly, what is meant by the claim that 'Cicero is Tully' is '*a posteriori*' may be that the sentence's truth is a fact of applied rather than pure semantics for English. The resulting claim—which is supposed to be a consequence of direct reference—that certain sentences, including 'Cicero is Tully', are necessary even though their truth is a fact of applied rather than pure semantics (i.e. synthetic yet necessary) may or may not be as surprising or remarkable in the present philosophical age as the

---

[24] I do not mean the phrase in the traditional sense, which rules out that the sentence in question describes an extralinguistic fact and is in that sense true partly by virtue of a feature of the world. Nor do I wish to be associated with the philosophical thesis, which has traditionally gone hand in hand with the analytic-synthetic distinction, that sentences like 'All husbands are married' are devoid of extralinguistic, factual content. Indeed, I think it is obvious that even logical validities like 'All married men are married', since they are contentful and true, describe facts—typically extralinguistic (albeit particularly unexciting) facts that are both necessary and knowable *a priori*. There is a natural and straightforward sense in which such a sentence is, like any contentful and true sentence, true 'in virtue of' both its meaning and the extralinguistic fact that it describes. A better phrase for the notion of analyticity that I am embracing here is 'true as a consequence of meaning alone'. An analytic sentence, in the sense in which I am using the term, is a contentful sentence which is true (and hence true in virtue of both its meaning and some fact about the world), and for which the very fact that it is true is itself a logical consequence entirely of purely semantic facts about the sentence.

[25] *Cf.* 'How *Not* to Become a Millian Heir', p. 172. This notion of analyticity differs slightly from that given in *Frege's Puzzle*, pp. 133–135. The latter is roughly the notion of a sentence whose proposition content is a logical truth. I argued there that sentences like 'Cicero is Tully' are analytic in the latter sense.

My distinction between pure semantics and applied semantics is loosely related to a distinction of Rudolf Carnap's, between what he called 'pure semantics' and 'descriptive semantics'—though the former distinction is free of many (not all) of the latter's controversial philosophical underpinnings. Carnap's notion of 'pure semantics' concerned only artificial languages whose semantics is stipulated; any semantical matter concerning a natural language—including its pure semantics, in my sense—was *ipso facto* a matter of 'descriptive semantics'. See his *Introduction to Semantics and Formalization of Logic* (Harvard University Press, 1942, 1943), volume I, section 5, pp. 11–13. My notion of a sentence whose truth is a fact of pure rather than applied semantics is closely related to Carnap's notion of '*L*-truth', although the latter corresponds more closely to the contemporary notion of *logical truth* as truth in all models for the language. See Carnap, *Introduction to Semantics and Formalization of Logic*, volume I, pp. 60–61, 79–80, 134–137; and *Meaning and Necessity* (University of Chicago Press, 1947, 1956), section 2, pp. 9–10. Carnap proposed *L*-truth as constituting an explication equally of analyticity and of necessity.

claim that some necessary truths are knowable only by means of experience. (Consider the mathematical equation, for example, or *a priori* principles of metaphysics.) But it is hardly devoid of philosophical significance.

Is it the case, though, that the fact that 'Cicero is Tully' is true is not a purely semantic fact about English? Certainly a speaker who is in full command of the language may nevertheless fail to know that 'Cicero is Tully' is true. Even a master logician who is fully competent in the use of 'Cicero', 'Tully', and the 'is' of identity may be in no position to infer that 'Cicero is Tully' is true from the purely semantic fact that 'Cicero is Tully' is true if Cicero is Tully. On the other hand, it is a purely semantic fact that 'Cicero' refers to Cicero, and it is also a purely semantic fact that 'Tully' refers to Tully. The latter, according to the Millian view, is identical with the fact that 'Tully' refers to Cicero. And it is a truth of logic that if 'Cicero' and 'Tully' both refer to Cicero, then there is something to which both names co-refer. Given the purely semantic facts for English, it follows that 'Cicero is Tully' is true. Alternatively, it is a fact of pure semantics for English that 'Cicero is Tully' is true if Cicero is Tully. According to Millianism, that Cicero is Tully is nothing more than the logical truth about Cicero that he is him. On the Millian theory, then, 'Cicero is Tully' is '*a priori*' even in the sense that its truth is logically settled by pure rather than applied semantics. It is true solely by virtue of meaning.

Why is the master logician unable to infer by *modus ponens* that 'Cicero is Tully' is true from his *a priori* knowledge concerning Cicero that he is him, if the latter is really nothing less than knowledge of the fact that Cicero is Tully? The answer is that if the logician does not already know that 'Cicero is Tully' is true, he or she knows the conditional fact about English that 'Cicero is Tully' is true if Cicero is Tully only by taking that proposition in a way that does not reveal the special logical status of its antecedent; the logician does not recognize the antecedent proposition, so taken, as the truism concerning Cicero that he is him. The logician is in the same boat as the speaker who understands 'Ketchup is catsup' without knowing that it is true.[26]

It is difficult for the direct-reference theorist to escape our conclusion: Identity sentences like 'Cicero is Tully' are neither informative nor *a posteriori*, nor *s*-aposteriori, nor is their truth a matter of applied rather than pure semantics. 'Cicero is Tully' and 'Ketchup is catsup' are birds of a feather. Both are *a priori* and *s*-apriori, uninformative and trivial. Indeed, both are equally analytic.[27]

---

[26] This general phenomenon is the central topic of 'Illogical Belief'. There is a brief discussion of the particular inability in question at pp. 259–261 and *passim*. See especially, p. 278*n*19. *Cf.* 'How *Not* to Become a Millian Heir', pp. 168, 174–175*n*11.

[27] The 'meter' and 'Newman-1' examples constitute an interesting anomaly. Given the manner in which the reference of 'Newman-1' is fixed, the fact that 'Newman-1' refers to the first child to be born in the 22nd Century, and hence also the resulting fact that the 'Newman-1' sentence is true, do indeed seem to be facts of pure rather than applied semantics. One might say, therefore, that the 'Newman-1' sentence is 'analytic'. This is a purely terminological matter of decision. Interestingly, the further fact that 'Newman-1' refers to Newman-1 seems to be a fact of applied rather than pure semantics, since it obtains only by virtue of the nonlinguistic fact that Newman-1 (i.e. that very future person) will be the first child to be born in the twenty-second Century. *Cf.* 'How to Measure the Standard Meter', pp. 200–201*n*10.

Even if the 'Newman-1' sentence is declared analytic, it is widely recognized nowadays that it does not follow that the sentence's content is necessary. Still, it is usually assumed that the content of any sentence that is true solely by virtue of meaning is *a priori*. I maintain that the 'meter' and 'Newman-1' sentences are both contingent and *a posteriori* in the sense that their contents are contingent and knowable only by means of experience. (Those sentences are counted synthetic under the alternative notion of analyticity given in *Frege's Puzzle*. They are also deemed synthetic on Kripke's alternative definition of analyticity—in *Naming and Necessity*, p. 39—though for a different reason. See especially pp. 56*n*, 122–123*n* of that work, and notes 22 and 24 above.)

Whereas the philosophical significance of the existence of propositions that are both contingent and *a priori* is apparent, the philosophical significance of the fact that such sentences as the 'Newman-1' and 'meter' sentences express contingencies even though their truth is a matter of pure semantics is less so. One consequence (noted by Kaplan, in 'Demonstratives', p. 540) is that W. V. Quine was wrong to see the 'second grade of modal involvement' as recasting analyticity, which is a meta-theoretic notion, as the object-language notion of necessity. Carnap was equally wrong to identify necessity with truth by pure semantics. If I am correct, another consequence is that analyticity, in this sense, is no guarantee of apriority (knowability independently of experience).

10

Analyticity and Apriority (1993)

The logical positivists invoked various notions of analyticity, or 'truth by convention', to explain the special modal and epistemological character of logic and mathematics, as well as of other nonempirically based assertions. The central idea of at least one version of the argument is that the postulates of, for example, arithmetic, do not describe independently existing fact, and instead constitute linguistic conventions, which represent decisions to use expressions in a certain way, with such-and-such meaning. Such decisions are 'conventions' in the sense that alternatives were available and furthermore the choices made among the alternatives do not require epistemic justification. Rather, they are to be justified on pragmatic grounds.[1]

On reflection, the fundamental claim that the postulates of arithmetic (or of any other subject) require no epistemic justification is really quite puzzling. In fact, conventionalism is based on serious philosophical errors. A linguistic convention which is supposed to be justified pragmatically rather than epistemically is not strictly a piece of cognitive information at all. It is not a truth or a fact; it is a decision, a commitment, a resolve. It is precisely because one's stipulations are in this way prescriptive rather than descriptive, that the justification for their adoption is pragmatic rather than epistemic. This feature already poses a significant challenge for the conventionalist account of the arithmetic postulates and of other *a priori* statements (statements whose contents are knowable independently of experience). The famous Peano Postulates, for example, describe paradigmatic facts concerning natural numbers; it is generally presumed that they state necessary facts that are knowable *a priori*. Linguistic conventions, while they are not themselves facts, do of course create, or give rise to, facts. That a particular expression, 'successor' for example, has the meaning it does—even when that meaning was secured by explicit stipulation—is every bit a knowable fact. But the linguistic convention *per se*, the resolve to use the expression with that meaning, is not the right sort of thing to be a piece of knowledge, properly speaking. Furthermore, the facts to which conventions give rise are, by the very nature of their source, contingent rather than necessary, and knowledge of those facts

---

The present chapter was presented as commentary on a paper by Richard Creath (cited in note 1 below) to the UCLA Carnap and Reichenbach Centennial Symposium, October 1991. An argument related to (though also significantly different from) one to be given below was presented by James Cain in 'Are Analytic Statements Necessarily *A Priori*?', *Australasian Journal of Philosophy*, 69, 3 (September, 1991), pp. 334–337. (I discovered Cain's article only after the present chapter had originally gone to press.)

[1] Richard Creath provides a sympathetic exposition of this version of the argument in 'Carnap's Conventionalism', delivered to the UCLA Carnap and Reichenbach Centennial Symposium.

is generally *a posteriori* (epistemically justified only by way of experience) rather than *a priori*. This poses a further, serious difficulty for the conventionalist's attempt to accommodate the necessary apriority of mathematics. I think it ultimately impossible that these pressing challenges to conventionalism can be satisfactorily met.[2]

There is a related problem with the conventionalist idea that the postulates of arithmetic, or of some other subject, are conventions for which a pragmatic rather than epistemic justification is appropriate, and with the related notion that, as David O. Brink put it, 'convention is the mother of necessity',[3] i.e. that the necessity of mathematics has its source in convention. I strongly suspect that these conventionalist ideas involve a conceptual confusion, one that remains widespread in contemporary analytic philosophy. Essentially, it is the failure to distinguish between the semantic cognitive content of a declarative sentence S and the logically independent, metatheoretic proposition that S itself is true.[4]

To take an example of a widely discussed linguistic convention, consider the sentence

(M) The Standard Bar (assuming it exists) is exactly one meter long at time t,

in the context of someone's having introduced the expression 'meter' as a word for a unit of length which is exactly the length at time t of a particular stick, the Standard Bar. We assume the Standard has a particular length at t. Let l be that length. The decision to use the word 'meter' as a name for l, together with the semantic facts created by this decision, must be sharply distinguished from the independent, pre-existing fact about the Standard Bar that it has the very length l at t. As we have seen, it is arguable—and indeed it is part of at least one version of the conventionalist account—that the decision to use 'meter' in this way is not a piece of knowledge, since it is not a natural, extralinguistic fact but a man-made convention, a resolve, and that therefore a pragmatic rather than an epistemic justification is appropriate. The stipulation creates or gives rise to the fact that the phrase 'one meter' designates the length l of the Standard at t, and hence also the fact that the sentence (M) is true. Nevertheless, the fact that the Standard has the particular length l at t is in no way a result of linguistic stipulation or decision. That fact, unlike the semantic facts concerning 'one meter' and (M), would have obtained regardless of whatever linguistic conventions one might have chosen to adopt. As Saul Kripke observed in opposition to Wittgenstein's cryptic remarks concerning this example, the fact that the Standard

---

[2] Perhaps the conventionalist is prepared to eschew the mathematical facts themselves in favor of the metamathematical facts created by linguistic convention. Creath, who sees this approach to the problem as far preferable to an epistemology that invokes Russellian-type nonempirical acquaintance with the subject matter of mathematics, endorsed the approach in response to my objection at the UCLA Carnap-Reichenbach symposium. But what becomes of the conventionally established meta-theoretic facts when the object-theoretic facts are discarded? If the best, or only, way of getting rid of the bath water involves throwing out the baby, one should probably give serious consideration to finding a use for grey water.

[3] See Alan Sidelle, *Necessity, Essence, and Individuation* (Cornell University Press, 1989), p. vi.

[4] In my book *Frege's Puzzle* (Atascadero, Calif.: Ridgeview, 1986, 1991), I highlight this distinction as a special case of the more general distinction between information *semantically contained* in a sentence and information merely *pragmatically imparted* by utterances of the sentence.

is one meter long at *t* is surely a statable piece of knowledge, and one that obtains only contingently.[5]

When philosophical questions concerning the epistemological status of a particular sentence are under investigation—whether it is a sentence from theoretical science, from mathematics, or from everyday life—our concern is not one of providing an historical or causal explanation of how the sentence came to be true (or perhaps I should say *assertable*), but one of providing a philosophical account of how one might come to know the proposition that is the cognitive content of the sentence. In particular, even if it is taken as settled that the decisions or conventions that resulted in the truth of (*M*) require only pragmatic justification, and even if it is taken as settled that the resulting fact that (*M*) is true is thereby knowable somehow *a priori*, we must consider anew the justification for the fact *semantically described* or *encoded* by (*M*).

How is knowledge of the fact semantically described or encoded by (*M*) to be justified? Sentence (*M*) and others like it have been offered by Kripke and David Kaplan, and discussed by many others, as nontrivial counterexamples to the thesis—which was the dominant view among the logical positivists—that any proposition that is knowable *a priori* is true by necessity.[6] The following similar, and in some respects purer, example of what is alleged to be the same phenomenon is due to Kaplan. If one introduces the expression 'Newman-1' as a name for the first child to be born in the twenty-second century, then the sentence

(*N*) If anyone will be the first child born in the twenty-second century, it will be Newman-1

is supposed to describe a fact that might have been otherwise yet is knowable *a priori* by the speaker who adopts this convention.[7] If Kaplan and Kripke are correct, one might try to make a case, along the conventionalist's lines, for the claim that (*M*) and (*N*) are justified pragmatically rather than epistemically. (I ignore for present purposes the significant fact mentioned above that a decision or convention that is justified pragmatically rather than epistemically is not properly termed '*a priori*', since it is not strictly a knowable fact at all.) However, Keith Donnellan and a few others, citing the distinction mentioned earlier between the semantic content of a sentence *S* and

---

[5] Kripke, *Naming and Necessity* (Harvard University Press, 1972, 1980), p. 54.

[6] Kripke, *Naming and Necessity*, pp. 54–56, 63, 79n; Kaplan, 'Demonstratives' and the 'Afterthoughts' thereto, in J. Almog, J. Perry, and H. Wettstein, eds, *Themes from Kaplan* (Oxford University Press, 1988), pp. 481–614, at 536–539, 550, 560, 597, 604–607. *Cf.* Kaplan, 'Dthat', in P. French, T. Uehling, and H. Wettstein, eds, *Contemporary Perspectives in the Philosophy of Language* (Minneapolis: University of Minnesota Press, 1979), pp. 383–400, at 397. Kripke has modified his view of the epistemological status of sentences like (*M*) and (*N*) (below) since the appearance of *Naming and Necessity*.

[7] The 'Newman-1' example first appeared in Kaplan's 'Quantifying In', in D. Davidson and J. Hintikka, eds, *Words and Objections: Essays on the Work of W. V. Quine* (Dordrecht: D. Reidel, 1969), pp. 206–242, at 228–229. There, however, Kaplan's intuitions were aligned much more closely with common sense. (*Cf.* also pp. 220–221 of that work.)

For some reason, in Kaplan's more recent writings (cited in the previous note) the description has become 'the first child to be born in the 21st Century'. Since the controversy concerning this sort of example is not likely to be settled during the current decade, we should do well to return to the original example, as I am doing here.

the metatheoretic proposition that S is true, criticized Kaplan's and Kripke's account of the epistemological status of sentences like (M) and (N).[8] Exposing a fallacy in Kripke's treatment of the matter, Donnellan argued persuasively that knowledge of the facts described by (M) and (N) are knowable only *a posteriori* (i.e. by means of experience), requiring a straightforwardly empirical justification.

I believe, with Donnellan and company, that (M) and (N) fail as examples of the contingent *a priori*.[9] The fact described by (M) is a nonlinguistic fact concerning the length of a particular object. That the Standard has length l is paradigmatically *a posteriori*. In fact, I propose to turn Kaplan and Kripke on their heads by taking these same examples a step further. It is my contention that these very same examples may be seen as demonstrating the falsity of an even more cherished thesis, virtually unchallenged in analytic philosophy: that all analytic sentences—or, if one prefers, all sentences that are true by convention—state facts that are knowable *a priori*.

Whether (M) and (N) qualify as genuinely analytic, or true by convention, depends in large measure on precisely what is meant in calling a sentence 'analytic' or 'true by convention'. A number of definitions or explications of analyticity have been proposed. My favorite is a proposal by Hilary Putnam. In an exposition of W. V. Quine's famous (if little understood) attack on the analytic–synthetic distinction, Putnam suggests that a sentence may be termed 'analytic' if it is deducible from the sentences in a finite list at the top of which someone who bears the ancestral of the graduate-student relation to Carnap has printed the words 'Meaning Postulate'.[10] This definition not only acknowledges the central importance of Carnap's contribution to the role of the analytic–synthetic distinction in analytic philosophy, but it has the additional virtue that it accords to those few among us who bear this special relationship to Carnap an authority that strikes me as only fitting. Unfortunately, there are those who fail to appreciate the virtues of Putnam's definition. For them I should like to propose a variation on Carnap's own explication of analyticity.

In his *Introduction to Semantics*, Carnap distinguished between what he called *pure semantics* and *descriptive semantics*.[11] Descriptive semantics was concerned with the

---

[8] Donnellan, 'The Contingent *A Priori* and Rigid Designators', in P. French, T. Uehling, and H. Wettstein, eds, *Contemporary Perspectives in the Philosophy of Language* (Minneapolis: University of Minnesota Press, 1979), pp. 49–60; Michael Levin, 'Kripke's Argument Against the Identity Thesis', *The Journal of Philosophy*, 72, 6 (March 27, 1975), pp. 149–167, at 152n2; Alvin Plantinga, *The Nature of Necessity* (Oxford University Press, 1974), at p. 8–9n1.

[9] I assume that the cognitive content of (or the fact semantically described by) (M) is the proposition (fact) that the Standard has the particular length l at t. For an account like Donnellan's, based on the theory of Russellian singular propositions as the semantic contents of sentences involving names and similar devices, but differing from Donnellan's in significant respects, compare *Frege's Puzzle*, pp. 140–142, and my 'How to Measure the Standard Meter', *Proceedings of the Aristotelian Society* (New Series), 88 (1987/1988), pp. 193–217. (I do not deny that there are examples of contingent *a priori* truths.)

[10] Putnam, 'The Meaning of "Meaning"', in K. Gunderson, ed., *Minnesota Studies in the Philosophy of Science, VII: Language, Mind, and Knowledge* (Minneapolis: University of Minnesota Press), pp. 131–193, at 174.

[11] Carnap, *Introduction to Semantics and Formalization of Logic* (Harvard University Press, 1942, 1943), volume I, section 5, at pp. 11–13.

semantical features of a natural language, with all its diachronic vicissitudes, while pure semantics was concerned exclusively with artificial languages ('semantical systems') whose semantics is stipulated. The former was an empirical science, whereas the latter consisted entirely of definitions for semantical expressions like 'designates-in-L' and 'true-in-L' and their logical consequences. Carnap's distinction between descriptive and pure semantics corresponds roughly to the distinction between a law of nature and a law passed by the legislature. Although Carnap did not explicitly propose doing so, his notion of pure semantics might have been extended to cover artificial bits of a natural language, as for example the name 'Newman-1' or, perhaps, certain legislative decrees by *L'Academie francaise*.

The definition of analyticity that I propose is based on a somewhat different distinction, between what I call *pure semantics* and *applied semantics*, analogous to the distinction between pure and applied mathematics. It is a purely semantic fact about English that the definite description 'the inventor of bifocals' designates (denotes, refers to) the inventor of bifocals. It is also a semantic fact about English that 'the inventor of bifocals' designates Benjamin Franklin. But the latter is a fact of applied semantics; it obtains partly in virtue of the nonlinguistic, historical fact that it was Benjamin Franklin who invented bifocals. Similarly, whereas it is a purely semantic fact about English that 'Snow is white' is true if and only if snow is white, it is an applied semantic fact that 'Snow is white' is true. As with Carnap's notion, pure semantics, in my sense, consists of appropriate recursive definitions for semantic expressions like 'true-in-L' and 'designates-in-L' and their logical consequences. For Carnap, however, any semantical matter concerning a natural language—including its pure semantics, in my sense—was *ipso facto* a matter of descriptive semantics. With my notion of pure semantics, the language L whose semantics is under consideration may be 'historically given', the product of natural evolution rather than of legislation. On the other side of the coin, the 'appropriateness' of the semantic definitions is crucial for my notion. A definition for truth-in-English that has the consequence that 'Snow is white' is true if and only if grass is green, while it may not involve any falsehood, is inappropriate. It has smuggled in some applied semantics.[12]

Certain sentences are special in that their truth value is settled entirely by pure semantics. It is a purely semantic fact about English for example that 'All married men are married' is true. For this fact is a logical consequence of the purely semantic fact that 'All married men are married' is true if and only if all married men are married. My proposal, finally, is that we call a true sentence 'analytic' if its truth is in this way a fact of pure rather than applied semantics.[13] This notion is related to Carnap's

---

[12] Thus while my distinction between pure and applied semantics is free of some of the controversial philosophical underpinnings of Carnap's distinction between pure and descriptive semantics, it is not free of all such. The same thing is true, for essentially the same reason, of Donald Davidson's program of providing a theory of meaning for a language by supplying a theory of truth.

[13] This notion of analyticity differs from that given in *Frege's Puzzle*, pp. 133–135. The latter is roughly the notion of a sentence whose proposition content is a logical truth. I argued there that sentences like 'Cicero is Tully' are analytic in the latter sense. In 'Relative and Absolute Apriority' (*Philosophical Studies* 1993; preceding chapter in this volume), I argue that 'Cicero is Tully' is also analytic in the sense proposed here.

notion of '*L*-truth', which he proposed as constituting an explication equally of analyticity and of necessity—although *L*-truth corresponds more closely to (and indeed is an important precursor to) the contemporary notion of *logical truth* as truth in all models for the language.[14]

The proposed definition includes certain sentences in addition to those that have the form of a logical validity. A sentence like 'All husbands are married', assuming 'husband' is synonymous with 'married man' also qualifies as analytic under the definition. For it is a purely semantic fact about English that the adjective 'married' (correctly) applies to all married individuals, and it is also a purely semantic fact that the noun 'husband' applies only to married men. In fact, assuming 'husband' and 'married man' are synonymous, the purely semantic fact that 'husband' applies only to husbands is identical with the fact that 'husband' applies only to married men. It is a truth of logic that if 'married' applies to all married individuals and 'husband' applies only to married men, then 'married' applies to any individual to which 'husband' applies. Given the further purely semantic fact that the English construction 'All *N*s are *A*' is true if and only if the adjective *A* applies to anything to which the NP *N* applies, it follows that 'All husbands are married' is true. Alternatively, it is a fact of pure semantics for English that 'All husbands are married' is true if all husbands are married. That all husbands are married is nothing more than the logical truth that all married men are married. The truth of 'All husbands are married' is thus logically settled by pure rather than applied semantics.

Let us return to sentence (*N*). Given the manner in which the designation of 'Newman-1' is fixed, the fact that 'Newman-1' designates the first child to be born in the 22nd Century, and hence also the resulting fact that (*N*) is true, are facts of pure rather than applied semantics. One may also say, therefore, that (*N*) is analytic; it is, in a straightforward sense, true by convention. Similarly for (*M*).[15] Indeed, the truth of either sentence is settled by 'pure semantics' in both Carnap's sense (as extended above to incorporate stipulated bits of natural language) and my own.

The notion of a sentence's truth being a logical consequence of pure rather than applied semantics is, roughly, a notion of 'truth solely by virtue of meaning'.[16] The

---

[14] *Introduction to Semantics and Formalization of Logic*, volume I, pp. 60–61, 79–80, 134–137; *Meaning and Necessity* (University of Chicago Press, 1947, 1956), section 2, at pp. 9–10.

[15] This is, of course, a purely terminological matter of decision. Those sentences are counted synthetic under the alternative notion of analyticity given in *Frege's Puzzle*. (See note 13 above.) They are also deemed synthetic on Kripke's alternative definition of analyticity—in *Naming and Necessity*, p. 39—though for a different reason. See especially pp. 56*n*, 122–123*n* of that work.

Interestingly, the further fact that 'Newman-1' designates Newman-1 is a fact of applied rather than pure semantics, since it obtains only by virtue of the nonlinguistic fact that Newman-1 (i.e. that very future person) will be the first child to be born in the twenty-second Century. *Cf.* 'How to Measure the Standard Meter', at pp. 200–201*n*10.

[16] I do not mean the phrase (or its cognates, e.g. 'true in virtue of meaning alone') in the traditional sense, which rules out that the sentence in question describes an extralinguistic fact and is in that sense true partly by virtue of a feature of the world. Nor (as will shortly become even more evident) do I wish to be associated with the philosophical thesis, which has traditionally gone hand in hand with the analytic–synthetic distinction, that sentences like 'All husbands are married' are devoid of extralinguistic, factual content. (*Cf.* note 12 above.) Indeed, I think it is obvious that even logical validities like 'All married men are married', since they are contentful and true,

epistemologically charged term '*a priori*' is less appropriate for this notion than the more semantic epithet 'analytic'. Nevertheless, I have often felt that this form of analyticity may be what is meant by particular uses of '*a priori*'.[17] The notion of truth-as-a-consequence-of-semantics-alone does have an epistemological dimension: for any sentence whose truth value is a logical consequence of pure semantics, anyone competent in the language is *ipso facto* in possession of sufficient information to determine that truth value by logic—never mind that knowledge of pure semantics for a natural language, and hence competence in the language, is gained only by means of experience. This might explain the Kaplan–Kripke stance with respect to (*M*) and (*N*). What originally prompted the claim that those sentences are *a priori* was the recognition that they belong, in some sense, with sentences for which knowledge of the meaning—however empirical that knowledge may be—is sufficient to establish their truth.[18]

Even if (*M*) and (*N*) are declared analytic, it is widely recognized nowadays that it does not follow that their contents are necessary truths. Still, it is usually assumed that the content of any sentence that is true solely by virtue of meaning is *a priori*. I maintain that (*M*) and (*N*), though analytic in the suggested sense, are both contingent and *a posteriori*; their contents are not only contingent but also knowable only by means of experience. Whereas the philosophical significance of the existence of propositions that are both contingent and *a priori* is apparent, the philosophical significance of the fact that such conventionally true sentences as (*M*) and (*N*) express contingencies even though their truth is a matter of pure semantics is less so. One consequence (noted by Kaplan, in 'Demonstratives', p. 540) is that Quine was wrong to see the 'second grade of modal involvement' as recasting analyticity, which is a meta-theoretic notion, as the object-language notion of necessity. Carnap was equally wrong to identify necessity with truth by pure semantics.

---

describe facts—typically extralinguistic (albeit particularly unexciting) facts that are both necessary and knowable *a priori*. There is a natural and straightforward sense in which such a sentence is, like any contentful and true sentence, true 'in virtue of' both its meaning and the extralinguistic fact that it describes. A better phrase for the notion of analyticity that I am embracing here is 'true as a consequence of meaning alone'. An analytic sentence, in the sense in which I am using the term, is a contentful sentence which is true (and hence true in virtue of both its meaning and some fact about the world), and for which the very fact that it is true is itself a logical consequence entirely of purely semantic facts about the sentence.

[17] *Cf.* my 'How *Not* to Become a Millian Heir', *Philosophical Studies*, 62, 2 (May 1991), pp. 165–177, at p. 172.

[18] Kripke says: 'What . . . is the *epistemological* status of the statement [(*M*)], for someone who has fixed the metric system by reference to [the Standard Bar]? It would seem that he knows it *a priori*. For if he used [the Standard Bar] to fix the reference of the term "one meter", then as a result of this kind of "definition" (which is not an abbreviative or synonymous definition), he knows automatically, without further investigation, that [the Standard Bar] is one meter long' (*Naming and Necessity*, p. 56). But what the reference-fixer knows automatically as a result of his reference-fixing definition is that (*M*) is true (in his own idiolect); he knows automatically without investigating the Standard Bar that however long it is, that length is designated by the phrase 'one meter'. He does not automatically know of that length that the bar is exactly (or even roughly) that long. For extended discussion see the articles by Donnellan and me cited in notes 8, 9, and 13 above.

If I am correct, another consequence is that analyticity, in this sense, is no more a guarantee of apriority (knowability independently of experience) than it is of necessity. In order to explain the special modal and epistemological status of necessary *a priori* sentences, it is not sufficient to assert (whether rightly or wrongly) that they are analytic, or true by convention.

Consider the following mathematical postulate:

(P) π is the ratio of the circumference of a circle to its diameter (if there is a fixed such ratio).

It is very plausible that the term 'π' is, in some sense, *defined* by (P). This is in fact significantly more plausible than the prospect that the expressions 'natural number', '0', and 'successor' are somehow implicitly but simultaneously defined by the Peano Postulates.[19] For (P) at least determines the extension of 'π'. Indeed, the truth of (P) is analogous in many ways to the truth of (M) and (N). To use Kripke's phrase, the definite description 'the ratio of the circumference of a circle to its diameter' *fixes the reference* of 'π', without thereby turning 'π' into a synonym for the description.[20] One point of disanalogy with the case of (M) and (N) is that the reference-fixing definite description involved here is a rigid designator; (P) contains a necessary truth. The various analogies with (M) and (N), however, amply demonstrate that the analyticity, or conventional truth, of (P) does not account for its necessity—otherwise (M) and (N) should be necessary as well. An alternative account is required.

A second striking disanalogy with the case of (M) and (N) is that it is not at all plausible that (P) is *a posteriori*. The epistemic justification of purely mathematical knowledge is very different from that concerning the lengths of bars and the birthdates of persons. On the other hand, the central point of analogy remains: the epistemic justification for the mathematical fact described by (P) is independent of the justification for the metamathematical fact that (P) is true. In order to know that (P) is true, one need only know how 'π' is defined. That is pure semantics. It is also *a posteriori*. To say that (P) is not *a posteriori*, however, is not yet to say that it is *a priori*. For it is arguable that the content of (P) is not knowable at all. Exactly what is involved in coming to know of the number, π, that it is the ratio of the circumference of a circle to its diameter (assuming there is such a ratio)—and even the question of whether it is possible for us to gain this purely mathematical, nonsemantic knowledge—are vexing matters that raise delicate issues in the philosophy of mathematics and epistemology generally.[21] The analyticity of (P) is of no help here.

---

[19] This prospect may have been first proposed by Richard Dedekind in '*Was Sind und Was Sollen die Zahlen?*' (section 10), one year before Peano proposed taking Dedekind's conditions as postulates for arithmetic. See William and Martha Kneale, *The Development of Logic* (Oxford University Press, 1962, 1986), at pp. 469–473. *Cf.* the position defended in Paul Benacerraf, 'What Numbers Could not Be', *The Philosophical Review*, 74 (1965), pp. 47–73.

[20] *Cf. Naming and Necessity*, p. 60.

[21] *Cf.* 'How to Measure the Standard Meter', pp. 211–212.

PART III
BELIEF

11

Illogical Belief (1989)

I

My purpose here is to present a defense against some criticisms that have been leveled against various doctrines and theses I advanced in *Frege's Puzzle*,[1] and to draw out some philosophically interesting applications and consequences of some of the central ideas utilized in my defense. The two principal objections I shall consider—one of which is offered by Saul Kripke and the other by Stephen Schiffer—as I reconstruct them, tacitly presuppose or assume one or both of a pair of closely related and largely uncontroversial principles concerning belief and deductive reasoning. The first is a normative principle, which I shall call *the belief justification principle*. It may be stated thus:

Suppose x is a normal, fully rational agent who consciously and rationally believes a certain proposition p. Suppose also that x is consciously interested in the further question of whether q is also the case, where q is another proposition. Suppose further that q is in fact a trivial deductive consequence of p. Suppose finally that x fully realizes that q is a deductive consequence of p and is fully able to deduce q from p. Under these circumstances, x would be rationally justified in coming to believe q on the basis of his or her belief of p (and its deductive relationship to q), or alternatively, if x withholds belief from q (by disbelieving or by suspending judgement) for independent reasons, x would be rationally justified in accordingly relinquishing his or her belief of p.

The second principle is similar to this, except that it is descriptive rather than prescriptive. I shall call it *the belief closure principle*:

Make the same initial-condition suppositions concerning x *vis a vis* the propositions p and q as given in the belief justification principle. Under these circumstances, if x consciously considers the question of whether q is the case and has adequate time for reflection on the matter, x will in fact come to believe q in addition to p on the basis of his or her belief of p (and its deductive relationship to q), unless x instead withholds belief from q (either by disbelieving or by suspending judgement) for independent reasons, and accordingly relinquishes his or her belief of p.

Part of the present chapter was presented to the Pacific Division of the American Philosophical Association on March 26, 1987. It has benefitted from discussion with Stephen Schiffer and with Scott Soames. Thanks go also to Keith Donnellan and the participants in his seminar at UCLA during Spring 1987 for their insightful comments on *Frege's Puzzle*, and to the participants in my seminar at UCSB during Fall 1986 for forcing me to elaborate on my response to Kripke's objection to my position regarding his puzzle about belief.

[1] Cambridge, Mass.: Bradford Books/MIT Press, 1986.

The belief justification principle, since it is normative rather than predictive, may seem somehow more certain and on sounder footing than the belief closure principle, but both principles are quite compelling. I shall claim that there are situations that present straightforward counter-examples to both principles simultaneously. Specifically, I claim that these principles fail in precisely the sort of circumstances to which my objectors tacitly apply the principles.

First, a preliminary exposition of the project undertaken in *Frege's Puzzle* is in order. The central thesis is that ordinary proper names, demonstratives, other single-word indexicals or pronouns (such as 'he'), and other simple (noncompound) singular terms are, in a given possible context of use, Russellian 'genuine names in the strict logical sense'.[2] Put more fully, I maintain the following anti-Fregean doctrine: that the contribution made by an ordinary proper name or other simple singular term, to securing the information content of, or the proposition expressed by, declarative sentences (with respect to a given possible context of use) in which the term occurs (outside of the scope of nonextensional operators, such as quotation marks) is just the referent of the term, or the bearer of the name (with respect to that context of use). In the terminology of *Frege's Puzzle*, I maintain that the *information value* of an ordinary proper name is just its referent.

Some other theses that I maintain in *Frege's Puzzle* are also critical to the present discussion. One such thesis (which Frege and Russell both more or less accepted) is that the proposition that is the information content of a declarative sentence (with respect to a given context) is structured in a certain way, and that its structure and constituents mirror, and are in some way readable from, the structure and constituents of the sentence containing that proposition.[3] By and large, a simple

---

[2] See Russell's 'Knowledge by Acquaintance and Knowledge by Description', Chapter X of Russell's *Mysticism and Logic and Other Essays* (London: Longmans, Green and Company, 1911), pp. 209–232, also in N. Salmon and S. Soames, eds, *Propositions and Attitudes* (Oxford University Press, Readings in Philosophy, 1988); and Russell's 'The Philosophy of Logical Atomism', in his *Logic and Knowledge*, R. C. Marsh, ed. (London: George Allen and Unwin, 1956), pp. 177–281; also in his *The Philosophy of Logical Atomism*, D. Pears, ed. (La Salle: Open Court, 1985), pp. 35–155.

[3] This separates the theory of *Frege's Puzzle* together with the theories of Frege, Russell, and their followers, from contemporary theories that assimilate the information contents of declarative sentences with such things as sets of possible worlds, or sets of situations, or functions from possible worlds to truth-values, etc.

Both Frege and Russell would regard declarative sentences as typically reflecting only *part of* the structure of their content, since they would insist that many (perhaps even most) grammatically simple (noncompound) expressions occurring in a sentence may (especially if introduced into the language by abbreviation or by some other type of explicit 'definition') contribute complex proposition-constituents that would have been more perspicuously contributed by compound expressions. In short, Frege and Russell regard the prospect of expressions that are grammatically simple yet semantically compound (at the level of content) as not only possible but ubiquitous. Furthermore, according to Russell's Theory of Descriptions, definite and indefinite descriptions ('the author of *Waverley*', 'an author', etc.), behave grammatically but not semantically (at the level of content) as a self-contained unit, so that a sentence containing such an expression is at best only a rough guide to the structure of the content. Russell extends this idea further to ordinary proper names and most uses of pronouns and demonstratives. This makes the structure of nearly any sentence only a very rough guide to the structure of the sentence's content. The theory advanced in *Frege's Puzzle* sticks much more closely to the grammatical structure of the sentence. (But see the following paragraph in the text concerning abstracted predicates.)

(noncompound) expression contributes a single entity, taken as a simple (noncomplex) unit, to the information content of a sentence in which the expression occurs, whereas the contribution of a compound expression (such as a phrase or sentential clause) is a complex entity composed of the contributions of the simple components.[4] Hence, the contents of beliefs formulatable using ordinary proper names, demonstratives, or other simple singular terms, are on my view so-called *singular propositions* (David Kaplan), i.e., structured propositions directly about some individual, which occurs directly as a constituent of the proposition. This thesis (together with certain relatively uncontroversial assumptions) yields the consequence that *de re* belief (or *belief of*) is simply a special case of *de dicto* belief (*belief that*). To believe *of* an individual x, *de re*, that it (he, she) is F is to believe *de dicto* the singular proposition about (containing) x that it (he, she) is F, a proposition that can be expressed using an ordinary proper name for x. Similarly for the other propositional attitudes.

There is an important class of exceptions to the general rule that a compound expression contributes to the information content of a sentence in which it occurs a complex entity composed of the contributions of the simple components. These are compound predicates formed by abstraction from an open sentence. For example, from the 'open' sentence 'I love her and she loves me'—with pronouns 'her' and 'she' functioning as 'freely' as the free variables occurring in such open sentences of the formal vernacular as '$F(a, x)$ & $F(x, a)$'—we may form (by 'abstraction') the compound predicate 'is someone such that I love her and she loves me'. Formally, using Alonzo Church's 'λ'-abstraction operator, we might write this '$(\lambda x)[F(a, x)$ & $F(x, a)]$'. Such an abstracted compound predicate should be seen as contributing something like an attribute or a Russellian *propositional function*, taken as a unit, to the information content of sentences in which it occurs, rather than as contributing a complex made up of the typical contributions of the compound's components.

In addition to this, I propose the sketch of an analysis of the binary relation of belief between believers and propositions (sometimes Russellian singular propositions). I take the belief relation to be, in effect, the existential generalization of a ternary relation, *BEL*, among believers, propositions, and some third type of entity. To believe a proposition p is to adopt an appropriate favorable attitude toward p when taking p in some relevant *way*. It is to agree to p, or to assent mentally to p, or to approve of p, or some such thing, when taking p a certain way. This is the *BEL* relation. I do not say a great deal about what the third relata for the *BEL* relation are. They are perhaps something like *proposition guises*, or *modes* of acquaintance or familiarity with propositions,

---

[4] There are well-known exceptions to the general rule—hence the phrase 'by and large'. Certain nonextensional operators, such as quotation marks, create contexts in which compound expressions contribute themselves as units to the information content of sentences in which the expression occurs. Less widely recognized is the fact that even ordinary temporal operators (e.g. 'on April 1, 1986' + past tense) create contexts in which some compound expressions (most notably, open and closed sentences) contribute complexes other than their customary contribution to information content. See my 'Tense and Singular Propositions', in J. Almog, J. Perry, and H. Wettstein, eds, *Themes from Kaplan* (Oxford University Press, 1989). The following paragraph in the text cites another largely overlooked class of exceptions.

or *ways* in which a believer may take a given proposition. The important thing is that, by definition, they are such that if a fully rational believer adopts conflicting attitudes (such as belief and disbelief, or belief and suspension of judgement) toward propositions p and q, then the believer must take p and q in different ways, by means of different guises, in harboring the conflicting attitudes toward them—even if p and q are in fact the same proposition. More generally, if a fully rational agent construes objects x and y as distinct (or even merely withholds construing them as one and the very same—as might be evidenced, for example, by the agent's adopting conflicting beliefs or attitudes concerning x and y), then for some appropriate notion of a way of taking an object, the agent takes x and y in different ways, even if in fact $x = y$.[5] Of course, to use a distinction of Kripke's, this formulation is far too vague to constitute a fully developed *theory* of proposition guises and their role in belief formation, but it does provide a *picture* of belief that differs significantly from the sort of picture of propositional attitudes advanced by Frege or Russell, and enough can be said concerning the *BEL* relation to allow for at least the sketch of a solution to certain philosophical problems, puzzles, and paradoxes—including those in the same family as Frege's notorious 'Hesperus'–'Phosphorus' puzzle.[6]

In particular, the *BEL* relation satisfies the following three conditions:

(*i*) A believes p if and only if there is some x such that A is familiar with p by means of x and $BEL(A, p, x)$;[7]

(*ii*) A may believe p by standing in *BEL* to p and some x by means of which A is familiar with p without standing in *BEL* to p and all x by means of which A is familiar with p;

---

[5] An appropriate notion of a way of taking an object is such that if an agent encounters a single object several times and each time construes it as a different object from the objects in the previous encounters, or even as a different object *for all he or she knows*, then each time he or she takes the object in a new and different way. This is required in order to accommodate the fact that an agent in such circumstances may (perhaps *inevitably will*) adopt several conflicting attitudes toward what is in fact a single object. One cannot require, however, that these ways of taking objects are rich enough by themselves to determine the object so taken, without the assistance of extra-mental, contextual factors. Presumably, twin agents who are molecule-for-molecule duplicates, and whose brains are in exactly the same configuration down to the finest detail, may encounter different (though duplicate) objects, taking them in the very same way. Likewise, a single agent might be artificially induced through brain manipulations into taking different objects the same way.

[6] The *BEL* relation is applied to additional puzzles in my 'Reflexivity', *Notre Dame Journal of Formal Logic*, 27, 3 (July 1986), pp. 401–429; also in N. Salmon and S. Soames, eds, *Propositions and Attitudes*.

[7] I do not claim that a sentence of the form ⌜A believes p⌝ is exactly synonymous with the existential formula on the right-hand side of 'if and only if' in condition (*i*). I do claim that condition (*i*) is a (metaphysically) necessary, conceptually *a priori* truth. (See two paragraphs back in the text concerning the contents of predicates. It may be helpful to think of the English verb 'believe' as a *name* for the binary relation described by the right-hand side of (*i*), i.e., for the existential generalization on the third argument-place of the *BEL* relation.) My claim in *Frege's Puzzle* (p. 111) that belief may be so 'analyzed' is meant to entail that condition (*i*) is a necessary *a priori* truth, not that the two sides of the biconditional are synonymous. (My own view is that something along these lines is all that can be plausibly claimed for such purported philosophical 'analyses' as have been offered for ⌜A knows p⌝, ⌜A perceives B⌝, ⌜A (nonnaturally) means p in uttering S⌝, etc.)

Illogical Belief

(*iii*) In one sense of 'withhold belief', *A* withholds belief concerning *p* (either by disbelieving or by suspending judgement) if and only if there is some *x* by means of which *A* is familiar with *p* and not-*BEL*(*A*, *p*, *x*).

These conditions generate a philosophically important distinction between withholding belief and failure to believe (i.e., not believing). In particular, one may both withhold belief from and believe the very same proposition simultaneously. (Neither withholding belief nor failure to believe is to be identified with the related notions of disbelief and suspension of judgement—which are two different ways of withholding belief, in my sense, and which may occur simultaneously with belief of the very same proposition in a single believer.)

It happens in most cases (though not all) that when a believer believes some particular proposition *p*, the relevant third relatum for the *BEL* relation is a function of the believer and some particular *sentence* of the believer's language. There is, for example, the binary function *f* that assigns to any believer *A* and sentence *S* of *A*'s language, the *way A* takes the proposition contained in *S* (in *A*'s language with respect to *A*'s context at some particular time *t*) were it presented to *A* (at *t*) through the very sentence *S*, if there is exactly one such way of taking the proposition in question. (In some cases, there are too many such ways of taking the proposition in question.)

This account may be applied to the comic-book legend of Superman and his woman-friend Lois Lane. According to this saga, Lois Lane is acquainted with Superman in both of his guises—as a mild-mannered reporter and dullard named 'Clark Kent' and as the superheroic defender of truth, justice, and the American way, named 'Superman'—but she is unaware that these are one and the very same person. Whereas she finds our hero somewhat uninteresting when she encounters him in his mild-mannered reporter guise, her heartbeat quickens with excitement whenever she encounters him, or even merely thinks of him, in his superhero guise. Consider now the sentence

(0) Lois Lane believes that Clark Kent is Superman.

Is this true or false? According to my account, it is true! For Lois Lane agrees to the proposition that Clark Kent is Superman when taking it in a certain way—for example, if one points to Superman in one of his guises and says 'He is him', or when the proposition is presented to her by such sentences as 'Clark Kent is Clark Kent' and 'Superman is Superman'. That is,

> *BEL*[Lois Lane, that Clark Kent is Superman, *f* (Lois Lane, 'Superman is Superman')].

Lois Lane also withholds belief concerning whether Superman is Superman. In fact, according to my account, she believes that Superman is not Superman! For she agrees to the proposition that Superman is not Superman when taking it in the way it is presented to her by the sentence 'Clark Kent is not Superman'. That is,

> *BEL*[Lois Lane, that Superman is not Superman, *f* (Lois Lane, 'Clark Kent is not Superman')],

and hence, since Lois Lane is fully rational, it is not the case that

BEL[Lois Lane, that Superman is Superman, f(Lois Lane, 'Clark Kent is Superman')].

II

It is evident that these consequences of my account do not conform with the way we actually speak. Instead it is customary when discussing the Superman legend to deny sentence (0) and to say such things as

(1) Lois Lane does not realize that Clark Kent is Superman.

According to my account, sentence (1) is literally false in the context of the Superman legend. In fact, (1)'s literal truth-conditions are, according to the view I advocate, conditions that are plainly unfulfilled (in the context of the Superman legend). Why, then, do we say such things as (1)? Some explanation of our speech patterns in these sorts of cases is called for. The explanation I offer in *Frege's Puzzle* is somewhat complex, consisting of three main parts. The first part of the explanation for the common disposition to utter or to assent to (1) is that speakers may have a tendency to confuse the content of (1) with that of

(1′) Lois Lane does not realize that 'Clark Kent is Superman' is true (in English).

Since sentence (1′) is obviously true, this confusion naturally leads to a similarly favorable disposition toward (1). This part of the explanation cannot be the whole story, however, since even speakers who know enough about semantics to know that the fact that Clark Kent is Superman is logically independent of the fact that the sentence 'Clark Kent is Superman' is true (in English, according to the legend), and who are careful to distinguish the content of (1) from that of (1′), are nevertheless favorably disposed toward (1) itself—because of the fact that Lois Lane bursts into uncontrollable laughter whenever the mere suggestion 'Clark Kent could turn out to be Superman' is put to her.

The second part of my explanation for (1)'s appearance of truth is that (1) itself is the product of a plausible but mistaken inference from the fact that Lois Lane sincerely dissents (or at least does not sincerely assent) when queried 'Is Clark Kent Superman?', while fully understanding the question and grasping its content, or (as Keith Donnellan has pointed out) even from her expressions of preference for the man of steel over the mild-mannered reporter. More accurately, ordinary speakers (and even most nonordinary speakers) are disposed to regard the fact that Lois Lane does not agree to the proposition that Clark Kent is Superman, when taking it in a certain way (the way it might be presented to her by the very sentence 'Clark Kent is Superman'), as sufficient to warrant the denial of sentence (0) and the assertion of sentence (1). In the special sense explained in the preceding section, Lois Lane withholds belief from the proposition that Clark Kent is Superman, actively failing to agree with it whenever it is put to her in so many words, and this fact misleads ordinary speakers, including Lois Lane herself, into concluding that Lois harbors no favorable attitude of agreement whatsoever toward the proposition in question, and hence does not believe it.

The third part of the explanation is that, where someone under discussion has conflicting attitudes toward a single proposition that he or she takes to be two independent propositions (i.e. in the troublesome 'Hesperus'–'Phosphorus', 'Superman'–'Clark Kent' type cases), there is an established practice of using belief attributions to convey not only the proposition agreed to (which is specified by the belief attribution) but also the way the subject of the attribution takes the proposition in agreeing to it (which is no part of the semantic content of the belief attribution). Specifically, there is an established practice of using such a sentence as (0), which contains the uninteresting proposition that Lois Lane believes the singular proposition about Superman that he is him, to convey furthermore that Lois Lane agrees to this proposition *when she takes it in the way it is presented to her by the very sentence 'Clark Kent is Superman'* (assuming she understands this sentence). That is, there is an established practice of using (0) to convey the thought that

BEL[Lois Lane, that Clark Kent is Superman, f(Lois Lane, 'Clark Kent is Superman')].

III

The last part of the explanation just sketched may be clarified by considering an objection raised by Schiffer.[8] Schiffer sees my theory as attempting to explain ordinary speakers' dispositions to utter or to assent to (1) by postulating that in such cases a particular mechanism, of a sort described by H. P. Grice,[9] comes into play. The mechanism works in the following way: A speaker deliberately utters a particular sentence where there is mutual recognition by the speaker and his or her audience that the speaker believes the sentence to be false. The speaker and the audience mutually recognize that the speaker is not opting out of Grice's conversational Cooperative Principle (according to which one should make one's conversational contribution such as is required, at the stage at which it occurs, by the accepted purpose or direction of the conversation) and hence that the speaker is subject to the usual Gricean conversational maxims. Yet the speaker and audience also recognize that there is a *prima facie* apparent violation of the first conversational *maxim of Quality*: 'Do not say what you believe to be false.' The audience infers, in accordance with the speakers intentions, that the speaker is using the sentence not to commit himself or herself to its literal content (which is taken to be false) but instead to convey, or to 'implicate', some saliently related proposition, which is easily gleaned from the context of

---

[8] 'The "Fido–Fido" Theory of Belief', in James Tomberlin, ed., *Philosophical Perspectives 1: Metaphysics* (Atascadero: Ridgeview, 1987), pp. 455–480. Schiffer's article includes a rejoinder, in an appended postscript, to many of the arguments of the present article. I think it is useful, however, to include in the present article my own statements of the arguments and replies that Schiffer is rejoining in his postscript. It is left to the reader to evaluate the relative merits of my replies to Schiffer's objections and Schiffer's rejoinder to my replies.

[9] 'Logic and Conversation', in P. Cole and J. L. Morgan, eds, *Syntax and Semantics*, volume 3 (New York: Academic Press, 1975), pp. 41–55; also in D. Davidson and G. Harman, eds, *The Logic of Grammar* (Encino: Dickenson, 1975), pp. 64–75; also in A. P. Martinich, ed., *The Philosophy of Language* (Oxford University Press, 1985), pp. 159–170.

the conversation. In the case of sentence (1), or this account, the speaker employs this mechanism to implicate that Lois Lane does not agree to the proposition that Clark Kent is Superman when she takes it in the way it is presented to her by the very sentence 'Clark Kent is Superman'. Schiffer's criticism is that this account flies in the face of the obvious fact that ordinary speakers do not believe (1) to be false, but believe it true.

This criticism is indeed decisive against the explanation described above for our propensity to say such things as (1). But this is not the explanation I proposed in *Frege's Puzzle*. Oddly, the very example of sentence (1) comes from a particular passage in *Frege's Puzzle* that explicitly precludes Schiffer's interpretation:

> Now, there is no denying that, given the proper circumstances, we say things like 'Lois Lane does not realize ... that Clark Kent is Superman' ... When we make these utterances, we typically do not intend to be speaking elliptically or figuratively; we take ourselves to be speaking literally and truthfully. (p. 81)

My pragmatic account of the appearance of truth in the case of such sentences as (1) is meant not only as an explanation of the widespread disposition to utter or to assent to (1), but equally as an explanation of the widespread intuition that (1) is literally true, and equally as an explanation of the widespread belief of the content of (1). What is needed, and what I attempt to provide (or at least a sketch thereof), is not merely an explanation of the disposition of ordinary speakers to utter or assent to (1) given the relevant facts concerning Lois Lane's ignorance of Superman's secret identity, but an explanation why ordinary speakers who understand (1) perfectly well, fully grasping its content, sincerely utter it while taking themselves to speaking literally and truthfully, without being exactly similarly disposed toward such synonymous sentences as

Lois Lane does not realize that Superman is Superman

when they also understand these sentences perfectly well and the common content of these sentences is something these speakers believe.[10] The particular Gricean mechanism that Schiffer describes is no doubt part of the correct explanation in *some* cases of how ordinary speakers may use certain sentences to convey what these sentences do not literally mean. But the particular mechanism in question cannot yield a coherent account of why ordinary speakers believe that a given sentence is true. How would the alleged explanation go? 'Here's why ordinary speakers believe that sentence S is true: They realize that it's false. This mutual recognition of its falsity enables them to use S to convey something true. Their use of S to convey something true leads them to conclude that S is true.' This alleged explanation is incoherent; it purports to explain ordinary speakers' belief that a given sentence is true by means of their belief that it is false. Clearly, no attempt to explain the widespread view that (1) is literally true can

---

[10] Contrary to a proposal Schiffer makes in his postscript, the observation that the content of (1) is something ordinary speakers believe, *per se*, does not yield an adequate explanation here. For ordinary speakers are not similarly disposed toward 'Lois Lane does not realize that Superman is Superman' although they fully grasp its content, which (on my view) is the same as that of (1).

proceed from the initial hypothesis that ordinary speakers typically believe that (1) is literally false!

Schiffer's criticism concerns only the third part of the explanation sketched in the preceding section: the hypothesis that there is an established practice of using such a sentence as (0) to convey that Lois Lane agrees to the proposition that Clark Kent is Superman when taking it in the way it is presented to her by the very sentence 'Clark Kent is Superman'. I do not claim that this practice came about by means of a special Gricean mechanism requiring the mutual recognition by the speaker and his or her audience that sentence (0) is literally true. Quite the contrary, I suppose that many ordinary speakers, and most philosophers, would take the proposition that they use the sentence to convey to be the very content of the sentence. That is why they would deem the sentence literally false. Schiffer describes a particular mechanism that allows speakers to use a sentence to convey ('implicate') what it does not literally mean by means of a mutual recognition that what is conveyed cannot be what the sentence literally means. I had in mind an alternative mechanism that allows speakers to use a sentence to convey something stronger than what it literally means, thereby creating a mutual misimpression that what is conveyed is precisely what the sentence literally means. There is nothing in the general Gricean strategy (as opposed to the particular strategy involving Grice's first conversational maxim of Quality) that requires ordinary speakers to recognize or believe that the sentence used is literally false. Grice describes several mechanisms that involve speakers' using a sentence mutually believed to be true to convey ('implicate') something further that the sentence does not literally mean, and Schiffer himself cites such a mechanism in the course of presenting his objection. Surely there can be such a mechanism that, when employed, sometimes has the unintended and unnoticed consequence that speakers mistake what is conveyed ('implicated') for the literal content. Consider, for example, the conjunction 'Jane became pregnant and she got married', which normally carries the implicature that Jane became pregnant before getting married. Utterers of this sentence, in order to employ it with its customary implicature, need not be aware that the sentence is literally true even if Jane became pregnant only after getting married. Some utterers may well become misled by the sentence's customary implicature into believing that the sentence literally means precisely what it normally conveys—so that, if they believe that Mary became pregnant only after getting married, they would reject the true but misleading conjunction as literally false. A similar situation may obtain in connection with certain English indicative conditionals ('If you work hard, you will be rewarded') and universal generalizations ('All white male cats with blue eyes are deaf'), which carry an implicature of some salient connection between antecedent and consequent that is more than merely truth-functional 'constant conjunction'. (The implicated connection need not be the temporal relation of earlier-later, as in the conjunction case.) It is this general sort of situation, or something very similar, that I impute to propositional-attitude attributions.[11]

---

[11] It is doubtful whether the conjunction and conditional cases, and the sort of situation I have in mind in connection with propositional-attitude attributions, qualify as cases of what Grice calls *particularized conversational implicature* (by far the most widely discussed notion of Gricean

Frege's Puzzle makes the suggestion that, in a certain type of case, a simple belief attribution ⌜*c* believes that *S*⌝ may be routinely used to convey the further information (not semantically encoded) that (assuming he or she understands his or her sentence for *S*) *x* agrees to the proposition *p* when taking it in the way it is presented to *x* by the very sentence *S*, where *x* is the referent of *c* and *p* is the content of the nonindexical sentence *S*.[12] The book does not include the much stronger claim that the manner in which such a belief attribution is routinely used to convey this further information must exhibit all of the features that characterize Gricean implicature—let alone does it include the highly specific claim that the phenomenon in question is an instance of Gricean particularized conversational implicature.

I have not thoroughly explored the relation of Grice's many rich and fruitful ideas to the sort of project undertaken in *Frege's Puzzle*; obviously, there is a great deal more to be investigated. It should be clear, however, that there is nothing in Grice's general apparatus that makes the sort of explanation I have in mind in connection with propositional-attitude attributions altogether impossible. Quite the contrary, some of the central ideas of the Gricean program are obviously directly applicable.

IV

In *Frege's Puzzle* I explicitly applied the various doctrines and theses sketched in Section I above to Kripke's vexing puzzle about belief.[13] Kripke considers a certain Frenchman, Pierre, who at some time t_1, speaks only French and, on the basis of

implicature); in a number of important respects, these cases better fit one or the other of Grice's two contrasting notions of *generalized conversational implicature* and *conventional* (nonconversational) *implicature*. Surely a great many speakers may be confused by the conventional or generalized conversational implicature of a sentence into thinking that the sentence literally says (in part) what it in fact only implicates. Grice's notion of particularized conversational implicature apparently precludes the possibility of this sort of confusion. (See the third essential feature of particularized conversational implicature cited *op. cit.* on p. 169 of Martinich.) In some cases, it may also be possible to cancel explicitly the conventional or generalized conversational implicature of a sentence. I am not suggesting that the case of propositional-attitude attributions is exactly analogous to the conjunction and conditional cases. (The issues here are quite delicate.)

[12] It might be thought that if ordinary speakers take a belief attribution ⌜*c* believes that *S*⌝ to express the assertion that *x* agrees to the proposition *p* when taking it in the way it is presented to *x* by the very sentence *S*, and they use the attribution to convey (or 'implicate') precisely this proposition, then this proposition cannot help but *be* (part of) the content of the attribution. The fact that the attribution does not literally mean what it is used to convey is attested to by the validity of the inference from the conjunction 'Floyd claims that Superman is mild-mannered, and Lois believes anything Floyd says concerning Superman' to 'Lois believes that Superman is mild-mannered'. The inference would be invalid if its conclusion literally meant that Lois agrees that Superman is mild-mannered when she takes this proposition in the way it is presented to her by the very sentence 'Superman is mild-mannered'. The premiss gives information concerning only what propositions Lois believes, not how she takes them in believing them. (Grice also insists, p. 169 of Martinich, that the supposition that an erstwhile implicature of a particular construction has become included in the construction's conventional meaning 'would require special justification'.)

[13] 'A Puzzle about Belief', in A. Margalit, ed. *Meaning and Use* (Dordrecht: D. Reidel, 1979), pp. 239–275; also in N. Salmon and S. Soames, eds, *Propositions and Attitudes*. Kripke's puzzle is addressed in appendix A of *Frege's Puzzle*, pp. 129–132.

deceptive travel brochures published by the London Chamber of Commerce and the like, comes to assent to the French sentence '*Londres est jolie*' (as a sentence of French), which literally means in French that London is pretty. At some later time t_2, Pierre moves to London and learns the English language by direct assimilation (not by translation in an ESL course). Seeing only especially unappealing parts of the city, and not recognizing that this city called 'London' is the very same city that he and his fellow French speakers call '*Londres*', Pierre comes to assent to the sentence 'London is not pretty' (as a sentence of English), while maintaining his former attitude toward the French sentence '*Londres est jolie*'. Kripke presses the following question: Does Pierre believe at t_2 that London is pretty? The puzzle arises from Kripke's forceful demonstration that both the assertion that Pierre does believe this, and the denial that he does, appear deeply unsatisfactory (for different reasons). Likewise, both the assertion that Pierre believes at t_2 that London is *not* pretty and the denial that he does appear deeply unsatisfactory.

What does my account say about Pierre's doxastic disposition at t_2 *vis à vis* the propositions that London is pretty and that London is not pretty? I maintain that he believes them both. For he understands the French sentence '*Londres est jolie*' when he assents to it, fully grasping its content. That content is the proposition that London is pretty. Since he agrees to this proposition when he takes it in the way it is presented to him by the French sentence, he believes it. Exactly the same thing obtains with regard to the negation of this proposition and the English sentence 'London is not pretty'. Hence he believes this proposition too. In fact, Pierre presumably also assents to the conjunctive sentence '*Londres* is pretty but London is not', as a sentence of Frenglish, i.e. French-cum-English (French-English 'word-salad'). And he understands this sentence in Frenglish. Hence he even believes the conjunctive proposition that London is pretty and London is not pretty. If he is sufficiently reflective, he will even know that he believes that London is pretty and London is not pretty. For given adequate time to reflect on the matter he can, with sufficient linguistic competence and ample epistemic justification, assent to the sentence 'You, Pierre, believe that *Londres* is pretty but London is not', taken as addressed to him as a sentence of Frenglish. The tri-part explanation sketched in Section II above may easily be extended to account for our propensity to say such things (in Frenglish) as 'Pierre does not realize that London is *Londres*' despite their falsity.

Kripke objects to the sort of account I offer of Pierre's situation with some trenchant remarks. I quote at length:

But there seem to be insuperable difficulties with [the position that Pierre believes both that London is pretty and that London is not pretty]... We may suppose that Pierre, in spite of the unfortunate situation in which he now finds himself, is a leading philosopher and logician. He would *never* let contradictory beliefs pass. And surely anyone, leading logician or no, is in principle in a position to notice and correct contradictory beliefs if he has them. Precisely for this reason, we regard individuals who contradict themselves as subject to greater censure than those who merely have false beliefs. But it is clear that Pierre, as long as he is unaware that the cities he calls 'London' and '*Londres*' are one and the same, is in no position to see, by logic alone, that at least one of his beliefs must be false. He lacks information, not logical acumen. He cannot be convicted of inconsistency: to do so is incorrect.

204 *Belief*

We can shed more light on this if we change the case. Suppose that, in France, Pierre, instead of affirming '*Londres est jolie*,' had affirmed, more cautiously, '*Si New York est jolie, Londres est jolie aussi*,' so that [according to this account] he believed that *if* New York is pretty, so is London. Later Pierre moves to London, learns English as before, and says (in English) 'London is not pretty'. So he now [allegedly] believes, further, that London is *not* pretty. Now from the two premises, both of which appear to be among his beliefs, (a) if New York is pretty, London is, and (b) London is not pretty, Pierre should be able to deduce by *modus tollens* that New York is not pretty. But no matter how great Pierre's logical acumen may be, *he cannot in fact make any such deduction, as long as he supposes that* 'Londres' *and* 'London' *may name two different cities*. If he *did* draw such a conclusion, he would be guilty of a fallacy.

Intuitively, he may well suspect that New York is pretty, and just this suspicion may lead him to suppose that '*Londres*' and 'London' probably name distinct cities. Yet if we follow our normal practice of reporting the beliefs of French and English speakers, *Pierre has available to him (among his beliefs) both the premises of a modus tollens argument that New York is not pretty*. ... (pp. 257–258)

... Pierre is in no position to draw ordinary logical consequences from the conjoint set of what, when we consider him separately as a speaker of English and as a speaker of French, we would call his beliefs. He cannot infer a contradiction from his separate [alleged] beliefs that London is pretty and that London is not pretty. Nor, in the modified situation above, would Pierre make a normal *modus tollens* inference from his [alleged] beliefs that London is not pretty and that London is pretty if New York is. ... Indeed, if he *did* draw what would appear to be the normal conclusion in this case ... , Pierre would in fact be guilty of a logical fallacy. (p. 262)

... The situation of the puzzle seems to lead to a breakdown of our normal practices of attributing belief... [The view that Pierre believes both that London is pretty and that London is not pretty] definitely get[s] it *wrong*. [That view] yields the result that Pierre holds inconsistent beliefs, that logic alone should teach him that one of his beliefs is false. Intuitively, this is plainly incorrect. ... [It is] *obviously wrong* ... [a] patent falsehood ... (pp. 266–267)

... when we enter into the area exemplified by ... Pierre, we enter into an area where our normal practices of interpretation and attribution of belief are subjected to the greatest possible strain, perhaps to the point of breakdown. So is the notion of the *content* of someone's assertion, the *proposition* it expresses.

... Pierre's [case] lies in an area where our normal apparatus for the ascription of belief is placed under the greatest strain and may even break down.   (pp. 269–270)

These passages indicate (or at least strongly suggest) that Kripke rejects as 'plainly incorrect' the view, which I maintain, that Pierre believes at t_2 both that London is pretty and that London is not pretty.[14]

---

[14] I believe that a careful reading of 'A Puzzle about Belief' reveals that Kripke probably ultimately rejects his schematic *disquotation principle* (pp. 248–249). The schema might be rewritten in the form of a single general principle (instead of as a schema), as follows: *If a speaker, on reflection, sincerely assents to a particular sentence S that he fully understands (as a sentence of his language), then he believes the content of S (in his language with respect to his context)*. By contrast with Kripke's original principle schema, in this variation the sentence *S* may contain indexical or pronominal devices, and need not be a sentence of English. Either version, if correct, would entail that, since Pierre is a normal English speaker who fully understands, and on reflection sincerely assents to, the English sentence 'London is not pretty', he believes that London is not pretty, and since Pierre is also a normal Frenglish speaker who fully understands, and on reflection sincerely assents to, '*Londres* is pretty', he also believes that London is pretty. It is this disquotation principle

V

Schiffer raises a second objection to the theory advanced in *Frege's Puzzle*—one that is evidently similar in certain respects to Kripke's, but focuses more on the *de re* mode than on the *de dicto*. Schiffer's second criticism concerns such nesting (or second-level) propositional-attitude attributions as

(2) Floyd believes that Lois Lane does not realize that Clark Kent is Superman.

Schiffer tells a little story according to which Floyd is an ordinary speaker who is fully aware that the mild-mannered reporter is none other than the man of steel himself, and who is also aware of Lois Lane's ignorance of this fact. Schiffer argues that, whereas sentence (2) is straightforwardly true in the context of this little story—since Floyd believes that sentence (1) is true (and knows that if (1) is true, then Lois Lane does not realize that Clark Kent is Superman)—I am committed by my adherence to my central thesis (which Schiffer calls 'the 'Fido'–Fido theory of belief') to the falsity of (2), and further by my account of the dispositions of ordinary speakers to utter or to assent to (1), to the erroneous claim that Floyd does not believe that sentence (1) is true, and instead believes it to be false.

We have seen in Section III above that, contrary to Schiffer's interpretation, the explanation I offer for Floyd's propensity to utter (1) does not involve the obviously false claim that Floyd believes (1) to be false. How is it that I am committed to the claim that Floyd does not believe that Lois Lane does not realize that Clark Kent is Superman, and hence to the falsity of (2)? Schiffer argues that I am thus committed by invoking a certain principle that concerns *de re* belief, and which he has elsewhere called 'Frege's Constraint'.[15] Actually, the principle Schiffer explicitly cites is inadequate for his purposes, and should be replaced by a pair of principles which together entail the cited principle. The first might be called 'Frege's Thesis' and may be stated (using Schiffer's theoretical apparatus and terminology) as follows:

If x believes y to be F, then there is an object m that is a mode of presentation of y and x believes y under m to be F.

The second principle, which I shall call 'Schiffer's Constraint', is the following (again stated using Schiffer's theoretical apparatus and terminology):

If a fully rational person x believes a thing y under a mode of presentation m to be F and also disbelieves y under a mode of presentation m' to be F, then $m \neq m'$ and x construes m and m' as (modes of) presenting distinct individuals.

Together these two principles pose a serious obstacle to my taking the position, which seems undeniably correct, that sentence (2) is true. For Floyd, whom we may

---

that is 'subjected to the greatest possible strain, perhaps to the point of breakdown'. In contrast to Kripke's skepticism, I endorse the disquotation principle and its consequences. In fact, the principle is virtually entailed by the first condition on the *BEL* relation given in Section I above.

[15] 'The Basis of Reference', *Erkenntnis* 13 (July 1978), pp. 171–206, at p. 180.

suppose to be fully rational, no doubt believes that Lois Lane realizes that Superman is Superman. Yet given that Floyd is aware of Superman's secret identity, there do not seem to be the two modes of presentation required by Frege's Thesis and Schiffer's Constraint in order for Floyd to believe furthermore that Lois Lane does not realize that Clark Kent is Superman.

VI

Let us consider first Kripke's argument against the view that Pierre believes at t_2 both that London is pretty and that it is not. I briefly addressed Kripke's objection in *Frege's Puzzle*. I shall elaborate here on certain aspects of my reply.[16]

Kripke's primary critical argument might be stated in full thus:

*P*1: Pierre sees, by logic alone, that the propositions (beliefs) that London is pretty and that London is not pretty are contradictory.

*P*2: If Pierre has the beliefs that London is pretty and that London is not pretty, then he is in principle in a position to notice that he has these beliefs.

Therefore,

*C*1: If Pierre has the beliefs that London is pretty and that London is not pretty, then he is in principle in a position to see both that he has these beliefs and that they are contradictory.

*P*3: But Pierre, as long as he is unaware that the cities he calls 'London' and '*Londres*' are one and the same, is in no position to see that the propositions (beliefs) that London is pretty and that London is not pretty are simultaneously beliefs of his and contradictory, and hence is in no position to see that at least one of his beliefs must be false.

Therefore,

*C*2: As long as Pierre is unaware that the cities he calls 'London' and '*Londres*' are one and the same, it is incorrect to say that he has the beliefs that London is pretty and that London is not pretty.

An exactly similar argument may be stated, as Kripke proposes, replacing the belief that London is pretty with the more cautious belief that London is pretty if New York is, and replacing the logical attribute of contradictoriness with that of entailing that New York is not pretty. Furthermore, in this case we may replace the epistemic state of being in a position to see that at least one of the first pair of beliefs must be false

---

[16] I treat logical attributes (such as the relation of deductive entailment and the property of contradictoriness) here as attributes of propositions, setting aside for the present purpose my contention that these attributes are primarily and in the first instance attributes of sentences in a language, and that whereas it is not incorrect, it can be quite misleading to treat them also as attributes of propositions.

with the disposition of being such that one would be logically justified in inferring that New York is not pretty from the second, more cautious pair of beliefs.

Both the displayed argument and the one obtained by making the suggested substitutions are extremely compelling. But they are fallacious. I do not mean by this that they proceed from false premisses. I mean that they are invalid: the premisses are all true, but one of the critical inferences is fallacious. Which one?

The fallacy involved may be seen more clearly if we first consider the following simpler and more direct argument:

If Pierre has the beliefs that London is pretty if New York is and that London is not pretty, then (assuming that he consciously considers the further question of whether New York is pretty, that he fully realizes that the proposition that New York is not pretty is a trivial and immediate deductive consequence of the propositions that London is pretty if New York is and that London is not pretty, that he has no independent reasons for withholding belief from the proposition that New York is not pretty, and that he has adequate time for reflection on the matter) he will come to believe that New York is not pretty on the basis of these beliefs, and he would be logically justified in doing so. But Pierre, as long as he is unaware that the cities he calls 'London' and '*Londres*' are one and the same, will not come to believe that New York is not pretty on the basis of his beliefs that London is pretty if New York is and that London is not pretty, and he would not be logically justified in doing so. Therefore, as long as Pierre is unaware that the cities he calls 'London' and '*Londres*' are one and the same, it is incorrect to say that he has the beliefs that London is pretty if New York is and that London is not pretty.

This argument is evidently at least very much like one of Kripke's, and it is valid. I have formulated it in such a way as to make obvious its reliance, in its first premiss, on the belief closure and justification principles. (Let p be the conjunctive proposition that whereas London is pretty if New York is, London is not pretty, and let q be the entailed proposition that New York is not pretty.) I maintain that Pierre's inability to infer that New York is not pretty presents a bona fide counter-example to these principles, so that the first premiss of this argument is false. The theses advanced in *Frege's Puzzle* show how Pierre's case may be seen as presenting a counter-example. Pierre fully understands the English sentence 'London is not pretty' and also the Frenglish sentence '*Londres* is pretty if New York is', grasping their content. In particular, he understands the Frenglish sentence to mean precisely what it does mean (in Frenglish): that London is pretty if New York is. (He does not misunderstand it to mean, for example, that *Rome* is pretty if New York is. If any French speaker who has never been to London can nevertheless understand French sentences containing the French name '*Londres*', Pierre understands the particular sentence '*Si* New York *est jolie, Londres est jolie aussi*' as well as its Frenglish translations.) When these sentences are put to him, he unhesitatingly assents; he agrees to the propositions that are their contents when he takes these propositions in the way they are presented to him by these very sentences. Hence he believes these propositions.

Pierre also fully understands the English sentence 'London is pretty if New York is', grasping its content. He is fully aware that the proposition so expressed, taken together with the proposition expressed by 'London is not pretty', collectively entail that New York is not pretty. Unfortunately for Pierre, he does not take this conditional proposition the same way when it is presented to him by the different sentences. He mistakes the proposition for two, logically independent propositions—just as he mistakes London itself for two separate cities. This is evidenced by the fact that he harbors conflicting doxastic attitudes toward the proposition. He believes it, since he agrees to it taking it one way (the way it is presented to him by the Frenglish sentence, or by its French translation), but he also withholds belief from it, in the sense specified in Section I above, since he does not agree to it taking it the other way (the way it is presented to him by the English sentence). It is this confusion of Pierre's—his lack of recognition of the same proposition when it is presented to him differently—that prevents Pierre from making the logical connection between his two beliefs and drawing the *modus tollens* inference. He fails to recognize that his belief that London is not pretty is the negation of the consequent of his belief that London is pretty if New York is.

It is precisely Pierre's sort of situation, in which there is propositional recognition failure, that gives rise to counter-examples to the belief closure and justification principles. The principles can, of course, be weakened to rescue them from vulnerability to this sort of counter-example. One way to do this is to adjoin a further initial-condition supposition: that x recognizes that q is a deductive consequence of his or her belief of p. That is, we must be given not only that x recognizes both that he or she believes p and that p entails q, but furthermore that x also recognizes that p is both a belief of his or hers and entailing of q. Since he is a logician, Pierre knows that the compound proposition that *whereas London is pretty if New York is, London is not pretty* entails that New York is not pretty, and he also knows (taking this proposition in a different way) that this proposition is something he believes, but since he fails to recognize this proposition when taking it differently, he does not recognize that this proposition is *simultaneously* something that entails that New York is not pretty and something he believes.[17]

---

[17] Suppose x does not have the belief that p entails q, because (for example) x does not have the concept of logical entailment, but that x believes p and can nevertheless reason perfectly well, etc. Surely in some such cases we should expect that x would still come to believe q on the basis of his or her belief of p, and that x would be justified in doing so. One reformulation of the belief justification principle that seems both invulnerable to the sort of counterexample at issue in Pierre's case and more to the point makes explicit reference to the third relata of the *BEL* relation:

Suppose x is a normal, fully rational agent who fully understands a particular sentence S (as a sentence of x's language) and that $BEL[x, p, f(x, S)]$, where p is the content of S (in x's context). Suppose also that x is consciously interested in the further question of whether q is also the case, taking q the way he or she does when it is presented to x by the particular sentence S' (of x's language). Suppose further that x also fully understands S' (as a sentence of x's language). Suppose finally that S' is uncontroversially a trivial deductive consequence of S (in x's language) by logical form alone (without the help of additional analytical meaning postulates for x's language). Under these circumstances, x would be rationally justified in coming to stand in *BEL* to q and $f(x, S')$ on the basis of his or her standing in *BEL* to p and $f(x, S)$ (and the deductive relationship between S and S'), or alternatively, if for independent reasons x does not stand in *BEL* to q and $f(x, S')$, x would be rationally justified in accordingly ceasing to stand in *BEL* to p and $f(x, S)$,

where f is the function that assigns to an individual speaker and a sentence of his or her idiolect, the corresponding third relatum of the *BEL* relation (e.g., the way the speaker takes the proposition

One might be tempted to defend these disputed instances of the belief closure and justification principles by arguing that if a normal, fully rational agent x knows both that a particular proposition p is something he or she believes and furthermore that p deductively entails another proposition q, then x can easily infer that p is simultaneously both something he or she believes and something that deductively entails q. Since the former conditions are already included as initial-condition suppositions in the belief closure and justification principles, the new initial-condition supposition would be entirely superfluous.

This purported defense of the belief closure and justification principles does not succeed. Notice how it is supposed to go. We might begin by noting that the argument form ⌜a is F and a is G; therefore a is both F and G⌝ is valid, since it is simply a special application of the 'λ'-transformation rule of *abstraction*, which permits the inference from a formula ϕ_a to ⌜$(\lambda_x)[\phi x](a)$⌝, i.e. to ⌜a is an individual such that ϕ_{it}⌝ (where ϕ_a is the result of uniformly substituting free occurrences of a for free occurrences of 'x' in ϕ_x—or for 'free' occurrences of the pronoun 'it' in ϕ_{it}). In particular, then, there is a valid argument from 'x believes p, and p deductively entails q' to 'p is something that x believes and that deductively entails q'. We then invoke the belief closure and justification principles to argue that if x believes the conjunctive proposition that he or she believes p and p deductively entails q, then (assuming the rest of the initial conditions obtain) x will infer that p is something that he or she believes and that deductively entails q, and x would be justified in doing so. This would be a *meta-application* of the belief closure and justification principles, an application to beliefs concerning inference and belief formation. But this meta-application of these principles is part of a purported justification of these very principles! The problem with this defense of the two principles is that, like the misguided attempt to defend induction-by-enumeration by citing inductive evidence of its utility, it presupposes precisely the very principles it is aimed at defending, and hence suffers from a vicious circularity. If we let x be Pierre, p be the conjunctive proposition that whereas London is pretty if New York is, London is not pretty, and q be the proposition that New York is not pretty, then the resulting instances of the belief closure and justification principles are precisely special instances whose truth is explicitly denied by the sort of account I advocate.

More generally, the theory advanced in *Frege's Puzzle* distinguishes sharply between a complex sentence ϕ_a and the logically equivalent sentence ⌜$(\lambda_x)[\phi x](a)$⌝ (or ⌜a is such that ϕ_{it}⌝) as regards their proposition content. I have argued elsewhere for this distinction in some detail in connection with sentences ϕ_a that involve multiple occurrences of the name a.[18] Thus, for example, Pierre no doubt believes

---

that is the content of the sentence when it is presented to him or her by that very sentence). *Cf.* note 14 above. I am assuming here that 'London is *Londres*' is not a logically valid sentence of Frenglish (Pierre's language), despite the fact that it is an analytic sentence of Frenglish. *Cf. Frege's Puzzle*, pp. 133–135.

An analogous principle may be given in place of the belief closure principle. These more cautious principles must be weakened even further to accommodate cases in which the function f is not defined, as in Kripke's 'Paderewski' case, pp. 265–266.

[18] 'Reflexivity'.

(putting it in Frenglish) that *Londres* is prettier than London, and (according to my view) he thereby believes the proposition (putting it in proper English) that London is prettier than London, but he does not thereby believe the unbelievable proposition that London exceeds itself in pulchritude (that London is something that is prettier than itself). Likewise, Pierre believes the conjunctive proposition that London is pretty and London is not pretty, but he surely does not believe that London has the unusual property of being both pretty and not pretty.

The fallacy in Kripke's argument, as reconstructed above, occurs in the inference from the subsidiary conclusion *C1* and the additional premise *P3* to the final conclusion *C2*. More specifically, the argument would apparently involve an implicit and invalid intervening inference from *C1* to the following:

C1': If Pierre has the beliefs that London is pretty and that London is not pretty, then he is in principle in a position to see that these propositions (beliefs) are simultaneously beliefs of his and contradictory, and hence in a position to see that at least one of his beliefs must be false.

This intervening subsidiary conclusion *C1'* together with premise *P3* validly yield the desired conclusion *C2*. The implicit inference from *C1* to *C1'* is, in effect, a meta-application of one of the disputed instances of the belief closure and justification principles. Pierre is indeed in a position to know that he believes that London is pretty and that London is not pretty. Being a logician, he certainly knows that the propositions that London is pretty and that London is not pretty are logically incompatible. But he believes these facts about these propositions only when taking one of them in different ways, believing it to be two logically independent propositions, failing to recognize it as a single proposition. He is in no position to see or infer that these two propositions are simultaneously believed by him and contradictory.

There is a serious residual problem with the account given so far of Pierre's situation. There is an extremely compelling reason to deny that Pierre believes that London is pretty: when the sentence 'London is pretty' is put to him (after t_2), he sincerely dissents from it in good faith, while fully understanding the sentence and grasping its content. The theoretical apparatus of *Frege's Puzzle* makes it possible to dispel at least some of the force of this sort of consideration. Using that apparatus, where 'f' refers to the function that assigns to a speaker and a sentence of the speaker's idiolect the corresponding third relatum of the *BEL* relation (e.g., the way the speaker would take the content of the sentence were it presented to the speaker at t_2 by that very sentence), we may say that at t_2

BEL[Pierre, that London is pretty, f(Pierre, '*Londres* is pretty')],

or in Frenglish,

BEL[Pierre, that *Londres* is pretty, f(Pierre, '*Londres* is pretty')],

whereas we must deny that at t_2

BEL[Pierre, that London is pretty, f(Pierre, 'London is pretty')].

Pierre believes the proposition that *Londres* is pretty, taking it as presented by those very words, but he also withholds belief from (in fact disbelieves) the proposition that London is pretty, taking it as presented by those very words. Pierre's doxastic disposition towards the proposition depends entirely on how the proposition is presented to him. The reason offered for denying that Pierre believes that London is pretty is a decisive reason for affirming that he disbelieves that London is pretty (and therefore that he withholds belief), but it is highly misleading evidence regarding the separate and independent question of whether he believes that London is pretty.[19]

VII

I turn now to Schiffer's criticism that I am committed to the falsity of the true sentence (2). I fully agree with Schiffer that sentence (2) is straightforwardly true in his little story involving Floyd, as long as Floyd understands sentence (1) when uttering it or assenting to it. In fact, far from being committed to the claim that (2) is false, the theory advanced in *Frege's Puzzle* is in fact committed to precisely the opposite claim that (2) is true! This virtually follows directly from the first condition on the *BEL* relation given in Section I above, according to which it is sufficient for the truth of (2) that Floyd should agree to the content of (1) when taking this proposition the way it is presented to him by the very sentence (1).[20] On my view, then, Floyd does believe that Lois Lane does not realize that Clark Kent is Superman. In addition, I also maintain (as Schiffer correctly points out) that Floyd believes that Lois Lane does

---

[19] A reply exactly similar to this can be offered to Steven Wagner's central criticism (in 'California Semantics Meets the Great Fact', *Notre Dame Journal of Formal Logic*, 27, 3, July 1986, pp. 430–455) of the theory advanced in *Frege's Puzzle*. Wagner objects (at pp. 435–436) that the theory is incorrect to characterize someone who knows that 'Samuel Clemens' refers (in English) to Samuel Clemens as thereby knowing that 'Samuel Clemens' refers (in English) to Mark Twain, since any rational agent who knows the latter, and the trivial fact that 'Mark Twain' refers (in English) to Mark Twain, is *ipso facto* in a position to infer that 'Mark Twain' and 'Samuel Clemens' are co-referential, and that therefore 'Mark Twain is Samuel Clemens', and all of its Leibniz's-Law consequences, are true. (Wagner, at pp. 445–446, acknowledges the effectiveness of the sort of reply I am offering here, but finds it excessively reminiscent of the Fregean account of propositional-attitude attributions. There is considerable tension, however, between this reaction and some of his remarks on pp. 431–432. *Cf.* also note 5 above and *Frege's Puzzle*, pp. 2–7, 66–70, and especially pp. 119–126.)

On a related point, I argued in *Frege's Puzzle* (pp. 133–138) that the sentence 'Hesperus, if it exists, is Phosphorus' expresses a truth (in English) that is knowable (by anyone sufficiently *en rapport* with the planet Venus) *a priori*, by logic alone. One may also know, by principles of (English) semantics alone, that *if Hesperus, if it exists, is Phosphorus, then the sentence 'Hesperus, if it exists, is Phosphorus' is true (in English)*. But knowing these things does not *ipso facto* place one in a position to infer (and thereby to know by logic and semantics alone) that 'Hesperus, if it exists, is Phosphorus' is true (in English). The inability to draw this *modus ponens* inference (justifiably) is an instance of essentially the same phenomenon as Pierre's inability to draw the *modus tollens* inference.

[20] In *Frege's Puzzle* I explicitly endorse (at pp. 129–130) Kripke's schematic disquotation principle. (Indeed, as pointed out in note 14 above, the principle is virtually entailed by the first condition on the *BEL* relation.) This disquotation principle (in turn) virtually entails the truth of (2) (in Schiffer's story), assuming Floyd fully understands (1) in assenting to it. *Cf.* also note 17 above.

realize that Clark Kent is Superman—since Floyd believes the proposition that Lois Lane realizes that Superman is Superman, and on my view this just is the proposition that Lois Lane realizes that Clark Kent is Superman. Thus, I maintain that Floyd both believes and disbelieves that Lois Lane realizes that Clark Kent is Superman.

Schiffer has uncovered a very interesting philosophical problem here. Before presenting my solution, I want to emphasize the generality of the problem. The general problem is not one that is peculiar to my own theory of propositional-attitude attributions (contrary to the impression created by Schiffer's presentation of his criticism), but is equally a problem for the orthodox, Fregean theory, and indeed for virtually any theory of propositional-attitude attributions.

Consider an analogous situation involving straightforward (strict) synonyms. Suppose that Sasha learns the words 'ketchup' and 'catsup' not by being taught that they are perfect synonyms, but by actually consuming the condiment and reading the labels on the bottles. Suppose further that, in Sasha's idiosyncratic experience, people typically have the condiment called 'catsup' with their eggs and hash browns at breakfast, whereas they routinely have the condiment called 'ketchup' with their hamburgers at lunch. This naturally leads Sasha to conclude, erroneously, that ketchup and catsup are different condiments, condiments that happen to share a similar taste, color, consistency, and name. He sincerely utters the sentence 'Ketchup is a sandwich condiment; but no one in his right mind would eat a sandwich condiment with eggs at breakfast, so catsup is not a sandwich condiment.' Now, Tyler Burge, who has a considerable knowledge of formal semantics and who is well aware (unlike Sasha) that 'ketchup' and 'catsup' are exact synonyms, would claim that Sasha believes that ketchup is a sandwich condiment but that Sasha does not believe that catsup is, describing his view in exactly so many words.[21] Clearly, Burge believes that Sasha believes that ketchup is a sandwich condiment. (See note 23 below.) When queried, 'Does Sasha believe that catsup is a sandwich condiment?', however, Burge sincerely responds 'No', while fully understanding the question and grasping its content. Given Burge's mastery of English, there would seem to be every reason to say, therefore, that he also believes that Sasha does not believe that catsup is a sandwich condiment. Yet by an argument exactly analogous to Schiffer's, we are apparently barred, by Frege's Thesis and Schiffer's Constraint, from acknowledging this. For we have granted that Burge believes ketchup to be something Sasha believes is a sandwich condiment. If, while remaining fully rational, Burge also believed catsup (i.e. ketchup) *not* to be something Sasha believes is a sandwich condiment, there would be a violation of the conjunction of Frege's Thesis with Schiffer's Constraint. There are no relevant modes of presenting ketchup that Burge construes as (modes of) presenting different stuff, as are required by Frege's Thesis together with Schiffer's Constraint. The conjunction of Frege's Thesis with Schiffer's Constraint thus apparently prohibits us from acknowledging that Burge does indeed disbelieve what he sincerely claims to disbelieve—that Sasha believes that catsup is a sandwich condiment.

---

[21] See his 'Belief and Synonymy', *Journal of Philosophy*, 75 (March 1978), pp. 119–138.

Some philosophers will conclude that, despite his insistence to the contrary, Burge really does not disbelieve that Sasha believes that catsup is a sandwich condiment, and when he protests that he does, he is operating under a misunderstanding of the phrase 'believes that'. What Burge really disbelieves, they claim, is something linguistic, for example that Sasha believes that the sentence 'Catsup is a sandwich condiment' is true in English, or that Sasha satisfies the sentential matrix '*x* believes that catsup is a sandwich condiment' in English (i.e. that the open sentence '*x* believes that catsup is a sandwich condiment' is true in English when Sasha is assigned as value for the free variable '*x*').[22] Yet this seems plainly wrong—and therein lies the problem. Burge correctly understands the sentence 'Sasha believes that catsup is a sandwich condiment.' He understands it to mean (in English) that Sasha believes that catsup, i.e. ketchup, is a sandwich condiment. He knows enough formal semantics to know that the sentence does not mean instead that Sasha believes that the sentence 'Catsup is a sandwich condiment' is true in English, nor that Sasha satisfies the sentential matrix '*x* believes that catsup is a sandwich condiment' in English. Burge sincerely dissents from this sentence (as a sentence of English) because of his philosophical views concerning belief (which assimilate the proposition so expressed with the false proposition that Sasha accepts, or would accept, the sentence 'Catsup is a sandwich condiment', understood in a certain way). Burge's sincere dissent surely indicates a belief on his part (even if it is confused) that Sasha does not believe that catsup is a sandwich condiment—in addition to his correct belief that Sasha does believe that ketchup is a sandwich condiment, and in addition to his (erroneous) linguistic belief that Sasha fails to satisfy the sentential matrix '*x* believes that catsup is a sandwich condiment' in English. The problem is that this apparently conflicts with Frege's Thesis in conjunction with Schiffer's Constraint.

This time the objection is not an objection to my theory of belief attributions in particular. If Schiffer's second criticism of my theory of belief attributions is sound, any reasonable theory of belief attributions, even a Fregean theory, would be required to deny that Burge believes that Sasha does not believe that catsup is a sandwich condiment.[23] Yet surely we are not barred by the demands of reasonableness (and

---

[22] *Cf.* the discussion of Mates's famous problem concerning nested propositional-attitude attributions in Alonzo Church, 'Intensional Isomorphism and Identity of Belief', in N. Salmon and S. Soames, eds, *Propositions and Attitudes*. Whereas I disagree with Church concerning Burge's beliefs, I fully endorse his argument that the sentences 'Burge disbelieves that Sasha believes catsup is a sandwich condiment' and 'Burge disbelieves that Sasha believes ketchup is a sandwich condiment' cannot differ in truth value in English if 'ketchup' and 'catsup' are English synonyms.

[23] There is one potential difference between this case and that of sentence (2): Burge's belief that Sasha believes that ketchup is a sandwich condiment is very likely based, to some extent, on Sasha's readiness to assent to the sentence 'Ketchup is a sandwich condiment.' But whereas it is clear that Lois Lane fully understands the sentence 'Superman is Superman', and grasps its content, it is arguable that Sasha does not fully understand the sentence 'Ketchup is a sandwich condiment', since he takes it to be compatible with 'Catsup is not a sandwich condiment.' See the final footnote of Saul Kripke's 'A Puzzle About Belief', concerning a 'deep conceptual confusion' that arises from 'misapplication of the disquotational principle' to speakers in situations like Sasha's. Kripke's view is that 'although the issues are delicate, there is a case for' rejecting the claim that Burge believes that Sasha believes that ketchup is a sandwich condiment, on the grounds that Burge apparently misapplies the disquotation principle to Sasha's assent to 'Ketchup is a sandwich condiment',

consistency) from acknowledging that Burge does indeed disbelieve what he claims to disbelieve. Since it proves too much, there must be something wrong with Schiffer's argument. What?[24]

It is perhaps natural to point an accusing finger at Schiffer's Constraint. Since this principle (in conjunction with Frege's Thesis) apparently bars us—Fregeans, Russellians, and other theorists alike—from acknowledging what is patently true about Burge's beliefs, it would appear that it must be incorrect.

I was careful in *Frege's Puzzle* to avoid particular commitments concerning the nature of what I call 'proposition guises' or 'ways of taking propositions' or 'means by which one is familiar with a proposition'. However, I am prepared to grant, for present purposes, that *something* along the lines of Frege's Thesis and Schiffer's Constraint is indeed correct.[25] Does this, together with the doctrines and theses I

---

thereby betraying a misunderstanding of the term 'believe'. (Kripke adds that he does not believe that his brief discussion of this sort of situation ends the matter.)

Against this, the following should be noted First, it is by no means obvious that Sasha fails to understand the term 'ketchup'; he has learned the term in much the same way as nearly everyone else who has learned it: by means of a sort of ostensive definition. If Sasha misunderstands the term 'ketchup', why does Lois Lane not similarly misunderstand the name 'Superman'? Second, even if Sasha's understanding of the term 'ketchup' is somehow defective, this does not make any difference to Burge's beliefs concerning Sasha's beliefs. Burge's philosophical views concerning belief allow that Sasha's grasp of the term 'ketchup', imperfect though it may be, is sufficient to enable him to form a belief that ketchup is a sandwich condiment. (See Burge's 'Individualism and the Mental', in P. French, T. Uehling, and H. Wettstein, eds, *Midwest Studies in Philosophy IV: Studies in Metaphysics*, Minneapolis: University of Minnesota Press, 1979, pp. 73–121.) Even if Burge's philosophical views are incorrect, they are views concerning belief. It would be implausible to claim that Burge's views in this connection *must* indicate a misunderstanding of the term 'believe' (as used in standard English), as opposed to advocacy of a somewhat controversial theory concerning (genuine) belief. Last but not least, even if Sasha's understanding of the term 'ketchup' is somehow defective, the claim that Sasha therefore fails to believe that ketchup is a sandwich condiment is fundamentally implausible. Suppose Sasha points to a bottle labeled 'KETCHUP', and sincerely declares, 'This stuff here is a sandwich condiment.' Does he nevertheless fail to believe that ketchup is a sandwich condiment, simply because he does not realize that 'ketchup' and 'catsup' are synonyms?

[24] The example of Sasha demonstrates that the difficulty involved is more general than it appears, arising not only on my own theory of propositional-attitude attributions but equally on a very wide range of such theories, including various Fregean theories. This feature is not peculiar to Schiffer's criticism. Although I cannot argue the case here, a great many criticisms that have been leveled against the sort of account I advocate—perhaps most—are based on some difficulty or other that is more general in nature than it first appears, and that equally arises on virtually any theory of propositional-attitude attributions in connection with the example of Sasha's understanding of the synonyms 'ketchup' and 'catsup'. The argument given here involving the terms 'ketchup' and 'catsup' is related to Kripke's 'proof' of substitutivity using two Hebrew words for Germany, and to his argument involving 'furze' and 'gorse', in the conclusion section of 'A Puzzle About Belief'. All of these arguments are closely related to Church's famous arguments from translation. (See especially 'Intentional Isomorphism and Identity of Belief'.) I hope to elaborate on this matter in later work.

[25] For several reasons, I do not accept the letter of Schiffer's Constraint as here formulated, though I do accept its spirit. I believe that Schiffer shares some of my misgivings over the principle, as here formulated. He mentions potential problems arising from the 'F' in the statement of the principle, and the need for 'modes of presentation' for properties. A related difficulty is noted below. In addition, I do not accept the Fregean notion of a purely conceptual *mode of presentation* of an entity as an adequate substitute for my notion of a *way of taking* the entity in question. See note 5 above.

advocate in *Frege's Puzzle*, lead to a commitment to the falsity of (2), as Schiffer argues? If so, then my position is strictly *inconsistent* since I also maintain that (2) is true.

Contra Schiffer, my granting that something along the lines of Frege's Thesis and Schiffer's Constraint is correct does not commit me to the falsity of sentence (2). For illustration, first instantiate the '*x*' to Floyd, the '*y*' to the fact (or proposition) that Clark Kent is Superman, and the '*F*' to the property of *being realized by Lois Lane*. On my theory, the fact (or proposition) that Clark Kent is Superman is just the fact that Superman is Superman. The relevant instances of the two principles entail that, since Floyd both believes and disbelieves this fact to be realized by Lois Lane, if he is fully rational he must grasp this fact by means of two distinct modes of presentation of it, he must take this fact in two different ways. I am happy to say that Floyd does. In fact, my theory more or less requires that he does. Unless Floyd himself believes with me what Schiffer calls 'the 'Fido–Fido theory of meaning', he may rationally proclaim 'The fact that Superman is Superman is trivial and something that Lois Lane realizes, whereas the fact that Clark Kent is Superman is neither; hence they are distinct facts.' As the discussion in Section I made clear, whatever else my notion of a *way of taking* an object is, it is such that if Floyd believes that a proposition p is distinct from a proposition q, then Floyd takes these propositions in different ways (even if $p = q$). If Floyd is sufficiently philosophical, he may mistake the singular proposition about Superman that he is him, when it is presented to him by the sentence 'Clark Kent is Superman', for some general proposition to the effect that the mild-mannered reporter having such-and-such drab physical appearance is the superhero who wears blue tights, a big 'S' on his chest, and a red cape, etc. Or instead he may mistake the proposition, so presented, for the singular proposition *taken in a certain way*, or what comes to the same thing, the singular proposition together with a certain way of taking it. This is how he takes the singular proposition when it is so presented. The fact that he knows this proposition to be true does not have the consequence that he sees it as the very same thing, in the very same way, as the corresponding thing (general proposition or singular-proposition-taken-in-a-certain-way) that he associates with 'Superman is Superman'.

Consider Frege in place of Floyd. On my view, Frege mistook the singular proposition about the planet Venus that it is it to be two different propositions ('thoughts'). He took this proposition in one way when it was presented to him by the sentence '*Der Morgenstern ist derselbe wie der Morgenstern*' (the German version of 'Morningstar is the same as Morningstar') and in another way when it was presented to him by the sentence '*Der Morgenstern ist derselbe wie der Abendstern*' ('Morningstar is the same as Eveningstar')—despite the fact that he was well aware that the names '*Morgenstern*' and '*Abenstern*' refer to ('mean') the same planet. That he took this proposition in two different ways is established by the fact that he took it to be two different propositions. Floyd is in a similar state with respect to the singular proposition about Superman that he is him—even if Floyd has not formed a specific view about the nature of propositions in general or about the nature of this proposition in particular, as long as he takes this proposition to be two different propositions. Anyone who does not consciously subscribe to the sort of theory advanced in *Frege's Puzzle* is likely to have different perspectives on a given singular proposition of the form *x is x* when it is presented in various ways, seeing it as a different entity each time.[26]

Let us return to Frege's Thesis and Schiffer's Constraint. Suppose instead that the '*y*' is instantiated this time to Superman (or to Clark Kent) and the '*F*' to the property of *being an individual x such that Lois Lane realizes that x is Superman*, or *being someone that Lois Lane realizes is Superman*. Surely Floyd believes Superman to have this property. (We ask Floyd, 'You know that man who calls himself "Superman". Does Lois Lane realize that he is Superman?' If Floyd understands the question, he should answer 'Yes'.) If at the same time Floyd disbelieves Superman to have this property, yet he remains fully rational, the conjunction of Frege's Thesis with Schiffer's Constraint will have been violated. As Schiffer points out, it will not do in this case to defend my theory by claiming that there are relevant modes of presentation *m* and *m'* of Superman that Floyd grasps but construes as (modes of) presenting different individuals, for there are no such modes of presentation in Schiffer's little story.

Does Floyd disbelieve Superman to be such that Lois realizes that he is Superman? Put another way, does Floyd believe Clark Kent to be someone that Lois Lane does not realize is Superman? I suspect that Schiffer assumed that if I were to concede that Floyd believes Lois Lane does not realize that Clark Kent is Superman, it would simply follow—according to my own theory—that Floyd believes Clark Kent to be someone that Lois Lane does not realize is Superman. That is, Schiffer's second criticism apparently involves an inference from

(2) Floyd believes that Lois Lane does not realize that Clark Kent is Superman

to

(3) Floyd believes that Clark Kent is someone that Lois does not realize is Superman.

On my theory, it virtually follows from (3) that Floyd believes Clark Kent not to be someone that Lois Lane realizes is Superman. The conjunction of Frege's Thesis with Schiffer's Constraint would thus bar me from acknowledging the truth of (2).

It is an essential part of the theory I advanced in *Frege's Puzzle*, however, that (3) does *not* follow from (2). The theory advanced in *Frege's Puzzle* distinguishes sharply between the proposition that Lois Lane does not realize that Clark Kent is such-and-such and the proposition that Clark Kent is someone that Lois Lane does not realize is such-and-such. These propositions differ in structure. Roughly put,

---

[26] In *Frege's Puzzle* I wrote: 'The means by which one is acquainted with a singular proposition includes as a part the means by which one is familiar with the individual constituent(s) of the proposition' (p. 108). Contrary to the interpretation advanced in Schiffer's postscript, I never suggested that the way an agent takes a structured complex object, such as a proposition, is made up *without remainder* of the ways the agent takes the separate constituents of the complex (with these ways-of-taking-objects structured in a similar way). The principal criticism of Schiffer's postscript challenges my contention that Floyd takes the singular proposition (or fact) about Superman that he is him in two different ways. It is difficult to understand, however, why Schiffer—who himself advanced (something along the lines of) Schiffer's Constraint in criticizing the theory of *Frege's Puzzle*—insists, as part of the same criticism, that the fact that a fully rational agent believes that whereas *p* is trivial, *q* is not, does not yield an adequate reason to conclude that this agent takes *p* and *q* in different ways (by means of different 'modes of presentation').

Clark Kent is the subject of the latter proposition, but not of the former. According to my account, Floyd believes that Lois Lane does not realize that Clark Kent is Superman but, at least very likely, he does not also believe of Superman that he is someone Lois Lane does not realize is Superman.

In fact, it is precisely in the implicit inference from (2) to (3) that Schiffer might be invoking the belief closure principle (and perhaps the belief justification principle as well). Here again, the relevant logical entailment is an instance of the inference rule of abstraction. And here again, we seem to have an example of someone believing a proposition while being in no position to infer a simple deductive consequence from the proposition. Worse, if Schiffer's apparent implicit inference from (2) to (3) is indeed based on an application of the belief closure principle, as it seems to be, it is a fallacious application. For one of the initial-condition provisos of the belief closure principle is that the agent is aware of the deductive relationship between his or her current belief and its deductive consequence. But it seems likely in Schiffer's little story that Floyd does not believe that the proposition that Clark Kent is someone that Lois Lane does not realize is such-and-such is a valid deductive consequence of the proposition that Lois Lane does not realize that Clark Kent is such-and-such.[27] Given his favorable attitude toward sentence (1), it is evident that Floyd believes that Lois Lane does not realize that Clark Kent is Superman, but he is in no position to infer that Clark Kent is someone that Lois Lane does not realize is Superman, and he would not be logically justified in doing so. For we may suppose that Floyd also believes that Superman is someone that Lois Lane realizes is Superman. On my view, this is just to say that Floyd believes the singular proposition about Superman, i.e. Clark Kent, that *he* is someone that Lois Lane realizes is Superman. Floyd is not about to relinquish this belief of his. He would indeed be less than fully rational, in the sense used in Schiffer's Constraint, if at the same time he also formed the belief of Superman (i.e. Clark Kent) that he is someone that Lois Lane does not realize is Superman.

Floyd would be less than fully rational, that is, *unless* he has gained a *new* mode of familiarity with Superman, an additional mode of presentation, by encountering Superman on another occasion and failing to recognize him, *or* he somehow mistakes the logically incompatible properties of being someone Lois Lane realizes is Superman and of being someone Lois Lane does not realize is Superman—which are properties that such individuals as you, me, and Superman either have or lack in an absolute *de re* way—for properties of *individuals-under-guises* (or equivalently, for binary relations between individuals and ways of conceiving them).[28] Either of these predicaments might rescue Floyd from irrationality even when he both believes and disbelieves Superman to be someone Lois Lane realizes is Superman. For present purposes,

---

[27] Furthermore, it is highly controversial whether the former is a valid deductive consequence of the latter, and indeed, Floyd's views entail a negative answer to this controversial question. This renders the alternative belief justification principle cited in note 17 above also inapplicable.

[28] The possibility of such confusion demonstrates a further difficulty with Schiffer's Constraint, as it is formulated here (see note 25), and that the principle should be stated more carefully—perhaps by adding a proviso concerning *x*'s lack of confusion in regard to the nonrelativity, and the consequent logical incompatibility, of the property of being F and that of not being F, and in regard to the sort of entities that are candidates for having either.

we may assume that Floyd has acquired neither a new mode of presentation nor this philosophically sophisticated confusion.

Suppose we queried Floyd, 'You know that man who calls himself "Superman" and "Clark Kent". Does Lois Lane realize that he is Superman, or does she fail to realize that he is Superman?' If he understands the question, he should answer 'She *does* realize that he is Superman.' If he were sufficiently philosophical, he might describe his pertinent beliefs by adding, 'Lois does not realize that *Clark Kent* is Superman. But if you're asking about the man himself (and not about the man-under-one-of-his-guises), she thinks he is two men. She *doubts* that he is Superman, but she also realizes that he is Superman. It all depends on the guise under which he is presented to her.' Floyd cannot fully rationally add to this stock of beliefs a further belief that he would express by 'That man, Clark Kent, is someone Lois does *not* realize is Superman.' If he added this belief to his present stock, without relinquishing any of his current beliefs, he would believe of Superman that he simultaneously is and also is not someone Lois Lane realizes is Superman, that he both is and is not such that Lois Lane realizes that he is Superman. That would indeed be less than fully rational, in the sense used in Schiffer's Constraint (unless Floyd is under the sort of confusion mentioned in the preceding paragraph). To use a piece of terminology recently introduced by Schiffer, Floyd, in both believing and disbelieving that Lois Lane realizes that Clark Kent is Superman, exhibits *the belief/disbelief phenomenon with respect to* the phrase 'that Clark Kent is Superman' (which he does not construe as standing for the same thing as the phrase 'that Superman is Superman').[29] However, since on my view Floyd (unless he is under the sort of confusion mentioned above) does not disbelieve Clark Kent to be someone that Lois realizes is Superman, he does not exhibit the belief/disbelief phenomenon with respect to the name 'Clark Kent' (which he rightly construes as standing for the same individual as the name 'Superman'). Hence, my theory does not conflict here with the conjunction of Frege's Thesis and Schiffer's Constraint.[30]

VIII

Although the general philosophical problem uncovered by Schiffer does not refute my theory of propositional-attitude attributions (or Frege's), it does pose a very serious difficulty for—in fact, a refutation of—a proposal originally made by W. V. Quine in 1956 in his classic 'Quantifiers and Propositional Attitudes',[31] and more

---

[29] *Cf.* Schiffer's 'The Real Trouble with Propositions', in R. J. Bogdan, ed., *Belief* (Oxford University Press, 1986), pp. 83–117, at p. 107*n*.

[30] Likewise, Burge believes ketchup, i.e. catsup, to be something that Sasha believes is a sandwich condiment, and he also believes ketchup to be something that Sasha disbelieves is a sandwich condiment. Furthermore, he disbelieves that Sasha believes that catsup is a sandwich condiment, but he does not disbelieve catsup to be something that Sasha believes is a sandwich condiment (I assume he is not under the sort of confusion mentioned in the preceding paragraph of the text)—otherwise he would not be fully rational in the relevant sense. Frege's Thesis and Schiffer's Constraint do not force us to deny that Burge disbelieves that Sasha believes that catsup is a sandwich condiment.

[31] In Quine's *The Ways of Paradox* (New York: Random House, 1966), pp. 183–194.

recently endorsed (and improved upon) by David Kaplan.[32] The proposal is one for translating (or in Quine's case, replacing) constructions involving quantification into intensional or content-sensitive operators by a certain type of construction—which Kaplan calls 'syntactically *de re*'—that avoids such quantifying in. In particular, a syntactically *de dicto* open sentence

$$c \text{ believes that } \phi_x,$$

where 'x' is the only free variable of the open sentence ϕ_x, and has only one free occurrence therein (positioned inside the scope of the content-sensitive syntactically *de dicto* operator 'c believes that'), is to be replaced by

$$c \text{ believes the property of being an object } y \text{ such that } \phi_y \text{ of } x$$

(Quine), or equivalently, to be translated into the syntactically *de re*

$$x \text{ is believed by } c \text{ to be an object } y \text{ such that } \phi_y$$

(Kaplan). The proposed substitutes artfully leave the free variable 'x' outside the scope of 'believe'.[33] Accordingly, on this proposal, the syntactically *de dicto* open sentence

(2′) Floyd believes that Lois Lane does not realize that x is Superman

is rewritten as

> Floyd believes the property of being an object y such that Lois Lane does not realize the property of being Superman of y, of x

(Quine), or as

> x is believed by Floyd to be an object y such that y is not realized by Lois Lane to be Superman

(Kaplan), or more colloquially as

(3″) Floyd believes x to be someone that Lois Lane does not realize to be Superman.

Now, in Schiffer's little story, (2′) is true when Superman is assigned as value for the variable 'x', i.e. Superman satisfies (2′). Yet Schiffer's argument demonstrates that (3″) is false when Superman is assigned as value for 'x', i.e. Superman does not satisfy (3″). If (3″) were true of Superman, Floyd would be less than fully rational, in the sense used in Schiffer's Constraint (unless he is under the confusion mentioned in the preceding section concerning the nature of the property of being someone Lois

---

[32] 'Opacity', appendix B, in E. Hahn and P. A. Schilpp, eds, *The Philosophy of W. V. Quine* (La Salle: Open Court, 1986), pp. 229–294, at pp. 268–272.

[33] The open sentence ϕ_y is the result of uniformly substituting free occurrences of the variable 'y' for free occurrences of the variable 'x' throughout ϕ_x. If 'x' has a free occurrence in ϕ_x inside the scope of a variable-binding operator on 'y', it will be necessary to use a different variable in place of 'y'. Kaplan's improvement on Quine's proposal introduces a somewhat more complicated translation, involving a procedure Kaplan calls *articulation*, in case ϕ_x contains more than one free occurrence of 'x' (as in 'x indulges x'). Such multiple-occurrence syntactically *de dicto* constructions will not concern us here.

Lane realizes is Superman), since he would then both believe and disbelieve Superman to be someone Lois realizes is Superman, while lacking the required 'modes of presentation' construed as (modes of) presenting distinct individuals. The proposed translation of (2') into (3") thus fails, and for precisely the same reason as Schiffer's implicit inference from (2) to (3).[34]

REFERENCES

J. Almog, 'Form and Content', *Nous*, 19, 4 (December 1985), pp. 603–616.

T. Burge, 'Belief and Synonymy', *Journal of Philosophy*, 75 (March 1978), pp. 119–138.

—— 'Individualism and the Mental,' in P. French, T. Uehling, and H. Wettstein, eds, *Midwest Studies in Philosophy IV: Studies in Metaphysics* (Minneapolis: University of Minnesota Press, 1979), pp. 73–122.

J. Barwise and J. Perry, 'Shifting Situations and Shaken Attitudes', *Linguistics and Philosophy*, 8 (1985), pp. 105–161.

A. J. Chien, 'Demonstratives and Belief States', *Philosophical Studies*, 47 (1985), pp. 271–289.

R. M. Chisholm, *The First Person* (Minneapolis: University of Minnesota Press, 1981).

A. Church, 'Intensional Isomorphism and Identity of Belief', *Philosophical Studies* (1954), pp. 65–73; also in N. Salmon and S. Soames, 1988.

—— 'A Remark Concerning Quine's Paradox About Modality', in N. Salmon and S. Soames, 1988.

M. J. Cresswell, *Structured Meanings: The Semantics of Propositional Attitudes* (Cambridge, Mass.: Bradford Books/The MIT Press, 1985).

K. Donnellan, 'Proper Names and Identifying Descriptions', in D. Davidson and G. Harman, eds, *Semantics of Natural Language* (Dordrecht: D. Reidel, 1972), pp. 356–379.

—— 'Speaking of Nothing', *The Philosophical Review*, 83 (January 1974), pp. 3–31; also in Schwartz, 1977, pp. 216–244.

G. Evans, 'Pronouns, Quantifiers and Relative Clauses (I)', in M. Platts, ed., *Reference, Truth and Reality* (London: Routledge and Kegan Paul, 1980), pp. 255–317.

G. Frege, '*Über Sinn und Bedeutung*', *Zeitschrift für Philosophie und Philosophische Kritik*, 100 (1893), pp. 25–50; in English in Frege, 1984, pp. 157–177; also in *Translations from the Philosophical Writings of Gottlob Frege*, translated by P. Geach and M. Black (Oxford: Basil Blackwell, 1952), pp. 56–78.

—— '*Der Gedanke*', in English in Frege, 1984, pp. 351–372; also in Frege, 1977, pp. 1–30; also in N. Salmon and S. Soames, 1988.

---

[34] No doubt, Superman himself agrees with Floyd concerning Lois Lane's ignorance of his secret identity, i.e. he believes with Floyd that Lois Lane does not realize that Clark Kent is Superman. But he also agrees with Floyd that Lois Lane realizes that he himself is Superman (since she realizes that Superman is Superman), and thus he believes himself to be someone Lois Lane realizes is Superman. Hence, being fully rational, he does not also believe himself to be someone that Lois Lane does not realize is Superman (although he believes himself to be someone that Lois Lane doubts is Superman). This refutes any attempt to analyze the so-called *de se* construction ⌜*a* believes that ϕ$_{\text{he-himself}}$⌝ by means of something along the lines of ⌜*a* self-ascribes the property of being someone *y* such that ϕ$_y$⌝. Such attempts are made by David Lewis, 'Attitudes *De Dicto* and *De Se*', *The Philosophical Review*, 88 (1979), pp. 513–543, and Roderick Chisholm, *The First Person* (Minneapolis: University of Minnesota Press, 1981), at pp. 34–37 and *passim*.

―― *Logical Investigations* (New Haven: Yale University Press, 1977).
―― *Collected Papers on Mathematics, Logic, and Philosophy*, B. McGuinness, ed., translated by M. Black, V. H. Dudman, P. Geach, H. Kaal, E.-H. W. Kluge, B. McGuinness, and R. H. Stoothoff (Oxford: Basil Blackwell, 1984).
―― *Philosophical and Mathematical Correspondence*, G. Gabriel, H. Hermes, F. Kambartel, C. Thiel, and A. Veraart, eds, abridged by B. McGuinness, translated by H. Kaal (University of Chicago Press, 1980); excerpts in N. Salmon and S. Soames, 1988.
P. French, T. Uehling, and H. Wettstein, eds, *Contemporary Perspectives in the Philosophy of Language* (Minneapolis: University of Minnesota Press, 1979).
P. T. Geach, *Reference and Generality* (Ithaca: Cornell University Press, 1962).
―― 'Logical Procedures and the Identity of Expressions', in Geach, *Logic Matters* (University of California Press, 1972), pp. 108–115.
H. P. Grice, 'Logic and Conversation', in P. Cole and J. L. Morgan, eds, *Syntax and Semantics*, volume 3 (New York: Academic Press, 1975), pp. 41–55; also in D. Davidson and G. Harman, eds, *The Logic of Grammar* (Encino: Dickenson, 1975), pp. 64–75; also in A. P. Martinich, ed., *The Philosophy of Language* (Oxford University Press, 1985), pp. 159–170.
L. R. Horn, 'Metalinguistic Negation and Pragmatic Ambiguity', *Language*, 61, 1 (1985), pp. 121–174.
D. Kaplan, 'On the Logic of Demonstratives', in French, *et al.* 1979, pp. 401–412; also in N. Salmon and S. Soames, 1988.
―― 'Demonstratives', in J. Almog, J. Perry, and H. Wettstein, eds, *Themes from Kaplan* (Oxford University Press, 1989).
―― "Opacity', in L. E. Hahn and P. A. Schilpp, eds, *The Philosophy of W. V. Quine* (La Salle, Ill.: Open Court, 1986), pp. 229–288.
S. Kripke, 'Identity and Necessity', in M. Munitz, ed., *Identity and Individuation* (New York: New York University Press, 1971), pp. 135–164; also in Schwartz, 1977, pp. 66–101.
―― *Naming and Necessity* (Harvard University Press and Basil Blackwell, 1972, 1980); also in D. Davidson and G. Harman, eds, *Semantics of Natural Language* (Dordrecht: D. Reidel, 1972), pp. 253–355, 763–769.
―― 'A Puzzle about Belief', in A. Margalit, ed., *Meaning and Use* (Dordrecht: D. Reidel, 1979), pp. 239–275; also in N. Salmon and S. Soames, 1988.
D. Lewis, 'Attitudes *De Dicto* and *De Se*', *The Philosophical Review*, 88 (1979), pp. 513–543.
―― 'What Puzzling Pierre Does Not Believe', *Australasian Journal of Philosophy*, 59, 3 (1981), pp. 283–289.
L. Linsky, *Oblique Contexts* (Chicago: University of Chicago Press, 1983).
B. Loar, 'Names in Thought', *Philosophical Studies*, 51 (1987), pp. 169–185.
R. B. Marcus, 'A Proposed Solution to a Puzzle About Belief', in P. French, T. Uehling, and H. Wettstein, eds, *Midwest Studies in Philosophy VI: The Foundations of Analytic Philosophy* (Minneapolis: University of Minnesota Press, 1981), pp. 501–510.
―― 'Rationality and Believing the Impossible', *Journal of Philosophy*, 80, 6 (June 1983), pp. 321–338.
T. McKay, 'On Proper Names in Belief Ascriptions', *Philosophical Studies*, 39 (1981), pp. 287–303.
J. Perry, 'Frege on Demonstratives', *The Philosophical Review*, 86 (1977), pp. 474–497.
―― 'The Problem of the Essential Indexical', *Nous*, 13 (1979), pp. 3–21; also in N. Salmon and S. Soames, 1988.

J. Perry 'Belief and Acceptance', in P. French, T. Uehling, and H. Wettstein, eds, *Midwest Studies in Philosophy V: Studies in Epistemology* (Minneapolis: University of Minnesota Press, 1980), pp. 533–542.

——— 'A Problem About Continued Belief', *Pacific Philosophical Quarterly*, 61 (1980), pp. 317–332.

H. Putnam, 'Synonymy, and the Analysis of Belief Sentences', *Analysis*, 14, 5 (April 1954), pp. 114–122; also in N. Salmon and S. Soames, 1988.

——— 'Meaning and Reference', *The Journal of Philosophy*, 70, (November 8, 1973): 699–711; also in Schwartz, 1977, pp. 119–132.

——— 'The Meaning of "Meaning"', in K. Gunderson, ed., *Minnesota Studies in the Philosophy of Science VII: Language, Mind, and Knowledge* (Minneapolis: University of Minnesota Press, 1975); also in Putnam's *Philosophical Papers II: Mind, Language, and Reality* (Cambridge University Press, 1975), pp. 215–271.

W. V. O. Quine, 'Reference and Modality', in Quine, *From a Logical Point of View* (New York: Harper and Row, 1953), pp. 139–159.

——— 'Quantifiers and Propositional Attitudes', *Journal of Philosophy*, 53, 5 (March 1, 1956): 177–187; also in Quine's *The Ways of Paradox* (New York: Random House, 1966), pp. 183–194.

M. Richard, 'Direct Reference and Ascriptions of Belief', *Journal of Philosophical Logic*, 12 (1983), pp. 425–452; also in N. Salmon and S. Soames, 1988.

——— 'Attitude Ascriptions, Semantic Theory, and Pragmatic Evidence', *Proceedings of the Aristotelian Society*, 1, 87 (1986/1987), pp. 243–262.

B. Russell, 'On Denoting', *Mind*, 14 (October 1905), pp. 479–493; also in Russell, 1956, pp. 41–56.

——— 'Knowledge by Acquaintance and Knowledge by Description', Chapter X of Russell's *Mysticism and Logic and Other Essays* (London: Longmans, Green and Company, 1911), pp. 209–232; also in N. Salmon and S. Soames, 1988.

——— 'The Philosophy of Logical Atomism', in Russell, 1956, pp. 177–281.

——— *Logic and Knowledge*, R. C. Marsh, ed., (London: George Allen and Unwin, 1956).

N. Salmon, *Reference and Essence* (Princeton University Press and Basil Blackwell, 1981).

——— *Frege's Puzzle* (Cambridge, Mass.: Bradford Books/The MIT Press, 1986).

——— 'Reflexivity', *Notre Dame Journal of Formal Logic*, 27, 3 (July 1986), pp. 401–429; also in N. Salmon and S. Soames, 1988.

N. Salmon and S. Soames, eds, *Propositions and Attitudes* (Oxford University Press, Readings in Philosophy, 1988).

S. Schiffer, 'Naming and Knowing', in P. French, T. Uehling, and H. Wettstein, eds, 1979, pp. 61–74.

——— 'The Basis of Reference', *Erkenntnis*, 13 (1978), pp. 171–206.

——— 'Indexicals and the Theory of Reference', *Synthese*, 49 (1981), pp. 43–100.

——— 'The Real Trouble with Propositions', in R. J. Bogdan, *Belief: Form, Content, and Function* (Oxford University Press, 1986), pp. 83–118.

——— 'The "Fido–Fido" Theory of Belief', in J. Tomberlin, ed., *Philosophical Perspectives 1: Metaphysics* (Atascadero: Ridgeview, 1987), pp. 455–480.

S. Schwartz, *Naming, Necessity, and Natural Kinds* (Cornell University Press, 1977).

S. Soames, 'Lost Innocence', *Linguistics and Philosophy*, 8 (1985), pp. 59–71.

——— 'Direct Reference, Propositional Attitudes and Semantic Content', in N. Salmon and S. Soames, 1988.

S. Wagner, 'California Semantics Meets the Great Fact', *Notre Dame Journal of Formal Logic*, 27, 3 (July 1986), pp. 430–455.

D. Wiggins, 'Identity, Necessity and Physicalism', in S. Korner, ed., *Philosophy of Logic* (University of California Press, 1976), pp. 96–132, 159–182.

―― 'Frege's Problem of the Morning Star and the Evening Star', in M. Schirn, ed., *Studies on Frege II: Logic and the Philosophy of Language* (Stuttgart: Bad Canstatt, 1976), pp. 221–255.

12

The Resilience of Illogical Belief (2006)

Although Professor Schiffer and I have many times disagreed, I share his deep and abiding commitment to argument as a primary philosophical tool. Regretting any communication failure that has occurred, I endeavor here to make clearer my earlier reply in 'Illogical Belief' to Schiffer's alleged problem for my version of Millianism.[1] I shall be skeletal, however; the interested reader is encouraged to turn to 'Illogical Belief' for detail and elaboration.

I have argued that to bear a propositional attitude *de re* is to bear that attitude toward the corresponding singular proposition, no more and no less. If this is right, then according to Millianism every instance of the following modal schema is true:

S: Necessarily, α Vs that ϕ_β iff α Vs of β (*de re*) that ϕ_{it},

where α is any singular term of English, V is any of a range of transitive English verbs of propositional attitude (including 'believe', 'disbelieve', and 'doubt'), β is any proper name or other Millian term of English, ϕ_{it} is any English 'open sentence' in which the pronoun 'it' occurs as a free variable—alternatively 'he', 'him', 'she', or 'her'—and ϕ_β is the same as ϕ_{it} except for having occurrences of β wherever ϕ_{it} has free occurrences of the relevant pronoun.[2]

Schiffer uses the epithet 'Frege's constraint' for a principle that entails the following:

FC: (Necessarily) if x rationally believes y to be F while also disbelieving (or merely withholding believing) y to be F, for some property or singular-functional concept F, then in so doing x takes y in differing ways, by means of distinct *guises* ('modes of presentation') m and m'; in so doing, x does not construe m and m' as separate ways of taking a single thing.

I have spent much of the past two decades arguing for a duly qualified version of (*FC*). The primary rationale is that if x rationally believes y to be F while disbelieving

---

I thank David Braun for comments on an earlier draft. I also thank the editors of *Noûs* for providing me this opportunity.

[1] In J. Tomberlin, ed., *Philosophical Perspectives, 3: Philosophy of Mind and Action Theory* (Atascadero, Calif.: Ridgeview, 1989), pp. 243–285, at part VII, pp. 264–273. Schiffer had presented his problem for Millianism in 'The "Fido"–Fido Theory of Belief', in J. Tomberlin, ed., *Philosophical Perspectives, 1: Metaphysics* (Atascadero, Calif.: Ridgeview, 1987), pp. 445–480. The earliest forum for our debate was a Pacific Division meeting of the American Philosophical Association in March 1987.

[2] The relevant pronoun occurrences are anaphoric, hence bound, within (*S*) itself. See my 'Pronouns as Variables', *Philosophy and Phenomenological Research*, forthcoming 2006.

z to be *F*, then *x*, in so doing, takes *y* and *z* to be distinct. Insofar as *x* is rational, he/she thereby takes *y* and *z* differently—even if, in fact, *y* = *z*. Similarly, if *x* rationally believes *y* to be *F* while also suspending judgment whether *z* is *F*, then ordinarily, in so doing *x* takes *y* and *z* differently.

Schiffer derives from these principles the conclusion that my Millianism is inconsistent with the possibility of a certain possible state of affairs (*a*): Jane's rationally believing, even while she is fully aware that 'George Eliot' and 'Mary Ann Evans' co-designate, both that Ralph believes that George Eliot was a man and that Ralph does not believe that Mary Ann Evans was a man. For according to Millianism, in situation (*a*), Jane rationally believes both the singular proposition about Eliot, that Ralph believes she was a man, and its denial. Putting 'Jane' for α in (*S*), 'George Eliot' for β, 'believe' for *V*, and 'Ralph believes *she* was a man' for ϕ_{it}, and performing a bit of logic, one obtains the result that, in (*a*) Eliot is believed by Jane to be such that Ralph believes she was a man. Now putting for β instead 'Mary Ann Evans' and for ϕ_{it} 'Ralph does *not* believe *she* was a man', and drawing analogous inferences, one obtains the additional result that in (*a*) Eliot is also rationally believed by Jane *not* to be such that Ralph believes she was a man. Thus, in (*a*) Jane believes Eliot to be *F* while also believing Eliot not to be *F*, for a particular property or concept *F*. It follows by (*FC*) that in (*a*) Jane, insofar as she is rational, takes Eliot in differing ways, by means of a pair of guises that Jane does not thereby take to be of a single individual. But Jane does not do this in (*a*).

The *reductio* derivation is in fact fallacious. Specifically, a fallacy is committed when Schiffer erroneously 'restates' the relevant half of the first premise as the thesis that every instance of the following alternative schema is true (putting 'believe' for *V*):

S' Necessarily, if α believes that ϕ_β, then β is believed by α to be (something/someone) such that ϕ_{it}.[3]

Contradiction is indeed derivable from (*S'*) taken together with Millianism, (*FC*), and the possibility of (*a*), exactly in the manner that Schiffer sets out. This is because the relevant instance of (*S'*) is inconsistent with the facts. The derivation might even be taken as demonstrating this—at least by the Millian's lights. Importantly, Millianism is in no way committed to (*S'*), not even a Millianism like my own, which is committed to (*S*). I am committed to the existence of counter-instances of (*S'*).

The distinction between the *de re* constructions ⌜α believes of β that ϕ_{it}⌝ and ⌜β is believed by α to be something such that ϕ_{it}⌝ may seem excessively subtle and delicate, but in the present instance it is crucial. The latter is the passive-voice transformation of a relational predication: **Believes**$_r(\alpha, \beta,$ to be something such that ϕ_{it}), where '**Believes**$_r$' is a triadic predicate for a ternary relation between a believer *x*, an object

---

[3] I have reformulated Schiffer's 'restatement' to conform to the present notation, in a manner that accords with the intent indicated by Schiffer's applications of the schema. Schiffer commits the fallacy precisely at his step (iii), when he derives his (c).
As I argued in 'Illogical Belief' (pp. 265–267), Millianism is inessential to Schiffer's alleged problem. With a change of example to one of a sort made famous by Benson Mates, a similar derivation can be constructed without any appeal to Millianism. This consideration alone bursts Schiffer's attempt to refute Millianism.

y, and importantly, a property or singulary-functional concept F that x attributes to y. Schema (S') is thus indeed a logical consequence of (S) in a special case: if the open sentence ϕ_{it} has monadic-predicational form, 'It' $+$ VP, where VP is a monadic predicate in which the pronoun 'it' does not occur free. The predicate VP is then a term for a particular property or singulary-functional concept F. If someone x believes the singular proposition expressed by 'It' $+$ VP under the assignment of a particular value y to the variable 'it', then the proposition believed—that y is F—has the simple structure, $<y, F>$, so that x indeed believes y to be F.[4]

Not all *de re* beliefs about y involve the attribution of a property to y. Many singular propositions involving y have considerably more structure than $<y, F>$. There are some propositions, expressed by complex sentences ϕ_β, such that someone might rationally believe the proposition even while doubting the consequence expressed by $\ulcorner \beta$ is something such that $\phi_{it} \urcorner$. Some of these propositions are witness to the fact that (S') is no logical consequence of (S).

One example is due to David Kaplan. If Quine's Ralph believes that *this man* [pointing at a fuzzy picture of Ortcutt, his face covered by a large brown hat] is taller than Ortcutt, then Ralph believes the singular proposition about Ortcutt, that he (Ortcutt) is taller than he (Ortcutt) is. According to (S), Ralph thus believes that Ortcutt is taller than Ortcutt. But Ralph does not thereby believe Ortcutt to be someone taller than himself; i.e., Ortcutt is not believed by Ralph to be something z such that z is taller than z. The proposition Ralph believes has the binary-relational form: $<$Ortcutt, Ortcutt, *taller-than*$>$—or perhaps, the special monadic-predicational form: $<$Ortcutt, $<$*taller-than*, Ortcutt$\gg$. It does not have the alternate monadic-predicational form: $<$Ortcutt, *being taller than oneself*$>$. Putting 'Ralph' for α, 'Ortcutt' for β, 'believe' for V, and '*He is taller than he is*' for ϕ_{it}, the resulting instance of (S) is true, the resulting instance of (S') false.[5]

Schiffer's central example employs another such sentence: 'Ralph does not believe that Mary Ann Evans was a man.' This expresses a singular proposition about Eliot, that Ralph does not believe that she was a man, represented by the ordered pair

---

[4] I assume here that (necessarily) x believes y to be F iff x believes of y, *de re*, that it (he, she) is F. For more on this assumed equivalence, see Kaplan, 'Afterthoughts' in J. Almog, J. Perry, and H. Wettstein, eds, *Themes from Kaplan* (Oxford University Press, 1989), pp. 565–614, at 605–606; and my 'Relational Belief', in P. Leonardi and M. Santambrogio, eds, *On Quine: New Essays* (Cambridge University Press, 1995), pp. 206–228, at 214–216, 219.

In contrast to $\ulcorner \alpha$ believes of β that $\phi_{it} \urcorner$, $\ulcorner \beta$ is believed by α to be something such that $\phi_{it} \urcorner$ is what David Kaplan calls a *syntactically de re* construction. *Cf.* his 'Opacity', in L. E. Hahn and P. A. Schilpp, eds, *The Philosophy of W. V. Quine* (La Salle, Ill.: Open Court, 1986), pp. 229–288, at 268. The former is equivalent to $\ulcorner(\lambda\gamma)[\alpha$ **believes** $\wedge\phi_\gamma\wedge](\beta)\urcorner$; the latter to $\ulcorner(\lambda\gamma)[\alpha$ **believes** $\wedge(\lambda\zeta)[\phi_\zeta](\gamma)\wedge](\beta)\urcorner$, where '$\wedge$' is a content-quotation mark. Given Millianism, (S') entails: $([\alpha$ **believes**$^\wedge\phi_\beta{}^\wedge \supset \alpha$ **believes**$^\wedge(\lambda\gamma)[\phi_\gamma](\beta)^\wedge])$, where β is any proper name or other Millian term.

[5] See Kaplan, 'Opacity', at pp. 269–272, and my 'Relational Belief', especially pp. 213–214. I investigated these matters in some detail in 'Reflexivity', *Notre Dame Journal of Formal Logic*, 27, 3 (July 1986), pp. 401–429, and 'Reflections on Reflexivity', *Linguistics and Philosophy*, 15, 1 (February 1992), pp. 53–63.

≪Ralph, *believing*, <Eliot, *having been a man*≫, *being false*>. Jane rationally believes this proposition, while also believing precisely what it denies, as expressed by 'Ralph believes that George Eliot was a man' and represented by <Ralph, *believing*, <Eliot, *having been a man*≫. But Jane does not thereby both believe and disbelieve the singular proposition about Eliot, that she is believed by Ralph to have been a man, as represented by <Eliot, *being believed by Ralph to have been a man*>. The following dialogue illustrates Jane's pertinent beliefs:

SOCRATES 'Does Ralph believe that Mary Ann Evans was a man?'
JANE   'No, he doesn't.'
SOCRATES 'Does Ralph believe that George Eliot was a man?'
JANE   'Yes.'
SOCRATES 'So George Eliot is someone Ralph believes was a man?'
JANE   'Yes.'
SOCRATES 'What about Mary Ann Evans, then? Does Ralph also believe *she* was a man?'
JANE   'Ralph doesn't believe that *Mary Ann Evans* was a man. But you're now asking about Mary Ann Evans herself. Mary Ann Evans and George Eliot are the same person, don't you know? And Ralph does indeed believe she was a man.'
SOCRATES 'Very well. Is Mary Ann Evans someone Ralph also *doesn't* believe was a man?'
JANE   'Of course not; that would be logically impossible. I just told you: Mary Ann Evans is someone Ralph *does* believe was a man.'
SOCRATES 'Is George Eliot someone Ralph *doesn't* believe was a man?'
JANE   'You're not listening to me: George Eliot and Mary Ann Evans are the same person. Ralph *does* believe she was a man.'

Jane's position is rational, sophisticated, even subtle. It is perfectly coherent (even if it is inconsistent, at least by Millian lights). It is part of a neo-Fregean theory that purports to analyze or explain *de re* constructions solely in terms of Fregean thoughts. Putting 'Jane' for α, 'George Eliot' for β, 'believe' for V, and 'Ralph believes *she* was a man' for ϕ_{it}, the resulting instance of (S) is true, the resulting instance of (S') false. Schiffer's *reductio* derivation fallaciously infers the latter from the former on its way to deriving a contradiction.

Schiffer's objection can make do without this fallacious inference if (FC) can be extended into the following:

FC': (Necessarily) if α rationally believes of β that ϕ_{it} while also disbelieving (or merely withholding believing) of β that ϕ_{it}, then in so doing α takes β in differing ways.

(Schiffer proposes a related generalization.) But as remarked earlier, there are complex singular propositions about y that one can rationally believe without attributing the corresponding property to y. Someone can rationally believe and disbelieve one of these propositions without taking y to be distinct things. Given the existence of such cases, there is no obvious rationale for (FC'). Indeed, the very situation (a) arguably yields a counter-instance. I maintain that in (a), Jane rationally both believes and disbelieves of George Eliot, *de re*, that Ralph believes she was a man—even though in so doing, Jane does not take Eliot to be two separate people. It is unclear how, or even whether, a neo-Fregean can plausibly avoid this conclusion.[6]

There remains a bit of a mystery: How *can* someone both believe and disbelieve a singular proposition about *y* without thereby taking *y* to be distinct things?

The solution is not far to find. There is a potentially sound substitute for Schiffer's fallacious *reductio*, an alternative derivation that relies on (*FC*) and (*S*) without fatally detouring through dubious generalizations. This time, putting for β the 'that'-clause 'that George Eliot was a man' and putting for ϕ_{it} the open sentence '*It* is something Ralph believes', the relevant half of the resulting instance of (*S*) states that necessarily, if Jane believes that (the proposition) that Eliot was a man is something Ralph believes, then Jane believes of (the proposition) that George Eliot was a man, *de re*, that it is something Ralph believes. In situation (*a*), it may be supposed, so Jane does. One similarly obtains the result that necessarily, if Jane believes that (the proposition) that Mary Ann Evans was a man is something Ralph does not believe, then Jane believes of (the proposition) that Mary Ann Evans was a man, *de re*, that it is something Ralph does not believe. In situation (*a*), it may be supposed, so Jane does. According to Millianism, the propositions to which Jane in (*a*) *de re* attributes complementary properties (being believed by Ralph and not) are one and the same. Reasoning from (*FC*), it follows that Jane, insofar as she is rational in (*a*), must take this proposition in differing ways.

In situation (*a*), it may be supposed, so Jane does. She evidently mistakes this singular proposition for two independent thoughts (or at least is committed to doing so), one that Ralph believes, the other (according to Jane) not. No contradiction is derived and no problem for Millianism generated. On the contrary, our conclusion solves the riddle of how, without mistaking Eliot for two distinct people, one can rationally both believe and disbelieve of Eliot, *de re*, that Ralph believes she was a man. Though Jane does not mistake Eliot for distinct people, she may nevertheless mistake the singular proposition that Eliot was a man for distinct thoughts.[7] With this new derivation, Jane has been outed as a proto- or closet neo-Fregean. With a little further Socratic questioning, she might be induced to embrace her neo-Fregeanism with pride.

Schiffer defends his objection to Millianism, asserting, '. . . the only reasonable construal of *propositional* modes of presentation is that they are structured entities whose basic components are modes of presentation of the basic components of the Russellian propositions of which the propositional modes of presentation are modes of presentation.' Since Jane does not have the requisite differing modes of presentation of Eliot (nor of the property or concept of *having been a man*), she also does not have differing modes of presentation of the (putatively singular) proposition that Eliot was a man, as would be required by (*FC*).

With all due respect, it is unreasonable to suppose that the only proposition guises are such composite constructions as Schiffer envisions. The rational neo-Fregean who takes the proposition that George Eliot was a man to be believed by Ralph and also

---

[6] See 'Relational Belief', pp. 217–218.   [7] See 'Relational Belief', pp. 218–219.

takes the proposition that Mary Ann Evans was a man not to be believed by Ralph takes a single proposition to be two thoughts, and thereby takes it differently. The proposition might be taken as invoking Ralph's concept of who George Eliot is, and alternatively, as not doing so. The former is a misconception, to be sure, but misconceiving is a way of taking.

13

Being of Two Minds: Belief with Doubt (1995)

I

Belief is systematically connected with a variety of psychological attitudes. Disbelief is, in a certain sense, the opposite of belief. But one may fail to believe something—say, that Ortcutt is a spy—without going so far as to disbelieve it. One may suspend judgment on the issue. For the purposes of the present discussion, let us agree to stipulate the following definition for the word 'doubt':

A doubts p $=_{\text{def}}$ (*A* disbelieves *p*) $\vee$ (*A* suspends judgment concerning *p*).

Notice that according to this definition, in order for Ralph to count as doubting whether Ortcutt is a spy, Ralph need not even believe it unlikely that Ortcutt is a spy. It is enough that Ralph have no opinion on the matter. This constitutes a departure from standard usage, but it is merely a stipulation concerning how the word 'doubt' will be used here.[1]

What, now, is the relationship among these five: belief, disbelief, failure to believe, failure to disbelieve, and suspension of judgment?

Here is one plausible way to make out the connections. Let us tentatively lay down the following additional definitions, treating the English verb 'believes' together with the standard truth-functional connectives as primitive:

A disbelieves p $=_{\text{def}}$ *A* believes $\sim p$.

A fails to believe p $=_{\text{def}}$ $\sim$(*A* believes *p*).

A fails to disbelieve p $=_{\text{def}}$ $\sim$(*A* disbelieves *p*).

A suspends judgment concerning p $=_{\text{def}}$ (*A* fails to believe *p*) $\wedge$ (*A* fails to disbelieve *p*).

I am grateful to the participants in my seminar at UCSB during Spring 1993 for acting as the initial sounding board for the material in this essay, which was also presented to the American Philosophical Association in March 1994, with comments by Keith Donnellan and Stephen Neale. I thank them, and Takashi Yagisawa, for their comments.

[1] One finds a similar usage elsewhere in the philosophical literature. See, for example, Bertrand Russell, 'Belief, Disbelief, and Doubt', in his *Theory of Knowledge* (London: Routledge, 1992).

Notice that disbelief is (unlike failure to believe, failure to disbelieve, and suspension of judgment) a form of belief: it is belief of the denial. Suspension of judgment is defined as the joint failure of both belief and its opposite, disbelief. This definition is objectionable on the ground that genuine suspension of judgment requires in addition, for example, that one have a grasp—some apprehension, perhaps even if imperfect—of the proposition in question. One might suppose furthermore that suspension of judgment, in Russell's words, 'represents the result of an attempt to decide between the two'—i.e. that in order to count as suspending judgment on some matter one must have at least consciously considered the question at issue.[2] The points I shall make below are not greatly affected if one adds such restrictions as these to the proposed definition. For the most part, the discussion will require only minor modification to take account of the further conditions (for example by restricting the range of the propositional variable 'p' to propositions that A apprehends). As we did for doubt, let us simply stipulate that as we use the phrase here, suspension of judgment does not require that one have consciously considered the question.

Some immediate consequences of the definitions should be noted. We have made doubt definitionally equivalent to the disjunction of disbelief with suspension of judgment, thereby making for two distinct ways of doubting something. The definitions, as given, yield an alternative equivalent disjunction: To doubt something is to disbelieve it, or alternatively, simply to fail to believe it. It is not that failure to believe is equivalent to suspending judgment, suspending judgment, as defined above, entails failing to believe, but not vice versa. In failing to believe something one either disbelieves it, thereby doubting by disbelieving, or failing that, one suspends judgment (by definition), which is the second way of doubting. But the definitions allow for at least the possibility of someone believing something while also disbelieving, and hence doubting, it. Having contradictory beliefs is depicted here as at least a logical possibility, even if it is an irrational possibility and even if, as some have argued, it is a psychological impossibility. With this in mind, one can see that doubt is not simply identified with failure to believe. It is logically possible for one to doubt something while still believing it, but only by believing it and disbelieving it at the same time. The only way to fail to doubt something is to believe it but without also disbelieving it, i.e. to believe it in the normal way.

Such consequences as these are more easily seen if our definitions are symbolized in a standard logical notation. Let upper-case 'P' symbolize 'Ralph believes that Ortcutt is a spy', and let upper-case 'Q' symbolize 'Ralph disbelieves that Ortcutt is a spy'. The following symbolizations for the notions of failure to believe, failure to disbelieve, suspension of judgment, and doubt are thereby generated:

Ralph fails to believe that Ortcutt is a spy: $\sim P$.

Ralph fails to disbelieve that Ortcutt is a spy: $\sim Q$.

Ralph suspends judgment concerning whether Ortcutt is a spy: $\sim P \wedge \sim Q$.

Ralph doubts whether Ortcutt is a spy: $Q \vee (\sim P \wedge \sim Q)$.

[2] Ibid., p. 143.

The decision to symbolize in this manner presupposes the logical independence of belief and disbelief. One may compensate for this, if one wishes, by laying it down as a special postulate that Ralph does not both believe and disbelieve that Ortcutt is a spy, $\sim(P \wedge Q)$. In the general case, let us call the following postulate 'A's Consistency':

$\sim(A$ believes $p \wedge A$ disbelieves $p)$.

Here now are several theorems, each of which is easily derived from the definitions in standard propositional logic:

T1: A believes $p \vee A$ doubts p.

T2: $\sim(A$ believes $p \wedge A$ suspends judgment concerning $p)$.

T3: $\sim(A$ disbelieves $p \wedge A$ suspends judgment concerning $p)$.

T4: A doubts $p \equiv \sim(A$ disbelieves $p \equiv A$ suspends judgment concerning $p)$.

T5: A doubts $p \equiv (A$ believes $p \supset A$ disbelieves $p)$.

T6: $(A$ believes $p \wedge A$ doubts $p) \supset A$ disbelieves p.

Theorem *T1* tells us of every proposition within the range of 'p', that A either believes it or doubts it, where A can be anyone at all. Theorem *T2* tells us that no one both believes and suspends judgment concerning the very same proposition, and theorem *T3* tells us that no one both disbelieves and suspends judgment concerning the very same proposition. Theorem *T4* indicates that doubting—which was defined as the inclusive disjunction of disbelief with suspension of judgment—is equivalent to the *exclusive* disjunction. This equivalence is an immediate corollary of *T3*. Theorem *T5* indicates an alternative equivalent of doubting p: if one believes p, then one also disbelieves p. This was foreshadowed in our observation that doubt is definitionally equivalent to the disjunction of disbelief with mere failure to believe. Theorem *T5* immediately yields the result, given in *T6*, that believing while at the same time doubting the same thing inevitably requires one also to disbelieve that same thing—a corollary that resonates with *T2*.

Taking A's Consistency as a postulate yields the following addenda to *T1* and *T2*:

C1: $\sim(A$ believes $p \wedge A$ doubts $p)$.

C2: $\sim(A$ believes $p \equiv A$ doubts $p)$.

A's Consistency thus tells us of every proposition within the range of 'p', that A either believes it or doubts it, but never both. We noted above that the logical possibility of believing while also disbelieving is all that prevents the identification of doubt with simple failure to believe. Consequence *C2* immediately yields the following additional consequence, as a strengthened replacement for *T5*:

C3: A doubts $p \equiv A$ fails to believe p.

It is easily shown that each of *C1*, *C2*, and *C3* is in fact equivalent to A's Consistency.

II

All of these theorems and consequences are questionable results. In effect, they exclude various combinations of doxastic attitudes and/or the lack of doxastic attitudes as logically impossible—or in the case of *A*'s Consistency, as perhaps impossible in some other manner (e.g. psychologically). In particular, *T2* through *T6* and *A*'s Consistency and its equivalents exclude as impossible various ways of being of two minds, combining belief with doubt. What shall we make of these results?

Whatever oddity there may be in *T1* results entirely from our decision to understand *suspension of judgment* in a passive way. If we bear in mind that, so understood, merely failing to believe something while also failing to disbelieve it qualifies as suspending judgment concerning it, and hence as doubting it, *T1* should not strike us as unacceptable—or at least it should not strike us as being unacceptable in some further way. The case is very different, however, with *T2* through *T6*, and with *A*'s Consistency and its equivalents. For the combinations of conflicting attitudes that they rule out are evidently combinations that one may nevertheless exhibit.

Is it possible, in a real sense, to have genuinely conflicting doxastic attitudes? One immediately thinks of the subconscious and of self-conscious ambivalence. It is arguable that such cases provide genuine counterexamples to *T2* through *T6* and/or to *A*'s Consistency and its equivalents. It is equally arguable that they do not. Let us set such cases aside. The philosophy of language has provided an altogether different kind of example of conflicting attitudes.

Nearly four decades ago in his classic 'Quantifiers and Propositional Attitudes', Quine made a significant case against *A*'s Consistency.[3] He there provided a now famous example in which it would be clearly correct to say that, because he has failed to recognize Ortcutt in his different personae, Ralph believes Ortcutt to be a spy while simultaneously believing Ortcutt not to be a spy. Being a Millian with respect to proper names, I accept Quine's example as a case of Ralph both believing that Ortcutt is a spy, and at the same time also disbelieving, and hence doubting, that Ortcutt is a spy. Quine himself evidently does not so construe the case, insisting instead on Ralph's Consistency and on the inaccuracy of characterizing Ralph as believing of Ortcutt that he is a spy. But his argument for this is confused and, in my judgment, very much mistaken.[4]

---

[3] In Quine's *The Ways of Paradox* (New York: Random House, 1966), pp. 183–194.

[4] *Cf.* my 'Relational Belief', in P. Leonardi and M. Santambrogio, eds, *On Quine*, Proceedings of the 1990 San Marino Conference on Quine's Contributions to Philosophy (Cambridge University Press, 1994), first note. Quine objects to the claim that Ortcutt is believed by Ralph to be a spy on the questionable grounds that 'if so, we find ourselves accepting a conjunction of the type *w* sincerely denies "..." & *w* believes that ... as true, with one and the same sentence ['Ortcutt is a spy'] in both blanks' (*op. cit.*, p. 185). Quine takes no notice of the fact that this involves the tacit assumption that if Ralph believes Ortcutt to be a spy, in virtue of believing that the man in the brown hat is a spy, then Ralph also believes *that Ortcutt is a spy*. This assumption is highly controversial. Perhaps a majority of philosophers of language reject it; Quine himself almost certainly does. By contrast, I accept it, together with the consequence that Ralph sincerely denies something

Even setting Quine's example alongside cases from the subconscious and ambivalence, similar sorts of examples are driving an increasing number of philosophers to the same conclusion that failure to recognize someone or something typically results in contradictory beliefs about that one or that thing. Nothing has done more to lend credence to this conclusion, and to foster its widespread acceptance, than Kripke's recent classic 'A Puzzle about Belief'.[5] Kripke himself concludes his trenchant essay by cautioning against drawing any significant theoretical conclusions from his arguments and examples.[6] And indeed, several remarks seem to indicate that he adamantly opposes this conclusion in particular.[7] In hindsight, however, his examples and arguments are today very often seen—perhaps even usually seen—as making an extremely strong case (however inadvertent) against *A*'s Consistency. Those examples and arguments also make an extremely strong case against claims like those made in *T2* through *T6*, when taken in their usual senses, or something close to it (as opposed to the nonstandard senses imposed on them by the proposed definitions). The case against the 'theorems' is in many respects quite similar to, even though significantly stronger than, Quine's (equally inadvertent) case against *A*'s Consistency and its equivalents.

Kripke's examples refute *A*'s Consistency by providing cases in which a rational believer, Pierre, is unknowingly of two minds concerning whether London is pretty. Although frequently overlooked, one of the most significant aspects of Kripke's examples is that the difficulties they raise for *A*'s Consistency and its equivalents are quite independent of the on-going debate between Millianism (or neo-Russellianism) and Fregeanism. Millians and Fregeans alike have concluded that Pierre is of two minds, harboring conflicting attitudes toward the single proposition that London is pretty. In the central example, Pierre both believes and disbelieves that London is pretty. Kripke also briefly considers a modified example in which Pierre instead both believes and suspends judgment without disbelieving (*op. cit.*, pp. 122–123). Although Kripke does not do so, one might also consider an alternative modified example in which Pierre disbelieves and suspends judgment without believing. In

---

he in fact believes. Indeed, he sincerely denies that Ortcutt is a spy precisely because he disbelieves it.

[5] In N. Salmon and S. Soames, eds, *Propositions and Attitudes* (Oxford Readings in Philosophy, 1988), pp. 102–148.

[6] At p. 136.

[7] At p. 122 (top paragraph). *Cf.* also pp. 131–136, especially 132. Some of these passages suggest that Kripke may endorse the postulate of Pierre's Consistency. However, this is very likely a misrepresentation of his position. Kripke argues vigorously that when we attempt to evaluate the English sentences 'Pierre believes that London is pretty' and 'Pierre disbelieves that London is pretty' as true or false, 'we enter into an area where our normal practices of interpretation and attribution of belief are subjected to the greatest possible strain, perhaps to the point of breakdown' (pp. 134–135). As I read him, Kripke thinks—unofficially, as it were—that both sentences are probably neither true nor false, in his example (owing to some sort of conceptual deficiency in the verb 'believes'). This would make their conjunction also neither true nor false, and hence also the negation of that conjunction—which is Pierre's Consistency. *Cf.* my *Frege's Puzzle*, pp. 129–132; and 'Illogical Belief', in J. Tomberlin, ed., *Philosophical Perspectives, 3: Philosophy of Mind and Action Theory*, 1989 (Atascadero, Calif.: Ridgeview, 1989), pp. 243–285, at pp. 255–256, 276–277n14.

fact, it is a simple matter to extend the original example into one in which Pierre is of three minds. Imagine that Pierre has learned not only English but also Italian by direct assimilation (not by translation into either French or English). He comes to believe that the city named '*Londra*' is a third city, distinct from both the pretty city named '*Londres*' and the ugly city named 'London'. When queried in Italian, '*Londra è graziosa?*', he neither assents nor dissents, explaining that he has no opinion on the matter. In this example, he believes, disbelieves, and also suspends judgment with respect to the same proposition that London is pretty! This and the other permutations on Kripke's original example, I contend, invalidate each of *T2* through *T6*, when taken in something like their standard senses, as well as *A*'s Consistency.[8]

Since each of these theorems follow logically from the proposed definitions, the examples thereby discredit those definitions. Our conclusion, then, is that, however plausible they seemed at first sight, at least one of our definitions has missed its intended target. Which one, or ones?

It is under the pressure applied by examples of someone being of two minds—combining belief with doubt—that I have suggested alternative accounts of belief and doubt.[9] Many commentators have thought that my alternative account is proposed as an *ad hoc* supplement to my advocacy of a Millian theory of names, in order to make the theory more palatable. Let me emphasize that the pressure to adopt some such alternative account does not come from my Millianism, except perhaps by a very circuitous route. If I were a Fregean, I would still advocate my alternative account of the doxastic attitudes, and for very much the same reasons. Even looking at the situation through Fregean lenses, one is drawn to the conclusion that someone in Pierre's state of confusion is, or at least can be, of two minds (or of three or more minds) with respect to one and the same proposition—or in Frege's preferred terminology, with respect to one and the same 'thought' (*Gedanke*).[10] To account for this anomaly, the Fregean need only turn to his/her notion of *indirect sense* (*ungerade Sinn*). The indirect sense of an expression is the sense that the expression allegedly takes on in positions in which it has indirect reference (*ungerade Bedeutung*), referring not to its customary referent but to its indirect referent, which is the sense customarily expressed. Indeed, although I do not know of anyone who has explicitly responded to Kripke's arguments by invoking the orthodox Fregean notion of indirect sense, that notion is tailor-made to explain predicaments like Pierre's.[11] The English 'London is pretty', the French '*Londres est jolie*', and the Italian '*Londra è graziosa*' all express the same proposition. Pierre fully understands each of the three sentences. Each of those sentences therefore expresses the very same thing even for Pierre. But he does not realize that. The sentences present their shared proposition

---

[8] For those who insist that issues of inter-language translation are importantly relevant to Kripke's examples, this case may be replaced, exactly as Kripke suggests, by one in which Peter believes, disbelieves, and suspends judgment concerning whether Paderewski has musical talent.

[9] *Frege's Puzzle* (Atascadero, Calif.: Ridgeview, 1986, 1989), in chapter 8, at pp. 103–118.

[10] Frege himself probably would not have accepted this conclusion regarding Pierre's particular circumstance. But see note 12 below.

[11] *Cf.* Alonzo Church's review of the famous Black/White exchange concerning the paradox of analysis, in *The Journal of Symbolic Logic*, 11 (1946), pp. 132–133.

content to Pierre in different ways. Though exactly alike in customary sense, the three sentences thus differ in indirect sense, at least for Pierre, as he understands them.[12]

Although I am not a Fregean, I have helped myself, enthusiastically, to certain aspects of Frege's notion of sense—or more specifically, to certain aspects of his notion of indirect sense.[13] I have done so not because my Millianism imposes a special requirement to do so, but because Pierre's predicament does. Pierre is of two (or more) minds concerning the proposition that London is pretty because he takes the proposition in different ways, mistaking it for two (or more) independent propositions—just as he mistakes London for two (or more) different cities. If a believer A treats a pair of propositions p and q as being distinct, then he or she takes p and q in different ways—even if, in fact, $p = q$. Thus if A mistakes p for two independent propositions, then he or she takes p in two different ways. I have proposed that we recognize a ternary relation, *BEL*, underlying the binary relation between believer and proposition believed. The *BEL* relation obtains among

---

[12] The indirect-sense solution just adumbrated is not necessarily Frege's own. In light of his remarks in the famous second footnote to '*Über Sinn und Bedeutung*' pertaining to the name 'Aristotle' and the sentence 'Aristotle was born in Stagira', Frege himself would have likely denied that the name 'London' is a part of English—or, at least, that it is a univocal part—and that the name '*Londres*' is a part of French, etc. Carried through to its natural conclusion, this denial would involve a refusal to apply the disquotational principle on which Kripke relies in developing his puzzle to sentences involving either name, on the grounds that such sentences occur only in individual idiolects and not in any public natural language. Pierre's sincere and reflective dissent from 'London is pretty' indicates his disbelief of the proposition ('thought') expressed by that sentence *in his own idiolect*. But according to Frege, we cannot report Pierre's attitude using the sentence 'Pierre disbelieves that London is pretty' unless we happen to attach the very same (customary) sense to 'London' as Pierre—an extremely unlikely coincidence, on Frege's view.

A couple of points should be made in this connection. First, the famous translation test advocated and successfully employed by Frege's most ardent follower, Alonzo Church, would seem to support the conclusion that the English 'London is pretty' and the French '*Londres est jolie*' express the same proposition. The proposed indirect-sense solution is the natural Fregean position, once this conclusion is conceded (contra Frege himself). More importantly, situations like Pierre's can be reproduced using general terms in place of genuine proper names. Kripke, in a slightly different connection, suggests examples using natural-kind terms (*op. cit.*, pp. 128–130; see also pp. 108–110, 115–117 for related discussion). I have elsewhere suggested examples using 'ketchup'/'catsup', 'color'/'colour', and even differing pronunciations of 'tomato'. See my 'A Millian Heir Rejects the Wages of *Sinn*', in C. A. Anderson and J. Owens, eds, *Propositional Attitudes: The Role of Content in Logic, Language, and Mind* (Stanford, Calif.: CSLI, 1990), pp. 215–247, at pp. 220–221; and 'Relative and Absolute Apriority', *Philosophical Studies*, 69 (1993), pp. 83–100, at p. 86. Frege's views about genuine proper names, however reasonable they may seem at first blush, cannot be plausibly extended to cover all of these examples. Where they cannot, the indirect-sense solution is the only appropriately Fregean response.

I should add that I believe the indirect-sense solution, although in some respects natural, is ultimately quite implausible. See my 'A Problem in the Frege–Church Theory of Sense and Denotation', *Noûs*, 27, 2 (June 1993), pp. 158–166. I thus sharply disagree with those who maintain that Kripke's examples pose no serious problem for the Fregean (as for example, William Taschek, 'Would a Fregean be Puzzled by Pierre?', *Mind*, 97, 385 (January 1988), pp. 99–104).

[13] I reject the charge that my doing so makes me a closet Fregean. As I said in the previous note, I believe the orthodox indirect-sense solution is ultimately quite implausible; I employ only certain aspects of Frege's notion of indirect sense. See João Branquinho, 'Are Salmon's "Guises" Disguised Fregean Senses?', *Analysis*, 50, 1 (January 1990), pp. 19–24; and my 'A Millian Heir Rejects the Wages of *Sinn*'.

a believer *A*, a proposition *p*, and a way *x* of taking *p*, when *A* is disposed to cognitive assent to *p*, taking it in way *x*. Or something along those lines. The important point is that *A* may stand in *BEL* to *p* and one third relatum *x* (one way in which *A* takes *p*), yet fail to stand in *BEL* to *p* and some other third relatum $x' \neq x$ (some other way in which *A* takes *p*). When one fails to recognize something or someone, one's attitude toward that thing or that one may depend on *how one takes it*, on which thing or which one it is taken to be.

The simple claim '*A* believes *p*' is analyzable as *A*'s standing in *BEL* to *p* and some way or other in which *A* takes *p*:

$(\exists x)[A \text{ takes } p \text{ in way } x \wedge BEL(A, p, x)]$.

A point that has escaped many of my commentators is that this analysis makes belief a binary, rather than a ternary, relation. One might view my reliance on the *BEL* relation as making for a relative notion of belief, one that obtains *relative to* ways of taking propositions. If one does, then ordinary belief is nothing other than the absolute notion naturally corresponding to this relative one. The English verb 'believes' may be regarded as a dyadic predicate for the relation between individuals and propositions defined by the expression displayed above (more accurately, for the relation defined by prefixing '$(\lambda A, p)$' to the expression displayed above).

Combining this analysis for belief with our earlier definitions, we arrive at the following analyses for '*A* disbelieves *p*', '*A* fails to believe *p*', and '*A* fails to disbelieve *p*', respectively:

$(\exists x)[A \text{ takes } \sim p \text{ in way } x \wedge BEL(A, \sim p, x)]$;

$\sim(\exists x)[A \text{ takes } p \text{ in way } x \wedge BEL(A, p, x)]$;

$\sim(\exists x)[A \text{ takes } \sim p \text{ in way } x \wedge BEL(A, \sim p, x)]$.

These constructions simply insert a negation sign at one place or another in the analysis for '*A* believes *p*'. There is at least one other position in which the negation sign might be sensibly placed. To account for situations like Pierre's, I offered an analysis of a supplementary notion, which is modeled in a certain sense after the notion of failure to believe, and which I called 'withheld belief'. '*A* withholds belief from *p*' is analyzed as:

$(\exists x)[A \text{ takes } p \text{ in way } x \wedge \sim BEL(A, p, x)]$.[14]

Notice that this notion is logically compatible not only with failure to believe and with disbelief, as analyzed above, but also with belief of the very same proposition *p*. Taken together with our analysis of belief it immediately yields the following theorem:

T7: $(\exists x)(A \text{ takes } p \text{ in way } x) \supset (A \text{ believes } p \vee A \text{ withholds belief from } p)$.

---

[14] *Frege's Puzzle*, p. 111. The analysis was inspired by an argument in David Kaplan, 'Quantifying In', in D. Davidson and J. Hintikka, eds, *Words and Objections: Essays on the Work of W. V. Quine* (Dordrecht: D. Reidel, 1969), pp. 206–242. See especially section XI, at pp. 233–235.

This tells us that anyone who apprehends a given proposition without believing it withholds belief from it. But refraining from believing an apprehended proposition is not the only way to withhold belief. One can both believe and withhold belief from the same proposition.

In place of the earlier definition for *suspension of judgment*, we now have the following analysis for '*A* suspends judgments concerning *p*':

$(\exists x)[A$ takes p in way $x \land {\sim}BEL(A, p, x) \land A$ takes ${\sim}p$ in way $Neg(x) \land {\sim}BEL(A, {\sim}p, Neg(x))]$,

where $Neg(x)$ is the corresponding way of taking the denial of the proposition that x is a way of taking.[15] This immediately yields the following theorems:

T8: *A* suspends judgment concerning $p \supset A$ withholds belief from p.

T9: *A* suspends judgment concerning $p \supset A$ withholds belief from ${\sim}p$.

These theorems, taken together with our new analysis of suspension of judgment, tell us that to suspend judgment concerning a proposition is to withhold belief both from that proposition and from its denial, but to do so in a special manner *via* a single way of taking the matter.

III

We have seen that failure to believe an apprehended proposition entails withholding belief from it, but not vice versa. What is the relationship among disbelief, withheld belief, suspension of judgment, and doubt?

To answer this question, I propose assuming three special postulates.[16] The first I shall call '*A*'s Comprehension':

A takes p in way $x \equiv A$ takes ${\sim}p$ in way $Neg(x)$.

This tells us that if *A* apprehends a certain proposition p, then *A* also apprehends its denial ${\sim}p$ in the appropriate way corresponding to the way in which *A* takes p, i.e. as the denial of p. It also tells us that if *A* apprehends a certain negative proposition ${\sim}p$ in an appropriate manner (i.e. as a negative proposition), then *A* also apprehends the proposition p that ${\sim}p$ negates in the appropriate way corresponding to the way in which *A* takes ${\sim}p$, i.e. as the proposition negated by ${\sim}p$. *A*'s Comprehension (in the left–right direction), taken alone, yields the following consequence:

C4: *A* withholds belief from $p \supset (A$ disbelieves $p \lor A$ suspends judgment concerning p).

---

[15] This is a minor modification of the analysis proposed in *Frege's Puzzle*, p. 172n1. The different analyses are rendered equivalent under the assumption, to be proposed shortly, of *A*'s Comprehension.

[16] Other postulates may be assumed in addition to these. A trivial case in point is what I call 'the BEL Principle': '$BEL(A, p, x) \supset A$ takes p in way x.' This merely encapsulates the triviality that if *A* believes p relative to a particular way x of taking p, then *A* takes p in way x. (It renders part of the proposed analysis of belief redundant.)

The second postulate I shall call 'the Negativity Principle':

A takes $\sim p$ in way $x \supset (\exists y)(x = Neg(y))$.

This tells us, in effect, that to any way of taking a negative proposition $\sim p$ there corresponds an appropriate way of taking the proposition p negated by $\sim p$. The third postulate, which I shall call 'A's Rationality', replaces the now discarded A's Consistency:

$\sim[BEL(A, p, x) \land BEL(A, \sim p, Neg(x))]$.[17]

Recall that A's Consistency, in its consequence $C3$, rendered doubt equivalent to failure to believe. Using the Negativity Principle and A's Comprehension (in the right–left direction only) in combination with A's Rationality, we may derive:

A disbelieves $p \supset A$ withholds belief from p.

Combining this consequence with $T8$ and $C4$ we have the following:

$C5$: A withholds belief from $p \equiv A$ doubts p.

Consequence $C5$ is our replacement for $C3$. Although the definition for 'doubt' has not been altered, the notion so defined has changed significantly. This is because doubt is defined in terms of suspension of judgment, and our new notion of suspension of judgment is significantly different from our old one. Consequence $C4$ yields a near entailment between the old notion and the new one:

$(\exists x)(A$ takes p in way $x) \supset [(A$ fails to believe $p \land A$ fails to disbelieve $p) \supset A$ suspends judgments concerning $p]$.

This tells us that if A apprehends p but neither believes it nor disbelieves it, then A suspends judgment. But we no longer have that if A apprehends p and suspends judgment concerning it, then A fails to believe it, and likewise we no longer have that if A apprehends p and suspends judgment concerning it, then A fails to disbelieve it. In short, the new notion of suspension of judgment is, in a sense, weaker than the old one. Most significantly, 'A suspends judgment concerning p' is now consistent both with 'A believes p' and with 'A disbelieves p'. In fact, even A's Rationality (with or without the other two postulates) does not exclude the joint truth of all three. This is all for the good, since on the amended example, Pierre believes, disbelieves, and suspends judgment with respect to a single proposition. The new, weaker notion of suspension of judgment yields a notion of doubt that is likewise weaker than the old one.

We have already seen our replacements for the discarded A's Consistency and its equivalents. But what has become of the previous theorems $T1$ through $T6$? In place of $T1$, as a direct consequence of $T7$ and $C5$ we now have:

$C6$: $(\exists x)(A$ takes p in way $x) \supset (A$ believes $p \lor A$ doubts $p)$.

---

[17] General claims to the effect that we form beliefs in accordance with the rules of logic have to be weakened in analogous ways. *Cf.* my 'Illogical Belief'.

Thus failing to believe an apprehended proposition remains one way of doubting it.

By contrast with *T1*, all of *T2* through *T6* simply go by the wayside.[18]

IV

I have stressed that my postulation of a ternary relation underlying the binary relation between a believer and the proposition believed is motivated primarily by considerations that are largely independent of the controversy between Millians and Fregeans. Recognition of the *BEL* relation allows for the natural definition of a relation of suspension of judgment that is compatible with both belief and disbelief of the same proposition, and with belief-with-disbelief. It also allows for a straightforward understanding of such notions as that of *believing the same thing in two different ways* or *believing the same thing twice over*, of *doubting the same thing twice over*, etc. Examples like Kripke's compel one to recognize these various doxastic notions, and the examples do so largely independently of one's theory of meaning. I have also relied on the presence of the *BEL* relation in the underlying structure of the belief relation to explain the prevailing intuitions against some of the consequences of Millianism concerning substitution.[19]

Other philosophers have looked to the *BEL* relation to do independent duty as part of a device that can rescue Millianism altogether from its untoward consequences. One strategy is to treat the grammatical complement clause in a belief attribution as specifying at one and the same time both the proposition, belief of which is being attributed, and with it also a specific third relatum for the *BEL* relation. For example, an English belief attribution of the form

α believes that φ,

where α is a singular term and φ is a declarative sentence, might be regarded as expressing a proposition about the referent of α, to the effect that he/she stands in *BEL* to p and w (or that he/she believes p 'relative to' w), where p is the proposition content of φ and w is a particular third relatum for the *BEL* relation carried by the very sentence φ for the referent of α. The complement clause φ is thus pressed to perform two separate roles, determining distinct relata in separate argument places of the *BEL* relation. Indeed, on this theory, the belief attribution may be regarded as a shorthand for something like the following:

$BEL(\alpha,\ \text{that}\ \varphi,\ W[\alpha, \varphi])$,

where 'W' is special operator, not appearing explicitly in the surface structure, such that the result of attaching it to a singular term α and a sentence φ in brackets refers to the way the referent of α takes the content of φ when that proposition is presented

---

[18] There are, of course, replacements for *T2* through *T6* involving '*BEL*' in place of 'believes'. Each is trivial.

[19] *Frege's Puzzle*, especially pp. 114–118; 'Illogical Belief', especially pp. 248–253.

to him/her by means of (his/her version of) the very sentence φ. Let us call this *the double-dipper theory*.[20]

Assuming that pairs of co-contentful sentences like 'Hesperus appears at dusk' and 'Phosphorus appears at dusk' provide speakers with distinct ways of taking their shared proposition content, the double-dipper theory offers a ready explanation for the appearance of a failure of substitution in problematic attributions like 'Jones believes that Hesperus appears at dusk': Whereas substituting 'Phosphorus' for 'Hesperus' preserves the attributed proposition, doing so does not also preserve the specified way of taking that proposition, and hence need not preserve truth value for the whole attribution. The double-dipper theory is in fact reminiscent of Fregeanism. One of the principal characteristics that distinguish the double-dipper theory from a mere notational variant of Fregeanism is that the thing said to be believed in 'Jones believes that Hesperus appears at dusk' (or the thing said to be doubted in 'Jones doubts whether Hesperus appears at dusk', etc.) is not supposed to be the proposition-cum-way-of-taking-it provided by the complement clause, but merely the proposition, in this case a singular proposition. As will become clear in due course, this feature of the double-dipper theory is significant. Another feature of the double-dipper theory that differentiates it from Fregeanism is that it is refuted by Alonzo Church's famous translation argument.[21]

Stephen Schiffer has proposed a close relative of the double-dipper theory, which he calls *the hidden-indexical theory*.[22] The hidden-indexical theory, or something extremely similar, has been defended by Mark Crimmins and John Perry.[23] The central idea is that an English belief attribution of the form

α believes θ,

with α a singular term and θ a term referring to a proposition, is indexical, expressing different propositions with respect to different contexts of utterance. With respect to

---

[20] I have argued that belief attributions are often used to convey precisely the information ascribed to them as their semantic content by the double-dipper theory, rather than the nonspecific, existential information that my own theory ascribes as semantic content. (See the previous note.) It is important to note that even if one succeeds in asserting the former sort of information in uttering a particular belief attribution, it does not follow that the attribution itself semantically contains this same information, rather than information of the latter sort, with respect to the context of utterance. See note 27 below.

[21] Alonzo Church, 'On Carnap's Analysis of Statements of Assertion and Belief', in L. Linsky, ed., *Reference and Modality* (Oxford University Press, 1971), pp. 168–170.

[22] Schiffer deems the hidden-indexical theory the best theory of the semantics of belief attributions that is predicated on the relatively uncontroversial assumption (which Schiffer himself rejects) that natural language 'has a correct compositional truth theory'. He first presented a version of the theory in 'Naming and Knowing', in P. French, T. Uehling, and H. Wettstein, eds, *Contemporary Perspectives in the Philosophy of Language* (Minneapolis: University of Minnesota Press, 1977, 1979), pp. 61–74, at pp. 65–67. See also his 'The "Fido"–Fido Theory of Belief', in J. Tomberlin, ed., *Philosophical Perspectives, 1, Metaphysics,* 1987 (Atascadero, Calif.: Ridgeview, 1987), pp. 455–480; and 'Belief Ascription', *Journal of Philosophy*, 89, 10 (October 1992), pp. 499–521. (I respond to the second mentioned article at some length in 'Illogical Belief, *loc. cit.*)

[23] Crimmins and Perry, 'The Prince and the Phone Booth: Reporting Puzzling Beliefs', *Journal of Philosophy*, 86, 12 (December 1989), pp. 685–711; Crimmins, *Talk About Beliefs* (Cambridge, Mass.: MIT Press, 1992). The latter work is the most thorough in its detailed development and defense of the theory.

a given context c, it expresses (or at least commonly expresses) a proposition about the referent of α with respect to c and the referent of θ with respect to c, to the effect that the former stands in *BEL* to the latter and w, where w is a particular third relatum for the *BEL* relation, one that is implicitly or tacitly referred to ('unarticulated', to use Perry's term) in, and determined only relative to, the context c. It is as if the attribution were shorthand for something like the following:

BEL(α, θ, *that* way of taking θ).

Here the third argument is a demonstrative phrase which is 'hidden' in the surface structure, and by means of which (or as if by means of which) the speaker refers, in his/her context, to a particular way of taking a proposition.[24]

---

[24] Schiffer refers to the third relata of the *BEL* relation by the Fregean epithet 'mode of presentation', but he defines modes of presentation essentially as whatever plays the role of third relata for the *BEL* relation. Crimmins and Perry take the third relata to be mental particulars. The objections to be raised below are independent of these matters. I shall continue to speak of the third relata as 'ways of taking propositions', but I mean this phrase to be neutral regarding the exact nature of the third relata (as with Schiffer's use of 'modes of presentation'). *Cf. Frege's Puzzle*, pp. 111, 119–120, 126–128.

The hidden-indexical theorists allow that belief attributions need not always involve implicit contextual specification of a particular third relatum for *BEL*, and may instead merely characterize a third relatum as being of a certain implicitly, contextually indicated kind (for example when simultaneously attributing belief to a plurality of believers rather than to a single individual). It is also allowed that, on comparatively rare occasion, there is neither contextual specification nor contextual characterization, but merely existential generalization—the last being precisely what I contend is the correct analysis for all belief attributions. In the general case, a belief attribution of the form 'α believes θ' is shorthand (or, in some way, as if it were shorthand) for something like: '($\exists x$)[x is a way of taking θ & x is of *that* kind & *BEL*(α, θ, x)].' Here the demonstrative '*that*' refers, with respect to a context, to a kind of way of taking a proposition (or to a property of ways of taking propositions). Typically, the kind in question may be uniquely specific to one way of taking a proposition, but in an extreme case, the kind in question may be utterly nonspecific, including every way of taking a proposition.

The theory thus appears to offer a great deal of flexibility. By the same token, however, it comes perilously close to being an ambiguity theory of belief attributions. (The ambiguity would presumably trace to a lexical ambiguity in the English verb 'believes'.) As such, the theory may be subject to special objections that do not arise with respect to the variant that treats belief attributions as always involving contextual specification. See for example Kripke's 'Speaker's Reference and Semantic Reference', in P. French, T. Uehling, and H. Wettstein, eds, *Contemporary Perspectives in the Philosophy of Language* (Minneapolis: University of Minnesota Press, 1977, 1979), pp. 6–27, at p. 19. The objections there adduced against ambiguity hypotheses may apply to a significant extent also to indexicality hypotheses of the sort proposed by the hidden-indexical theory. (Is there a significant difference between the usual view that the English word 'bank' is ambiguous, and the 'rival' theory that 'bank' univocally means 'object of *that* kind', where the implicit demonstrative always refers either to the kind *Financial Bank* or to the kind *River Bank*, as determined by the context?)

For simplicity, in the text I consider only the less flexible uniquely-specific version of the theory. This simplification invites the worry that the more general theory might have been originally motivated, in part, by some of the very considerations to be adduced below. But my central objections might be extended to the theory in its full generality, provided the hypothesized variability of specificity (or the alleged ambiguity) is systematic to a sufficient degree. Extending the objections in this way is a somewhat delicate matter, since the theory's defenders might respond that the particular example at hand cannot involve the typical sort of case, and instead necessarily involves one of the relatively rare occasions on which the third relatum is neither specified nor

Both the double-dipper and the hidden-indexical theories, as well as my own theory, are compatible with, and even strongly suggest, the thesis that a 'that'-clause ⌜that φ⌝, with φ a declarative sentence, is a singular term (or at least a term much like a singular term) referring to the proposition content of φ. As I have noted elsewhere, independently of the rivalry among these theories, this thesis regarding 'that'-clauses is both natural and plausible.[25] It provides the best explanation, for example, for the validity of inferences like the following:

(*I*): Pierre believes everything Jean-Paul says about London.
Jean-Paul says (about London) that London is pretty.
Therefore, Pierre believes that London is pretty.

Indeed, Schiffer cites this observation as yielding a very important consideration in favor of the hidden-indexical theory over alternative theories that preclude treating 'that'-clauses as singular terms for propositions.[26] Notice furthermore that the hidden-indexical theory provides an analysis for belief attributions of the form '*A* believes θ' even when the proposition term θ does not take the form 'that φ', with φ a declarative sentence, and instead takes the form of a definite description ('the proposition to which our nation is dedicated', 'what Jean-Paul said') or a name ('Church's Thesis', 'functionalism'). It is questionable whether the double-dipper theory can be plausibly extended to cover attributions of the more general form. The hidden-indexical theory may thus afford significantly greater flexibility in this regard.

There is considerable intuitive evidence, however, that typical belief attributions do not semantically specify (or even constrain) particular third relata for the *BEL*

---

substantively characterized but merely existentially generalized upon. The theory may have to be judged ultimately by the plausibility, or implausibility, of this additional claim.

[25] *Cf. Frege's Puzzle*, p. 5.

[26] 'The "Fido"–Fido Theory of Belief', at pp. 458–461; 'Belief Ascription', at pp. 504–505. The account presented in Kaplan, 'Quantifying In', in connection with *de re* constructions like 'Pierre believes of London that it is pretty' is the forerunner, and perhaps the best known instance, of the sort of theory that Schiffer is arguing against. *Cf.* my 'A Millian Heir Rejects the Wages of *Sinn*', at pp. 239–242. I should note, however, that the hidden-indexical theory is primarily a theory of *de dicto* constructions. A hidden-indexical theorist need not treat the 'that'-clause in a *de re* attribution as a term for a proposition, as my own theory does (though he/she may).

While expressing sympathy for most of the ideas defended here, Neale argued in his comments at the American Philosophical Association session that an alternative explanation for the validity of (*I*) is provided by the rival hypothesis that the phrase 'that London is pretty' is a compound quantifier, perhaps synonymous with 'some unique proposition expressed [in English] by "London is pretty"'. Neale argued further that evidence for the superiority of this rival hypothesis is provided by the difficulty that otherwise arises in interpreting 'that'-clauses that are bound by a quantifier (as in 'Every man believes that he is moral'). Contra Neale, quantification into a 'that'-clause, even when the latter is taken to be a singular term, presents no special problem of interpretation. Open singular terms (including variables) refer only under an assignment of values to their free variables. Open 'that'-clauses ('that *x* is moral' with its free '*x*', or 'that he is moral' with its free pronoun), when evaluated with respect to assignments of values to their free variables, simply refer to singular propositions. It is as much a confusion to ask for the referent of a *bound* occurrence of a 'that'-clause as it is to ask for the referent of the bound occurrence of its variable or pronoun. (*Cf. Frege's Puzzle*, pp. 2–6.) Moreover, the particular hypothesis mentioned here is again refuted by Church's translation objection, cited above in connection with the double-dipper theory.

relation—whether explicitly or implicitly, whether contextually or noncontextually. The point at issue parallels in many respects the much-debated question of whether so-called indefinite descriptions, like 'a man', are singular terms or instead nonspecific existential-quantificational constructions.[27] For example, suppose Peter utters the attribution,

𝒫: Pierre believes that London is pretty

based on the erroneous assumption that Pierre, on reflection, is disposed to assent sincerely to the sentence 'London is pretty'. To press the case even further, suppose that the background for Peter's utterance of 𝒫 includes special attention to the matter of

---

[27] See Charles Chastain, 'Reference and Context', in K. Gunderson, ed., *Minnesota Studies in the Philosophy of Science VII: Language, Mind, and Knowledge* (Minneapolis: University of Minnesota Press, 1975), pp. 194–269; Keith Donnellan, 'Speaker Reference, Descriptions, and Anaphora', in P. French, T. Uehling, and H. Wettstein, eds, *Contemporary Perspectives in the Philosophy of Language* (Minneapolis: University of Minnesota Press, 1977, 1979), pp. 28–44, at pp. 38–39; Kripke, 'Speaker's Reference and Semantic Reference', at pp. 17, 24n24, 26n32; Peter Ludlow and Stephen Neale, 'Indefinite Descriptions: In Defense of Russell', *Linguistics and Philosophy*, 14 (1991), pp. 171–202. It is my view that many, perhaps most, of the positive arguments offered by the hidden-indexical theorists commit a special fallacy, one that is also committed in many arguments for the thesis that indefinite descriptions are singular terms (and indeed is prevalent in much recent philosophy of language). See my 'The Pragmatic Fallacy', *Philosophical Studies*, 63 (1991), pp. 83–97, especially p. 96n15. The sort of inference to which I object is virtually demanded by a particular conception of semantics which fails to distinguish sharply between properly semantic ideas and those pertaining primarily to speech acts—for example, between the semantic content of a sentence with respect to a given context and the content of the assertion, or assertions (statements, utterances), made by the speaker in uttering the sentence in that context. I believe this *speech-act centered conception* presents a seriously distorted picture of what semantics is—as does the analogous *thought centered conception*. (*Cf. Frege's Puzzle*, p. 174n2.) It very often happens that what certain words express or refer to diverges in various ways from what a speaker expresses or refers to in uttering those same words. The conception of semantics reflected in the work of Crimmins, Perry, Schiffer, and many others, is unable to draw this distinction correctly. The speech-act centered conception fuels a host of questionable theories in philosophical semantics, including the double-dipper theory as well as the hidden-indexical theory. (*Cf.* Crimmins and Perry, p. 711, final paragraph; Crimmins, p. 7n.)

Although I largely steer clear of these broader foundational issues in the text, I believe they lie at the heart of the matter with regard to the double-dipper and hidden-indexical theories. I note here that the intuitive case to be presented against those theories—especially the examples concerning the intuitive correctness of certain inferences—also applies to a significant extent against the conception of semantics that drives those theories. By the same token, anyone who is theoretically committed to, or otherwise under, that misconception may for that very reason lack the intuitions on which I shall rely, and hence may not find the case particularly troubling. My arguments are addressed not so much to my partisan opponents as to the neutral agnostic—such indeed is the nature of philosophical debate in general. On the other hand, as I note below, Schiffer, in the very course of defending his hidden-indexical theory, explicitly endorses the major premise of my principal objection, evidently unaware that it conflicts with the theory.

I learned as the present paper was going to press that Mark Richard has criticized the hidden-indexical theory on some grounds very similar to (even if not exactly the same as) those to be presented here—especially in connection with the intuitive validity of certain types of inferences counted invalid by the theory, and more generally with regard to the dependence of the hidden-indexical theory on what I am calling 'the speech-act centered conception of semantics'. See his 'Attitudes in Context', *Linguistics and Philosophy*, 16 (1993), pp. 123–148, at 143–147. (But see also note 31 below.)

what sort of impression one forms of London based primarily on an exposure to its slums. There is some temptation to judge that 𝒫 is false, as uttered by Peter under these circumstances. And this is exactly the verdict delivered by the hidden-indexical theory.[28] Yet (as Kripke forcefully demonstrates), on reflection there is a solid intuitive basis for the contrary judgment that 𝒫 is literally true in English, with respect to Peter's context, even though Peter's basis for it is seriously flawed. For Pierre does indeed assent to the proposition that London is pretty when it is presented to him by means of the French sentence '*Londres est jolie*'; he thus believes the proposition in at least one way ('relative to' some way or other). One might rightfully say that Peter spoke incorrectly; perhaps one may even say that Peter said something false about Pierre. But none of this overturns the thesis that the sentence Peter used is literally true.[29] The situation here is exactly analogous to the debate concerning whether 'I met a man this afternoon' is true in English even if the man the speaker has in mind was in fact met that morning—the speaker's watch was mistakenly set an hour ahead—when the speaker also met some man or other that afternoon, even though the speaker has forgotten all about it. A sentence that is true by sheer accident or dumb luck is no less true than one whose iron-clad support is still fresh in one's mind.

If there is a genuine clash of reflective intuitions here, then it is no defect in the hidden-indexical theory (or indeed in any other theory) that it fails to accommodate all of the relevant intuitions. However, a much more serious problem arises from the fact that the hidden-indexical theory makes the additional, distinctly counterintuitive claim that 𝒫 is literally true with respect to some contexts, while also being not merely misleading or otherwise infelicitous but literally false with respect to others (like the one described above)—this even though Pierre's relevant opinions remain unshakably firm.[30]

Perhaps the most compelling intuitive evidence against the hidden-indexical theory is provided by valid inferences that the theory declares invalid. Crimmins and Perry discuss a special version of Leibniz's Law:

α believes θ

$\alpha = \beta$

Therefore, β believes θ.

---

[28] *Cf.* Crimmins, *op. cit.*, pp. 160, 176, 198–199.

[29] In my view, the hidden-indexical theory here declares a true attribution not true. The theory also declares some intuitively false attributions not false. See Crimmins, p. 184. (The view expressed there differs significantly from Crimmins and Perry, pp. 702–704.)

[30] Crimmins and Perry, pp. 687, 706–707. Crimmins, p. 163; see also p. 199. Crimmins ascribes to Kripke the view that 𝒫 is literally true with respect to some contexts and literally false with respect to others (p. 141), claiming that this verdict is recommended by intuition (pp. 28, 145). I believe this is a serious misrepresentation of Kripke's view. (See note 7 above.) I would also emphasize that one's having an intuition that 𝒫 is true with respect to a particular context c and also a second intuition that 𝒫 is false with respect to a different context c' does not preclude one from having a third intuition, which may be stronger than either of the first two, that 𝒫 cannot be simultaneously true with respect to one context and false with respect to another context unless Pierre changes his mind between the two. Indeed, there is an obvious sense in which Kripke's puzzle turns on just such intuitions as these, especially the third.

Crimmins and Perry argue that this inference is logically invalid, in the sense that there are instances for which there is a single context with respect to which the premisses are true and the conclusion false.[31]

The claim that this inference is invalid on the hidden-indexical theory is, at best, misleading. The issue is complicated. Inspection of the case discussed by Crimmins and Perry reveals that, on their view of the matter, the substitution performed on the first premiss necessarily alters the context, thereby shifting the reference of the hidden indexical between the relevant (minor) premiss and the conclusion, providing a different 'unarticulated constituent'. If this were indeed the case, we would not have a situation in which truth fails to be preserved when the premisses and conclusion are all evaluated with respect to a single context. Rather, what Crimmins and Perry seem to be claiming is that truth fails to be preserved when the premisses are evaluated with respect to a single context and the conclusion is evaluated with respect to a different context, one just like the context of the premisses except for the presence of different words being uttered. It is precisely this shift in context that is supposed to explain the difference in 'unarticulated constituents' between premiss and conclusion.[32] Compare: Giorgione was called by *that name* because of his size. Giorgione = Barbarelli. Therefore Barbarelli was called by *that name* because of his size.

Where indexicals are involved, the classical notion of logical validity must be adjusted to take account of context. But truth preservation under shifting contexts does not constitute the proper notion of validity. Rather, what is at issue is truth

---

[31] Crimmins and Perry, pp. 708–709, 710; Crimmins, pp. 30–32. The particular example they discuss is from Mark Richard's phone-booth example, in 'Direct Reference and Ascriptions of Belief', in *Propositions and Attitudes*, pp. 169–196:

The man watching you believes that you are in danger. I am the man watching you.

Therefore, I believe that you are in danger.

Richard assumed, correctly, that the inference is valid. (Nevertheless, I believe Richard may be re-evaluating his position on this issue.)

[32] This is explicitly acknowledged by Crimmins and Perry, at p. 709. This acknowledgement, however, is in tension with remarks on p. 710 (and with Crimmins, pp. 30–32). The text, and especially the accompanying note (p. 710*n*), suggest that Crimmins and Perry may be using the word 'context' in such a way that a single context may be said to undergo changes in its semantically relevant features. The changes that a context (in this sense) undergoes depend not on the passage of time (each context has a particular time built into it), but, mysteriously enough, on which expression is being evaluated with respect to that context. Crimmins and Perry also seem to argue that a more useful notion of context for the purposes of semantics would be such that a context is unchangeable but includes the expression under evaluation (or a possible utterance of that expression) among its semantically relevant features. Schiffer makes some related unconventional remarks concerning the semantic nature of contexts, in 'Belief Ascription', p. 505*n*6. All of these unorthodox remarks represent a concession to the speech-act centered conception of semantics. In my judgment, they constitute further evidence of the extent to which that conception is a misconception. (See note 27 above.) A proper conception of semantics must allow for the evaluation of any expression with respect to any context. It must therefore allow for the evaluation of different expressions with respect to the same context, and also for the evaluation of expressions with respect to contexts in which those very expressions are not uttered, and in which perhaps completely different expressions are uttered. (There must be contexts, for example, with respect to which the sentence 'I am speaking' is false; otherwise the sentence becomes logically valid.)

preservation under fixed contextual parameters (in every model).[33] This notice accommodates the classically valid inference form '$\varphi \therefore \varphi$'. It also validates the above inference involving Barbarelli. Furthermore it declares logically inconsistent the illusionist's trademark slogan 'Now you see it; now you don't'. To accommodate the slogan and lose the inference involving Barbarelli, one may define a complementary notion for the assessment of arguments, one that looks at such phenomena as the shifting of contexts that occurs, or may occur, in the actual utterance of an argument. One might then reject even repetition inference of the form '$\varphi \therefore \varphi$'—for example, replacing 'I am seeing a flash now; therefore I am seeing a flash now' with 'I am seeing a flash now; therefore, I *was* seeing a flash *then*.' (Notice that the latter is semantically invalid.) Let us call this speech-act centered notion *pragmatic cogency*, to distinguish it from semantic validity.[34] It is not the proper notion of logical validity, but it is not a useless notion. With it one can see a genuine aberration in the hidden-indexical theory: Whereas, *pace* Crimmins and Perry, the theory in fact accommodates the semantic validity of Leibniz's Law when applied to belief attributions, it fails to accommodate its pragmatic cogency. The willingness of the theory's adherents to embrace this consequence, or their possible willingness to do so, does not alter the fact that the consequence is decidedly counterintuitive.[35]

Perhaps the most compelling evidence that belief attributions do not semantically specify (or constrain) any way of taking a proposition in addition to the proposition itself is provided by the validity of inference (*I*) displayed above. Ironically, in the proper sense of 'valid', the hidden-indexical theory fails to accommodate inferences of the very sort that Schiffer cites in defense of that theory. According to the theory, the conclusion of inference (*I*), $\mathcal{P}$, will (typically) specify, with respect to any given context *c*, the same way of taking the proposition that London is pretty that is specified with respect to *c* in the minor premiss 'Jean-Paul says that London is pretty'. Indeed, if either the double-dipper theory or the hidden-indexical theory were correct, the

---

[33] I am indebted here to the penetrating work of David Kaplan. See his 'Demonstratives' and its 'Afterthoughts', in J. Almog, J. Perry, and H. Wettstein, eds, *Themes from Kaplan* (Oxford University Press, 1989), pp. 481–563, 565–614. In this connection see especially pp. 522, 546, 584–585. See also notes 27 and 32 above.

[34] Notice that the sentence 'I am speaking', though not logically valid, may well be deemed pragmatically cogent, since there can be no context in which it is uttered falsely. See note 32 above.

[35] Perhaps the hidden-indexical theorists discard such intuitions as irrelevant. But Crimmins dismisses the sort of account I advocate, saying that 'the obvious criticism of this view is that it seems clearly to fail as a truth-conditional analysis of belief reporting: it makes predictions about substitutivity and so on that simply do not correspond to our intuitions about the truth values of reports' (p. 205). This same criticism may be made of his own version of the hidden-indexical theory, and with at least as much force.

In addition to the counterintuitive consequences already noted, and a further one to be noted below in the text, Crimmins, like Schiffer, endorses latitudinarianism with respect to exportation—the inference from the *de dicto* reading of a belief attribution to the *de re*—even while acknowledging (p. 86) that latitudinarianism is clearly counterintuitive. And indeed, latitudinarianism plays a crucial role in Crimmin's richly developed version of the hidden-indexical theory. For Schiffer's endorsement of a version of latitudinarianism, see his 'The Basis of Reference', *Erkenntnis*, 13 (1978), pp. 171–206. (The paper, however, involves a curious inconsistency on that point. *Cf.* my 'How to Measure the Standard Meter', *Proceedings of the Aristotelian Society*, 88 (1987/1988), pp. 193–217, at p. 199*n*.)

conclusion of (*I*) would contain more information than one would be warranted in inferring on the basis of the premisses. Far from supporting the hidden-indexical theory as Schiffer argues, the evident validity of such inferences thus intuitively refutes both the double-dipper theory and the hidden-indexical theory.

14

Relational Belief (1995)

I

When faced with a philosophically problematic locution, Quine has proposed replacing the offending construction with one better suited to his philosophical temperament and point of view. At first sight this replacement strategy seems a profitable move. But on closer scrutiny the strategy can be somewhat puzzling. If the replacement means the same thing as the original construction, then surely nothing is to be gained in the substitution of the one by the other. But even if the replacement construction does not mean the same thing as the original, what is to be gained in the substitution—other than obfuscation? The problematic locution has merely been replaced with something less problematic; it has not been obliterated. It still exists; it just does not occur where it used to. Philosophical problems are not solved by diverting attention from them.

Part of the answer sometimes lies in the fact that the original locution is not only replaced, but also repudiated. It is deemed ill-formed nonsense. The replacement is made to fill the void left by the expulsion of the meaningless.

Such is the case with part of Quine's proposed solution to his famous puzzle concerning Bernard J. Ortcutt from his classic article 'Quantifiers and Propositional Attitudes' (Quine, 1956). Quine imagines a character, Ralph, who believes someone is a spy. Ralph believes this in both of two very different senses. Like all of us, Ralph believes that someone or other is a spy, i.e., that there are spies. This is the notional sense of believing someone is a spy. But more than this, Ralph believes someone in particular to be a spy. This is the relational sense of believing someone is a spy. Ralph believes that a certain man he saw under suspicious circumstances, wearing a brown hat, is a spy. Ralph also happens to believe that a certain pillar of the community named 'Bernard J. Ortcutt', whom he remembers having seen once at the beach, is not a spy. What Ralph does not realize is that the man at the beach and the man in the brown hat are one and the same. Consider this man Bernard Ortcutt. Does Ralph believe that he is a spy? One may be inclined to say that Ralph does, since he believes

---

This chapter was written just prior to the birth of my daughter, Simone Salmon, to whom it is dedicated. It was written for the University of San Marino International Center for Semiotic and Cognitive Studies conference on W. V. Quine's Contribution to Philosophy, May 1990. Portions were delivered there and to the Tel Aviv University/Van Leer Jerusalem Institute conference on the New Theory of Meaning, also in May 1990. I am grateful to Alonzo Church, Earl Conee, Graeme Forbes, and Timothy Williamson for their comments on an earlier draft.

that the man in the brown hat is a spy, and that man is Ortcutt. But Ralph does not believe that the man at the beach is a spy, and that man is also Ortcutt.

The problem concerns the sentence

0*a* Ralph believes of Ortcutt that he is a spy.

To bring the problem into its sharpest focus, consider the following quasiformal sentence, which seems to assert the same thing as 0*a*:

(λx) [Ralph believes that x is a spy] (Ortcutt).

By the conventional semantic rules governing Alonzo Church's 'λ'-abstraction operator, this sentence is true if and only if the open sentence

1 Ralph believes that x is a spy

is itself true under the assignment of Ortcutt as value for the variable 'x'. Is 1 true under this assignment or is it false? To pose the same question in the terminology of Tarski, does Ortcutt satisfy 1? There does not seem to be a satisfactory answer. When the variable is replaced by the phrase 'the man seen wearing the brown hat', the resulting sentence is true. When the variable is replaced by the phrase 'the man seen at the beach', however, the resulting sentence is false. Whether Ralph believes Ortcutt to be a spy or not depends crucially on how Ralph is conceiving of Ortcutt. It seems impossible to evaluate 1 under the assignment of Ortcutt himself, as opposed to various ways of specifying him, to the variable. Quantification (or any other sort of variable binding) into a nonextensional context like 'Ralph believes that ...' is thus senseless. These considerations seem to bar us from saying anything along the lines of

2 Ralph believes that he is a spy

with reference to Ortcutt (so that the pronoun 'he' in 2 plays the same role as the variable 'x' in 1)—as, for example, in the context 'As regards Ortcutt, ...'. And this bars us from 0*a*. How, then, shall we express the obvious fact that Ralph believes someone is a spy in the relational sense?

It is important to notice that this problem, unlike Kripke's famous puzzle about belief (Kripke, 1979), primarily concerns the object that the belief is about, i.e., Ortcutt. Ralph and his notional beliefs (as represented by the sentences he accepts), considered in abstraction from Ralph's fellows, present no special difficulties. He is simply in a state of partial ignorance. He does not realize that the suspicious looking man wearing the brown hat is the man at the beach; he erroneously believes that the man in the brown hat is someone other than Ortcutt. The crucial philosophical question is whether Ortcutt, independently of any particular specification of him, satisfies a certain relational condition: Is he believed by Ralph to be a spy? The grounds for an affirmative answer—that Ralph does indeed believe that the man in the brown hat is a spy—seem perfectly counterbalanced by equally good (or equally bad) grounds for the opposite answer. One is invited to conclude that the question of whether Ortcutt himself, in abstraction from any particular conception of him, is believed by Ralph to be a spy makes no sense—or at least that it has no sensible answer.[1]

The puzzle can be made out especially forcefully from the perspective of a Fregean philosophy of semantics. As Frege would have noted, although the expressions 'the man seen wearing the brown hat' and 'the man seen at the beach' both refer to Ortcutt, they differ in sense. They present Ortcutt by means of different individual concepts. In any belief attribution, such as

3a Ralph believes that the man in the brown hat is a spy

every expression following the phrase 'believes that' occurs in an indirect or oblique context, and refers in that position not to the expression's customary referent but to its customary sense. In this theoretical framework, quantification into an oblique context poses a special difficulty. The 'x' in 1, taken under the assignment of Ortcutt as value, is supposed to refer in that position to its customary sense. But 'x', under the assignment of a particular value, has no sense. (Alternatively, it ambiguously expresses infinitely many different senses, viz., every sense that determines its value as referent.) It would seem that 1, under the assignment of Ortcutt to 'x', must therefore also lack sense. Once again, we seem driven to the conclusion that the question of whether Ortcutt himself satisfies 1 has no sensible answer—or at best, that Ortcutt satisfies neither 1 nor its negation, so that no one can ever believe of anyone that he or she is either spy or nonspy. How, then, do we express the fact that Ralph believes someone is a spy in the relational sense?

Quine proposed as a way out of this puzzle that, corresponding to the distinction between two senses of believing someone is a spy, we recognize a lexical ambiguity in 'believes' (and 'wishes', 'hopes', 'fears', etc.). There is the ordinary notion of belief expressed in a sentence like 3a. We may call this *n-belief* (for notional belief), so that 3a may be rewritten as:

3b Ralph *n*-believes that the man in the brown hat is a spy.

Quine urged that we also recognize an alternative kind of belief, which we might call *r-belief* (for relational belief). Grammatically, whereas one n-believes (or fails to n-believe) that such-and-such, one *r*-believes someone (or something) to be thus-and-so.[2] Ralph does not *n*-believe that Ortcutt is a spy, but he does *n*-believe that the man in the brown hat is a spy, and he thereby *r*-believes Ortcutt to be a spy. The sentence

---

[1] Quine himself may not have been clear on this matter. In presenting the puzzle, he objects to the (correct!) claim that Ortcutt is indeed believed by Ralph to be a spy, on the questionable grounds that 'if so, we find ourselves accepting a conjunction of the type "w sincerely denies '...' & w believes that ..." as true, with one and the same sentence ['Ortcutt is a spy'] in both blanks' (1956: 185). In the first place, this involves the controversial assumption that if Ralph believes Ortcutt to be a spy, in virtue of believing that the man in the brown hat is a spy, then Ralph also believes that Ortcutt is a spy. (Who, besides one or two diehard Millians, would accept this assumption? Quine? If so, why does he not simply endorse Russell's solution to the problem?) In the second place, Quine's focus emphasizes the wrong set of issues, as if the main problem were to make Ralph come out consistent. The primary issues in Quine's puzzle are not those in the philosophy of psychology raised by Ralph's predicament; they are those in the philosophy of logic raised by Ortcutt's.

[2] Quine's preferred phrasing was somewhat more awkward. In place of 0b he wrote 'Ralph believes $z(z$ is a spy) of Ortcutt', which is perhaps best glossed as: Ralph ascribes being a spy to

0*b* Ralph *r*-believes Ortcutt to be a spy

does not present the same difficulties as 0*a*, since 0*b* remains true whether the name 'Ortcutt' is replaced by either 'the man at the beach' or 'the man in the brown hat'—or by any expression that refers to Ortcutt. By contrast, the true sentence 3*b* is transformed into a falsehood when 'the man at the beach' is substituted for 'the man in the brown hat'. Consequently, replacement of the latter by a variable in the style of 1 is to be disallowed as ill-formed nonsense. Presumably, the same would hold for 2, and hence for 0*a*.

Quine did not rest content, however, with the distinction between n-belief and r-belief. For sentence 3*b* entails the existence not only of Ralph but of an additional entity, that the man in the brown hat is a spy, and 0*b* likewise entails the existence of being a spy. The former entity is a proposition, the latter a property. Quine devoutly disbelieves in such 'intensions' (for reasons that are largely independent of the issues concerning relational belief). Quine proposed replacing 3*b* with

3*c* Ralph believes-true 'The man in the brown hat is a spy'

and likewise replacing 0*b*—which was itself a replacement for 0*a*—with

0*c* Ralph believes-true 'is a spy' of Ortcutt.[3]

Whereas the former constructions employing '*n*-believes' and '*r*-believes' involve a commitment to the existence of intensions, these new, wholly artificial constructions involve a commitment merely to the existence of sentences and predicates. This is a meager commitment that Quine is prepared to accept (however reluctantly). Thus, these replacements portend ontological dividends. They portend conceptual dividends as well. For the substitutes apparently replace unclear notions like that of belief of a proposition with far less dubious notions like that of truth (which might even be mathematically definable in the style of Tarski).

Quine's solution thus consists in a chain of replacements. An 'unregimented' belief attribution

I*a* β believes that φ

where φ is a closed sentence, may be perspicuously formalized as

I*b* B_n(β, that φ)

Ortcutt. (Both occurrences of '*z*' in '*z*(*z* is a spy)' are bound by a nonextensional variable-binding operator. Whereas Quine objects to occurrences of variables in 'nonreferential position', and the second occurrence of '*z*' here is evidently not in referential position, Quine's objection, properly understood, is actually to bindable free variable occurrences in nonreferential position.)

[3] The particular formulation of 0*c* is extrapolated from a combination of Quine, 1956, and Quine, 1979. In the former work, the moves from attributes to expressions is accompanied by a switch from an abstracted attribute name (see the previous note) to an open sentence, whereby 0*a* is replaced with 'Ralph believes "y is a spy" satisfied by Ortcutt' (which is perhaps best glossed as: Ralph believes-true '*y* is a spy' under the assignment: '*y*' → Ortcutt). The rationale for the switch from an abstract to an open sentence is unclear, and in any event in the later work the open sentence has been dropped in favor of a predicate.

where 'B_n' is a dyadic predicate for notional belief and 'that' is a nonextensional operator that forms a term for the proposition expressed by the attached sentence. This construction is replaced directly with

Ic Believes-true(β, 'ϕ')

in which the sentence that forms the 'that' clause of *Ia* is taken out of the scope of 'that' and placed within quotation marks instead. By contrast, an unregimented sentence of the form

IIa β believes of α that ϕ_{it}

where the pronoun 'it' ('he', 'she') occurs anaphorically in ϕ_{it}, undergoes a two-stage modification. In the first stage it is replaced with

β *r*-believes α to be such that ϕ_{it}

This may be formalized as:

IIb $B_r(\beta, \alpha, (\mu\gamma)[\phi_\gamma])$

where ϕ_γ is the same expression as ϕ_{it} except for containing free occurrences of a variable γ where ϕ_{it} contains 'free' occurrences of the pronoun 'it'. Here 'B_r' is a triadic predicate for relational belief, and the 'μ' in its third argument is a nonextensional variable-binding operator that allows for the abstraction of an attribute name from an open sentence. (See note 2 regarding Quine's alternative notation.) This formalization makes it obvious why the relevant notion is called 'relational'; α occurs all alone in a 'purely referential' argument position, where it is open to substitution and to quantification from without.[4] In the second stage, *IIb* is replaced further by

IIc Believes-true-of $(\beta, '(\lambda\gamma)[\phi_\gamma]', \alpha)$.

In the more recent discussion of 'Intensions Revisited' (Quine, 1981: 115, 119), the move between *IIa* and its final replacement is described as a 'translation', one by means of which relational belief is explained in terms of 'believes-true'.

II

Owing largely to Quine's impressive rhetorical gift and persuasive skill, a great many philosophers of language today—perhaps most—are under the impression that quantification into a nonextensional context is dubious business, and that such innocent looking constructions as *0a* are, from the point of view of philosophical logic, deeply problematic. This is ironic.

A few critics (Kaplan, 1986: 264–266; Kazmi, 1987: 95–98; Forbes, 1985: 52) have objected to Quine's argument by noting that an analogous situation arises out of certain temporal constructions, where the corresponding claim analogous to Quine's

---

[4] The relation asserted to hold between Ralph and Ortcutt may be defined as: $(\lambda xy) [B_r(x, y, (\mu z) [z$ is a spy$])]$.

in connection with 1 would be completely unwarranted. For example, the open sentence

S In 1978, *x* was a Republican

is true when the variable is replaced by the name 'George Bush' but false when the variable is replaced by the phrase 'the United States President', despite the fact that these two expressions refer to the same individual. (That is, they refer to the same individual with respect to the present time.) It hardly follows that *S* cannot be evaluated under the assignment of Bush as value for '*x*'—let alone that we are forced to acknowledge a distinction between a notional and a relational concept of being the case in 1978 (whatever that would mean). The open sentence *S*, as it stands, is straightforwardly true under the assignment of Bush to '*x*', since he (independent of any particular specification of him) was indeed a Republican in 1978. Quine's argument in connection with 1 is fallacious.

One may respond by rejecting the treatment of the phrase 'in 1978' as a sentential operator attachable to open sentences, insisting instead that *S* ultimately involves a dyadic predicate 'is a Republican at', which expresses a binary relation between individuals and times. (Very well. Suppose we invent an artificial, temporally neutral monadic predicate 'Republicanize' for the property of being a Republican—which applies with respect to any time *t* to exactly those individuals who are Republicans at *t*—and a sentential temporal operator 'During 1978' + past tense. What of that?) Fortunately, there is an alternative way of showing that Quine's argument against the logical intelligibility of 1 is fallacious, one that does not depend on any allegedly nonextensional context other than 'Ralph believes that . . .'.

A half century before Quine's influential discussion, Russell was able to draw a very general distinction, of which Quine's distinction between the notional and relational sense of believing (or wishing, etc.) some *F* is *G* is merely a special case.[5] Russell's distinction between primary occurrence and secondary occurrence applies to constructions involving any 'denoting phrase', i.e., any definite or indefinite description, in place of Quine's 'some *F*'—for example, 'Ralph believes every foreigner he meets is a spy', 'Ralph believes no friend of his is a spy', 'Ralph believes the union president is a spy', 'Ralph believes most Russians are spies', and so on. In fact, Russell's more general distinction is not merely twofold, but $(n + 1)$-fold where *n* is the number of operator occurrences in which the description ('denoting phrase') is embedded. For example, in addition to predicting its straightforwardly relational reading, Russell distinguished two notional readings for the complex attribution

Quine said that Ralph believes someone is a spy

Whereas the small-scope reading correctly reports the content of Quine's assertion when he attributes to Ralph a notional belief that someone is a spy (e.g., were Quine to utter the sentence 'Ralph believes that there are spies'), the intermediate-scope reading correctly reports the content of Quine's assertion when he instead attributes relational belief ('There is someone whom Ralph believes to be a spy').

[5] 'On Denoting', in Russell (1956: 39–56).

More significantly, Russell was able to explain his more general distinction as itself a special case of an even more general phenomenon: scope ambiguity On the theory of 'On Denoting', it is not in the least problematic that 1 is true when '*x*' is replaced by 'the man in the brown hat' and false when '*x*' is replaced by 'the man at the beach'. The resulting 'that' clauses 'denote', i.e. refer to, different propositions, one of which Ralph believes and the other one of which he does not. By contrast, the original 'that' clause

that *x* is a spy

refers, under the assignment of Ortcutt to '*x*', to yet a third proposition, one in which Ortcutt himself 'occurs as a constituent'. This is the singular proposition about Ortcutt that he is a spy. Logically, the question of whether Ralph believes this singular proposition is quite independent of whether he believes either, both, or neither of the other two.

Quine's philosophical bias precluded him from endorsing Russell's elegant account of the notional/relational distinction. The evidence suggests that, even while entertaining the theory of propositions as objects of belief, Quine dismissed out of hand the Russellian idea of a singular proposition as an object of belief.[6] Where Russell saw syntactic ambiguity Quine posited semantic ambiguity. One may quarrel over the

---

[6] Kaplan (1986) is a thorough and penetrating critique of Quine's argument against the logical coherence of quantification into nonextensional contexts. Quine is probably correct, however, to protest (in Quine, 1986) against Kaplan's reconstruction (233–235) of his central argument as one involving a fallacy. (Kaplan admits that his reconstruction is speculative; *cf.* 277 n15; *cf.* also Kazmi [1987: 90–93].) Quine's main argument is for the conclusion that no singular-term position in an opaque context in an (open or closed) sentence can be occupied by a bindable free occurrence of an objectual variable. (See note 2.) I believe that the failure of the argument (or at least of later versions of it) should be traced to a largely implicit premiss (which was probably at least vaguely intended even in the earliest versions of the argument). This is the Fregean thesis that the referent of (i.e., the contribution made to the truth value of the containing sentence by) a singular-term occurrence that is not itself in purely referential position (i.e., that is in the scope of a nonextensional operator) is not, and does not involve, the term's customary referent. (An exception may be made in the rare case of a self-referential term whose customary referent is not a nonlinguistic object like Ortcutt but is rather the term's own meaning, or the term itself, etc.—like 'the meaning of the description quoted in note 6 of "Relational Belief" '.) This generalization, and Quine's conclusion, seem plausible when one considers the case of a term occurring within quotation marks. (Is an otherwise unbound variable occurrence within quotation marks free?) It breaks down in other sorts of cases. The treatment of 1 in Russell's semantic theory directly conflicts with Quine's Fregean thesis.

Kaplan (1986: 235, 244) replaces Quine's thesis that only free variable occurrences that are in purely referential position are bindable with the slightly different thesis (the denial of which he describes as incoherent) that only free variable occurrences that are themselves purely referential (i.e., that 'solely refer' to the variable's value, thereby preserving substitution of co-valued variables) are bindable. This thesis also breaks down in certain cases, however, even if only artificial ones. Ironically, Kaplan's notion of associative valuation, introduced on page 244, provides one such counterexample. (*Cf.* Richard [1987].) What, then, does account for the unbindability of otherwise unbound variable occurrences within quotation marks? Something significantly weaker than either Quine's or Kaplan's theses may be true: that only free objectual variable occurrences whose referent (contribution to truth value) involves the variable's value in a special manner are bindable. (An occurrence of '*x*' within quotation marks, even under the assignment of '*x*' itself as value, does not refer to '*x*' in the appropriate manner.)

relative merits of a theory that posits lexical ambiguity over one that posits singular propositional belief. Still, there is nothing in the logic (as opposed to the psychology) of the situation that precludes the theory of singular propositions. One may reject singular-proposition theory as false, as implausible, even as outrageously so. My own view is that one would be dead wrong in doing so, but there is room for debate. One may not similarly reject singular-proposition theory as logically incoherent. Indeed, Russell's theory is virtually inevitable. Wherever there is quantification into a propositional-attitude context, the idea of a singular proposition cannot be very far behind.[7] The mere coherence of Russell's 1905 theory was already sufficient to demonstrate that any argument for the thesis that quantification into the context 'Ralph believes that . . .' is logically or semantically incoherent is itself mistaken.[8] Given Russell's theory, it is puzzling that Quine and his many followers could have thought that quantification into this context creates any logical difficulty.

Although Quine's critics are correct to point out that his (apparent) argument against the legitimacy of quantification into notional belief contexts is fallacious, pointing this out does not constitute a demonstration that Quine's solution to his puzzle is not a viable alternative to Russell's. It can be shown, however, that insofar as one is prepared to accept Russellian singular propositions, Quine's proposal to translate sentences of form *IIa* into sentences of form *IIb* does not work. In fact, whether or not singular propositions are countenanced, Quine's proposal fails.

III

One immediate difficulty for Quine's account is that, as it stands, it does not accommodate such evidently valid inferences as the following:

> Everything Ralph believes is true (doubted by Quine, plausible, etc.).
>
> Ralph believes Ortcutt to be a spy.
>
> Therefore, Ortcutt is truly (doubted by Quine to be, etc.) a spy.

The problem is that, on Quine's account, the major premiss involves the notion of notional belief and the minor premiss instead involves the distinct notion of relational belief. One might hope to accommodate this inference within Quine's framework by adopting an analysis of the relational in terms of the notional, perhaps along the lines of David Kaplan's earlier commentary in 'Quantifying In'. Recent results in the theory of meaning and reference, however, leave little promise for the success of this type of an analysis, and Kaplan himself has abandoned the project. (The matter remains highly controversial.) In any event, Kaplan's original scheme does not validate all inferences of this type, and it is none too clear how to give an analysis within the spirit of Quine's philosophical views that does. (Indeed, Quine would probably reject such inferences, or at least many of them.)

---

[7] *Cf.* Salmon (1986a: 2–5) and Salmon (1989a: 212–215).
[8] *Cf.* Kaplan (1986: especially 239–241).

Another serious flaw in Quine's proposal was uncovered by Kaplan in 'Opacity' (268–272). Following Quine, Kaplan proposes a distinction among propositional attributions (whether attributions of propositional attitude, of modality, or whatever), between what Kaplan calls the *syntactically de dicto* and the *syntactically de re*. The syntactically *de dicto* is illustrated by such attributions as 1, 2, and 3a—each of which involves the 'believes that' construction. Syntactically *de dicto* belief attributions would be formalized along the lines of *Ib*, where φ may be either open or closed. The syntactically *de re* is illustrated by 0b, which involves the 'believes ... to be' construction. Syntactically *de re* belief attributions would be formalized along the lines of *IIb*. Kaplan sees Quine as proposing a method for translating an (apparently) *de re* (relational) belief attribution that is syntactically *de dicto* (such as 0a) into a pure *de re* form, i.e., something that is both semantically and syntactically *de re*. Kaplan pointed out, however, that Quine's method of translation is insensitive to subtle distinctions in content involving the phenomenon that I call 'reflexivity'.[9] The problem arises in the case of sentences of the form *IIa* where there are multiple (two or more) free occurrences of the pronoun 'it' in φ_{it}. Thus suppose Ralph is under the illusion that the man in the brown hat is taller than the man at the beach. It would seem then that the following sentence is true:

Ralph believes of Ortcutt that he is taller than he.

Quine's procedure translates this sentence into

B_r(Ralph, Ortcutt, $(\mu x)[x$ is taller than $x]$)

which may be read: Ralph *r*-believes Ortcutt to be a thing that is taller than itself. Unless Ralph is insane this is false. Kaplan improved upon Quine's scheme by employing a procedure that Kaplan calls 'articulation'. Kaplan translates the problem sentence instead into something along the lines of:

B_r(Ralph, <Ortcutt, Ortcutt>, $(\mu xy) [x$ is taller than $y]$).

This may be read: Ralph *r*-believes Ortcutt and himself to be so related that the former is taller than the latter.[10]

Unlike Quine, Kaplan sees no logical difficulty with 0a as it stands. Nevertheless, in 'Opacity' he apparently accepts Quine's contention that all such mixed (syntactically *de dicto* semantically *de re*) belief attributions can be paraphrased into the pure *de re* form using the syntactically *de re* 'believes ... to be' construction—as long as articulation is employed wherever possible. On this view, Quine's proposal to replace 0a with 0b (when stripped of the proposal's philosophical underpinnings) is neither superior nor inferior to Russell's account of quantifying in. In the long run, Quine's translation, modified to incorporate articulation, is simply a rephrasing of Russell's account.

---

[9] These differences in content are of a sort highlighted in Salmon (1986b): e.g., the difference in content between 'Ortcutt loves Ortcutt' and 'Ortcutt is a person who loves himself'.
[10] Kaplan's procedure of articulation is introduced independently in Church (1989).

More recently, in 'Afterthoughts' (605–606), Kaplan suggests instead that the pure *de re* construction is significantly stronger than the mixed (syntactically *de dicto* semantically *de re*). On his more recent view, the mixed 0*a* does not say that Ralph believes Ortcutt to be a spy (although this may well be what we generally mean when we utter 0*a*). The difference, according to Kaplan, is that if Ralph were to introduce a new name by means of some definite description that, unknown to Ralph, happens to refer to Ortcutt (say 'the world's shortest spy'), then Ralph could believe of Ortcutt that he is a spy even if Ralph has had no epistemic contact with Ortcutt and, to use Russell's phrase, knows him only by description.[11] By contrast, according to Kaplan, in order for Ralph to believe Ortcutt to be a spy, Ralph must be, in a certain epistemological and perhaps interest-relative sense, *en rapport* with Ortcutt.[12] On this view, Quine's proposal (even when modified to incorporate articulation) fails, since 0*b* is significantly stronger than 0*a*.

This view does not reject all translation between the mixed form and the pure *de re*. It is just that the translation will have to be complicated. Presumably, the epistemologically stronger *IIb* would analyze into something like the following:

β is *en rapport* with α and β believes of α that ϕ_{it}, grasping the proposition about α that ϕ_{it} in such-and-such a manner by means of β's acquaintance with α,

where 'it' has only one free occurrence in ϕ_{it}. (If the pronoun has multiple occurrences, *IIb* must be replaced by an articulated expansion.) In this way, the pure *de re* form is equivalent to a complex mixed form that entails the simple mixed form.

The problem is to specify that special 'manner' in which the belief is held. Kaplan says that this particular problem with translating between the mixed form and the pure

> involves understanding the conditions under which we correctly ascribe to [Sherlock] Holmes, for example, the *de re* attitude that there is someone whom he believes to have committed the murder [as opposed to asserting merely that there is someone such that Holmes believes *that* he committed the murder]. It seems clear that the mere fact that the murderer has given himself a *nom de crime* and leaves a message using this name should not suffice. (In fact, I suspect that there are no fixed conditions, only conditions relative to the topic, interests, aims, and presuppositions of a particular discourse.) (605–606n)

Here Kaplan is surely mistaken. Quite the contrary, it seems clear that the mere fact that Holmes has drawn inferences from clues gathered at the scene of the crime suffices in order for Holmes to form relational beliefs concerning the murderer—even without a *nom de crime* to facilitate Holmes's expression of those beliefs. ('Elementary, Watson. On the basis of my preliminary investigation, I believe our quarry to be

---

[11] Do not confuse this with the very different claim (which I accept) that introducing a name by means of a description in this manner is sufficient to enable Ralph to say of Ortcutt that he is a spy. Kaplan's claim concerns believing the singular proposition thereby asserted. He makes the same latitudinarian claim concerning Ralph's merely apprehending the singular proposition.

[12] The text of 'Afterthoughts' is somewhat obscure on this point. Kaplan has confirmed in conversation that this is his current view. In some respects Kaplan's notion of being *en rapport*, though not nearly so restrictive, is a descendant of Russell's notion of acquaintance. *Cf.* Kaplan (1969).

an elderly bachelor who is fond of pasta and owns a sheep dog.') Kaplan has evidently confused two potential states of Holmes: (*i*) *r*-believing someone to be the murderer; and (*ii*) having an opinion as to who the murderer is. The second notion is far more plausibly regarded as interest-relative. Whereas obtaining the murderer's *nom de crime* does not suffice (in most ordinary contexts) to place Holmes in the second state, it is overkill for the first. Of course, in the special case of Holmes, the first state is invariably followed by the second, but this is a matter of Holmes's powers of deduction, not of ours.[13]

Whether Kaplan has confused (i) and (ii) or not, I have to confess to not knowing exactly what he means by a sentence like 0*a*. As I use 0*a*, it is straightforwardly equivalent to 'Ralph believes Ortcutt to be a spy'. Each requires that Ralph have some (albeit perhaps minimal) epistemic connection to Ortcutt—and neither requires that Ralph know, or even have any opinion about, who Ortcutt is (in any nonvacuous sense).[14] Perhaps Kaplan means instead that there is some sentence *S* satisfying the conditions that: *S*'s content is the singular proposition about Ortcutt that he is a spy; Ralph knows what *S*'s content is, though perhaps only by description; and Ralph believes *S* to be true. To be sure, this does not require Ralph to be epistemically connected to Ortcutt in any manner beyond knowledge by description, but it also has nothing to do with relational belief concerning Ortcutt. It involves only relational belief concerning *S*.[15]

Beware of wanting too much to have one's cake and eat it too. Kaplan offers little or no evidence on behalf of the nonequivalence of 0*a* and 0*b*. In my view, the contrary claim that the latter is indeed equivalent to, and even definable by means of, the former is so intuitive, and so theoretically smooth, that a great deal of evidence indeed should be required to warrant its rejection. The definition I have in mind is captured neither by Quine's schema nor by Kaplan's. It is the following:

$$B_r(\beta, \alpha, (\mu\gamma)[\phi_\gamma]) =_{\text{def.}} (\lambda\delta)[B_n(\beta, \text{that } (\lambda\gamma)[\phi_\gamma](\delta))](\alpha).$$

Notice that this definition does not provide for a translation of an arbitrary mixed belief attribution into one that is pure *de re*. In some sense, what it provides is precisely the opposite.[16]

In any event, there are examples that simultaneously refute Quine's original proposed translation, Kaplan's improved method invoking articulation, and Kaplan's more recent view that 0*b* is stronger than 0*a* in the manner suggested. One such example is obtained by a natural extension of Quine's story concerning Ralph and Ortcutt. Perhaps the most straightforward version of the argument assumes the theory of Russellian singular propositions—a theory that Kaplan accepts, even if

---

[13] *Cf.* Salmon (1987/1988). Ironically, Kaplan himself entreats us to keep the epistemic analogues of these doxastic notions sharply distinct. *Cf.* 'Opacity' (258–260) and 'Afterthoughts' (607).
[14] *Cf.* Salmon (1987/1988).
[15] *Cf.* Donnellan (1979) and Salmon (1987/1988).
[16] The internal occurrence of 'λ' in the definiens is every bit as critical as the external occurrence. Kaplan makes the mistake of equating the definiendum instead with the simpler '$(\lambda\delta)[B_n(\beta, \text{that } \phi_\delta)](\alpha)$'.

Quine does not—but this assumption can be weakened considerably, to an extent evidently acceptable even to Quine.

IV

My aim is first to show, by example, that a sentence of the form *IIa* will often (typically) attribute a different belief from that attributed in the corresponding sentence of the form *IIb*. Suppose Ralph has a reflective but commonsensical friend, Kevin, who realizes what Ralph does not: that the suspicious-looking man that Ralph saw wearing the brown hat is none other than Bernard Ortcutt, the pillar of the community whom Ralph saw that time at the beach. (Like Ralph, Kevin knows fully well who Ortcutt is.) When asked whether Ralph believes that Ortcutt is a spy, Kevin responds as follows:

No, Ralph does not believe that Ortcutt, the man he saw at the beach, is a spy. In fact, he believes that Ortcutt is not a spy. But he also believes that the man he saw wearing the brown hat is a spy, and although Ralph does not know it, the man in the brown hat is Ortcutt.

So far, so good. Now we press Quine's puzzle question: 'Very well, consider this man Ortcutt. Does Ralph believe that he is a spy?' Suppose Kevin replies, cautiously and philosophically, as follows:

Well, as I said, Ralph doesn't believe that the man seen at the beach is a spy. But if you are asking about Ortcutt himself—as opposed to various ways of conceiving of him—yes, Ralph believes that he is a spy. Ralph believes that the man he saw wearing the brown hat is a spy. Thus Ralph believes of Ortcutt that he is a spy, without believing that Ortcutt is a spy. Of course, Ralph also believes that the man he saw at the beach is not a spy. He therefore also believes of Ortcutt that he is not a spy. So if you're asking about Ortcutt himself, Ralph believes that he is a spy, but Ralph also disbelieves that he is a spy. It all depends on how Ralph is conceiving of him.

Well spoken. Kevin's position is coherent, rational, well considered, and very plausible. Although the matter remains controversial, no doubt many readers (and many more nonreaders)—perhaps even Quine—are in perfect agreement with Kevin.[17]

We consider the following complex sentence:

4*a* Kevin believes of Ortcutt that Ralph does not believe that he is a spy

Is this sentence true? Support for an affirmative response begins with the truth of the following sentence:

5 Kevin believes that Ralph does not believe that Ortcutt is a spy

---

[17] I am not. I agree with everything Kevin says except that Ralph does not believe that Ortcutt is a spy. Ralph does not believe the man at the beach is a spy, and Ralph does not believe that the man called 'Bernard J. Ortcutt' is a spy, but on my view, however strongly and sincerely he may deny it, Ralph believes that Ortcutt is a spy. Moreover, he even knows that he believes that Ortcutt is a spy. *Cf.* Salmon (1986a) and note 1. The argument that follows does not require any particular decision with regard to these matters.

One argument for the truth of 4a comes by way of the theory of singular propositions. Assuming that the contribution made by the name 'Ortcutt' to the propositional content of sentences containing the name is Ortcutt—the man himself—sentence 5 says that Kevin believes that Ralph does not believe the singular proposition about Ortcutt that he is a spy. On this same assumption, the proposition (which is believed by Kevin) that Ralph does not believe the singular proposition about Ortcutt that he is a spy is itself a complex singular proposition about Ortcutt, to wit, the proposition about Ortcutt that Ralph does not believe the proposition that he is a spy. Thus, since 5 is true, Kevin believes the singular proposition about Ortcutt that Ralph does not believe that he is a spy. Therefore, Ortcutt himself is such that Kevin believes that Ralph does not believe that he is a spy.

Not everyone subscribes to the theory of singular propositions. But it should be clear that even without singular propositions, a similar line of reasoning will quickly lead to the same conclusion that 4a is true.

Consider in particular the theory advanced in 'Intensions Revisited' (Quine, 1981: 120–121). There Quine declares that the following form of exportation is valid:

β believes that ϕ_α
$(\exists \gamma)[\beta$ believes of γ that it $= \alpha]$
Therefore, β believes of α that ϕ_{it}

Quine also suggests that the second premiss might be taken instead as

β knows who α is[18]

In the case at hand, there is indeed someone whom Kevin believes, and even knows, to be Ortcutt—and Kevin knows who Ortcutt is. Given 5, it follows by either of Quine's suggested forms of exportation that 4a is true.

In its simplest terms, the argument for the truth of 4a is this: If 5 is true, then Kevin stands in a certain relation to Ortcutt, by virtue of Kevin's believing that Ralph does not believe that Ortcutt is a spy. That relation is the relation that a bears to b when a believes that Ralph does not believe that b is a spy. Thus if 5 is true, then Kevin has a certain belief about Ortcutt: that Ralph does not believe that he is a spy. And 5 is true.

If there is a more direct argument for Kevin believing of Ortcutt that Ralph does not believe that he is a spy, it can only be this: So what else does it take if not 5?

Applying Quine's proposal to the present case, in the first stage, 4a is to be replaced with (or 'translated' into):

4b Kevin believes Ortcutt to be such that Ralph does not believe him to be a spy

---

[18] Quine discusses only the special instances in which β is 'Ralph', α is either 'Ortcutt' or 'the shortest spy', and ϕ is '_____ is a spy'. Presumably, the discussion is meant to generalize to arbitrary α, β, and ϕ (where ϕ_α is the same expression as ϕ_γ except for having free occurrences of α wherever ϕ_γ has free occurrences of γ).

Evidently a third premiss '$(\exists \gamma)[\gamma = \alpha]$' is also required. Although Quine rejects (1981: 119–120) the simplest form of exportation (which results from the deletion of the second premiss), in part, on the grounds that α may be nonreferring, he fails to consider this possibility in attempting a corrected version of the inference.

The rub is that 4*b*, unlike 4*a*, is false. When asked whether Ortcutt himself was such that Ralph believed that he was a spy, Kevin answered that Ortcutt was indeed. Kevin thus believes Ortcutt to be such that Ralph does believe him to be a spy. This evidently precludes the truth of 4*b*.

One might respond by pointing out that, as we have seen, it is possible for Kevin to believe Ortcutt to be thus-and-so even while disbelieving Ortcutt to be thus-and-so (that is, even while believing Ortcutt not to be thus-and-so)—just as Ralph does—so that the fact that Kevin believes Ortcutt to be believed by Ralph to be a spy does not prove that Kevin does not also believe Ortcutt not to be such.

Quite so. But assuming Kevin is sane and rational, he will not believe Ortcutt to be thus-and-so while also disbelieving Ortcutt to be thus-and-so unless he somehow mistakes Ortcutt to be two different people—just as Ralph does. In order for Kevin to form a belief about Ortcutt that he is not believed by Ralph to be a spy, without altering his opinion that Ortcutt is believed by Ralph to be a spy, Kevin must encounter Ortcutt under different circumstances, and failing to recognize him, come to believe that he is someone Ralph does not believe is a spy. Kevin does no such thing. It is because Kevin is not thus confused that his believing Ortcutt to be someone Ralph believes is a spy precludes the truth of 4*b*.[19]

There is an interesting complication: Kevin does indeed have inconsistent beliefs about Ortcutt. For it is part of Kevin's view that Ralph believes of Ortcutt that he is a spy. This belief of Kevin's concerning Ralph is also a belief concerning Ortcutt, to the effect that Ralph believes that he is a spy. Thus, even though Kevin has not mistaken him for two different men, Ortcutt is such that Kevin both believes and disbelieves that Ralph believes that he is a spy. How is this possible if Kevin is rational?

The matter is controversial. My own answer (see note 17) is that Kevin has indeed mistaken a single thing for two different things—or is at least committed to doing so. That thing is not Ortcutt himself but the singular proposition that he is a spy. Kevin's incompatible beliefs concern this proposition; he believes it to be something that Ralph believes, but he also believes it to be something that Ralph does not believe. In judging that Ralph does not believe that Ortcutt is a spy, Kevin does not recognize the proposition in question, the belief of which he thereby denies to Ralph, as the very same proposition the belief of which he ascribes to Ralph in maintaining that Ralph believes of Ortcutt that he is a spy. Kevin does not have similarly inconsistent beliefs concerning Ortcutt, to the effect that he is thus-and-so and he is not thus-and-so. In particular, Kevin is in no position to see that it would follow from his (mistaken) belief that Ralph does not believe that Ortcutt is a spy, that Ortcutt is not believed

---

[19] Alternatively, Kevin may rationally come to believe that Ortcutt is someone Ralph does not believe to be a spy without mistaking Ortcutt to be two different people (and without relinquishing his belief that Ortcutt is someone Ralph believes to be a spy) by mistaking the logically incompatible properties of being someone Ralph believes is a spy and of being someone Ralph does not believe is a spy—which are properties that such individuals as you, I, and Ortcutt either have or lack in an absolute de re way—for properties of individuals-under-guises (or equivalently, for binary relations between individuals and ways of conceiving them). This philosophically sophisticated confusion would rescue Kevin from irrationality even when he both believes and disbelieves Ortcutt to be believed by Ralph to be a spy, if only he were so confused.

by Ralph to be a spy. Kevin does not recognize that in dissenting from the attribution 'Ralph believes that Ortcutt is a spy', he commits himself to something he explicitly rejects, Ortcutt's being someone Ralph does not believe is a spy.[20]

The example also demonstrates that Kaplan's more recent view (as I have reconstructed it) concerning the import of the pure de re form must also be incorrect. Consider the following variant of 4*b* (replacing the pure de re 'Ralph does not believe him to be a spy' with the allegedly stronger 'Ralph does not believe that he is a spy'):

6   Kevin believes Ortcutt to be such that Ralph does not believe that he is a spy

On Kaplan's view, 6 says something like the following: Kevin is acquainted with Ortcutt and believes the singular proposition about Ortcutt that Ralph does not believe that he is a spy, when grasping that proposition in a special [such-and-such] manner by means of Kevin's aforementioned acquaintance with Ortcutt. If that were what 6 meant, it evidently would be true (as the entirety of facts underlying the truth of 4*a* would seem to attest) instead of false.

What has gone wrong? The defect in Quine's original scheme that Kaplan's articulation was introduced to correct stems from the fact that in moving from the syntactically *de dicto* semantically *de re*

β believes of Ortcutt that ϕ_{he}

to the pure *de re*

β believes Ortcutt to be an individual such that ϕ_{it}

(formalized by *IIb* with $\alpha = $ 'Ortcutt'), one reparses the attributed belief into two components—an objectual component and a qualitative component—by simultaneously isolating the individual the belief is about and abstracting a property from the complement 'open sentence' ϕ_{he}. That is, one consolidates the internal propositional structure of the complement clause into a single property. One then depicts the referent of β as ascribing this property to Ortcutt. Thus Ralph's complex belief of Ortcutt that he is taller than he is erroneously rendered as the absurd belief about Ortcutt that he is a thing-that-is-taller-than-itself. The reparsing into objectual and qualitative components alters the nature of the belief attributed to Ralph, and Quine's translation fails to capture any relational belief of Ralph's. Articulation more discriminantly consolidates the propositional structure into a relation, in a manner that is sensitive to beliefs that (unknown to the believer) involve a reflexive structure. But articulation remains a method of reparsing and abstraction, whereby the structure of the belief attributed in the untranslated construction is fundamentally altered in the course of translation. The general problem remains: One's relational belief may have the propositional structure indicated by the sentence ϕ_{he} without the believer also ascribing to Ortcutt the corresponding attribute (property or relation), as the proposed translation requires. Kevin's belief about Ortcutt reported in 4*a* has a complex structure; it is the denial of an attribution to Ralph of a particular belief involving Ortcutt. The belief attributed to Kevin in 4*b* has a very different structure; it is the

---

[20] For further details, see Salmon (1989b).

attribution of a certain property to Ortcutt. Kevin has the first belief and not the second.[21]

The example demonstrates that no such attempt to reduce the allegedly problematic mixed form to the pure form can succeed, since reparsing into an objectual and a qualitative component is required by the very form of the syntactically *de re*—to fill the second and third argument places of 'B_r' in *IIb*.

V

Quine's ultimate goal is to replace the 'that' clauses of belief attributions with quotations, thereby replacing a field of unruly weeds with neatly arranged fruit trees. Since the problem we have noted with the attempt to reduce the syntactically *de dicto* semantically *de re* form to the pure *de re* arises from the abstraction on the open sentence occurring in the 'that' clause of the former, Quine's ultimate goal might be attained by simply bypassing the intermediate stage and moving directly from 4*a* to

4*d* Kevin believes 'Ralph does not believe that x is a spy' satisfied by Ortcutt

In general, the allegedly problematic *IIa* may now be replaced with

IId Believes-satisfied-by(β, 'ϕ_γ', α)

in which the open sentence that forms the 'that' clause of *IIa* is quoted directly without first abstracting a predicate from it.[22]

At first sight, the replacement of 4*a* by 4*d* does not seem an improvement over the earlier replacement by 4*b*. Kevin does not believe Ortcutt to be someone that satisfies the open sentence 'Ralph does not believe that x is a spy', any more than he believes Ortcutt to be someone Ralph does not believe is a spy. Indeed, the new replacement

---

[21] The propositional objects of these two potential beliefs are, on my view, equivalent. That does not alter the fact that Kevin believes only one of them. Indeed, it is (in some sense) part of Kevin's view that the assertion that Ralph does not believe that Ortcutt is a spy is not equivalent to the assertion that Ortcutt is not believed by Ralph to be a spy.

The example can also be adjusted to refute certain contemporary theories of so-called *de se* belief attributions, i.e., attributions of first-person belief concerning oneself. Specifically, the example can be made to refute any attempt to analyze a *de se* attribution of the form ⌜α believes that $\phi_{he-himself}$⌝ by means of something along the lines of ⌜α self-ascribes the property of being someone γ such that ϕ_γ⌝. Such attempts are made in Lewis (1979) and inn Chisholm (1981: 34–7 and *passim*). Simply let Kevin be Ortcutt himself, and let him express the belief reported in 4*a* by means of the first-person 'Ralph does not believe that I am a spy'. ('What Ralph believes', he adds 'is that the man in the brown hat is a spy. The man in the brown hat is in fact me, but Ralph doesn't realize that.' It may help for this purpose to suppose that Ortcutt subscribes to Frege's theory of the first-person pronoun, on which it expresses a particular private sense in Ortcutt's idiolect.) Ortcutt may nevertheless believe himself to be someone that Ralph believes to be a spy. (He is such a person after all.) Being fully rational, Ortcutt would not also believe himself to be someone that Ralph does not believe is a spy (although he may believe himself to be someone that Ralph also disbelieves is a spy). Thus Ortcutt would not self-ascribe the property of not being believed by Ralph to be a spy.

[22] It should be noted again here that this is indeed how things end up in Quine (1956) where for some unexplained reason, the abstraction that occurred at the intermediate stage is dropped at the final stage. It is restored in Quine (1979). See note 3.

seems even worse than the old. Even if Kevin were to come to believe of Ortcutt (say, by failing to recognize him in his new black hat) that he is someone Ralph does not believe is a spy, Kevin need not conclude that Ortcutt satisfies the open sentence in question. Kevin may know nothing of formal semantics. A similar concern arises in connection with Quine's proposed replacement of 3*a* by 3*c*. Ralph may believe that the man in the brown hat is a spy without believing 'The man in the brown hat is a spy' to be true—for example, if Ralph speaks no English.

In a revealing passage, Quine acknowledges (in effect) that his terminology is misleading:

> This semantical reformulation [of *Ia* into *Ic*] is not, of course, intended to suggest that the subject of the propositional attitude speaks the language of the quotation, or any language. We may treat a mouse's fear of a cat as his fearing true a certain English sentence. This is unnatural without being therefore wrong. ... [If] anyone does approve of speaking of belief of a proposition at all and of speaking of a proposition in turn as meant [i.e., expressed] by a sentence, then certainly he cannot object to our semantical reformulation ...; for [*Ic*] is explicitly definable in *his* terms as ['β believes the proposition expressed by "ϕ"']. Similarly for the semantical reformulation [of *IIb* into *IIc*].   (Quine, 1966: 192–193)[23]

Despite appearances, believing-true ϕ is something very different from believing ϕ to be true (which is something the mouse cannot do). Truth is not involved in any way in Quine's concept of 'believing-true'. Indeed, the concept would be more perspicuously written 'believes-the-content-of'. For the propositionalist (such as myself), this concept involves not truth, but the relation, usually called 'expressing', between a sentence and its propositional content. For Quine, it involves neither.[24]

Quine's terminology in the passage quoted remains misleading. For Quine, the 'semantical reformulations' are more pragmatic than semantic. The supposed point of writing 3*c* in place of 3*a* is precisely that the former allegedly avoids the latter's commitment to Ralph's belief of a proposition. Believing-true, for Quine, is evidently a relation that a subject bears to a sentence by virtue of a certain kind of match between the subject's psychological state and some ontologically thrifty feature of the sentence—perhaps its associated assent-producing and dissent-producing stimuli (in Quine's jargon, its stimulus meaning) or its conventional use in communication, where this is taken as not involving the assignment of a proposition as semantic content. If this thin notion is deemed semantical, our concern is with 'semantics' in a very loose sense. In its more restrictive sense as a term for the formal study of the symbolic nature of language—a subject that essentially involves the assignment of semantic values (truth values, or 'intensions', etc.)—believing-true, for Quine, is about as semantical as True Value Hardware Stores or *The Plain Truth* magazine. It is semantical in name only. Any comfort or security derived from the use of the words 'true' or 'satisfy' in Quine's proposal is based on illusion.

---

[23] Although the matter is somewhat unclear, in the last sentence quoted here Quine evidently means that *IIc* may be defined for the intensionalist along the lines of 'β ascribes the property expressed by "(λγ)[ϕ$_γ$]" to α'.

[24] In Quine (1979), the syllable 'true' is dropped altogether from the predicate 'believes-true'.

Since it is an attempt to eliminate propositions and the like from propositional-attitude attributions in favor of expressions, Quine's proposal faces Alonzo Church's powerful objection from Church, 1950. Church points out that typical purported analyses that seek to do away with propositions in favor of such things as sentences 'must be rejected on the grounds that [the analysans] does not convey the same information as [the analysandum]' (97–98). In the present case, 3a conveys the content of Ralph's belief—specifying that it is a belief whose content is that the man in the brown hat is a spy—whereas 3c specifies certain words that express that content 'without saying what meaning is attached to them'. Adapting Church's objection to the present case, he argues that

> (3c) is unacceptable as an analysis of (3a). For it is not even possible to infer (3a) as a consequence of (3c), on logical grounds alone—but only by making use of the item of factual information, not contained in (3c), that 'The man in the brown hat is a spy' means in English that the man in the brown hat is a spy.
>
> Following a suggestion of Langford [in *Journal of Symbolic Logic*, 2, 1937: 53] we may bring out more sharply the inadequacy of (3c) as an analysis of (3a) by translating into another language, say German, and observing that the two translated statements would obviously convey different meanings to a German (whom we may suppose to have no knowledge of English). (Church, 1950: 98)[25]

Quine, by way of response, concedes Church's point but dismisses the objection as inapplicable to his proposed replacements, since 3c and 1c are offered as materially equivalent substitutes, and not as meaning-preserving analyses, for the constructions they replace. He writes:

> a systematic agreement in truth value [between *Ic* and *Ia*] can be claimed, and no more. This limitation will prove of little moment to persons who share my skepticism about analyticity. (194)

This response makes it extremely difficult to understand just what is going on in the last seven paragraphs of Quine, 1956. Church (1950) begins with the following observation:

> For statements such as *Seneca said that man is a rational animal* and *Columbus believed the world to be round*, the most obvious analysis makes them statements about certain abstract entities which we shall call 'propositions' ..., namely the proposition that man is a rational animal and the proposition that the world is round; and these propositions are taken as having been respectively the object of an assertion by Seneca and the object of a belief by Columbus. ... [Our] purpose is to point out what we believe may be an insuperable objection against alternative analyses that undertake to do away with propositions in favor of such more concrete things as sentences.

Church may thus be seen as issuing a challenge: A true propositional-attitude attribution like 3a expresses a fact that appears to require not only a believer but also a

---

[25] I have altered the wording to adapt the argument to the present case. Notice that the deficiency that Church notes remains even after 'believes-true' is defined (for the propositionalist) as 'believes the proposition expressed in English by'. At most, 3c merely describes the content of the belief attributed to Ralph (as the content, in English, of a certain sentence); it does not actually provide that content, in the fashion of 3a.

proposition for the believer to believe. (Consider, for example, the intuitively valid inference from 3*a* to 'That the man in the brown hat is a spy is something Ralph believes' or to 'There is something that Ralph believes, which is that the man in the brown hat is a spy'.) If you reject propositions, then propose an analysis of 3*a* that avoids them (and that explains, or otherwise accommodates, such phenomena as the intuitive validity of the two inferences just mentioned), while also avoiding the apparently insuperable objection noted above. In admitting that 3*c* is put forward only as a substitute and not as an analysis, Quine fails to address—let alone to meet—this serious challenge.

Perhaps Quine rejects any notion of analysis that such a challenge might presuppose, and therefore respectfully declines. He motivates his proposal to substitute 3*c* for 3*a* on the ground that this is sufficient to avoid the latter's commitment to Ralph's belief of a proposition. He admits 3*a*'s commitment to a proposition; it is for that very reason that he proposes replacing it with something less extravagant.

At this juncture the question posed at the start of this essay arises with overwhelming force. Given Quine's admission that *Ia* and *Ic* are alike in truth value, how can the replacement of the former by the latter serve his purpose? Specifically, what can be the point of writing 3*c* 'instead of' 3*a* if it is granted that the latter, though not equivalent to its proposed replacement, is literally true and entails the existence of a proposition? One cannot avoid the ontological commitments of a theory merely by refraining from asserting the theory, if at the same time one concedes the theory's truth. If Quine's proposal to replace 3*a* with 3*c* is not simply an attempt at subterfuge, it can only be a confusion. In making the substitution one may camouflage the commitment to an 'intension', but the commitment remains. Indeed, given Quine's admission of 3*a*'s truth as well as its commitment to a proposition, his own commitment to that proposition remains quite visible.

This is a curious inconsistency. The only viable remedies are three. Quine could recant his concession that 3*a* involves a commitment to an 'intension'. Alternatively, he could recant his concession that 3*a* is true, and renounce 3*a* along with 1*a*. Similarly for 1*b*, and indeed for all attributions of either the syntactically *de dicto* form *Ia* or the syntactically *de re* form *IIb*.

The second alternative must be regarded as extremist; as Quine himself has insisted, both the theory and practice of psychology—not to mention our ordinary conceptions of everyday human affairs and of what it is to have a cognitive life—depend heavily on just such attributions. The first alternative is perhaps even less attractive. For it would obligate Quine to rise to Church's challenge; it remains highly doubtful whether that challenge will ever be met in a completely satisfactory way.

The third alternative is to admit propositions. There are problems here as well, but it seems likely that their solution lies within our grasp. To make the conversion to intensionalism as painless as possible, one might begin with Russellian singular propositions. Admitting singular propositions has the additional feature that Quine's proposed replacements, one and all, may be discarded in favor of an extremely resilient and satisfying account of relational belief, the essentials of which have been with us since 1905.

REFERENCES

Burge, T., 1977. 'Belief *De Re*', *The Journal of Philosophy*, 74, June: 338–362.

Chisholm, R., 1981. *The First Person*, Minneapolis: University of Minnesota Press.

Church, A., 1950. 'On Carnap's Analysis of Statements of Assertion and Belief', *Analysis*, 10, 5: 97–99.

──── 1989. 'Intensionality and the Paradox of the Name Relation', in *Themes from Kaplan*, J. Almog, J. Perry, and H. Wettstein, eds, Oxford: Oxford University Press, pp. 151–165.

Donnellan, K., 1979. 'The Contingent *A Priori* and Rigid Designators', in *Contemporary Perspectives in the Philosophy of Language*, P. French, T. Uehling, and H. Wettstein, eds, Minneapolis: University of Minnesota Press, pp. 45–60.

Fine, K., 1990. 'Quine on Quantifying In', in *Propositional Attitudes: The Role of Content in Logic, Language, and Mind*, C. Anthony Anderson and J. Owens, eds, Stanford: Center for the Study of Language and Information, pp. 1–25.

Forbes, G., 1985. *The Metaphysics of Modality*, Oxford: Oxford University Press.

Kaplan, D., 1969. 'Quantifying In', in *Words and Objections: Essays on the Work of W. V. Quine*, D. Davidson and J. Hintikka, eds, Dordrecht: Reidel, pp. 206–242.

──── 1986. 'Opacity', in *The Philosophy of W. V. Quine*, L. E. Hahn and P. A. Schilpp, eds, La Salle: Open Court, pp. 229–289.

──── 1989. 'Demonstratives', in *Themes from Kaplan*, J. Almog, H. Wettstein, and J. Perry, eds, Oxford: Oxford University Press, pp. 481–565.

──── 1989. 'Afterthoughts', in *Themes from Kaplan*, J. Almog, H. Wettstein, and J. Perry, eds., Oxford: Oxford University Press, pp. 565–614.

Kazmi, A., 1987. 'Quantification and Opacity', *Linguistics and Philosophy*, 10: 77–100.

Kripke, S., 1979. 'A Puzzle About Belief', in *Meaning and Use*, A. Margalit, ed., Dordrecht: Reidel, pp. 239–283; also in *Propositions and Attitudes*, N. Salmon and S. Soames, eds, Oxford: Oxford University Press, 1988, pp. 102–248.

Lewis, D., 1979. 'Attitudes *De Dicto* and *De Se*', *The Philosophical Review*, 88: 513–543.

Quine, W. V., 1956. 'Quantifiers and Propositional Attitudes', *The Journal of Philosophy*, 53: 177–187, reprinted in Quine (1966: 183–194).

──── 1960. *Word and Object*, Cambridge, Mass.: MIT Press.

──── 1966. *The Ways of Paradox*, New York: Random House.

──── 1969. 'Reply to Kaplan', in *Words and Objections: Essays on the Work of W. V. Quine*, D. Davidson and J. Hintikka, eds, Dordrecht: Reidel, pp. 341–345.

──── 1979. 'Intension Revisited', in *Contemporary Perspectives in the Philosophy of Language*, P. French, T. Uehling, and H. Wettstein, eds., Minneapolis: University of Minnesota Press, pp. 268–274; also in Quine (1981: 113–123).

──── 1981. *Theories and Things*, Cambridge, Mass.: Harvard University Press.

──── 1986. 'Reply to David Kaplan', in *The Philosophy of W. V. Quine*, L. E. Hahn and P. A. Schlipp, eds, La Salle: Open Court, pp. 290–294.

Richard, M., 1987. 'Quantification and Leibniz's Law', *The Philosophical Review*, 96, 4: 555–578.

Russell, B., 1956, *Logic and Knowledge*, Robert C. Marsh, ed., London: George Allen and Unwin.

Salmon, N., 1986a. *Frege's Puzzle*, Cambridge, Mass.: MIT Press (a Bradford Book).

──── 1986b. 'Reflexivity', *Notre Dame Journal of Formal Logic*, 27, 3: 401–429; also in Salmon and Soames (1988: 240–274).

──── 1987/1988. 'How to Measure the Standard Meter', *Proceedings of the Aristotelian Society*, 88: 193–217.

____ 1989a. 'How to Become a Millian Heir', *Nous*, 23, 2: 211–220.

____ 1989b. 'Illogical Belief', in *Philosophical Perspectives, 3: Philosophy of Mind and Action Theory*, J. Tomberlin, ed., Atascadero, Calif.: Ridgeview, pp. 243–285.

____ 1990. 'A Millian Heir Rejects the Wages of *Sinn*', in *Propositional Attitudes*, C. A. Anderson and J. Owens, eds, Stanford, Calif.: Center for the Study of Language and Information, pp. 215–247.

Salmon, N., and Soames, S., eds, 1988. *Propositions and Attitudes*, Oxford: Oxford University Press.

15

Is *De Re* Belief Reducible to *De Dicto*? (1998)

I

Yes and no. It depends on the meaning of the question. Traditionally, those on the affirmative side—predominantly neo-Fregeans—hold that Ralph's believing about Ortcutt, *de re*, that he is a spy is identical with, or otherwise reducible to, Ralph's believing some proposition or other of the form *The such-and-such is a spy*, for some concept *the such-and-such* that is thoroughly conceptual or qualitative (or perhaps thoroughly qualitative but for the involvement of constituents of Ralph's consciousness or of other mental particulars), and that uniquely *determines*, or is uniquely a *concept of*, Ortcutt (in Alonzo Church's sense of 'determines' and 'concept of').[1] Concerns over Ralph's believing that whoever is shortest among spies is a spy while not suspecting anyone in particular have led some neo-Fregeans (not all) to qualify their affirmative response by requiring that the concept *the such-and-such* and its object bear some connection that is epistemologically more substantial than that between *the shortest spy* and the shortest spy. For example, in his classic 'Quantifying In', David Kaplan required that the concept be (among other things) *vivid* in a certain sense.[2] If the question is whether a *de re* belief attribution like

(1) Ralph believes of Ortcutt that he is a spy,

logically entails in English, and is logically entailed by, the claim that for some thoroughly conceptual or qualitative concept *such-and-such* that uniquely determines Ortcutt in an epistemologically special manner, Ralph believes that the such-and-such is a spy, I believe the answer is unequivocally 'No'. (Kaplan also no longer endorses this theory.) If the question is instead whether it is in the nature of human cognition, rather than by logic, that (1) is true iff for some epistemologically special, thoroughly qualitative concept *such-and such* of Ortcutt, Ralph believes that the such-and-such

---

I am grateful to the Santa Barbarians Discussion Group for its comments on some of the arguments presented here. Anthony Brueckner and Francis Dauer made particularly helpful observations.

[1] See for example Daniel Dennett, 'Beyond Belief', in A. Woodfield, ed., *Thought and Object* (Oxford University Press 1982), 1–95 (e.g., at 84); John Searle, 'Are There Irreducibly *De Re* Beliefs', in *Intentionality* (Cambridge University Press 1983), ch. 8, §2, 208–217.

[2] In D. Davidson and J. Hintikka, eds, *Words and Objections: Essays on the Work of W. V. Quine* (Dordrecht: D. Reidel 1969), 178–214; reprinted in L. Linsky, ed., *Reference and Modality* (Oxford University Press 1972), 112–144. All page references herein are to the latter printing.

is a spy, the answer is still 'No'. If there is a Twin Earth in the great beyond, and my *Doppelgänger* there believes his wife to be beautiful, I nevertheless have no *de re* judgment concerning her pulchritude (how could I?), even though he and I share all the same thoroughly qualitative beliefs of the form *The such-and-such is beautiful*, and neither of us possesses any thoroughly qualitative concept that uniquely determines his wife.[3]

There is a significantly weaker sense in which *de re* belief may correctly be said to be reducible to *de dicto*. It is that Ralph's belief about Ortcutt (a *res*) that he is a spy is identical with, or otherwise reducible to, Ralph's belief of some proposition (a *dictum*) to the effect that Ortcutt is a spy—though not necessarily a proposition of the form *The such-and-such is a spy* where *such-and-such* is a special, thoroughly qualitative concept of Ortcutt. This weaker thesis is fairly modest as far as reducibility claims go. Nevertheless, it too has been challenged. Indeed, philosophers who make one or another of the more full-blooded reducibility claims typically reject my claim that *de re* belief is analyzable into belief of a proposition, as I intend the analysis.

The classic case against reducibility of *de re* belief to *de dicto* was made in Quine's 'Quantifiers and Propositional Attitudes'.[4] He described a scenario, which I shall call 'Act I', in which Ralph has witnessed a man, his face hidden from view by a brown hat, engaged in clandestine activity that prompted Ralph to conclude that he was a foreign spy. What Ralph does not realize is that the man wearing the hat is Ortcutt, whom Ralph remembers having seen once at the beach and whom Ralph regards as a patriotic pillar of the community, hence no spy. Ralph has conflicting views concerning Ortcutt, separately believing and disbelieving him to be a spy. On the basis of Act I, Quine argued that true *de re* belief attributions like (1) and

(2) Ralph believes of the man seen at the beach that he is a spy,

stand in need of regimentation. Clearly (2) should not be viewed as imputing to Ralph a *de dicto* belief that the man seen at the beach is a spy. Using 'B_{dd}' as a symbol for belief of a proposition, the sentence

(3) Ralph B_{dd} that the man seen at the beach is a spy,

says something very different from (2), indeed something that is false with respect to Quine's example.[5] A crucial feature of a *de re* construction like (2), distinguishing it sharply from (3), is that the occurrence of 'the man seen at the beach' is open

---

[3] The Twin Earth thought experiment is due to Hilary Putnam. See his 'Meaning and Reference', *Journal of Philosophy* 70 (1973), 699–711. For a similar argument, see Tyler Burge, 'Individualism and the Mental', in P. French, T. Uehling, and H. Wettstein, eds, *Midwest Studies in Philosophy IV: Studies in Metaphysics* (Minneapolis: University of Minnesota Press 1979), 73–121.

[4] *Journal of Philosophy* 53 (1957) 177–187; reprinted in Quine's *The Ways of Paradox* (New York: Random House 1967), 183–194; also in L. Linsky, ed., *Reference and Modality* (Oxford University Press 1971), 101–111, and elsewhere. All page references herein are to the Linsky printing. See also Tyler Burge, 'Kaplan, Quine, and Suspended Belief', *Philosophical Studies* 31 (1977) 197–203, and 'Belief De Re', *Journal of Philosophy* 74 (1977) 338–362.

[5] Kaplan symbolizes (3) as Ralph **B** ⌜the man seen at the beach is a spy⌝. While I have altered his symbol for *de dicto* belief I am preserving elements of his syntax, which is aptly suited to clarifying the issues under discussion. (See especially note 22 below.)

to substitution of 'the man in the brown hat'. It is tempting to provide (2) a quasi-formalization in:

(4) $(\exists x)[x = $ the man seen at the beach $\&$ Ralph $\mathbf{B}_{dd}$ that x is a spy$\,]$,

thus removing 'the man seen at the beach' from the scope of 'Ralph believes that'. This is equivalent to something familiar to readers of Russell:

(4′) $(\exists x)[(y)(y$ is a man seen at the beach $\leftrightarrow x = y)\ \&$ Ralph $\mathbf{B}_{dd}$ that x is a spy$\,]$.

Either way, it would seem therefore that (2) is true if and only if the component open sentence,

(5) Ralph $\mathbf{B}_{dd}$ that x is a spy,

is true under the assignment to the variable 'x' of the individual who uniquely satisfies 'y is a man seen at the beach', i.e. of Ortcutt. The meaning of '$\mathbf{B}_{dd}$' is such that a sentence of the form $\ulcorner \alpha\ \mathbf{B}_{dd}$ that $\phi \urcorner$ is true if and only if the referent of the subject term α believes the proposition expressed by ϕ (the proposition referred to by the argument $\ulcorner$ that $\phi \urcorner$). But, Quine reasoned, this yields a truth condition for (2) that is essentially incomplete. Whether it is fulfilled depends not only on *what* the value of the variable in (5) is but also on *how* that value was assigned, since Ralph believes that the man in the brown hat is a spy but does not believe that the man at the beach is. If the variable receives its value by means of the particular description 'the man seen at the beach' rather than 'the man in the brown hat'—as it seems to have done—then under that assignment, performed that way, (2) should simply recapitulate (3), and consequently should be false rather than true.

Quine concluded that (2) should not be seen as attributing *de dicto* belief at all. Instead Quine counseled that (4) and (4′) be scrapped, and that (2) be seen as ascribing to Ralph a different relation—that of *de re* ('relational') belief—to the beach man and the property of being a spy:

(6) Ralph $\mathbf{B}_{dr}$ (the man seen at the beach, to be a spy).

In Quine's words, (6) 'is to be viewed not as dyadic belief between Ralph and the proposition *that* Ortcutt has [the attribute of being a spy], but rather as an irreducibly triadic relation among the three things' (*op. cit.*, p. 106). The proposal thus echoes Russell's 'multiple-relation' theory of belief.[6] Also true with respect to Act I is the following:

(7) Ralph $\mathbf{B}_{dr}$ (the man seen at the beach, $\sim$[to be a spy]).

Quine emphasized that the joint truth of (6) and (7) does not indicate an inconsistency on Ralph's part.

---

[6] See 'On the Nature of Truth and Falsehood', in Russell's *Philosophical Essays* (New York: Simon and Schuster 1968), pp. 147–159; *Our Knowledge of the External World* (New York: New American Library 1956), pp. 52–53; D. Pears, ed., *The Philosophy of Logical Atomism* (La Salle: Open Court 1985), pp. 79–93.

Quine writes (6) as 'Ralph believes $z(z$ is a spy) of the man seen at the beach', Kaplan as 'Ralph **Bel** ('x is a spy', the man seen at the beach)'.

I have argued against Quine that any sweeping proposal to parse ⌜Ralph believes of α that ϕ_{he/she/it}⌝ into a ternary-relational assertion is doomed.[7] My objection focused on specific instances involving a complicated substituend for ϕ (specifically, a belief ascription). This leaves open the question of whether a less ambitious proposal might fare better, at least when restricted to gentler ϕ like 'He is a spy'. Is there anything problematic about regimenting (2) and its ilk, rewriting it in the style of (6) as 'Ralph believes the man seen at the beach to be a spy'?

There is. Quine conjectured that (6) should be seen as a logical consequence of (3).[8] Kaplan labeled the inference pattern 'exportation', and argued against it through his example of the shortest spy. Quine recanted, and later recanted his recant.[9] Still, it would appear that the predicates for *de dicto* and *de re* belief are not logically independent. Whatever the final decision with regard to exportation, the logical validity of the following inference is difficult to resist:

(*I*) Every proposition Ralph believes, Kevin disbelieves. Ralph believes the man seen at the beach to be a spy. Therefore, Kevin believes the man seen at the beach not to be a spy.

But if the first premiss is symbolized by means of 'B_{dd}' and the second by means of 'B_{dr},' then a middle term is missing and the validity remains unexplained.

II

In 'Quantifying In', Kaplan proposed a full-blooded reducibility thesis for modality as well as belief and other propositional attitudes. He proposed first (p. 130) that

N_{dr} (the number of planets, to be odd),

i.e., 'The number of planets is such that it is necessary for it to be odd', be analyzed into:

$(\exists \alpha)[\Delta_N(\alpha, \text{the number of planets}) \ \& \ N_{dd} \ulcorner \alpha \text{ is odd}\urcorner]$.[10]

The variable 'α' may be taken as a first approximation as ranging over singular terms, but should ultimately be regarded as ranging over thoroughly conceptual or qualitative individual concepts, with the quasi-quotation marks accordingly

---

[7] 'Relational Belief', in P. Leonardi and M. Santambrogio, eds, *On Quine: New Essays* (Cambridge University Press 1995), pp. 206–228

[8] 'Quantifiers and Propositional Attitudes', p. 106

[9] The recant is made in 'Replies', in D. Davidson and G. Harman, eds, *Words and Objections*, pp. 337–338, 341–342; the recant of the recant in 'Intensions Revisited', in P. French, T. Uehling, and H. Wettstein, eds, *Contemporary Perspectives in the Philosophy of Language* (Minneapolis: University of Minnesota Press 1979), pp. 268–274, at 272–273, reprinted in Quine's *Theories and Things* (Harvard University Press 1981), pp. 113–123, at 119–121.

[10] I must note that exportation cannot be generally valid for all propositional attributions. Otherwise, from the empirical premiss that there are in fact exactly nine planets, and the philosophical observation that there might instead have been an even number of (or more specifically, eight or ten) planets, one could validly infer that nine might have been even (or eight or ten).

interpreted either standardly or as quasi-sense-quotation marks.[11] The first conjunct '$\Delta_N(\alpha,$ the number of planets)' says that α necessarily determines the object that *actually* numbers the planets—in effect, that α rigidly designates that number, in the sense of Kripke. Analogously, Kaplan proposed (p. 138) that (6) be analyzed thus:

(K6) ($\exists\alpha$)[R(α, the man seen at the beach, Ralph) & Ralph $\mathbf{B}_{dd}$ ⌜α is a spy⌝].

The first conjunct says that α provides a *de re* connection for Ralph to the man seen at the beach. In Kaplan's terminology, α 'represents' the man seen at the beach for Ralph. Kaplan provides an analysis for his epistemologically special notion of representation, whereby 'R(α, the man seen at the beach, Ralph)' entails, but is strictly stronger than, '$\Delta(\alpha,$ the man seen at the beach)' (i.e., α determines the man seen at the beach). It has not been established, however, that this further step is properly a matter of philosophical logic—rather than, for example, of philosophical psychology.[12] Beyond the mentioned entailment, the exact analysis of Kaplan's 'R' will not concern me here.

Kaplan's ingenious reductive analysis of *de re* propositional attribution might be interpreted as a proposal for dealing with any propositional attribution that involves an open sentence. One might regard an open 'that'-clause, like 'that x is a spy', as having no meaning in isolation, but as contributing indirectly to the meanings of sentences in which it occurs. A contextual definition for 'that x is a spy' is provided as follows: First, analyses are provided for atomic formulae ⌜$\Pi^n(\beta_1, \beta_2, \ldots,$ that x is a spy$, \ldots, \beta_{n-1})$⌝ containing the 'that'-clause among its argument expressions. The most common cases are: those where $n = 1$ and Π^1 is a predicate for a *de dicto* modality, i.e. a modal predicate of propositions ('necessarily true', 'probably true', etc.); and those where $n = 2$ and Π^2 is a predicate for a *de dicto* propositional attitude ('believes', 'doubts', 'hopes', 'fears', 'wishes', etc.). In the latter case,

$\beta\ \Pi_{dd}$ that x is a spy

is analyzed as:

($\exists\alpha$)[R(α, x, β) & $\beta\ \Pi_{dd}$ ⌜α is a spy⌝].

---

[11] An *individual concept* is a concept for (i.e. a concept whose function is to determine) an individual, and may thus serve as the semantic content of singular term.

[12] Evidently on Kaplan's account, the following sentence is alleged to be an analytic truth:

If Ralph believes the man seen at the beach to be a spy, then there is a vivid individual concept α that determines, and is for Ralph a name of, the man seen at the beach such that Ralph believes ⌜α is a spy⌝.

Similarly for its converse. I believe, on the contrary, that neither the conditional nor its converse is analytic. Even if the conditional were both necessary and *a priori*, the inference from antecedent to consequent, or vice versa, does not feel to me like one that is licensed strictly as a matter of the principles governing correct reasoning and the meanings of 'believe', 'vivid', 'name of', etc. As a matter of fact, the Twin Earth considerations mentioned in the first paragraph of this article demonstrate that the conditional need not even be true. By contrast, the mutual inference between (4) (or (2)) and (6) does feel to me to be licensed by pure logic. *Cf.* my remarks concerning the modal-propositional-logical system T as compared with stronger systems, in 'The Logic of What Might Have Been', *The Philosophical Review* 98 (1989), pp. 3–34.

Plugging this contextual definition of 'that x is a spy' into (4) yields (K6), or rather, something classically equivalent to it. More complicated constructions involving the analysandum are then subject to scope ambiguities exactly analogous to those found in Russell's Theory of Descriptions. The negation $\ulcorner\sim(\beta \, \Pi_{dd}$ that x is a spy $)\urcorner$, for example, may be analyzed as involving a 'primary occurrence' of the 'that'-clause, or alternatively as involving a 'secondary occurrence', where the latter corresponds to the genuine negation of the original, un-negated analysandum:

$(\exists\alpha)[R(\alpha, x, \beta) \, \& \, \sim(\beta \, \Pi_{dd} \ulcorner\alpha \text{ is a spy}\urcorner)]$

$\sim(\exists\alpha)[R(\alpha, x, \beta) \, \& \, \beta \, \Pi_{dd} \ulcorner\alpha \text{ is a spy}\urcorner].$[13]

One virtue of Kaplan's analysis is that it may reduce the inference (I) to a valid argument of first-order logic. Declining any analysis of *de re* belief into *de dicto* leaves few alternatives. One may take 'B_{dd}' and 'B_{dr}' as primitives, for example, and propose Carnapian 'meaning postulates' for them that would enable one to derive (I). Perhaps one may save the inference instead through an analysis of the former predicate in terms of the latter.[14] Or one may reject inferences like (I) as invalid.

Kaplan argued on somewhat different grounds that leaving the *de re* form unanalyzed into the *de dicto* is inadequate (pp. 140–143). His argument invokes a later development in Quine's example:

In Quine's story, [(7) holds]. But we can continue the story to a later time at which Ralph's suspicions regarding even the man at the beach have begun to grow. Not that Ralph now proclaims that respected citizen to be a spy, but Ralph now suspends judgment as to the man's spyhood. At this time (7) is false. (pp. 141–142)

In Act II, Ralph has not changed his mind concerning whether the man in the brown hat is a spy. Thus (1), (2), and (6) are all still true. While (3) is still false— Ralph still does not believe that the man seen at the beach is a spy—Ralph no longer believes that the man seen at the beach is not a spy.

The important feature of Act II is that Ralph's suspension of judgment is not only *de dicto* but *de re*. Ralph's attitudes towards Ortcutt still conflict, but not in the straightforward manner of believing him to be a spy while also believing him not to be a spy. Concerning Ortcutt, Ralph believes him to be a spy while also actively

---

[13] *Cf.* my 'A Millian Heir Rejects the Wages of *Sinn*', in C. A. Anderson and J. Owens, eds, *Propositional Attitudes: The Role of Content in Logic, Language, and Mind* (Stanford: CSLI 1990), pp. 215–247, at 239–240. Kaplan does not explicitly regard (K6) as a consequence of a contextual definition for open 'that'-clauses; I suggest this merely as a possibly enlightening interpretation of his program. He proposes (K6) specifically as an analysis of (6), rather than of (4), which Quine had found improper. Kaplan does, however, suggest (114 *n*3) that instead of repudiating (4) altogether, it might be taken as analyzed by (6). Quine later came around to this same view, in 'Intensions Revisited', pp. 268, 274 *n*9.

[14] Quine appears to prefer this option. *Cf.* 'Quantifiers and Propositional Attitudes', section II. He there takes 'B_{dr}' to be *multi-grade*, i.e. 'letting it figure as an *n*-place predicate for each $n > 1$' ('Intensions Revisited', p. 268). This allows one to say that Ralph believes of the man in the brown hat and the man at the beach that the former is taller than the latter by writing 'Ralph B_{dr} (the man in the brown hat, the man at the beach, $\ulcorner\lambda xy[x \text{ is taller than } y]\urcorner$)'. The *de dicto* predicate 'B_{dd}' may then be taken to be the limiting case of 'B_{dr}' where $n = 2$. But how exactly does this give us (I)?

suspending judgment. Using 'SJ' as a predicate for suspension of judgment, both of the following are true in Act II:

Ralph B_{dd} that the man in the brown hat is a spy
Ralph SJ_{dd} that the man seen at the beach is a spy.

The consequences of the latter regarding belief are given by the following conjunction, which provides a kind of analysis of at the least the core meaning:

$\sim$[Ralph B_{dd} that the man seen at the beach is a spy] & $\sim$[Ralph B_{dd} that $\sim$(the man seen at the beach is a spy)].

Indeed, the truth of this conjunction with respect to Act II may simply be taken as stipulated.[15] Also true, partly in virtue of the foregoing, are the following:

(6) Ralph B_{dr} (the man seen at the beach, to be a spy)

(8) Ralph SJ_{dr} (the man seen at the beach, to be a spy).

Without analyzing *de re* belief in terms of *de dicto*, rendering (8) in terms of withheld belief poses a special difficulty. One is tempted to write:

$\sim$[Ralph B_{dr} (the man seen at the beach, to be a spy)] & $\sim$[Ralph B_{dr} (the man seen at the beach, $\sim$[to be a spy])].

But the first conjunct flies in the face of the continued truth of (6) in Act II. Not to mention that the second conjunct (which is the negation of (7)) is unjustified. We have no guarantee that Ralph is not acquainted with Ortcutt in some third way. The problem is to express the withheld belief of Ralph's new doxastic situation indicated by (8) consistently with (6).

The difficulty, according to Kaplan, is that the left conjunct above—the apparent negation of (6)—is ambiguous. He writes:

Cases of the foregoing kind, which agree with Quine's intuitions, argue an inadequacy in his regimentation of language. For in the same sense in which (7) and (6) do not express an inconsistency on Ralph's part, neither should (6) and ⌜$\sim$(6)⌝ express an inconsistency on ours. Indeed it seems natural to claim that ⌜$\sim$(6)⌝ is a consequence of (7). But the temptation to look upon (6) and ⌜$\sim$(6)⌝ as contradictory is extremely difficult to resist. The problem is that since Quine's 'B_{dr}' suppresses mention of the specific name [or concept] being exported, he cannot distinguish between

$(\exists\alpha)[R(\alpha,$ the seen man at the beach, Ralph$)$ & $\sim($Ralph B_{dd} ⌜α is a spy⌝$)]$

and

$\sim(\exists\alpha)[R(\alpha,$ the man seen at the beach, Ralph$)$ & Ralph B_{dd} ⌜α is a spy⌝$]$.

If ⌜$\sim$(6)⌝ is read as [the former], there is no inconsistency with (7); in fact on this interpretation ⌜$\sim$(6)⌝ is a consequence of (7) (at least on the assumption that Ralph does not have

---

[15] I criticize this analysis (which is Kaplan's, not mine) of suspension of judgment as being too strong, in my 'Being of Two Minds: Belief with Doubt', *Noûs* 29 (1995), pp. 1–20. There is no doubt in this case, however, that the conjunction is indeed true with respect to Act II.

contradictory beliefs). But if ⌜∼(6)⌝ is read as [the latter] (Quine's intention, I suppose) it is inconsistent with (6) and independent of (7).

So long as Ralph can believe of one person that he is two, as in Quine's story, we should be loath to make either [reading of ⌜∼(6)⌝] inexpressible.[16]

Analyzing *de re* suspension of judgment in terms of *de dicto* in the style of (*K*6) yields the following Kaplanesque analysis of (8):

(∃α)[**R**(α, the man seen at the beach, Ralph) & Ralph **SJ**$_{dd}$ ⌜α is a spy⌝].

The principal consequences of this regarding belief are summed up by:

(*K*8) (∃α)[**R**(α, the man seen at the beach, Ralph) & ∼(Ralph **B**$_{dd}$ ⌜α is a spy⌝) & ∼(Ralph **B**$_{dd}$ ⌜∼(α is a spy)⌝)].

This represents Kaplan's way of laying bare the withholding of belief expressed in (8). It is perfectly compatible with (*K*6). Both may be true so long as the two α's are different, as are *the man in the brown hat* and *the man seen at the beach*.

The ambiguity that Kaplan sees in ⌜∼(6)⌝ is precisely the Russellian primary-occurrence/secondary-occurrence ambiguity that arises in ⌜∼(5)⌝ on the contextual-definition interpretation of his project. The important point is not whether the reader (or the current writer) agrees that the alleged primary-occurrence reading is legitimate. Kaplan's principal point is that if ⌜∼(6)⌝ is interpreted so that it is the genuine negation of (6), then without analyzing *de re* suspension of judgment ultimately in terms of *de dicto* belief the withheld belief in (8) becomes inexpressible.

III

Tyler Burge has responded to Kaplan's argument, claiming (in effect) that Quine can analyze (8) as follows:

(∃α)[Ralph **B**$_{dr}$ (the man seen at the beach, ⌜(λz)(z = α)⌝) & Ralph **SJ**$_{dd}$ ⌜α is a spy⌝].

The consequences of this for belief may then be summarized by:

(*B*8) (∃α)[Ralph **B**$_{dr}$ (the man seen at the beach, ⌜(λz)(z = α)⌝) & ∼(Ralph **B**$_{dd}$ ⌜α is a spy⌝) & ∼(Ralph **B**$_{dd}$ ⌜∼(α is a spy)⌝)].[17]

That is, there is some individual concept *the such-and-such* whereby Ralph believes the man seen at the beach to be the such-and-such, but Ralph believes neither that the such-and-such is a spy nor that the such-and-such is not a spy. This existential claim is made true by the very concept, *the man seen at the beach*. Comparison of (*B*8) with (*K*8) reveals that, in effect, Burge rewrites Kaplan's representation clause '**R**(α, the man seen at the beach, Ralph)' in terms of *de re* belief. For Kaplan, this puts the cart

---

[16] *Ibid.*, 141. Here as elsewhere I have slightly altered the text for the purpose of matching numbered expressions with the numbers used in the present paper.

[17] In 'Kaplan, Quine, and Suspended Belief', p. 198. I have expanded on Burge's actual proposal, keeping to both its letter and spirit, in order to secure the full force of suspension of judgment as opposed to mere failure to believe.

before the horse; he invokes representation precisely to analyze *de re* belief in terms of *de dicto*. But reduction of *de re* to *de dicto* is precisely what Burge rejects. Burge offers (*B*8) as a Quinean analysis of *de re* suspension of judgment in terms of both *de dicto* and *de re* belief, with *de re* treated as primitive, or at least as unanalyzable in terms of *de dicto*.[18]

Ironically, the idea of replacing '$R(\alpha$, the man seen at the beach, Ralph)' with 'Ralph B_{dr} (the man seen at the beach, $\ulcorner(\lambda z)(z = \alpha)\urcorner)$' is originally due to Kaplan. He had suggested replacing (*K*6) with

(*B*6) $(\exists\alpha)$[Ralph B_{dr} (the man seen at the beach, $\ulcorner(\lambda z)[z = \alpha]\urcorner$) & Ralph $B_{dd}\ulcorner\alpha$ is a spy$\urcorner$].

Acknowledging that this is not equivalent to the supplanted notion, at least when (*B*6) is taken as analyzed by means of **R**-representation, Kaplan went on to say, 'Still this new notion of representation, when used in place of our current **R** in an analysis of the form of [(*K*6)], leads to the same relational sense of belief.'[19]

If Kaplan was correct about this, then he inadvertently showed the way to refutation of his argument against Quine. But he was not correct; the new notion does not strictly 'lead to the same sense' as the old. Analyzing (*B*6) in the style of Kaplan, one obtains (something equivalent to):

(*B*6*K*) $(\exists\beta)(\exists\alpha)$[$R(\alpha$, the man seen at the beach, Ralph) & Ralph $B_{dd}\ulcorner\alpha = \beta\urcorner$ & Ralph $B_{dd}\ulcorner\beta$ is a spy $\urcorner$].

This does not strictly entail (*K*6). Likewise, analyzing (*B*8) *à la* Kaplan in terms of '**R**', one obtains:

---

[18] Whereas Burge aims to refute Kaplan's argument for reducibility, he does not himself endorse the proposal he makes on Quine's behalf, and instead says that the conjunction of (6) with (8) may be formulated along the lines of something like:

Ralph believes the man seen at the beach to be *this man* and a spy, and Ralph neither believes the man seen at the beach to be *that man* and a spy nor believes the man seen at the beach to be *that man* and not a spy,

as spoken with three references to Ortcutt, in his guises as *this man* (in the brown hat) and as *that man* (seen at the beach). This proposal seriously distorts the very *de re* locutions it employs. Indeed, it contains a contradiction, its first conjunct expressing about Ortcutt exactly what the second conjunct denies.

[19] 'Quantifying In', p. 139 *n*30. Quine proposes (in 'Intensions Revisited', at pp. 272–273) taking $\ulcorner(\exists x)$[Ralph $B_{dr}(x, \ulcorner(\lambda z)(z = \alpha)\urcorner)]\urcorner$—e.g., 'There is someone whom Ralph takes to be the shortest spy'—as the further premiss required to validate the exportation inference from $\ulcorner$Ralph B_{dd} that α is a spy$\urcorner$ to $\ulcorner$Ralph B_{dr} (α, to be a spy)$\urcorner$. See note 10 above. Influenced by Jaakko Hintikka, Quine incorrectly glosses this proposed premiss as $\ulcorner$Ralph has an opinion as to who α is$\urcorner$. Even this stronger premiss, however, is not up to the task; suppose, for example, that Ralph is of the erroneous opinion that the shortest spy is none other than Ortcutt. See Igal Kvart, 'Quine and Modalities De Re: A Way Out?', *Journal of Philosophy* 79 (June 1982), pp. 295–328, at 298–302; and my 'How to Measure the Standard Meter', *Proceedings of the Aristotelian Society* (New Series) 88 (1987/1988) pp. 193–217, at 205–206, 213–214. Quine's intent may be better captured by taking the additional premiss to be instead $\ulcorner$Ralph B_{dr} ($\alpha, \ulcorner(\lambda z)(z = \alpha)\urcorner)\urcorner$—e.g., 'Ralph believes the shortest spy to be the shortest spy.' This move, in turn, suggests an analysis of (6) *à la* Kaplan/Burge into (*B*6) (perhaps as part of a general analysis of attributions of *de re* beliefs other than identity beliefs). The alternative premiss Kvart proposes, by comparison, suggests instead an analysis more along the lines of Kaplan's original (*K*6).

($B8K$) $(\exists\beta)(\exists\alpha)[R(\alpha,$ the man seen at the beach, Ralph) & Ralph $\mathbf{B}_{dd}\ulcorner\alpha = \beta\urcorner$ & $\sim$(Ralph $\mathbf{B}_{dd}\ulcorner\beta$ is a spy$\urcorner$) & $\sim$(Ralph $\mathbf{B}_{dd}\ulcorner\sim(\beta$ is a spy)$\urcorner$)],

which does not entail ($K8$). From Kaplan's perspective, the new notions are weaker than the old ones.

Why, then, does Kaplan say that the new notion of representation 'leads to the same relational sense'? As Burge notes (p. 199), ($K8$) is derivable from ($B8K$) using the additional premiss:

(9) $(\alpha)(\beta)$[Ralph $\mathbf{B}_{dd}\ulcorner\alpha = \beta\urcorner \rightarrow$ (Ralph $\mathbf{B}_{dd}\ulcorner\alpha$ is a spy$\urcorner \leftrightarrow$ Ralph $\mathbf{B}_{dd}\ulcorner\beta$ is a spy$\urcorner$) & (Ralph $\mathbf{B}_{dd}\ulcorner\sim(\alpha$ is a spy)$\urcorner \leftrightarrow$ Ralph $\mathbf{B}_{dd}\ulcorner\sim(\beta$ is a spy)$\urcorner$)].

This additional premiss also suffices to obtain ($K6$) from ($B6K$). No matter. If Kaplan leaned on some premiss like (9)—and it is unclear whether he did—Burge clearly does not. Instead, he objects that 'if Ralph is Everyman, (9) cannot be guaranteed' (p. 199). Burge does not specify the sort of circumstance he has in mind in which (9) fails, but there is no need for him to do so. Even the most thorough of logicians (let alone Everyman) does not draw all logically valid inferences from all his/her beliefs. Otherwise there would be no theorems of mathematics left to prove. Nothing as sweeping as (9) is even close to being true.

How, then, can Burge rely on the replacement strategy? He is not strictly committed, as Kaplan was, to analyzing ($B6$) into ($B6K$) and ($B8$) into ($B8K$). Nevertheless, he contends (evidently with Kaplan) that ($B8K$) successfully captures ($K8$), so that one attracted to Kaplan's analysis cannot object to ($B8$) on the ground that it does not render (8) equally as well as ($K8$) does. Burge cites the following considerations in support of this contention:

Now an obvious candidate for fulfilling the role of β [in ($B8K$)] is α itself. If we approve the candidate, and assume that Ralph believes $\ulcorner\alpha = \alpha\urcorner$, then ($B8K$) and ($K8$) indeed become strictly equivalent. ... The claim that everyone believes the self-identity statement for each 'representing' singular expression in his repertoire is fairly plausible. Even more plausible—and equally adequate in yielding equivalence between ($B8K$) and ($K8$)—is the Frege-like view that everyone believes *some* identity statement for each representing singular expression in his repertoire. (p. 199)

This argument is multiply flawed. To begin with, contrary to Burge the mentioned 'Frege-like view' is woefully inadequate to the task of yielding an implication of either ($K8$) by ($B8K$) or vice versa. It is unclear what Burge means by the obscure phrase 'approve a candidate for fulfilling the role of β'. Both ($K8$) and ($B8K$) follow from the assumption that Ralph believes $\ulcorner\alpha = \alpha\urcorner$ while believing neither $\ulcorner\alpha$ is a spy$\urcorner$ nor $\ulcorner\sim(\alpha$ is a spy)$\urcorner$, for some concept α that represents Ortcutt—such as perhaps the concept, *the man Ortcutt, whom I saw that time at the beach*. In this sense, one may derive ($B8K$) from the premiss that Ralph suspends judgment concerning whether the man at the beach is a spy and the further premiss that Ralph believes that the man at the beach is the man at the beach, by casting *the man at the beach* in the roles of both α and β in ($B8K$) (more precisely, by two judicious applications of Existential Generalization on an appropriately expanded variant of ($K8$)). But when going in the other direction, attempting to derive ($K8$) from ($B8K$), the latter is given and may be true in virtue of a pair of distinct concepts α and β. The roles of α and β

have already been cast; the task is to establish that Ralph lacks further relevant beliefs. Not only the 'Frege-like view', but even the stronger claim that Ralph believes the particular identity $\ulcorner \alpha = \alpha \urcorner$ whenever α is representing is inadequate to yield (K8) from (B8K) without the intervention of something like (9). In particular, the mere assumption that Ralph believes $\ulcorner \alpha = \alpha \urcorner$ in no way permits the replacement of (B8K) by the special case where α and β are the same.

To establish this, I submit Act III: A more decisive Ralph has become convinced that the man in the brown hat and the man at the beach are working in tandem. As regards Ortcutt, Ralph no longer suspends judgment whether he is a spy. On the contrary, Ralph believes him a spy twice over, as it were. Further, Ralph also happens to believe $\ulcorner \alpha = \alpha \urcorner$ for every individual concept α in his repertoire. In particular, Ralph believes that the man seen at the beach is the man seen at the beach. When queried, 'Which one, if any, is the most trusted man in town?' Ralph points to Ortcutt. As it turns out, Ralph is wrong about this; Wyman is more trusted than Ortcutt. When asked whether whoever is more trusted than every other man in town is a foreign spy, Ralph hesitates momentarily and wonders, ever so briefly, before inferring (much to his dismay) that the most trusted man is indeed a spy. Until he is through hesitating and finally makes the substitution—however brief the period of hesitation may be—Ralph suspends judgment whether the most trusted man in town is a spy, even while believing both that Ortcutt is most trusted and that he is a spy. (Burge presumably will not object to this hypothesis, given his rejection of (9). The hypothesis is in any case unobjectionable.)

Ralph's suspension of judgment whether the most trusted man is a spy cannot of itself constitute *de re* suspension of judgment about Ortcutt. Indeed, it does not even involve reference to Ortcutt. Since *the most trusted man in town* is a concept of (determines) Wyman and not Ortcutt, it cannot represent Ortcutt for Ralph in the requisite manner. With respect to Act III, (K8) remains false despite the truth of (B8K). Burge's response to Kaplan thus fails.

The significance of Act III extends beyond the fact that it yields a counter-model to Burge's contention that (K8) and (B8K) are alike in truth value if Ralph believes $\ulcorner \alpha = \alpha \urcorner$ for each of his representing concepts α. (K8) and (B8K) are Kaplan's analyses, respectively, of (8) and of (B8), the latter being Burge's proposal for capturing (8) without analyzing *de re* belief in terms of *de dicto*. But the general point does not specifically concern Kaplan's particular manner of analyzing *de re* into *de dicto*. Act III also directly refutes Burge's account of *de re* suspension of judgment. The principal difference between Act II and Act III is that in the former there is *de re* suspension of judgment concerning Ortcutt on the part of Ralph and in the latter there is not. Sentence (8) differentiates between the two acts, being true with respect to one and false (its negation true) with respect to the other. But (B8) is true with respect to both acts. Since it can be true even when (8) is false, Burge's attempt at capturing (8) through (B8) fails.

Strengthening Burge's clause 'Ralph B_{dr} (the man seen at the beach, $\ulcorner (\lambda z)(z = \alpha) \urcorner$)' to assert that Ralph has correct *de re* belief (or *de re* knowledge) does not solve the problem. Even if Ralph were correct in thinking that Ortcutt was the most trusted man, he may still hesitate before inferring that the most trusted man is a spy, thus satisfying the new formulation without thereby engaging in *de re* suspended judgment—unless one who believes that the shortest spy is a spy thereby engages in *de re* belief.[20]

IV

Burge's primary concern is to reject Kaplan's full-blooded reducibility. He objects that 'if one uses "denote" strictly, it is implausible that in all cases of *de re* belief, one of the believer's beliefs contains a thought symbol or individual concept that denotes the *res*' ('Belief *De Re*,' p. 351). By 'thought symbol or individual concept', Burge means a thoroughly conceptual or qualitative concept. The 'strict use of "denote" ' Burge intends is essentially Church's use of 'determines' for the binary relation (which is not context-relative) between a concept and its object.

On this point Burge and I are in complete agreement. The Twin-Earth considerations raised in the first paragraph are sufficient to demonstrate the point. But this point does not weaken Kaplan's argument, which is aimed at establishing that *de re* belief is reducible to *de dicto*. Even if the argument succeeds, it does nothing to establish Kaplan's particular, full-blooded way of carrying out the reduction. On the contrary, as I shall argue in the next section, with a certain modification the same argument can be redirected against Kaplan's reduction.

My own version of modest reducibility is this: that *de re* belief about an object x is nothing more or less than belief of the corresponding *singular proposition* (singular *dictum*)—a proposition that is about x by including x directly as a constituent, instead of a conceptual or intensional representation of x. Ironically, the principal argument in favor of this form of modest reducibility begins, and proceeds, nearly the same as Quine's argument against reducibility. It is this: The logical form of a *de re* attribution like (1) is better revealed by rewriting it as:

About Ortcutt, Ralph believes that he is a spy.

This is true in English if and only if its component open sentence,

(5′) Ralph believes that he is a spy,

(or 'Ralph B_{dd} that he is a spy') is true as spoken with reference to Ortcutt. That is, (1) is true if and only if (5′) is true under the assignment of Ortcutt to the pronoun 'he'. Indeed, the pronoun functions in (5′) exactly as the free variable does in (5). It is precisely this that disturbs Quine about (1). The variable/pronoun stands in a position in which what matters is not what is referred to but how it is referred to. By

---

[20] *Cf.* my *Frege's Puzzle* (Atascadero, Calif.: Ridgeview 1986, 1991), pp. 171–2. An alternative scenario is also possible in which Ralph believes (on the basis of general suspicions) that the most trusted man in any town is a spy, and knows Ortcutt to be the most trusted man in town, while not yet concluding about Ortcutt that he in particular must be a spy. Such a case refutes the analysis suggested in note 19 above. Intuitively, one who believes that whoever is most trusted among men in town is a spy does not *ipso facto* believe of the most trusted man, *de re*, that he is a spy. (Notice that the description 'the most trusted man in town', like 'the shortest spy', qualifies neither as *vivid*, nor as a *name of* its referent, in Kaplan's quasi-technical senses.)

pure English semantics alone, (1) is true if and only if Ralph believes the proposition expressed by 'He is a spy' under the assignment of Ortcutt to 'he'. This is also the proposition expressed by the open sentence 'x is a spy' under the assignment of Ortcutt to 'x'. Quine could not make sense of this because of a severe limitation he implicitly imposed—following Frege, and to a lesser extent, Russell—on the range of propositions potentially believed by Ralph, no one of which by Quine's reckoning has yet been singled out. Granted, the proposition expressed by 'He is a spy' under the assignment of Ortcutt to 'he' is neither that the man seen at the beach is a spy nor that the man in the brown hat is a spy. It is a third proposition, I say, independent of these others and dismissed by Frege, Russell, and Quine as no possible object of belief by Ralph. Following Russell, we may say that the variable/pronoun in (5)/(5') functions as a 'logically proper name' of its assigned referent. The open sentence expresses a singular proposition about Ortcutt, the proposition that *he* is a spy.[21]

Accordingly, I have suggested that (2), and hence also (6), should be analyzed in terms of propositional belief not by ($K6$) but instead by means of (something trivially equivalent to):

(S6) (λx)[Ralph $\mathbf{B_{dd}}$ that x is a spy](the man seen at the beach).

This may be read, 'The man seen at the beach is such that Ralph believes that he is a spy.' (S6) is classically equivalent to (4). Whereas (4) provides for a logical form that in some respects mirrors that of ($K6$), the underlying idea is very different. It is that (2) ascribes to Ralph belief of a singular proposition about the man seen at the beach. *De re* belief is *de dicto* belief of a singular *dictum* about the *res*.[22]

In addition, I have suggested that a propositional-belief attribution like (3) be analyzed as follows by means of the existential generalization of a ternary relation, **BEL**, which holds among a believer, a proposition, and something like a *proposition guise* or *way of taking* the proposition when the believer agrees to the proposition taking it that way:

($\exists x$)[Ralph **BEL** (that the man seen at the beach is a spy, x)].[23]

Putting these two proposals together, I analyze (6) as:

(S6') $(\lambda x)[(\exists y)$(Ralph **BEL** [that x is a spy, y])](the man seen at the beach).

---

[21] Cf. *Frege's Puzzle*, 2–7. See also my 'How to Become a Millian Heir', *Noûs* 23 (1989), pp. 211–220; and 'A Millian Heir Rejects the Wages of *Sinn*', pp. 223–227.

[22] 'Relational Belief', p. 216. The analysis is broadly Russellian in spirit. However, Russell himself embraced an epistemology that prevented him from accepting the analysis (and which may be part of the original motivation for his multiple-relation theory of *de re* belief). Quine also rejects it. Indeed, this is what led Quine to propose replacing (2) with something along the lines of (6). His objections, however, are dubious. See Kaplan, 'Opacity', in L. E. Hahn and P. A. Schilpp, eds, *The Philosophy of W. V. Quine* (La Salle: Open Court 1986), pp. 229–289; and my 'Relational Belief'.

Identifying the singular proposition about Ortcutt that he is a spy with the corresponding ordered pair, the proposed analysis of (6) might be revealingly reformulated as: 'Ralph $\mathbf{B_{dr}}$ (the man seen at the beach, to be a spy) $=_{def.}$ Ralph $\mathbf{B_{dd}}$ <the man seen at the beach, to be a spy>.'

[23] More exactly, my view is that the dyadic predicate '$\mathbf{B_{dd}}$' is definable as: '$(\lambda x p)[(\exists y)(x \; \mathbf{BEL}[p, y])]$.'

That is, the man seen at the beach is such that Ralph agrees to the proposition that he is a spy, taking it in at least one way in which he grasps it. Like Kaplan's rival analysis, this analysis also accommodates inference (*I*).

Analyzing (*B6*) in the manner I propose, at the first stage one obtains:

(*B6S*) $(\exists \beta)[(\lambda x)[\text{Ralph } \mathbf{B}_{dd} \ulcorner x = \beta \urcorner]$ (the man seen at the beach) & Ralph $\mathbf{B}_{dd} \ulcorner \beta$ is a spy $\urcorner$].

Just as (*B6K*) does not strictly yield (*K6*), (*B6S*) is weaker than (*S6*). An additional premiss like (9) (except with its bound variable 'α' interpreted as ranging over singular-term-contents, construed as including individuals as well as individual concepts) is required in order to derive (*S6*) from (*B6S*).[24]

V

I analyze (8) thus:

(*S8*) $(\lambda x)[(\exists y)[\text{Ralph grasps the proposition that } x \text{ is a spy by means of } y \ \&\ \sim(\text{Ralph } \mathbf{BEL}$ [that x is a spy, y]) & $\sim$(Ralph **BEL** [that $\sim$(x is a spy), y])]](the man seen at the beach).

There are numerous similarities between (*K6*) and (*S6'*), as well as between (*K8*) and (*S8*). In particular, the analyses claim to uncover a hidden existential quantifier, which may joust with a negation sign for dominant position. This *existentialism* (to coin a term) is brought out in cases of *de re* suspended judgment, in which the negation is inserted after the existential quantifier. Despite his decidedly differing philosophical outlook, Burge's (*B8*) also capitalizes on Kaplan's discovery of the existential quantifier internal to *de re* suspended judgment. Like (*K8*), (*S8*) is true with respect to Act II but false with respect to Act III. Hence (*B8*), which is true with respect to Act III, is not equivalent to (*S8*), nor is (*S8*) derivable from (*B8*) together with the premiss that Ralph believes $\ulcorner \alpha = \alpha \urcorner$ for every individual concept α that he grasps.

These similarities obscure the important differences that remain between Kaplan's analysis and mine. Foremost, where my existential quantifier ranges over proposition guises, or ways of taking propositions, Kaplan's ranges over thoroughly conceptual or qualitative individual concepts (or over singular terms expressing such concepts). It is essentially this feature of Kaplan's analysis that both Burge and I (and Kaplan today) find objectionable. (See note 12 above.) Kaplan located the hidden existential quantifier in the use of open 'that'-clauses, like 'that he is a spy' and 'that x is a spy', which have no meaning in isolation even under the assignment of a value to its free pronoun/variable. In effect, Kaplan found existentialism in the very nature of *de re* propositional attribution. By contrast, I locate it in the particular phenomenon of belief. By my account, there is no logical reason to expect an analogous existentialism

---

[24] Alternatively, something like Kaplan's full-blooded reducibility thesis might be invoked as a third premiss in addition to (9), thus removing (*B6S*) still further from (*S6*). Alternatively, the 'α' may be replaced by an objectual variable. Analogously, Kaplan may have intended a version of (9) in which 'α' ranges only over 'representing' names, in his sense, while 'β' is not similarly restricted. Burge's objection that the relevant version of (9) is not guaranteed is appropriate regardless.

to occur in connection with all propositional attributions—including for example in 'Ralph proved that' or 'It is necessary that'.[25] Indeed, if there is a primary-occurrence/secondary-occurrence ambiguity in ⌜∼(5)⌝ under the assignment of the man at the beach as value for the variable 'x', there is no like ambiguity in 'It is not necessary that there be n planets' under the assignment of the number of planets to the variable 'n' (nor in '∼[N_{dr} (the number of planets, to number the planets)]').

On the other side of the coin, on my account there is also no logical reason why the competition for dominance between the existential quantifier and negation should not occur also with *de dicto* belief. In fact it does. Kripke's famous puzzle about belief includes such a case.[26] Before presenting the puzzle Kripke emphasizes that it concerns *de dicto* belief rather than *de re*. He says:

> the *de dicto* or 'small scope' reading ... is the *only* reading, for belief contexts ... that will concern us ... *de re* beliefs—as in 'Jones believes, *of* Cicero (or: *of* his favorite Latin author), that he was bald'—do *not* concern us in this paper. Such contexts, if they make sense, are by definition subject to a substitutivity principle for both names and descriptions. Rather we are concerned with the *de dicto* locution expressed explicitly in such formulations as, 'Jones believes that: Cicero was bald' (or: 'Jones believes that: the man who denounced Catiline was bald'). The material after the colon expresses the *content* of Jones's belief. Other, more explicit formulations are: 'Jones believes the proposition—that—Cicero—was—bald', or even in the 'formal' mode, 'The sentence "Cicero was bald" gives the content of a belief of Jones.' (pp. 105–6)

In Kripke's original example, a Frenchman, Pierre, comes to believe on the basis of cleverly crafted travel brochures that London is pretty—or as he would put it, that '*Londres est jolie*'. Later he is hijacked to an unattractive part of London, and after learning the native language through assimilation (not through an ESL class or a French–English dictionary), he comes to believe that London is not pretty, without realizing that the cities he knows by the names 'London' and '*Londres*' are one and the same. Even now that he is disposed, on reflection, to assent sincerely to 'London is not pretty', Pierre continues to assent sincerely and reflectively also to '*Londres est jolie*'. Kripke constructs a puzzle by pressing the question: Does Pierre believe that London is pretty? The question is not whether Pierre believes *of* London, *de re*, that it is pretty. That issue is easily settled. Like Ralph with respect to Ortcutt and his possible hidden agenda in Act I, Pierre both believes London to be pretty and disbelieves London to be pretty. But as Kripke has emphasized, his question is not this. Using our notation, we may say that Kripke is concerned not with

Pierre **B**$_{dr}$ (London, to be pretty),

which (along with 'Pierre **B**$_{dr}$ [London, ∼(to be pretty)]') is undoubtedly true with respect to the example, but with

(10) Pierre **B**$_{dd}$ that London is pretty.

---

[25] *Cf.* 'A Millian Heir Rejects the Wages of *Sinn*', especially pp. 234–247.
[26] Saul Kripke, 'A Puzzle about Belief', in N. Salmon and S. Soames, eds, *Propositions and Attitudes* (Oxford University Press 1988), pp. 102–148.

Kripke forcefully argues that any possible response to the question of whether (10) is true is beset with serious conceptual difficulties.

Kripke argues further that it is imprudent to draw any conclusions, positive or negative, with respect to the question. Nevertheless perhaps most commentators—including myself—are persuaded that (10), as well as

(11) Pierre $\mathbf{B}_{dd}$ that $\sim$(London is pretty),

are indeed true with respect to Kripke's example. In short, I and others charge Pierre not merely with inconsistency, but with believing a contradiction. One lesson of Kripke's puzzle is that not all contradictory beliefs subject the believer to justifiable censure.[27]

Finding this conclusion unwarranted, Kripke considers a modified case for which such a conclusion is ruled out by hypothesis:

> Suppose Pierre's neighbors think that since they rarely venture outside their own ugly section, they have no right to any opinion as to the pulchritude of the whole city. Suppose Pierre shares their attitude. Then, judging by his failure to respond affirmatively to 'London is pretty', we may judge, from Pierre's behavior as an *English* speaker, that he lacks the belief that London is pretty: never mind whether he disbelieves it, as before, or whether, as in the modified story, he insists that he has no firm opinion on the matter.
>
> Now ... we can derive a contradiction, not merely in Pierre's judgments, but in our own. For on the basis of his behavior as an English speaker, we concluded that he does *not* believe that London is pretty (that is, that it is not the case that he believes that London is pretty). But on the basis of his behavior as a *French* speaker, we must conclude that he *does* believe that London is pretty. This is a contradiction.   (pp. 122–3)

As with Ralph in Act II, Pierre now both believes London to be pretty and suspends judgment. Despite the *déjà vu* of this second act, the transition from one act to the next in Kripke's drama raises at least one very significant issue not raised in Kaplan's continuation of Quine's tale. As Kripke has laid out the problem, it is not to reconcile Pierre's *de re* belief about London with his *de re* suspension of judgment. Kaplan has indicated one way to do this. The new problem is that Pierre seems for all the world to have a *de dicto* belief that London is pretty, on the one hand, but equally seems for all the world to harbor *de dicto* suspended judgment. With respect to Kripke's new act, it would appear that (10) is true together not with (11) (which is clearly false) but with:

(12) Pierre $\mathbf{SJ}_{dd}$ that London is pretty.

(Compare (6) and (8) above.) Kaplan's treatment of suspension of judgment expresses the withheld belief in (12) by:

(K12) $\sim$[Pierre $\mathbf{B}_{dd}$ that London is pretty] & $\sim$[Pierre $\mathbf{B}_{dd}$ that $\sim$(London is pretty)].

But as Kripke emphasizes, this directly contradicts (10).

---

[27] I respond to Kripke's puzzle, and to his objections to the solution I propose, in *Frege's Puzzle*, pp. 129–132; and in 'Illogical Belief', in J. Tomberlin, ed., *Philosophical Perspectives, 3: Philosophy of Mind and Action Theory* (Atascadero, Calif.: Ridgeview 1989), pp. 243–285.

As I see it, Kripke's puzzle is a problem of reconciliation. (Kripke sees it somewhat differently.) In this version of the puzzle, the problem is this: How can Pierre's belief that London is pretty be reconciled with his suspended judgment? In this respect, it is like the reconciliation problem in Kaplan's Act II. The difference is that Kaplan's problem concerned *de re* belief where Kripke's concerns *de dicto*. Although the two reconciliation problems are variants of one another, Kaplan's solution to the *de re* version does not extend in any straightforward manner to the *de dicto*. For Kaplan's analysis of (8) into (*K*8) does not yield a straightforward analogue for (12); and indeed, his account of suspended judgment leads directly from (12) to (*K*12), whose differences with (10) are irreconcilable. What is wanted is a uniform solution to both the *de re* and the *de dicto* versions of the general reconciliation problem.

Kripke also notes (in connection with his Paderewski example) that the general problem does not in the end turn on issues concerning translation between languages. Nor does the general problem turn on a peculiarity of proper names. The same problem arises in connection with some general terms. Elsewhere I have proposed the strange case of Sasha, who believes that the condiment called 'ketchup' is supposed to be used with certain sandwiches, while the condiment called 'catsup', which he wrongly takes to be distinct from ketchup, is supposed to be used instead with scrambled eggs. Suppose Sasha is persuaded that ketchup tastes good on hamburgers but claims to have no opinion concerning whether catsup does. Or again consider the confused native Santa Barbaran who sincerely declares, 'When I was in England I tasted a terrific sauce made from toe-**mah**-toes. I wonder whether toe-**mae**-toes could be made into as good a sauce.' Whether Kaplan's strategy for dealing with *de re* suspension of judgment is successful or not, it has no obvious extension to this case of *de dicto* suspended judgment. The almost exact analogy between the problems posed by suspension of judgment in the *de re* and *de dicto* cases strongly suggests that a correct solution to any should apply to each.[28]

Pierre's suspended judgment does not pose the same problem for my account that it does for Kaplan's. I propose analyzing (10) and (12) into the following:

(*S*10) $(\exists x)$[Pierre **BEL** (that London is pretty, x)]

(*S*12) $(\exists y)$[Pierre grasps that London is pretty by means of y & $\sim$(Pierre **BEL** [that London is pretty, y]) & $\sim$(Pierre **BEL** [that $\sim$(London is pretty), y])].

No contradiction follows from (*S*10) and (*S*12). The desired reconciliation is achieved. What does follow is that the x and the y are distinct proposition guises. In the example these are given to Pierre by the distinct sentences '*Londres est jolie*' and 'London is pretty', respectively.

The reconciliation is made possible through the limited commitments of (*S*12) as compared to those of (*K*12). Following the originator of the reconciliation problem, one might argue as follows:

---

[28] 'A Millian Heir Rejects the Wages of *Sinn*', pp. 220–222. It is difficult to see how one can maintain that the belief that tomatoes make a good sauce is not a belief of a certain proposition (but instead a relation to various entities) without committing oneself to the conclusion that no belief is of a proposition.

Cases of the foregoing kind, which agree with Kaplan's intuitions, argue an inadequacy in his regimentation of language. For in the same sense in which (10) and (11) do not express a censurable inconsistency on Pierre's part, neither should (10) and (12) express an inconsistency on ours. But the temptation to look upon (10) and (K12) as contradictory is extremely difficult to resist. So long as Ralph or Pierre can believe of one person or city that it is two, as in Quine's, Kaplan's, and Kripke's stories, we should be loath to make either (S8) or (S12) inexpressible.

If examples like Kaplan's involving belief combined with suspension of judgment argue that *de re* belief is reducible to *de dicto*, they equally argue that the existentialism in terms of which the reduction proceeds is not peculiar to the *de re* notion, but internal to the *de dicto* notion. Recognition of this fact paves the way for modest reducibility in lieu of the more full-blooded variety. Through reconciliation comes insight.[29]

[29] *Cf. Frege's Puzzle*, pp. 92–128.

PART IV
SEMANTICS AND PRAGMATICS

16

Assertion and Incomplete Definite Descriptions (1982)

I

In a recent paper, Howard Wettstein has argued that Donnellan's referential–attributive distinction is a genuinely semantic distinction and not merely a pragmatic one.[1] I shall argue here that Wettstein does not succeed in establishing his thesis. In so doing, I shall offer certain examples which tend to show that the common phenomenon of so-called indefinite (Donnellan) or incomplete (Tyler Burge) or contextually (David Lewis) definite descriptions—i.e., improper descriptions like 'the table' which, on a given occasion of use, denote a specific object underspecified by the description itself—have a more complex semantics than is sometimes supposed.

Wettstein correctly notes that Donnellan's original, and for some reason controversial, idea that referential uses of definite descriptions succeed in referring to the intended individual regardless of whether that individual in fact satisfies the description, is inessential to the main idea behind the referential–attributive distinction. Given the current dispute over the issue of reference to an individual not satisfying the description, the best way to approach the question of whether the referential–attributive distinction is of semantic significance is precisely as Wettstein proposes: we may sidestep this apparently irrelevant controversy by confining our attention to cases where the intended referent *does* satisfy the description, or to use a terminology employed by both Donnellan and Kripke, cases where, as it happens, speaker's reference and semantic reference coincide.[2] Following Wettstein, then, I

---

[1] 'Demonstrative Reference and Definite Descriptions', *Philosophical Studies* 40 (1981), pp. 241–257. The present chapter was originally delivered as commentary on Wettstein's paper at a meeting of the Pacific Division of the American Philosophical Association on March 28, 1980. For an argument similar in outline to Wettstein's, see Michael Devitt, 'Donnellan's Distinction', in French, Uehling, and Wettstein (eds), *Midwest Studies in Philosophy VI: The Foundations of Analytic Philosophy* (University of Minnesota Press, Minneapolis, 1981), pp. 511–524.

[2] See Keith Donnellan, 'Speaker Reference, Descriptions, and Anaphora', and Saul Kripke, 'Speaker's Reference and Semantic Reference', in French, Uehling, and Wettstein (eds), *Contemporary Perspectives in the Philosophy of Language* (University of Minnesota Press, Minneapolis, 1979) pp. 6–27, and 28–44, respectively. Donnellan's use of the term 'speaker's reference' does not quite coincide with Kripke's; Donnellan reserves the term for the so-called 'referential' case, in which there is someone in particular to whom the speaker intends to refer, whereas Kripke applies the term also to cases in which the speaker has only the general intention to refer to whoever is the semantic referent. I shall conform to Kripke's usage throughout.

shall restrict my investigation to sentences like 'Smith's murderer is insane', as uttered with the intention of predicating insanity of someone in particular, who, it happens, really is Smith's actual murderer. In such cases, of course, the individual referred to, and consequently the truth-value of what is expressed, are ordinarily unaffected by the fact of whether the description is used referentially or attributively. The question of reference and/or truth-value with respect to the actual world becomes irrelevant. The referential–attributive distinction will show itself, if at all, in the matter of which proposition is expressed. If the distinction is a genuine semantic distinction, different uses of the description will result in different propositions, in the straightforward sense that the truth-conditions of the sentence, as uttered by the speaker, will depend on whether the description is used referentially or attributively. If the distinction is one with genuine semantic import, then the sentence 'Smith's murderer is insane', when its contained description is used attributively, should express a (partly) general proposition true with respect to a possible world w just in case exactly one person murdered Smith in w and that murderer in w is insane in w; whereas this same sentence, with the description used referentially, should express a singular proposition true with respect to a possible world w just in case the particular individual Jones, Smith's *actual* murderer, is insane in w, whether or not he murders Smith in w.[3]

Wettstein rightly recognizes that it is indeed this alleged difference in propositional content—in the straightforward sense of a divergence in truth-conditions—that lies at the heart of the notion of a semantically significant referential–attributive distinction. Is there really such a divergence? Nobody disagrees that the sentence, when used attributively, expresses a (partly) general proposition which is true if and only if some unique murderer of Smith is insane. But if the sentence is used referentially, will the singular proposition about Jones result instead of the (more) general proposition? That is the question. Let us call it *the question of semantic significance of the referential use*. The *thesis of semantic significance* is the thesis that sentences involving definite descriptions are semantically ambiguous, in the sense that the proposition expressed is either singular or general, in the relevant sense, according as the description is used referentially or attributively.

Wettstein's argument for semantic significance, briefly, is this. Modifying Donnellan's original example slightly, a speaker may use a sentence like 'The murderer is insane' to make a determinate statement about a contextually relevant murderer, Jones. It is implausible to suppose that the expression 'the murderer' must function here as a shorthand or abbreviation for some one proper (i.e., uniquely identifying) description of Jones, such as 'Harry Smith's murderer' or 'the murderer of Sally Smith's husband'. For the speaker need not have intended any one such fuller specification of Jones to the exclusion of all the other possible specifications. Several different possible specifications may have equal claim to conformity with

---

[3] The terminology of 'singular' and 'general' propositions is David Kaplan's. See his 'Dthat' in French *et al.*, pp. 383–400. I call the first proposition *partly* general because even it is singular with respect to the position occupied by Smith, though it is general with respect to the position occupied by Smith's murderer. To use Russellian jargon, Smith does, but his murderer does not, *occur as a constituent* of the first proposition. This situation is reversed in the second proposition.

the speaker's intentions, each yielding a different general proposition to the effect that some unique murderer satisfying such-and-such a specification is insane. Yet the speaker's remark is not multiply ambiguous; a fully determinate assertion was made. How can this be possible? The speaker must have used the incomplete specification 'the murderer' referentially, Wettstein argues, and the proposition expressed is the singular proposition about Jones that he is insane. Nevertheless, in another sort of case, a speaker may utter the very same sentence, 'The murderer is insane', using the description attributively to refer to Jones. In this case, the description involves implicit reference to the victim, and has the force of '*his* murderer'. The proposition expressed here is the singular proposition about the victim to the effect that some unique murderer of him is insane. Hence, there is a referential–attributive distinction for expressions like 'the murderer' and 'the table', and the referential use of such expressions is semantically significant.

Incomplete or contextually definite descriptions like 'the table' provide the most difficult case for one, such as myself, who wishes to maintain that the content, or truth-conditions, of a sentence involving a term which, at least at the level of surface syntax, would appear to be a singular definite description, are unaffected by the fact of whether the description is used referentially or attributively. Donnellan (*op. cit.*) urged consideration of incomplete definite descriptions in support of his thesis of semantic significance, arguing that it is not always plausible to regard these phrases as elliptical for some more fully specified descriptive phrase to be supplied by presumed shared background assumptions in the context of use, or something similar. Even Kripke, perhaps the staunchest opponent of the thesis of semantic significance of the referential use in the case of complete definite descriptions, softens his opposition considerably in the case of incomplete descriptions. In 'Speaker's Reference and Semantic Reference' he writes:

Although [Russell's] theory does a far better job of handling ordinary discourse than many have thought, and although many popular arguments against it are inconclusive, probably it ultimately fails. The considerations I have in mind have to do with the existence of 'improper' definite descriptions, such as 'the table', where uniquely specifying conditions are not contained in the description itself. Contrary to the Russellian picture, I doubt that such descriptions can always be regarded as elliptical with some uniquely specifying conditions added. And it may even be the case that a true picture will resemble various aspects of Donnellan's in important respects...[4].

... It seems to me likely that 'indefinite' definite descriptions such as 'the table' present difficulties for a Russellian analysis. It is somewhat tempting to assimilate such descriptions to the corresponding demonstrative (for example, 'that table') and to the extent that such a temptation turns out to be plausible, there may be new arguments in such cases for the intuitions of those who have advocated a rigid vs. non-rigid ambiguity in definite descriptions, or for Donnellan's intuitions concerning the referential case, or for both.[5]

These remarks are hedged, but they strongly suggest that the thesis of semantic significance may prevail, at least with regard to the case of incomplete definite descriptions, for just the reasons urged by Donnellan, Wettstein, and others.

[4] pp. 6–7.   [5] Ibid., p. 22.

This would be an important concession. By far and away the most common use in ordinary discourse of phrases constructed from the definite article is one that relies on supplementation by the context to secure a definite reference. As Wettstein notes, it would seem that this use is often intended even in cases where, by chance, the form of words chosen already happens to fit something uniquely, without further reliance on the context. Kripke's contention that the referential use has only pragmatic significance rings hollow if it has to be restricted to a class of rarely used, if not entirely artificial, expressions.

II

Does the case of incomplete definite descriptions show that the referential use is semantically significant, in the sense defined earlier? H. P. Grice draws a distinction between what he calls *utterer's meaning* and *sentence meaning*.[6] The former notion is pragmatic: what the speaker means in uttering a particular sentence. The latter notion is semantic: what the sentence itself means. Following Grice, Kripke has distinguished between speaker's reference and semantic reference in arguing against the existence of a semantic referential–attributive ambiguity. Kripke's arguments, however, are aimed at least to some extent against the stronger thesis that referentially used definite descriptions denote the intended individual—the speaker's referent—even if that individual does not actually satisfy the description, i.e., even if that individual is not the semantic referent. We have agreed to set aside such cases in order to investigate the more restricted question of semantic significance, as I have defined it. With respect to our question—whether referential use results in a singular proposition about the referent—a distinction such as Grice's in terms of sentence meaning, or propositional content, is the relevant one. Let us distinguish between what I shall call the *speaker assertion* and the *semantic content* of a particular sentence utterance. The semantic content of an utterance may be identified with the proposition expressed by the uttered sentence with respect to the context of the utterance. If the sentence contains demonstratives or other context-sensitive items, it will express a different proposition with respect to different contexts of use. Hence, the general notion of semantic content is relativized to the context of use. The speaker assertion of an utterance is whatever proposition, if any, the speaker succeeds in asserting by performing the utterance. Speaker assertion is a pragmatic notion.

Of course, one hopes and expects that speaker assertion and semantic content will ordinarily bear a close relation to one another. In particular, one hopes and expects that on at least some occasions, in fact in any ordinary circumstances, if a speaker utters a sentence, he or she thereby asserts the very same proposition which is the semantic content of the sentence with respect to that context of use. But the fact that speaker assertion and semantic content may diverge is a familiar one. Rhetorical questions express no declarative proposition as semantic content, though that does not

---

[6] See his 'Utterer's Meaning, Sentence-Meaning and Word Meaning', *Foundations of Language* 4 (1968), pp. 225–242.

prevent the speaker from asserting some declarative proposition in the utterance. If a parent disciplines her child by yelling at him, 'You will eat your spinach', or better, 'You will eat your spinach and like it!', the semantic content may be false, though the parent may have intended to be construed as issuing a directive, and not as making a true-or-false prediction. In cases of irony or sarcasm, the speaker may succeed in asserting the very negation of the semantic content of his or her words. More importantly for the present purpose, in uttering a sentence with only a single proposition as semantic content, the speaker may nevertheless succeed in asserting several different propositions simultaneously. I believe, for example, that ordinarily, in asserting the general proposition that the so-and-so is such-and-such, the speaker may be plausibly regarded as having automatically also asserted the materially equivalent, but not strictly equivalent, singular proposition about the so-and-so that it (he or she) is such-and-such.[7] If I am correct, then in many utterances, speaker assertion and semantic content must be distinguished, if only because the former outnumber the latter. In case of semantic ambiguity, this situation is precisely reversed: semantic contents outnumber speaker's assertion.

Insofar as speaker assertion and semantic content diverge, the question of semantic significance of the referential use is concerned primarily with semantic content and not speaker assertion. The question is whether a sentence like 'Smith's murderer is insane' expresses the singular proposition about Jones as its content with respect to a context in which the sentence is used referentially, rather than the (more) general proposition true with respect to a possible world w just in case Smith's murderer in w is insane in w. This question is concerned primarily and directly with the content of *the very words* 'Smith's murderer is insane', and at least not directly with what the speaker may succeed in asserting or conveying to his or her audience. Wettstein's discussion, like Donnellan's original paper and most other discussions of these and related issues, suffers from a failure to keep separate the notions of speaker assertion and semantic content. Our main concern is with what the *words* express as their semantic content *with respect to* the relevant context of use. In order to establish the thesis of semantic significance of the referential use, it will not do simply to show that in using a sentence referentially one thereby asserts the relevant singular proposition. For the speaker may

---

[7] *Cf.* John Searle, 'Referential and Attributive', *Monist* 62 (1979), pp. 190–208, where a distinction is drawn between primary and secondary illocutionary acts performed in a single utterance by way of (what Donnellan calls) a referential use of a definite description. Searle rejects the referential–attributive distinction, as it is drawn by Donnellan. His objections are extended also to the *de re–de dicto* distinction, as it is sometimes drawn, and would no doubt be meant to apply to the referential–attributive distinction as it is drawn by Wettstein in his attempt to resurrect the semantic significance thesis. I do not accept Searle's objections to either the referential–attributive distinction or the *de re–de dicto* distinction (taken as a distinction between types of propositions), but I find the independent idea of a distinction between primary and secondary speaker assertions in a single utterance both plausible and a serious obstacle to Wettstein's argument for the semantic significance thesis. Unlike Searle, I maintain that one of the speaker assertions—what Searle calls the primary one—made by means of a referential use is a singular proposition, rather than some further general proposition independent of the semantic content literally expressed.

also assert a relevant general proposition simultaneously. In any case, the relevant question is not what the speaker manages to assert, but what his or her words express.

Wettstein's argument for semantic significance of the referential use by way of incomplete definite descriptions can be reformulated to focus explicitly on semantic content. But when the issue is sharpened in this way, much, if not all, of the intuitive force behind his argument seems to vanish. Consider again Wettstein's example of the speaker's utterance of 'The murderer is insane', using the incomplete description 'the murderer' referentially to refer to Jones. It is plausible to maintain that the speaker asserts (at least) the singular proposition about Jones that he is insane. But I, for one, find it much less plausible to suppose that the proposition expressed by the sentence, as completed by the contextual factors of the occasion of use—i.e., the semantic content of the sentence—is this same singular proposition rather than some more general proposition to the effect that the murderer relevant to certain interests or to a certain *situation*, as delineated by the context, is insane. A proponent of the semantic significance thesis such as Wettstein, must maintain that the sentence 'The murderer is insane', as used on this occasion, is true with respect to any possible world in which Jones is insane, even if Smith is alive and well, Jones is no murderer at all, and in fact, no murders are committed by anyone anywhere. It seems quite clear, however, that the sentence 'The murderer is insane' is not true with respect to such a world, and indeed, it seems quite clear that the phrase 'the murderer' does not denote anyone, not even Jones, with respect to such a world.

Consider also the following kind of example. Suppose that the speaker, upon taking a closer look at the suspect, recognizes him to be his child's babysitter, Jones. He may exclaim with great terror and alarm 'My gosh! The murderer is *Jones*; Jones is the babysitter; the murderer and the babysitter are one and the same!' We may suppose that in each occurrence the singular terms involved are used referentially. Notice here that the two descriptions 'the murderer' and 'the babysitter' are incomplete. Now I believe that a case can be made for the hypothesis that among the things accomplished by the speaker in his outburst were three consecutive assertings of a certain singular proposition about Jones, namely, the necessary truth about Jones that he and himself are identical. But even so, that has to do with speaker assertion, rather than with the primary question of semantic content. A proponent of the semantic significance thesis should maintain that each of the three identity statements uttered expresses this same singular proposition as its semantic content with respect to the relevant context. That would mean that the three sentences express necessary truths, (or at least propositions true with respect to every possible world in which Jones exists). But it is quite clear that *none* of the three sentences express necessary truths. While it may be true that the murderer and the babysitter are in fact Jones, surely it is not a *necessary* truth that the murderer is one and the same person as the babysitter. The sentence 'The murderer and the babysitter are identical' cannot be true with respect to a possible world in which the speaker has no children, Smith has no murderer, and Jones, though he exists, is neither murderer nor babysitter. In fact, a proponent of the thesis of semantic significance must make the implausible claim that the sentence 'The murderer and the babysitter are identical' is true even with respect to a possible world in which there are no murderers or babysitters, as long as Jones exists there.[8] Faced with examples such as these, and backed against the distinction between speaker assertion and semantic content, I see no convincing defensive strategy for the thesis of semantic significance.

III

One important question raised by these examples remains unanswered. How do incomplete descriptions such as 'the murderer' and 'the babysitter' manage to secure a definite reference when their content is incomplete, and therefore inadequate to do the job alone? As Donnellan, Kripke, and Wettstein all note, it is not always plausible to regard such phrases as elliptical for some more fully specified yet thoroughly descriptive phrases floating in reach just overhead. Yet my examples suggest that descriptive content is crucial in securing reference, at least to the extent that nothing failing to satisfy what little descriptive content there is to be found in the wording may count as the semantic referent. What then supplements this meager descriptive content to achieve the definite reference? This is the keenest and most pressing question raised in Wettstein's paper. What I should want to suggest is, in effect, a certain unified account, which combines the differing accounts offered by Wettstein of the referential and attributive uses of incomplete descriptions like 'the murderer' into a single semantic treatment of incomplete descriptions. It is important to notice in this connection that, despite Wettstein's argument against the strategy of regarding incomplete descriptions as elliptical for complete ones, his own account of the attributive use of 'the murderer' seems to involve something very much like treating it as elliptical for '*his* murderer' or 'the murderer of *that* one'. But I leave the details of such an alternative account for another time.

---

[8] Another sort of example that presents difficulties for the thesis of semantic significance is the following: Suppose that the speaker, cautioning against letting the accused man in the dock off too easily on grounds of insanity, reminds his audience of the seriousness of the crime by asserting referentially 'Let us not forget that the murderer has killed someone'. Again, it can be plausibly maintained that in uttering this sentence, the speaker asserted a singular proposition about Jones, the man in the dock, one which is true with respect to all and only those possible worlds in which Jones has killed someone. But this concerns speaker assertion rather than semantic content. A proponent of the semantic significance thesis must maintain that the sentence 'The murderer has killed someone' also expresses this very same singular proposition as its semantic content with respect to the relevant context. But this singular proposition about Jones is entirely contingent and *a posteriori*. If Jones had not been insane, it might not have come to pass that he would become a killer. On the other hand, it seems difficult to maintain that the sentence 'The murderer has killed someone' does not express a (nearly) *analytic* truth, or at least one true with respect to every possible world in which Smith is murdered by a lone killer, whether or not that killer is Jones. Nevertheless, I believe that the latter view can be plausibly and consistently maintained while denying the thesis of semantic significance. Although I myself sometimes have some inclination towards this line, I shall not defend it here. For present purposes, it is sufficient to point out that the question of *rigidity* of incomplete definite descriptions, which is at issue here, though entailed by the thesis of semantic significance, does not *depend* on it. Incomplete descriptions may *turn out* to be rigid in much the same way that some complete descriptions do, e.g., 'the even prime integer'.

17
The Pragmatic Fallacy (1991)

I present here a contribution to the continuing debate over the alleged semantic significance of Keith Donnellan's referential–attributive distinction, especially in connection with so-called incomplete definite descriptions, i.e., improper definite descriptions like 'the table' that, on a given occasion of use, refer to a specific object underspecified by the description itself. My broader purpose, however, is to highlight a fallacious form of reasoning that has led many a language theorist to erroneous conclusions.

I

First the background to the particular issue under dispute: Jones, acting alone, killed Smith in cold blood. A few of the townsfolk rightly suspected Jones of the crime, but most erroneously suspected Johnson. A few even began referring to the unfortunate Johnson behind his back as 'Smith's murderer', or sometimes simply as 'the murderer'. Keith Donnellan was understood to offer the following hypothesis:[1]

Whereas the description 'Smith's murderer' may refer with respect to a context in which the speaker uses the description *attributively* (without the specific intention to refer to some particular individual, believing that individual to be Smith's lone killer) to whomever acted alone in murdering Smith, the same description refers with respect to a context in which the speaker uses the description *referentially* (intending to refer specifically to a particular individual that the speaker has in mind, believing that individual to be Smith's lone killer) to the individual the speaker intends—even if that individual did not kill Smith.

While the police scratched their heads, other philosophers objected that it is implausible to regard the phrase 'Smith's murderer' as referring to someone who did not actually kill Smith. It is far more plausible, they argued, to suppose that the phrase refers to ('denotes', 'designates', etc.) whoever murdered Smith, even as used by a speaker who intends someone else.[2] Saul Kripke supported this intuition

---

The present chapter is based to some extent on letters written in 1988 to William K. Blackburn concerning his article 'Wettstein on Definite Descriptions', *Philosophical Studies* 53 (1988), pp. 263–278.

[1] 'Reference and Definite Descriptions', *The Philosophical Review* 75, 3 (1966), pp. 281–304.
[2] *Cf.* for example, H. P. Grice, 'Vacuous Names', in D. Davidson and J. Hintikka, eds, *Words and Objections: Essays on the Work of W. V. Quine* (Dordrecht: D. Reidel, 1969), pp. 118–145, at pp. 141–143; Michael Lockwood, 'On Predicating Proper Names', *The Philosophical Review*, 84 (1975), pp. 471–498, at p. 485n21; David Wiggins, 'Identity, Designation, Essentialism, and

by distinguishing between *speaker's reference* and *semantic reference*. The first is whomever or whatever the speaker refers to, or intends to refer to, assuming the speaker has some particular person or thing in mind. The second is whomever or whatever the speaker's *words* refer to as a matter of the semantic rules governing the language, irrespective of whomever or whatever the speaker has in mind.[3] Donnellan presented a compelling case that speakers can use 'Smith's murderer' to refer to someone who did not actually kill Smith, but, Kripke argued, this pragmatic phenomenon does not refute the semantically natural thesis that the words 'Smith's murderer' semantically refer to Smith's actual killer. The very same phenomena of misdescription and misinformed speaker's reference would arise regardless of the words' semantic reference (and indeed, even if Russell's theory is correct and such phrases are not semantic units at all, and hence do not have semantic reference).[4]

Kripke demurred, however, when it came to incomplete descriptions. Donnellan had objected to the idea that the context supplies implicit descriptive content to complete an 'incomplete' description, arguing that, whereas this seems plausible with respect to attributive uses, it is much less so with respect to descriptions that fit a great many individuals. Such incomplete descriptions, Donnellan pointed out, are commonly used referentially:

Asked to make his description more precise, [the speaker] may have to think about how best to do it. Several further descriptions may come to mind, not all of which are actually correct. Which, then, shall we say is the full but implicit one? Once we see the function of a referential description, however, we need not suppose that there is any one description recoverable from the speech act that is supposed uniquely to apply to the object referred to. The audience may through the partial description and various clues and cues know to what the speaker refers without being in possession of a description that uniquely fits it and which was implicit all along in the speaker's speech act.   ('Putting Humpty Dumpty Together Again', *The Philosophical Review*, 77 (1968), pp. 203–215, at p. 204*n*)

In a similar spirit Kripke (pp. 6–7, 22) suggested that an incomplete description might be assimilated to the corresponding demonstrative phrase ('that table'). Subsequently, Michael Devitt, Howard Wettstein, and others argued that the assimilation of incomplete descriptions to demonstratives is correct.[5] Although Wettstein

---

Physicalism', *Philosophia*, 5 (1975), pp. 1–30, at p. 28*n*9; R. M. Sainsbury, *Russell* (London: Routledge & Kegan Paul, 1979), pp. 126–133; and John Searle, 'Referential and Attributive', *Monist*, 62 (1979) pp. 190–208.

[3] When words are used by a speaker to a certain pragmatic end (e.g., to refer to something in particular), there may be an indirect nonsemantic relation that obtains between the words used and some (typically nonlinguistic) entity or entities – for example, the relation between expressions and objects of *being used by the speaker to refer to*. It would be incorrect to count the resulting feature of the words themselves as semantic rather than pragmatic.

[4] 'Speaker's Reference and Semantic Reference', in P. French, T. Uehling, and H. Wettstein, eds, *Contemporary Perspectives in the Philosophy of Language* (Minneapolis: University of Minnesota Press, 1979), pp. 6–27.

[5] Michael Devitt, 'Donnellan's Distinction', in P. French, T. Uehling, and H. Wettstein, eds, *Midwest Studies in Philosophy VI: The Foundations of Analytic Philosophy* (Minneapolis: University of Minnesota Press, 1981), pp. 511–524; Howard Wettstein, 'Demonstrative Reference and Definite Descriptions', *Philosophical Studies*, 40 (1981), pp. 241–257.

does not share Donnellan's view that a description refers with respect to a referential-use context to the intended individual even when the description does not fit that individual (p. 255n9), he argued that one can maintain that the referential–attributive distinction is semantically significant without maintaining this controversial aspect of Donnellan's view. Even if the literal referent is always answerable to the description, on Wettstein's view it remains that whenever an incomplete definite description is used referentially the proposition expressed will not incorporate the descriptive content (what little there is) of the description.

Suppose Brown, who rightly suspects Jones, utters the sentence

S: The murderer is insane,

using the incomplete description 'the murderer' referentially to refer to Jones. Let us call the context of Brown's utterance '*C*'. Then the following is an instance of the *semantic ambiguity hypothesis*:[6]

With respect to any context in which the speaker uses the description 'the murderer' attributively, sentence *S* expresses as its semantic content some proposition to the effect that the such-and-such murderer is insane, where supposedly one murderer and no one else is a such-and-such murderer. With respect to any context in which the speaker instead uses the description referentially to refer to the individual who in fact murdered Smith, the sentence expresses the singular proposition about Smith's murderer that *he* or *she* is insane.

The critical component of this claim is an instance of what I call the *thesis of the semantic significance of the referential use*:

Curiously, nearly every discussion since Russell's fails to take note of the fact that at the beginning of his discussion of 'the' in 'On Denoting', Russell explicitly considers the case of incomplete definite descriptions and proposes an account for them other than (and perhaps even incompatible with) the ellipsis account often attributed to him. He suggests that an incomplete definite description 'the such-and-such', where there is obviously more than one such-and-such in the world, is to be analyzed as a (complete) indefinite description 'a such-and-such'. Although this theory is not at all easy to disprove, it suffers from a defect that Russell in the same work attributed to Frege's rival account of 'the son of So-and-so' when So-and-so has a fine family of ten: 'This procedure, though it may not lead to actual logical error, is plainly artificial, and does not give an exact analysis of the matter.'

[6] As in 'Assertion and Incomplete Definite Descriptions', in *Philosophical Studies*, 42 (1982), pp. 37–45, I here use the phrase 'semantic ambiguity' in an artificially broad sense, to cover both ordinary ambiguity and the distinct phenomenon of *indexicality*, in which the semantic content of an expression varies with context even when there is univocality of semantic meaning. I also use the term 'context' to cover not only those parameters with respect to which the content of an indexical expression may vary, but also those features of an utterance of an ambiguous sentence that serve to disambigate, making only one reading operative. Francois Recanati, in 'Referential/Attributive: A Contextualist Proposal', *Philosophical Studies*, 56 (1989), pp. 217–249, at 224–225 and *passim*, proposes that definite descriptions are properly seen as indexical, rather than strictly ambiguous, with their content in a given context depending on whether the phrase is used referentially or attributively. But this is almost certainly exactly what Donnellan proffered in his original discussion, which explicitly denies that descriptions are semantically ambiguous (*op. cit.*, p. 297). Donnellan's notion of *pragmatic ambiguity* (*ibid.*) has puzzled a number of philosophers. *Cf.* Kripke, *op. cit.*, pp. 12–13; John Searle, *op. cit.*, at p. 208n6; and Stephen Neale, *Descriptions* (Cambridge, Mass.: MIT Press, 1990), at pp. 104n7, 110–112n36. One natural construal of the notion, however, simply identifies it with indexicality (or perhaps with a special kind of indexicality).

ST: Sentence *S* expresses the singular proposition about Jones that he is insane as its semantic content with respect to Brown's context *C*.

Wettstein argued in favor of thesis *ST*; I argued against it.

II

Wettstein's central argument for *ST* is the following:

P1: For any proposition to the effect that the such-and-such murderer is insane, where Jones and no one else is a such-and-such murderer, there are other such propositions that accord equally well with Brown's intentions in uttering *S* in *C*, and none of these is precisely intended as such, to the exclusion of the others, by Brown in his utterance.

P2: In uttering *S* in *C*, Brown does not assert each of, or somehow indeterminately assert any one of, a loose cluster of propositions; he determinately asserts one single proposition making reference to Jones and attributing insanity to him.

Therefore,

C1: In uttering *S* in *C*, Brown does not assert any proposition to the effect that the such-and-such murderer is insane.

Therefore,

C2: In uttering *S* in *C*, Brown asserts the singular proposition about Jones that he is insane.

Perhaps there are additional, tacit premises. In any event, the argument need not be regarded as deductive.

My own view is that the sub-conclusion *C1* of this argument is straightforwardly false.[7] While premiss *P1* is true by hypothesis, I maintain that the second conjunct of *P2* is false. My criticism of the argument for *C2*, however, was not that it relies on a false premiss. It was that, taken as an argument for *ST*, it is simply a *non sequitur*. I also maintain that the main conclusion *C2* is straightforwardly true (even though the argument for it from *C1* is unsound). Still *ST* does not follow. To think otherwise is to equate *C2* with *ST*, or to assimilate *C2* with *ST*, or at least, to make an implicit inference from *C2* to *ST*. This move is based on a confusion between what I call *speaker assertion* and *semantic content*.

---

[7] In 'Assertion and Incomplete Definite Descriptions', I suggested (p. 42) that Brown asserts the proposition that the murderer relevant to certain interests, or to a certain situation, is insane. *Cf.* my *Reference and Essence* (Princeton University Press, 1981), at p. 18*n*16. Another possibility, which I now favor, is the proposition that the murderer among *K* is insane, where '*K*' is a plural term (like 'them') directly referring to the members of the domain over which quantifiers (or quantifier-like operators such as 'everyone') range—or what comes (for most purposes) to the same thing, where '*K*' is a singular term referring to the domain in question.

In his reply to my criticism, Wettstein protests that his argument focuses on speaker assertion to the exclusion of semantic content.[8] Yet even in his restatement of his argument, Wettstein says that 'speakers often manage to assert *truths* despite the fact that the descriptions they utter fail to uniquely denote [in Russell's sense]'. He asks 'How then does the speaker refer and assert a determinate proposition?' and 'How are we to account for the fact that in such cases determinate references are made and determinate propositions asserted?' (p. 189). His answer, in the case of Brown: 'what was asserted was that *that one, Jones, is insane*, a singular proposition' (p. 190). Thus even in Wettstein's response, the argument is aimed at C2. Moreover, Wettstein's reconstruction of my criticism (p. 193) is stated entirely in terms of 'convey', rather than 'assert', despite my explicit objection that the notion of speaker *assertion* is irrelevant. All of this suggests that Wettstein was so firmly convinced of the obvious legitimacy of inferring semantic content from speaker assertion that he misunderstood me to be objecting instead that C2 does not follow from

C2′: In uttering S in C, Brown conveys the singular proposition about Jones that he is insane[9]

My criticism that ST does not follow from C2 targets a different fallacy, that of inferring semantic content from speaker assertion. Roughly speaking, someone's uttering a sentence (in appropriate circumstances) whose semantic content (with respect to the context of utterance) is *p* typically entails the speaker's asserting *p*, *but not vice-versa*. Likewise, asserting *p* typically entails conveying *p*, but not vice-versa.

Wettstein objects (*op. cit.*, p. 195n12) that my distinction between speaker assertion and semantic content 'rides roughshod' over H. P. Grice's distinction between saying and implicating. I must emphasize, therefore, that I am entirely sympathetic to Grice's distinction. I am drawing a different distinction, between two different notions. The Gricean terminology for his distinction between 'saying' and 'implicating' or 'meaning' is to some extent technical—as Grice himself would doubtless have conceded, or even have insisted. He writes: 'In the sense in which I am using the word "say", I intend what someone has said to be closely related to the conventional meanings of the words (the sentence) which he has uttered' ('Logic and Conversation', in D. Davidson and G. Harman, eds, *The Logic of Grammar*, Encino, Calif.: Diskenson, 1975, pp. 64–75, at p. 66). One may choose to use the words 'say' or 'assert' (we here use the two interchangeably) roughly in the sense of the phrase 'utter some expression that has as its literal semantic content, in the speaker's context, ...'. This is a perfectly acceptable use of these words, and it may be one on which the inference from C2 to ST is valid—by the very definition of 'assert'. We might call this *literally saying*, or (following Bishop Joseph Butler) saying or asserting *in the strict and philosophical sense*. If so, then this use of 'say' and 'assert' has no claim to correspond

---

[8] 'The Semantic Significance of the Referential–Attributive Distinction', *Philosophical Studies*, 44 (1983), pp. 187–196. The claim is made at p. 196n14.

[9] *Cf.* also Wettstein, p. 195n12. I believe that Blackburn, pp. 277–278n1, and in correspondence, may be subject to the same, or similar, confusion.

exactly with the use of 'say' or 'assert' in English—with saying *in the loose and popular sense*. My distinction between speaker assertion and semantic content is concerned entirely with saying in the latter sense—the concept expressed in ordinary English by 'say' or 'assert', in their use to give not the actual words used by a speaker (what in the Fregean tradition is called *direct discourse*) nor even the semantic content of those words, but the—or I should say *a*—content of the speaker's speech act.[10]

Nor is it my view that English speakers use the words 'say' and 'assert' in a very wide sense that covers both literally saying and 'implicating' in Grice's technical sense. (I suspect that the English words 'say' and 'assert' are somewhat narrower than that, yet rather wider than Grice's special use.) It is my considered view that, as 'say' and 'assert' are used in English, for any individual x, if x is the such-and-such and someone utters a sentence whose semantic content is that the such-and-such is thus-and-so, then it is typically correct to report the speaker as having said (asserted) that x is thus-and-so. This is not because we often use 'say' when we mean *implicate*, in Grice's sense; it is because it is typically correct to report the speaker as having said *of* the such-and-such that it (he, she) is thus-and-so—even when the description was used attributively—and on my view, saying of x, *de re*, that it is thus-and-so just *is* asserting the singular proposition that x is thus-and-so.[11] In the case at hand, it certainly would seem to be allowable in English to report Brown as having said of Jones that he is insane. To use the contemporary jargon, a version of *latitudinarianism* with regard to exportation seems to be correct for assertion, even if latitudinarianism for belief and other propositional attitudes has been fairly thoroughly refuted (by the shortest spy, *et al.*)[12]

---

[10] In fact, it is not in the least clear that Grice's use of 'say' is as artificially strict as Wettstein's understanding of it. Grice amplifies his explanation of his special use of 'say' with the following remark: 'This brief indication of my use of "say" leaves it open whether a man who says (today) [i.e. in 1975] "Harold Wilson is a great man" and another who says (also today) "The British Prime Minister is a great man" would, if each knew that the two singular terms had the same reference, have said the same thing' (*loc. cit.*). If each knew that 'the British Prime Minister' (or better: 'the present Prime Minister of Great Britain') referred with respect to 1975 to Harold Wilson, then the description was (likely) used referentially rather than attributively. Although the semantic content ('conventional meaning') of 'The British Prime Minister is a great man' is evidently very different from that of 'Harold Wilson is a great man', Grice's use of 'say' (in 1975) evidently does not preclude the possibility that the man who used the former sentence nevertheless said (asserted the proposition) that Harold Wilson is a great man.

[11] I invoke the qualifier 'typically' because of certain cases in which we apparently would not report one's assertion in the manner described, e.g. if someone utters a sentence of the form 'The such-and-such is the such-and-such'. *Cf.* Searle, *op. cit.*, at p. 207.

[12] The matter remains highly controversial. *Cf.* my *Frege's Puzzle* (Cambridge, Mass.: MIT Press/Bradford Books, 1986), at pp. 179–180n19, and 'How to Measure the Standard Metre', *Proceedings of the Aristotelian Society*, New Series, 88 (1987/1988), pp. 193–217, especially at p. 199n8. Some sort of latitudinarianism with regard to *de re* assertion has the bonus feature that the otherwise puzzling phenomenon that Kaplan calls the *pseudo de re* is fully explicable. Kaplan's example (from his 'Demonstratives', in J. Almog, J. Perry, and H. Wettstein, eds, *Themes from Kaplan* (Oxford University Press, 1989), pp. 481–563, at p. 555n71) is the following angry report of John's claim when he utters the words 'The man I sent to you yesterday is honest': *John says that the lying S.O.B. who took my car is honest*. Kaplan evidently believes that such reports are straightforwardly false, and that they pose no theoretically interesting issues. By contrast,

In any event *C2*, taken in its usual sense in English, does not logically entail *ST*. Indeed, I believe *C2* is true and *ST* false. Conversely, if 'assert' is used in a special sense according to which the inference from *C2* to *ST* is trivially valid (Wettstein says that he is so using the term), it is also used in a sense according to which the prior sub-conclusion *C1* (on which *C2* is based) means, in effect, that sentence *S* does not express, as its literal semantic content with respect to *C*, any proposition to the effect that the such-and-such murderer is insane. This conclusion certainly does not follow from *P1* and *P2*, construing 'assert' so that the latter premiss is true. The inference presupposes that where one's explicit words in a given utterance are incomplete, the semantic content of the sentence uttered is strongly governed by one's intentions, to the peculiar extent that in order for such a sentence to contain, unambiguously, the descriptive proposition that the such-and-such is thus-and-so, the speaker must consciously intend precisely that proposition to the exclusion of all others, even though such finely discriminating intentions are not required in order for the sentence to contain unambiguously the singular proposition *about* the such-and-such that *it* (he or she) is thus-and-so. Why should discriminating intentions be required in one case but not the other? I submit that *C2* derives whatever plausibility it may have from the ordinary sense of 'assert', or perhaps from equivocation between two (or more?) senses.

With 'assert' construed in Wettstein's strict sense, his conclusions *C1* and *C2* are at best highly suspect. Everyone is accustomed to using determiners like 'any', 'every', 'some', 'no', 'few', etc., with a restricted domain (just as the word 'everyone' is used in this very sentence). No one would argue that general or quantified propositions disappear as a result of the restrictions. The sentence 'Everyone is here' may express the proposition that everyone among *K* is here, where '*K*' refers to a relevantly restricted class of persons. (Notice that the class *K* itself would thus emerge as a constituent of the proposition expressed, so that the proposition, though 'general'—that is to say quantificational—would be singular with respect to *K*.) Or it may express the proposition that everyone who generally attends this seminar is here, or that everyone who is supposed to be here is here, etc. It certainly does not express a conjunctive singular proposition lacking all semblance of quantification (*Tom is here and Dick is here and Harry is here and* . . .). The incomplete sentence contains a general proposition even if the speaker—and even if we—are unable to decide among various candidate quantificational propositions. We should require extremely compelling evidence

---

Wettstein argues ('Has Semantics Rested on a Mistake?', *Journal of Philosophy*, 83, 4 (April 1986), pp. 185–209, at pp. 205–208) from the phenomenon of the *pseudo de re* to the dramatic conclusion that propositional-attitude predicates of the form ⌜*V*'s that *S*⌝ (e.g., 'believes that Smith's murderer is insane') do not attribute the attitude expressed by the attitude verb *V* to the proposition content of the complement sentence *S*. Far more plausible than either of Kaplan's or Wettstein's diametrically opposed conclusions is the view, strongly supported by ordinary assertion reports, that the so-called pseudo *de re* is not pseudo at all; it is genuine *de re*. (Kaplan sketches an argument that *pseudo de re* substitutions license completely unacceptable assertion reports. But the argument assumes that such assertion reports are *de dicto*, so that the substitutions are made within the scope of a nonextensional phrase ⌜α says that⌝.) The speaker in Kaplan's example is evidently reporting, correctly, that John says *of* the lying S.O.B. in question that he is honest.

before we conclude that 'the' is not also used with suppressed or tacit restrictions. With respect to Brown's context C, S may express the proposition that the murderer among K is insane, where 'K' directly refers to a highly restricted domain of salient individuals. (See note 7 above.) It does not seem to express, as its literal semantic content, a singular proposition completely lacking the generality contributed by the operator 'the'.

It is ironic that Wettstein should cite Grice's distinction between literally saying and merely implicating in defense of his version of Donnellan's view that referential use of a definite description has semantic ramifications. Grice himself opposed the semantic-significance thesis (as Wettstein notes in his earlier discussion); in fact, he invoked his distinction in opposing the thesis. Brown did say of Jones in the loose and popular sense of 'say' that he is insane. In that sense, then, Jones is someone whom Brown said is insane. In the strict and philosophical sense, however, Jones is not someone Brown said is insane; Brown did not 'say', in that sense, that he is insane. Nor did Brown literally say that *Jones* is insane. What Brown literally said was that *the murderer* is insane.

Grice's opposition to the semantic-significance thesis extended to cases involving incomplete definite descriptions.[13] Discussing a case in which a referentially used description misdescribed the intended referent, he wrote:

If in [such a] case the speaker has used a descriptive phrase ... which in fact has no application, then what the speaker has *said* will, strictly speaking, be false; the truth-conditions for a [statement involving a referential use of a definite description], no less than for [one involving an attributive use], can be thought of as being given by a Russellian account of definite descriptions (with suitable provision for unexpressed restrictions, to cover cases in which, for example, someone uses the phrase 'the table' meaning thereby 'the table in this room'). But though what, in such a case, a speaker has *said* may be false, what he *meant* may be true... ('Vacuous Names', p. 142)

If what the speaker said in such a case is automatically false because nothing fits the description when it is taken literally—even allowing for suppressed or tacit restrictions—then the speaker did not assert the relevant singular proposition. To repeat, Grice is here using 'say' in a technical and artificially strict sense. He need not deny that in the ordinary, everyday sense, the speaker not only meant (i.e. implicated), but even said, something true of the intended referent.

III

Wettstein's apparent inference of *ST* from *C2* may be seen as a special case of the following inference pattern:

Speaker α, in using expressing e in context c, expresses concept κ.

---

[13] And even when he evidently used the word 'say' in Wettstein's artificially narrow sense on which Brown did not 'say' (but merely implicated) of Jones that he is insane (so that *C2*, so understood, is false). See note 10 above.

Therefore, e expresses κ as its semantic content with respect to c.

The inference from what the speaker expresses to what his or her words express (as their semantic content) is closely related to the two following extensional variations on the theme:

Speaker α, in using expression e in context c, refers to β.
Therefore, e semantically refers to (designates, denotes, stands for) β, with respect to c.

Speaker α, in using sentence S in context c, is correct (speaks the truth, says something true).
Therefore, S is semantically true with respect to c.

The general pattern exhibited in these inferences is invalid. I call it *the Pragmatic Fallacy*.[14] The Pragmatic Fallacy embodies the idea that if the use of a particular expression fulfills a certain illocutionary purpose of the speaker's, then that purpose must also characterize the expression's semantic function with respect to the speaker's context. The purpose fulfilled by the use of an expression, of course, often indicates the expression's semantic function, but not invariably so. One should proceed with special caution in inferring purely semantic attributes from such illocutionary acts as asserting that such-and-such or making reference to so-and-so. Despite the efforts of Grice and others to guard us against various instances of the Pragmatic Fallacy, it remains pervasive in contemporary discussions in the theory of reference and meaning.[15]

IV

I also proposed independent evidence, from possible-world semantics, against *ST*. If *ST* were true, then 'the murderer' would have to be a rigid designator (with respect to *C*). It would refer to Jones with respect to any possible world whatsoever (in which Jones exists)—even a world in which (Jones exists but) there are no murders. This, I submit, is every bit as counter-intuitive as Donnellan's controversial view, which even Wettstein does not share, that the complete description 'Smith's murderer' refers to poor Johnson with respect to contexts in which the speaker uses this description referentially with Johnson in mind.

Indeed, my point is precisely a modal-semantical extension of the original objection to Donnellan's hypothesis that the semantic referent of a referentially

---

[14] This is evidently not exactly the same fallacy that Wettstein calls by the same name (in 'The Semantic Significance of the Referential–Attributive Distinction', at p. 194).

[15] One classic example is Charles Chastain, 'Reference and Context', in K. Gunderson, ed., *Language, Mind, and Knowledge* (Minneapolis: University of Minnesota Press, 1975), pp. 194–269. Although I cannot argue the case here, I would cite as two recent examples in which erroneous, or at least highly suspect, conclusions seem to be supported through some form or other of the Pragmatic Fallacy: David Kaplan's intriguing (and in other respects insightful) discussion of Donnellan's example of 'the man drinking champagne', in Kaplan's 'Afterthoughts', to his 'Demonstratives', *op. cit.* at pp. 583–584; and Mark Crimmins's and John Perry's motivating remarks for the theory proferred in their 'The Prince and the Phone Booth: Reporting Puzzling Beliefs', *Journal of Philosophy*, 86, 12 (December 1989): pp. 685–711.

used description is not answerable to the description—an objection that Wettstein attempts to accommodate in his effort to revive a semantically significant referential–attributive distinction. Whereas Wettstein is correct that Donnellan's controversial hypothesis is not essential to the very idea of a semantically significant referential use, a modal variant of the hypothesis is virtually a consequence of the semantic-significance thesis. One cannot defend the semantic-significance thesis while fully accommodating the widely shared semantic intuition, which Wettstein evidently shares, that 'the such-and-such' never refers to (denotes, designates) something that is not a such-and-such.[16]

Wettstein's reply to this criticism (pp. 191–193) seems to betray a misunderstanding—or perhaps a deep mistrust—of the enterprise of possible-world semantics. I do not see how it can be a mistake to talk about the reference (denotation, designation, etc.) of a singular term *with respect to* a possible world, any more than it can be a mistake to talk about the truth value of a sentence with respect to a possible world, etc.[17] But the argument can be made without doing so.

Consider the following, less formal formulation of the objection: Suppose that the police have been discussing various scenarios concerning Smith's murder. On one of these scenarios, Johnson is perfectly sane and murdered Smith in cold blood while Jones is insane and had no part in the murder. In discussing this contrary-to-fact scenario, they say things like 'Johnson committed the murder. The murderer then washed his hands and returned to his desk at work. The murderer seemed perfectly sane to his co-workers', etc. Brown overhears some of the discussion—enough to realize that a potentially contrary-to-fact scenario is under discussion but not enough to know who was stipulated to be the murderer and whether he was stipulated to be sane or not. On the basis of some of the remarks made, Brown surmises, erroneously, that they are discussing a scenario on which Jones is both the murderer and insane. (For whatever it is worth, recall that in reality, Jones is the actual murderer.) Brown bursts into the discussion uttering sentence S, intended as a contribution to the discussion of the scenario in question. The semantic-significance thesis has the consequence that, in discourse about this Johnson-guilty scenario, the phrase 'the murderer' refers, with respect to Brown's context C, to Jones even though Jones is not a murderer on that scenario. But this is clearly wrong, and it goes against the very sorts of intuitions that

---

[16] Neale says (*op. cit.*, at pp. 92–93) that he is sympathetic to my modal argument against Wettstein's defense of the thesis of semantic significance, but doubts that the principal premiss—that sentence S, as used by Brown in context C, is not true with respect to a possible world in which no murderer is insane (say, because there are no murders)—will be accepted by an advocate of the thesis it aims to debunk. This is very likely correct, but it is a feature shared by most philosophical arguments against controversial doctrines. The point here is that Wettstein concedes that 'the such-and-such' never semantically refers to something that is not a such-and-such; but it is this very intuition that defeats the semantic-significance thesis.

[17] A parallel argument can be made using time in place of modality. Unlike the name 'Jones', the phrase 'the murderer', even when used referentially, does not semantically refer to Jones, or to anyone else, with respect to times before Jones committed murder. This is one respect in which incomplete definite descriptions differ also from most occurrences of pronouns, other than pronouns of laziness and perhaps so-called E-type anaphoric pronouns, which are not c-commanded by their antecedents. (When Wettstein showed me the typescript of his reply, I informed him that, contrary to his claim on p. 192, I regard most pronoun occurrences as directly referential.)

Wettstein attempts to accommodate. In discourse about the Johnson-guilty scenario, 'the murderer' refers to Johnson, not Jones. The mere fact that the same phrase correctly applies to Jones in ordinary discourse about reality is completely irrelevant. Equally irrelevant is the fact that Brown intends Jones by his use of the phrase. Even if there is some sense in which Brown, in his state of partial ignorance, asserted something true about the scenario under discussion, and in so doing referred to Jones, the sentence he used makes no reference to Jones, and is clearly false, taken as a contribution to the operative discourse.

Wettstein's stance might indicate a more general skepticism, perhaps a global rejection of all extensional formal semantics *a la* Tarski. The main idea may be something like the following (associated with Strawson and his followers): Singular terms do not refer; speakers *use* singular terms to refer. This is compatible with Wettstein's endorsement of *C2*. But it is difficult to understand how ST can be maintained if the phrase 'the murderer' is held not to refer to Jones with respect to C. It would be far more natural to follow this skeptical idea all the way and claim that S itself does not express any proposition with respect C as its semantic content; Brown *uses* S to make a statement. (Brown does so use S.) This would be to concede that ST is false.

A blanket rejection of extensional formal semantics is a radical stance; Wettstein's arguments do not support such global semantic skepticism. Reasoning in accordance with the Pragmatic Fallacy is very often an indication of a misunderstanding concerning the nature of semantics generally, and especially concerning the contrast between pragmatics and matters that are properly semantic. It is no trivial task to set out criteria that differentiate semantics proper from pragmatics, and in the case of natural languages especially there are doubtless important connections between the two, but this should not blind us to the distinction.[18]

---

[18] *Cf. Frege's Puzzle*, pp. 12–13, 58–59, 78–79.

18

The Good, the Bad, and the Ugly (2004)

I

One of the most important achievements in philosophy in the latter half of the last century was a movement in the philosophy of language, spilling over into metaphysics, epistemology, and the philosophy of mind. This movement has come to be known as *the theory of direct reference*. Keith Donnellan's 1966 classic 'Reference and Definite Descriptions'—spotlighting its famous distinction between the referential and the attributive use of definite descriptions—is an early and important precursor to the direct-reference theory, in its contemporary incarnation.[1] Ironically, that article argues for a direct-reference theory on its least promising turf. During the first half of the twentieth century, a broadly Fregean account of meaning and reference was generally held for all linguistic terms. Then the direct-reference theorists began exposing how badly the Fregean picture fit certain sorts of terms. Especially and most obviously, the Fregean account failed for the logician's individual variables. But it failed also for such common expressions as proper names, indexicals, pronouns, natural-kind terms, and more besides (phenomenon terms like 'heat', color words like 'red', artifact terms like 'pencil')—perhaps most, or even all, simple (or single-word) terms. Even after this chip, chip, chipping away of once cherished doctrine into scrap, one might still suppose that, if there are any terms for which the traditional, Fregean perspective is at least more-or-less correct, they are definite descriptions. One might suppose this, that is, but for Donnellan's ground-breaking article. Donnellan argues instead that even definite descriptions are routinely used in a manner that 'comes closer to performing the function of Russell's [logically] proper names' (1956: 303), hence a use sharply out of sync with the traditional Fregean picture.[2]

As a student I had the privilege through most of the 1970s of taking a number of courses and seminars in philosophy from Keith Donnellan, in whose honor the present chapter was written. I am grateful to the participants in my seminar at UCSB during Fall 1993 (especially Ilhan Inan) for fruitful discussion of the issues presented here, and to Alan Berger for comments. I am grateful to Donnellan both for correspondence in connection with the seminar and more generally for his many contributions to my own philosophical development.

[1] See also Donnellan (1968, 1978). A pioneering direct-reference theorist, Donnellan has made additional important contributions to the literature on the theory, especially in Donnellan (1972, 1974).

[2] If definite descriptions go the way of direct reference, is there anything left for the Fregean account to cover? Yes: the comparatively rare attributive uses of descriptions. Also, multi-worded

A number of direct-reference theorists—including Barwise and Perry (1983: 149–156 and *passim*), Devitt (1981), Kaplan (1979, 1989*b*: 583–584), Recanati (1989, 1993: 277–299), and Wettstein (1981, 1983)—have favored the broad outlines of Donnellan's account. Others—notably Kripke (1977), in a farsighted and still under-appreciated critique—have balked at Donnellan's attempt to extend the notion of direct reference that far, seeing the distinction between referential and attributive use as fundamentally pragmatic in nature, with no special semantic significance.[3] Interestingly, however, Kripke (1977: 6–7, 22) concedes, in effect, that he too is inclined to embrace a direct-reference theory for the most common type of definite description by far: the so-called incomplete definite description. Taking the hard line, I have argued (with special reference to Wettstein's arguments) that going even this far is a mistake.[4] I maintain that definite descriptions in English (and in Hebrew, Italian, Japanese, etc.), even referentially used incomplete ones, are not Russellian logically proper names. I say they are more like Fregean terms—or perhaps generalized quantifiers (as Russell thought)—but, I claim, devices of direct reference they are not. So goes the controversy within a controversy within a controversy.

It is not to my purpose here to rehearse the arguments that I have given elsewhere against the thesis of semantic significance. Rather I shall explore a host of philosophical issues raised by the semantic-significance thesis itself, by Donnellan's endorsement of it, by Kripke's criticism of it, and more generally by various attempts to characterize the distinction between referential and attributive. These issues, which concern such things as *de re* belief and related matters, have applications in the theory of knowledge and the philosophy of mind that go well beyond the philosophy of language.

First up: What is this controversial thesis of semantic significance? Suppose that a speaker, Brown, utters the sentence 'Smith's murderer is insane'. For some versions of the debate, the description 'Smith's murderer' should be replaced by its 'incomplete' variation 'the murderer'. In either case, the central question concerns whether Brown's use of the description ('Smith's murderer' or 'the murderer') affects which proposition is semantically expressed by the sentence with respect to Brown's context. There is no (relevant) quarrel if Brown uses the description attributively. The

---

phrases, like 'middle-aged, stocky man with horn-rimmed glasses, a greying beard, and a balding head', and ... whole sentences! But if sentences may be fruitfully thought of as designating truth-values—as Frege and others have taught us—is it not so that they are typically used referentially, rather than attributively? Something to ponder.

[3] See also Donnellan (1978). Putting the controversy in terms of the presence or absence of 'semantic significance' may be misleading. As Kripke (1977: 21) suggests, speaker reference like anything else can become 'semantically relevant simply by virtue of being conversationally salient—whenever an expression (such as a deictic pronoun) is invoked that relies on conversational salience to secure reference. The point of the thesis of semantic significance is this: When a definite description is used referentially (at least if the description is 'proper', in the Russellian sense, and used referentially for the object 'denoted', in Russell's sense), the fact that it is so used is what *directly* determines that its semantic content is the object referred to by the speaker—by contrast with this being indirectly determined by means of some interceding phenomenon, like conversational salience, which directly determines semantic content. This is the sense in which, according to the thesis, the referential–attributive distinction has *special* semantic significance.

[4] In addition to Wettstein (1981, 1983), see W. Blackburn (1988) and Salmon (1982, 1991).

consensus is that the sentence then expresses the proposition about Smith (at least indirectly about him), that whoever murdered him single-handedly is insane. The controversy turns on the question of what the semantic content of the sentence is if Brown uses the description referentially, but correctly (let us say) for Smith's lone killer. According to the thesis of semantic significance, 'Smith's murderer is insane' then semantically expresses a proposition not at all about Smith, but instead a proposition about the murderer, that *he* is insane. Those of us who maintain that Donnellan's distinction has no special semantic significance contend that the semantic content of the sentence, with respect to the relevant context, is completely unaffected by Brown's referential use. It still expresses the proposition about Smith.

Donnellan and his followers thus endorse something along the lines of the following theses:

(SS_a) If a speaker utters 'Smith's murderer is insane' in an appropriate manner in a context c, then the speaker uses 'Smith's murderer' attributively in c iff 'Smith's murderer is insane' expresses the proposition that whoever single-handedly murdered Smith is insane as its English semantic content with respect to c.

(SS_r) If a speaker utters 'Smith's murderer is insane' in an appropriate manner in a context c, then the speaker uses 'Smith's murderer' referentially for x in c iff 'Smith's murderer' semantically refers in English to x with respect to c and 'Smith's murderer is insane' expresses the singular proposition about x that he/she is insane as its English semantic content with respect to c.

Here the phrase 'to utter in an appropriate manner' means to utter a sentence as a sentence of a particular language in a normal way with assertive intent—by contrast with reciting a line in a play, conveying a message by secret code, etc. A singular proposition about an individual x is an 'object-involving' Russellian proposition that is about x by virtue of x's occurring directly as a constituent. Let us call the conjunction of the two theses '*SS*'. It is a thesis to the effect that a definite description is indexical, expressing different semantic contents with respect to different contexts, depending (at least in some instances) on whether it is used referentially or attributively.

Donnellan (1966) was not completely clear on this last point, leaving some readers to speculate that he conceived of his distinction as a lexical ambiguity rather than as a type of indexicality. This has led to some misplaced criticism. It should be noted that Donnellan (1966: 297) explicitly denied that definite descriptions are semantically ambiguous. And indeed, his contrasting notion of 'pragmatic ambiguity' seems to correspond very closely to the contemporary notion of indexicality, or perhaps to a special kind of indexicality.[5] Donnellan's account may thus be insulated to some extent against Kripke's (1977: 18–20) appeal to H. P. Grice's Modified Occam's Razor principle that one should avoid 'multiplying senses beyond necessity'.[6] On the other hand, there is probably a worthy objection, analogous to Kripke's plea

---

[5] Donnellan has confirmed in personal correspondence (October 1993) that the indexicality conception has always been his view of the matter.

[6] See Grice (1969: 142–143; 1978: 118–120).

for semantic economy, against positing indexicality beyond necessity—or at least beyond what is sufficiently plausible on independent grounds.[7]

One of Kripke's central objections is easily adjusted to target the indexical rather than the lexical-ambiguity version of the semantic-significance thesis.[8] So modified, it runs something like this: Donnellan's distinction generalizes to cover proper names in addition to definite descriptions. For example, just as one may use the description 'Mary's husband' referentially for someone who is not in fact legally married to Mary, one may also mistakenly use the name 'Jones' in reference to Smith, having mistaken him in the distance for Jones. Yet it is not plausible in the least that a proper name shifts in semantic reference with the context, depending on whether there is, over and above the speaker's general intention always to use that name for the person so named, a particular person (or other object) whom the speaker has in mind and whom, on this particular occasion, the speaker means by the use of the name. Just as the fact that a name may be misapplied on a given occasion does not mean that the semantic reference of the name shifts to erase the mistake, nor does the semantic reference of a description shift to accommodate misapplication of the description.

II

It is important to note that the thesis of semantic significance primarily concerns the semantic content of definite descriptions (or what is sometimes called the contribution toward 'truth conditions', or the 'intension'), rather than the semantic reference. It is the thesis that the proposition expressed by a sentence containing a definite description (or the question of whether the sentence is true with respect to a given possible world), as opposed to the reference (with respect to the actual world) of the description itself, depends crucially on the use made of the description. Donnellan contends that the referent of a definite description ⌜the φ⌝ shifts with the context even when its matrix φ is indexical-free. Specifically, he maintains that a referentially used definite description refers (with respect to the context of utterance) to the person or object meant by the speaker even if that person or object does not fit the description. This has proved highly controversial. But as Wettstein (1981) pointed out, the thesis of semantic significance does not actually require Donnellan's controversial contention. It is enough if the proposition semantically expressed when a definite description is used referentially for the right entity is the corresponding singular proposition about that entity. And indeed, Wettstein (1981: 243–244) maintains that the referential–attributive distinction is semantically significant while not endorsing Donnellan's more controversial claim. One can maintain a version of

---

[7] *Cf.* Recanati (1989, 1993: 277–299) and Salmon (1991: 95 n. 6).

[8] Kripke first presented the objection, targeting the lexical-ambiguity version of the semantic-significance thesis, in Kripke (1980: 25 n.)—in what is easily seen, in retrospect, to be a compressed summary of the not yet written 'Speaker's Reference and Semantic Reference'. See Kripke (1977: 13–21). Kripke's formulations speak of ambiguity where the version presented here speaks instead of reference shifting with the context.

the semantic-significance thesis that does not make Donnellan's additional claim by weakening the controversial thesis SS_r into the following:

(SS'_r) If a speaker utters 'Smith's murderer is insane' in an appropriate manner in a context c, then the speaker uses 'Smith's murderer' referentially for Smith's murderer in c iff 'Smith's murderer' semantically refers in English to Smith's murderer with respect to c and 'Smith's murderer is insane' expresses the singular proposition about Smith's murderer that he/she is insane as its English semantic content with respect to c.

Let SS' be the conjunction of theses SS_a and SS'_r. It is neutral on the question of what happens when the speaker uses 'Smith's murderer' referentially for someone other than Smith's murderer. Donnellan's thesis SS_r supplements SS' to provide an answer to that question. Indeed, I believe SS_r is the only natural complement to SS'_r with regard to the question at hand. But SS_r represents Donnellan at his most defiant, prompting at least one follower to retreat to the neutral version of the semantic-significance thesis.

The mere possibility of the more neutral version of the thesis of semantic significance demonstrates that the objection from Kripke sketched at the end of the previous section stands in serious need of repair. First let us calibrate the referential–attributive distinction more finely. One should distinguish among three types of uses of definite descriptions: (i) correctly applied referential uses, that is, the use of a definite description ⌜the φ⌝ referentially for the person or object that satisfies φ (or the person or object that satisfies a suitable expansion of φ, in case the description is incomplete); (ii) incorrectly applied referential uses, that is, the use of ⌜the φ⌝ referentially for someone or something that does not uniquely satisfy (a suitable expansion of) ϕ; and (iii) attributive uses. Donnellan's distinction is between (i)-cum-(ii) on the one hand, and (iii) on the other. The distinction-within-a-distinction between (i) and (ii) reveals a further interesting distinction, perpendicular to the referential–attributive distinction. Let us say that a use of either type (i) or type (iii) is a *Good* use, and that a use of type (ii) is *Bad*. The point made above may now be rephrased by saying that the thesis of semantic significance does not require Donnellan's complementary claim that a definite description, when used Badly, semantically refers to the entity meant by the speaker. A less defiant version of the thesis confines itself to Good uses, holding that the semantic content of a description with respect to such a use depends on whether that use is of type (i) or of type (iii). An effective objection to the semantic-significance thesis must expose some difficulty with the latter claim.

Kripke's Jones/Smith argument is aimed at Donnellan's more full-blooded version of the thesis of semantic significance which asserts SS_r. In the example, a misapplied use of a proper name is contrasted with a correctly applied use of the name, where the former is analogous to a Bad use of a definite description, the latter to a Good use. It is argued that the Bad use cannot affect the semantic reference of the name. This pays no attention to the question of semantic content, and hence inevitably misses the neutral version of the semantic-significance thesis.

Even when evaluated in this light, however, the argument is flawed—and not merely because it leaves the door open for the neutral version of the semantic-significance thesis. The principal defect is that Kripke has not succeeded by his

Jones/Smith example in extending the referential/attributive distinction to proper names. His discussion presupposes that typical correctly applied uses of a name are the analogue of the attributive use of a definite description. Correct uses of names are indeed Good, but they typically bear a much stronger kinship to Good uses of type (i) than to those of type (iii). The contrast between the correct use and the misuse of 'Jones' is roughly analogous to the distinction among referential uses between (i) and (ii). Since Kripke has not demonstrated a genuinely *attributive* use for a name, his Jones/Smith example does not adequately replicate the full grounds for the semantic-significance thesis. For the purposes of Kripke's objection, it still needs to be shown that a proper name can have contrasting uses analogous to, and as different as, the referential use of a definite description (encompassing (i) + (ii)) and the attributive.

As we shall see in Section V below, what Kripke actually provides is a distinction between uses that are, in a certain sense, automatically Good, and uses that are either Bad or only accidentally Good. This comes close, but still falls significantly short of capturing Donnellan's distinction. Inevitably, there are competing, non-coextensive ways of generalizing Donnellan's distinction for definite descriptions to extend it to proper names. My point is not that one of these extensions is right and the rest are wrong. (This way of putting things threatens to ignite a dispute that is largely terminological.) The point is rather that a natural and plausible extension—one that aspires to capture and respect what is conceptually and philosophically at the core of Donnellan's distinction—will cast our commonplace uses of ordinary names on the referential side rather than the attributive. And this is something Kripke's generalized distinction evidently fails to do.

I believe it is relatively uncontroversial that proper names are at least normally used referentially. Indeed, in his initial characterization of the distinction, Donnellan likened the referential use of a definite description to the use of a name, or at least of a 'logically proper name':

Furthermore, on Russell's view the type of expression that comes closest to performing the function of the referential use of definite descriptions turns out, as one might suspect, to be a proper name (in 'the narrow logical sense'). Many of the things said about proper names by Russell can, I think, be said about the referential use of definite descriptions without straining senses unduly. (Donnellan 1966: 282)

The crucial question for the purpose of Kripke's argument is: Can a proper name be used instead in something more like the manner of an attributively used definite description?

In order to construct a plausible and relatively clear-cut example of such a use, one is naturally led to consider the sort of cases that Kripke (1980: 54–60, 70, and *passim*) discusses under the rubric of *fixing the reference of a name by a description*, that is, examples like Kaplan's (1969: 228–229) introduction of the term 'Newman 1' as a name for whoever will be the first child born in the twenty-second century.[9] Very well, here is a proper name that is used attributively (if used at all). But can *this*

---

[9] I owe the point that such reference-fixing 'definitions' plausibly give rise to attributive uses for names to my former student, Ilhan Inan.

name be used referentially? It can, though presumably not by us. Unless and until we take ourselves to have someone in mind who Newman 1 will be, we are powerless to bestow upon the proper name so defined what Russell (1988: 21) described as 'the direct use which it always wishes to have, as simply standing for a certain object, and not for a description of the object'.[10] Imagine, then, that Newman 1's future parents will be avid followers of the philosophical debates of the latter half of the twentieth century, and will decide that Kaplan has spared them the anxiety of finding the right name for their child. They will be able to use the name referentially. *Voilà*: a referential–attributive distinction for proper names.

But now Kripke's intended argument encounters a serious obstacle. The problem is that some philosophers would maintain, and indeed it is not at all implausible, that the parents' future use of 'Newman 1' and our present use differ in semantic content. In fact, judging from his more recent writings, it is not clear that Kripke himself is prepared to insist (as I am) that, despite the obvious difference in flavor between the two uses, the name 'Newman 1' is semantically univocal.[11]

Finally, suppose this roadblock is somehow circumvented. Even if the case is successfully made that 'Newman 1' retains the same semantic content regardless of whether it is given a Good referential use or an attributive use, it is still open to the semantic-significance theorist to argue, not implausibly, that this precisely reflects the semantic gulf—which Kripke himself (1980: 55–58 and *passim*) insists upon—that separates the name from the description that fixes its reference.

III

There is no dispute concerning the legitimacy of the referential/attributive distinction. The bone of contention concerns its significance, or lack of significance, for semantics. Given the existence of this controversy, one cannot simply take (an appropriate generalization of) the conjunction of theses *SS*—or alternatively, the conjunction of theses *SS'*—as a neutral characterization of the distinction. Fortunately (and wisely), Donnellan (1966) provides distinct characterizations of the distinction.

In the opening section, he characterizes it in terms of another distinction, that between the Russellian 'denotation' of a definite description and what a speaker refers to in using an expression. In 'On Denoting', after presenting his theory of descriptions, Russell explains his notion of denotation for definite descriptions as

---

[10] In Kaplan's later writings, 'Newman 1' has been changed into a name for the first child to be born in the twenty-first century rather than the twenty-second. See e.g. Kaplan (1979: 397). No reason for the change was given. Perhaps having recognized Inan's point (see the immediately preceding note), an indulgent Kaplan was simply growing impatient to give the name the direct use which it always wishes to have. (The change in example is accompanied by a radical change in view regarding what one can do with the name; see below.) Since the various controversies that surround reference-fixing stipulations were not resolved before the turn of the century, I am granting us a small reprieve by reverting to Kaplan's original example. I shall alter some quotations below accordingly.

[11] I have in mind certain passages in the preface to Kripke (1980: 20–21), and especially in Kripke (1988: 146–147 n. 43 and 44). Kripke explicitly proclaims his neutrality on such issues.

follows (using the word 'proposition' where nowadays we would probably use the word 'sentence'):

> Every proposition in which 'the author of *Waverley*' occurs being explained as above, the proposition 'Scott was the author of *Waverley*' (i.e. 'Scott was identical with the author of *Waverley*') becomes 'One and only one entity wrote *Waverley*, and Scott was identical with that one' ... Thus if '*C*' is a denoting phrase [i.e. definite description], it may happen that there is one entity *x* (there cannot be more than one) for which the proposition '*x* is identical with *C*' is true, this proposition being interpreted as above. We may then say that the entity *x* is the denotation of the phrase '*C*'. Thus Scott is the denotation of 'the author of *Waverley*'. (Russell 1905: 169)[12]

Similarly, then, the Russellian denotation of the description 'Smith's murderer' is defined as being the person who actually murdered Smith, if there is exactly one such person, and nothing otherwise—irrespective of whom the speaker might have in mind and mean, on a particular occasion, in using the phrase. The referential–attributive distinction may then be explained by saying that in a referential use of a definite description, but not in an attributive use, there is someone or something the speaker has in mind and to which the speaker refers using the description (and which the speaker's assertion is thereby directly about), independently of its satisfying, or its not satisfying, the particular conditions that would make it the denotation, in Russell's sense, of the description used.

Interestingly, Donnellan's initial characterization of the referential–attributive distinction thus closely parallels Kripke's later characterization of a more general distinction, of which Donnellan's is supposed to be a special case, in terms of the Gricean distinction between *speaker reference* (what the speaker refers to) and *semantic reference* (what the expression refers to). The parallel is striking, but it is also very likely misleading. It is my impression—based on numerous lectures and discussions, as well as his writings—that Donnellan presupposes what I call the *speech-act centered conception of semantics*. On the speech-act centered conception, semantic attributes of expressions—like a singular term's referring to an object, or a sentence's expressing a proposition—somehow reduce to, are to be understood by means of, are derived from, or at least are directly determined by, the illocutionary acts performed by speakers in using those expressions, or perhaps the illocutionary acts that would normally be performed in using those expressions. This contrasts with an *expression centered conception*, which I favor, according to which the semantic attributes of expressions are not conceptually derivative of the speech acts performed by their utterers, and are thought of instead as intrinsic to the expressions themselves, or to the expressions *as* expressions of a particular language and as occurring in a particular context.

---

[12] An important aspect (all too often ignored) of Russell's theory in 'On Denoting' is that a definite description ⌜the φ⌝, though allegedly having no 'meaning in isolation', is nevertheless said to 'denote' the object that satisfies its matrix φ, when there is only one such object, and to 'denote' nothing otherwise. This semantic relation is not simply an idle wheel in Russell's philosophy; it carries a vitally important epistemological payload. It is through denoting, in this sense, that we are supposed to form beliefs and other thoughts 'about'—and thereby to gain crucial cognitive access to—the many and varied objects so important in our lives but with which we are not *directly acquainted* (in Russell's sense). See especially the first two paragraphs of Russell (1905).

The expression centered conception takes seriously the idea that expressions are *symbols*, and that as such, they have a semantic life of their own. The expression centered conception need not deny that semantics, at least for a natural language, may be ultimately a result or product of speech acts, rather than (or more likely, in addition to) the other way around. But the expression centered conception marks a definite separation between semantics and pragmatics, allowing for at least the possibility of extreme, pervasive, and even highly systematic deviation between the two. The speech-act centered conception is more reductionist in spirit.

The expression centered conception is the received conception in the tradition of Frege and Russell. With their emphasis on artificial or idealized languages, it is they more than anyone else who deserve credit for cultivating the expression centered conception among contemporary philosophers of language. Wittgenstein focused, in contrast, on spoken, natural language in his impenetrable but seemingly penetrating diatribe against the expression centered conception. Whether or not he himself subscribed to the speech-act centered conception, it is he—with his influential slogan that 'meaning is use'—who must bear the brunt of responsibility for that rival conception.

If Donnellan subscribes to the speech-act centered conception, he is not alone. I fear it may be the dominant conception—especially among philosophers with a propensity toward nominalism, physicalism, anti-realism, or other reductionisms, and among those, like Donnellan, who trace their scholarly lineage to Wittgenstein. Anyone whose lineage traces back to Wittgenstein can trace it a step further to Russell. And there are indeed clear elements of both traditions manifest in Donnellan's thought on reference and related matters. Still, his commitment to the speech-act centered conception might explain Donnellan's unwavering endorsement of the stronger version of the semantic-significance thesis. The speech-act centered conception cannot distinguish correctly between the semantic content of a sentence with respect to a given context and the content of the assertion, or assertions (statements, utterances), normally made by a speaker in uttering the sentence in that context. If this interpretation (which is somewhat speculative) is correct, then Donnellan conceives of speaker reference as, at least implicitly, a semantic, rather than a pragmatic, notion. Furthermore, he then conceives of Russell's notion of denotation for definite descriptions as a *non-semantic* notion, since it does not concern (at least not directly) acts of speakers' reference normally performed with descriptions. This interpretation seems to be confirmed by the subsequent discussion in Donnellan (1978). There he adopts Kripke's terminology of 'speaker reference' and 'semantic reference', but he does not equate what he means by the latter with Russellian denotation, vigorously arguing instead that 'semantic reference' depends on, and is determined by, speaker reference, which may be other than the Russellian denotation.[13]

---

[13] Donnellan sometimes appears to allow for semantic reference in the absence of speaker reference. On the one hand, Donnellan (1978: 30, 32) says that in using a definite description attributively, the speaker does not refer to anything even if the description happens to be proper, in the Russellian sense. But he also seems to say (on the same p. 32, and in the same paragraph)

It is the expression centered conception, and the general Frege–Russell tradition, that is the natural habitat of the distinction between speaker reference and semantic reference (as well as such other Gricean distinctions as that between speaker meaning and sentence meaning). My own view—well within the Frege–Russell tradition—is that Donnellan's apparent cataloging of speaker reference as semantic and of Russellian denotation as non-semantic gets matters exactly reversed. It is just one piece of evidence of the extent to which the speech-act centered conception presents a seriously distorted picture of what semantics is, enough so that I am tempted to say that those in the grip of that conception, when applying such semantic terms as 'refer' and 'express' to expressions, are not talking about anything semantic at all.[14] In any event, from the perspective of the expression centered conception it would be dangerous to take Donnellan's characterization of the referential/attributive distinction in terms of speaker reference and denotation at face value.

IV

Donnellan (1966: s. III, 285–289) alternatively characterizes the referential–attributive distinction in terms of what a speaker asserts (states, says) and the *de-re/de-dicto* distinction. He does not use the actual terms '*de re*' and '*de dicto*', nor any other arcane terminology for the latter distinction, but he clearly appeals to it. The central idea may be illustrated by a pair of theses paralleling those comprised by SS. Let us call the conjunction of the following theses '*DT*', for 'Donnellan's Thesis':

(DT_a) If a speaker utters 'Smith's murderer is insane' in an appropriate manner in a context c, then the speaker uses 'Smith's murderer' attributively in c iff the speaker, in uttering 'Smith's murderer is insane' in c, asserts *de dicto* that whoever single-handedly murdered Smith is insane (and does not assert of anyone, *de re*, that he/she is insane).

(DT_r) If a speaker utters 'Smith's murderer is insane' in an appropriate manner in a context c, then the speaker uses 'Smith's murderer' referentially for x in c iff the speaker, in uttering 'Smith's murderer is insane' in c, refers to x and asserts of x, *de re*, that he/she is insane (and does not assert *de dicto* that whoever single-handedly murdered Smith is insane).[15]

---

that an attributively used description itself refers to its Russellian denotation. This leads to the curious position that when a speaker uses a proper description attributively, the description refers but the speaker does not. And this does not fit well the speech-act centered conception of semantics. But coupled with Donnellan's more central position that when a description is used referentially for something x, both the description and the speaker refer to x even if x is not the Russellian denotation, nor does this curious position exactly fit the expression centered conception—or any other conception that I can think of. Though I am uncertain what to make of Donnellan's assertions here, I believe that a careful reading reveals that appearances are deceptive, and that Donnellan (through a carefully placed occurrence of the subjunctive 'would') deliberately avoids any commitment to the claim that an attributively used proper description has semantic reference. I may be wrong.

[14] See Salmon (1995: 18–19 n. 27).

[15] Donnellan has confirmed in correspondence (see n. 5) that he endorses both of these theses in addition to SS. There are passages in Donnellan (1966) in s. III and again in s. VIII, suggesting, contra *DT*, that one makes a *de re* assertion when using a proper description (in the Russellian sense) attributively. Donnellan says that any such suggestion was unintended.

I believe that many philosophers—including many who reject *SS*—would take *DT* to be analytic, by means of an appropriate generalization that literally *defines* the referential–attributive distinction in terms of *de re* and *de dicto* illocutionary acts (stating, asking, etc.). For example, in a criticism of Donnellan on the semantic-significance thesis, Scott Soames characterizes the distinction by saying that

> a referential use of a description to refer to an individual o is a use in which the speaker *says of* o that o is such and such. What, we might ask, is it to *say of* an individual that it is such and such? The answer, it seems to me, is that to say of an individual that it is such and such is to assert the singular proposition that predicates such and such of that individual . . . In short, referential uses of definite descriptions are cases in which the speaker asserts a singular proposition about the individual the description is used to refer to. (Soames 1994: 149–152)[16]

Soames's remark alludes to an intimate relationship that obtains, on the direct-reference theory, between the *de-re/de-dicto* distinction, on the one hand, and the distinction between singular and general propositions, on the other. To assert (or deny, believe, disbelieve, etc.) that such-and-such is to assert (deny, etc.) a certain proposition, the proposition that such-and-such. So to assert *about* (or to assert *of*) someone or something *x* that he/she/it is thus-and-so is to assert the proposition *about* *x* that *he/she/it* is thus-and-so. The latter is a singular proposition. *De re* assertion (or denial, etc.) is nothing more nor less than assertion (denial) of a singular proposition.[17] Recognizing this relationship, an equivalence between *DT* and *SS* can be seen to follow from a general principle governing the separate phenomena that I distinguish under the epithets of 'speaker assertion' and 'semantic content' (Salmon 1982: 40–41).

(*AC*) If a speaker utters an English sentence *S* in an appropriate manner in a context *c*, then *S* expresses proposition *p* as its English semantic content with respect to *c* iff the speaker, in uttering *S* in *c*, asserts *p*.

This assertion/content principle is plausible. Some might even hold it to be analytic, true solely as a consequence of the meanings of 'assert', 'semantic content', and 'utter in an appropriate manner'.[18] And especially those under the spell of the speech-act centered conception of semantics tend to embrace the principle as trivial. Soames, on the other hand, must deny *AC*. For it is logically true that if *AC*, then (*DT* iff *SS*). Donnellan and his followers may have arrived at *SS* precisely via the assertion/content principle *AC* in combination with an implicit definition or characterization of the referential/attributive distinction in terms of *de re* and *de dicto* assertion. But taking *DT* to be true, let alone analytic, is a mistake. In fact, I contend that both theses *DT*$_a$ and

---

[16] Compare also Neale (1990: 85). Though some of the general conclusions reached by Soames are friendly to the views expressed both here and in my previous writings on the subject, most of the arguments he uses to reach those conclusions are not (as will shortly become clearer).

[17] I provide an argument for this in Salmon (1986: 2–6) and a more detailed treatment in Salmon (1990).

[18] The word 'assert' is used throughout the present chapter in its usual sense, which is strict enough to allow for the distinction—highlighted by Grice—between what a person asserts (or 'says') and what he/she *means* ('implicates') by what was actually asserted. Not everything that a speaker means is asserted, nor vice versa. *Cf.* Salmon (1991: 88).

DT_r have straightforward counter-examples. Indeed, I believe all are false: AC. DT. and SS.

The case against DT and AC is probably best seen in the light of a phenomenon that Kaplan (1989a) has called *the pseudo de re*:

A typical example is 'John says that the lying S.O.B. who took my car is honest'. It is clear that John does not say, 'The lying S.O.B. who took your car is honest'. Does John say ⌜δ is honest⌝ for some directly referential term δ which the reporter believes to refer to the lying S.O.B. who took the car? Not necessarily. John may say something as simple as, 'The man I sent to you yesterday is honest'. The reporter has simply substituted his description for John's. What justifies this shocking falsification of John's speech? Nothing! But we do it, and often recognize—or don't care—when it is being done. The form lends itself to strikingly distorted reports. As Church has shown, in his *Introduction to Mathematical Logic* (Princeton: Princeton University Press, 1956), on page 25, when John says 'Sir Walter Scott is the author of *Waverley*' use of the *pseudo de re* form (plus a quite plausible synonymy transformation) allows the report, 'John says that there are twenty-nine counties in Utah'! I do not see that the existence of the *pseudo de re* form of report poses any issues of sufficient theoretical interest to make it worth pursuing. (Kaplan 1989a: 555–556 n. 71)

The Church argument mentioned by Kaplan is principally concerned with the question of whether sentences should be said to refer ('denote'). The argument shows under relatively minimal assumptions that 'Scott is the author of *Waverley*' and 'There are 29 counties in Utah' refer to the same thing, thus supporting Frege's doctrine that sentences refer to their truth-values. Adapting Church's original argument to embeddings of such sentences within the non-extensional phrase 'John says that', Kaplan tacitly considers the following chain of assertion attributions (where we may let the first be true by hypothesis):

(i) John says that Scott = the author of *Waverley*

(ii) John says that Scott = the man who wrote 29 Waverley Novels altogether

(iii) John says that the number n such that Scott = the man who wrote n Waverley Novels altogether = 29

(iv) John says that the number of counties in Utah = 29.

Here both (ii) and (iv) are obtained from their immediate predecessors by the liberal sort of substitution characteristic of the so-called *pseudo de re*, whereas (iii) is obtained from (ii) by the mentioned 'plausible synonymy transformation'—in this case the assumption that 'Scott = the man who wrote 29 Waverley Novels altogether' and 'The number n such that Scott = the man who wrote n Waverley Novels altogether = 29' are synonymous (or at least sufficiently close in meaning that if John asserted the content of the first, then he may be accurately reported as having asserted the content of the second). The final attribution (iv) intuitively does not follow from (i). Following Church, Kaplan considers a further attribution obtained from (iv) by a second application of the synonymy transformation, though this is strictly unnecessary to the argument. Indeed, even (iv) is unnecessary, since (iii) already goes well beyond what may be validly inferred from (i).

Kaplan's apparent conclusion—based at least in part on his liberal adaptation of Church's argument—is that *pseudo de re* substitutions are not in general truth-preserving. It is presumably for that very reason that they are supposed to pose no interesting theoretical issues. Wettstein (1986) has argued that the phenomenon in question leads, on the contrary, to a highly significant conclusion:

> In many, many contexts of reporting what other people say, think, believe, and so on, substitutions of embedded singular terms preserve truth, and so do substitutions of names for other names, even names for definite descriptions, definite descriptions for names, or definite descriptions for definite descriptions, as the following examples illustrate.
> ... Tom, a new faculty member, is told about all the new funding that the dean has arranged for faculty research. He says, not having any idea of who the dean is, 'The dean is obviously very smart'. I report to Barbara that Tom believes that Mike is very smart or that Jonathan's soccer coach is very smart (in case Barbara, say, characteristically refers to the relevant individual as 'Mike' or is most familiar with him in his role as Jonathan's soccer coach).
> Such substitutions, at least in the sorts of contexts indicated [like Kaplan's], are perfectly acceptable. Nor do we, in making such substitutions, have to worry about preserving or reporting the Fregean sense of the original remarks. In such contexts at least, the truth or falsity of the report depends not upon accurately capturing the Fregean thought believed, but simply upon correctly formulating who it is the believer has a belief about and what the believer believes about him. ...
> ... Belief reports are extremely resistant to neat theoretical treatment—and this is so on either the Fregean or the anti-Fregean orientation. Perhaps a neat treatment is not even possible. (Wettstein 1986: 205–208)

Wettstein adds in a footnote that truth-preserving substitutions of nonsynonymous expressions in assertion or belief reports, etc., 'are particularly interesting, since not only Fregeans but just about everyone has assumed that such substitutions ought not to preserve truth. This shows, I think, that we've virtually all had the wrong idea about the semantics of attitude reports.' In sharp contrast to Kaplan's summary dismissal of the so-called *pseudo de re* as theoretically uninteresting, Wettstein says that the phenomenon, in combination with other data, 'suggests that what is reported is not (at least not exclusively) propositional content believed'. Wettstein adduces this data to motivate an unorthodox and highly controversial theory of the meanings of attitude reports. (Since he does not address Kaplan's discussion, Wettstein does not respond to Kaplan's adaptation of Church's argument.)

Wettstein's example involving Tom and the dean is sufficiently similar to Kaplan's involving John and the lying S.O.B. that both obviously qualify as instances of the general phenomenon that Kaplan means by his phrase 'the *pseudo de re*'. One significant difference between the two cases, however, or at least a potentially significant difference, is that John presumably uses the description 'the man I sent to you yesterday' referentially for the liar in question, whereas Tom uses 'the dean' attributively. This is supported by (and may be the main point of) Wettstein's remark that Tom has no idea who the dean is. But this difference does not matter as regards the overall pattern. In fact, the attributive use in Wettstein's example makes it a purer example, in some sense, of the phenomenon that Kaplan has in mind. The main point is: it seems we readily accept the reporter's substitution of his own description in either case.

The position I take with regard to the *pseudo de re* steers a middle course between the diametrically opposed conclusions of Kaplan and Wettstein, and has more to recommend it than either of these other treatments. I agree with Wettstein, as against Kaplan, that such substitutions are truth-preserving. But I do not agree that they call for an unconventional account of attitude attributions. The central characteristic of the *pseudo de re*—and the precise reason for the presence of the words '*de re*' in the phrase—is that, as Wettstein puts it, 'the truth or falsity of the report depends not upon accurately capturing the Fregean thought believed, but simply upon correctly formulating who it is the believer has a belief about and what the believer believes about him'. One can put this without begging the crucial question by talking about the *acceptability* or *unacceptability* of the report instead of its truth or falsity. The defining feature of the *pseudo de re* is that such reports behave in ordinary discourse as if they were *de re*. They do this, I contend, for a very simple reason: they are *de re*. I mean that they are not 'pseudo' at all; they are genuine, ordinary, conventional, authentic, bonafide, run-of-the-mill, barnyard-variety, par-for-the-course *de re*, nothing more and nothing less. In Russell's terminology, the relevant description occurrence is a *primary occurrence* rather than a *secondary occurrence*, the description has *wide scope* rather than *narrow scope*. Kaplan's term '*pseudo de re*' is a seriously misleading misnomer.

In Wettstein's example, Tom believes the proposition that *whoever* is dean is very smart. This is *de dicto* rather than *de re*, general rather than singular. But, and in part in virtue of this general belief, Tom also believes *of* the dean, that is, of Jonathan's soccer coach Mike, that *he* is very smart. It is this latter *de re* belief that I contend Wettstein is reporting when he says, 'Tom believes that Jonathan's soccer coach is very smart'. In any event, that report must be interpreted *de re* rather than *de dicto*—with the description 'Jonathan's soccer coach' taking wide rather than narrow scope—if it is to have any hope of being a sincere attempt at accurate reporting (assuming that Wettstein does not believe that Tom has independently formed the opinion, after watching Jonathan play, that he has been cleverly coached). It would also seem that the report, so interpreted, is indeed true. Tom's having no idea who the dean is does not prevent him from forming a favorable opinion about the dean's intelligence. Likewise in Kaplan's example, the report 'John says that the lying S.O.B. who took my car is honest' must be interpreted *de re* rather than *de dicto* if it is to have any hope of being accurate—the *de dicto* reading being ruled out of court as a gratuitous attribution of inconsistency. And interpreted *de re*, the report is quite accurate, even if not completely faithful. (Indeed, the truth of the *de re* report is perhaps even more evident in Kaplan's example, despite his misgivings, due to John's referential use of the relevant description.)

One may object that in uttering the words 'The man I sent to you yesterday is honest', what John *literally says* is that whichever man he had sent the day before is honest. This observation is indeed correct. But it should not be lodged as a protest. For again I say that it is precisely *by* literally saying that whichever man he had sent the day before is honest that John says *of* the liar in question, *de re*, that he is honest. (A faithful report would presumably report what John *literally* asserts, rather than what he *indirectly* asserts by virtue of his literal assertion.) This is by no means a singular or unusual case. Nor does it take essential advantage of the fact that the original speaker used a description referentially. There is also someone whom Tom says is very smart (namely of course, the dean/coach), even when using the description 'the dean' only attributively. Virtually *whenever* one asserts that the such-and-such is thus-and-so, one thereby asserts *of* the such-and-such, if there is exactly one, that he/she/it is thus-and-so. Whether for good or bad, this evidently is how our notion of *de re* assertion works.[19]

This position (unlike Wettstein's) easily blocks Kaplan's adaptation of Church's argument. In the succession of assertion reports (i)–(iv), each must be read either *de dicto* or *de re*. If the transition from (i) to (ii) is to be an instance of the same general phenomenon as we find in the lying S.O.B. case and the dean/coach case, then (i) is to be interpreted *de re*, reporting that John says *of* the author of *Waverley* that Scott is *him*. Interpreted *de re*, (ii) then straightforwardly follows (assuming that Scott wrote exactly twenty-nine Waverley Novels). Similarly, if the transition from (iii) to (iv) is to be an instance of the same phenomenon, then both are to be interpreted *de re*, as reporting that John says *of* a certain number that *it* is twenty-nine. So interpreted, however, the transition from (ii) to (iii) cannot be justified as a 'plausible synonymy transformation'. Indeed, so interpreted, (iii) does not even appear to follow from (ii); if John is sufficiently taciturn, (iii) may be false, interpreted *de re*, even when (ii) is true (interpreted either way). The transition from (ii) to (iii) can be justified as a mere synonymy transformation only if both are interpreted *de dicto* rather than *de re*. It thus emerges that Kaplan's adaptation of Church's argument turns on the fallacy of equivocation—where the crucial ambiguity is not lexical but an ambiguity of scope.[20]

Invoking the connection between the *de re* and singular propositions, the position I am defending is tantamount to the claim that in asserting a general proposition to the effect that the such-and-such is thus-and-so, one typically also asserts the corresponding singular proposition. In a single utterance John asserts at least two different things: that the man sent the day before is honest, and the singular proposition about the liar in question that *he* is honest. More generally, in uttering a sentence ⌜ψ(the φ)⌝, one thereby typically asserts two propositions: the general proposition which is the semantic content of the sentence (this is one's literal assertion); and indirectly (and non-literally), in virtue of the first assertion, also the corresponding singular proposition about the person or object that uniquely satisfies φ, if there is one. The speaker buys two propositions for the price of one. This is so, I contend, whether the definite description ⌜the φ⌝ was used referentially or attributively, *and even if the*

---

[19] *Cf.* Salmon (1982: 1–2; 1991: 88). It is not implausible that exceptions arise in cases where ⌜such-and-such⌝ trivially entails ⌜thus-and-so⌝, as e.g. in 'The shortest spy is a spy'. See Searle (1979*b*: 207); and Salmon (1982: 45 n. 7). I am strongly inclined to believe, however, that these are not genuine exceptions to a fully encompassing latitudinarianism with respect to assertion.

[20] Church's original argument commits no fallacy; in my judgment, its soundness is unimpeachable. It is Kaplan's adaptation of Church's argument that commits the fallacy of equivocation.

description was used Badly, that is, even if it was used referentially for someone who does not satisfy φ. In this special case, the speaker may have asserted no less than three propositions—all for the price of one. It is precisely this possibility of multiple assertion by a single utterance that defies principle *AC* and both DT_a and DT_r.

The availability of this simple, straightforward account of the so-called *pseudo de re* has not been widely recognized.[21] There are a number of sources for this oversight. First, there is the familiar (if still somewhat controversial) observation that *de re* belief does not follow from *de dicto*, even assuming the relevant person or object exists. In the now hackneyed example, Kevin may believe, solely on the basis of reflection on the concepts, that whoever is shortest among spies is a spy, without thereby suspecting anyone in particular of being a spy. That is to say, *latitudinarianism*—the doctrine that the inference from the *de dicto*, together with an existence premiss, to the *de re* is valid—is mistaken. In order to graduate from *de dicto* belief to *de re*, one must bear some epistemically substantial *connection* to the person or object in question. Notoriously, there is no consensus concerning the precise nature of *de re* connectedness, but there is widespread (even if not unanimous) agreement that it is cognitively more 'real' than the mere coincidence that obtains between Kevin's apprehension of the concept *he/she who is shortest among spies* and the person whom that concept happens to fit. To use Kaplan's (1969) phrase, one must be *en rapport* with the entity in question. Russell held that one must be *directly acquainted* with the entity, in his peculiar sense. This requirement is easily seen to be excessive, and more recent philosophers have substituted various weaker acquaintance relations for Russell's. Many embrace the view that one must merely *know who* the person is, or *know what object* it is, in an ordinary sense. Some say instead—or in addition—that one must have the person or object 'in mind' sufficiently to be able to use a term referentially for him/her/it.[22] It is assumed furthermore that *de re* assertion has an analogous prerequisite, one appropriate to assertion in lieu of belief. For example, it is held that the subject must possess and use a special sort of singular term—a 'vivid name' perhaps, or a directly referential, logically proper (Millian) name, or at least a term used referentially rather than attributively.[23] In addition to all of the above, there is a general pre-evidential bias in favor of the tenet that a speaker is allowed only one assertion per utterance of an unambiguous sentence (perhaps as a consequence of the assertion/content principle *AC*).

These are myths. The example of the shortest spy does indeed show that latitudinarianism with regard to belief is mistaken. But *de re* belief does not require anything

---

[21] One possible exception is Sosa (1970: 890). See also Searle (1979*b*).

[22] For an example of the first view, see Quine (1981: 272–273); Soames (1994: 159–162) is similarly flawed by presupposition of an admixture of both the first and second view.

[23] Kaplan (1969) seems to have required the use of a vivid name (among other things). Later in Kaplan (1979) and also in his brief discussion (quoted above) of the so-called *pseudo de re* in Kaplan (1989*a*), he evidently presupposes instead that use of a directly referential term is both necessary and sufficient. Still later, in Kaplan (1989*b*: 583 n. 36), he appears to move toward the less restrictive view that a referential use is sufficient. As should already be clear, I believe this permissive trend in Kaplan's thought is entirely positive and ought to be followed to its natural, and plausible, conclusion.

as stringent as knowing who the person is or having the object 'in mind', in a Donnellanian sense. An eyewitness distinguishing the culprit from the decoys in a police lineup has a *de re* belief, but may not 'know who' that person is, in the usual sense. And when the investigating homicide detective utters 'Smith's murderer is insane' using the description attributively, there is indeed someone of whom the detective suspects insanity, though not someone he has in mind (in the relevant sense). The detective need not even be 'acquainted' with the murderer, in any ordinary sense; his knowledge of the murderer is *by description*, in Russell's phrase. Never mind; he still manages to pull off a *de re* belief. It is enough that the believer is appropriately cognitively connected to the person or object. The *de re* connection need not be direct and intimate; it may be remote and indirect, perhaps consisting of a network of causal intermediaries interposed between the cognizer and the object.[24]

Donnellan (1979: 58) suggested that in order to assert something *de re* about a person or object, there is no requirement, of the sort Kaplan (1969) laid down, that the speaker use a vivid term or even that the speaker use a term that denotes the entity in question. Interestingly, Donnellan suggested instead that Kaplan's third and final condition is both necessary and, by itself, sufficient: that one use a term that is a *name of* the entity for the speaker—analogous to the sense in which a bad photograph may be a *picture of* an object that it does not resemble, and fail to be a *picture of* another object to which it bears an uncanny resemblance (Kaplan 1969: 227–229). That is, Donnellan suggested that it is necessary and sufficient that the entity enter properly into the 'genetic' account of how the speaker came to learn the term he/she uses to refer to it. I am suggesting that some such condition (perhaps one involving 'mental names'?) may be operative in the formation of *de re* beliefs, thus blocking Kevin from suspecting anyone in particular of espionage while allowing the homicide detective to form his *de re* diagnosis of insanity. But *pace* Donnellan, any such condition seems to me overkill for the making of a *de re* assertion. Kaplan's well-documented change of attitude toward the *de re* is also accompanied by a shift in which attitude is alleged to be *de re* (see n. 10 above). Kaplan (1969: 228–229) says, 'I am unwilling to adopt any theory of proper names which permits me to perform a dubbing in absentia, as by solemnly declaring "I hereby dub the first child to be born in the twenty-second century 'Newman 1' ", and thus grant myself standing to have beliefs about that as yet unborn child.' Kaplan (1979: 397) recants:

All this familiarity with demonstratives has led me to believe that I was mistaken in 'Quantifying In' in thinking that the most fundamental cases of what I might now describe as a person having a propositional attitude (believing, asserting, etc.) toward a singular proposition required that the person be *en rapport* with the subject of the proposition. It is now clear that I can assert *of* the first child to be born in the twenty-first century that *he* will be bald, simply by assertively uttering 'Dthat ("the first child to be born in the twenty-first century") will be bald'.

I say that Kaplan was right on both counts. Where he goes wrong is in thinking that his second observation shows that his first was mistaken. Saying something

---

[24] *Cf.* Sosa (1970). See also Salmon (1986: 179–180 n. 19; 1987/88: 199 n. 8, 204 n. 11, 213 n. 17).

about Newman 1 is a piece of cake. Forming a belief about him/her, by contrast, requires some degree of cognitive connection, however sparing. *De re* connectedness is required for *de re* belief, not for *de re* assertion.

We must guard against deciding at the outset, before considering the evidence, that all of the propositional attitudes behave as one—especially if something that makes as little cognitive demand on the subject as mere assertion is counted as one of the attitudes. Perhaps one must apprehend propositions in order to believe them. And perhaps one must apprehend propositions in order to make assertions. But it is doubtful that one must apprehend what one is asserting in order to assert it. Whereas latitudinarianism fails in the case of belief, some form seems to govern assertion. This conclusion does not reflect an idiosyncratic theoretical bias. Regardless of one's views on the controversial issues, there seems every reason to admit that, intuitively, when Tom says 'The dean is very smart' he thereby says *of* the administrator in question that he is very smart, and when John says 'The man I sent to you yesterday is honest' he thereby says *of* the liar in question that he is honest. There is even some intuition that when I say 'Newman 1 is unconnected to us', I thereby assert something *of* a particular future individual.

Ironically, evidence in favor of my proposal comes indirectly from Donnellan (1979). The burden of that article is to challenge Kripke's famous examples of allegedly contingent *a priori* statements. Kripke's examples are trivial consequences of stipulations that fix the reference of a new name or other term by means of a definite description—sentences like 'Assuming Newman 1 will exist, he or she will be born in the twenty-second century.' The overall structure of Donnellan's argument is that the sort of knowledge contained in such sentences is *de re*. Yet one typically cannot gain such *de re* knowledge merely on the basis of the reference-fixing introduction of the name, without further experience of the object. In the course of the argument, Donnellan applies a pair of general principles to show that one has not gained the relevant *de re* knowledge. The principles—let us call them '$K1$' and '$K2$'—are stated by Donnellan as follows:

($K1$) If one has a name for a person, say 'N', and there is a bit of knowledge that one would express by saying 'N is φ' then if one subsequently meets the person it will be true to say of him, using the second-person pronoun, 'I knew that you were φ',

($K2$) If an object is called by one name, say 'N', by one group of people and by another name by a second group, say 'M', and if, in the language of the first group 'N is φ' expresses a bit of knowledge of theirs and if 'is ψ' is a translation of 'is φ' into the language of the second group then if the relevant facts are known to the second group, they can say truly that the first group 'knew that M is ψ'. (Donnellan 1979: 55)[25]

Here the 'you' and the 'M' are to be taken as occurring within the scope of the non-extensional operator 'knew that'. Donnellan adds that

---

[25] In an endnote Donnellan recognizes that for the purposes of his argument, he does not need to defend these principles even for cases in which the user of the name 'N' also uses a second name for the same person or object, believing the two names to refer to different entities. But Donnellan also there expresses a temptation to extend the principles to some of these cases as well. (My own view is that they should be extended across the board to all such cases.)

essentially the same considerations that were adduced for denying that there was knowledge of an entity just in virtue of the sort of stipulation that introduces a rigid designator by means of a description can be applied to the other propositional attitudes. It would, for example, seem to me just as incorrect to say to John who turns out to be the first child born in the [twenty-second century], 'I believed about you some [one hundred and] twenty-five years before your birth...'. (Donnellan 1979: 56–57)

Donnellan evidently endorses the following analogues of his stated principles:

(A1) If one has a name for a person, say 'N', and one makes an assertion (in the ordinary way) by uttering 'N is φ' then if one subsequently meets the person it will be true to say of him, using the second-person pronoun, 'I said that you were φ',

(B1) If one has a name for a person, say 'N', and one believes what one would express by saying 'N is φ' then if one subsequently meets the person it will be true to say of him, using the second-person pronoun, 'I believed that you were φ'; etc.

These various principles, in effect, licence the substitution, under appropriate circumstances, of a name or of a simple indexical ('you') for a co-referential name in an attribution of an assertion or other propositional attitude. The basis for these principles is the fact that such sentences as 'You were φ', 'N is φ', and 'M is ψ', with 'N' and 'M' being names, semantically contain singular propositions (in the relevant languages), so that one who utters them assertively makes a literal *de re* assertion about the referent of the name or indexical, and any knowledge or belief of the propositions they contain is *de re* knowledge or belief.[26] This suggests certain more fundamental principles:

(A1') If an expression, say 'φ', expresses a property (state, condition) F in one's language, then one asserts about a person, *de re*, that he/she is F iff, if one were subsequently to meet the person, it would be true to say to him, using the second-person pronoun, 'I said that you were φ'.

(B1') If an expression, say 'φ', expresses a property (state, condition) F in one's language, then one believes about a person, *de re*, that he/she is F iff, if one were subsequently to meet the person, it would be true to say to him, using the second-person pronoun, 'I believed that you were φ'; etc.

Indeed, it is difficult to imagine a justification for A1 that does not go by way of the notion of *de re* assertion, or some closely related notion. In any event, I think it is clear that Donnellan bases his principles on more fundamental principles like these.[27] Earlier, Ernest Sosa also implicitly relied on principles like these in making

---

[26] Donnellan (1974) more or less endorses the idea that 'predicative statements' (those predicating properties other than existence, or its cognates) involving names semantically express singular propositions.

[27] Strictly speaking, only one of the two conditionals making up the biconditional in B1' is needed for Donnellan's argument, though I believe it is clear that he would endorse the full biconditional. Just before formulating his general principles, Donnellan (1979: 54) says, 'I am assuming, to use the jargon, that if we now have any knowledge (other than about linguistic matters) just as a result of the stipulation concerning the sentence, "Newman I will be the first child born in the [22nd] century" it would have to be knowledge *de re*. That is, it would have to be knowledge *about* an individual in the sense that there is (or will be) an individual about whom we now know something and if that individual turns out to be John we now know something about John.'

a determination concerning whether one has a given *de re* belief about someone or something, or has made a *de re* assertion, etc.[28] I shall call this 'the Donnellan–Sosa test'. Illustrating how the test applies to the case of Newman 1, Donnellan observes,

> If the first child born in the [twenty-second century] comes to be named 'John' it would not be correct to say then that although we had a different name for him we knew [one hundred and] twenty-five years beforehand that John would be the first child born in the [twenty-second century] ... I suggest that the reason is that the stipulations have not given rise to any knowledge (other than of linguistic matters). And so not to any knowledge *a priori*. (1979: 55)

My principal concern here is not with the thorny question of whether Kripke's alleged examples of the contingent *a priori* hold up under such careful scrutiny.[29] Our concern is instead with the more immediate matter of whether there is *de re* belief or assertion present in the sort of examples that Kaplan has labeled the *pseudo de re*. And here the more fundamental principles $A1'$ and $B1'$ are the ones to employ. By contrast to the Newman 1 case, John in Kaplan's example, having sincerely uttered the sentence 'The man I sent to you yesterday is honest', surely could truthfully address the man in question with the words 'I said that you were honest', and even with 'I believed that you were honest'. Hence, applying $A1'$ and $B1'$, John did assert and believe of the man, *de re*, that he was honest. And just as certainly, Tom in Wettstein's example could address the dean truthfully (if shamelessly) with the words, 'I told Wettstein that you were very smart', and with 'Even before I learned who you were, I had already formed the opinion that you were very smart, based on the wonderful things you have done for the faculty.' Consequently, Tom made the relevant *de re* assertion, and had the corresponding *de re* belief.

The contrast between Kaplan's example and Wettstein's now looms large. Recall that Tom, unlike John, uses his description attributively. Since Donnellan endorses DT_r as well as the principles $A1$, etc., in order to avoid inconsistency he must deny that Tom can truthfully say to the dean 'I said, and believed, that you were very smart'. It is not surprising, therefore, to find that he says of the Newman 1 case, 'It would ... seem to me just as incorrect to say to John who turns out to be the first child born in the [twenty-second century], "I believed about you some [one hundred and] twenty-five years before your birth ...", "I asserted about you some [one hundred and] twenty-five years before your birth ...", etc.'[30] In fact, however,

---

[28] See Sosa (1970: 890–891). Others besides may have also used the test. I believe Sosa may be the first to have done so, and to have concluded, correctly, that in some cases, one may have a *de re* belief (or other attitude) about someone without knowing who it is.

[29] I discuss this issue at length in Salmon (1987/88). In a lecture presented in 1984 at a conference at Stanford University, Kripke responded to Donnellan's criticism, arguing that what I am calling 'the Donnellan–Sosa test' does not support Donnellan's contentions in the case of Leverrier's introduction of 'Neptune' as a name for whatever planet it is causing particular perturbations in the orbit of Uranus. *Cf.* Kripke (1980: 79 n.). Notice that 'Neptune' was already a *name of* the planet (in Kaplan's sense) for Leverrier when he so named it, even before it was located in the sky. The case is quite different with 'Newman 1', where Donnellan's criticism of Kripke seems significantly stronger. In the Stanford lecture, Kripke developed and modified his position on the contingent *a priori*. See Salmon (1987/88: 203 n.).

[30] Similar remarks, explicitly echoing Donnellan, occur in Soames (1994: 165).

these two sentences seem significantly different. It is indeed dubious that Newman 1's future contemporaries could truthfully utter 'Some philosophers of the late twentieth century believed that you would not be born until the twenty-second century.' For despite Kaplan's heroic efforts, we simply are not sufficiently *en rapport* to have *de re* beliefs about Newman 1. The *de re* connection is lacking. By contrast, there is no reason why Newman 1's contemporaries could not truthfully utter 'Some philosophers of the late twentieth century had a name for you, and using that name, they said about you that you were not knowable by them (that you would be born in the twenty-second century, etc.).' They might add, 'Of course, they did not know (or even believe) that they were talking about *you*—how could they?—but you are the one they were talking about.' The case of Tom and the dean is clearer. The analogue of Donnellan's remark is plainly incorrect, for both belief and assertion. Worse, since Donnellan also endorses DT_a, he must also deny that John said that the man he had sent the day before was honest. But surely that is exactly what John did say.

The Donnellan–Sosa test does not conclusively settle all such questions. There are some very hard cases. Inevitably individual intuitions in particular applications of the test will sometimes clash. But they often converge, or tend to converge, as in the case of Kevin and the shortest spy. It is fair to say that intuition in applying the Donnellan–Sosa test is not squarely on Donnellan's side. In many cases—especially cases of attributive use where there is also an epistemically 'real' (e.g. causal) connection—it seems clear that intuition is squarely on the other side. (See again n. 29.) Thus, in an article coincidentally published in the same year as Donnellan's article in which he proffers the Donnellan–Sosa test, Searle says:

if I know the sheriff said 'attributively', 'Smith's murderer is insane' and I know Jones is Smith's murderer I might indeed tell Jones, 'Jones, the sheriff believes you are insane', or even report, 'About Jones, the sheriff believes he is insane'. Furthermore even where I know that Jones is not Smith's murderer and I know that Ralph said 'referentially' 'Smith's murderer is insane', and I know he had Jones in mind, I can still report his speech act by saying, 'Ralph said that Smith's murderer is insane', for he did indeed say just that. (Searle 1979: 207)

V

A correct characterization of Donnellan's distinction remains neutral with regard to the theses *AC. DT*, and *SS*. And this requires that the distinction be given in overtly pragmatic terms. As noted, Kripke has made the tantalizing claim that one distinction characterized in just this way covers the referential/attributive distinction and applies more generally to proper names and other non-descriptive terms. We saw in section II above that one of Kripke's arguments in this connection is flawed in that he did not provide an example of a genuinely attributive use of a proper name, and that he misclassifies our routine, everyday uses of names as attributive rather than as referential. But we also saw that attributive uses of names do genuinely exist. Let us consider Kripke's more general distinction in greater detail. He writes:

In a given idiolect, the semantic referent of a designator (without indexicals) is given by a *general* intention of the speaker to refer to a certain object whenever the designator is used.

> The speaker's referent is given by a *specific* intention, on a given occasion, to refer to a certain object. If the speaker believes that the object he wants to talk about, on a given occasion, fulfills the conditions for being the semantic referent, then he believes that there is no clash between his general intentions and his specific intentions. My hypothesis is that Donnellan's referential/attributive distinction should be generalized in this light. For the speaker, on a given occasion, may believe that his specific intention coincides with his general intention for one of two reasons. In one case (the 'simple' case), his specific intention is simply to refer to the semantic referent: that is, his specific intention *is* simply his general semantic intention. (For example, he uses 'Jones' as a name of Jones—elaborate this according to your favorite theory of proper names—and, on this occasion, simply wishes to use 'Jones' to refer to Jones.) Alternatively—the 'complex' case—he has a specific intention, which is distinct from his general intention, but which he believes, as a matter of fact, to determine the same object as the one determined by his general intention. (For example, he wishes to refer to the man 'over there' but believes that he *is* Jones.) In the 'simple' case, the speaker's referent is, *by definition*, the semantic referent. In the 'complex' case, they may coincide, if the speaker's belief is correct, but they need not. (The man 'over there' may be Smith and not Jones.) To anticipate, my hypothesis will be that Donnellan's 'attributive' use is nothing but the 'simple' case, specialized to definite descriptions, and that the 'referential' use is, similarly, the 'complex' case. (Kripke 1977: 15)

One discerns in this passage the source (or at least a source) of Kripke's generalizing Donnellan's distinction into a conceptually separate distinction. He explicitly catalogues what seems a perfectly ordinary use of the name 'Jones' as a 'simple' case, and hence, on his proposal for generalizing Donnellan's distinction, as a generalized attributive, rather than a generalized referential, use. But it is not clear from Kripke's wording that such uses really exemplify the simple rather than the complex case. I have a 'general' intention to use the name 'Donnellan' generally as a name for Keith Donnellan. On a particular occasion when I use the name, I also have a 'specific' intention to refer to Donnellan by my use of the name (as opposed to a specific intention to refer to Kripke, or to the man 'over there', etc.). Are these intentions of mine the same intention, or are they different? How is one supposed to tell? Must I be conceiving of Donnellan as *he whom I generally mean by the name* in my specific intention in order for it to be the same as my general intention? If so, then my general intention is an intention generally to mean by the name he whom I generally mean by the name. How can such an intention succeed in determining a semantic referent for the name, as Kripke claims?

Kripke evidently presupposes that the intentions are one and the same. But how can a standing intention generally to do such-and-such be strictly the *very same* intention as an occurrent intention on a particular occasion to do such-and-such *on that occasion*? Or is the relevant intention supposed to be not an intention to refer to Donnellan *generally* by one's use of the name, nor to do so *now*, nor to do so *at time t*, nor to do so *sometime or other*, but simply to do so (period)? Do we have temporally nonspecific intentions? Can intentions even *be* temporally nonspecific in this way?

One ought to feel uneasy, maybe even annoyed, with these questions, at least in the present context—much as we do when the philosophically uneducated ask for the sound of one hand clapping, or when the philosophically miseducated make equally ridiculous demands. It is preferable to minimize the extent to which the legitimacy and intelligibility of Donnellan's distinction is made to depend on the identification and differentiation of intentions in such contexts. More importantly, if commonplace uses of ordinary names fall under Kripke's notion of a *simple* case (as he evidently believes), then as noted above, his distinction between simple and complex cases fails to generalize Donnellan's distinction for definite descriptions in the most natural and plausible manner.

Notice, by contrast, that typical uses of names whose reference was fixed by an attributive use of a definite description seem more clearly to fall squarely within the parameters of what Kripke means by 'the simple case'. We have the general intention to refer by 'Newman 1' to the first child to be born in the twenty-second century. Kripke would say that our specific intention in connection with our use of the name on a given occasion is this very same intention. Either that, or else barnyard-variety attributive uses of definite descriptions will exemplify the complex case, contrary to Kripke's intent. One may raise skeptical questions in this connection—like those I have already posed, and more—but it is clear, or at least relatively clear, that in this case, there is no potentially conflicting, non-semantic intention to refer specifically to this person or that, in addition to our pre-set semantic intention to refer to whoever is born first on New Year's Day, AD 2100 (or is it AD 2101?) The problem with Kripke's characterization is not that it is off the wall. It is simply off target.

It is at least arguable, as we have seen above, that there is (and there will be) no one for whom we now have a *de re* intention to use 'Newman 1' as a name. This observation—and not the differentiation of intentions—provides the key to Donnellan's distinction and its most natural generalization to other sorts of terms. It will not do, however, to say that a use of a term is referential whenever there is an occurrent specific *de re* intention concerning some particular person or thing, to refer to him/her/it by the term. As we have seen, the homicide detective investigating Smith's murder may be said not only to make *de re* assertions but also to have *de re* beliefs concerning the murderer (e.g. that he is insane), even at the earliest stage of the investigation before the detective is in a position to use the description referentially. (Recall the Donnellan–Sosa test and the quote from Searle in Section IV above.) Intention is sufficiently like belief that it would seem correct to say that, even at that stage, the detective also has the specific *de re* intention, concerning Smith's murderer, to refer to him/her by the phrase 'Smith's murderer'. The required *de re* connection has already been established.

The same phenomenon can arise with proper names. A case in point may be the name 'Deep Throat', coined by Washington *Post* reporters Bob Woodward and Carl Bernstein for a highly placed, confidential source in their famous investigation of the Watergate scandal. (This example is mentioned by Donnellan 1978: 38–39.) It seems correct to say of typical readers or viewers of the work, *All the President's Men*, that there is indeed someone whom they mean, *de re*, by 'Deep Throat', and about whom they are expressing their views when discussing the *Post*'s coverage of Watergate—even though the readers do not know, and may even have no guess concerning, that person's actual identity. Here again, the Donnellan–Sosa test seems to bear this out. On a given occasion of use, the typical reader has a specific intention to refer to this same person. In this respect, 'Deep Throat' is more like 'Jack the Ripper' (or 'Smith's murderer') than 'Newman 1'. A typical reader who does not have even a hunch as to Deep Throat's identity, however, does not have anyone in mind, in Donnellan's sense, when reading and using the name. That is, the reader does not have anyone in mind sufficiently to be able to use a definite description referentially. A similar situation arises when one encounters someone's name for the first time without being adequately introduced (even if only *in absentia*) to the person so named—say by looking at a new class-enrollment list or a luggage identification tag. If one then uses the name to state something about the person so named, while still having no idea whose name it is, one makes a *de re* assertion and expresses a *de re* belief. ('This belongs to one Byron Mallone. Mr Mallone, whoever he is, has traveled to Israel and was very recently around someone who smokes cigars.') Such uses are not referential.

Donnellan's notion of *having an individual in mind*—the notion of having-in-mind that is a requirement for using a definite description referentially—seems to fall somewhere closer to the notion of knowing who someone is, or perhaps to that of having an opinion as to who someone is (the doxastic analogue of the epistemic notion of knowing-who), than to the distinct notion of having *de re* beliefs, intentions, or other cognitive attitudes concerning the person in question. To be sure, the notions of having someone in mind and of knowing-who are not the same. One can use a description referentially for someone while having no opinion, let alone knowledge, concerning that person's identity, in the usual sense. But the notions seem connected or similar, more so than the notion of having-in-mind is similar to that of having *de re* attitudes. I believe that the relevant notion of having-in-mind, like the notions of knowing-who and having-an-opinion-as-to-who, is best thought of as a cognitive relation between a cognizer and a content appropriate to a singular term.[31] In nearly all of the cases discussed by Donnellan and others in connection with referential use, what one has in mind is an individual person or object that the description is supposed to fit. Donnellan (1966: 290–291) provides an example in which a speaker uses the description 'the king' referentially for someone whom he believes to be a usurper, but whose claim to the throne is known to be unquestioned by the people with whom he is conversing. In such a case, the speaker does not believe the description used actually fits the object he/she has in mind, but is adopting the pretense that it does. In still other cases, one might instead have in mind not a particular individual but what Church (following Carnap) calls an *individual concept*, that is, a descriptive content appropriate to a definite description. The latter type of situation

---

[31] *Cf.* Salmon (1987/88: 213 n. 17, 214 n. 19). I now think that, in so far as there is a difference (however subtle), I should have used the phrase 'knows what F' instead of 'knows which F' for the generic notion of which knowing-who is a species. It seems likely that the notion of knowing-who is, at least to some extent, interest relative; someone whose epistemic or cognitive situation remains unchanged might be correctly described in one context (setting one range of interests) as knowing who someone else is, and in another context as not knowing who the other person is. The notion of having someone in mind does not seem interest relative—at least not in exactly the same way and to exactly the same extent as is the notion of knowing-who. It is possible that Donnellan's notion of having an individual in mind is logically related to the semantic content of the phrase 'knows what F'—or more likely, 'knows which F'—with respect to one sort of context or range of interests. (I do not feel confident about how to resolve these issues.)

is characteristic of an attributive use. When the homicide detective says 'Smith's murderer is insane', he has no one in particular in mind; what he has in mind is the individual concept *that person, whoever he or she is, who single-handedly murdered Smith*.

In pointing out the existence of the referential use of a definite description, Donnellan highlighted the possibility of using a description while having a particular person or object in mind that the description may not denote, in Russell's sense. There is an analogous possibility, which has not been generally recognized, of using a definite description while having a particular individual concept in mind that the description does not semantically express. It very often happens that what a speaker has primarily in mind in using a definite description is *neither* the concept conventionally contained in the description used nor an individual that the description is supposed to fit, but a *different description* (or at least a different descriptive content), one that the speaker can only use attributively. To modify Donnellan's king example slightly, consider that the speaker does not have any idea who the usurper is, believing only that the rightful king has been wrongly deposed by someone or other. What he primarily thinks when he says 'the king' is: *whoever it is that is taken to be king*.[32] Or again, suppose that the investigating detective is completely convinced that Johnson was murdered by the same culprit, so far still unidentified, who committed the recent, very similar murder of Smith. The homicide department has no suspects, no witnesses, and no leads in either case; the detective's firm belief is based entirely on the common MO. When the detective uses the phrase 'Smith's murderer' at the scene of the later crime, he primarily means: *the guy, whoever he is, who murdered Johnson*. The detective does not actually have the murderer in mind, in the relevant sense; otherwise, he could use the phrase referentially. Instead the detective thinks of Johnson's murderer by description.

Such uses as these are a kind of pseudo or mock referential use. In a sense, the mock referential use is what you get when you cross referential with attributive. In many such uses, there is even someone or something that the speaker intends (*de re*) to refer to by the description. The only thing preventing the use from being bona-fide referential is the exact nature of the user's cognitive access to the individual. In this respect, mock referential uses are more attributive than referential. But in other respects, they are so much like genuine referential uses that they ought to have been included in previous discussions of the referential use, and ought to be included in subsequent discussions.

A referential use of a definite description is Good or Bad, according as the individual that the speaker has in mind is, or is not, denoted (in Russell's sense) by the description. A mock referential use of a definite description is either Good or Bad, depending on whether the individual concept that the speaker has in mind is, or is not, coextensive with the concept conventionally expressed by the description. Let us say that a Good mock referential use is a *Pretty* use, and that a Bad mock referential use is *Ugly*. Recall in this connection that Donnellan allows that Russell's theory of descriptions may give the correct analysis for attributive uses of definite descriptions,

---

[32] This modification of Donnellan's original example is due to Ilhan Inan.

though not for referential uses. Whatever reasons Donnellan may have for withholding Russell's analysis from referential uses seem to extend straightforwardly to mock referential uses. When the detective says 'Smith's murderer left a smudge print here' at the scene of Johnson's murder, someone of Donnellan's ilk might argue that, in some sense, the detective will have stated something true as long as the smudge was made by *Johnson's* murderer, whether or not he also murdered Smith. More revealing, such a philosopher would argue further that, in some sense, the detective will have stated something *false* as long as Johnson's murderer did not make the relevant smudge print—even if the detective's belief that Smith and Johnson were murdered by the same person is incorrect and, purely by happenstance, Smith's murderer coincidentally left the smudge there sometime prior to Johnson's murder. An Ugly use of a definite description is a very close facsimile of a Bad referential use.

We have seen that Kripke's attempt at generalizing Donnellan's distinction casts the ordinary use of proper names on the attributive side when they are more at home on the referential side. There is a further difficulty, but opposite in kind. Other uses of terms are miscast as referential when they are attributive, or at least more attributive than referential. This is due to the fact that Kripke's notion of the complex case does not include as a necessary condition that the speaker have a particular someone in mind, in the relevant sense. It is sufficient that the speaker have an occurrent specific intention distinct from, and in addition to, his/her standing general intention. Mock referential uses satisfy this condition. On a particular occasion when the homicide detective uses the phrase 'Johnson's murderer', he may have the occurrent specific intention to refer to the repeat murderer responsible for the deaths of both Smith and Johnson. This is clearly different from his background semantic intention always to use the phrase with its usual English meaning. His use therefore exemplifies the complex case. The two intentions may even conflict. If Johnson's murderer is a copycat, the detective's use of the phrase 'Johnson's murderer' is Ugly. It does not fit the paradigm for a referential use, since there is still no one whom the detective has in mind. Otherwise, he should also be able to use 'Smith's murderer' referentially. But he cannot (even though he has various *de re* beliefs concerning Smith's murderer, e.g. that he murdered Johnson).

VI

Kripke distinguishes between standing ('general') intentions always to use a term in such-and-such a way and occurrent ('specific') intentions to use the term in such-and-such a way on a particular occasion, saying that semantic reference is given by the first kind of intention and speaker reference by the second. This distinction among intentions seems an excessively delicate basis for the comparatively firm distinctions between semantic reference and speaker reference, and between referential and attributive use. If I have the occurrent intention to use 'Smith's murderer' to mean the man 'over there' on this occasion, because I genuinely believe that man murdered Smith, do I not also form a standing intention *always* to use the phrase for that man? Conversely, it seems rather likely that standing intentions in connection with our use of language typically (if not invariably) give rise to occurrent intentions on particular occasions. This may even be built into the notion of a standing state.

I believe it may be more helpful to replace Kripke's distinction between standing and occurrent linguistic intentions with a different one: the distinction between linguistic intentions that are *purely semantic* in nature and those that are not. We who speak English intend to use our words generally with their conventional meanings. Our knowledge of what those words mean allows us to form more specific semantic intentions. Thus I intend to use the word 'guitarist' in whatever is its usual English sense. Given my knowledge of what the word means in English, I form the additional intention to use the word specifically as a term for one who plays the guitar. The first is a general background intention, one that specifies the intended meaning only as *whatever the term means in English*; the second identifies a particular meaning for the term. Both are purely semantic intentions, in that they are meant to govern not merely which individuals the word 'guitarist' *happens to* apply to, but what the word applies to *as a matter of the semantics of my idiolect*. Indeed, they are also meant to govern what the word is to *mean*. The second intention may be termed an *identifying semantic* intention. If I believe that all and only guitarists keep their fingernails short on one hand and longer on the other, I may form the additional linguistic intention to use the word to apply to individuals of exactly that class. Such an intention would also be an identifying semantic intention, in the sense I intend, since it identifies a particular extension for 'guitarist' (in contrast with an intention to use the word to apply to exactly the things to which it correctly applies in English). But it would not be a purely semantic intention; it depends on an extra-linguistic belief of mine, one which is (and which I recognize to be) non-semantic in nature.

In using a singular term the speaker typically has a purely semantic, identifying intention of the form ⌜By my use of this term, I intend to refer to α⌝. And it is arguably this intention, rather than some non-semantic standing linguistic intention, that governs semantic reference for the term in the speaker's idiolect. The metalinguistic variable 'α' here may be a stand-in for a definite description—or if the quasi-quotation marks are interpreted as content-quotation marks, rather than as syntactic quotation marks, the 'α' may be a stand-in for an individual concept. For example, one may have the purely semantic intention expressed by 'By my use of the phrase "Smith's murderer", I intend to refer to whoever single-handedly murdered Smith.' In this case, the intention is a product of more fundamental identifying semantic intentions: to use 'Smith' to mean Smith, to use 'murderer' as a term for murderers, etc. But the α might instead stand in for a proper name of a person or object. In the case of a typical proper name, the relevant purely semantic, identifying intention is 'singular' or *de re*: 'By my use of "Smith", I intend to refer to Smith [*that very guy*].' By contrast, in the case of a name whose reference is fixed by an attributive use of a definite description, the purely semantic, identifying intention is 'general' or *de dicto*: 'By my use of "Newman 1", I intend to refer to whoever is born first in the twenty-second century.' This is not the same as an intention to use 'Newman 1' specifically as a name for *that particular future individual,* Newman

1. The Donnellan–Sosa test would seem to indicate that we do not have the latter intention. No *de re* connection has been established.[33]

Before attempting to extend Donnellan's distinction to proper names and other terms in a natural and plausible way, a further point must be made. Our use of a particular term is often accompanied by a plurality of identifying semantic intentions, each of the form ⌜By my use of this term, I intend to refer to α⌝. It may happen that the speaker regards one or more of these as essential to what he or she means, and the rest as so much window dressing, mere accoutrement. Suppose the speaker is asked, ⌜Consider a hypothetical scenario in which your intention to refer to α by the term and your separate intention to refer to β conflict, because these are different individuals. In such a case, which do you mean by your use of the term?⌝ In reply the speaker may cite one intention as the superseding, decisive intention. We may call this the speaker's *primary* linguistic intention.

One may come close to generalizing Donnellan's distinction, then, by invoking the various notions of purely semantic intentions, primary linguistic intentions, and identifying semantic intentions. Let us distinguish between *generalized referential* and *generalized attributive* uses as follows. In a g-attributive use of a singular term, the speaker has a primary, identifying, purely semantic intention of the form ⌜By my use of this term, I intend to refer to α⌝, where α is a definite description. This intention is general, as opposed to singular; it is a *de dicto* intention.[34] Further, the speaker does not have in addition a supplementary primary linguistic intention of the form ⌜By my use of this term, I intend to refer to β⌝ that is not purely semantic in nature, or where β is a directly referential, Millian term (e.g. a name) for an individual person or object that the speaker 'has in mind', in the relevant sense. Here there is no potential conflict (from the point of view of pure semantics) with the primary *de dicto* linguistic intention, and speaker reference is therefore governed by that purely semantic intention. In a g-referential use of a term, by contrast, the speaker has a primary linguistic intention (either purely semantic or not) of the form ⌜By my use of this term, I intend to refer to α⌝, where this time α is a directly referential term for an individual person or object (rather than a definite description), one whom the speaker 'has in mind' in forming this intention. The speaker's primary linguistic intention is a *de re* intention concerning the person or object for which the speaker is using the term g-referentially. In this case, speaker reference may be governed by both this primary linguistic intention and a separate purely semantic intention. It may even happen that the speaker inadvertently refers simultaneously to two (or more) entities by a single use of a term.

This distinction aims at capturing conceptually critical elements of the referential and the attributive use of a definite description. The generalized distinction has several noteworthy features. First, it seems clear that a use of a definite description is referential if it is g-referential, and attributive if g-attributive. The distinction between

---

[33] *Cf.* also Salmon (1993*a*; 1993*b*: 99–100 n. 27).

[34] I do not mean by this to rule out the possibility that the intention is also *de re* or singular. Some intentions, beliefs, etc. are both *de dicto* and *de re*. The detective's belief that whoever single-handedly murdered Smith is insane, e.g. is *de re* (singular) with regard to Smith and *de dicto* (general) with regard to his murderer. *Cf.* Salmon (1982: 44–45 n. 3).

g-referential and g-attributive use is mutually exclusive, or nearly enough so; no use of a term can be both g-referential and g-attributive except (perhaps) where a speaker has linguistic meta-intentions that create a duality of use by giving equal weight to conflicting linguistic intentions, neither one of which supersedes the other. Donnellan seems to have originally intended his more restrictive distinction also to be mutually exclusive (at least to this same extent).

Kripke (1977: 8) says that he does not regard Donnellan's distinction as exclusive. In his example of a use that might be regarded as simultaneously partially referential and partially attributive (1977: 25–26 n. 28), a speaker utters 'Smith's murderer is insane' based both on the grisly condition of Smith's body and also on the peculiar behavior of the person whom the speaker has in mind and is observing (believing him to be Smith's murderer), where 'neither consideration would have sufficed by itself, but they suffice jointly'. I believe Donnellan would probably say that this is simply a referential use and not attributive, and I do not see a compelling reason to dispute this verdict. Indeed, if Kripke's case is to be regarded as somehow involving an attributive use in combination with a referential use, it raises the specter that most (or at least a great many) uses that are generally taken to be referential and not attributive will turn out to be combined referential–attributive. This would run counter to how we ordinarily conceive of the distinction.[35] While the generalized distinction is exclusive, it is not exhaustive. Many uses of definite descriptions are neither g-referential nor g-attributive. Mock referential uses, for example—which are common in ordinary speech—have elements of both referential use and attributive use. For that very reason they do not fit the paradigm for either use, as Donnellan set out the original distinction.[36]

---

[35] In so far as it is desirable to allow for such a thing as a combined referential–attributive use, the generalization proposed here might be adjusted to accommodate Kripke's intuitions about the case (perhaps by deleting the condition on g-attributive use that there be no primary purely semantic intention concerning someone or something that the speaker has in mind and/or the condition that there not be a second, non-semantic intention). Kripke's attempt at generalizing Donnellan's distinction—in terms of the identification or differentiation of 'general' and 'specific' linguistic intentions and the distinction between 'simple' and 'complex' cases—does not straightforwardly allow for combined uses. Furthermore, since strict identity is a clear-cut, all-or-nothing affair, it is by no means obvious how to adjust Kripke's distinction to accommodate combined (partially simple, partially complex) uses—and especially how to do so without making most referential uses into combined uses. Perhaps this can be done.

[36] Neale (1990: 202–203) describes a case similar to the detective's use of 'Johnson's murderer', as set out above, declaring that it is attributive, by Donnellan's criterion, and not referential. Inan independently gave a similar example, judging it to be attributive, and concluding, more carefully, that Donnellan's explicit criterion for attributive use fails to capture the intent. An informal survey of many of the cognoscenti showed that, aside from one explicit abstention, all nine remaining respondents unanimously regard the detective's use of 'Johnson's murderer' as: (*a*) attributive; and (*b*) not referential. I continue to believe that the use is neither referential nor attributive, as Donnellan intended these terms. It is a mock referential use in which the detective primarily intends *whoever single-handedly murdered both Smith and Johnson*, rather than *whoever single-handedly murdered Johnson (whether or not he also single-handedly murdered Smith)*. I believe Donnellan would therefore withhold Russell's analysis from it, by contrast with a genuine attributive use. (Two respondents, Anthony Brueckner and Genoveva Marti, supplemented their vote with unsolicited remarks showing a sensitivity to the sort of considerations raised in the text in connection with Ugly uses, like the detective's use of 'Smith's murderer' for whoever murdered Johnson, where Johnson's

More interestingly, uses of proper names whose reference has been fixed by an attributive use of a definite description are typically g-attributive. Some other unusual uses of names are also g-attributive, as in the 'Deep Throat' example. But commonplace uses of ordinary names are typically g-referential.

Perhaps most importantly, one of Kripke's principal criticisms of Donnellan is upheld. Especially telling, and to the point, is Kripke's observation—made forcefully with the aid of a variety of postulated languages (1977: 15–17)—that the pragmatic phenomena involving speaker reference, speaker assertion, and the like adduced by Donnellan in connection with the referential use are no evidence for the thesis of semantic significance. The generalized distinction is neutral regarding controversial theses like SS and SS'. Using that characterization of the referential–attributive distinction, it is possible to provide an account of the referential use, and more generally of the g-referential use, that attributes to it no special semantic significance, while accommodating, and even predicting, the circumstances and frequency of its occurrence in everyday speech. The latter therefore has no bearing on the question of semantic significance.

REFERENCES

Barwise, J. and Perry, J. (1983). *Situations and Attitudes* (Cambridge, Mass.: MIT Press).
Blackburn, W. (1988). 'Wettstein on Definite Descriptions', *Philosophical Studies*, 53: 263–278.
Devitt, M. (1974). 'Singular Terms', *Journal of Philosophy*, 71: 183–205.
Donnellan, K. (1966). 'Reference and Definite Descriptions', *Philosophical Review*, 75: 281–304.
—— (1968). 'Putting Humpty Dumpty Together Again', *Philosophical Review*, 77: 203–215.
—— (1972). 'Proper Names and Identifying Descriptions', in D. Davidson and G. Harman (eds), *Semantics of Natural Language* (Dordrecht: Reidel), 356–79.
—— (1974). 'Speaking of Nothing', *Philosophical Review*, 83: 3–32.
—— (1978). 'Speaker Reference, Descriptions and Anaphora', in P. Cole (ed.), *Syntax and Semantics, ix. Pragmatics* (New York: Academic Press), 47–68.
—— (1979). 'The Contingent *A Priori* and Rigid Designators', in P. French, T. Vehling, and H. Wettstein (eds), *Contemporary Perspectives in the Philosophy of Language* (Minneapolis: University of Minnesota Press), 45–60.
Grice, H. P. (1969). 'Vacuous Names', in D. Davidson and J. Hintikka (eds), *Words and Objections: Essays on the Work of W. V. Quine* (Dordrecht: Reidel), 118–145.
—— (1978). 'Further Notes on Logic and Conversation', in P. Cole (ed.), *Syntax and Semantics, 9 Pragmatics* (New York: Academic Press), 113–127.
Kaplan, D. (1969). 'Quantifying In', in D. Davidson and J. Hintikka (eds), *Words and Objections* (Dordrecht: Reidel), 206–242.
—— (1979). 'Dthat', in P. French, T. Vehling, and H. Wettstein (eds), *Contemporary Perspectives in the Philosophy of Language* (Minneapolis: University of Minnesota Press), 338–400.

murderer turns out to be a copycat.) Attributive or not, as already noted, the fact that the use is clearly not referential even though it exemplifies the 'complex case' shows that Kripke's attempt to generalize Donnellan's distinction for definite descriptions does not get matters exactly right.

—— (1989a). 'Demonstratives', in J. Almog, J. Perry, and H. Wettstein (eds), *Themes from Kaplan* (Oxford: Oxford University Press), 481–563.
—— (1989b). 'Afterthoughts', in J. Almog, J. Perry, and H. Wettstein (eds), *Themes from Kaplan* (New York: Oxford University Press), 565–614.
Kripke, S. (1977). 'Speaker Reference and Semantic Reference', in P. French, T. Vehling, and H. Wettstein (eds), *Contemporary Perspectives in the Philosophy of Language* (Minneapolis: University of Minnesota Press), 6–27.
—— (1980). *Naming and Necessity* (Cambridge, Mass.: Harvard University Press).
—— (1988). 'A Puzzle about Belief', in N. Salmon and S. Soames (eds), *Propositions and Attitudes* (Oxford: Oxford University Press), 102–148.
Neale, S. (1990). *Descriptions* (Cambridge: MIT Press).
Quine, W. V. O. (1981). 'Intensions Revisited', in P. French, T. Vehling, and H. Wettstein (eds), *Contemporary Perspectives in the Philosophy of Language* (Minneapolis: University of Minnesota Press), 268–274.
Recanati, F. (1989). 'Referential/Attributive: A Contextualist Proposal', *Philosophical Studies*, 56: 217–249.
—— (1993). *Direct Reference: From Language to Thought* (Oxford: Blackwell).
Russell, B. (1905). 'On Denoting', *Mind*, 14: 479–493.
—— (1956). 'The Philosophy of Logical Atomism', in R. C. Marsh (ed.), *Logic and Knowledge: Essays 1901–1950* (London: George Allen & Unwin), 175–281.
—— (1988). 'Knowledge by Acquaintance and Knowledge by Description', in N. Salmon and S. Soames (eds), *Propositions and Attitudes* (Oxford: Oxford University Press), 16–32.
Salmon, N. (1982). 'Assertion and Incomplete Definite Descriptions', *Philosophical Studies*, 42: 37–45.
—— (1986). *Frege's Puzzle* (Cambridge, Mass.: MIT Press).
—— (1987/88). 'How to Measure the Standard Meter', *Proceedings of the Aristotelian Society*, 88: 193–217.
—— (1990). 'A Millian Heir Rejects the Wages of *Sinn*', in C. A. Anderson and J. Owens (eds), *Propositional Attitudes: The Role of Content in Logic, Language and Mind* (Stanford, Calif.: CSLI Publications), 215–247.
—— (1991). 'The Pragmatic Fallacy', *Philosophical Studies*, 63: 83–97.
—— (1993a). 'Analyticity and Apriority', in J. Tomberlin (ed.), *Philosophical Perspectives*, vii. *Language and Logic* (Atascadero, Calif.: Ridgeview), 125–134.
—— (1993b). 'Relative and Absolute Apriority', *Philosophical Studies*, 69: 83–100.
—— (1995). 'Being of Two Minds: Belief with Doubt', *Noûs*, 29: 1–20.
Searle, J. (1979a). *Expression and Meaning* (Cambridge: Cambridge University Press).
—— (1979b). 'Referential and Attributive', *The Monist*, 62: 190–208.
Soames, S. (1994). 'Donnellan's Referential/Attributive Distinction', *Philosophical Studies*, 73: 149–168.
Sosa, E. (1970). 'Propositional Attitudes *De Dicto* and *De Re*', *Journal of Philosophy*, 67: 883–896.
Wettstein, H. (1981). 'Demonstrative Reference and Definite Descriptions', *Philosophical Studies*, 40: 241–257.
—— (1983). 'The Semantic Significance of the Referential/Attributive Distinction', *Philosophical Studies*, 44: 187–196.
—— (1986). 'Has Semantics Rested on a Mistake?', *Journal of Philosophy*, 83: 185–209.

19
Two Conceptions of Semantics (2004)

Ever since Charles W. Morris distinguished among syntax, semantics, and pragmatics, those of us who attempt to teach philosophy of language to undergraduates have agonized over the boundary between the latter two. The distinction is typically explained in terms of the concept of *use*: pragmatics is the study of the way signs or symbols are used in context, whereas semantics concerns the meaning of a symbol in abstraction from its use. But this is more of a slogan than a clarification or explanation. How are we supposed to understand the difference between semantics and pragmatics when the meaning of an expression is so closely bound to the manner in which that expression is used? An expression is used a certain way because of its meaning, and yet the expression came to have the meaning it does through usage. Each of meaning and use seems to be a direct product of the other. Wittgenstein went so far as to identify the meaning of a word in a large proper class of cases with its use (*Philosophical Investigations*, §43). Many regard this identification as one of the deepest philosophical insights of the twentieth century.[1]

Anguish over the semantic–pragmatic distinction has become especially acute since it emerged in the work of such writers as David Kaplan that even the *pure* semantics of some expressions—like 'here', 'this', and other indexicals—necessarily involves 'indexing', or relativizing, standard semantic attributes, like truth value, content, and designation (reference, denotation), to contexts of use.[2] Some writers have mistaken this as demonstrating that semantics (at least the semantics of indexicals) includes some pragmatics, or even is wholly contained within the latter. The various roles played in semantics by a speaker's use of an expression, and also the highly systematic, rule-governed interaction between meaning and use—these have made the correct characterization of pragmatics, as distinct from semantics, into a particularly thorny problem. This difficulty, however, is no excuse for blurring the distinction. However deep and pervasive are the interconnections between meaning and use, the fundamental character of the relationship between the two has been greatly overstated by some of Wittgenstein's admirers.

I thank the editor of *Semantics and Pragmatics* and a referee for their comments.

[1] It is significant that Wittgenstein did not go so far in §43 as to identify the meaning of a sentence or phrase with its use.

[2] D. Kaplan, 'Demonstratives', in J. Almog, J. Perry, and H. Wettstein (eds), *Themes from Kaplan* (Oxford: Oxford University Press, 1989), 481–563. In unpublished material Kaplan has argued in connection with expressions like 'hello' and 'ouch' for an even broader assimilation between meaning and use.

Michael Dummett presents the following argument:

The meaning of a mathematical statement determines and is exhaustively determined by its *use*. The meaning of such a statement cannot be, or cannot contain as an ingredient, anything which is not manifest in the use to be made of it, lying solely in the mind of the individual who apprehends that meaning: if two individuals agree completely about the use to be made of the statement, then they agree about its meaning. The reason is that the meaning of a statement consists solely in its rôle as an instrument of communication between individuals, just as the powers of a chess-piece consist solely in its rôle in the game according to the rules. An individual cannot communicate what he cannot be observed to communicate: if one individual associated with a mathematical symbol or formula some mental content, where the association did not lie in the use he made of the symbol or formula, then he could not convey that content by means of the symbol or formula, for his audience would be unaware of the association and would have no means of becoming aware of it ... there must be an observable difference between the behavior or capacities of someone who is said to have [implicit knowledge constituting understanding of the language of mathematics] and someone who is said to lack it. Hence it follows, once more, that a grasp of the meaning of a mathematical statement must, in general, consist of a capacity to use that statement in a certain way, or to respond in a certain way to its use by others.[3]

Dummett's argument, if it is correct about mathematical statements, is equally applicable to statements made in non-mathematical language. Dummett's observation that only an observable act by a speaker can succeed in communicating, even if correct, in no way yields the conclusion that an expression's meaning is secured by, or understood by observing, the use of the expression—whether actual or potential uses.[4] The meanings of most sentences of natural language, in fact, *cannot* lie in their actual use.

---

[3] M. Dummett, 'The Philosophical Basis of Intuitionistic Logic', in H. E. Rose and J. C. Shepherdson (eds), *Logic Colloquium '73* (Amsterdam: North-Holland, 1975), 5–40; repr. in Dummett, *Truth and Other Enigmas* (Cambridge, Mass.: Harvard University Press, 1978), 215–247.

[4] Though this is at least close to Dummett's conclusion, it is unclear exactly what Dummett means in speaking of the use *to be made* of a sentence. Is this the use that has actually been made of the sentence? Is it the actual (immediate) future use? Is it the union of the actual past, the actual present, and the actual future use? Is it a possible future use? Is it perhaps the *semantically correct* use, a use that accords with the literal meaning (a use by the speaker to express the content that the expression itself semantically expresses with respect to the speaker's context)? Among the various conclusions that result by substituting one of these more explicit phrases for Dummett's 'the use to be made', none follows from the observation that communication requires observation.

Dummett's view expressed elsewhere (*cf.* *The Logical Basis of Metaphysics* (Cambridge, Mass.: Harvard University Press, 1991), 223–225) is that the meaning of a typical sentence is determined compositionally, whereas the meaning of the ultimate sentence components is determined by past use of special sentences—the lexical meaning givers—whose meanings are themselves determined by their own actual past use, rather than compositionally. The meaning of 'fragile', for example, is supposed to be gotten by observing the use of particular 'simple predications' (the meaning givers) like 'That plate is fragile'. It is difficult to reconcile this view with Dummett's argument quoted in the text, which is not restricted to the allegedly meaning-giver sentences and instead covers every mathematical sentence. The meaning of any typical mathematical sentence (e.g. '$e^{\pi i} + 1 = 0$', etc.) is secured and understood compositionally. For this very reason, one need not observe a use of the sentence in order to understand it. Indeed, in the absence of a prior understanding of its component expressions ('e', 'i', '+', exponentiation, etc.), observation of a particular use of the sentence will typically leave the observer clueless as to the meaning.

This is a simple logical consequence of the fact that at any given time, only finitely many sentences have actually been used, whereas natural language includes infinitely many meaningful sentences. And indeed, very many, probably nearly all, of the sentences that are actually used are immediately understood by both the speaker and the audience despite the fact that the sentence has not been used in their presence before, and even its potential use has not been contemplated.[5] We typically and routinely understand sentences on hearing or reading them for the first time. (Consider, for example, the sequence of sentences that make up this very chapter.) Even on hearing or reading a previously used sentence, we do not understand it by remembering how it was used in the past. The fact that we understand sentences independently of any previous use, and we do this routinely, is not particularly mysterious. For we have observed actual uses of the individual words that make up the sentences of novel utterances, and have also learned (presumably at least partly through observation) how these words are composed to form sentences, and also how to understand a sentence on the basis of the meanings and the mode of composition of the words themselves. Observation of use undoubtedly plays a very significant role in understanding. But the conclusion that we understand an expression only through observation of actual uses of that very expression is incorrect. We definitely do not understand the sentences that give expression to the thoughts that fill our lives on the basis of previous uses of those sentences.

The point is not merely that the meaning of a sentence or phrase is not determined by its actual past uses. It should be even more obvious that the meaning of an expression is also not determined by its actual future uses, let alone by its possible future uses. Many expressions will actually come to be used to express contents that those expressions do not presently express. And *any* expression *might* yet come to be so used. There is no backward road from future use to present meaning, much less is there a trans-modal road from possible use to actual meaning. The meaning of a sentence or phrase is in fact determined *independently* of its actual or potential use, but by its semantic composition, by the meanings of the words and the manner in which the words are combined to form the sentence or phrase.

Even the converse thesis that the meaning of an expression determines its use is significantly overstated. Many sentences are commonly used only to convey something other than their literal content, or would be so used if they were used at all. Such uses deviate from the meaning, but they are uses all the same. The connection between meaning and use is not a matter of historical anthropology. It is a normative matter,

---

Some of the considerations to be made shortly apply straightforwardly to the allegedly meaning-giver sentences. We do not understand what 'That plate is fragile' expresses in a given use simply by observing the utterance. A non-French-speaker, for example, does not observe what Pierre expresses by 'Cette assiette là est fragile' when the plate that Pierre is demonstrating remains entirely intact. Rather, we understand what is expressed (namely, that a particular plate is easily broken) in the standard way, by a kind of compositional computation on the basis of a prior understanding of each of the words.

[5] This generalization may not extend to sentences of a purely mathematical language. Nevertheless, the manner in which such sentences are understood is essentially the same compositional–computational manner as in the case of non-mathematical language.

not merely descriptive but also prescriptive. Perhaps it may be said that the meaning of a sentence (or other type of expression) determines its *correct* use. But even this formulation requires due caution. Many sentences are sufficiently unnatural, inappropriate, insulting, offensive, or bizarre, etc., that they would essentially never be used to convey the information they literally contain. In any normal sense, it would be *incorrect* to use some sentences to assert what the sentence literally expresses. There are sentences such that to use them with their literal meaning—to assert what the sentence literally expresses (and not as part of a parody, or in an attempt at offensive humor, etc.)—would violate every condition on civilized human society as we know it. There is indeed a dimension of evaluation on which the use of an expression may be deemed correct if and only if the expression is used with its literal meaning. But this does not provide for an illuminating identification or assimilation of meaning with use in any philosophically significant manner (e.g. a conceptual reduction of meaning to use). For the dimension of evaluation in question is peculiarly within the realm of semantics proper: an expression is used correctly *from the point of view of pure semantics* if and only if it is used with its literal meaning. Along any genuinely distinct, non-semantic dimension of evaluation, some expressions, if they are used with their literal meaning, are counter-recommended in even a minimally civilized society, if not outright prohibited by the dictates of common human decency, i.e. they are not used correctly in the relevant non-semantic way. (The publisher prefers that specific examples of outlandishly offensive sentences be left to the reader's imagination.) The claim that meaning determines correct use is true only if it is vacuous.

The problem of correctly characterizing the semantic–pragmatic distinction remains open. It is accompanied by competing conceptions of the very enterprise known as *semantics*. Some writers conceive of semantics as concerned with what a speaker *says* or *asserts* in uttering a declarative sentence, as contrasted with what the speaker *means* or *accomplishes* by means of the utterance, and/or with how the audience interprets, or how the audience correctly interprets, the utterance (these being matters of pragmatics). I believe these distinctions are properly seen as distinctions wholly *within* pragmatics, distinctions that do not so much as touch on semantics properly so-called (except in so far as semantics provides one source, among many, for what the speaker asserts in the utterance). To conceive of semantics as concerned with speaker assertion (i.e. with what the speaker who uses the sentence thereby asserts) is not merely to blur the distinction between semantics and pragmatics. It is to *misidentify* semantics altogether, and to do so sufficiently badly that those who conceive semantics in this way, when using semantic expressions like 'denote', 'content', or 'true', are often fruitfully interpreted as not speaking about the notions of denotation, content, or (semantic) truth at all, but about other notions entirely—specifically various pragmatic notions.

To clarify this point, I want to distinguish here between two radically opposing conceptions of semantics. The rivalry between these conceptions has seriously exacerbated the problem of maintaining the conceptual integrity of the semantic–pragmatic distinction. One or the other of these competing conceptions of semantics seems to be presupposed by virtually everyone who has worked in the philosophy of language. The gulf that separates the two conceptions came forcefully before my mind while reflecting on the current debate among such writers as Keith Donnellan, Saul Kripke, Howard Wettstein, myself, and others, concerning the alleged semantic significance of Donnellan's *referential–attributive* distinction—although numerous contemporary controversies in the philosophy of language equally illustrate the fundamental difference between the two rival ways of conceptualizing semantics. A definite description, 'the *such-and-such*', is *used referentially* for a particular object *x* if the use in question is relevantly connected to *x* in the right way—paradigmatically, the speaker has that particular object in mind and believes of the object that it uniquely answers to the description (i.e. that it is a unique *such-and-such*)—and the speaker uses the description as a name or label for that object. By contrast, a definite description is *used attributively* if no object is relevantly connected to the use and instead the speaker means something to the effect that whoever or whatever is uniquely *such-and-such* is . . . The central controversy concerns whether a referential use of a definite description results in a different semantic content from an attributive use. The *thesis of semantic significance*, which Donnellan holds, is that a referential use, unlike an attributive use, results in a proposition directly about the relevantly connected object—typically, the object that the speaker has in mind.

On the *speech-act centered conception* of semantics, semantic attributes of expressions—like a singular term's designating an object, or a sentence's containing or expressing a proposition—somehow reduce to, are to be understood by means of, are derived from, or at least are directly determined by, the illocutionary acts performed by speakers in using those expressions, or perhaps the illocutionary acts that would normally be performed in using those expressions. Theorists who embrace the speech-act centered conception typically ascribe semantic attributes to such things as expression tokens or utterances, or to possible utterances.

The speech-act centered conception yields a serious misconceptualization of the semantic–pragmatic distinction. That distinction is properly understood by recognizing signs or expression-types (not tokens) as genuine *symbols*. Symbols symbolize; i.e. they represent. Speakers, of course, also represent. We represent things, we represent ways for things to be, and we represent things as being one way rather than another. We routinely do these things, and we routinely do these things by producing symbols *which also do these same sorts of things*. The symbols we use, or at least many of them, represent in the way they do by means of, or in accordance with, a highly systematic assignment of representations to symbols. This systematic assignment of representations is semantics. And it is aptly representable by means of inductive (recursive) definitions for concepts like *designation*, *truth*, and *content*. This is how, and why, semantics is a formal discipline employing mathematical methodologies, rather than, say, psychological methodologies or anthropological methodologies—even though the semantics of a natural language is an *a posteriori* discipline. However deep the influence of actual usage on the representational nature of our symbols may be, it remains that the symbols themselves (including complex symbols like sentences) have specific representations systematically assigned to them, some of these assignments being a function of context.

As we have seen, our understanding of certain complex symbols is not, as it were, on a case-by-case basis, by one-at-a-time learning and rote memory. Instead we achieve an understanding of the atomic symbols, perhaps in a case-by-case one-at-a-time way, and we learn the system through which we are enabled to work out for ourselves on a case-by-case basis exactly what any given molecular symbol represents or means. What we represent with the symbols we produce need not be the very same as what the symbols themselves represent. We are constrained by the symbols' system of representation—by their semantics—but we are not enslaved by it. Frequently, routinely in fact, what we represent by means of a symbol deviates from the symbol's semantics. Most obviously this occurs with the sentences we utter, whereby we routinely assert something beyond what the sentence itself semantically expresses. Irony, sarcasm, and figurative language may be cases in point. Even in non-figurative discourse, we routinely use sentences to assert more than they semantically express. One such phenomenon that is frequently misunderstood is instanced by the following sort of case: The words 'My daughter is 12 years old' express with respect to my present context something tantamount to my having a 12-year-old daughter (more accurately, following Russell, that someone or other is both uniquely my daughter and 12 years old), whereas in uttering those same words I thereby assert something more directly about my daughter: that *she* is 12 years old. What I additionally assert—not merely that I have some 12-year-old daughter or other but specifically that *she (that very girl)* is 12 years old—is not semantically expressed by my words. This is exactly the sort of phenomenon that the speech-act centered conception does not adequately characterize.[6]

The principal rival to the speech-act centered conception of semantics is what I call *the expression centered conception*. According to this alternative conception, the semantic attributes of expressions are not conceptually derivative of the speech acts performed by their utterers, and are thought of instead as intrinsic to the expressions themselves, or to the expressions *as* expressions of a particular language (and as occurring in a particular context). The expression centered conception takes seriously the idea that expressions are symbols, and that, as such, they have a semantic life of their own. The expression centered conception need not deny that semantics, at least for a natural language, may be ultimately a result or product of speech acts, rather than (or more likely, in addition to) the other way around. But the expression centered conception marks a definite separation between semantics and pragmatics, allowing for at least the possibility of extreme, pervasive, and even highly systematic deviation. The speech-act centered conception is more reductionist in spirit.

The expression centered conception is the received conception of semantics in the tradition of Frege and Russell. With their emphasis on artificial or idealized languages, it is they more than anyone else who deserve credit for cultivating the expression centered conception among contemporary philosophers of language. Wittgenstein focused, in contrast, on spoken natural language in his impenetrable but seemingly penetrating diatribe against the expression centered conception. Whether or not he himself subscribed to the speech-act centered conception, he is

---

[6] The phenomenon in question lies at the heart of what David Kaplan has misnamed the *pseudo de re* in 'Demonstratives', 555–556 n. 71. *Cf.* my 'The Good, the Bad, and the Ugly', in A. Bezuidenhout and M. Reimer (eds), *Descriptions and Beyond* (Oxford University Press, 2004).

largely responsible for the preeminence of that rival conception in contemporary philosophy of language. I fear that the speech-act centered conception may currently be the dominant conception of semantics—especially among philosophers with a propensity toward nominalism, physicalism, functionalism, anti-realism, or various other philosophically timid doctrines, and also among those who trace their scholarly lineage to Wittgenstein.

Anyone whose lineage traces to Wittgenstein can trace it a step further to Russell. Elements of both traditions are clearly manifest in Donnellan's thought on reference and related matters. Still, his commitment to the speech-act centered conception might explain Donnellan's unwavering endorsement of a particularly strong version of the semantic-significance thesis according to which a referentially used description semantically designates the speaker's intended designatum regardless of whether the description actually fits. The speech-act centered conception cannot distinguish correctly between the semantic content of a sentence with respect to a given context and the content of the assertion, or assertions (statements, utterances), normally made by a speaker in uttering the sentence in that context. If this interpretation (which is somewhat speculative) is correct, then Donnellan conceives of *speaker reference* (i.e. a speaker designating an object through the use of an expression) as, at least implicitly, a semantic, rather than a pragmatic, notion. Furthermore, he then conceives of Russell's notion of denotation for definite descriptions as a *nonsemantic* notion, since it does not concern (at least not directly) acts of speakers' reference normally performed with descriptions.[7] This interpretation seems to be confirmed by Donnellan's subsequent discussion in 'Speaker Reference, Descriptions, and Anaphora'.[8] There he adopts Kripke's terminology of 'speaker reference' and 'semantic reference', but he does not equate what he means by the latter with Russellian denotation, vigorously arguing instead that 'semantic reference' depends on, and is determined by, speaker reference, which may be other than the Russellian denotation.[9]

---

[7] For present purposes, Russell's notion of *denotation* for definite descriptions may be defined by saying that a definite description ⌜the α: φ_α⌝ *R-denotes* (with respect to semantic parameters, such as context) the individual that uniquely satisfies its matrix φ_α (with respect to those same parameters), if there is such an individual; and otherwise, it *R*-denotes nothing. Though it may be obvious that the relation of *R*-denotation between a definite description and the object that uniquely answers to it is fundamentally a semantic relation, Russell's use of John Stuart Mill's term 'denotation' is highly misleading. As is well known, Russell regarded definite descriptions as complex quantificational phrases that have neither semantic content ('no meaning in isolation') nor semantic designation (reference). The description's relation to the object uniquely answering to it *simulates* semantic designation on his theory. Russell should have called the notion 'quasi-denotation', or even 'simulated denotation'. *Cf.* my 'On Designating', *Mind* (October 2005 issue celebrating the centennial of the original publication of 'On Denoting', ed. Stephen Neale).

[8] In P. French, T. Uehling, and H. Wettstein (eds), *Contemporary Perspectives in the Philosophy of Language* (Minneapolis: University of Minnesota Press, 1979), 28–44.

[9] Donnellan sometimes appears to allow for semantic designation in the absence of speaker designation. On the one hand, he says in 'Speaker Reference, Descriptions, and Anaphora' (pp. 30, 32) that in using a definite description attributively, the speaker does not designate anything even if the description happens to be proper, in the Russellian sense. But he also seems to say (on the same p. 32, and in the same paragraph) that an attributively used description itself designates its Russellian denotation. This leads to the curious position that when a speaker uses a proper description attributively, the description designates but the speaker does not. And this does not fit

It is the expression centered conception of semantics, and the general Frege–Russell tradition, that is the natural habitat of the distinction between speaker designation and semantic designation (as well as such other Gricean distinctions as that between speaker meaning and sentence meaning). Donnellan originally characterized the referential–attributive distinction in terms of speaker reference and denotation. It would be dangerous, however, to take Donnellan's characterization at face value. My own view—well within the Frege–Russell tradition—is that Donnellan's apparent cataloging of speaker reference as semantic and of Russellian denotation as non-semantic obviously gets matters exactly reversed. It is just one piece of evidence of the extent to which the speech-act centered conception presents a seriously distorted picture of what semantics is, enough so that I am tempted to say that those in the grip of that conception, when using such semantic terms as 'designate' and 'express'—especially when applying such terms to such things as utterances rather than expressions—are not talking about anything semantic at all.[10]

Confronted with the two rival conceptions of semantics, those in the grip of the speech-act centered conception will typically protest that the distinction merely reflects a purely terminological difference, superimposed on a biased preference for one sort of theoretical investigation over another. Indeed, I have offered these arguments in favor of the expression centered conception over the speech-act centered conception in several venues, invariably invoking the response that the issue is merely terminological. This response misjudges the extent of disagreement that has been registered in numerous controversies in the philosophy of language during the past several decades. Again, the debate over the alleged semantic significance of the referential use is illustrative of the general point. Proponents of the semantic-significance thesis have not claimed merely that referential use issues in a *de re* assertion by the speaker. They have claimed furthermore that the resulting *de re* assertion reflects the semantics—the content and truth value—that the sentence uttered takes on when the description therein is given such a use. I have argued elsewhere against the semantic-significance thesis.[11] It is not to my present purpose to rehearse those arguments. It is sufficient here to note that the two rival conceptions of semantics differ sharply over substantive issues: the question of the designation of particular definite descriptions and the question of the truth values of particular sentences. No less significant is the current controversy concerning whether co-designative names are inter-substitutable in attributions of belief or other

---

well the speech-act centered conception of semantics. But coupled with Donnellan's more central position that when a description is used referentially for something *x*, both the description and the speaker designate *x* even if *x* is not the Russellian denotation, neither does this curious position exactly fit the expression centered conception—or any other conception that I can think of.

Though I am uncertain what to make of Donnellan's assertions here, I believe that a careful reading reveals that appearances are deceptive, and that Donnellan (through a carefully placed occurrence of the subjunctive 'would') deliberately avoids any commitment to the claim that an attributively used proper description has semantic designation. I may be wrong.

[10] See my 'Being of Two Minds: Belief with Doubt', *Noûs*, 29/1 (1995), esp. 18–19 n. 27.
[11] See 'Assertion and Incomplete Definite Descriptions', *Philosophical Studies*, 42/1 (July 1982), 37–45; 'The Pragmatic Fallacy', *Philosophical Studies*, 63 (1991), 83–97; 'The Good, the Bad, and the Ugly'.

propositional attitudes. It is doubtful that those (perhaps the vast majority) who insist that such substitutions fail, on the basis of what is imparted by uttering the result of such a substitution, would be prepared to grant that, nevertheless, such substitutions preserve truth value in every admissible model in which the names co-designate. While the debate over substitution might be fueled to some extent by terminological confusion or equivocation, the two competing conceptions of semantics tend to support competing judgments concerning the truth values of certain sentences, as they do also in the semantic-significance controversy. The different choices of terminology are accompanied, at least sometimes, by different verdicts concerning the truth values of particular sentences.

The battle cry 'It's all just terminology' is the last refuge of the speech-act centered conception. To be sure, there is a legitimate enterprise of investigating and cataloging the systematic correlation of speakers' utterances or other speech acts with, say, the propositions thereby asserted or the objects to which the speaker thereby refers. Such an enterprise raises issues and questions of a philosophical nature. What are the conditions on which a speaker makes a *de re* (or *relational*) assertion? Must the speaker, for instance, use a directly referential, logically proper name? Are these conditions systematically related to the conditions on which a speaker forms or harbors a *de re* belief? Can a speaker inadvertently refer to distinct objects in a single utterance? If so, is one of the referents the primary referent, to which all other referents are subordinate? If so, in what sense is it primary, and how is it determined which referent is the speech act's primary referent? Can a speaker make two statements in a single utterance? Several? When a speaker makes a statement, is the proposition semantically expressed by the uttered sentence *ipso facto* at least one of the propositions asserted in the speech act? Is it the primary assertion? Can a speaker assert a proposition that he or she does not grasp or understand? Do we learn the meaning of a word from its usage even when the meaning determines an infinite extension and we have only observed a finite number of applications? If so, how do we do this? What kind of fact is it about me that I mean a particular concept with an infinite extension, rather than some other concept with a different extension, one that overlaps with the one I do mean on those applications that I have observed?

These questions and more like them cry out for exploration. Their answers may reveal deep insights into the nature of cognition and the human mind. They are notoriously difficult. Some may be intractable. They are philosophically legitimate, even important questions. They are questions in the philosophy of language, broadly construed. But they do not belong to the philosophy of logic and semantics. They do not address, for example, whether the semantic content of a demonstrative is the object demonstrated or something more perceptual or conceptual. Their answers do not specify the logical form of a belief attribution. They do not say whether quantification into a non-extensional context is semantically coherent. They do not say whether definite descriptions are indexicals. The attempt to derive properly semantic conclusions from pragmatic observations in any simple, straightforward manner is doomed to failure. It is at best misleading and confusing to use semantic jargon when talking about utterances or speech acts—to characterize utterances using terms like 'semantic content' and 'semantically express', 'true with respect to context' and 'true under an assignment of values to variables'. It is perfectly legitimate and instructive to observe that a speaker would typically assert or convey or impart p in uttering sentence S in a context c. It is at best misleading to put this observation by saying that an utterance of S in c 'expresses' p. Such formulations invite a construal as an observation—immediate, straightforward, obvious—that S semantically contains p with respect to c. It is perforce wrong to suppose that the observation has any direct bearing whatsoever on the issues concerning S's truth value. Observing that we typically use descriptions in conveying or imparting different propositions from those Russell assigns as semantic content cannot refute Russell's semantic theory of descriptions.[12] It only confuses the issue to formulate the observation in terms of what propositions various *utterances* 'express'. Nor can the question of logical validity for a proposed inference be settled by appeal to a general willingness or readiness to draw the inference, or conversely to a general unwillingness or reluctance.[13] For the very same reason, neither can Frege's semantic theory of proper names be supported by observing that we have general, non-singular thoughts in mind when we use names. Here again reformulating the irrelevant observation, focusing on an utterance of a sentence using a proper name and looking for the thought thereby 'expressed' (i.e. pragmatically imparted), engenders no genuine support, only confusion. Semantic issues may be obfuscated, but cannot even be addressed, let alone settled, by making non-semantic observations using a semantic-sounding formulation. Calling a sow's ear a *silk purse* is not a way to make it so.

[12] *Cf.* my 'The Pragmatic Fallacy'.
[13] This would include substitutivity arguments in the logic of propositional attribution like $\ulcorner O(\text{that } \varphi_\alpha).\ \alpha = \beta \therefore O(\text{that } \varphi_\beta)\urcorner$, where α and β are logically simple constants. (Let O represent 'it is necessary' or, more controversially, 'Jones believes'.)

Bibliography of Nathan Salmon, 1979–2006

BOOKS

Essentialism in Current Theories of Reference (1979 UCLA doctoral dissertation, University Microfilms International, 1980).

Reference and Essence (Princeton University Press, 1981; and Basil Blackwell, 1982).

Frege's Puzzle (Cambridge, Mass.: Bradford Books, MIT Press, 1986).

Propositions and Attitudes, Co-edited (with Scott Soames) (Oxford: Oxford University Press, Oxford Readings in Philosophy, 1988).

Frege's Puzzle (Second Edition) (Atascadero, Calif.: Ridgeview, 1991).

Reference and Essence, Korean translation by Joonho Park, Chonbuk National University, Korea (Korea: Hankook, 2000).

Reference and Essence (Second Edition) (Prometheus Books, 2005).

† *Metaphysics, Mathematics, and Meaning: Philosophical Papers I* (Oxford University Press, 2005).

†† *Content, Cognition, and Communication: Philosophical Papers II* (Oxford University Press, 2006).

ARTICLES

Note: Articles marked † appear in Volume I, those marked †† in Volume II.

Critical Review of Leonard Linsky, *Names and Descriptions*, *The Journal of Philosophy*, 76, 8 (August 1979), pp. 436–452.

'How *Not* to Derive Essentialism from the Theory of Reference', *The Journal of Philosophy*, 76, 12 (December 1979), pp. 703–725.

†† 'Assertion and Incomplete Definite Descriptions', *Philosophical Studies*, 42, 1 (July 1982), pp. 37–45.

'Fregean Theory and the Four Worlds Paradox: A Reply to David Over', *Philosophical Books*, 25, 1 (January 1984), pp. 7–11.

† 'Impossible Worlds', *Analysis*, 44, 3 (June 1984), pp. 114–117.

†† 'Reflexivity', *Notre Dame Journal of Formal Logic*, 27, 3 (July 1986), pp. 401–429; reprinted in *Propositions and Attitudes* (Oxford Readings in Philosophy, 1988), pp. 240–274.

'Modal Paradox: Parts and Counterparts, Points and Counterpoints', in Peter French, Theodore Uehling, Jr., and Howard Wettstein, eds, *Midwest Studies in Philosophy XI: Studies in Essentialism* (Minneapolis: University of Minnesota Press, 1986), pp. 75–120.

† 'Existence', in James Tomberlin, ed., *Philosophical Perspectives, 1: Metaphysics* (Atascadero, Calif.: Ridgeview, 1987), pp. 49–108.

† 'The Fact that $x = y$', *Philosophia* (Israel), 17, 4 (December 1987), pp. 517–518.

† Critical Review of David Lewis, *On the Plurality of Worlds*, *The Philosophical Review*, 97, 2 (April 1988), pp. 237–244.

†† 'How to Measure the Standard Meter', *Proceedings of the Aristotelian Society*, New Series, 88 (1987/1988), pp. 193–217.

'Introduction' to *Propositions and Attitudes* (co-authored with Scott Soames, Oxford Readings in Philosophy, 1988), pp. 1–15.

† 'The Logic of What Might Have Been', *The Philosophical Review*, 98, 1 (January 1989), pp. 3–34.

'Reference and Information Content: Names and Descriptions', in Dov Gabbay and Franz Guenthner, eds, *Handbook of Philosophical Logic IV: Topics in the Philosophy of Language* (Dordrecht: Springer, 1989), Chapter IV.5, pp. 409–461.

'How to Become a Millian Heir', *Noûs*, 23, 2 (April 1989), pp. 211–220.

'Tense and Singular Propositions', in Joseph Almog, John Perry, and Howard Wettstein, eds, *Themes from Kaplan* (Oxford University Press, 1989), pp. 331–392.

†† 'Illogical Belief', in James Tomberlin, ed., *Philosophical Perspectives, 3: Philosophy of Mind and Action Theory* (Atascadero, Calif.: Ridgeview, 1989), pp. 243–285.

†† 'A Millian Heir Rejects the Wages of *Sinn*', in C. Anthony Anderson and Joseph Owens, eds, *Propositional Attitudes: the Role of Content in Logic, Language, and Mind* (Stanford, Calif.: Center for the Study of Language and Information, Stanford University, 1990), pp. 215–247.

'Temporality', in William Bright, ed., *Oxford International Encyclopedia of Linguistics* (Oxford University Press, 1990).

'Singular Terms', in Hans Burkhardt and Barry Smith, eds, *Handbook of Metaphysics and Ontology* (Munich: Philosophia Verlag, 1990).

†† 'How *Not* to Become a Millian Heir', *Philosophical Studies*, 62, 2 (May 1991), pp. 165–177.

†† 'The Pragmatic Fallacy', *Philosophical Studies*, 63, 1 (July 1991), pp. 83–97.

†† 'Reflections on Reflexivity', *Linguistics and Philosophy*, 15, 1 (February 1992), pp. 53–63.

† 'On Content', *Mind*, 101, 404 (October 1992; special issue commemorating the centennial of Gottlob Frege's '*Über Sinn und Bedeutung*'), pp. 733–751.

†† 'Relative and Absolute Apriority', *Philosophical Studies*, 69, (1993), pp. 83–100.

† 'This Side of Paradox', *Philosophical Topics*, 21, 2 (Spring 1993), pp. 187–197.

† 'A Problem in the Frege–Church Theory of Sense and Denotation', *Noûs*, 27, 2 (June 1993), pp. 158–166.

†† 'Analyticity and Apriority', in J. E. Tomberlin, ed., *Philosophical Perspectives, 7: Language and Logic* (Atascadero, Calif.: Ridgeview, 1993), pp. 125–133.

'Sense and Reference', in Robert M. Harnish, ed., *Basic Topics in the Philosophy of Language* (Prentice-Hall and Harvester Wheatsheaf, 1994), pp. 99–129.

'*Frege's Puzzle* (excerpts)', in Robert M. Harnish, ed., *Basic Topics in the Philosophy of Language* (Prentice-Hall and Harvester Wheatsheaf, 1994), pp. 447–489.

†† 'Being of Two Minds: Belief with Doubt', *Noûs*, 29, 1 (January 1995), pp. 1–20.

†† 'Relational Belief', in Paolo Leonardi and Marco Santambrogio, eds, *On Quine: New Essays* (Cambridge University Press, 1995), pp. 206–228.

'Reference: Names, Descriptions, and Variables', in Marcelo Dascal, Dietfried Gerhardus, Kuno Lorenz, and Georg Meggle, eds, *Handbuch Sprachphilosophie: Volume 2* (Berlin: Walter De Gruyter & Co, 1996), pp. 1123–1152.

'Trans-World Identification and Stipulation', *Philosophical Studies*, 84, 2–3 (December 1996), pp. 203–223.

† 'Wholes, Parts, and Numbers', in J. E. Tomberlin, ed., *Philosophical Perspectives, 11: Mind, Causation, and World* (Atascadero, Calif.: Ridgeview, 1997), pp. 1–15.

† 'Nonexistence', *Noûs*, 32, 3 (September 1998), pp. 277–319.

Bibliography of Nathan Salmon 353

†† 'Is *De Re* Belief Reducible to *De Dicto*?' in A. A. Kazmi, ed., *Meaning and Reference*, *Canadian Journal of Philosophy*, Supplementary Volume 23, 1997, (University of Calgary Press, 1998), pp. 85–110.

'Kripke', entry in the *Cambridge Dictionary of Philosophy*, Second Edition (Cambridge University Press, 1995, 1999), p. 476.

'Preface' to the Korean Translation of *Reference and Essence*, Korean translation by Joonho Park (Korea: Hankook, 2000).

† 'The Limits of Human Mathematics', in J. E. Tomberlin, ed., *Philosophical Perspectives, 15: Metaphysics, 2001* (Oxford: Blackwell, 2001), pp. 93–117.

† 'Mythical Objects', in J. Campbell, M. O'Rourke, and D. Shier, eds, *Meaning and Truth*, Proceedings of the Eastern Washington University and the University of Idaho Inland Northwest Philosophy Conference on Meaning (Seven Bridges Press, 2002), pp. 105–123.

'Puzzles about Intensionality', in Dale Jacquette, ed., *Blackwell Companion to Philosophical Logic* (Oxford: Blackwell, 2002), pp. 73–85.

† 'The Very Possibility of Language: A Sermon on the Consequences of Missing Church', C. A. Anderson and M. Zeleny, eds, *Logic, Meaning and Computation: Essays in Memory of Alonzo Church* (Boston: Kluwer, 2001), pp. 573–595.

† 'Identity Facts', in C. Hill, ed., *Philosophical Topics*, 30, 1 (Spring 2002), pp. 237–267.

†† 'Demonstrating and Necessity', *The Philosophical Review*, 111, 4 (October 2002), pp. 497–537.

'Naming, Necessity, and Beyond', *Mind*, 112, 447 (July 2003), pp. 475–492.

† 'Tense and Intension', in A. Jokic, ed., *Time, Tense, and Reference* (Cambridge University Press, 2003), pp. 107–154.

'Reference and Information Content: Names and Descriptions' (revised), in Dov Gabbay and Franz Guenthner, eds, *Handbook of Philosophical Logic, Second Edition, 10* (Boston: Kluwer, 1989, 2003), pp. 39–85.

'*Wei man ein Millianer wird*' (German translation of 'How to Become a Millian Heir'), in Mark Textor, ed., *Neue Theorien der Referenz* (*New Theories of Reference*, Paderborn, Germany: Mentis Publishing Co., 2004), pp. 38–47.

'*Die Krux von Freges Rätsel*' (German translation of an excerpt from *Frege's Puzzle*), in Mark Textor, ed., *Neue Theorien der Referenz* (*New Theories of Reference*, Paderborn, Germany: Mentis Publishing Co., 2004), pp. 60–71.

†† 'The Good, the Bad, and the Ugly', in A. Bezuidenhout and M. Reimer, eds, *Descriptions and Beyond* (Oxford University Press, 2004), pp. 230–260.

†† 'Two Conceptions of Semantics', in Zoltan Szabo, ed., *Semantics versus Pragmatics* (Oxford University Press, 2005), pp. 317–328.

†† 'Are General Terms Rigid?', *Linguistics and Philosophy*, 28, 1 (2005), pp. 117–134.

'Proper Names and Descriptions', in Donald M. Borchert, ed., *Encyclopedia of Philosophy* (Second Edition) (New York: Macmillan, 2005).

'Letter to Teresa Robertson', in *Reference and Essence* (2nd Edition), pp. 369–375.

† 'On Designating', *Mind*, 114, 456 (October 2005), pp. 1069–1133.

† 'A Father's Message', Preface to *Metaphysics, Mathematics, and Meaning*.

† 'Modal Logic Kalish-and-Montague Style', in *Metaphysics, Mathematics, and Meaning*, chapter 4.

† 'Personal Identity: What's the Problem?' in J. Berg, ed., Proceedings of the University of Haifa International Conference on the Work of Saul Kripke: *Naming, Necessity, and More* (forthcoming).

†† 'The Resilience of Illogical Belief', *Noûs* 40, 2 (June 2006), pp. 369–375.

'Terms in Bondage', *Philosophical Issues, 16, Philosophy of language* (2006), pp. 263–274.

†† 'A Theory of Bondage', *The Philosophical Review* 115, 4 (October 2006), pp. 415–448.
† 'Pronouns as Variables', *Philosophy and Phenomenological Research*, symposium on Alan Berger's *Terms and Truth* (2006).
'Semantics *vs*. Pragmatics', in Richard Schantz, ed., *What is Meaning?* (New York: de Gruyter, forthcoming 2007).
'Quantifying Into the Unquantifiable: The Life and Work of David Kaplan', to appear in a festschrift for David Kaplan edited by J. Almog and P. Leonardi, eds; available online at http://www.humnet.ucla.edu/humnet/phil/Lectures/DavidFest/DavidFest.htm.
'Three Perspectives on Quantifying In', *Pacific Philosophical Quarterly* (forthcoming 2007).
'Points, Complexes, Complex Points, and a Yacht', in N. Griffin and D. Jacquette, eds, the proceedings of the McMaster University conference on Russell *vs*. Meinong: 100 Years after 'On Denoting' (forthcoming 2007).
'Constraint with Restraint', to appear in G. Ostertag, ed., Festschrift for Stephen Schiffer.
'What is Existence?' to appear in H. Deutsch and A. Everett, eds (forthcoming 2007).
'On Sense and Direct Reference', forward to Matthew Davidson, ed., *On Sense and Direct Reference* (McGraw-Hill, 2007).
' "Must" and "Might" ', for a chapter on modal logic to appear in D. Kalish, R. Montague, G. Mar, and N. Salmon, *Logic: Techniques of Formal Reasoning* (Third Edition), Oxford University Press.

Index

a priori knowledge 141, 142–143, 144 n, 146, 148, 149 n, 154, 174, 181
abstract entities 149
abstraction operator 65
Abstraction Operator theory 62 n, 63–64, 65 n
accidental property 141
'actually' 80, 84
alethic modal attributes 99
alethic modality 22
All the President's Men 331
Almog, Joseph 32
American English 172 n
analyticity 180, 182 n, 183, 186–190
  see also truth by convention
anaphoric expressions, incompleteness of 61
anaphorically referring singular terms 52–53
anti-realism 343
aposteriority, traditional notion of 169, 173–177, 175
  see also s-aposteriority
applied semantics 179–181
apriority 164–168
  sentence-relative 173–174
  traditional notion of 175
  see also s-apriority
articulation, method of 25n, 219n, 257–259, 263
  see also syntactically *de dicto*; syntactically *de re*
assertion/content principle 319, 324
Austin, J. L. 172 n

Bare Bones theory of indexicals, the 81–82, 86–87, 88 n, 91, 96 n
Barwise, Jon 32–34, 36, 48, 51, 52, 310
Beatty, Warren 113
Bedeutung 19, 21n, 117, 119, 68, 70 n, 74
  ungerade 117, 119, 123, 235
  customary 117
  see also Sinn; indirect referent; indirect sense
BEL relation 16–19, 45–46, 47 n, 48, 50, 55, 174, 176, 195–196, 236–237, 240, 242
belief:
  de dicto 4, 156 n, 195, 257, 271–272, 277–282, 284–285, 324
  de re 4, 28, 90 n, 156 n, 195, 205, 226, 257, 270–271, 273, 276, 277–278, 280–282, 284–287, 310, 322–326, 328–329, 331–332, 334, 345
  reduction to belief of a singular proposition 4, 156 n, 270–287
  'Fido'–Fido theory of 205
  notional 249–256
  relational 249, 251–254, 256–259, 263, 267
belief attribution 240–243
belief closure principle 193–194, 208, 217
belief contexts, quantification into 43–44, 48, 53–54, 56–57
belief justification principle 193–194, 208 n, 217
Berger, Alan 98 n, 100, 113, 135 n, 309
Bernstein, Carl 331
Bertolet, Rod 169, 173–174, 177 n
Boer, Stephen 156 n
bondage designatum 123–124
bondage extension 119–123, 128, 130–131, 136, 138
bondage semantics 118, 124, 138
Borg, Emma 96 n
Bound Variable Theory, the 64–66
Brando, Marlon 113–114, 117–118, 124
Branquinho, Julio 236 n
Braun, David 75 n, 83 n, 84 n, 90 n, 96 n, 99 n
bridge principle 162–163
  aposteriority of 163
Brink, David O. 184
Brueckner, Anthony 337
Burge, Tyler 14, 69–72, 73 n, 212–214, 218 n, 277–281, 283, 286, 291
Burley, Walter 132
Bush, George H. W. 132
Bush, George W. 114–115

Cain, James
canonical names
  see standard names
Caplan, Ben 67, 88 n
Carnap, Rudolph 67, 180 n, 186–189, 332
c-command 58, 60, 62–63, 65
Chaplin, Charlie 133–134, 136
character 68–69, 72, 74–79, 80 n, 81–83, 84 n, 85 n, 87, 91–93, 96 n
character-building content rule 75, 76 n, 79, 80 n, 81, 91–93

character-building content rule (*cont.*)
  as mode of presentation of content 76 n, 92
Chastain, Charles 244 n
Chomsky, Noam 65
Church, Alonzo 5 n, 8 n, 25 n, 32, 43–44, 48, 53–57, 72–73, 87–89, 92, 100, 113, 117, 124, 127 n, 137, 195, 213 n, 214 n, 236 n, 249, 250, 266–267, 270, 281, 320–321, 323, 332
Church's Thesis 243
Church–Langford translation argument 162
circumstance of evaluation 68–71, 72 n, 73, 78–81, 83–84, 86, 90 n, 95
classical semantics 113–115, 118, 126
Clemens, Samuel 211 n
cognitive information content 5, 144
  see also information content
cognitive value 75–77, 81, 93
Cohen, Stewart 156 n
color predicates 102
compositionality, principle of 114, 116, 124
compound predicates 195
conceptual content 6
Conee, Earl 249
constants 10, 13
content 67–69, 70 n, 71, 73–84, 85 n, 86–87, 89–98
  eternal nature of 66 n
content base 68 n, 69 n, 86 n
  see also program; proposition matrices
content operators 80, 95–96
content-demonstratum distinction 82
content-sensitive operators:
  quantification into 219
Context Principle 114–117, 124, 127 n
contingent *a priori* 99 n, 142–143, 145 n, 148 n, 186, 326, 328
conventional implicature 202
conventional linguistic meaning 70
conventionalism 183–184
conversational maxim of Quality 201
Creath, Richard 183 n
Cresswell, M. J. 50, 52, 58
Crimmins, Mark 241, 242 n, 244 n, 245–247
customary sense 117, 119, 124, 127 n, 236, 251
customary-sense value assignments 121–124

Davidson, Donald 115 n
de re assertion 90 n, 318 n, 319, 324–328, 331–332, 344
de re connection 274
  see also belief *de re*
de re constructions, semantics of 15, 23–24, 26, 28

de re knowledge 90 n, 145 n, 156 n, 280
de re propositional attitude attribution 10, 12 n, 205, 264, 270–271
de se belief attribution 264
Deep Throat 331–332, 338
definite descriptions 4 n, 11, 19–20, 24, 25 n, 41 n, 69, 77 n, 78–79, 83, 88, 91 n, 94, 96 n, 100 n, 103–104, 107–111, 114, 118, 127–134, 136, 148 n, 179, 187, 190, 194 n, 243, 258, 291–294, 295 n, 296, 297 n, 298, 300, 305, 307 n, 309–317, 319–321, 323, 326, 330–338, 341, 343–345
  attributive use of 146, 292–293, 309, 313–315, 317 n, 323, 331, 334, 341
  Bad use of 313–314, 324, 333–334
  context-dependent 69
  context-specific 76, 92
  first-order 100 n, 104–108
  Good use of 313–315, 333
  improper 291
  incomplete 291, 293–294, 296–297
  indexical 78
  mock referential use of 333–334, 337
  Pretty use of 333
  referential use of 146, 309–314, 316, 318–319, 321–324, 329–334, 336–338
  Russellian denotation of 315–318
  second-order 110 n
  Ugly use of 333–335, 337 n
demonstrations 69, 72, 73 n, 78, 80–82, 84 n, 87, 89–93, 97
  Fregean theory of 78, 82, 93
demonstrative expressions:
  incompleteness of 61
demonstrative semantics 67
demonstratives 67–99
  complex 79 n, 94, 96–98
  supplemented 72, 76 n, 78, 80–81, 83, 84 n, 86–87
Dennett, Daniel 270 n
denoting phrases 254
descriptive name 147 n
descriptive semantics 180 n
designation:
  customary 117 n, 118 n, 119, 120 n, 124, 126, 129–131, 137
  indirect 117, 123, 126, 127 n
  non-anaphoric 61
  relativized to context of use 337
  rigid 101–102, 134
  semantic 343 n, 344
  simulated 343 n
  speaker 343, 344
Devitt, Michael 310

direct acquaintance 316 n, 324
disbelief 230–232, 237–240
disquotation principle 204 n, 211 n, 213
does-anybody-really-know-what-time-it-is
    skepticism 154–155
Donnellan, Keith 18, 34, 143 n, 145 n, 146,
    147 n, 148 n, 156 n, 170–171, 173,
    177–178, 179 n, 185–186, 189 n, 193,
    198, 230, 291–293, 295, 297, 309–319,
    325–334, 338, 341, 343–344
Donnellan's Thesis 318
Donnellan–Sosa test 328–329, 331
double-dipper theory 241, 243, 244 n,
    247–248
    see also hidden-indexical theory
doubt 230–233, 235, 240–241
doxastic attitudes 233, 235
'*dthat*'-operator 76 n, 78–80, 82–84, 85
    n, 88, 89 n, 93–95
    syncategorematicity of 83
    see also '*zat*'-operator
Dummett, Michael 338
Dyadic-Predicate Operator Theory 61, 63

epistemic justification 142, 147, 148 n, 149 n,
    151
Erkenntniswerte 5, 75–76, 91
    see also cognitive value
E-type pronouns 63 n, 65, 132, 134, 135
    n, 136, 137 n
Evans, Gareth 19 n, 20 n, 21 n, 25 n, 51 n,
    52 n, 128 n, 132, 133 n, 134, 136,
    144 n, 145 n
existence predicate 47
existentialism 283, 287
    see also BEL relation; belief
exportation 42, 247 n, 261, 273, 278 n, 303
    unrestricted rule of 41 n
expression-based conception of
    semantics
    see semantics, expression-centered
        conception of
extension 68–69, 75 n, 77 n, 79 n, 84 n,
    94 n, 95 n, 96
    metaphysical 101 n, 110 n, 111 n
    semantic 101, 106, 114, 117, 126 n, 129
extensionality:
    restricted principle of 126
    universal principles of 114, 116, 124

Fine, Kit 121 n
Forbes, Graeme 3, 19 n, 23, 25–26, 29, 249,
    253
Franklin, Benjamin 179, 187
free logic 144 n, 145 n
Frege, Gottlob 3–7, 34, 45, 67–75, 77–78,
    81–83, 85, 87, 91–93, 159–162, 167,
169, 194, 196, 215, 218, 235 n, 236
    n, 251, 310 n, 317–318, 320, 342
Frege's Constraint 205, 224–228
Frege's Law 5, 7–8, 15 n, 16 n, 159
Frege's Puzzle 3–4, 6–7, 8 n, 10 n, 15–16,
    18–19, 21 n, 26 n, 27 n, 143, 148
    n, 149, 153 n, 155 n, 169–170, 171 n,
    173–174, 176 n, 177, 180 n, 182 n,
    281 n, 282 n, 285 n, 287 n
Frege's Puzzle 67, 74–75, 77, 81–82, 86–87,
    91–93
Frege's Thesis 205–206, 212–216, 218
    see also Schiffer's Constraint
Fregean name 144 n
Fregean philosophy of semantics 72, 251
Fregean sense 20 n, 21, 24, 26, 28
Fregean thoughts 26, 28, 227, 321–322
Fregeanism 25 n, 29, 241
Frege–Russellian occurrence-based
    semantics 124–125
functionalism 243–343

gappy expressions 63–64
    treated as open formulae 64
Geach, Peter 51 n, 62, 64–65, 88 n,
    118–119, 128 n, 132, 134, 135 n
general proposition 11, 124, 146, 149 n, 215,
    292–293, 295–296, 305, 319, 323
    see also quantificational proposition; singular
        proposition
general terms 100–105, 108–112
    biological-taxonomic 102
    descriptional 111
    chemical-compound 102
    natural-phenomenon 103 n
    non-descriptional 103 n
    non-rigid 110 n, 111
    rigid 111
generalized quantifiers
    see restricted quantifiers
George IV 43–44, 53–56
Gödel, Kurt 25
Godel-numbering 144
Goldman, Alvin 156 n
Graff, Delia 100, 104 n
'Gray's *Elegy*' argument 123 n
Grice, H. P. 201–202, 294, 311, 319 n

hidden-indexical theory 241, 243, 244,
    245–248
Higgenbotham, James 107
Hirsch, Eli 141 n, 149 n
Hume, David 53

identifying semantic intention 335–336
identity statements 12, 15 n, 16, 19, 24 n,
    25–26, 27 n, 28, 100, 107

illocutionary acts 316, 319
importation 41
Inan, Ilhan 309, 314 n, 315, 333, 337
incomplete symbols 19, 71–72, 83–84, 86
  see also syncategorematic expressions
indefinite descriptions 4 n, 105 n, 108, 194 n, 244, 254, 300 n
  predicative 108
Indexical Theory of demonstratives, the 81, 91, 93
  see also Bare Bones Theory, the
indexicality 69, 86, 242 n, 300 n, 311–312
  temporal 67
indexicals 3, 33, 68–71, 73–75, 77–78, 82–83, 89–91, 166 n, 194, 246, 309, 329 n, 337, 345
indicative conditionals 201
indirect reference 235
indirect sense 77 n, 117 n, 122, 126, 127 n, 235–236
  hierarchy of 120
  see also Sinn ungerade
Indiscernability of Identicals 43, 50
  see also Leibniz's Law
individual concepts 117, 274 n, 277, 280–281, 283, 332–333, 336
individuals-under-guises 217, 262n
information content 3–5, 8–11, 13 n, 32–33, 35–40, 43, 48 n, 50, 51 n, 52 n, 53, 57, 144, 159, 194–195
  set-of-circumstances theory of 36, 38, 43–44, 47–51
  structured-singular proposition theory of 38, 43, 48, 52 n
information value 3, 5 n, 6–14, 19–20, 21 n, 28, 33, 52 n, 57, 155 n, 194
intensionalism 67, 267
intensions 252, 265

Kalish, Donald 113
Kamp, Hans 86
Kaplan, David 4, 32, 60, 67–70, 84, 85 n, 86–91, 93, 95–96, 99 n, 110 n, 113, 144, 145 n, 148 n, 156 n, 173 n, 178, 182 n, 185–186, 189, 195, 219, 226, 243 n, 247 n, 253, 255, 257–259, 263, 270–271, 272 n, 274–281, 282 n, 283, 285–287, 292, 310, 314–315, 320–325, 328–329, 337, 342 n
Kazmi, Ali 253, 255
Keaton, Buster 133, 136
Kennedy, Ralph 150 n
Kent, Clark 34, 45–46, 50, 198, 200–201, 205–206, 211–212, 215–218, 220 n
King, Jeffrey 94 n, 128, 136–138
knowledge by acquaintance 76 n

knowledge by description 76 n, 92, 154
knowledge-which 155–156, 158
  interest-relativity of 156
knowledge-who 155, 325, 328 n, 332
Kripke, Saul 3, 7, 8 n, 13, 16, 34, 45, 67, 72 n, 84 n, 98 n, 99 n, 102 n, 103, 106, 111–112, 113, 127 n, 131, 141–144, 145 n, 146 n, 148–150, 151 n, 152, 153 n, 156 n, 159, 169–175, 177 n, 178–179, 182 n, 185–186, 188 n, 189–190, 193, 196, 202–207, 209 n, 210, 211 n, 213 n, 214 n, 234–235, 236 n, 240, 242 n, 244 n, 245, 250, 274, 284–287, 291, 293–294, 297, 310–317, 326, 328–335, 337–338, 341, 343
Kvart, Igal 278
λ-abstraction operator 64–65

Lane, Lois 34, 198, 200–201, 205–206, 211–220
language-game 142, 151–153, 155, 157–158
latitudinarianism 90 n, 145 n, 146 n, 247 n, 323 n, 324, 326
laws of epistemology 153, 157
  universality of 153
Leibniz's Law 8, 43, 50, 105, 108–109, 245, 247
Lepore, Ernest 94 n
Levin, Michael 143 n
Lewis, David 264, 291
lines-of-communication 59, 60 n
  see also Linked Anaphor Theory
linguistic intentions 335–337
  de dicto 336–337
  de re 336–337
  primary 336
  purely semantic 335–336, 337 n
Linked Anaphor Theory 59–61, 64
Linsky, Bernard 103, 111 n
Linsky, Leonard 145 n
logical content 106
logical validity:
  classical notion of 246–247
logically proper names 77 n, 111 n, 124, 282, 309–310, 314, 345
  see also Millian terms
L-truth 180 n, 188
Ludwig, Kirk 94 n
Lycan, William 156 n

MacLaine, Shirley, 113–114, 117, 123–124
Marcus, Ruth Barcan 48–50, 162
mass terms 107, 110 n
Mates, Benson 94 n, 95 n, 127–131, 136–138
mathematical statements 338

mathematics:
  necessary apriority of 184
  special modal and epistemological character of 184
May, Robert 100, 107–108
McKay, Thomas 58–66
McKinsey, Michael 98 n, 133, 134 n
Meaning and Necessity 67, 126 n, 180 n, 188 n
measuring, institution of 152–153
mere expressions 71
meter rule:
  language-game of measuring with 151–153, 155, 157–158
meter sentence 142–144, 145 n, 146 n, 147–148, 150
  assertability of 142
  epistemic justification of 142
  contingent apriority 142–143, 145 n, 148
Mill, John Stuart 169, 173
Millian names
  see Millian term
Millian term 59, 77 n, 224, 324
Millianism 3–5, 10, 13 n, 15 n, 19–21, 23–26, 159–164, 169–170, 181, 224–225, 228, 234–236, 240
modal intension 106
modal operators 80, 116, 133
modes of acquaintance 16, 45, 48, 154, 195
  see also proposition guises; ways-of-taking propositions
mode of presentation 92, 205, 214 n, 217–218, 242 n
  see also Fregean sense
Mont Blanc 20, 21 n, 29
Montague, Richard 61, 100 n, 107, 115 n
Morris, Charles W. 337
Morti, Genoveve 337
multiple-relation theory of belief 272, 282 n

naïve set theory 44
name of 274 n, 281 n, 325, 328 n
Naming and Necessity 67, 99 n, 169–170, 173 n, 178 n, 179 n, 182 n
natural-kind
  phrase 102 n
  predicates 101 n, 102
  terms 93, 102–103, 172, 254 n, 309
Neale, Stephen 94 n, 133, 230, 243 n, 244, 319 n, 337 n
necessary *a posteriori* 169, 177
Negativity Principle 239
neo-Fregeanism 10, 19, 20 n, 21, 23–29, 227–228, 270
neo-Russellianism 19–20, 25 n, 234
  see also Millianism

'Newman-1' 76 n, 178–179, 181 n, 182 n 185, 187–188, 314–315, 325–326, 328–329, 331–332, 335
nominalism 317, 343
non-extensional contexts 10, 108 n, 250, 253–254, 255 n
  quantification into 10, 250, 255 n
non-extensional operators 3, 10, 33, 38, 159, 326
non-referring singular terms 36
non-reflexive pronouns 51 n

object-involving sense 27 n
Occam's Razor 87, 91, 93
Ortcutt, Bernard J. 50, 52, 79, 84, 86, 88, 230–233, 234 n. 249–253, 255–265, 270, 272, 275–276, 278 n, 279–282, 284
ostension 69–70
ostensive definition 171–172

paradoxes of material implication 56
Paris 141
Partee, Barbara 115
particularized conversational implicature 201 n, 202
Perry, John 19 n, 25 n, 32–34, 36, 48 n, 51 n, 52 n, 76 n, 241, 242 n, 244 n, 245–247
phenomenon terms 309
Philosophical Investigations 141, 155 n, 158
physicalism 317, 343
Plantinga, Alvin 143 n
Polyadic-Predicate Operator Theory 61–63, 65 n
possible-world semantics 100 n, 306, 307
pragmatic ambiguity
  Donnellan's notion of 311
pragmatic cogency 247
pragmatic fallacy 244 n, 308
pragmatically imparted information 9–10, 163 n, 184 n, 346
pragmatics 337, 340
Predelli, Stefano 96 n
primary qualities 144
Principia Mathematica 105
pro-clause of laziness 135
program 68 n
pronouns of laziness 63 n, 65, 67, 88 n
proposition guises 45, 92, 93, 195–196, 214, 282–283, 286
proposition matrices 68 n
propositional attitude attribution 3, 5, 10–14, 18, 21–23, 26, 32–33, 38, 201–202, 205, 212, 214, 218
  apparent failures of substitutivity in 3, 11, 15–16, 34

propositional attitude attribution (*cont.*)
  de dicto 29 n
  de re 12 n
propositional functions 116, 124
propositional recognition failure 208
pseudo *de re* 320–322, 324, 328, 342 n
psychological attitudes 230
pure indexicals 69, 77, 90 n, 91
Putnam wires
  see lines-of-communication
Putnam, Hilary 5 n, 6, 26, 177 n
puzzle of reflexives in propositional attitude contexts 43, 46, 48, 50, 51 n, 53, 56–57

quantificational proposition 304
quantified modal logic 44, 55 n
quantifier phrases
  binding 135
  non-extensionality of 113, 116
  non-truth-functionality of 113
Quine, W. V. 37, 145 n, 156 n, 182 n, 186, 189, 218–219, 226, 233–234, 272–273, 275–278, 281–282, 285, 287

Recanati, Francois 310, 312 n
Reference and Essence 102, 145 n
referential/attributive distinction 291–297, 310 n, 312–313, 314–316, 318–319, 329–330, 337–338, 341
  alleged semantic significance of *see* semantic significance thesis
  extended to proper names 312–315, 331, 334–336, 338
  generalized attributive use 336–338
  generalized referential use 336–338
reflexive pronouns 52–53, 56–57, 61–62, 63 n
reflexive properties 40, 43, 50–52, 60, 62–63
reflexivity 57, 59, 257
Reinhart, Tanya 62, 65
representation
  intensional 281
  Kaplan's notion of 274–279
restricted quantifiers 127, 130, 134–135, 310
Richard, Mark 3, 29 n, 32–34, 36–37, 47 n, 48 n, 51 n, 52 n, 244 n, 246 n
Richard–Soames problem 32, 34, 36–38, 40, 43, 45–46, 48, 51 n, 56–57
Russell, Bertrand 17, 19–20, 24, 28, 33–34, 38, 45, 67, 76, 77 n, 78 n, 96 n, 100, 105, 107, 145 n, 154, 194, 196, 251, 254–256, 258, 272, 275, 282, 309–311, 314–318, 322, 324–325, 333–334, 337 n, 342–343, 346
Russell's paradox 44, 107 n

Russellian genuine proper names
  see logically proper names
Russellian intensional semantics 124

Salmon, Nathan 21 n, 35 n, 58, 59 n, 60 n, 61, 63, 107 n, 164, 256 n, 257 n, 259 n, 260 n, 310 n, 312 n, 318 n, 319 n, 323 n, 328 n, 332 n, 336 n
Salmon, Simone 159n, 249
s-aposteriority 175–177
s-apriority 174–177
Schiffer, Stephen 2, 193, 200–201, 211–220, 224–228, 241–243, 244 n, 246 n, 247–248
Schiffer's Constraint 205–206, 212–219
Scott, Sir Walter 43–44, 54–56, 316, 319–320, 323
Searle, John R. 172 n, 323 n, 324 n, 329, 331
second-order singular terms 107
semantic attributes, standard 337, 341–342
semantic extension 101, 106
semantic reference 291, 312–313, 316–318, 334–335, 343
  see also speaker reference
semantic significance thesis 292–297, 310–313, 317, 338, 341, 343–344
  indexical version of 311–312
  lexical-ambiguity version 311–312
semantic value 68, 72, 74, 84 n
semantically contained information 9–10
  see also pragmatically imparted information
semantic–pragmatic distinction 337, 340–341
semantics
  expression-centered conception of 115–116, 125–126, 316–318, 342, 344
  Frege–Russell tradition of 344
  occurrence-based 115–117, 124–126, 131, 337, 340
  pure 179–181
  Russell–Tarski 125
  speech-act centered conception of 244
Simple Anaphor Theory 58–61
simple singular terms 3, 12 n, 13 n, 24, 29, 33, 36, 38, 41 n, 48
singular propositions 4, 10, 13 n, 16, 19, 24 n, 25–28, 47 n, 48 n, 52 n, 75–76, 81–82, 84, 89 n, 91–92, 116, 124–125, 137, 144, 148 n, 149 n, 156 n, 170–171, 191 n, 195, 215, 217, 237–256, 281–282, 311–313, 323, 325, 327
singular-term rigidity 102, 112
singular-term contents 283
Sinn 19, 27 n, 59, 68
  ungerade 77n, 235
  see also Fregean sense

skeptical paradox 154, 156
Soames, Scott 32–34, 36–38, 40, 46, 47 n, 48 n, 58, 60 n, 63, 54, 65 n, 100, 102–105, 112 n, 133, 193, 319, 324 n, 328 n
Sosa, Ernest 145 n, 156 n, 324 n, 325 n, 327–329, 331, 336
speaker assertion 319, 338, 340
speaker reference 291, 310 n, 316–318, 334, 336, 338, 343–344
Standard Meter, the 99, 141–143, 153–154, 155 n, 157–158
standard names 149, 154, 156–157
Stanley, Jason 128 n, 137–138
Stein, Gertrude 90 n
Strawson, P. F. 68, 70 n, 77 n
strong compositionality principle 81, 124, 126
subconscious 233–234
Substitution of Equality
 see Leibniz's Law
Superman 34, 45–47, 50, 198–201, 202, 205–206, 211–220
supplemented expressions 71
supplemented indexicals 71, 73 n
suspension of judgment 230–233, 238–240, 275–278, 280, 285–287
syncategorematic expressions 71, 83–84, 86, 93, 97
synonymy transformation 316, 323
syntactic incompleteness thesis 71, 74, 77, 81, 86, 91
syntactically *de dicto* 257–259, 263–264, 267
syntactically *de re* 219, 226, 257, 264, 267
synthetic sentences 91 n
syntheticity 169
Szabó, Zoltán Gendler 113

Tarski, Alfred 10, 113–114, 125, 137, 251, 252

Taschek, William 60, 236 n
Taylor, Barry 94 n
temporal operators 38 n, 116
tense 67, 69
Theory of Descriptions, the 11 n, 20, 194 n, 275, 315, 333, 346
Tomberlin, James 151 n, 156 n
truth by convention 183
T-sentences 75 n
Twain, Mark 211
 see also Clemens, Samuel

variable-binding
 occurrence-based semantics of 116–117
variable-binding operators 118–126
vivid term 270, 274 n, 281 n, 324–325

Watergate scandal 331
Waverley 43–44, 54, 56, 316, 320, 323
ways-of-taking propositions 16–17, 21–22, 23 n, 25, 28, 174–177, 214–215, 237, 283
Wettstein, Howard 83 n, 160–163, 170 n, 291–297, 341, 310, 312, 321–323
Whitehead, Alfred North 105
Wiggins, David 51 n, 52
Williamson, Timothy 3, 249
Wilson, George 104 n
Wittgenstein, Ludwig 184, 141–143, 150, 154–155, 158, 317, 337, 342–343
Wong, Kai-Yee 160, 164–167
Woodward, Bob 331

Yagisawa, Takashi 230

'*zat*'-operator 95